MAGILL'S
LITERARY ANNUAL
2008

# MAGILL'S
# LITERARY ANNUAL
# 2008

*Essay-Reviews of 200 Outstanding Books
Published in the United States During 2007*

*With an Annotated List of Titles*

Volume Two
Lit-Z

*Edited by*
JOHN D. WILSON
STEVEN G. KELLMAN

**SALEM PRESS**
**Pasadena, California    Hackensack, New Jersey**

LIBRARY OF CONGRESS CATALOG CARD NO. 77-99209
ISBN (set): 978-1-58765-416-9
ISBN (vol. 1): 978-1-58765-417-6
ISBN (vol. 2): 978-1-58765-418-3

FIRST PRINTING

PRINTED IN CANADA

# CONTENTS

CONTENTS

# COMPLETE ANNOTATED LIST OF TITLES

## VOLUME 1

COMPLETE ANNOTATED LIST OF TITLES

COMPLETE ANNOTATED LIST OF TITLES

COMPLETE ANNOTATED LIST OF TITLES

COMPLETE ANNOTATED LIST OF TITLES

COMPLETE ANNOTATED LIST OF TITLES

COMPLETE ANNOTATED LIST OF TITLES

COMPLETE ANNOTATED LIST OF TITLES

# COMPLETE ANNOTATED LIST OF TITLES

# COMPLETE ANNOTATED LIST OF TITLES

# MAGILL'S
# LITERARY ANNUAL
## 2008

# LITTLE BOAT

*Author:* Jean Valentine (1934-    )
*Publisher:* Wesleyan University Press (Middletown,
    Conn.). 67 pp. $22.95
*Type of work:* Poetry

*Valentine uses her spare style and oblique images to
take her readers into a world of dream and mystery where
she considers love and death*

A number of commenters on contemporary poetry in
America have noted that the last few decades have produced a trend toward accessibility. Writers such as Billy
Collins, Ted Kooser, and Sharon Olds, to name only a few,
have contributed to the trend, which has resulted in events
such as poetry slams and Collins's radio readings on *Prairie Home Companion.* There's a comfort in such accessibility.

Jean Valentine, however, is not in the accessibility school. Her stripped-down
poems (one critic has said they seem more like notebook jottings than poems) demand
that readers give to each of her few words the same careful attention she used to select
them. Her spare style, her slant images, her unconventional punctuation (which sometimes includes extra spaces between words in a line) may remind one of Emily
Dickinson and explain why many call Valentine a "poet's poet." The minimalist
poems of *Little Boat*, like those in Valentine's earlier books, draw the reader into a
fragile and dreamlike world where the poet considers subjects such as love and death.
Poems like these do not offer the reader many conclusions about their subjects;
instead, they invite the reader to participate intuitively to discover the author's vision.

The opening poem of the volume, "La Chalupa, the Boat," offers a sample of
Valentine's approach. In the opening lines, the speaker is a young person drifting in
"la chalupa." The little blue boat is painted with flowers, roses, and lilies. The second
stanza revises: "No, not drifting, I am poling/ my way into my life. It seems/ like
another life." From this point on, the poem exchanges present tense for past. Evi-
dently the life the speaker poled herself into was some time ago. The third stanza suggests past obstacles in that life by listing "walls of the mind" and even "cliffs of the
mind," "seven deaths" and finally "seven bread-offerings." The last image seems to
evoke more worship, even blessing, than frustration. The explanation may lie in the
vessel that carried the speaker into life, the boat that the last line identifies as the little
boat "you built once, slowly, in the yard, after school." The presence of that "you"
in the last line gives the poem a surprising direction that often appears at the end
of Valentine's poems. Here it suggests how the speaker was able to deal with life's
walls and cliffs, for she has set out in a craft that "you" built carefully, long before.
Such reading is a little like what a hiker might do if he or she discovers a skeleton—
dry, bleached bones—in the woods and reimagines the animal with flesh and hide.

~

*Jean Valentine has published ten books of poetry. Her first volume of poems,* Dream Barker, *won the 1965 Yale Younger Poets Series award.* Door in the Mountain: New and Collected Poems, 1965-2003, *won the National Book Award for 2004.*

~

Valentine's poems give enough of bone and sinew that the discoverer will understand the omitted flesh; at the same time, they offer the stark beauty of the bare bone itself.

Several of the poems in this volume allude to graphic artists. "The Artist in Prison" is designated "for Ray Materson," whose work as an embroiderer of miniatures during his prison sentence has brought him considerable public attention. Valentine writes the poem in Materson's voice, but it becomes a statement of how all artists work, poets included. The speaker begins by offering to trade cigarettes for other prisoners' socks, so that he can use the threads to embroider tiny pictures, as in fact Materson has done. He then goes on to trade days of his freedom and even "red shadow/ on the inside of my skull" for the socks that are the medium of his art. The poem thus becomes not only a tribute to Materson but also a description of how all artists work, trading their freedom for whatever they need to bring the red shadows of their artistic vision to life.

Several of the poems in the first section of this book deal with loss, prison, and death. "Photographs at her Wake," for example, pictures the life of the dead woman through images as small as the tortoiseshell combs she wore, as tiny as hair under a page of a phone book. In "Lord of the world!" one whose hand has been found to be "caught in the prisoner's hand" prays for protection. Many of the poems of this section suggest the speaker responding to loss. In "The father was a carrier," the speaker laments the loss of a man who carried everything—perhaps all the burdens of his life—in five buckets. By the end of the poem, he has morphed into all men who are heavy-laden. In "The Eleventh Brother (2)," Valentine builds on the Hans Christian Andersen story of the sister who must weave shirts for all her eleven brothers to return them from swan to human form. The sister leaves one shirt without a completed sleeve, and in Valentine's version the one-winged brother loses control of his car on a bridge. He cannot be recalled to life, even after the sister dives into the dark water to deliver the missing arm. "'Remote Objects of Intense Devotion'" uses the objects in the miniature box installations of the surrealist artist Joseph Cornell as representations of loss in the way it is felt by ordinary people—"A guy smoking, in his chair."

The second section of *Little Boat* is titled "Jesus Said," drawing some of its subject and form from the Gospel of Thomas, one of the so-called Gnostic gospels, which attribute to Jesus a number of sayings not found in the New Testament canon. The subtitle to the section quotes one of these sayings: "Jesus said, Split a piece of wood, and I am there." In this section, "Annunciation Poem" suggests a love poem from mother to longed-for child, "the eye of my eye." "The Teacher's Poem" begins with an epigraph from Pablo Picasso: "If you don't have red, use green." It then opens with a saying of Jesus: "Jesus said, Fix anything." As the poem progresses, however, it lists things that cannot be fixed, not a granddaughter's sorrow or the end of life or even a stovepipe. Is all this in answer to Jesus' command or part of what Jesus himself said?

Either reading is possible; in the end, neither red nor green can remedy what is wrong. The poem seems tied to the one that follows it, "Death Poem." Here Jesus tells his hearer that neither his life nor his death has been of use to the one who has moved against him. The section concludes with "The Afterlife Poem." In it, Jesus is quoted again: "But I *am* 'alive'!" He then goes on almost whimsically to define that life in afterlife: "It's the same material,/ but lighter,/ summer stuff."

The "Strange Lights" section of the volume is composed of five poems, each with "Hospital" as part of its title. Their reference to hospitals is mostly oblique; "doctor" shows up in one, however, and "MRI." In "Hospital: It was euphoria," the speaker describes how little veins of euphoria sent a "burst to the brain," which showed like fireworks on the MRI. Euphoria happened also "when you stove my boat/ & brought me over/ listing in the racing foam." Here, as in the opening poem, the boat seems to suggest the speaker's soul.

In the section titled "A Bowl of Milk," several poems seem to address the dead. "This Side" illustrates the oracular quality of much of Valentine's work. It begins by describing "window-eyes" that seem to observe the world from across the street. The speaker prays and waits, even extends an antenna wrapped in aluminum foil. Still waiting for the message, she carries the aerial with her, caduceus she calls it, the two-winged staff of Hermes the messenger. In the last section of the poem, the speaker leaves a bowl of milk on the threshold so that the dead may return to drink. With a powerful picture of grief, she concludes "& in the morning/ licked it where he licked." "His White Jade Eggs" describes the dislocation the grieving one can feel after a death; it is the strange sense of uncertainty one has when the train begins to move, or perhaps the train next to one's own. It is the elusive sense of trying to watch the floaters in one's own eye.

The section "From the Questions of Bhanu Kapil" draws on the questions that the British Punjabi poet Bhanu Kapil Rider used to create her work *The Vertical Interrogations of Strangers* (2001), a work in which she posed a sequence of twelve questions, ordered variously, to strangers. Those questions form the titles of these poems to which Valentine has built her own answers.

The "Maria Gravida, Mary Expectant" section draws its image from the icon described in "Maria Gravida" where the "gold mother," the pregnant Mary, draws the speaker into the icon. Its images of goldfinches and peacocks suggest death and immortality. The very earth seems pregnant: "Not a casket but a darkroom for our love," mysteriously impregnated by the silver fertility image, the herma. Here, as in many of these poems, mystery is a dominant theme.

In "Moose and calf," Valentine begins with a picture of the moose and calf of the title, eating willow shoots beside an Alaskan highway, "looking for you" she adds ambiguously, as if the moose and speaker are both seeking "you." The next stanza continues the idea; the seeker is also thirsting for something she cannot name "before I can't remember you any more," suggesting the common fear of the bereaved, that the memory of the dead will fade to nothingness. In the poem's third stanza, however, the implications that the "you" is a human are transmuted to suggest Christ, often portrayed with a broken heart and here with a wound in his side as well, a wound that becomes wide enough *"to offer refuge for all."* The line is quoted from the fourteenth century English mystic, Julian of Norwich, whose visions suggested to her a mystic unity of all the world in God's love.

The volume's last poem, "The Rose," seems to draw on traditional associations of the rose with both human and divine love. The poem's first lines seem to deny this, however. It looks like the sort of labyrinth that might reveal God, but at its center it is merely a rose. The poem continues to describe the rose as growing in "us," nourishing us in life and love; "only flesh itself" Valentine adds, reminding the reader of Christianity's view of the connection between God and flesh. The concluding stanza pictures "god the mother" comforting Jim and inviting him with the homely image of her knees as a country porch on which he can rest.

Reading Jean Valentine's poems is like stepping into a landscape from which some road markers have been removed; although the land remains familiar, the task of travel requires new, perhaps unaccustomed, attentiveness from the reader. The reward for that attention, however, is a journey into a dreamscape more lovely, more evocative than the usual journey into the common suburbs where the roads are full of signs identifying the street names and telling us matter-of-factly when to merge.

*Ann D. Garbett*

## Review Sources

*Booklist* 104, no. 2 (September 15, 2007): 16.
*Library Journal* 132, no. 13 (August 1, 2007): 92.
*Publishers Weekly* 254, no. 33 (August 20, 2007): 48.

# A LONG WAY GONE
## Memoirs of a Boy Soldier

*Author:* Ishmael Beah (1980-     )
*Publisher:* Farrar, Straus and Giroux (New York).
   229 pp. $22.00
*Type of work:* Memoir
*Time:* 1993-1998
*Locale:* Sierra Leone

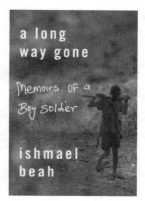

*The author describes his experience as a child soldier in Sierra Leone's civil war, where he was driven to kill by hunger, fear, and drugs*

*Principal personages:*
   ISHMAEL BEAH, a boy whose family is
      killed in his country's civil war and who
      becomes a child soldier
   JUNIOR, his brother
   ESTHER, a nurse who helps Beah begin to heal after he is
      rescued from military service
   UNCLE TOMMY, Beah's uncle, who gives him a home
   LAURA SIMMS, an American storyteller who adopts Beah

While readers in the United States might occasionally read a news report that mentions child soldiers or encounter statistics about the fate of children in war zones, few can imagine how average people, and especially children, could take part in the atrocities. Ishmael Beah's memoir, *A Long Way Home: Memoirs of a Boy Soldier*, tells how an ordinary boy became a ruthless soldier and then overcame his terrible experiences. The memoir not only highlights the complexity of human nature under stress but also adds an important voice to political and policy discussions on the effects of war on children.

Beah acknowledges in the prologue (dated New York City, 1998) that readers will probably be emotionally distant from the subject matter. For part of a page, he provides details that set up a contrast with what will follow. The narrator describes speaking with high school friends who are curious about the war in his home country. They think it is "cool" that Beah "saw people running around with guns and shooting each other." He promises to tell them about it sometime.

The prologue anchors the story as one told after the fact by a storyteller to friends. Although many of the details in the memoir are horrific, Beah helps the reader through it by maintaining the tone of a storyteller somewhat distanced from what has happened. Though many of Beah's memories include tragedy, personal loss, and extreme violence, he lets the facts speak for themselves.

Beah begins the main narration in chapter 1 by explaining that, at the beginning of the war, he knew about it only through stories told by others fleeing the fighting.

~

*Ishmael Beah has had writing*
*published in* Vespertine Press *and* LIT.
*He is a member of the Human Rights*
*Watch Children's Rights Division*
*Advisory Committee and has spoken*
*widely about children affected by war,*
*including several speeches at the*
*United Nations. His memoir has met*
*with wide acclaim, both in literary*
*publications and the popular press.*

~

In this way, he opens the memoir by forming connections with the readers, who are likewise learning about the war through a story told by someone else: "There were all kinds of stories told about the war that made it sound as if it was happening in a faraway and different land." While Beah observes that the refugees telling the stories have been strongly affected by what they have seen, his own experience with war, like that of American readers', is formed through popular culture. He mentions books and movies such as *Rambo: First Blood* (1982). Those works of fiction produced in other countries at first seem more real than the war in his own country. As the fighting moves into his area, getting together with his friends and listening to rap music remain the twelve-year-old's immediate concerns.

When their village is invaded by rebel soldiers, Beah and his brother Junior are visiting friends in town. Separated from their family and not knowing if any of them are alive, they and their friends wander from village to village trying to stay away from the soldiers. Most people are too afraid of teenage boys to help them. They encounter other homeless boys in their travels, but there is no system in place to help them. In fact, all semblance of normal society has fallen apart. It is not clear what the fighting factions stand for, and no governmental services remain. There are no police officers protecting anyone, no one to feed or shelter the war orphans, and no one to help children separated from their families to find them or to find food while they search.

After being separated from Junior and his friends, Beah spends time alone, lost in a forest, and eventually meets up with another group of boys, some of whom he knew before the war. After months of roaming, he meets someone from his former village who knows where his parents and brother Junior are. As they approach the village where the family is staying, gunshots break out. They hide in the jungle until the fighting ends, but by that time everyone in the village is dead.

While much of the memoir is narrated in a fairly neutral tone, the description of the village after the slaughter is one of the most detailed in the book, and Beah includes his intense emotions in the narration. "I screamed at the top of my lungs and began to cry as loudly as I could, punching and kicking with all my might into the weak walls that continued to burn. I had lost my sense of touch. My hands and feet punched and kicked the burning walls, but I couldn't feel a thing." His grief gives way to anger, and he hits the friend who brought him to the village.

Around the time Beah calms down, soldiers return to the village. From where he is hiding, he can hear them casually discussing their attack on three villages, killing everyone in the one where Beah's family was staying. Their conversation shows no compassion for the people they killed and no remorse for their actions. They laugh as they talk and sit playing cards in the middle of the carnage. The horror of soldiers who have lost all sense of humanity is clear.

By the time Beah and his friends become soldiers, their lack of options is clear. They have lost their families and their homes; they have no source of food or shelter; the few people who are willing to help them risk their lives to do so. When the boys are taken to a village where they are given food and a place to sleep, they feel safe for the first time in a long time. However, when their safety is threatened by the rebels, whom the soldiers blame for killing their families, their willingness to join the fight comes as no surprise to the reader. When the boys are called up for their first military encounter, they have spent the day in typical childhood activities—playing soccer and swimming.

Beah's tent companions are so young that that they have trouble holding up their guns. The outing is an emotionally charged part of the memoir, reflecting the boys' terror at meeting the armed enemy in the forest. Beah watches one of his tent mates die, and he loses other friends as well. His description of Josiah's death is poignant in its detail, and its effect on the narrator is evident from the strength of the prose: "As I watched him, the water in his eyes was replaced by blood that quickly turned his brown eyes into red. He reached for my shoulder as if he wanted to hold it and pull himself up. But midway, he stopped moving. The gunshots faded in my head, and it was as if my heart had stopped and the whole world had come to a standstill."

The following chapters narrate Beah's acceptance of killing, helped by constant access to marijuana, cocaine, and other drugs. The boys' lives as soldiers consist of watching war movies, taking the drugs that stave off fear and prevent them from thinking clearly about the horrors of what they are doing, and remorselessly slaughtering soldiers and civilians. Beah and his friends become like the soldiers who casually discussed their day's work after killing Beah's family and everyone else in the village.

Unlike most war memoirs, which are often written by military leaders or adult soldiers with some knowledge of the strategy and politics involved, Beah's is a first-person account by a child with little understanding of the reasons for the war. In fact, Beah's memoir describes a society in so much chaos that it is not clear that even the military leaders have a good understanding of what the war is about. Young boys are given guns and drugs and persuaded to fight because they want to avenge the deaths of their families and because they have no other way to get food. The boys hear rumors about political developments but have no real understanding of the war.

Once Beah is rescued from the fighting and taken to a center for rehabilitating the young soldiers, it becomes clear that the boys who fought for the opposite side have no better understanding of the reasons for the war and endured horrors just as extreme. In the end, the book gives no evidence that one side had greater moral authority than the other. At the rehabilitation center, the boys fight with those from the other side, destroy the buildings and furniture, beat up the workers, and steal food from the kitchen and drugs from the health center. The center's administrators are patient and do not punish them; their repeated refrain is "this isn't your fault." As the drugs slowly work out of his system, Beah begins to trust the center's nurse Esther and other workers. He begins to tell her what has happened to him and to return to more civil behavior.

After learning details about his life and family, the workers at the center find Beah's uncle, Tommy, who lives in the same city, based only on his first name and occupation. Beah's uncle and his family welcome him into their home. Despite the constant dangers of the war, Beah is able to attend school.

Beah is invited to interview to be one of two children from Sierra Leone to speak at the United Nations at a conference about children affected by war. Children from around the world attend the conference, and Beah recognizes how his story fits into the larger issue of how children are taken advantage of and suffer because of war.

Beah humorously describes his initial reaction to New York City. He says that his expectations came from rap music, but he resorts to Shakespeare to try to make sense of what he sees. When he learns that it is dark so early in the afternoon because it is winter, he thinks, "I knew the word 'winter' from Shakespeare's texts and I thought I should look up its meaning again." He never imagined that it could be so cold, and he has only summer clothes.

At the conference, Beah meets an American storyteller named Laura Simms. After he returns to Sierra Leone, his uncle dies, and the fighting in the city escalates. Beah asks Simms if he can stay with her if he can get to New York, and she later adopts him. After escaping the country, he finishes high school in the United States, where the prologue's conversation with his friends takes place.

*Joan Hope*

## Review Sources

*Booklist* 103, nos. 19/20 (June 1, 2007): 112.
*Chicago Tribune*, February 11, 2007, p. 4.
*Denver Post*, March 4, 2007, p. F14.
*Kirkus Reviews* 75, no. 5 (March 1, 2007): 3.
*Library Journal* 132, no. 4 (March 1, 2007): 91.
*The New York Times Book Review* 156 (February 25, 2007): 12.
*Publishers Weekly* 253, no. 50 (December 18, 2006): 55.

# LOST CITY RADIO

*Author:* Daniel Alarcón (1977-    )
*Publisher:* HarperCollins (New York). 257 pp. $24.95
*Type of work:* Novel
*Time:* Undetermined
*Locale:* A nameless South American country

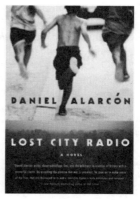

*A narrative about a country torn apart by a civil war, told through the tragedies and hardships that its civilians have undergone*

*Principal characters:*

NORMA, the host of a radio program that tries to reunite those separated by the war
VICTOR, a boy sent from his village, 1797, with a mission to read the names of his village's missing on Norma's show
ELMER, Norma's nervous station manager
LEN, Norma's engineer at the station
ELIJAH MANAU, a teacher sent from the city to teach in Victor's village who later takes Victor to Norma
ADELA, Victor's deceased mother
REY, Norma's missing husband and suspected Illegitiment Legion member
NICO, Victor's friend who leaves 1797 to join the army
TRINI, Rey's uncle and former police chief
MARDEN, Rey's underground contact in the Illegitiment Legion
YEREVAN, a disc jockey at Norma's station who disappears after appearing sympathetic to the Illegitiment Legion
ZAHIR, an elder in Victor's village who lost his hands at a Tadek rite

Bearing striking resemblances to dystopian novels such as George Orwell's *Nineteen Eighty-Four* (1949) and Aldous Huxley's *Brave New World* (1932), Daniel Alarcón's *Lost City Radio* describes an anonymous South American country torn apart by a decade of civil war, of which no citizen remembers its beginning or its purpose. The war resulted in a new totalitarian government, which is committed to obliterating the native cultures and allegiances by renaming all villages using a numbering system (odd numbers indicate the village is near water, and the higher the number the more remote and mountainous the village), quelling native Indians' languages and dialects and replacing them with politically approved languages like Orwell's newspeak, and rewriting the history, geography, and culture of the country. *Lost City Radio*, however, is not about political strife or the effects of war on a country, but rather about the effects of war on the individual. The novel interlaces the stories of three main characters as it jumps from character to character, village to city, and decade to decade.

Lost City Radio *is Daniel Alarcón's first novel. He previously published a collection of short stories,* War by Candlelight, *a finalist for the 2006 Hemingway Foundation/PEN Award. In 2001, he won a Fulbright scholarship, which allowed him to write an anthropological study of San Juan de Lurigancho, in his native Lima, Peru. He is associate editor of* Etiqueta Negra, *a monthly Peruvian magazine.*

The novel's first protagonist is Norma, a woman who has become a national treasure through her voice, yet her face is unknown to her fellow countrymen. Working at the only radio station in the capital city, Norma prepares news stories to be approved by the government and reads them the following day. Any mention of the war or of any dissident is strictly forbidden. This rule is reinforced when one of Norma's coworkers, a classical music host named Yerevan, disobeys the rules, then disappears, never to be heard from again. What has brought Norma celebrity, however, is not her reading of the daily headlines but her program *Lost City Radio*.

Every Sunday evening, Norma hosts *Lost City Radio*, with the goal of reuniting families and friends who have been separated and have had their lives torn apart by the civil war. The program highlights the stories of the hundreds of thousands of missing, who came from Indian villages and poor barrios and were recruited by the army or relocated to the city in hopes of finding work. Perhaps dead, rotting in a military prison, or devoured by the city, the missing have never returned to their homes, leaving their loved ones to listen to *Lost City Radio*, hoping for Norma to reinstate their families, homes, and lives. Her listeners send her gifts and photos of their missing, while other listeners pretend to be the missing. At first, these impostures angered Norma, but over the years she has come to realize that "there are people out there who think of themselves as belonging to someone. To a person who, for whatever reason, has gone. And they wait years: They don't look for their missing, they *are* the missing." Thus, Norma invites her callers not only to search for loved ones but also to share their memories, to re-create the feel and scents of their villages. In doing so, the callers construct a new community, and Norma's voice helps to heal a "country [that] had slipped, fallen into a nightmare, now horrifying, now comic, and in the city, there was only a sense of dismay at the inexplicability of it."

Norma also has personal reasons for hosting the weekly radio program. Besides helping those in desperate need, Norma too is missing someone. One year before the end of the war, Norma's husband, Rey, went on a routine trip into the jungle and never came back. Norma had long suspected that Rey had been involved with the underground Illegitimet Legion (IL), who were opposed to the regime in power and were therefore tortured and often killed when captured. The night Norma had met Rey, before the war, he was arrested and taken to a dissident torture camp known as The Moon. A year later, when he was released, he would rarely speak of his time there but would wake up screaming from nightmares.

Rey, the second protagonist, was a college professor of botany and specialized in medicinal usages of jungle plants. He regularly ventured into the jungle, performing research and interviewing the Indians about plant usages. Rey was particularly interested in psychoactive plants and wrote an article about the practice of Tadek, used to find and punish criminals. After a crime was committed, villagers fed a young boy hallucinogens, then set him loose in the village to identify the culprit. Once discovered, the culprit was tied to a tree and both hands were chopped off. Much to Norma's horror, Rey published this Tadek article, something outlawed in the government's quest to stamp out all ties to native customs and beliefs. Rey further angered authorities by not denouncing the practice, even claiming Tadek as "the antique precursor to the absolutely modern system of justice now being employed in the nation" and "applauded a few well-publicized cases of tortured union leaders and missing students as successful, contemporary versions of Tadek, whereby the state assigned guilt based on outward signifiers." The article placed Rey on the government's radar as an insurgence collaborator once again. Throughout his life, whether safely at home, in the jungle, or working with the IL, Rey wonders how he became so entwined in a war he knew nothing about. Remembering the beginning of the war and his involvement, Rey reflects, "Even then anyone paying attention should have known what was coming. But they had stepped together into this chaos, the insurgency and the government, arm in arm, and for nine violent years, they'd danced." On a research trip into the jungle, nine years into the war, Rey does not come back. Ten years later, Norma continues to hold out hope that he will hear her voice and return.

The novel jumps yet again to another character and time, as Norma's life is altered when a scrawny eleven-year-old boy from the jungle, Victor, appears at the radio station one morning looking for Norma. Victor, the third protagonist, is from the village 1797, the last place Rey had been seen. Victor, who "was slender and fragile and [whose] eyes were too small for his face," has brought with him a list of his village's missing. The villagers wrote the names of their loved ones and trusted Victor to travel to the city, read their names, and help bring their loved ones home. Taking pity on the boy, Norma takes Victor in and begins to learn of 1797. She reads the note and is shocked to find Rey's name on Victor's list.

With new hope and determination, Norma and Victor track down Elijah Manau, Victor's teacher who had left the city to teach in 1797 and had returned, almost retreated in surrender, to his hometown under the excuse of bringing Victor to Norma. Manau sought refuge in his parents' house after returning to the city, considering his experience in 1797 as being "exiled . . . to teach in this humid backwater," a "testament to his consistent mediocrity." When Norma finds him, she presses Manau for information about how Rey's name got placed on the list of missing. Reluctantly, Manau shows Victor and Norma a drawing that will forever change their lives and relationship to one another.

The drawing, which was created by an artist who traveled among villages drawing the missing based on descriptions from those they left behind, is of Rey. It was given to Manau by Victor's mother, Adela, who recently died in the village river. Manau reveals that he and Adela had been lovers and that Adela confided a great deal to Manau, perhaps sensing her immanent death. One of her secrets was that of her love for a scientist who would visit the village to study the local plants and their medicinal implications. As Norma listens to the stranger talk of her husband as described by his deceased lover, it is nearly more than she can bear. She forces herself to listen in hopes of finding a clue to Rey's location, or to his demise. Manau explains that Rey and Adela had a son eleven years ago, and Norma's focus shifts to Victor. Upon learning this, she feels the need for "some explosive act of violence: for the rending and tearing of some heirloom or photograph, the destruction of a meaningful item, some article of clothing," but instead must listen and ask only her unanswerable question as to what became of Rey—is he alive? She now must struggle to redefine herself and her relationship with Victor.

In a graceful and effortless fashion, Alarcón is able to switch from the big city to the remote 1797, and from era to era, with each chapter. The author takes the reader inside each character's mind to reveal his or her thoughts, emotions, and the true effects the war has had on each of them. He describes the atrocities of war through the havoc wreaked on the characters rather than through describing the battles themselves. Alarcón also exposes war's futility when he writes that none of the characters could remember how or when the war started or could ever tell who was winning. At one point, the desperate and exhausted villagers of 1797 look to Rey to explain this war that they are not a part of yet are devastated by. One villager asks, "'Tell us, sir,' . . . already speaking of the war in the past tense, 'who was right in all of this?'" Rey, like so many of his countrymen, has no answer.

With great tenderness, Alarcón writes of the emptiness and endless longing Norma and others feel as they search for their missing, of the perhaps naïve hope that their loved ones will return. In a poignant line, Norma admits, "The person [she] missed most of all in Rey's absence was not Rey but the person she had been when she was with him." This admission reinforces a theme throughout the novel: that the war not only separated families from one another but also separated people from themselves.

*Sara Vidar*

### Review Sources

*Booklist* 103, no. 8 (December 15, 2006): 20.
*Chicago Tribune*, April 1, 2007, p. 3.
*Harper's Magazine* 314 (February, 2007): 86.
*Kirkus Reviews* 74, no. 22 (November 15, 2006): 1139.
*Library Journal* 131, no. 20 (December 1, 2006): 105.
*The New York Times Book Review* 156 (March 25, 2007): 19.
*The Washington Post*, January 28, 2007, p. BW15.

# THE LUCIFER EFFECT
## Understanding How Good People Turn Evil

*Author:* Philip Zimbardo (1933-    )
*Publisher:* Random House (New York). 551 pp. $27.95
*Type of work:* Psychology, current affairs

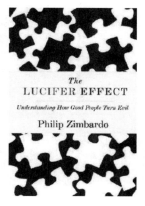

The
LUCIFER EFFECT

*Understanding How Good People Turn Evil*

Philip Zimbardo

*A research-based account of how larger forces influence human beings to choose evil, as well as some suggestions for resisting pernicious influences*

*Principal personages:*
> PHILIP ZIMBARDO, a Stanford psychology professor who led the Stanford prison experiment
> "JOHN WAYNE," an everyday college student turned abusive prison guard
> CHRISTINA MASLACH, a psychology student and Zimbardo's partner who brought an end to the experiment
> CARLO PRESCOTT, an ex-convict who served seventeen years in prison and who influenced Zimbardo's perspective on prisons
> IVAN "CHIP" FREDERICK, a U.S. Army soldier who abused Iraqi prisoners in Abu Ghraib prison and whose defense was supported by Zimbardo's expert testimony

In exploring human morality and temptation, Philip Zimbardo's *The Lucifer Effect: Understanding How Good People Turn Evil* labors in a field that has been tilled by almost every important figure in the Western canon, from the writers of the Old Testament to modern philosophers and psychologists. According to Zimbardo, the dominant modern perspective on evil is "dispositional": People commit evil because of some flaw in their characters, morals, or personalities, and therefore the only one at fault for an evil deed is the one who commits it. To Zimbardo, the Western emphasis on personal responsibility provides the basis for theory and practice in fields as diverse as education, medicine, psychiatry, religion, and criminal justice.

As Zimbardo contends, the emphasis on personal responsibility for evil is flawed for several reasons. First, almost a century's worth of research in social psychology demonstrates that people can be led to do a wide range of previously unthinkable actions when the conditions are right. Second, dispositional approaches lessen the responsibility of others to create social conditions that are fair, just, and workable. Also, the dispositional approach does very little to prevent future evil; removing bad apples from a barrel does not stop other apples from rotting. Finally, the dispositional approach does little to explain how ordinary people often commit acts of good in spite of pernicious social forces.

The title of *The Lucifer Effect* refers to an angel turned archfiend, a figure in Judeo-Christian religious thought whose story was described in the first few books of the landmark poem *Paradise Lost* (1667), by John Milton (1608-1674), the eminent

*Professor emeritus at Stanford University, Philip Zimbardo has published scholarly work, including numerous peer-reviewed articles and books. He has also hosted a public television series on psychology and testified as an expert witness in prisoner-abuse trials.*

seventeenth century English poet. Basing his poem on both canonical and apocryphal books of the Bible, Milton writes that Lucifer was once God's most beautiful and favored angel but became disgruntled by God's preferential love for humanity. In his pride, Lucifer rebelled, was cast out of heaven, and was transformed into the devil. Frustrated in his exile from heaven and aware that he could not win in open revolt against God, the devil's plans changed, to warp humanity into rejecting God. By secretly working on human beings, tempting them with half-truths and illusions, the archfiend works behind the scenes, subverting God's providence.

In offering this figure as symbolic, Zimbardo observes that each of us can easily become transformed into someone we would hardly recognize, choosing evil when before we would have considered ourselves wholly good. Similarly, the symbol illustrates Zimbardo's second point: People must remain watchful of the temptation to consider themselves stronger than their circumstances. These circumstances include letting the desire to be a part of a group outweigh our moral compasses, when we are led to believe that others will take responsibility for our actions, when we believe that we can act anonymously, and when we believe that those who suffer are not as important as ourselves.

In making the argument that circumstances matter, Zimbardo is not claiming that those who commit evil should not be blamed for it. In fact, he repeatedly expresses his belief that those who do wrong should face the consequences of their misdeeds. In addition to personal accountability, however, Zimbardo makes the commonsense claim that conditions influence personal choice and that we are all responsible for changing abusive, inhuman circumstances.

To support this claim, Zimbardo offers a wealth of evidence from social psychology. One of Zimbardo's more compelling examples of the power of situations to influence action comes from an experiment at Princeton University in 1973. Theology students at Princeton were asked by experimenters in the psychology department to deliver a sermon on the parable of the Good Samaritan from the Gospel of Luke in the New Testament. The parable describes the moral duty of good people to help others when they are in need.

The experiment, however, demonstrated the power of time pressures to make us ignore others' needs. Some theology students were told that they were late for the videotaping session and would have to hurry; other theology students were told they had a little more time; still others were told they had plenty of time. During the walk across campus, each theology student was confronted by a distressed stranger, calling for help. The vast majority of theology students in a hurry ignored the stranger, despite seemingly obvious parallels between the situation and the sermon they were pondering. This is the evil of inaction; the students in a hurry failed to help. In contrast, those students who believed they had more time were more likely to help. If theology students thinking about the Good Samaritan failed to resist time pressures, the rest of us are equally likely to let situations influence our actions.

Other, more dramatic studies in *The Lucifer Effect* go into greater detail about the blended guilt of those who do evil and those with power who allow it to continue. One example is Zimbardo's own Stanford prison experiment (SPE). As an experiment in the social sciences, the SPE was poorly designed and executed. As an example of how easily people can be led to commit evil and how evil those in power can be, however, the SPE warrants summary.

The idea for the SPE came at a time in America when abusive prison conditions were front-page news. Guards were frequently represented in popular literature and movies as natural sadists, prisoners as attractive antiheroes. In 1971, Zimbardo and colleagues decided to construct an experimental prison. They wanted to see whether the allegedly abusive conditions in prisons were due to supposed character traits of guards and criminals or inherent in the system itself.

For his part, Zimbardo believed and continues to believe that penal systems in the United States are inherently abusive, and his sympathies are with prisoners, reasons for incarceration notwithstanding. Usually, social scientists work to minimize such biases; for example, in this case, bias could have been minimized by using multiple small jails across the country to lessen the impact of Zimbardo's own preconceptions. This easy, if more expensive, step was not taken. In fact, experimenter bias was built into the experiment. In the months leading up to the SPE, Zimbardo cotaught a course in the psychology of imprisonment with Carlo Prescott, a San Francisco-area personality who had served seventeen years in prison for attempted murder. In an opinion piece he wrote for the *Stanford Daily* in 2005, Prescott claims that he gave Zimbardo the idea for many abusive techniques months before the SPE took place. Prescott claims that he took part in the SPE because he wanted to transform it into an indictment of the California prison system.

After building their own prison, Zimbardo and his colleagues placed advertisements in local newspapers, offering $15 per day for a two-week simulated study of prison life. Those who responded were given tests and interviews to weed out any violent tendencies, mental illness, or extreme points of view. The goal was to find as absolutely average a group of young men as possible. Those selected were randomly grouped into prisoners or guards.

Although some have suggested that the guards became abusive, the truth is Zimbardo required them to abuse from day one. There were no toilets in the prison, so guards were told to hood and chain prisoners before escorting them to the toilet in another part of the building. If given the ability to choose on their own, perhaps the guards would have decided on other, more ethical toileting techniques.

With abuse built into the system, it is not surprising that some guards took matters further. One third of the guards, especially one nicknamed "John Wayne," became creatively abusive, depriving the prisoners of self-respect, sanitation, nutrition, and adequate sleep. The threat of physical force was ever present. Zimbardo says that he prohibited physical violence, but he armed his guards with clubs. Throughout the experiment, Zimbardo and colleagues watched the guards use these clubs to intimidate the prisoners. It is doubtful the prisoners knew they would not be hit; certainly Zimbardo never told a guard to stop menacing the prisoners.

As some guards ramped up the abuse, some prisoners developed stress-related emotional problems, including psychotic symptoms. Within six days, the experiment had to be ended—not out of concern for the subjects but because Zimbardo's partner rightly pointed out that the SPE was inherently immoral. As he describes it, Zimbardo came to his senses and devoted his subsequent work to helping others break free of mental prisons of their own or others' making.

While the SPE fails as an experiment, it surely supports Zimbardo's claim that those who create abusive systems bear responsibility for what takes place within. He never hit, threatened, or deprived a student prisoner of sleep; but he designed the experiment, he failed to institute proper controls, and he failed to rein in the more abusive guards. He had the power to make things better and failed to do so.

Zimbardo's awareness of the power of abusive systems leads to his two final points in *The Lucifer Effect*. First, based on his awareness of guilt in creating the SPE, Zimbardo lays considerable blame on those who have power in the real world to harm or to heal. Much of the second half of *The Lucifer Effect* documents the guilt of members of the U.S. government, all the way up to President George W. Bush, for abuses that have been perpetrated in Iraqi prisons that first came to light in 2004. In that year, media around the world presented the dramatic news that American soldiers serving as prison guards at Abu Ghraib prison near Baghdad had been subjecting Iraqi prisoners to extreme physical and mental torture. Like most Americans, Zimbardo was repulsed by the news, angered about the abuse, about the conditions that led to abuse, and about the military's plans to scapegoat individual soldiers. One soldier, Ivan "Chip" Frederick, a country boy from Virginia with an almost pristine military record, was being represented as a particularly "bad apple." After reviewing available records and conducting interviews, Zimbardo served as an expert defense witness for Frederick, arguing that intolerable and stressful living conditions, an overcrowded prison, unclear guidelines, and malevolent leadership had to be taken into account when considering this one soldier's guilt.

To Zimbardo's credit, he does not end his book with a lengthy diatribe against the Bush administration or the military establishment, nor does he leave readers without suggestions for increasing their own capacity to perceive situational influence and resist it. Quite often, he claims, we are led to make bad choices when others we respect tell us a series of lies, including the lies that we are anonymous, that others will take responsibility for our actions. These others could be teachers, doctors, scientists, or military superiors. They can push us and lie to us, but we must never allow them to convince us that our actions are free of consequences.

*Michael R. Meyers*

## Review Sources

*Booklist* 103, no. 16 (April 15, 2007): 6.
*Discover* 28 (April, 2007): 68-69.
*Library Journal* 132, no. 5 (March 15, 2007): 83.
*The New Republic* 236, no. 16 (May 21, 2007): 51-55.
*Publishers Weekly* 254 (February 12, 2007): 74.
*The Times Higher Education Supplement*, April 6, 2007, p. 21.
*The Times Literary Supplement*, October 19, 2007, pp. 3-5.

# A MAGNIFICENT CATASTROPHE
## The Tumultuous Election of 1800,
## America's First Presidential Campaign

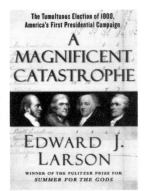

*Author:* Edward J. Larson (1953-    )
*Publisher:* Free Press (New York). 352 pp. $27.00
*Type of work:* History
*Time:* 1776-1801
*Locale:* The United States

*In the first contested election in U.S. history, and amid predictions of doom if the other won, Thomas Jefferson led radical Republicans to victory over Federalist incumbent president John Adams in a close contest decided in the House of Representatives*

Principal personages:
JOHN ADAMS (1735-1826), president of
    the United States, 1797-1801
THOMAS JEFFERSON (1743-1826), president of
    the United States, 1801-1809
AARON BURR (1756-1836), vice president of
    the United States, 1801-1805
CHARLES COTESWORTH PINCKNEY (1746-1825), Adams's
    Federalist running mate, 1800
THOMAS PINCKNEY (1750-1828), Adams's Federalist
    running mate, 1796
ALEXANDER HAMILTON (1755-1804), Federalist leader,
    secretary of the Treasury, 1789-1795
GEORGE WASHINGTON (1732-1799), president of
    the United States, 1789-1797
ABIGAIL ADAMS (1744-1818), Adams's wife

John Adams and Thomas Jefferson had been close collaborators and friends during the American Revolution, but in 1800 each headed opposing political parties. In 1776, both urged the Continental Congress to declare independence, and Adams served with Jefferson on the committee to write the Declaration of Independence, suggesting improvements to Jefferson's draft. As American diplomats in Europe after the peace, they supported each other's efforts, and the two families grew close. Abigail Adams aided Jefferson's daughter while Jefferson introduced young John Quincy Adams to the niceties of European diplomacy. Absent from the 1789 Constitutional Convention while serving in Europe, each supported the new Constitution with reservations; as Adams phrased it, he feared the rise of an aristocracy while Jefferson worried about the possibility of monarchy.

By 1800, what had seemed differences in emphasis had become unbridgeable chasms. The divergence began during George Washington's presidency, when Secretary of State Jefferson objected to the domestic policies of Secretary of Treasury Hamilton, which Jefferson thought favored wealthy, urban investors to the detriment of rural Americans. As Edward J. Larson points out, disagreements over domestic policy became highly emotional when they intersected with different reactions to the French Revolution. To Jeffersonians, it was a continuation and validation of the American Revolution as a world-altering event. Those who became the Federalists shuddered at French Revolutionary excesses, blaming extreme democracy. With one group favoring France in the European wars and the other England, each could accuse the other of treasonable conduct that threatened the survival of American independence.

~

*Edward J. Larson is professor of history and law at Pepperdine University. His previous books have dealt with issues of science and religion from a historical perspective, including* Trial and Error: The American Controversy over Creation and Evolution *(1985),* Evolution's Workshop: God and Science on the Galápagos Islands *(2001), and* Summer for the Gods: The Scopes Trial and America's Continuing Debate over Science and Religion *(1997), which won the 1998 Pulitzer Prize for history.*

~

Emotions became even more intemperate in 1798 when French depredations against American ships and requests that U.S. negotiators bribe their French counterparts led to an undeclared war with France. Congress appropriated funds to build warships. It increased the size of the army; George Washington accepted command and chose Hamilton as his deputy, putting him in charge. In the name of national security, a Sedition Act made criticism of the government and its officials a crime, but prosecution of opposition newspaper editors backfired, creating in the eyes of their supporters honorable martyrs for freedom of the press. In the 1798 election, war fever elected a large Federalist majority to the House of Representatives. Larson stresses that partisans on each side insisted the public faced a choice between order and liberty.

When news of Napoleon Bonaparte's 1799 coup d'etat reached the United States early in 1800, as Americans began to think about the coming presidential election, it confirmed prejudices on each side. Federalists, Larson notes, viewed the development as proving the weakness of excessive democracy; Jeffersonians stressed the dangers of a standing army, implicitly pointing to Hamilton's command of the U.S. Army.

Adams and Jefferson had been the leading candidates in 1796 when Washington retired. Adams received 71 votes from the 139 electors, Jefferson 68. Under the original Constitution, which did not separate votes for vice president from presidential votes, Jefferson became vice president. Hamilton, who thoroughly disliked Adams, covertly tried to sabotage his candidacy by urging electors to withhold votes for Adams, thereby putting his running mate, Thomas Pinckney, in the presidential chair. The plot backfired when New Englanders, angered over news of his plan, dumped Pinckney, permitting Jefferson to come in second. Parties were still evolving, and one elector in both Virginia and North Carolina deviated from otherwise solid Jeffersonian blocs by voting for Adams. Larson points out that Jefferson would have won if he had received the two votes, a possibility noted by his partisans, who determined to prevent such defections in the future.

Larson goes into great detail describing the variety of ways states organized in 1800. Republicans in Virginia created state and local campaign committees, the first signs of true party organization; similar groups appeared in Maryland and New Jersey.

In ten states, legislatures chose the electors. Of five states permitting voter choice, three (North Carolina, Kentucky, and Maryland) divided the state into districts, each selecting one elector, while two (Virginia and Rhode Island) asked voters to choose between statewide party lists. The Pennsylvania legislature, where the two houses were dominated by opposing parties, deadlocked over how to choose electors and nearly failed to participate in the election. Virginia switched from using separate districts to a general list for the entire state, to ensure that this time all its electoral votes would be cast for Jefferson. Massachusetts responded in kind, switching from separate districts to legislature choice to eliminate dissident votes.

Aaron Burr created an extensive organization in New York City, with groups in every precinct set to bring Republican voters to the polls in the April, 1800, legislative election. Winning the city's thirteen assembly seats created a Republican majority in the state legislature, guaranteeing that New York would vote for Jefferson in 1800, not Adams as it had in 1796. Larson points out that equally as important as Burr's machine in achieving that result was his success in getting eminent New Yorkers, including an ex-governor and a Revolutionary War general, to run for the lower house of legislature. In sharp contrast, Hamilton sponsored a Federalist slate of undistinguished personal loyalists.

Hamilton's opposition to Adams, covert in 1796, became overt in 1800. In May, convinced there was no danger of a French invasion, Adams disbanded the additional Army troops under Hamilton's command. He finally dismissed two cabinet members he had continued from the Washington administration, even though they were followers of Hamilton. Hamilton was furious. He decided to write an open letter virulently attacking Adams's fitness to be president, calling for Federalist electors to dump Adams in favor of his running mate, Charles Cotesworth Pinckney of South Carolina. Supposedly addressed only to Federalist worthies, the October letter (which ran fifty-four pages in a pamphlet edition) was widely reprinted in newspapers and hailed with glee by Republican editors who used it to discredit both author and target.

Partisans shamelessly launched personal attacks on their opponents. Republicans accused Adams of wanting to replace the republic with a monarchy and of moral misconduct in the White House. Abigail Adams never fully forgave Jefferson for the way his partisans slandered her husband. Federalists endlessly assailed Jefferson as an atheist who threatened the morals of the nation and was unfit to occupy the presidential chair.

Larson keeps a running total of the voting as states finally choose their electors. He calculates that by November 19, when Rhode Island voters chose four Federalist electors, Adams and Pinckney had 58 votes pledged to them, Jefferson and Burr 57. Pennsylvania's legislature was still deadlocked, and South Carolina's would not meet until

November 24, nine days before the electoral deadline of December 3. Pennsylvanians finally compromised and split their votes, eight for Jefferson and Burr, seven for Adams and Pinckney, leaving the four tied at 65 votes each. South Carolina, where party loyalties were still fluid, would decide the election.

In 1796, South Carolina's legislature had chosen electors committed to voting for Jefferson and Adams's Federalist running mate, South Carolinian Thomas Pinckney. If this year they chose Jefferson and favorite son Charles Cotesworth Pinckney, Adams and Burr would be eliminated, and Jefferson and Pinckney would each have 73 votes, with the final decision left to the House of Representatives. Hamilton's letter now had the reverse of his intended effect: It led Pinckney to insist that, as a matter of personal honor, he wanted votes only from electors pledged to both Adams and himself. The legislature bowed to his wishes, and South Carolina's eight votes went to Jefferson and Burr.

The electoral votes would not be officially counted until Congress convened in March, but as word of what electors had actually done trickled into Washington, it became apparent that Republicans had blundered by failing to differentiate their presidential and vice presidential candidates. Federalist electors had withheld one vote from Pinckney, giving Adams 65 votes to Pinckney's 64, but Republicans cast 73 votes for both Jefferson and Burr.

The Constitution provided that in case of a tie, the House would vote by states, each state casting one vote, with a majority of states necessary to win. The House in March, 1801, was still the one elected in 1798; the winners of the 1800 election, dominated by Republicans, would not take office until December. Jefferson needed to carry nine of the sixteen states, but Republicans were a majority in only eight. Two states (Maryland and Vermont) were equally divided and could not cast a vote. The six states with a Federalist majority all supported Burr.

At first, Burr congratulated Jefferson on his victory, but when he learned of the electoral tie he became strategically silent. Larson believes most Federalists despised Burr as an unprincipled adventurer, but they hated Jefferson. Hamilton tried to intervene against Burr, but he had little credibility left. The deadlock lasted thirty-four ballots. Rumors had Pennsylvania and Virginia militias poised to descend on Washington if Congress failed to confirm Jefferson's victory. When it became clear that Burr would make no promises, the sole congressman from Delaware decided to abstain, and Federalists in Maryland and Vermont followed his lead, delivering those two states to Jefferson, who received ten votes on the thirty-fifth ballot. No Federalist voted for Jefferson—the Connecticut, Massachusetts, New Hampshire, and Rhode Island delegations voted for Burr to the bitter end while other Federalists abstained rather than vote for their detested opponent.

Larson provides a clear, detailed narrative of this crucial election. He did not engage in archival research, but made very effective use of the many scholarly editions of letters and documents dealing with the early republic now available. Unfortunately, Larson's stress on details tends to drain away the drama from the events he records; the highly emotional reactions of the participants are mentioned, rather than shown.

There are two minor slips in *A Magnificent Catastrophe: The Tumultuous Election of 1800, America's First Presidential Campaign*. The United States did not send ambassadors to foreign countries in the eighteenth or early nineteenth centuries as Larson assumes, but chose the more republican title of minister for its emissaries. Surprising for a law professor is his assertion that the Constitution provides for the president pro tempore of the Senate to become acting president in the absence of a president and vice president; in fact, the succession when there is no vice president is set by act of Congress.

For Larson, the major significance of the 1800 election is the arrival of a two-party system. Equally important is the example set. For the first time, an opposition peacefully replaced an administration in power—despite apocalyptic rhetoric, no one had to be killed, no one sent into exile—a precedent the American republic would follow for succeeding centuries.

*Milton Berman*

## Review Sources

*The American Scholar* 76, no. 4 (Fall, 2007): 129-131.
*Booklist* 103, no. 21 (July 1, 2007): 24.
*The Christian Science Monitor*, September 18, 2007, p. 14.
*Entertainment Weekly*, no. 957 (October 5, 2007): 75.
*Kirkus Reviews* 75, no. 12 (June 15, 2007): 593.
*Library Journal* 132, no. 12 (July 15, 2007): 103-104.
*The New York Times Book Review* 157 (December 16, 2007): 28.
*The New Yorker* 83, no. 27 (September 17, 2007): 94-98.
*Publishers Weekly* 254, no. 21 (May 21, 2007): 43-44.

# THE MAIAS
## Episodes from Romantic Life

*Author:* José Maria Eça de Queirós (1845-1900)
*First published: Os Maias: Episódios da vida romântica,*
  1888, in Portugal
Translated from the Portuguese by Margaret Jull Costa
*Publisher:* New Directions (New York). 628 pp. $17.95
*Type of work:* Novel
*Time:* The end of the 1800's
*Locale:* Portugal

*Eça de Queirós traces three generations of a wealthy
Portuguese family, as they cease to hold on to their moral
and principled roots and sink into idleness and decadence,
to metaphorically illustrate a similar movement throughout Portugal and nineteenth century Europe*

*Principal characters:*
  CARLOS DA MAIA, a wealthy young Lisbon doctor
  ALFONSO DA MAIA, his grandfather, who raises him
  PEDRO DA MAIA, Carlos's father, who committed suicide
  MARIA MONFORTE DA MAIA, Carlos's mother, who abandoned him
    as a child
  JOÃO DA EGA, Carlos's best friend
  MARIA EDUARDA, Carlos's lover and sister
  DÁMASO SALCEDE, Carlos's pompous enemy
  VILACA, the Maias' family financial administrator

Margaret Jull Costa's translation of José Maria Eça de Queirós's *The Maias: Episodes from Romantic Life* has been hailed by such literary critics as Harold Bloom as infinitely more readable than the other versions of this nineteenth century Portuguese masterpiece available in English. They agree that it will no doubt become the standard translation.

Set in Lisbon at the close of the nineteenth century, *The Maias* can be viewed as a classic bildungsroman, or coming-of-age novel. Carlos da Maia, the novel's young hero and the heir to one of Portugal's greatest fortunes, has been living a petty, idle life of parties, fine wine, and romantic intrigue. Suddenly, he is forced to learn that all the money in the world cannot buy happiness and to accept the fact that actions have consequences, even though it might take generations for the results of irresponsible conduct to come to light.

Carlos grows up under the tutelage of his illustrious, highly principled and loving grandfather, Alfonso da Maia, after his father Pedro da Maia commits suicide in "romantic" desperation upon the departure of his beautiful and mysterious wife, Maria Monforte, with a man simply called the Italian. Maria takes with her Carlos's

*José Maria Eça de Queirós, who has been called one of the leading intellectuals of his era, wrote twenty books and introduced naturalism and realism to Portuguese literature. He founded literary reviews and worked as a diplomat throughout his life, living in Havana, London, and Paris. In 1878, while serving in the Portuguese consulate in England, he began work on his masterpiece,* The Maias. *He died of tuberculosis in 1900.*

sister, Maria Eduarda, whom she favors, but leaves Carlos behind in the care of his father. Knowing full well the horrific family drama, and in time coming to learn that his sister has died, Carlos grows up and flourishes at the hands of his attentive grandfather, who takes solace in his grandson as the youngster grows in kindness and character.

Although he is heir to one of Portugal's largest family fortunes, Carlos applies himself to his education and decides on a career in medicine to help his fellow human beings. However, despite his high intelligence and his well-meaning plans, after his return from the University of Coimbra to Lisbon, he soon falls into the opulent lifestyle of the city's upper crust. Sleeping until all hours, dressing luxuriously, lunching for hours, dining and drinking well into the night, attending the theater, and conducting casual sexual rendezvous in carriages with the wives of the local nobility take up all his time. He never gets around to establishing a list of patients, not to mention writing medical treatises or helping his fellow man. His offices in time become merely well-decorated meeting places for his long list of dandified acquaintances.

Chief among these friends is João da Ega, who, after being cast aside by the love of his life, spends most of his time at the Maias' richly decorated compound known as Ramalhete in the neighborhood of Janelas Verdes on the outskirts of Lisbon. Another friend, Dámaso Salcede, uses women for social gain. When these young, fashionable men tire of women, they coldly cast them aside and get angry when the women make a scene or have the effrontery to tell them they love them. Despite numerous affairs, Carlos has never been in love and looks askance at men who feel passion and devotion. However, this is shortly to change.

Meanwhile, Carlos's grandfather feels deeply disappointed by his grandson's behavior but remains patiently waiting in the family dwelling, in Olivas, for his sole heir to put aside childish things and grow up. Although he may not be ready, life will soon hit Carlos da Maia over the head and he will fall down hard.

The main plot of the novel begins one night when Carlos spies a beautiful, sophisticated-looking woman who, his pompous friend Dámaso tells him, is Maria Gomez, newly arrived from Brazil with her husband, Castro Gomez, and young daughter, Rosa. The boastful Dámaso promises Carlos an introduction but fails to deliver. When Carlos is called to attend the Gomez family's governess, Miss Sarah, Maria and Carlos instantly connect and begin an affair after the husband returns to Brazil. Carlos buys an idyllic summer home in the forest, and Maria and Rosa move in. The couple are ecstatically happy and plan to run away together—that is, until Castro returns and informs Carlos that Maria is merely his mistress, not his wife, and that, in fact, she was earlier the mistress of another man named MacGren.

Carlos is deeply angry and swears to have nothing to do with Maria until he hears the story of Maria's wretched life.

Earlier, in Brazil, young Maria had sunk into poverty in the company of her mother, who had led a fast life of luxury with a variety of men until her good looks and health failed her. Literally left with nothing to eat, Maria is forced to live with an Irish military man named MacGren, to whom she becomes engaged. She gives birth to Rosa before MacGren can marry her, and he dies in action, leaving her penniless. Forced then to take up with Castro Gomez, she pretends to be his wife to make social encounters easier. Carlos is deeply saddened by Maria's story, and, after his anger disappears, he asks her to marry him. The happy couple plan to leave Portugal permanently, but Carlos is troubled by how this decision will affect his grandfather. Soon, critical remarks about Maria begin to appear in the local gossip newspapers, and Carlos is forced to confront his jealous former friend Dámaso for planting the salacious items. A duel is proposed, but Ega manages to negotiate for a written retraction instead. Dámaso must explain in writing that when he made the accusations against Maria he was drunk and, furthermore, that he comes from a family of drunks.

One evening, with Ega in tow, Carlos attends the theater to hear a friend's vocal performance and here meets Dámaso's uncle, who has taken offense at his nephew's written remarks about his drunken family. Ega manages to soothe the uncle, and soon they begin a friendly conversation about the da Maia family. At the end of the evening, Dámaso's uncle, who heartily dislikes his nephew, asks Ega to return a box of papers given to him years before by Carlos's mother. He mentions to Ega that he is making this request because he had seen young Maria and her brother in a carriage and that he was glad the two were finally reconciled. At first, Ega is puzzled. Then the dreadful truth dawns on him.

After checking that the older man could not possibly be mistaken about the identities of those involved, Ega is forced to accept the fact that his best friend has unknowingly been having an incestuous affair with his own sister. He ponders how to tell Carlos without having him commit suicide like his father. Finally, Ega confides in Vilaca, the Maias' financial administrator, and both men approach Carlos with the news and the evidential box of papers that includes a note verifying the truth from Carlos and Maria's own mother.

Carlos is beyond despair. At first he attempts never to see Maria, the sister whom he believed to be dead. However, he gives in to his passion and sleeps with her, knowing full well that she is his sister. Worse still is the realization that his grandfather knows the truth. Carlos is devastated after his deeply saddened grandfather is found dead in the garden. After a while, Maria is made aware of the truth, and it is she— far wealthier now since she is entitled to half the da Maia estate—who takes matters into her own hands by returning to Brazil with her daughter. Carlos and Ega and friends begin an extended journey around the world.

It takes an aging Carlos ten years to find the courage to return to Lisbon, the site of all his youthful troubles. He is worn out with traveling and finally acknowledges that all he wants is peace.

At the end of the novel, in the year 1887, the world of horse-drawn carriages is dying out and the twentieth century is burgeoning. Despite their unlimited opportunities, neither Carlos nor Ega have fulfilled their youthful ambitions. Ega has not become a famous writer or literary critic; Carlos has wasted his medical education. He no longer treats patients and has even failed to write his promised medical treatise. As the now middle-aged friends ponder the past, a tram passes, and the men run frantically, hoping they might still catch it. The reader is left wondering whether Carlos and Ega will be able to catch up, not only to the modern-world tram but also with their lives. Will they grab the only chance they have left, or will they fail yet again and remain stuck in the regret of what might have been?

In his comprehensive portrayal of nineteenth century Portuguese politics and social history, Eça de Queirós, Portugal's greatest nineteenth century novelist, was influenced by both naturalism and Romanticism. The author, who sought to bring about social reform through writing literature, utilizes satire and an air of detached irony to dissect, layer upon decadent layer, the social strata of his day by brilliantly evoking, and simultaneously condemning, slow-to-change Portuguese society.

Thematically, *The Maias* deals with regret, not just in the sense of Carlos's impossible love for his sister but also over the fact that Portugal, once a great imperial power, has declined in glory in the eyes of the world. Gradually undermined by duplicity, complacency, and sexual license, the Maia fortune has continued to diminish over three generations. Similarly, Portugal has, as Eça de Queirós would argue, sunk from grandeur into scarcity.

Overall, the novel illustrates the debauched lifestyle of the well-to-do in nineteenth century Portugal. It criticizes the decadent manner of living that did not confine itself solely to Portugal but spread insidiously throughout most of Europe and culminated in the rise of totalitarianism, both world wars, and the emergence, in this case, of Portugal's fascist dictator, António de Oliveira Salazar (1889-1970).

Footnotes to help decipher the Portuguese history and cultural references would have proved helpful. Otherwise, readers might benefit from reading a brief overview of nineteenth century Portuguese history before beginning the novel.

*M. Casey Diana*

## Review Sources

*Kirkus Reviews* 75, no. 9 (May 1, 2007): 410.
*Library Journal* 132, no. 13 (August 1, 2007): 66.
*London Review of Books* 30, no. 1 (January 3, 2008): 13-14.
*The Nation* 285, no. 18 (December 3, 2007): 23-28.
*The New York Times Book Review* 156 (September 2, 2007): 6.

# MAKING MONEY

*Author:* Terry Pratchett (1948-    )
*Publisher:* HarperCollins (New York). 394 pp. $25.95
*Type of work:* Novel
*Locale:* Ankh-Morpork, the largest, dirtiest, and oldest
city on Discworld

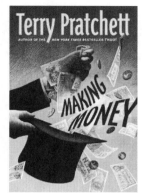

*Moist von Lipwig is a former con artist and current
postmaster of the city-state of Ankh-Morpork when he reluctantly becomes the city's leading banker and head of the
mint, where he revolutionizes the city's economy by introducing the concept of paper money*

*Principal characters:*
 MOIST VON LIPWIG, postmaster general of
   Ankh-Morpork
 ADORA "SPIKE" BELLE DEARHEART, von Lipwig's fiancé
 LORD HAVELOCK VETINARI, ruler of Ankh-Morpork
 TOPSY TURVY LAVISH, owner of 50 percent of the Royal Bank
 MR. FUSSPOT, friendly mongrel dog, owner of 1 percent of the
   Royal Bank, and heir to Topsy's share
 MAVOLIO BENT, chief cashier of the Royal Bank
 COSMO LAVISH, Topsy's nephew by marriage
 PUCCI LAVISH, Topsy's niece by marriage
 CRIBBINS, con artist masquerading as a priest of Om
 HUBERT TURVY, the bank's chief economist and Topsy's nephew
   by blood
 IGOR, Hubert's assistant
 PROFESSOR FLEAD, ghost of a three-hundred-years-dead wizard
   who was an expert on golems
 GLADYS, a female golem

Before J. K. Rowling introduced the enormously successful Harry Potter series,
Terry Pratchett was the best-selling author in the United Kingdom and is best known
for his Discworld fantasy series. There have been more than thirty books in the series
since the first novel, *The Colour of Magic*, was published in 1983. The authors parodied in the various books include J. R. R. Tolkien, Robert E. Howard, H. P. Lovecraft,
William Shakespeare, Ayn Rand, and many others. *Making Money* is the second
novel in the series to feature Moist von Lipwig, introduced in *Going Postal* (2004),
and there is a hint at the end of *Making Money* that he will return in a future book.
Normally, each of the Discworld books stands on its own and can be read in any order.
However, in this case, readers would be better served if they read *Going Postal* first.
*Going Postal* and *Making Money* are also atypical Discworld books in that they are
divided into chapters.

*Terry Pratchett's novels have sold more than forty-five million copies worldwide in thirty-five languages. His first short story was published when he was thirteen and his first book when he was twenty.* Making Money *is the thirty-sixth novel in the Discworld series.*

Discworld is a satirical fantasy universe in which the world is flat and disk-shaped. It is balanced on the backs of four gigantic elephants who themselves stand on the back of an even more gigantic turtle, Great A'Tuin, who swims through space. In this universe, magic works, and there are magical creatures such as golems, werewolves, trolls, and vampires. In *Making Money*, a group of wizards, called the Department of Postmortem Communications at the Unseen University, summon the ghost of Professor Flead, a wizard who has been dead for three hundred years. This ghost takes a lecherous interest in von Lipwig's girlfriend and likes to haunt the Pink Pussycat Club, Ankh-Morpork's leading exotic-dancing club, where he occupies seat number seven in the center of the front row.

Golems, creatures created from clay, play a particularly important role in both *Going Postal* and *Making Money*. On Discworld, they are traditionally slaves who do not require food, drink, sleep, sex, or vacations. They cannot die of natural causes and are extremely difficult to kill. Anghammarad, a golem in *Going Postal*, for example, is 19,000 years old. Although there is a strong golems' rights movement to grant them freedom and equality, they still compete with humans for jobs at the low end of the pay scale, if only to raise the money to buy other golems their freedom. In *Going Postal*, the most prominent golem is Mr. Pump, who received his name after tending a water pump one hundred feet underground for twenty-four hours a day, seven days a week, for 240 years without a break. His only job is to be von Lipwig's parole officer. Adora Belle Dearheart (nicknamed "Spike"), von Lipwig's girlfriend, works for the Golem Trust, a charity that finds golems, sets them free, and ensures that they have decent working conditions. She makes sure that Mr. Pump and the other golems get at least one day off each week, even if they do not know what to do with their leisure time.

In *Making Money*, the most prominent golem is Gladys, first introduced in *Going Postal*. In the earlier novel, Miss Maccalariat, the senior female post office employee, insisted that only a female golem be allowed to clean the ladies' restroom. (Miss Maccalariat also objects to hiring female dwarfs, because their beards make them impossible to distinguish from the male dwarfs, who might then sneak into the restroom for a peak at half-dressed human females.) The problem with determining golem gender is that golems do not have any sex organs; they are neither male nor female. Traditionally, they are referred to as male. Von Lipwig, as head of the post office, addresses the problem by selecting a seven-foot-tall golem, renaming it Gladys, and having it wear a dress. By *Making Money*, Gladys has acquired female gender by reading publications such as *Ladies' Own Magazine*, studying women's fashions, learning to cook, and listening to the conversations that women have among themselves. She also acts as a mother figure to von Lipwig, making sure that he eats regularly and gets enough sleep. However, her one attempt at giving von Lipwig a backrub almost kills him, because she does not know her own strength.

*Making Money* is one of the many Discworld books set primarily in Ankh-Morpork, a city-state known for its pollution and corruption and the largest on Discworld. Pratchett patterned it after Tallinn and Prague, with elements of eighteenth century London, nineteenth century Seattle, and twentieth century New York City. Its nickname is the "Big Wahoonie." It is also home to the Unseen University, where wizards learn magic.

The Machiavellian ruler of Ankh-Morpork is Lord Havelock Vetinari, called the Patrician. He is a tyrant in the sense that there are no laws to restrain him. His only restraint is his own intelligence, which tells him that instead of ordering people around, it is better in the long run to persuade them that they really want what he wants. An example is von Lipwig in both *Going Postal* and *Making Money*. In the first book, Vetinari makes him an offer he cannot refuse, a choice between death by hanging and becoming postmaster general of Ankh-Morpork. (Capital punishment for relatively minor offenses such as swindling is normal for Ankh-Morpork.) Vetinari felt that von Lipwig's experience as a con artist was good preparation for becoming a government official. Although von Lipwig tries to find a third alternative, he is eventually convinced that he will live at least a little longer if he becomes postmaster. He is successful in introducing the concept of postage, thereby spawning the hobby of stamp collecting and reinstituting the practice of actually delivering the mail to the people to whom it is addressed. As a sign of his office, he wears a golden suit, which also has significance at the end of *Making Money*.

At the beginning of the latest novel, von Lipwig is still the postmaster of Ankh-Morpork, but his success has left him bored with his life. Before the events in *Going Postal*, he was a swindler—a thrilling livelihood, since the smallest mistake could cost him his life. Through the manipulations of Vetinari, von Lipwig now becomes Master of the Royal Mint and the effective head of the Royal Bank. The mint is in especially bad shape because it costs more than a penny to manufacture one. Von Lipwig revolutionizes the economy by introducing the concept of paper money, for which he has to set up a printing and engraving operation in the bank. One challenge is that the city's best artist is on death row for counterfeiting stamps, so von Lipwig arranges for his escape and hides him in the bank. One of von Lipwig's opponents is Mavolio Bent, the bank's chief cashier, who believes that only gold is real money. Bent lives in a modest room in a boarding house, dislikes the theater, poetry, music, or any other art, and has no sense of humor or social life. Some of his subordinates at the bank suspect him of being a vampire, but he has a secret that he considers to be even more shameful.

Near the beginning of the book, Topsy Turvy Lavish, matriarch of the Lavish banking family, is visited by Death, a recurring character in the series who takes people's souls to the afterlife. In her will, she leaves a controlling interest in the Royal

Bank to her dog, Mr. Fusspot, the smallest and ugliest dog Lipwig has ever seen. Her will also makes von Lipwig the dog's guardian. Von Lipwig has two incentives to accept the post. First, there is an annual fee, and von Lipwig has no aversion to taking money. Second, Ms. Lavish placed a deposit with the Assassins' Guild for them to kill von Lipwig if Mr. Fusspot dies of unnatural causes.

Cosmo and Pucci Lavish, Topsy's nephew and niece, respectively, both live lavish lifestyles and were the reason Topsy always kept two loaded crossbows on her desk. They are to inherit Mr. Fusspot's share of the bank if the dog dies and would not grieve were von Lipwig to meet an untimely death. Cosmo also has ambitions to replace Lord Vetinari as the city tyrant.

Von Lipwig causes some trouble for himself when he accepts the bank's valuation of its gold reserve on face value, and the authorities discover that there is much less gold in the vault than there is supposed to be. Another problem arises with the appearance of Cribbins, a man who knew von Lipwig ten years ago when he went by the alias of Albert Spangler. Masquerading as a priest of Om, Cribbins intends to blackmail von Lipwig, as he needs money to replace his malfunctioning set of false teeth.

Pratchett satirizes economists by introducing the Glooper, a mechanical model of the Ankh-Morpork economy that is so accurate that it causes economic change. Pratchett based it on the Phillips Economic Computer, built in 1949 and based on hydraulics. The Glooper is tended by Hubert Turvy, who is portrayed as a mad scientist, and his assistant, Igor. Igors, creatures made from dead people's body parts, are recurring characters in the series. They are all named Igor, talk in lisps, limp, and sneak up behind people. They also tend to get nervous if their masters display any signs of sanity or rationality.

One of Pratchett's techniques is to provide background information on the world by means of footnotes. In this novel, he uses them to explain a tabloid, the Blind Letter Office, dwarfs, a fee, assassin clothing, the kind of people who employ Igors, a food called minced collops, an offense called "wasting watch time," lawyers, guarding, the advantage of committees over the iron maiden, crossword puzzles, and costs.

Pratchett writes in the tradition of Jonathan Swift, P. G. Wodehouse, Evelyn Waugh, and other British satirists. In this book, he satirizes modern concepts of money and banking. The series is also in the tradition of nineteenth century English novels such as those by Anthony Trollope, with their detailed descriptions of urban landscapes. However, this novel does not have the narrative drive of other books in the series. Furthermore, there is very little character development. Except for Gladys, all the major characters are essentially the same people at the end of the book as they were at the beginning.

*Thomas R. Feller*

## Review Sources

*Booklist* 103, no. 22 (August 1, 2007): 9.
*Kirkus Reviews* 75, no. 15 (August 1, 2007): 749.
*Library Journal* 132, no. 17 (October 15, 2007): 60.
*Publishers Weekly* 254, no. 32 (August 13, 2007): 43.
*USA Today*, November 8, 2007, p. D5.
*The Washington Post*, September 20, 2007, p. C5.

# THE MAYTREES

*Author:* Annie Dillard (1945-      )
*Publisher:* HarperCollins (New York). 216 pp. $24.95
*Type of work:* Novel
*Time:* About 1945 to 2000
*Locale:* Provincetown, Massachusetts, and Camden,
Maine

*The story of one couple's lifelong relationship amid the
artistic community of Provincetown, Massachusetts*

Principal characters:
TOBY MAYTREE, poet and carpenter
LOU BIGELOW MAYTREE, his wife
DEARY HIGHTOE, his second wife

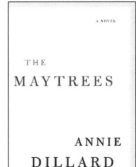

Annie Dillard has consistently held a high place in American letters since the publication of her first book, *Tickets for a Prayer Wheel* (1974), when she was still in her twenties. This is despite the fact that her publications tend to be brief, infrequent, and distributed over a wide range of genres, in both fiction and nonfiction. What is common to all of them is a poet's skill in the use of figurative language, a passion for the natural world, and a philosopher's sense of humanity's place in the cosmos. In her best-known work, *Pilgrim at Tinker Creek* (1974), Dillard chronicled the wonder and terror of the natural world at the edge of civilization in Roanoke Valley, Virginia. Like her literary predecessor, Henry David Thoreau at Walden Pond, Dillard is obsessed with humanity's intersection with nature as she observes the process from the margins of society. This is no less true of *The Maytrees*, a novel set among the bohemians of Provincetown, Massachusetts, in the decades following World War II. *Pilgrim at Tinker Creek* revealed her fascination with Thoreau's life in a cabin at the edge of town; *The Maytrees* demonstrates that this idea is still a potent stimulus for her imagination.

In their shack by the sea, Toby and Lou Bigelow Maytree are outsiders in bohemian Provincetown, which is itself a repository of outsiders. In her portrayal of this independent community, Dillard emphasizes that these characters bring the same sense of originality to their lives that they invest in their art. This is implied in the naming of her characters. On one side of the spectrum, there are writers for whom a character's name evokes little interest beyond its utilitarian value: a signifier for someone who plays a role in a story. At the opposite end of the literary continuum are the writers who employ naming as a means of revealing a character's role or his or her inner life. Ishmael, for example, is an appropriate name for the narrator of Herman Melville's *Moby-Dick* (1851) because he, like the biblical character of the same name, is an outcast. Dillard, on the other hand, takes a somewhat different approach. The singular nature of the inhabitants of this artistic community is embodied in their names: Deary Hightoe, Reevadare Weaver, Cornelius Blue, Sooner Roy.

The oddness of the names is also due in part to their high vowel content—not a minor matter to a poet as skilled as Dillard.

Indeed, Dillard brings a poet's sensibility to the overall structure of the novel. At just over two hundred pages in length, *The Maytrees* is a lightweight in the world of modern fiction; if it were any shorter, it would qualify as a novella. In spite of its brevity, however, Dillard imposes a formal structure on her novel worthy of an epic narrative. In addition to the prologue, there are three numbered parts and a concluding epilogue. In formal terms, Dillard appears to be building a modest cottage with walls as thick as a fortress. It serves a function, but it initially seems out of proportion to the narrative she seeks to relate. This can be partly accounted for by the fact she often brings a skewed sense of proportion to her best writing. In *Pilgrim at Tinker Creek*, for example, the devouring of a tiny toad by a large insect triggers a wave of shock and horror in the narrator that permeates much

*Annie Dillard gained early fame in 1974 with the publication of the poetry collection* Tickets for a Prayer Wheel *and* Pilgrim at Tinker Creek, *which won the Pulitzer Prize and became the first volume in a trilogy that includes* Holy the Firm *(1977) and* For the Time Being *(1999). Dillard was elected to the American Academy of Arts and Letters in 1999.*

of the rest of the book. Again, the key to understanding Dillard's reasoning lies in the fact that this is a prose work by an accomplished poet. One should keep in mind that in a poem—even a brief poem—structure is both visually and aesthetically important, from the lines within a stanza to the grouping of stanzas into named sections. The density of the prose, moreover, often belies the brevity of the book. Thus, the initial impression of an oversized structure for such a small book is one that soon dissipates.

The plot itself is simple enough: A prologue follows the Maytrees as their romance progresses into marriage and a child; part 1 focuses on the breakup of the relationship as Toby Maytree falls in love with Deary Hightoe; part 2 finds Lou living alone and Toby in his second marriage; part 3 and the epilogue find Toby and Lou back together again. All of this sounds like a cliché, like a typical popular romance really, and it does not do justice to Dillard's carefully crafted prose.

What enables Dillard's work to succeed and hold the reader's attention is the power and originality of her language. When Toby first meets Lou, Dillard reveals the signal importance of the event in words so poetic they could easily be set into a stanza: "She was young and broad of mouth and eye and jaw, fresh, solid and airy, as if light rays worked her instead of muscles." It is a striking image of the character, one that works on more than one level. On the surface, it is a physical description of Lou Bigelow, one that captures some essential aspects of her appearance. Dillard is letting the reader know that, far from being the musings of an omniscient narrator, the passage implies that this is a view of Lou as perceived by the poet Toby Maytree. The succeeding passage confirms this: "Oh, how a poet is a sap; he knew it." Given Dillard's skill as a poet, it is also a deliciously ironic comment regarding her own craft.

On a deeper level, one can recognize some significant characteristics of Dillard's writing, telltale points that recur throughout her prior works as well as *The Maytrees*. Note that the comment on the broadness of Lou's facial features proceeds to the simile that likens her to light rays. Upon first reading, this perception of Lou seems flawed in its contradictory union of the concepts of solidity and airiness. In one sense, the description works within the context of the scene because its contradictory nature seems to capture the tumultuousness of love at first sight, but Dillard has consistently used such oppositional imagery throughout her long career. In *Pilgrim at Tinker Creek*, for example, she says of a monarch butterfly that it "climbed a hill by falling still." The key to understanding the description about Lou lies in the simile to which it is tied. The invocation of light undoubtedly reflects Toby's budding affection, but it also calls to mind the fundamental properties of light itself: It exhibits the characteristics of both waves (airiness) and particles (solidity). Unlike many poets, Dillard does not make a distinction between art and science. In her best works, the facts of modern science often form the basis for much of her imagery. In preparing for the writing of *Pilgrim at Tinker Creek*, she read widely in the physical sciences and frequently invoked statistics when describing nature. Of course, a bare recitation of facts and figures would be out of place in a novel. Even so, Dillard has thoroughly immersed herself in the formal study of the physical world, and it is something that suffuses the novel.

Her intensive study in the sciences often produces imagery so startling that it threatens to overpower the very story it is intended to relate. Early in the novel, Dillard tries to convey Toby's growing affection for the beautiful young Lou. When describing Toby's attraction to her, Dillard states that in Lou's absence he "felt like one of two pieces of electrical tape pulled part." This is a risky approach to writing fiction, one that proves beyond question that Dillard is more concerned with her craft than with pleasing the masses. It is such an arresting image that, rather than just conveying Toby's feelings, it focuses the reader's attention more on the simile than on what it is intended to represent. The same effect occurs late in the book when Toby returns to Provincetown and Lou after an absence of twenty years. Rather than simply indicate that he is now wrinkled with age, the text states that Lou "saw parallel lines in his cheeks like presliced bacon." Not only does the imagery tend to overwhelm these somewhat shadowy characters, it also makes them seem less human at times. Dillard is too skilled a writer for this to be an oversight, and it is obvious that she never intended to dash off a conventional romance.

If there is a certain flatness to Dillard's characters, it can be explained in part by the role of nature in the novel. In *For the Time Being* (1999), references to sand and clouds appear with such frequency that they almost function as recurring characters. A similar effect also occurs in *The Maytrees*, where once again nature seems to vie for equal attention with the novel's protagonists. Although the book is nominally set in Provincetown, what action there is mostly takes place on the beach, a beach so isolated that it offers a perfect view of sand, ocean, clouds, and stars, but nothing of the town itself. Nature is always in a state of flux, but under such conditions one is confronted with an ever-mutating panorama of color, light, water, and earth. Conversely, if the scene is perpetually in motion, it also presents the viewer with the antithetical property of stasis. As Dillard herself succinctly states, "Each offshore surf line contained commotion but got nowhere, like someone's reading the same line over and over." Given this majestic backdrop of the larger forces of nature, the usual conflicts that drive fiction—particularly romantic fiction—tend to pale in comparison. This is apparent when Toby abandons his wife and young child for another woman after some fourteen years of marriage. In most fictional renderings of the subject, a writer would seek to wring every last particle of emotion from the breakup and follow the shock waves as they impact both major and minor characters. Dillard, however, creates a character in Lou who bears no malice toward her former husband, and their prior relationship resumes as though no breakup ever occurred. To Dillard, the pattern of relationship formation and severance is no different than the ever-repeating patterns of nature.

Even though the plot revolves around the relationship between Lou and Toby, and the novel devotes about equal time to each of them when they live separate lives, it is Lou who emerges as the central character in the novel. As taciturn as she is beautiful, it is she rather than her poet husband who absorbs the lessons of nature and accepts the vicissitudes of life with philosophical calm. That Dillard succeeds so well in treading such difficult ground is a tribute to her formidable talent as a writer. With its deep wisdom and memorable imagery, *The Maytrees* will appeal to serious readers everywhere.

*Cliff Prewencki*

## Review Sources

*The Atlantic Monthly* 300, no. 2 (September, 2007): 130.
*Booklist* 103, no. 11 (February 1, 2007): 4.
*The Christian Century* 124, no. 21 (October 16, 2007): 45-46.
*Entertainment Weekly*, no. 939 (June 15, 2007): 81.
*Library Journal* 132, no. 5 (March 15, 2007): 56.
*London Review of Books* 30, no. 1 (January 3, 2008): 34-35.
*The New York Times Book Review* 156 (July 29, 2007): 12-13.
*People* 67, no. 24 (June 18, 2007): 50.
*Publishers Weekly* 254, no. 6 (February 5, 2007): 36.

# MIYAZAWA KENJI
## Selections

*Author:* Kenji Miyazawa (1896-1933)
Translated from the Japanese by Hiroaki Sato
Foreword by Geoffrey O'Brien
*Publisher:* University of California Press (Berkeley).
248 pp. $19.95
*Type of work:* Poetry
*Time:* The 1920's to the early 1930's
*Locale:* Japan

*The Buddhist poems of Kenji Miyazawa capture the imagination of the reader with their moving promotion of mental tranquility in the face of personal suffering, their modern evocation of humanity's place in the cosmos, often exemplified by the landscape of northeast Japan, and their reflections on human folly*

Principal characters:
THE PERSONA, an often autobiographical alter ego of the poet
TOSHIKO, sister of the poet who dies of tuberculosis

*Miyazawa Kenji: Selections* offers new translations by Hiroaki Sato of the poems of one of Japan's most celebrated early twentieth century poets. Even though Kenji Miyazawa published just one anthology of his poetry during his lifetime, *Haru to shura* (1924; spring and asura), the efforts of his friends to publish his works after his death assured him a place in the canon of contemporary Japanese poetry.

The English-speaking reader who encounters the poetry of Kenji Miyazawa for the first time in this anthology is struck quickly by Miyazawa's modernism. Miyazawa deftly combines classical Japanese themes and Buddhist beliefs with images and words taken from the industrial age that entered Japan in force by the later years of the Meiji era (1868-1912) when Miyazawa was a boy. Thus "Proem" opens with a modern view of the fragility of the self: "The phenomenon called 'I'/ is a blue illumination/ of the hypothesized, organic alternating current lamp" that also casts flickering landscapes and creates a whole universe that may be nothing but an illusion of the mind. The modern image of an electric lamp is complemented further by the persona's use of scientific geological and meteorological terms such as "the glittering frozen nitrogen/ at the top stratum of the atmosphere" that contributes to his observed reality.

"Spring and Asura," the popular title poem of Miyazawa's sole lifetime anthology, presents the persona as "Asura incarnate" who is "spitting, gnashing, pacing back and forth." As Hiroaki Sato's excellent introduction tells the reader, an Asura is a Buddhist demon who loves to quarrel. An Asura lives just below the realm of the humans in Buddhist cosmology. Japanese critics have stated that for Miyazawa, the world of the Asura most closely resembles that of real life full of war and struggle, where Buddhist compassion is needed most.

Though even what the Buddha spoke is absent in his world for now, for "(the True Words are not here,/ Asura's tears fall on the earth)," Miyazawa's Asura uses his eyes to observe a world that takes scant notice of him. Life can be a struggle in Miyazawa's poems, but like the angry and sad little Asura, humanity is well advised to persist. The spiritual reward may be such life-affirming visions as that described in the optimistic poem "Daybreak." Reflecting on a winter sunrise, the persona observes, "The rolling snow/ gets bright peach juice poured into it" as darkness recedes.

∼

*During his lifetime, Kenji Miyazawa self-published only one collection of poetry,* Haru to shura *(1924), and a collection of children's and fairy tales,* Chūmon no ōi ryōriten *(1924), while working as teacher of agriculture. Other poems were published in magazines. Based on his posthumous popularity, by 2004 there existed in Japanese eight complete and one unfinished* zenshū, *complete collections of his works also based on his unpublished manuscripts.*

∼

The cycle of poems written on November 27, 1922, the day Miyazawa's beloved sister Toshiko died from tuberculosis, "The Morning of the Last Farewell," "Pine Needles," and "Voiceless Grief" as well as the later "White Birds" are among to the most moving elegies of modern Japanese poetry. The first poem opens with the haunting realization of the persona that "Before the day ends/ you will be far away, my sister." After observing the incongruity of brightness on a dark November day with sleet falling, the poet interjects the voice of Toshiko in brackets as she asks her brother for a last favor: "(Please get me some rain-snow)."

As the persona obliges this request that is repeated as a motif later throughout the poem, he gathers "two chipped ceramic bowls/ with blue water-shield designs" to gather the sleet. He approaches a snow-laden pine branch to gather drops of snow that, like Toshiko lingering in the state between life and death, "maintain the pure-white two-phase system of snow and water." Again, Miyazawa intersperses modern scientific terms into his poetry before giving expression to the paradox that "From that terrifying, disturbed sky/ this beautiful snow has come." Similarly, in Buddhism, death can be occasion for achieving heavenly happiness beyond all suffering. This is exactly what the persona wishes for his sister to achieve at the end of the poem.

With "Pine Needles," the next poem of the Toshiko cycle, as is the case with other key poems of this anthology, Sato chose to juxtapose some of his own translations of Miyazawa's poems with previous ones, most often those by American poet Gary Snyder done in the early 1960's. This technique calls the reader's attention to the fact that any translation, and especially that of poetry, remains a somewhat subjective act.

What Snyder rendered as "some raindrops still clinging/ —I brought you these pine boughs" for Miyazawa's opening lines, Sato translated as "Here's the beautiful pine branch/ I took the sleet from." While the next lines show more convergence with Snyder's "—you look like you'd jump up/ & put your hot cheek against this green" and Sato's "Oh, you almost leap to it/ pressing your hot cheeks to its green leaves," the reader easily realizes that each translation has its own flair.

The courage with which Sato highlights this difficult aspect of translating poetry in *Miyazawa Kenji* can be applauded critically because it acknowledges that there is hardly a final authorized version possible that exactly and immutably conveys the Japanese original into another language. Nevertheless, the reader is offered powerful choices of experiencing key poems of Miyazawa.

Sato brings home again his point of incertitude in translation with Kenji Miyazawa's most famous poem, "November 3rd." After the quotation of many other alternatives, Sato freshly translated the poem so that the opening lines read *"neither yielding to rain/ nor yielding to wind/ yielding neither to/ snow nor to summer heat."*

This poem expresses the persona's wish for an exemplary Buddhist life of quiet self-reliance and constant readiness to help and support others in need. It became especially popular during Japan's dark days at the end of World War II. Sato's excellent introduction relates that after the war, the occupation authorities took exception even to the persona's meager daily diet of *"eating one and a half pints of brown rice."* Miyazawa's line was changed and the amount of rice cut by one fourth. Only after this censorship was "November 3rd" published in a postwar textbook. The incident casts a telling light at the intersection of poetry and politics in postwar Japan.

In his poems selected by Sato, Miyazawa's landscapes are rendered in vivid colors. Miyazawa often used scientific or nontranslated Western words in his poems to give them a modern, cosmopolitan touch. At the same time, natural objects are ironically personified. Thus, "The Tsugaru Strait," about the channel separating the Japanese islands of Honshū and Hokkaidō, opens with "In the south black shelves of cumulostratus have formed/ and the two antiquated verdigris-colored peninsulas/ mutually shed afternoon fatigue."

In a similar vein, in the opening lines of "Volcano Bay: A Nocturne," Miyazawa includes a modern scientific explanation for the color of the vegetation observed: "Dextrin, the green gold of young peas,/ where do they come from, and shine so?" Here, even though the glucose polymer Dextrin is named as being responsible for the poetically rendered color, the question as to the reason for its existence is left open. The poem creates a conscious fissure between scientific observation and philosophical questions.

Many of Miyazawa's poems selected by Sato also include a poetic commentary on humanity's place in the natural world the poet describes. The world of Miyazawa's poems is generally that of the farmers and small-city dwellers, who labor and live close to the land. In "Okhotsk Elegy," the persona observes that "I know the man is all right/ because on that empty street corner/ when I asked him, Where's the busiest section of the shore?/ he said, It must be over there/ because I've never been there."

Yet the poems of Miyazawa do not hide the hardship experienced by the farmers and laborers he observed at work. In "Distant Work," Miyazawa's persona mercilessly exposes the pain behind the apparent idyll. The noise emanating from a brick factory appears pleasant enough from afar, yet for workers it is a different experience: "But at night Chūichi returns from there,/ tired, furious."

Often, Miyazawa pokes fun at human folly. His poems ironically expose the false sense of self-importance affecting upper members of the rural and small-town society he lived in. "Mr. Pamirs the Scholar Takes a Walk," "Colleagues," "The Landowner," and "Hateful Kuma Eats His Lunch" are wonderful examples of Miyazawa's keen, but ultimately empathic, portrayals of people caught at the cusp of tradition and modernity.

Similarly, "An Opinion Concerning a Proposed National Park Site" ironically describes the efforts to develop a tourist attraction to embody a fake version of the Buddhist Hell. Ingenious technology is envisioned to create special effects, such as "As a finale, blast off real shots electrically/ from two field cannons." About the majestic natural mountainside of the proposed park, the poem's interlocutor laconically explains "that, you see, will be the backdrop."

For Miyazawa, it was often the animals of his poetry that appear to embody best the spirit of undaunted perseverance valued in some branches of Buddhism. In the poem "The buckets climb," "A moth lies flat/ From the smooth powerful surface tension" of a pond, yet by the end of the poem it manages to break free and fly up and escape in "the indeterminate forms of clouds."

For all his occasional sarcasm directed at the folly of his fellow humanity, and animals surpassing humans in inner wisdom, Miyazawa's poems also treasure his community. Perhaps this is conveyed best in the untitled poem beginning with the lines "The man I parted from, below." Here, the persona confesses that "I feel a mysterious, helpless/ love for our land." It is lines like these that help the reader to understand why Miyazawa's poetry is so popular in his native land of Japan.

*Miyazawa Kenji* concludes with poems written by Miyazawa during periods of illness all the way to the last day of his life before succumbing to sickness. There is agony in Miyazawa's descriptions of his sick, failing body. Even though death could bring enlightenment and absence of pain for a devout Buddhist, in "Night" Miyazawa admits that even though his mind understands this idea, he is not yet ready to die: "new blood wells up and/ once again pale-white I become frightened." Yet in the last poem Miyazawa wrote, in the morning on the day of his death on September 21, 1933, his persona expresses hope that he may die in possession of "the dharma," the Buddhist concept of the right way of life.

Aptly, to introduce the poet Kenji Miyazawa to his English-speaking audience, Sato opens his edition with a perceptive foreword by poet Geoffrey O'Brien that illustrates the quintessential modernism of Miyazawa. Sato's own introduction contains a substantial biography of the poet that focuses on his life, his Buddhist beliefs, and key elements of his poetry. The excellent, substantial selection of Miyazawa's poetry is followed by three perceptive essays by two Japanese poets, Shuntarō Tanikawa and Gōzō Yoshimasu, who tell of Miyazawa's influence on their own work. A final short essay by Michael O'Brien compares Miyazawa's poetry to Western poets and writers.

It is to be hoped that *Miyazawa Kenji* will help to familiarize more English readers with the outstanding poetry of Miyazawa. Miyazawa's work strongly influenced Japanese postwar national self-consciousness and can serve to make a Western reader understand this topic.

Thus, overall, *Miyazawa Kenji* opens to the English reader a fresh window into the work of an important modern Japanese poet who captured much of the soul of his country in the brief years in which he was active. Miyazawa's poems have been given a perceptive translation by Hiroaki Sato. In English, too, they do not fail to show their perceptive power. Miyazawa's poems offer a deep insight into humanity's modern condition.

*R. C. Lutz*

## Review Source

*Booklist* 103, no. 18 (May 15, 2007): 16.

# MOTHER TERESA
## Come Be My Light—The Private Writings of the "Saint of Calcutta"

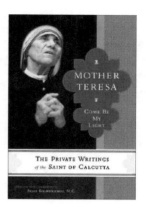

*Author:* Mother Teresa (1910-1997)
Edited and with commentary by Brian Kolodiejchuk
*Publisher:* Doubleday (New York). 416 pp. $22.95
*Type of work:* Letters, religion, biography
*Time:* 1928-1997
*Locale:* Primarily Calcutta, India

*This partial biography of Mother Teresa focuses on her interior life through her letters and other writings, as she labored to establish a new religious order while struggling with devastating spiritual doubt*

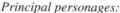

*Principal personages:*
MOTHER TERESA, founder of the
Missionaries of Charity
CELESTE VAN EXEM, her spiritual director beginning in 1944
FERDINAND PÉRIER, archbishop of Calcutta from 1924 to 1960
LAWRENCE TREVOR PICACHY, her spiritual director after 1956
JOSEPH NEUNER, the theologian in whom she confided

*Mother Teresa: Come Be My Light—The Private Writings of the "Saint of Calcutta,"* published on the tenth anniversary of the nun's death, reveals her inner life in her own words, as well as through the testimony of those who knew her. The book is meticulously documented by editor Brian Kolodiejchuk, a Catholic priest of the Missionaries of Charity Fathers and official postulator of the cause for her canonization. Kolodiejchuk, who met Mother Teresa in 1977 and was associated with her until her death twenty years later, also provides an essential narrative that places the various writings in context.

He spends little time on Mother Teresa's early life. She was born in Skopje, Ottoman Empire (now in Macedonia), on August 26, 1910, and baptized as Agnes Gonxha Bojaxhiu. Her first language was Albanian; her second, Serbo-Croatian, which she spoke at school. English came much later, after she realized that she had a vocation to serve the poor and traveled to Ireland to join the Sisters of Loreto, a missionary order dedicated to educating the young. In 1928, she took as her religious name that of her patron saint, the Carmelite nun Thérèse of Lisieux. The new Sister Teresa began her novitiate in India in 1929, making her first profession of vows two years later. Appointed to teach at Saint Mary's School for girls in Calcutta, where she would eventually be named principal, she also became an Indian citizen. After she made her final vows in 1937, she was addressed as Mother Teresa.

The editor focuses his attention on three distinct aspects of Mother Teresa's interior life: a private vow she made while still a Loreto nun, the subsequent mystical events that inspired her to found the Missionaries of Charity, and the spiritual dark-

⁓

*Mother Teresa authored several volumes of speeches, prayers, and meditations. She received many humanitarian awards, including the Jawaharlal Nehru Award, the Ramon Magsaysay Award, and the 1979 Nobel Peace Prize. In 2003, she was beatified by Pope John Paul II as Blessed Teresa of Calcutta.*

⁓

ness that plagued her for most of her lifetime. With the permission of her confessor, the Jesuit priest Celeste Van Exem, Mother Teresa made a private vow in April, 1942 (similar to one by Saint Thérèse), binding herself under pain of mortal sin never to refuse God anything, no matter what He asked of her. It was an attempt to hold herself to absolute, unquestioning obedience as proof of her intense love for Jesus, a promise she would faithfully keep, albeit with difficulty. No one knew of this vow except her spiritual advisers.

On September 10, 1946, as she traveled by train from Calcutta to the Loreto convent in Darjeeling for an annual retreat, Mother Teresa underwent a mystical experience, a calling to give up her life in Loreto and go directly into the streets "to bring Souls to God—and God to Souls." Her notes and letters, often with erratic punctuation, describe a voice, imploring her to *"come—carry me into the holes of the poor.— Come be My light,"* and urging her to dedicate herself to the abject poor in the slums of Calcutta. She believed this to be the voice of Jesus, which would continue to speak to her intimately for several months, entreating her to become a Missionary Sister of Charity, dressed simply in a sari and living in absolute poverty with the Indian poor, sharing their lives and ministering to them. The voice told her, *"There are plenty of Nuns to look after the rich and well to do people—but for My very poor, there are absolutely none. For them I long—them I love. Wilt thou refuse?"* She could not.

This experience marked the genesis of the Missionaries of Charity, the society Mother Teresa ultimately founded. She reported these events to Father Van Exem when she returned to Calcutta. However, she could not act without the consent of her superiors, including Van Exem and Archbishop Ferdinand Périer, both of whom were cautious. Finally, with Van Exem's permission, she wrote an impassioned letter to the archbishop, detailing her plans for this proposed society of missionary nuns and requesting permission to live beyond the convent walls so that she could go freely to the poor and sick of Calcutta's slums.

Archbishop Périer questioned whether her call to do God's work was genuine. She wrote to him reassuringly, "[God] will do all. . . . I am only a little instrument in His hands." She sent further accounts of her dialogues with Christ and of three visions of Jesus on the cross that she experienced, adding, "If the work be all human, it will die with me, if it be all His it will live for ages to come." She continued to hear the voice through the summer of 1947. Then it ceased.

Early in 1948, Pope Pius XII granted Mother Teresa's petition to begin her new mission in the slums. Alone, she left Loreto to obtain the basic nurse's training she would require to serve the poor. The Missionaries of Charity was officially established in Calcutta on the third floor of a private home, and by mid-1950 the community of one had grown to twelve. Nuns taught the children, nursed the sick, and comforted the dying. In spiritual terms, the society's mission was "to quench the thirst of Our Lord Jesus Christ for the salvation of souls" and "bring about their conversion and sanctification." In every Missionaries of Charity chapel, Christ's penultimate words on the cross, "I thirst" (John 19:28), would appear next to the crucifix as a reminder of this call. For herself, Mother Teresa wrote, "I want . . . to drink *only* from His chalice of pain and to give Mother Church real saints." Although she saw the words of Jesus being fulfilled, she told Périer, "One part [is] still left . . . that I would have to suffer much."

Most shocking to those who admired Mother Teresa is her revelation of an inner darkness that no one suspected. "There is such terrible darkness within me," she wrote. "It has been like this more or less from the time I started 'the work.'" In 1955, she mentioned to Périer an inner loneliness so intense that she could not speak about it even to Van Exem: "I used to get such help and consolation from spiritual direction—from the time the work has started—nothing. . . . Pray for me—for within me everything is icy cold."

Two Jesuit priests were especially helpful to Mother Teresa. After she was deeply moved by a 1956 retreat led by Lawrence Trevor Picachy (later, Cardinal Picachy), she began a correspondence that revealed how abandoned by God she felt, even as her love for Him increased. Except for the archbishop and her confessors, she offered up her suffering in silence for the poor she served: "I want to smile . . . at Jesus and so hide . . . the pain and the darkness of my soul even from Him." After the death of Pius XII, the darkness in her heart briefly disappeared, but within a month it returned.

Father Picachy encouraged her to write to Jesus what she could not say: "My God—how painful is this unknown pain. . . . What are You doing My God to one so small?" Perhaps her bitterest cry of doubt appears in another letter to Him: "What do I labour for? If there be no God—there can be no soul.—If there is no soul then Jesus—You also are not true. Heaven, what emptiness. . . ." Still, she was faithful. In the same letter she added, "Your happiness is all that I want. . . . I am ready to wait for You for all eternity."

Mother Teresa was aware of her contradictions. Nevertheless, she had great difficulty comprehending the purpose of this darkness, although she accepted it as God's will. After theologian Joseph Neuner conducted a 1961 retreat in Calcutta, she began to speak to him also about her interior life. What she could not deal with was the feeling of abandonment; she had been so close to God, and now there was nothing. Neuner too asked her to write down her feelings. She wrote of "this terrible sense of loss—this untold darkness—this loneliness—this continual longing for God."

Neuner was particularly supportive by giving Mother Teresa new insight into her darkness, as a silent sharing in Christ's agony on the cross. She began to view it as a "very small part of Jesus' darkness and pain on earth" and was then able to welcome it. To Neuner she wrote: "For the first time in this 11 years—I have come to love the darkness. . . . If I ever become a saint—I will surely be one of 'darkness.' I will continually be absent from heaven—to light the light of those in darkness on earth."

Her good works were many. When the Missionaries of Charity first began, people were dying in the streets, cases so hopeless that hospitals would not accept them. Mother Teresa wanted to create a shelter where they could receive basic medical care and die with peace and dignity, and the city of Calcutta provided her with such a place. She also built orphanages, schools, and homes for AIDS, leprosy, and tuberculosis patients. Archbishop Périer gave her permission to open new missions outside of Calcutta and appointed her superior general of the society, a position she held until shortly before her death. In 1965, she began to establish missions worldwide.

Mother Teresa included lay coworkers in the society, men and women who wished to join and work with her but were prevented by illness or disability. These became "spiritual twins" of the nuns who served the poor, each group offering encouragement and prayers for the other. She founded the Missionaries of Charity Brothers, the first male branch of the society, followed by a contemplative branch of priests and brothers, and by the Missionary of Charity Fathers.

Frequent travel for speeches and awards only made Mother Teresa feel more isolated. An increasingly public life was a trial for her, for she did not like to be in the public eye. Even as she inspired others, her own spiritual aridity persisted. She suffered from chronic headaches, and in later years a serious heart condition required a pacemaker, but she kept up normal activities as much as possible. She died September 5, 1997, at eighty-seven. At that time, the society consisted of more than 600 missions in 123 countries, with 4,000 sisters, 300 brothers, and 100,000 volunteers.

Kolodiejchuk's book has engendered controversy. Mother Teresa wished all her correspondence to be destroyed to avoid focusing interest on herself rather than on Jesus, yet some critics are angered that Kolodiejchuk and others chose to ignore this request. Others have charged that money she collected was not spent on the poor, that she had no interest in eliminating poverty, and that she was a hypocrite. Writing in *Newsweek*, Christopher Hitchens dismisses her as "a confused old lady" who "suffered from . . . self-hatred."

Kolodiejchuk argues that Mother Teresa endured not a crisis but a trial of faith and that without the pain of her interior darkness and the extended test of faith that followed, she could never have achieved such absolute identification with the poor. He concludes that it was not her suffering that made her a saint but her intense love for God and her fellow humans. Clearly, his intent in this book is to support her canonization, but his evidence, in her words, remains impressive.

*Joanne McCarthy*

## Review Sources

*America* 197, no. 8 (September 24, 2007): 14-17.
*Booklist* 104, no. 3 (October 1, 2007): 27.
*Newsweek* 150, no. 11 (September 10, 2007): 41.
*Time* 170, no. 10 (September 3, 2007): 36-43.
*The Washington Post*, September 5, 2007, p. A21.

# THE MURDER OF REGILLA
## A Case of Domestic Violence in Antiquity

*Author:* Sarah B. Pomeroy (1938-    )
*Publisher:* Harvard University Press (Cambridge, Mass.).
    249 pp. $24.95
*Type of work:* History
*Time:* The second century C.E.
*Locale:* Rome and Athens

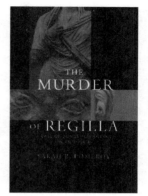

*A classical scholar uses a wide range of evidence to piece together the circumstances surrounding the life and death of a Roman woman in the second century* C.E.

Principal personages:

REGILLA (APPIA ANNIA REGILLA CAUCIDIA
    TERTULLA), the Roman wife of the
    Greek Herodes Atticus, the mother of his six children, and the
    victim, in Greece, of a violent death that is the focus of this
    investigation
HERODES ATTICUS (LUCIUS VIBULLIUS HIPPARCHUS TIBERIUS
    CLAUDIUS ATTICUS HERODES), one of the wealthiest men in
    the Roman Empire and both tutor and friend of the emperor
    Marcus Aurelius
BRADUA (APPIUS ANNIUS ATILIUS BRADUA), Regilla's younger
    brother who brought a charge in Rome against Herodes Atticus
    for the murder of his sister

More than a million people annually visit the Acropolis in Athens, Greece, and inevitably look down from the Acropolis on the well-preserved remains of the massive odeon or theater, with a seating capacity of about five thousand, built in 161 C.E. by Herodes Atticus in memory of his wife Regilla. Many of these tourists learn that Herodes Atticus, one of the richest men in the Roman Empire of the second century C.E., was a major benefactor of building projects throughout his native Greece, and especially in Athens. What is less well known is that this Greek philanthropist was probably responsible for the violent death of his pregnant Roman wife in 160. In *The Murder of Regilla: A Case of Domestic Violence in Antiquity*, Sarah B. Pomeroy, a prominent scholar of the history of women in the ancient Greek and Roman world, makes a noble effort to fill this unfortunate knowledge gap and uses her vast knowledge of the social history of the Roman Empire to piece together from meager evidence the biography of Regilla and the circumstances surrounding her death at the relatively young age of thirty-five.

Unfortunately, no words of Regilla herself have survived to communicate her feelings and experiences directly to posterity. To understand Regilla and her difficult position as the wife of Herodes Atticus, Pomeroy employed varied and often wide-

*Distinguished Professor Emerita of
Classics and History at the City
University of New York, Sarah B.
Pomeroy has been a pioneer in
women's studies in the ancient world
with works like* Goddesses, Wives,
Whores, and Slaves *(1975),* Families in
Classical and Hellenistic Greece
*(1997), and* Spartan Women *(2002).*

ranging evidence: letters between Marcus Aurelius (121-180) and his friend, Marcus Cornelius Fronto (c. 100-c. 166), a prominent grammarian and lawyer; a biography of Herodes Atticus by Flavius Philostratus (c. 170-245); archaeological remains of monuments associated with Herodes and Regilla in Italy and Greece; and inscriptions written to commemorate husband and wife, as well as other family members. Illustrations include many of these monuments and inscriptions. In addition to such material evidence directly related to Herodes and Regilla, Pomeroy appropriately cites ancient sources and evidence on the lives of Roman women in Regilla's time in order to fill out the picture of her subject's probable daily life and experiences.

Almost no full-length biographies of Greco-Roman women exist in antiquity, when only the poet Sappho of Lesbos received such attention. More recently, modern historians have begun to provide biographies of prominent ancient women such as Cleopatra VII and Livia, the wife of Augustus. Pomeroy's study of Regilla goes further by focusing on the life of a woman who lived a quieter life on the fringe of the powerful and famous.

The importance of Regilla's pedigree is suggested by the significance of her full Roman name: Appia Annia Regilla Caucidia Tertulla. The longer a name in Roman society, the more important the person was or wanted to appear. Appia associates Regilla with the Appii Claudii, an ancient Roman dynasty associated with the Appian Way, on which Regilla's own family owned an estate. Her father's family, the Annii Regilli, prominent in their own right, gained further importance as close relatives of Annia Galeria Faustina, wife of the emperor Marcus Aurelius. Regilla, the name by which she was commonly known, means "little queen" in Latin. From her mother, Atilia Caucidia Tertulla, Regilla bears the name Caucidia, suggesting that her maternal ancestors claimed descent from the Etruscans, who ruled Rome in its early days. From her mother she also inherited the name Tertulla, literally "little third daughter."

Pomeroy's investigation is both an inquest into the death of one specific Roman woman and the examination of the kind of life such women lived in the second century C.E. Thus, lacking facts about Regilla's own childhood, Pomeroy describes the typical life of a wealthy, upper-class Roman girl of that era. A girl such as Regilla would have lived a sheltered and happy life, surrounded by slaves who catered to her every wish. She would have been well-educated at home by slaves and would have learned Greek at an early age. Her upbringing groomed her to become the wife of a prominent Roman husband.

Regilla was married to Herodes Atticus around 140, when she was about fifteen years old. She probably had little say in the selection of her husband, chosen by her father, who was undoubtedly delighted to create by marriage a tie with such a wealthy man and close acquaintance of the emperor. It would have mattered little to her father or to Roman society that Herodes was old enough to be Regilla's father.

Within the year, Regilla bore Herodes his first child, a son who died in infancy. The death of this child is, in fact, mentioned in the extant correspondence between the emperor Marcus Aurelius and his friend Fronto. Their next child, a girl, was born within the next year, as Herodes prepared to move his family back to his native Greece. Regilla gave birth to at least three more children in Greece, including one son who died in childhood. At her death, she was pregnant with her sixth child, who may have died in the trauma of her death or shortly afterward. Of her six children, only three lived to adulthood, two daughters and a son. Unfortunately, this son, named Bradua (Tiberius Claudius Marcus Appius Atilius Bradua Regillus Atticus) was such a great disappointment to his father that he was disinherited in Herodes' will, although Bradua probably inherited substantial wealth from his mother. Despite Regilla's fecundity, it was, perhaps, her inability to produce a satisfactory male heir for her husband that soured the marriage. Pomeroy also notes Herodes' preference, possibly sexual, for several male foster children, which may have further distanced him from his Roman wife.

In Greece, Regilla lived at Herodes' ancestral estate at Marathon in Attica. Herodes gave (or sold) his wife a substantial portion of this estate. The remains of a formidable entrance gateway, known as the Gate of Eternal Harmony, suggest that Regilla's portion of this estate was completely surrounded by that of Herodes. Such a division of an estate between spouses was highly unorthodox in the period and may further suggest an unusual, if not troubled, marriage.

The wife of a prominent and wealthy Greek would have been expected to lead a public life in Greece as well. Unfortunately, her Roman ancestry disqualified Regilla from the most obvious and coveted roles open to women in Greek society, namely priestesses of one of the religious cults in Athens. Consequently, her husband seems to have used his considerable wealth to purchase for his wife the priesthood of Demeter Chamyne at the sanctuary of Olympia. Evidence of the couple's generosity at Olympia includes an aqueduct built by Herodes and a prominent nymphaeum or public fountain, of which a statue of a bull survives with a record of Regilla's donation inscribed on its flank. This fountain was also decorated with statues of Regilla and her children. Fragments of some of these statues also survive.

Herodes also created a public role in Athens for his wife by establishing the Roman cult of Fortuna (Tyche in Greek) and making Regilla priestess of Tyche. The Temple of Tyche was built above the Panathenaic Stadium, which Herodes restored between 139-140 and 143/144, a stadium still visible in its reconstructed form in the modern city. During her lifetime, a statue of Regilla was also erected by the public council of the city of Corinth at the famous Peirene Fountain, perhaps, as Pomeroy suggests, because she was the benefactor who paid for its renovation. Regilla's headless statue and an accompanying inscription survive on the site. A similar dedicatory statue in her memory has also been found at Delphi and may commemorate another act of munificence.

Regilla died in 160. From the surviving legal charge leveled later by her brother Bradua against Herodes in Rome, Regilla's death was the result of a blow to her abdomen inflicted, at her husband's direction, by his freedman Alcimedon. Bradua suggested in his deposition that the beating was "for trivial reasons." While Alcimedon might have been acting independently when he beat Regilla, Pomeroy suggests that it was much more likely that the freedman did so at the explicit or implicit direction of Herodes. Pomeroy leaves no doubt that Herodes, who was known for his violent temper and was philosophically opposed to *apatheia*, the repression of personal feelings advocated by the Stoics, was responsible for his wife's death. The trial in Rome was conducted before a jury of Roman senators. By custom, the accuser, Regilla's brother, served as prosecutor. Herodes spoke in his own defense and denied that he had ordered his freedman to beat his wife. Despite an inevitable senatorial bias in favor of Bradua, who was one of their own, Herodes was acquitted, probably because of imperial influence.

Following his wife's death, Herodes expressed his grief publicly, most conspicuously with the magnificent Odeon in Athens. At his wife's family estate on the Via Appia, he also built a temple-like cenotaph in his wife's memory (now the church of San Urbano). In these and many other memorials, including his own Greek poetry and a lengthy poem in Latin commissioned from the poet Marcellus of Side, the distraught husband repeatedly refers to his wife's virtues as well as his own conjugal affection. In all of these efforts, Pomeroy suggests, Herodes was attempting to placate the avenging spirit of his dead wife by transforming her into a gracious and benevolent heroine.

Regilla's life is particularly interesting because she married not a fellow Roman but a Romanized Greek and spent most of her married life in her husband's native Greece. Examination of Regilla's biography provides an almost unique opportunity to consider the challenges a Roman woman would face living in Greece during the Roman Empire. Many of the details of her life in Greece are unknown, but much may be deciphered from the situation itself. Regilla, whose native language was Latin, not only would probably have had to use Greek in her husband's home but also would have faced major differences in cultural expectations. In her native Rome, she would have had significant freedom and power as a married woman, while in Greece, even in the second century C.E., the life of a married woman was circumspect, restricted, and tied to the authority of her husband.

Modern readers might assume that the Roman Empire in the second century C.E. was a tranquil, homogeneous society. The history of the marriage of Regilla and Herodes Atticus reveals the flaws and the realities of life in that Roman world. In particular, in *The Murder of Regilla*, Pomeroy reveals the fragile and possibly dangerous status of even wealthy, aristocratic women like Regilla. If a woman like Regilla could have experienced a marriage and a death like hers, what, one imagines, was life like for her humbler female contemporaries?

*Thomas J. Sienkewicz*

## Review Sources

*The Chronicle of Higher Education* 54, no. 6 (October 5, 2007): 14.
*The New Yorker* 83, no. 39 (December 10, 2007): 113.
*Publishers Weekly* 254, no. 23 (June 4, 2007): 41-42.

# THE MUSEUM OF DR. MOSES
## Tales of Mystery and Suspense

*Author:* Joyce Carol Oates (1938-    )
*Publisher:* Harcourt (Orlando, Fla.). 229 pp. $24.00
*Type of work:* Short fiction
*Time:* 1950's to the 2000's
*Locale:* Western upstate New York, Philadelphia, New
   Jersey, and the Midwest

*A collection of ten previously published stories of vio-*
*lence, gore, and horror featuring serial killers, other mur-*
*derers and psychopaths, their family members, and their*
*victims*

*Principal characters:*
   ANONYMOUS MALE, victim of jogger's rage
   SETH M. NIORDE, prison inmate under suicide watch
   LAURENCE C. NIORDE, his visiting father
   COLUM "THE KID" DONAGHY, mid-level boxer found dead
   PATRICK HASSLER, his best friend
   DARYLL, puffed-up young humanities professor
   BENJAMIN S. "BAD HABITS" HASLIT, JR., serial killer
   DOLORES,
   TREVOR, and
   ALBERT, his children
   DEREK "DERRIE" KNIGHT, a child who turns feral
   KATE and STEPHEN KNIGHT, his parents
   LIAM GAVIN, a serial lover and killer of women
   HANNAH, MRS. "EVVIE" KNUDSEN, and
   OLIVE LUNDT, his victims
   B—— and C——, identical twins and rivals
   DR. A——, their manipulative father
   ANONYMOUS KILLER, a man who murders a prostitute
   DR. MOSES HAMMACHER, a retired family doctor and coroner
   VIRGINIA "GINNY" HAMMACHER, the divorcée who marries him
   ELLEN "ELLA" MCINTYRE, Ginny's daughter by her first marriage

It is hard to say where Joyce Carol Oates gets the ideas for such gruesome subjects and images as those featured in *The Museum of Dr. Moses: Tales of Mystery and Suspense*—a jogger who shoots another in the face, a poached baby, a humanities professor who turns his decaying corpse into a valentine, a chubby little boy who returns to the wild, a man who appreciates the infinite variety of women before he kills them, and a dotty old doctor who creates a museum of medical horrors. The stories in this collection are not for the queasy or weak at heart or for before- or after-dinner reading.

*The Museum of Dr. Moses* is also prob-ablynot among the best works in this pro-lific author's fifty-year writing career. (For Oates's best, readers should go to such novels as 1969's *them* and 1996's *We Were the Mulvaneys* and such story collections as 2006's *High Lonesome*.) A couple of the collection's stories are little more than sketches, some characters and actions are not well devel-oped, and Oates overdoes the gory details and ambiguous endings. Significantly, the collec-tion is still high-quality work: fascinating, gripping, imaginative, and morbidly enter-taining. Oates is equally good at entering the minds of both children and psychopaths, and she is such a practiced and accomplished craftsperson/stylist that she can hold the reader's attention much like a snake charmer. To students and scholars, the stories are also useful for what they reveal about Oates and her work.

~

*Joyce Carol Oates has written almost fifty novels and thirty collections of short stories, plus novellas, poetry, plays, criticism, and young adult and children's books. She has won many awards, including the 1996 PEN/ Malamud Award for short fiction and the 1970 National Book Award for the novel* them *(1969).*

~

For one thing, the stories tap into elemental, archetypal human fears that run through folklore and fairy tales and that help shape the American urban landscape, with its ghettos, suburbs, and gated communities. Almost any newspaper or news report shows that these fears are not just imaginary or psychological but realistic (even if often exaggerated or sensationalized): Violence is endemic to American life, both on a personal and societal basis, and is obsessively reenacted in movies, television shows, and games. It is not surprising that the sensi-tive and highly intelligent Oates, who grew up poor in rural upstate New York, was a teenager in the repressed 1950's, was valedictorian of her two-thousand-strong grad-uating class at Syracuse University, and taught college English in or near decaying Detroit during the troubled 1960's and 1970's, should take an interest in violence.

In addition, it is not surprising that she would depict violence realistically but also be drawn to Gothic forms and conventions, with their evocation of fear and horror. Both realism and the Gothic element are parts of the American literary tradition, and the well-read Oates had plenty of models to look to. The Gothic element, for example, enters into the work of such modern writers as William Faulkner (1897-1962) and Flannery O'Connor (1925-1964) and the earlier writers Nathaniel Haw-thorne (1804-1864) and Edgar Allan Poe (1809-1849). Another contemporary writer who makes use of the Gothic is Cormac McCarthy (b. 1933). It seems to be the point of both McCarthy and Oates that, too often in American life, the realistic and the Gothic tend to converge.

Among nonliterary influences apparent in *The Museum of Dr. Moses* are feminism and Freudianism. In the title story, for example, old Dr. Moses Hammacher wants his new middle-aged wife to get a face-lift—and even performs the operation himself, using staples—so that she will look young again as he remembers her. From the context, the author makes clear what she thinks of face-lifts, women who get them, and men who push women into getting them (Dr. Moses comes over like a Nazi Frankenstein). The stories also feature sexual predators and battered women. Nevertheless, some feminists apparently reject Oates, perhaps because she is not feminist enough or is also influenced by Freudianism. The influence of Freudianism can be seen in her depiction of pathological minds.

The destructive effect of poor parenting on children, both actual and alleged, is a repeated pattern in the stories. In "Suicide Watch," for instance, Seth M. Niorde blames lack of attention from his father for his own drug addition, self-destruction, and violence, but Seth is hardly one to cast stones, since he tells a horrible story (maybe not true) of how he accidentally poached his own two-year-old son by leaving hot water running in the bathroom while taking a nap. In "The Hunter," Liam Gavin similarly blames his mother, who abandoned him at birth, for his predatory hunting out, loving, and killing of women who are already maimed. In "Feral," parents who fail to investigate the near-drowning of their son watch him turn wild and take to the woods. Only in "Bad Habits" do the damaged children of a serial killer show signs of recovering, led by their hopeful mother, who represents the positive side of Oates's theme.

Some of the stories, like "Feral," challenge credibility. What parents would not inquire into the near-drowning of their son, especially if foul play is suspected? Can his near-drowning be the cause of his return to the wild or just another post hoc fallacy? How about turning feral in the first place? Still, one advantage of the Gothic tradition is that the rules of credibility are looser, if not nonexistent: Challenges to credibility are commonplace, even expected. Rather than the usual credibility, the stories take on a psychological, symbolic, or allegorical credibility. For example, "Feral," whose ending is reminiscent of Hawthorne's story "Young Goodman Brown," could be read as an allegory of the loosening strings of parenthood as kids grow up and, say, leave home for college.

Even the flimsier and more realistic stories are, like "Feral," carried along by the power of Oates's writing. "Hi! Howya Doin!" is the opening story, about joggers in a university setting. The main character is a big, unnamed athletic man who startles or irritates other joggers by shouting "Hi! Howya Doin!" as he blasts by. Finally, one day, an irritated jogger pulls a pistol and shoots him between the eyes. This incredible story seems grimly comic until one recalls similar shootings on university campuses, sometimes places of tension that draw out psychopathic personalities. Oates tells the story in one long six-page sentence that captures these tensions, mimics the breathless effects of jogging, and builds to the violent climax. A similar story is the even sketchier "Stripping," a stream-of-consciousness aria in the shower by a former teacher at St. Ignatius Middle School who is cleaning up after butchering a prostitute.

The most bizarre and gory story is "Valentine, July Heat Wave," narrated by a university humanities professor, Daryll, whose wife has left him. Daryll is a priggish, snobbish, egotistical, totally demented academic whose "most original work" in his thirties propelled him into a senior professorship. Specializing in philosophy of mind, he clarified Descartes' mind/body dichotomy:

> . . . "mind" inhabits "body" but is not subsumed in "body." For the principles of logic, as I have demonstrated by logical argument, in a systematic geometry in the mode of Spinoza, transcend all merely "bodily" limitations. All this, transmuted into the most precise symbols.

He also married the department secretary, a disastrous mismatch: She was incapable of understanding his work, and he was incapable of understanding her little gestures of love, like leaving a valentine for him. Now she has left him entirely but plans to return briefly for her things. In a bizarre application of his philosophical thesis, Daryll plans to leave her an elaborate valentine of his eight-day-old corpse rotting in their bed.

A couple of stories reflect Oates's special interests in boxing and in twins. In the short nonfiction work *On Boxing* (1987), Oates characterized boxing as a relic of the cult of masculinity. This feminist perspective is not as strong in "The Man Who Fought Roland LaStarza," although Colum "The Kid" Donaghy, the protagonist, does womanize and abuse his wife (who seems to hold her own). Instead, a working-class 1950's atmosphere prevails: Donaghy is depicted sympathetically as a well-liked mid-level boxer who is trying to rise in the corrupt boxing world and who pays with his life. The long realistic story also focuses on personal relationships, especially between Donaghy and his best friend Patrick Hassler, and has some surprises at the end. Oates's interest in twins recurs in a number of her works and is explored here in "The Twins: A Mystery." This somewhat confusing story (but perhaps intentionally so) looks at mature mirror twins who are rivals manipulated by their old father. Complaining that "nothing [on TV] to challenge the intellect is ever on," the decrepit Dr. A—— inserts a DVD of his twins that symbolizes how he plays and replays them. The DVD and reality in the story seem to overlap.

Dr. A—— previews the title story's Dr. Moses, another mean, mad old man. However, "The Museum of Dr. Moses" returns emphatically to the Gothic mode, recognizable by the title, the setting, and the grisly contents of the doctor's museum. The doctor's forbidding old stone house, isolated in the country in fictional Eden County, western upstate New York, could have been the setting for the movie *Psycho*, while the gracious host Dr. Moses (though he does once lose his temper and bang on the dinner table) seems like an elderly combination of Dr. Frankenstein and Dracula. The story also features twenty-six-year-old feminist Ellen "Ella" McIntyre, who, at 5 feet 9 inches and 180 pounds, has come to duke it out with Dr. Moses and rescue her mother, who for some strange reason married him and is "clearly a woman in distress, in thrall to a tyrannical male." Both of the story's main characters suggest some interesting autobiographical possibilities: Ella, a returning hometown product proud to have escaped the confining circumstances of her upbringing, could easily be a stand-in for the younger Oates, while Dr. Moses and his museum suggest the archive at Syracuse University where Oates began storing her writings, manuscripts, and letters in 1990.

Much as Dr. Moses' museum is a collection of legitimate if sometimes gruesome medical artifacts and specimens, except for the horrors in the Red Room, so Oates's writings are far more than a collection of Gothic horrors. The ten stories in *The Museum of Dr. Moses* demonstrate her enormous range and versatility in short fiction, and the striking similes she keeps reaching for are a reminder of her prodigious work in poetry and other genres. Even the stories here with Gothic elements evoke subtle meanings lurking below the surface, like the disturbed minds at work in "Suicide Watch" and "Stripping," the satire of academia in "Valentine, July Heat Wave," the satire of the media in "Bad Habits," the allegory in "Feral," and the autobiographical tensions in "The Museum of Dr. Moses."

*Harold Branam*

## Review Sources

*Booklist* 103, no. 17 (May 1, 2007): 36.
*The Boston Globe*, August 26, 2007, p. D5.
*Kirkus Reviews* 75, no. 11 (June 1, 2007): 535.
*Los Angeles Times Book Review*, August 26, 2007, p. 9.
*Publishers Weekly* 254, no. 26 (June 25, 2007): 31.
*School Library Journal* 53, no. 11 (November, 2007): 160.
*The Washington Post*, October 28, 2007, p. BW04.

# MUSICOPHILIA
## Tales of Music and the Brain

*Author:* Oliver Sacks (1933-     )
*Publisher:* Alfred A. Knopf (New York). 381 pp. $26.00
*Type of work:* Music, medicine, science

*A collection of discussions of the many ways that music can affect the brain for good or for ill drawn primarily from cases and patients with whom the author has worked in his profession as a neurologist*

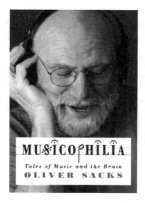

In recent years, the fields of neuroscience and neurobiology have expanded greatly. The technological resources of many different and sophisticated types of brain imaging have aided this expansion. Now insights from neuroscience are contributing to almost every area of human activity and aspect of the human condition. This knowledge of neuroscience is not limited to a minority of scientists. Increasingly popular scientific literature is making the advances of neuroscience available to a wider audience.

Music is one area of human life that has engaged the interest, attention, and imagination of people throughout history. The title of Oliver Sacks's book *Musicophilia: Tales of Music and the Brain* addresses this very issue. In the preface, Sacks states: "This propensity to music shows itself in infancy, is manifest and central in every culture, and probably goes back to the very beginnings of our species." By the term "musicophilia" he means that music "lies so deep in human nature that one must think of it as innate."

However, the question about music has always concerned how we apprehend music. How do our brains integrate the complex aspects of musical experience? Music engages many areas of the brain. Music activates the auditory sense. We perceive its structure. It is deeply embedded in memory. Even listening involves and evokes motor responses. Most famously and mysteriously, music stirs deep and varied emotions. In addition, if music is so central to our whole being, why do some people have such prodigious musical talents while others seem to be lacking these abilities? Neuroscience is a field that is well suited to make significant new contributions toward addressing these central questions about music and the human mind.

In *Musicophilia*, Sacks does not tackle these big questions directly. Rather, the subtitle of his book indicates his approach. Much as in his other nine books, he colects narratives of cases that he has encountered as a neurologist that demonstrate varying aspects of the effects of music on the brain. This presentation has advantages and disadvantages. One positive aspect is that, unlike other books in which neuroscience takes center stage with illustrative case examples, Sacks is able to bring a human face to the sometimes arcane neurobiology of music. Indeed, many of the people that the reader meets through Sacks's stories have inspiring tales of the power of music to ameliorate suffering and to help overcome disabilities. At the same time, disadvan-

*Oliver Sacks is a physician and professor of clinical neurology and psychiatry at Columbia University. He is the author of ten books, most of which examine case studies of neurological phenomena, including* Awakenings *(1973), which led to an Oscar-nominated film;* The Man Who Mistook His Wife for a Hat *(1985); and the autobiographical memoir,* Uncle Tungsten *(2001).*

tages include the fragmentary organization and lack of broader analytical perspective.

Sacks presents his material in twenty-nine chapters. Most of the chapters address a topic with several cases illustrating the individual variations on the basic theme. For instance, in "Part II: A Range of Musicality," Sacks devotes one chapter to the phenomenon of synesthesia and music. Synesthesia refers to a true mixing of the senses. With music, one manifestation of synesthesia is the way some people see or perceive color as integral to the experience of music. Thus, one musician specifically associates a color with a musical key. Another person who is not a musician associates color with light, shape, and position. She says of this imagery: "A chord will envelop me." Sacks also discusses scientific work on synesthesia but reaches no conclusions. Rather, he leaves the chapter open-ended about the neurobiology of synesthesia and the varying attitudes of synesthetes toward the role of this phenomenon in their lives.

Although none of the chapters are lengthy, most of them leave the reader with some food for thought. Some of the chapters are less satisfying, and a few are so brief that one wonders about the reason for their inclusion. An example is chapter 17, "Accidental Davening: Dyskinesia and Cantillation," which is only two pages in length. Sacks does not explain what dyskinesia and cantillation are. The example goes nowhere. This interlude seems puzzling and discordant.

Although there is some mixture of more positive aspects of music and the brain, the first two parts of the book, "Part I: Haunted by Music" and "Part II: A Range of Musicality," focus on the ways that musicophilia can become an affliction. Sacks tells of several cases that show how music can provoke seizures, a condition called musicogenic epilepsy. Sacks cites the case of the nineteenth century music critic Nikonov, who, after his first major seizure at a performance of an opera, became so sensitive to music that he developed a phobia of music and had to give up his profession. Sometimes music can go beyond the irritating mental replaying of musical tunes and phrases to full-blown musical hallucinations where a person cannot escape the music that constantly plays unbidden through his or her mind. In part 1, these troubling conditions are balanced with the opening chapter about a man who was struck by lightning and was subsequently seized with a passion for classical music, to which he had previously paid scant attention. Over the following years, he became a talented amateur pianist and composer.

In part 2, Sacks explores the neurological basis for the extensive variance in musical ability and responsiveness to music that is encompassed within the concept of musicophilia. On one end of the spectrum, there are a number forms of "amusia," the inability to perceive certain aspects of music. For some people, the amusia has to do with tone deafness and lack of apprehension of melody, sequences of notes, or pitch.

For others, the amusia falls into the category of rhythm and meter. Still others have minimal emotional response to music. In some instances, neuroscientists are beginning to identify damage or abnormalities in areas of the brain that seem to correspond with certain types of amusia. Still, therapeutic interventions for these conditions do not yet exist.

Two of the chapters in this section focus on problems stemming from the auditory sensory function. In "Pitch Imperfect: Cochlear Amusia," Sacks explains that because of the extreme complexity and delicacy of the ear, many things can impair hearing. The next chapter, "In Living Stereo: Why We Have Two Ears," he further elaborates on the importance of the way we "hear" music. These two chapters could have benefited from a more extensive discussion, perhaps with illustrations or diagrams, of the auditory canal in relation to the brain. Still, an important cautionary point is the vulnerability of the ear, especially its delicate hair cells, to loud noises, with which we are bombarded constantly. As Sacks points out, "once the hair cells are destroyed, it has been long thought, they are lost forever."

On the opposite side of the spectrum, Sacks discusses several aspects of unusual musical ability. He devotes one chapter to absolute pitch, and other chapters look at people who compensate for other deficiencies, disabilities, and losses by the intensive development of musical talents. Examples include musical savants and blindness. In the case of absolute pitch, which is actually independent of musical inclination, neuroscientists have found "an exaggerated asymmetry between the volumes of the right and left planum temporale" in people with absolute pitch. This centrality of the planum temporale for the perception of both speech and music among other things has led researchers to examine intriguing questions about the interrelationship and origins of both linguistic and musical abilities.

Citing the German Romantic writer Novalis—"Every disease is a musical problem; every cure is a musical solution"—in the third and fourth parts of this book Sacks highlights the ways that music can become an effective therapeutic intervention. Sacks makes an important distinction between music therapy that is directed toward problems with movement and motor coordination and music therapy that requires not just music itself but also the empathetic and relational skills of the therapist to help the patient with memory loss. In connection with movement, one chapter is devoted to the role of music therapy in Parkinson's disease. The "right" kind of music, usually legato with a clear rhythm, can help patients with Parkinsonian symptoms "entrain" their movement, particularly walking, with the steady rhythm of the music.

Sacks discusses even more dramatic and inspiring instances where music can become a lifeline for people with amnesia or dementia. One chapter focuses on the well-documented case of Clive Wearing, an English musician and musicologist who suffered devastating amnesia as a result of a brain infection, herpes encephalitis, that affected the memory parts of his brain. He exists only in the moment, with no past memories and no way to hold on to new memories. Wearing has said: "It's like being dead." However, when he plays music or conducts his procedural memory along with the structure and momentum of the music, he comes alive again. Once the music stops, he returns to a "lost place."

Regarding working with patients who have varying types of dementia, music therapy can have more global effects. It can immediately and dramatically bring patients out of an inner world to which they have retreated or calm patients who are excessively agitated. Beyond this, Sacks points out that the reason for the effectiveness of music therapy is that "musical perception, musical sensibility, musical emotion, and musical memory can survive long after other forms of memory have disappeared." Music can improve their quality of life and restore some sense of self. Sacks notes that "improvements of mood, behavior, even cognitive function" can continue for extended periods of time after the therapeutic encounter with music.

One of the most affecting chapters addresses music and emotion. Sacks speaks of personal experiences when music pulled him out of states of grief and depression. Whether it is grief or joy, music has the power to stimulate emotional response and release when nothing else can. Interestingly, this moving chapter is almost devoid of any connections with neurobiology. Sacks summarizes the emotional effects of music by saying that music "has a unique power to express inner states or feelings. Music can pierce the heart directly; it needs no mediation." This major topic could benefit from more integration of neurobiology and emotional states that has been developed, for example, in works such as Daniel Siegel's *The Mindful Brain* (2007), where experiential and neuroscientific knowledge come together in illuminating ways.

*Musicophilia* has much to offer. At the same time, the reader is left with a sense of missed opportunities. Sacks presents many topics that arouse curiosity about the ways that the human brain and mind process music. However, each topic and each case remain rather discrete. Many ideas are put forward; few are developed fully. Sacks successfully shows that musicophilia is a crucial part of being human. He points the way toward a greater neurological understanding of how and why music is such an integral part of the human experience and why it can be so devastating to an individual when the facility for music goes awry. In the end, music retains an affective power that neuroscience may never be fully able to explain.

*Karen Gould*

## Review Sources

*Booklist* 104, no. 1 (September 1, 2007): 4.
*The Chronicle of Higher Education* 54, no. 10 (November 2, 2007): 63.
*Commentary* 124, no. 5 (December, 2007): 73-77.
*Entertainment Weekly*, no. 961 (October 26, 2007): 71.
*Kirkus Reviews* 75, no. 16 (August 15, 2007): 843.
*Library Journal* 132, no. 15 (September 15, 2007): 76.
*New Statesman* 137 (October 29, 2007): 55-56.
*The New York Times Book Review* 157 (October 28, 2007): 16.
*Science News* 172, no. 19 (November 10, 2007): 303.
*Time* 170, no. 17 (October 22, 2007): 89.

# NADA

*Author:* Carmen Laforet (1921-2004)
*First published: Nada*, 1944, in Spain
Translated from the Spanish by Edith Grossman
Introduction by Mario Vargas Llosa
*Publisher:* Modern Library (New York). 244 pp. $22.95
*Type of work:* Novel
*Time:* The 1940's
*Locale:* Barcelona, Spain

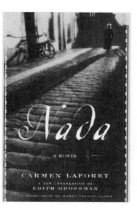

*A coming-of-age novel about an eighteen-year-old girl who travels to Barcelona to attend a university and live with her deceased mother's relatives as she searches for her identity in her new family, school, and society, which mirror the emptiness and confusion that many Spaniards felt in the wake of the Spanish Civil War*

*Principal characters:*
> ANDREA, the eighteen-year-old protagonist, who moves to Barcelona to attend a university and live with maternal relatives
> HER GRANDMOTHER, the religious matriarch of the family
> ANGUSTIAS, her aunt
> GLORIA, Juan's wife
> JUAN, Andrea's uncle
> ROMÁN, Andrea's uncle
> ENA, Andrea's friend at the university
> JAIME, Ena's boyfriend
> PONS, Andrea's friend at the university, who introduces her to bohemian culture
> GERARDO, a schoolmate who takes an interest in Andrea
> ANTONIA, the ornery maid of Calle de Aribau
> DON JERÓNIMO SANS, Angustias's boss and secret lover
> GUÍXOLS, a bohemian artist with a studio that serves as a haven for other young artists and Andrea
> ITURDIAGA, a bohemian artist
> CALLE DE ARIBAU, the house where Andrea's family lives

Sixty years after its original publication in Spain in 1944, *Nada* has been translated and published in English, bringing not only the coming-of-age story of one young girl but also the story of a country coming out of a civil war and into a fascist regime to a new audience. A longtime classic in Spain, Carmen Laforet's *Nada* captured the void, the nothing (*nada*) that many Spaniards felt under Francisco Franco's rule in the years immediately following the civil war (1936-1939) and hinted of the artistic revolution that was to occur by paralleling the struggles Spaniards experienced with the pain of an adolescent girl. Twenty-three-year-old Laforet wrote *Nada* in a style that is

*Carmen Laforet entered the Spanish canon at a time when literature was dominated by men.* Nada, *Laforet's first novel, received the Premio Nadal award in 1944. She also was awarded Spain's National Prize for Literature in 1955. Laforet wrote five additional novels, including* Al volver la esquina *(2004; around the block),* La mujer nueva *(1974; the new woman), and a collection of short stories.*

simultaneously calming and unnerving, that elicits pity and unease, as she shares the heart-breaking tale of eighteen-year-old protago-nist Andrea. *Nada* begins with Andrea alone at a Barcelona train station after traveling to the city to attend a university. Orphaned as a child, Andrea has moved from relative to rel-ative across Spain and travels to Barcelona to find an education, freedom, and herself. What she does not anticipate finding is a demented and depressing family waiting to welcome her, and potentially destroy her, with their dysfunctional structure.

The family is made up of the maternal grandmother matriarch, "a black-white blotch of a decrepit little old woman," Andrea's un-cle Juan, whose "face was full of hollows, like a skull in the light of the single bulb in the lamp," Juan's baby and his wife, Gloria, who is "thin and young, her disheveled red hair falling over her sharp white face," Andrea's uncle Román, "with curly hair and an amia-ble, intelligent face," and her Aunt Angustias, whose "expression revealed a certain contempt. She had graying hair that fell to her shoulders and a certain beauty in her dark, narrow face." They inhabit an over-crowded apartment that Andrea's grandparents purchased new. After the grandfather died, they divided their once-large flat into two, selling one half and forcing them-selves and their possessions into the other. The result is a macabre environment, a gothic labyrinth filled with antiques and oppressive furniture precariously stacked and rich yet tattered curtains that keep the sun out and the dust thick. Andrea reflects on the factors that attracted her grandparents and herself to the city and muses, "They came to Barcelona with a hope contrary to the one that had brought me: They wanted rest, and secure, methodical work. The city I thought of as the great change in my life was their safe haven." Barcelona more than changes Andrea's life, it offers her one for the first time and serves as a sometimes emotionally painful backdrop for her rites of passage.

The apartment on Calle de Aribau becomes its own character—reserved, oppres-sive, and cold, reflecting the Franco regime, with its isolationist and oppressive con-trol over its inhabitants. The dysfunction that occurs on Calle de Aribau is not limited to the mountains of possessions in various stages of disrepair but extends to the family members themselves. The grandmother is aware only of what she wishes through her dementia. Juan and Román fight nearly to the death regularly, Juan taking breaks only to beat Gloria, who supports the family by running an illegal gambling den out of her sister's house and secretly selling off pieces of furniture to local ragmen. Aunt

Angustias judges the other occupants with a puritanical strictness and attends church regularly—not to pray but to criticize how others are praying and dressing. Finally, the bitter maid Antonia, about whom Andrea remarks that "no other creature has ever made a more disagreeable impression on me," is kind only to her dog Trueno and sneaks around the house taking pleasure in everyone's pain. Andrea describes the bizarre human menagerie and their oppressive setting as "a thousand odors, sorrows, stories, rose from the paving stones, climbed to the balconies or entrances along Calle de Aribau. . . . A mix of lives, qualities, and tastes—that's what Calle de Aribau was. And I: one more element on it, small and lost." Such is the overall theme of *Nada*: one girl feeling obsolete and unaccepted, along with a country waking up from a bloody civil war to discover its citizens too were small and lost.

In the midst of the familial madness, Andrea quietly tries to go unnoticed, so as not to encounter a lecture, a possible flying hatchet, or an attack on her lifestyle from Angustias, who threatens, "If I'd gotten hold of you when you were younger, I'd have beaten you to death"—to have prevented her from growing up to be wicked and without morals. Andrea finds a degree of refuge at the university, where, awkward and introverted, poor and shabbily dressed, she draws the attention of her classmates and is pitied by Ena, a beautiful, wealthy, and popular girl. Ena and Andrea become fast inseparable friends, studying together at Ena's house and socializing with Ena's friends. The time Andrea spends with her are the only moments of happiness that Andrea has; she is so intoxicated by Ena that at times she doubts whether their friendship truly exists. Yet through this relationship and others she develops, Andrea is constantly reminded of what she does not have; she spends her meager monthly allowance in just days to impress her friends, then goes hungry for the remainder of the month, resorting to drinking the water used to boil vegetables. In fact, Andrea lacks more than money; she lacks the family, love, and confidence her friends possess, increasing her feelings of separation and casting her into deep despair.

The one almost normal aspect of Andrea's life is shattered when Ena develops a friendship with Román that excludes Andrea. Out of fear for her friend's well-being, and motivated by personal jealousy, Andrea tries to end the relationship; in doing so, she discovers secrets about Ena's mother and witnesses an unsettling side of Ena. Andrea makes other friends to fill the void left by Ena, but each relationship only reminds her that she does not truly fit in. Pons, a friend from school, introduces Andrea to the bohemian art scene by taking her to his friend Guíxols's studio. Although his friends welcome her, it is more out of a curiosity than acceptance. Poor and alone, she is never able to relate fully to their conversations and experiences. Her feelings of isolation climax when Pons invites her to a dance at his parents' house. Feeling as if she were Cinderella, Andrea arrives at the dance to find that she is grossly underdressed (although in her finest clothes), and, after Pons declares his feelings for another girl, she leaves the party embarrassed and ashamed. It is at that moment when Andrea "began to realize that it is much easier to endure great setbacks than everyday petty annoyances." Andrea has plenty of both.

Laforet parallels the feelings of isolation, political conformity versus nonconformity, and sexual and artistic repression that followed the civil war through the life-changing events that Andrea experiences in *Nada*. The characters of Calle de Arbrau are isolated in their fortress of an apartment, with little interaction with outsiders, and what interaction they have is frequently negative. Andrea too suffers from feelings of isolation and alienation, both within her relatives' home and with her friends at the university. Although she has family and friends for the first time in her life, she still feels as if she is an outsider and never truly assimilates. Many citizens of Spain experienced similar feelings under Franco's regime, as if they no longer belonged within their country, their home.

Andrea, in her quest to create a new life for herself, struggles between conformity and nonconformity. She conforms to Angustias's strict laws, silently takes the abuse from her uncles, and goes through her university invisible. Ultimately, she ignores Angustias's rules, stating, "I realized I could endure everything: the cold that permeated my worn clothes, the sadness of my absolute poverty, the dull horror of the filthy house. Everything except her control over me." She rebels against her uncles as well. Andrea also seeks out nonconformity at school by socializing with the Barcelona bohemian sect, discussing art and politics (even if only as an outsider). As in Andrea's world, such decisions to conform or revolt took place throughout Spain, as many Spaniards rebelled against the fascist rule and created an artistic revolution, their own coming-of-age.

Laforet draws further parallels between Spain's sexual repression and sexual tensions surrounding *Nada*'s characters. Throughout the novel, there are subtle references to and innuendo about incest and adultery. Gloria had a relationship with Román while carrying Juan's baby. The current status of this relationship is unknown. At the same time, Román makes several uncomfortable comments toward Andrea and blatant advances toward young Ena, while carrying on a secret affair with the maid Antonia. There are also undertones of feelings of more than friendship between Ena and Andrea, which are interrupted by Ena's boyfriend Jaime, who takes Andrea on the couple's outings. Even Aunt Angustias's skeletons are exposed, as her love affair with her married boss, Don Jerónimo Sans, is revealed, forcing her to join a convent.

After a difficult and emotionally uncomfortable coming-of-age of a girl and a nation, Laforet allows Andrea to realize that "*perhaps the meaning of life for a woman consists solely in being discovered like this, looked at so that she herself feels radiant with light.* Not in looking at, not in listening to the poisons and stupidities of others, but in experiencing fully the joy of her own feelings and sensations, her own despair and happiness. Her own wickedness or goodness." This revelation gives Andrea meaning and strength and was a daring sentiment for Laforet to write under Franco, since it not only went against the government by empowering women but also suggested that meaning for Spaniards was not defined by what the government deemed acceptable but by what uniquely constituted the individual during a time when individuality was discouraged.

*Sara Vidar*

## Review Sources

*The Guardian*, June 23, 2007, p. 16.
*Kirkus Reviews* 74, no. 23 (December 1, 2006): 1192.
*New Statesman* 136 (March 5, 2007): 59.
*The New York Times Book Review* 156 (April 15, 2007): 8.
*The Times Literary Supplement*, March 16, 2007, p. 21.
*The Washington Post*, February 18, 2007, p. BW15.

# THE NAMING OF THE DEAD

*Author:* Ian Rankin (1960-    )
*First published:* 2006, in Great Britain
*Publisher:* Little, Brown (New York). 452 pp. $24.99
*Type of work:* Novel
*Time:* July 1-July 9, 2005
*Locale:* Scotland, mainly Edinburgh

*The sixteenth novel in the well-known series featuring Detective Inspector John Rebus finds Rebus facing multiple challenging cases just when world leaders are gathered for the G8 summit near Edinburgh*

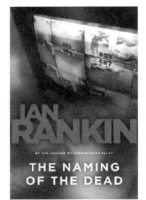

*Principal characters:*
> JOHN REBUS, an aging detective inspector with the Edinburgh police, officially the Lothian and Borders Police
> SIOBHAN "SHIV" CLARKE, the detective sergeant who works with Rebus and is placed in charge of a serial killer case, even though Rebus outranks her
> JAMES CORBYN, the new chief constable of Lothian and Borders Police who puts Rebus and Clarke on suspension so their case will not embarrass Scotland during the G8 summit
> ELLEN WYLIE, a woman connected with the serial killer case to whom Rebus turns for information
> MAIRIE HENDERSON, a newspaper reporter and acquaintance who wants information from Rebus and vice versa
> DAVID STEELFORTH, a London-based Special Branch (SO12) commander overseeing the police during the G8 summit
> GARETH TENCH, a former preacher, now a popular Edinburgh councilor
> KEITH CARBERRY, a young thug who seems close to Councilor Tench
> MORRIS GERALD "BIG GER" CAFFERTY, a longtime gangster leader in the Edinburgh underworld who also knows Carberry
> TEDDY CLARKE, Siobhan's father, an aging hippie activist who has come with his wife to join the protestors and demonstrators surrounding the G8 summit
> EVE CLARKE, Siobhan's mother, who is physically assaulted while in the demonstrators' Peace Camp
> SANTAL, a young woman at the camp who attaches herself to Siobhan's parents

Ian Rankin's *The Naming of the Dead* takes its title from a ceremony organized by protesters at the G8 summit of world leaders in Gleneagles, Scotland, in July, 2005. The marchers climbed to the top of Calton Hill in Edinburgh and solemnly read the names of lives lost during the Iraq War as a dramatic feature of their antiwar demonstration.

Rankin's sixteenth novel in the Detective Inspector John Rebus series is set during the week of the summit, and the ceremonial reading of names captures some of the political resonance of the hundreds of thousands of people who came to Edinburgh during that week. The title also signals other deaths, such as the victims whose killer Rebus is seeking, and others murdered during the course of the novel. The novel opens with Rebus at the funeral of his younger brother, Michael, who had apparently died of a massive stroke at age fifty-four. On a much broader level, the naming of the dead suggests remembering all losses and the lament voiced by Rebus that often one can do little except name them. Despite that, Rebus is determined to seek justice and prevent further murders by at least one killer, a serial killer in the case at hand.

*Ian Rankin has won Edgar and Gold Dagger Awards and the Cartier Diamond Dagger award for lifetime achievement. In 2007, he received the Edinburgh Award and was named a Deputy Lieutenant of Edinburgh. The Naming of the Dead won a British Book Award and was named the Worldbooks Crime Thriller of the Year.*

Rebus has been with the Crime Investigation Department (CID) of the police in Edinburgh (the Lothian and Borders Police) for many years. He is nearing mandatory retirement, which he does not want to contemplate. Work is essentially his only interest, other than smoking and drinking too much and knowing a lot about popular music. Most of his superiors and some of his fellow officers, however, would be glad not to have him around. Except for his colleague and protégée Detective Sergeant Siobhan "Shiv" Clarke, he is basically a loner, antithetical to supervision, an unpredictable "rogue" cop who follows his own rules. That he is obsessively dedicated and solves his cases has made him a legend, but that too serves to distance him from most of the others. More than once it is suggested to him that he just coast through his last year on the force. Rebus is weary, depressed about his brother's death, frustrated with his superior officers, and more introspective than ever, but he will not slack in his work. He does not even want to know how to.

Despite the many hundreds of extra police and law enforcement personnel from different agencies who have been assigned duties connected with the G8 summit meeting, his superior, Chief Constable James Corbyn, specifically excludes Rebus as a troublemaker and orders him to stay behind at the police station. Rebus gets involved anyway, when a call comes in that the body of a Labour member of Parliament, Ben Webster of Scotland, has been found on the ground below the walls of Edinburgh Castle during a high-level political meeting and party. The word is that Webster committed suicide. Rebus thinks it equally likely that he was pushed rather than jumped, especially when Rebus learns that Webster was campaigning against the arms trade.

Also going on at the same time is a case involving the murders of at least three men, all of whom were recently released from prison for rape or sexual-assault crimes. Siobhan Clarke has been assigned the case, with Rebus to work with her, even though he outranks her. The top police are not particularly interested, considering who the victims are. Now new evidence has been found at Coolie Well, where possible clothes of the victims have been left displayed in a wooded grove, as though the killer is leaving clues and daring the police to catch him or her. Chief Constable Corbyn orders Clarke and Rebus not to work on the case because he does not want the media to report such local embarrassments when the world is focusing on Edinburgh and the G8 summit. When he learns that they are still pursuing it, he suspends them from duty. They continue anyway.

Rebus learns that there is a Web site that provides alerts about sexual-assault criminals being released from prison. It seems designed to encourage the unidentified killer to find new victims. One of the people who apparently helps maintain the site is Ellen Wylie, who for personal reasons clearly has no sympathy for such criminals. Rebus has a heavy task trying to persuade Wylie to reveal what she knows and how much she is involved. The detective team also suspects a local crime figure, Morris Gerald "Big Ger" Cafferty, because one of the murder victims was formerly working as his muscle man. This brings Rebus into contact with Mairie Henderson, a well-known newspaper reporter who had ghostwritten a biography of Cafferty. Rebus wants information from her, and she wants information from him about the serial killer case, but he does not know if he can trust her regarding splashing the news in the headlines in the midst of the summit.

Others who seem to be involved include an Edinburgh councilman, Gareth Tench, who before he entered politics had been a popular evangelical preacher, well known in the city for his work with wayward boys. Keith Carberry, a young hooligan, seems to be close to Tench but also close to Cafferty. Rebus suspects that Tench may be trying to take over the territory that Cafferty claims as his own section of the city and that Tench's motives may be as self-serving as those of the current crime boss. The situation becomes more critical when another murder occurs, though this one is not of a released sex offender. A further complication arises when David Steelforth, the Special Branch commander in charge of security, approaches Rebus about the case but is unwilling to explain his interest.

Throughout all this interaction with an intricate cast of well-drawn characters, another problem arises. Siobhan Clarke's parents, both of whom have a long history of demonstrating and working for various causes—the peace movement, feeding the hungry, and others—have come to Edinburgh to join the multitude who are using the summit to gain publicity for their political action issues. Teddy and Eve Clarke had not approved of their only child becoming a police officer, a role they consider too conformist to the establishment. Siobhan has distanced herself from them but wants to see them. When she locates them in the Peace Camp, they are glad to see her, but they seem more engaged in what is taking place at the moment. They also seem more interested in a young woman who goes by the name of Santal, who has attached herself to them, than they are in their daughter.

As the daily television reports show, a ring of police surround the Peace Camp, primarily to keep the protesters from getting closer to the big eight world leaders.

Some of those inside the camp become too noisy and confrontational, or the police become confrontational, and physical assaults occur. Word comes that Eve Clarke has been hit in the head, and she has to be taken to a hospital. Suddenly, nothing else matters to Siobhan except her mother's welfare and finding out who hit her. It galls her to think that this was probably the work of a fellow police officer. In her attempt to locate video footage that might include the attack and to identify the attacker, she arranges a meeting with Big Ger Cafferty to get his help—the last thing she would want her superiors (or even Rebus) to know about.

As if there were not enough stress and anxiety going on that week in Scotland, on July 7, the second day of the summit meeting, multiple severe terrorist bombs wreak havoc, creating fear and causing considerable loss of life, in London.

The series of subplots that make up the overall plot are carefully interwoven and ultimately lead toward a common theme, that of the omnipresence of evil. Criminal acts, especially those based on greed and a fundamental lack of humanity toward others, abound at all levels. No one is safe. World leaders often add to the corruption and deceit rather than try to eliminate it, but the "common person" may be equally part of the problem rather than the solution. Police officers and others who work in law enforcement may also be criminals themselves; preachers may be as guilty as mobsters; those who are victimized may in turn victimize others.

Ian Rankin is often labeled the originator of "Tartan Noir," detective fiction by authors from Scotland and set in Scotland. *The Naming of the Dead* is firmly set in Edinburgh and the immediate surrounding area, and the city itself becomes a rounded character with many facets. However, in terms of crime, the setting could be any large urban area. The novel, especially by invoking the actual event of the summit meeting of eight world leaders, clearly implies a global perspective. Rankin is considered the number-one best seller of crime fiction in the United Kingdom, and *The Naming of the Dead* was named the Worldbooks Crime Thriller of the Year, as was the novel that preceded it, *Fleshmarket Close* (2004). This testimony to his popularity is equaled by his high praise from critics. Rankin's writing is considered superb, including his use of dialogue and his attention to characters and character development.

What Rankin accomplishes in *The Naming of the Dead* is to demonstrate again that some of the finest writing in contemporary literature is in the genre of detective fiction. His police procedural portrays a world that seems to capture well the spirit and realities of the times. *The Naming of the Dead*, by depicting the work and dedication during one week in the life of Rebus and Siobhan Clarke, also keeps alive the idea of justice and the need for compassion and individual responsibility.

*Lois A. Marchino*

## Review Sources

*Booklist* 103, no. 11 (February 1, 2007): 6.
*Library Journal* 132, no. 2 (February 1, 2007): 55.
*The New York Times* 156 (April 2, 2007): E1-E6.
*Publishers Weekly* 254, no. 4 (January 22, 2007): 155-156.
*The Times Literary Supplement*, November 10, 2006, p. 21.
*The Washington Post*, April 23, 2007, p. C7.

# NANCY CUNARD
## Heiress, Muse, Political Idealist

*Author:* Lois Gordon (1938-    )
*Publisher:* Columbia University Press (New York).
   447 pp. $32.50
*Type of work:* Biography
*Time:* 1896-1965
*Locale:* Europe, America

   *The turbulent life of modernist poet and publisher
Cunard, Jazz Age socialite turned journalist and political
activist*

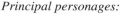

   *Principal personages:*
   NANCY CUNARD, wealthy daughter of an
      English baronet who spent her life and
      her fortune in the pursuit of literary and social causes
   MAUD CUNARD, Nancy's mother, American heiress (Lady
      "Emerald") and premier London society hostess who
      disinherited her daughter for publicly advocating black rights
   GEORGE MOORE, Irish writer, an early and lasting influence, and
      (as one of Maud's lovers) possibly Nancy's natural father
   HENRY CROWDER, African American jazz pianist and Nancy's
      lover in the 1930's
   JANET FLANNER, Paris-based columnist for *The New Yorker*,
      Nancy's longtime friend and correspondent

To readers having more than a nodding acquaintance with literary modernism, Nancy Cunard will be something of a known figure. Her achievements as publisher, anthologist, poet, and general bad girl of letters have secured her a firm if secondary place in the genealogy of early twentieth century arts and culture. Even those unfamiliar with the literary history of this period and unaware of her actual achievements might well recognize Cunard from the by-now iconic photographs made of her by Man Ray and Cecil Beaton in the 1920's. With her close-cropped hair and hard, chiseled features, the thin arms braceletted to the elbow with dozens of her signature ivory bands, she appears like some kind of fierce flapper siren, an embodiment of Jazz Age glamour, all edge and intensity, the image of insouciant daring and primitivist yearning. Lois Gordon's new biography, *Nancy Cunard: Heiress, Muse, Political Idealist*, however, suggests that Cunard was considerably more than this modernist pinup. Gordon sees Cunard not only as a vivid emblem of the new twentieth century aesthetic but also as a deeply involved political activist, a progressive campaigner for black rights, and intransigent foe of fascism in all of its forms. The biography mounts a persuasive case for making a principal player of a woman whom other commentators on the period have so often made a colorful figure in the background.

~

*A distinguished professor of English at Fairleigh Dickinson University, Lois Gordon is a critic of drama and American culture, having published several books on Harold Pinter and Samuel Beckett.*

~

Certainly she was colorful. Socially and sexually rebellious, with a history of headlong passions and furious enthusiasms, Cunard was a dazzling figure of avant-garde bohemianism, a high-profile, high-energy critic of artistic conventions and moral orthodoxies. She slept little, ate less, and seemed perpetually on the move, devouring experience with a gusto that delighted and shocked her peers and tortured and scandalized her parents. She was a prodigious drinker and defiant drunk and was promiscuous on a positively epic scale. Yet these excesses went hand in hand with a fastidious set of manners and real delicacy of feeling; she had an air of elegance at odds with her acts of violence. What any writer about Nancy Cunard must try to explain are the causes that fueled such extremes of behavior. What drove this mercurial aristocrat to her obsessive pursuit of unpopular causes and constructive social action while pushing her with equal force toward a systematic program of self-destruction? What made her a consummate "lost generation" insider in the immediate post-World War I years and made her such a curious outsider, an eccentric anachronism, in the decades thereafter? What linked her selfless martyrdom and her selfish manias? Gordon goes some way toward delivering satisfying answers to these crucial questions, supplying a persuasive psychological profile that clearly had its roots in a difficult, even scarring childhood.

Nancy Cunard was the only child of Sir Bache Cunard and the American millionaire Maud Burke, distant and unloving parents—the father benignly absent, the mother actively antagonistic. While born an heiress to the shipping fortune and spending her childhood in a bona fide castle, her life was scarcely that of a storybook princess. It was lonely, regimented, chill. Abandoned to cold and repressive governesses, restricted in diet and dress, drilled in relentless studies, she quickly formed a hatred of tyranny and a fiery resistance to upper-class authority. Her mother, for decades a brilliant society hostess and patroness of the opera (as well as longtime mistress of its conductor, Sir Thomas Beecham), epitomized to Nancy the fossilized conventions and false pieties of the belle époque world she was expected to embrace. Though she did not rebel at the time, she would later define herself precisely through this lifelong rebellion against a smug antiegalitarian ethos she forever associated with "her ladyship." She was also a deeply romantic young girl, influenced by another of her mother's lovers, the Irish writer George Moore, and inspired by her own solitary reading of lyric poetry. By 1914, her coming-out year, she was not just another wealthy debutante, she was a fully formed romantic idealist and at least a closet anarchist. Her life would be forged around these identities.

The years 1913-1919 were teeming with activities for Cunard. She was a charter member of the "Corrupt Coterie," young aristocrats and artists and writers who met regularly at London's Eiffel Tower Restaurant, and later the Café Royal, for monumental bouts of drink and talk and sex. She became intimate with Ezra Pound and the Imagists, Wyndham Lewis and the Vorticists, Bloomsbury and the Omega Workshop designers. New movements in art were bursting forth, and these "Bright Young Things" were in the thick of it all. Cunard was writing poetry by day and making history—or at least headlines—by night. When the war started, the volume was turned up even higher: a romance with a soldier who was killed, a rebound marriage with another that was dissolved, a breakdown after the whole awful bloodbath was over. Given the epidemic of disillusionment among the young generation, her collapse was not really surprising. Besides, since childhood Cunard had regularly experienced disappointment in her restless pursuit of an ideal that would make her feel whole, satisfied, secure. She tried to find it romantically with men, then politically with social causes, but, as Gordon makes clear, it never did and never could materialize. The pattern had been set early on: She needed something important to do, a quest worthy of her talents and energies, but she inwardly questioned the possibility of success and was too often frustrated by the outcomes. She launched grand adventures in spite of their futility. Her life of relentless, frenetic travel suggests a flight from loneliness as much as a search for stimulation and meaningful work. Hers is a history of undeflected recklessness that, while producing clear casualties on all sides, ultimately allowed her to achieve some extraordinary things.

The achievements began in Paris, where Cunard arrived in 1920 to find an artistic and intellectual home in the expatriate community there. She had affairs with Tristan Tzara and Louis Aragon, godfathers of Dadaism and Surrealism. She inspired novels and poems, sculptures, paintings, and photographs—from Ernest Hemingway to Aldous Huxley, Constantin Brancusi to Cecil Beaton. She published three volumes of her own poetry—passionately confessional verse, with hints of T. S. Eliot in the fragmented imagery. She founded The Hours Press, publishing experimental writing (the first work of Samuel Beckett) and producing hand-crafted books with a distinctively modernist design. Most important, she found her purpose: In the jazz clubs of Paris, just as later in the dance halls of Harlem, she discovered her passion for black culture and began a long campaign to make it better known. She took a black lover, jazz pianist Henry Crowder, and wrote a scathing exposé of her mother's racist response to their relationship. For this she was disinherited, and for the rest of her life money would be increasingly difficult to come by. She now had to produce an income by her pen, and she did, throwing herself into political and social issues and writing about them with the same uncompromising passion she had focused on the world of literature. She researched and assembled the vast anthology *Negro* (1934), which was the first ever compendium of black culture studies—an 800-page volume from 150 writers, with some 200 entries covering everything from the history of the slave trade to the trial of the Scottsboro Boys. This mix of scholarship and personal recollection, music, poetry, and photography was a breakthrough publication and seen as such among black communities on three continents, though it generated little but hatred for her as a race traitor in her own country.

Crucial as the quest for racial justice was to Cunard, her involvement in the Spanish Civil War was an even more defining struggle, and its failure was the great lingering catastrophe of her life. She immersed herself in the Republican cause, seeing it as the front line of the fight against fascism; and she spent the war years as a correspondent for the *Manchester Guardian*, walking where troops walked, living where they lived, eating what they ate. She endured staggering deprivations and dangers and wrote about it all. She enlisted other writers too, producing the 1937 volumes *Los poetas del mundo defienden al pueblo español* (*The Poets of the World Defend the Spanish People*) and *Authors Take Sides on the Spanish War*. Even after the war, she never really abandoned her resistance to the Francisco Franco regime in Spain. She organized food relief, coordinated resettlement plans, worked tirelessly and gave generously until she was officially ejected from the country and barred from reentry.

By this time, the 1950's, Cunard was living part of the year in an isolated cottage in France's remote Dordogne region and traveling nonstop the rest of the year to visit friends. It is not a pretty story. Alone much of the time, in alarmingly bad health (emphysema from the eternal Gauloise at her lips, emaciated and anemic from the herculean drinking and infrequent meals), she eked out a living as she had during World War II in London, surviving on tinned meats, biscuits, and whiskey, and banging out an endless stream of poems, manifestos, translations, letters, and prospectuses for antifascist projects. Finally, having miraculously gotten herself to Paris after an enforced commitment to a London psychiatric hospital, she flung herself, barely able to walk, from hotel to taxi to the street, where she was found ill and unconscious three days later. She died alone, in a common ward, burned out but somehow splendid, even heroic, in her refusal to give up a life lived on her own terms.

There has already been one telling of this life, Anne Chisholm's award-winning *Nancy Cunard* (1979), and in many important respects that earlier account has not been surpassed, in spite of additional material being available. Certainly, Chisholm is the more engaging, the better writer. Gordon, by comparison, can be flat and seems singularly at odds with the throb and hum of her subject's story. Readers do not need to experience on every page the propulsive energy, the tense and dizzying drama that characterized Cunard's life, but surely some of that pace and its breathtaking vibrancy should make its way into the text. It does not. Gordon is more a coordinator of biographical material than a writer of gripping narrative. Instead of a fluid string of events and figures mingling to create a riveting story, we too often get a series of chronological entries of the sort more appropriate to literary encyclopedias. On Imagism, say, she gives definitions, descriptions, principal practitioners, relation to Cunard; on Bloomsbury, definitions, descriptions, principal achievements, principal anecdotes, relation to Cunard; on World War I, principal causes, principal outcomes, relation to Cunard. Chapters begin with a kind of overview and then backtrack to fill in the details. It makes for a jumpy narrative, full of first-rate factual material (extensive revelatory passages from various Cunard diaries, for instance), but lacking imaginative shape and evocative power.

Nevertheless, a clear picture does emerge here, and it is an irresistibly striking one. If she was not, in Gordon's sweeping phrase, "one of the most unusual women of the twentieth century and perhaps of all time," Nancy Cunard was still a personality of fascinating range and astonishing ambition, a genuine eccentric whose hypnotic character inspired individual artists and whole communities. In her fevered pursuit of a few cherished ideals (whether of romantic love or racial equality or political freedom) she blazed a path that only the bravest and most high-minded have had the courage to follow.

*Thomas J. Campbell*

## Review Sources

*American Book Review* 28, no. 6 (September/October, 2007): 21-22.
*Biography: An Interdisciplinary Quarterly* 30, no. 3 (Summer, 2007): 420-421.
*Booklist* 103, no. 12 (February 15, 2007): 28-29.
*The Nation* 285, no. 5 (August 13, 2007): 30-35.
*The New York Times Book Review* 156 (April 1, 2007): 1-11.
*Publishers Weekly* 254, no. 4 (January 22, 2007): 172.
*The Times Literary Supplement*, July 6, 2007, p. 34.

# NATURE'S ENGRAVER
## A Life of Thomas Bewick

*Author:* Jenny Uglow
*Publisher:* Farrar, Straus and Giroux (New York).
  Illustrated. 458 pp. $30.00
*Type of work:* Biography, fine arts
*Time:* 1753-1828
*Locale:* England, primarily Northumberland

*Uglow's biography describes the life and work of Thomas Bewick, a gifted engraver whose charming but accurate wood engravings provided the ordinary people of his age with their first lessons in natural history*

*Principal personages:*
  THOMAS BEWICK, English engraver and
    book illustrator
  RALPH BEILBY, jeweler and engraver who was Bewick's
    master and subsequently his partner
  REVEREND CHRISTOPHER GREGSON, vicar of Ovingham and
    cleric who tutored and guided Bewick
  ISABELLA BEWICK, née ELLIOT, Bewick's wife
  GILBERT GRAY, freethinking bookbinder who influenced
    Thomas Bewick

Whether they know it or not, most Americans and Canadians have seen the works of Thomas Bewick. His small, intriguing, seemingly anonymous wood engravings have been reproduced so many times—in books and magazines, on pieces of advertising ephemera, and on greeting cards—that they have become practically invisible. Yet these modest images were once revolutionary, a contradiction that Jenny Uglow explores in the engaging biography *Nature's Engraver: A Life of Thomas Bewick.*

Bewick was born on August 10 or 11, 1753, near the village of Eltringham in the northeastern English county of Northumberland. The River Tyne runs beside the village, and the Scottish border lies just a few miles north. Growing up on his parents' farm of Cherryburn, Bewick was a rowdy boy who might have come to nothing had the Reverend Christopher Gregson, who ran a school in nearby Ovingham, not taken him under his wing.

It was while he was in school that Bewick began to pursue what had already become his two overriding interests—drawing and nature. He also began to turn against the crueler aspects of "sport" as enjoyed by his neighbors. A particular incident that stuck in Bewick's memory illustrates both the tenor of the times and the boy's developing attitudes. He had caught a panic-stricken hare that was being chased by dogs and turned it over to a farmer who promised to protect it. Instead, the farmer

*Jenny Uglow is an editor with English publisher Chatto & Windus. Her other books include* The Lunar Men: Five Friends Whose Curiosity Changed the World *(2002), which won the James Tait Black Memorial Prize for biography and the Hessell-Tiltman Prize for History, and* A Little History of British Gardening *(2004).*

broke one of the animal's legs and set it loose again to give the dogs a few more minutes' enjoyment.

When he was fourteen, Bewick was apprenticed to jeweler and engraver Ralph Beilby, who lived upriver in the bustling town of Newcastle upon Tyne. Significantly enough, the last drawing he made before leaving home showed a horse tethered to a tree. Although the apprenticeship allowed Bewick to learn the basics of engraving on copper and silver, he felt that he was being denied the opportunity to learn the finer points of the craft. The young man also found his master somewhat overbearing. By this time, however, he had developed an interest in engraving on wood, a technique that he would eventually transform into an art.

Bewick and his contemporaries had grown up with woodcuts, crude images produced from cutting designs into pieces of wood along the grain. Bewick's particular achievement lay in producing "wood engravings" on the end of the block of wood, cut across the grain. This technique allowed for much finer detail, particularly since Bewick used precision metalworking tools that he himself had adapted.

At the time, Great Britain was experiencing an increasing demand for books and a growing sophistication in popular taste. Bewick capitalized on these trends by seeking out a broad range of models for his engravings, many from the Continent, and many by such noted artists as Albrecht Dürer. Although he remained apprenticed to Ralph Beilby until 1774, Bewick established a reputation in the printing world and was soon commanding handsome prices for his little blocks of wood. Among the first important books that he illustrated were an edition of *The New Lottery Book of Birds and Beasts* (1771) and a version of Aesop's fables. A more ambitious and sophisticated project, undertaken by Newcastle printer Thomas Saint, was an edition of *Fables by the Late Mr. Gay* (1778). The "Mr. Gay" in question was versifier Thomas Gay.

Newcastle bookbinder Gilbert Gray was to have a profound influence on Bewick. During his apprentice days, Bewick spent evenings and early mornings reading through Gray's collection of books. He also absorbed much of the radical philosophy of Gray's circle of friends and apprentices, signing a petition against the conflict that Americans know as the Revolutionary War. In 1776, Bewick visited Scotland, whose freedom-loving ways he admired, and the British capital of London, which he found stultifying and disease-ridden.

Bewick gladly returned to Northumberland in 1777. The same year, after some hesitation, he agreed to become Beilby's partner, overseeing the engraving business while Beilby branched out into making and selling watchmaking tools and parts. Bewick took on his brother John as the first of many apprentices but continued his wood engraving. He had learned to eliminate the borders with which illustrators routinely framed their works, and as a result the open air seemed to permeate his works.

Bewick lost both his parents in 1785. He was a shy man and had long resisted the idea of marriage, but the following year he proposed to and married Isabella Elliot. Isabella's sister became their housekeeper, and their first daughter, Jane, was born in 1787.

As a man, Bewick was both practical and ambitious. With his business and domestic affairs set firmly in order, he set out to produce his own books with his own illustrations. His first such work was *A General History of Quadrupeds* (1790), which he had contemplated for nearly a decade. There had been other such studies, but Bewick found their illustrations unconvincing and felt that he could do better. He was right. Whenever possible, he produced his etchings from drawings he had made directly from nature. Some were actual portraits of particular animals whose owners lived in the area. In the case of rarer animals, which he knew only from others' pictures, he acknowledged his sources. Bewick's partner Beilby wrote the accompanying texts, which Bewick quietly corrected as necessary.

The first edition of the work, which described 260 wild and domestic animals, was produced in two sizes. Fifteen hundred copies were printed in a smaller format, and one hundred in a larger and more expensive one. The work was widely praised, particularly for its etchings, and sold out within a few months. A second edition, with eleven new animals, appeared in 1791, and a third the following year. Bewick was uncomfortable with fame, but the profits from the work allowed him and Beilby to move their offices to a better location.

Bewick followed his book on quadrupeds with *A History of British Birds*, which, like the earlier project, he had been considering for years. For this work, nascent naturalists throughout the country sent him untold specimens, while he himself traveled to County Durham to study a unique collection of more than eight hundred stuffed birds. Although restricting his subject to the British Isles, Bewick found that he needed two volumes to do the subject justice. The first, devoted to land birds, appeared in 1797, but not without a serious misunderstanding. Years before, Beilby had attempted to claim credit for the quadruped volume, although the matter had been worked out amicably. Here again the issue arose, with Beilby, who had written the work's text, intent on identifying himself as author. The partners presented the issue to an informal panel, which recognized Bewick as the sole author. It was to be their last major project together, and the partnership was dissolved at the end of the year.

Bewick's volume on waterbirds appeared in 1804, and although it cost him great effort to produce both the engravings and the text, he ultimately was rewarded. Like its companion, it sold well, and solidified its author's reputation as one of the leading naturalists of his time.

By this time, Bewick found his workshop deluged with work. He added entries to new editions of *A General History of Quadrupeds*, filled orders (with the help of his apprentices) for etchings from all over Great Britain, and even went into the exacting business of producing plates for banknotes. In the meantime, he was preparing *A Supplement to the History of British Birds*, which eventually appeared in 1821.

Two other major projects occupied Bewick in the 1820's—his autobiography, *A Memoir of Thomas Bewick, Written by Himself*, which was destined to appear only in

1862, and a natural history of British fishes. The latter was never finished, as Bewick died after a short illness on November 8, 1828.

As Jenny Uglow makes clear, Thomas Bewick's success was the result of several complementary factors. The first was his undoubted talent, which he displayed from an early age, filling every available flat surface with drawings. The second factor, which came in his apprentice years, was his recognition of wood engraving as the best medium for his talent. The third was at once the simplest and the most complex— his ability to see the world around him. Bewick saw particular trees where others saw only undifferentiated forest; he recognized individuals where others saw only types. As a boy, he had spent hours looking, and as a young man he learned to reproduce faithfully what he looked at. Many of the wood engravings that he produced were no larger than postage stamps or thumbprints, yet his inclusion of tiny, telling particulars sets them apart from similar works of the period. As a grown man, Bewick renewed his contact with nature by walking for hours through the countryside and by fishing.

In writing about Bewick, Jenny Uglow has produced an ideal biography. She draws much of her material from Bewick's autobiography, but in addition she brings a wide-ranging knowledge to her subject. She clearly knows the geography of Northumberland and is thoroughly at home with the age in which Bewick lived and worked. The latter point is particularly important, as most American readers will be unfamiliar with the context in which Bewick produced his modest masterpieces. Attractively printed and copiously illustrated with examples of Bewick's works, *Nature's Engraver* is the finest imaginable tribute to its subject.

*Grove Koger*

## Review Sources

*Booklist* 103, nos. 19/20 (June 1, 2007): 32.
*The Economist* 383 (May 26, 2007): 98-99.
*The Guardian*, September 30, 2006, p. 9.
*Kirkus Reviews* 75, no. 5 (March 1, 2007): 214.
*New Statesman* 135 (November 13, 2006): 57.
*The New York Times Book Review* 156 (June 17, 2007): 8.
*The New Yorker* 83, no. 17 (June 25, 2007): 93.
*Publishers Weekly* 254, no. 12 (March 19, 2007): 52.
*The Times Literary Supplement*, October 6, 2006, p. 36.
*The Washington Post*, June 24, 2007, p. BW10.

# NEW ENGLAND WHITE

*Author:* Stephen L. Carter (1954-    )
*Publisher:* Alfred A. Knopf (New York). 556 pp. $26.95
*Type of work:* Novel
*Time:* Spring, 2003, to summer, 2004
*Locale:* The fictional New England city of Elm Harbor

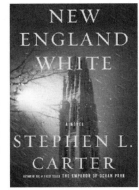

*Three murders, one thirty years old, draw a university president's wife into a web of past and present secrets, scattered clues, and dangerous episodes that expose forces and fault lines in her own life as well as in race relations in America*

*Principal characters:*
> LEMASTER CARLYLE, former White House counsel and recently appointed president of the Ivy League university in Elm Harbor
> JULIA CARLYLE, his wife, a deputy dean of the university's divinity school
> VANESSA CARLYLE, their troubled seventeen-year-old daughter
> KELLEN ZANT, an internationally known professor of economics at the university
> BRUCE VALLELY, the university's chief of safety
> TREVOR LAND, the university's old WASP secretary and fixer
> CAMERON KNOWLAND, a rich alumnus, benefactor, and fund-raiser for the current president of the United States
> MONA VEAZIE, Julia's mother, an expatriate leftist academic
> BYRON DENNISON, a powerful, now dying, former congressman and Lemaster's mentor

Like Stephen L. Carter's first novel *The Emperor of Ocean Park* (2002), *New England White* is a mystery in which an African American academic from the unnamed Ivy League university located in the fictional New England city of Elm Harbor becomes a detective. This time, that character is Julia Carlyle, a deputy dean of the divinity school, who is the daughter of a prominent black feminist professor, the wife of a powerful black lawyer and former judge who has recently become president of the university, the granddaughter of leading figures of Harlem's aristocracy in the first half of the twentieth century, the descendant of a family that has been a leading member of the Clan—the informal name for the oldest families of the black elite—since before the Civil War, and the mother of two daughters and two sons. Raised in Hanover, New Hampshire, where her mother taught at Dartmouth and she earned her undergraduate degree, she was a biology teacher for several years before attending the divinity school in Elm Harbor, where she met and married her husband, who was also a student there.

The novel begins on the night of the second Friday in November, 2003, as Julia and Lemaster Carlyle are driving home from a fund-raising event, talking about their evening and about their seventeen-year-old daughter Vanessa. In February, she had set fire to her father's midnight blue Mercedes on the Town Green in Tyler's Landing, the nearly all-white bedroom community where the family is living while the president's house at the university is being renovated. Since then, Vanessa has been in therapy, but they are not sure whether it is helping, and they still do not understand why she did it. Taking a shortcut on a back road, Lemaster loses control of their Cadillac Escalade on the ice, and they have an accident. When they get out to survey the damage, Julia sees something in the woods next to the road. It turns out to be the dead body of Kellen Zant, a professor of economics at the university—and Julia's lover more than twenty years ago, before she met Carlyle.

When it becomes clear that Zant has been murdered, and that he had been asking questions about the same thirty-year-old story of another death on another snowy night in Tyler's Landing that has been obsessing their daughter, Julia soon finds herself trying to uncover the truth about both murders. Ulti-

*Stephen L. Carter was a clerk for Associate Justice Thurgood Marshall before becoming a professor of law at Yale University in 1982. He is the author of seven books of nonfiction,* including Reflections of an Affirmative Action Baby *(1991),* The Culture of Disbelief *(1993),* Integrity *(1996),* Civility *(1998),* God's Name in Vain: The Wrongs and Rights of Religion in Politics *(2000), as well as the best-selling novel* The Emperor of Ocean Park *(2002).*

mately, her search will reveal more secrets than she is sure she wants to know—about her lover, her husband, and her daughter, but also about the president of the United States, a Democratic senator who is running against him in 2004, and about hidden currents of power in the black and white communities of Tyler's Landing, Elm Harbor, and the America beyond. "Time covers truth like snow," she will write to her mother on the novel's last page. "The best part of New England life is that it is a very long time before the snow melts."

Carter first came to prominence with his *Reflections of an Affirmative Action Baby* (1991), which combined memoir with a cultural analysis of racial attitudes in America. He has since gone on to write books about religion, politics, law, integrity, civility, and loyalty. In *New England White*, he touches on all of these themes in a tale that is, at once, a detective story, a novel of manners, and a family drama, as well as an exploration of upper-class black characters seldom seen in the fiction of other African American writers. It is hardly surprising, then, that his novel is more than five hundred pages long; what is surprising, perhaps, is that Carter manages to hold his readers' interest until that last page. He knows how to weave and satisfyingly complicate a plot; to end episodes and chapters with cliff-hangers that make the reader want to turn the page; to create main characters who engage his readers' curiosity and sympathy

and develop in intriguing ways; to introduce minor characters who are quickly defined and just as effectively used to advance, retard, confuse, divert, and resolve the
action; to use humor to lighten the mood and reveal a character; and how to tie up
all—well, most—of the loose ends, while exploring the manners and mores, textures
and tones, aspirations and foibles, of the black and white, urban and suburban, academic and political worlds he treats. Like John le Carré or Scott Turow, he offers the
satisfactions of first-class genre writing, and something more.

Thirty years ago, when Lemaster Carlyle was himself an undergraduate at the university he now heads, he lived with three white roommates from wealthy and powerful families: One was a rich playboy who died several years ago; another became the
current president of the United States (nicknamed "Scrunchy"), and the third became
the Democratic senator who now seeks to defeat him. They were known as the Four
Horsemen, and Carlyle was the only serious student in the group: His gravity, sense of
duty, and responsibility led the others to nickname him "Big Brother." Ever since, he
has managed to remain close to both the president and the senator who are now running against one another. While these young men were at the university, the body of
Gina Joule, the seventeen-year-old daughter of a faculty member who lived in Tyler's
Landing, was found raped and murdered at the town beach. A black teenager from the
Elm Harbor ghetto, DeShaun Vinney, who had stolen a BMW the night she died and
was reportedly the last person seen with her, was suspected of the crime; when he was
pursued by the police and shot, the case was closed.

Julia Carlyle reopens it because she senses it is somehow connected both to her
daughter's behavior and Zant's death. At the same time, the university's chief of security, an ex-special forces soldier named Bruce Vallely, is asked to begin his own
investigation of Zant's murder on behalf of the school by a senior member of the administration, Trevor Land. Carlyle and Vallely each uncover connections between the
two murders, and Carter skillfully moves back and forth between them as they pursue
their investigations. Along the way, they meet a wide range of characters, including
Jeremy Flew, Lemaster's multitalented and shadowy assistant; Mary Mallard, an
investigative reporter on the trail of a big story; Cameron Knowland, a rich man who
is used to getting exactly what he wants; Tricky Tony Tice, a shady lawyer; Arthur
Lewin, an economist who sees the world through his own peculiar lens; Representative Byron Dennison, the dying Machiavel who was, and still is, Lemaster's mentor;
Tonya Montez, chief sister lady of the local chapter of the Clan's women's society,
the Ladybugs; Terry Vinney, DeShaun's mother; and Roderick Ryan Rutherford, the
keeper of the keys to the divinity school's archives. Carter gives each of these characters his or her own particular angle of vision and distinctive voice.

The clues that keep Julia, Bruce, and the reader guessing are every bit as ingenious
as any mystery fan could ask and include messages in mirrors, two broken driveway
lampposts, a Broadway show poster, a dented fender, a cell phone's records, a stale
box of maple walnut fudge, spyware on a computer, a buried police report, an insurance claim, a secret shrine, a business card, a missing term paper, chocolate smears on
a file folder, hidden envelopes, a train ticket, a plane ticket, a diary, and several ana-
grams. In addition, this novel about the murder of a world-famous economist uses

terms from economics—utility function, inventory risk, all-in auctions, supply curve, market clearing—as both metaphors and clues to understanding.

As a novel of manners, *New England White* focuses on the university and the black upper crust, both of which Carter seems to know intimately. He lightly satirizes the academy's bureaucratic infighting, the officiousness of people given a small amount of power over others, the rumor mills that operate in any organization, the poses of administrators and faculty, and political correctness. (A faculty plan for a no-confidence vote on President Carlyle for his decision to merge gender and women's studies is forgotten when he "ascended to a new status, that most beloved of campus figures, the victim.") The manners and self-importance of the Clan and Carter's fictional versions of its social organizations—the Ladybugs, the Little-bugs, the Empyreals—are also gently mocked, while the historical reasons for their creation and their importance to some African Americans who live their public lives in worlds where they are a minority are clearly explained. The reality that wealth, status, and education do not prevent a black person from experiencing racism in contemporary America is vividly reflected in several incidents in Julia's story, and the fact that problems of race and poverty are more often than not placed at the bottom of the national agenda becomes a critical point in the plot as well as a prime motive for the behavior of several characters.

The novel also manages to present a contemporary family's life in a wholly believable and sympathetic way. Julia juggles the tasks that so many women do—working, helping her husband in his work, dropping off and picking up her children, managing the household, dealing with an often uncommunicative teenager, and trying at the same time to get a husband who is distracted, uncomfortable with emotion, and reluctant to express his feelings to communicate with her. (One of Carter's inside jokes occurs early in the novel, when Lemaster lies in bed flipping channels when Julia wants to talk to him and settles for a few moments on *Book TV*, "where a famous novelist was explaining why men should never write in women's voices." Carter has clearly ignored the advice.) Vanessa is beautifully drawn—from her monosyllabic responses to direct questions to the way she drops her head so that her braids cover her face when her mother tries to talk to her, from her acts of rebellion to her pride in her mother's growing strength, from her angry outbursts to her sudden displays of warmth and affection, from her surprising knowledge of unexpected subjects to her obvious insight into her parents. Lemaster Carlyle, the powerful, and powerfully buttoned-up, enigma at the heart of the family and the story, is an equally impressive creation.

In his second novel, Stephen L. Carter demonstrates that the success of his first was not a matter of luck. While teaching law and writing serious books about important public issues, he has also found the time and imagination to develop his own version of the mystery genre and focus in it on a social landscape that few of his contemporaries have explored.

*Bernard F. Rodgers, Jr.*

## Review Sources

*Booklist* 104, no. 5 (November 1, 2007): 72.
*The Boston Globe*, July 15, 2007, p. E5.
*The New York Times Book Review* 156 (July 8, 2007): 11.
*The New Yorker* 83, no. 18 (July 2, 2007): 74-75.
*Publishers Weekly* 254, no. 19 (May 7, 2007): 40.
*Time* 169, no. 27 (July 2, 2007): 82.
*USA Today*, July 4, 2007, p. D4.
*The Washington Post*, July 8, 2007, p. BW03.

# NIXON AND KISSINGER
## Partners in Power

*Author:* Robert Dallek (1936-    )
*Publisher:* HarperCollins (New York). 740 pp. $32.50
*Type of work:* Biography, history
*Time:* 1969-1974
*Locale:* Washington, D.C.

*A brilliant examination of the relationship between Richard M. Nixon and Henry Kissinger that explains their decisive impact on American foreign policy*

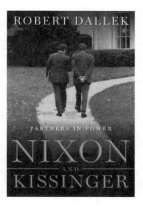

*Principal personages:*
RICHARD M. NIXON (1913-1994), president
of the United States, 1969-1974
HENRY KISSINGER (b. 1923), national
security adviser and secretary of state,
1973-1977
LEONID BREZHNEV (1906-1982), leader of the Soviet Union, 1966-1982
ZHOU ENLAI (CHOU EN-LAI; 1898-1976), premier of the People's
Republic of China, 1949-1976
H. R. "BOB" HALDEMAN (1926-1993), White House chief of staff
under Nixon
WILLIAM P. ROGERS (1913-2001), secretary of state, 1969-1973

Richard M. Nixon remains one of the most enigmatic and interesting of all of the twentieth century presidents. From humble beginnings in Southern California to his disgrace and resignation with the Watergate scandal, Nixon embodied key elements American politics. During his presidency, he fashioned a close working relationship with his national security adviser and later secretary of state Henry Kissinger. Their interaction and what it meant for the world throughout the early 1970's is the subject of Robert Dallek's fascinating book *Nixon and Kissinger: Partners in Power.*

An acclaimed biographer of Franklin D. Roosevelt, Lyndon B. Johnson, and John F. Kennedy, Dallek has tackled another high-profile presidential subject with his customary skill. Throughout his career as a prize-winning author and popular teacher at the University of California, Los Angeles, Dallek has displayed a continuing adroitness at making the presidents about whom he writes come alive on the page. His access to John F. Kennedy's previously closed medical records helped make that biography a national best seller.

Dallek has hit pay dirt once again with this study of the unlikely team of the introverted, tormented national politician Richard Nixon and the German refugee turned world strategist Henry Kissinger. Using the extensive transcripts of Nixon-Kissinger telephone conversations in Kissinger's papers at the Library of Congress plus the Nixon tapes in the National Archives, Dallek reconstructed with precision what the

*Robert Dallek is an award-winning
biographer of American presidents who
has published studies of Franklin D.
Roosevelt, Lyndon B. Johnson, and
John F. Kennedy. He taught for many
years at the University of California,
Los Angeles.*

two men said to each other about foreign policy and the international personalities involved. Their remarks are candid, frank, and often damning to the reputation of the president and his most intimate adviser. Neither of the principals expected that their words would be made public in this fashion. The result is an inside look at how foreign policy was really made during the Vietnam conflict and the Cold War.

Many facets of the characters of both men are troubling. Nixon was in private a coarse, crude individual who delighted in emphasizing how tough he was toward his enemies. Dallek accurately labels the president "a cultural anti-Semite" for his disparaging remarks about Jews and their effect on American foreign relations. That Kissinger, himself a Jew, listened to this rhetorical bilge without protest and often with tacit agreement illustrates the toadying quality that granted him so much sway with Nixon.

Richard Nixon was obsessed with being regarded as a strong president during his administration and later in history. As Dallek reveals, Nixon spent ample time every day making sure that his aides told the press just how resolute and determined he was. Through his chief of staff, H. R. "Bob" Haldeman, Nixon ran a sophisticated public relations campaign to make the case for his presidential excellence. He would not be the last president who emphasized an image of toughness over actually making tough decisions for their own sake. While Nixon prided himself on his focus and discipline, Dallek's analysis indicates that the president often wasted his time with trivial matters designed to feed his ego rather than making policy choices. The self-absorption and narcissism that characterized the mature Nixon are developed with great narrative skill in Dallek's gripping pages.

Kissinger, on the other hand, comes across as the deft courtier, always ready to chime in with the fulsome praise that Nixon coveted. Dallek shows that Kissinger trashed the president in private and to the friendly journalists that he ensnared with leaks and exclusives. Nixon was smart enough to realize how Kissinger was behaving but tolerated the methods of his valuable subordinate nonetheless. There are portions of this book that read as though Dallek had transcribed passages from the script of the television series *The Sopranos* rather than revealed the wise conduct of American foreign policy at the highest levels.

Both of these leaders had a deep disdain for the institutions by which Americans had chosen to govern themselves. Nixon came into office with a contempt for the Department of State and an intention to run foreign policy out of the White House. Secretary of State William P. Rogers was a marginal figure in Nixon's calculations, yet Dallek shows that often the bureaucrats at the State Department had a wiser comprehension of the complexities of foreign policy than the men in charge had. For all their high estimate of their own abilities, Nixon and Kissinger needed the counsel of individuals with more experience in specific areas of the world.

The president and Kissinger had an equally powerful loathing for the role of Congress in foreign policy. Nixon regarded Capitol Hill as a burdensome nuisance and believed that his judgment was far better than that of any of the lawmakers interested in international affairs. As a result, he tried to deny legislators any meaningful part in the shaping of foreign relations. If Nixon had devoted even a small portion of the time he spent getting around Congress to the more productive task of working with senators and representatives, he might have achieved more positive outcomes for the nation.

Throughout the narrative of the book, Dallek traces the corrosive effect of the war in Vietnam on the decisions that Nixon and Kissinger made. Though he never said that he had a secret plan to end the conflict in Southeast Asia, Nixon had campaigned in 1968 as though he intended to wind down American involvement in South Vietnam. In that way, he said, the United States could achieve peace with honor. Mindful of what had happened to destroy Lyndon Johnson, the new president did not wish to see his presidency collapse over the Vietnam issue, so he wanted to convey the impression that the war was ending.

At the same time, Nixon resisted the idea that his nation should concede defeat in Vietnam. He believed that such an outcome would undermine the world position of the United States and embolden the Soviet Union and China. The problem was, as Dallek shows again and again, that there was no viable strategy for victory in Southeast Asia. The government in Saigon lacked the political will to sustain itself against the unrelenting pressure from the Communist north. Nixon and his administration hoped that over time their strategy of Vietnamization would enable the South Vietnamese to establish a credible government. The United States could draw down its troop commitment to reduce domestic discontent with the war while at the same time the South Vietnamese would stand up to assume the burden of defense. Such an approach assumed that there was a real nation in South Vietnam, a proposition that proved false as the Nixon presidency went forward.

Nixon's policy thus went back and forth between a recognition that the war could not be won and an equal unwillingness to accept an American defeat. In the process, thousands of American troops continued to lose their lives in the conflict. Dallek makes a strong case that Nixon and Kissinger could have gotten the same terms for a settlement in 1969 that they agreed to in 1973. His work raises the question of whether the devastating military casualties incurred during those four years served any useful purpose. It is a stern indictment of the cynical leadership that Nixon offered to the nation in foreign affairs.

The overriding problem that influenced these decisions in Southeast Asia was the persistent tension with the Soviet Union amid the Cold War. The Nixon presidency evolved the concept of détente in dealing with Moscow, and Dallek traces the interaction of the two superpowers with insight and perceptive analysis. Nixon sought to have Moscow and its leader Leonid Brezhnev help secure a settlement in Vietnam without success and pursued other means of reducing strains in the East-West relationship.

To that larger end, Nixon and Kissinger crafted the opening to Communist China as the most famous diplomatic initiative of the Nixon years. Of course, one obstacle in the way of previous Democratic presidents taking similar steps had been the adamant opposition of Republican conservatives, led by Nixon, to any engagement with Beijing. Since no one could question Nixon's credentials as an anticommunist leader, he had the political leverage to take actions that he would have decried if a Democrat had initiated them. Dallek effectively presents how Nixon and the Chinese diplomatic leader Zhou Enlai interacted in this area.

The chance to take such a bold move in a clandestine manner also appealed to the side of Nixon and Kissinger that preferred to conduct diplomacy in secret and without much influence from the established bureaucracy or the Congress. When these two men could conspire out of the public view and with few restraints on them, they were in their element as leaders. In the case of China, this approach paid large dividends. However, Dallek also indicates that the secrecy could spill over into unwise actions such as the bombing of Cambodia in 1969 and 1970. One of the great strengths of the book is the balance that Dallek shows in dealing with these very controversial historical issues.

The reader knows that Nixon will run afoul of the Watergate scandal as Dallek's story progresses. While Kissinger was not involved in the criminal events that led to Nixon's impeachment, he shared the perspective that impelled the men around the president toward illegal acts. Like Nixon, Kissinger believed that political enemies were out to frustrate the administration's initiatives. As national security adviser, Kissinger approved wiretapping of journalists suspected of being the recipients of leaks of inside information. From these actions and others taken to punish political opponents, it became easier and easier for Nixon and his other aides to justify extreme measures as part of fighting back against their adversaries. The reader gets a good sense of how fragile civil liberties and the rule of law were in the hands of Richard Nixon when he was bent on victory.

Dallek explains a large body of complicated information with great deftness. Readers should be prepared for an intense immersion in the operations of American foreign policy during these years. Dallek's work sheds new light on the conduct of American foreign policy in the Middle East, the tensions between India and Pakistan, and the United States' involvement in the 1973 overthrow of the government of Chile. The roots of many of the contemporary issues that now divide Americans over the nation's role in the world are explained in Dallek's lucid analysis.

At the end of the epic tale of Nixon and Kissinger, readers will have a new appreciation for the difficulties that face historians of the recent past. The mass of sources that Dallek had to traverse, the intricacy of the issues to be understood, and the human fascination of men such as Nixon and Kissinger would test the talents of any scholar. Dallek has overcome these obstacles in a story that should become a standard source for understanding these two troubled and talented men.

*Lewis L. Gould*

## Review Sources

*The Economist* 383 (May 19, 2007): 87.
*The Journal of American History* 94, no. 2 (September, 2007): 652-653.
*Kirkus Reviews* 75, no. 5 (March 1, 2007): 204.
*Los Angeles Times*, April 24, 2007, p. E1.
*The New York Times* 156 (April 24, 2006): E1-E6.
*The New York Times Book Review* 156 (May 13, 2007): 29.
*Newsweek* 149, no. 20 (May 14, 2007): 47.
*Washington Monthly* 39, no. 6 (June, 2007): 58-61.
*The Washington Post*, May 13, 2007, p. BW07.

# NIXON AND MAO
## The Week That Changed the World

*Author:* Margaret MacMillan (1943- )
*Publisher:* Random House (New York). Illustrated.
404 pp. $27.95
*Type of work:* History
*Time:* 1972
*Locale:* The United States and China

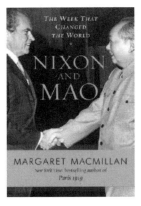

*Nixon's visit to China was a pivotal moment in world history and a step toward world peace, but the devil was in the details*

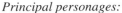

*Principal personages:*
RICHARD M. NIXON (1913-1994), president
of the United States, 1969-1974
MAO ZEDONG (MAO TSE-TUNG; 1893-1976),
chairman of the Chinese Communist Party, 1935-1976
HENRY KISSINGER (b. 1923), Nixon's national security adviser
ZHOU ENLAI (CHOU EN-LAI; 1898-1976), Mao's foreign minister, 1949-
1958, and premier of the People's Republic of China, 1949-1976
H. R. "BOB" HALDEMAN (1926-1993), Nixon's chief of staff
JIANG QING (CHIANG CH'ING; 1914-1991), Mao's actress wife
and political activist, member of the "Gang of Four"

Margaret MacMillan's *Nixon and Mao: The Week That Changed the World* depicts the meeting of two of the world's most powerful and enigmatic leaders that changed the international political situation favorably. The meeting could easily have failed, leaving relations between the United States and China even worse than before.

There were significant misunderstandings of their common past. Americans saw themselves as China's historical friend and protector, its ally during World War II; Chinese saw Americans as part of a West that had treated them as inferiors through the era of imperialism, as backers of the hated Kuomintang that was now in Taiwan and was pretending to be the legitimate government of all China, and as the embodiment of modern capitalism. The Korean and Vietnam Wars had intensified mutual fears and mistrust.

The time had come to change this situation. The unpopularity of the Vietnam War was isolating the United States, while China's rigorous efforts to shape a new, more egalitarian society had managed to alienate even much of the communist world. President Richard M. Nixon was widely regarded as a dangerous ideologue and warmonger, Mao Zedong as a mass murderer of his own people and destroyer of their traditions. Both were, however, basically practical men—realists, in a sense, who believed that morality was inappropriate in power politics. Both also wanted to do good, as they understood it, and were seeking to advance their national interests while avoiding what seemed to be an inevitable war. If they succeeded, history would look on them as great men. Most importantly, Nixon was the only American politician who could have brought conservatives to trust him. Communists took him seriously, and even liberals could dismiss him only at their own cost. He had his enemies, his personality flaws, his impossible hopes and his psychological contradictions, but he saw an opportunity to divide the communist bloc and make China into an ally.

~

*Canadian-born Margaret MacMillan was provost of Trinity College at the University of Toronto from 2002 to 2007, when she took up a new post at Oxford University. Her book* Paris 1919: Six Months That Changed the World *(2001) won numerous prizes for academic and literary excellence.*

~

Mao's peasant background, his tumultuous personal and political life, and his habit of dealing ruthlessly with enemies had sharpened natural habits of cunning and paranoia. What he said now and did later often had little in common. What were his motives for inviting a hated enemy to China?

Even historians who are skeptical of psychohistory see few other ways of approaching either Nixon or Mao. Both were very private, even secretive. Both had clawed their way up from the bottom, and both believed their hold on power was tenuous. Nixon puzzled everyone who met him—his insecurity, his fears bordering on paranoia, his great talents and insights, his ability to rebound from defeat and humiliation. Mao was a powerful despot with the power of life and death over the most populous nation in the world, but he had two serious problems, neither well-understood inside or outside of China. First, he was not well—he could barely walk and sometimes could not get out of bed; second, his government was unstable, but he refused even to appoint a successor. Experts analyzed the personality and motives of each leader but could not make much sense of either one. The Americans had almost no information from which to work; the Chinese were fearful of failing to follow the party line.

Thus it was that when Nixon's plane taxied to the reception committee in China, no one knew exactly what would happen. Nixon's people even looked out the window to see whether the president should wear an overcoat when he stepped out to shake the hand of Chinese premier Zhou Enlai. Pat Nixon wore a vivid red coat, ignoring warnings that in China only prostitutes wore red.

Many of the officials in the reception party were acting ministers or deputy ministers. This was not intended to be an insult: So many prominent men had fallen from favor in the recent Cultural Revolution that inexperience and confusion reigned in every bureau. The great exception was Zhou, born to a Mandarin family during the Boxer Rebellion, who was well educated and urbane. During his youth, China fell increasingly into powerless confusion and under foreign domination. Studying in Japan, Zhou encountered the works of Karl Marx; in 1920, he went to France, two years later helping found the Chinese Communist Party. When he came home, he was among the nation's foremost experts on the West; when he joined Mao in 1935, he became so valuable that in 1949 he was named the victorious communists' first foreign minister. He was soon internationally known as a capable and subtle negotiator.

Zhou's American counterpart was Henry Kissinger, a former Harvard professor who agreed with Nixon that diplomacy was a critical and enjoyable art, best conducted by individuals who could judge situations with little regard for morality or political pressures. He had come to the United States as a teenager, escaping from Nazi Germany at almost the last moment; as a scholar he demonstrated extraordinary brilliance at analysis and argument. He could not be Nixon's friend, but they had much in common—insecurity, sensitivity to insults, a love of the pomp and ceremony of office, and joy in the slippery world of politics. As national security adviser, he was to eclipse the colorless secretary of state, William P. Rogers; it helped that Nixon mistrusted all career diplomats, who were too cautious, too bureaucratic, and unable to see the big picture as he did.

The first meeting of the two leaders had little planning. Mao, wanting to meet Nixon immediately, was barely persuaded to allow the visitors to go to their villa and refresh themselves. Unable to restrain himself long, however, he ordered the president brought to him immediately. The ensuing conversation was a stunning success, each of the men even making fun of Kissinger, but they discussed nothing of significance. Zhou remained largely silent, looking anxiously at this watch, concerned both about Mao's strength and the banquet scheduled for the evening.

Each side knew that the world was watching. Consequently, the emphasis was always on the positive—jovial photographs, toasts at banquets, and visits to tourist sites. Zhou remembered the snub by John Foster Dulles who, in 1954, refused to shake his hand; he was determined to avoid a repetition of that insult. There were serious issues, such as avoiding nuclear war, that Nixon wished to discuss, but Mao and Zhou preferred to develop personal relationships first.

Indeed, there was a great deal of history that lay behind this encounter, and the Chinese leaders were unwilling to ignore it. Their subordinates, meanwhile, had no more idea what was happening than did the American delegation. All four leaders were secretive by nature, and all enjoyed springing surprises.

This very visit had been such a surprise. Nixon, the arch-anticommunist, had used Pakistani contacts to arrange a visit by Kissinger the previous July. Kissinger had sensed that Taiwan was the principal stumbling block to good relations and assistance in bringing the Vietnam War to an end. This issue might be bypassed by a general agreement that the United States would detach itself from Taiwan if China would vow not to attack. China wanted freedom on its southern frontiers in order to confront an increasingly bellicose Soviet Union. All this was very indirect and tentative, but enough for Nixon to risk his reputation on the visit. He later summarized his goals: Taiwan was the most crucial, Vietnam the most urgent. These were important distinctions, because one was long-term, the other immediate.

What the world knew was the picture presented by White House chief of staff H. R. "Bob" Haldeman, who micromanaged every image and word about the historic meeting. Given the large number of reporters present, this meant providing them with something to send home every day. Below that surface were mundane meetings, meaningless banquets, and endless discussions of trivial matters. Zhou warned, obliquely, that Jiang Qing, Mao's wife, could ruin everything if she wished.

Jiang had risen from obscurity to become a major force in the Cultural Revolution; she hated foreign ideas, foreign practices, and foreigners in general. She selected one of her operas, *The Red Detachment of Women*, for the visitors' entertainment. Some worried that its bold propaganda would insult the guests, but Jiang herself was more worried about whether or not to wear a dress, which the Americans would expect but which had been banned; in the end, she wore neither a dress nor a proletarian costume but a suit. Nixon enjoyed the show and applauded lustily.

What had this visit produced? That was the problem. The very language of the joint summary, the Shanghai Communiqué, was so vague as to bother Secretary of State Rogers. While trade, exchanges, the India-Pakistan conflict, and Taiwan were all mentioned, other subjects, such as world revolution, were not. There were even disagreements as to whether the participants should have their middle initials in their names. How would Nixon handle the shocked reactions in Moscow, Tokyo, and other world powers?

After a week, the principals were too tired to continue talks. They had inched toward one another on basic matters, each evening breaking for long and elaborate banquets, and they had visited cities and tourist sites. Most of the work fell to Kissinger and Zhou. The details were few and unimportant. The visit's significance was in establishing a new relationship between the two nations. Optimism was the prevailing feeling in both countries. The potential for peace could be sensed by all.

Nixon received a hero's welcome at home, the last he would enjoy. When North Vietnam immediately launched an offensive into the South, Nixon ordered heavy bombing that provoked only a mild protest from Beijing. Although the Soviet Union signed a major arms limitation treaty and American forces were being withdrawn from Vietnam, Nixon's reelection had been followed by the Watergate hearings. When impeachment seemed certain, Nixon resigned.

The Chinese watched all this with bewilderment. Mao did not understand it at all, but his health was failing too rapidly for that to matter. Since he mistrusted all doctors, he agreed only reluctantly to allow medical specialists to see him; no one dared recommend treatment, and in any case he would have refused it.

Mao's courtiers began intriguing for the succession. Jiang seemed best poised to seize power, although Zhou helped make Deng Xiaoping vice premier, Deng had to take refuge in the south, protected by the army. Zhou's death was followed shortly by Mao's. A month later, the army struck, arresting Jiang and her closest collaborators (the "Gang of Four").

The gains for America were less immediate: South Vietnam and Cambodia fell, but relations with the Soviet Union improved; Taiwan became less of a problem. The gains for China came equally slowly, but more surely: The Chinese Communist Party abandoned its efforts at social engineering, reached out increasingly to the West, and became an industrial giant. The relationship had been bound to change, but it took four men to begin the process.

*William L. Urban*

## Review Sources

*The Atlantic Monthly* 299, no. 5 (June, 2007): 122-123.
*Biography: An Interdisciplinary Quarterly* 30, no. 3 (Summer, 2007): 438.
*Current History* 107, no. 701 (September, 2007): 299.
*International Herald Tribune*, February 24, 2007, p. 13.
*The New York Times Book Review* 156 (February 25, 2007): 14-15.
*Publishers Weekly* 253, no. 48 (December 4, 2007): 47.
*The Spectator* 303 (March 3, 2007): 55-56.
*Washington Monthly* 39, no. 4 (April, 2007): 43-45.

# NOTEBOOKS

*Author:* Tennessee Williams (1911-1983)
Edited with notes by Margaret Bradham Thornton
*Publisher:* Yale University Press (New Haven, Conn.).
Illustrated. 828 pp. $40.00
*Type of work:* Diary
*Time:* 1936-1958 and 1979-1981
*Locale:* Principally St. Louis, New Orleans, New York
City, and Rome

*In almost eight hundred entries written in thirty note-
books covering twenty-five years, Williams records the oftentimes agonizing process of writing his poetry, fiction,
and plays while coming to terms with his homosexuality
and dependence on drugs and alcohol*

*Principal personages:*
TENNESSEE WILLIAMS, a leading American dramatist
  of the mid-twentieth century
EDWINA DAKIN WILLIAMS, his mother
ROSE ISABEL WILLIAMS, his sister and model for many of his heroines
FRANK MERLO, his lover for fourteen years
DONALD WINDHAM, his friend and one-time collaborator
PAUL BOWLES, his close friend and composer of incidental
  music for Williams's plays
AUDREY WOOD, his longtime agent
ELIA KAZAN, a leading director for film and theater, including
  several of Williams's plays

During much of Tennessee Williams's playwriting career, including the extraordinarily prolific period from *The Glass Menagerie* (pr. 1944) through *The Night of the
Iguana* (pr. 1961) when he wrote almost a dozen enduring works for the stage that
established his reputation as one of America's foremost dramatists, he kept a series
of private journals as well. Unlike what might be expected, these journals, now finally
in print under the collective title *Notebooks*, almost never contain working ideas or
plot outlines for his fiction or character sketches or fragments of dialogue for his
plays. Rather, they tell a personal story, even generally more revealing than the one
found in his *Memoirs* (1975). While that admittedly commercial publishing ven-
ture arrived with great public fanfare, Williams was ambivalent over whether these
*Notebooks* should ever be read by others, sometimes indicating that they were for
his eyes only as a potentially therapeutic confessional. Indeed, when he later goes
back and rereads them and sometimes even reacts to them, his second thoughts
about his earlier entries, reproduced here in his own handwriting, assume a startlingly
poignant immediacy.

~

*One of the most prolific authors to emerge from the American South, Tennessee Williams wrote poetry, fiction (both short stories and a novel), screenplays, essays, and autobiography. He remains best known as the playwright of such classic dramas as* The Glass Menagerie *(pr. 1944),* A Streetcar Named Desire *(pr. 1947), and* Cat on a Hot Tin Roof *(pr. 1955), the last two of which were awarded the Pulitzer Prize.*

~

The preponderance of the *Notebooks* cover two periods: what might be called his apprenticeship period, the eight years from November, 1936, through November, 1943, that saw the disastrous Boston tryout of what was to have been Williams's first Broadway play, *Battle of Angels* (pr. 1940), but also the writing of the prison drama *Night About Nightingales*, composed in 1939 but only very belatedly produced by the National Theatre in London and New York to posthumous praise sixty years later; and the two years from June, 1953, through September, 1955, the first of which witnessed the Broadway failure of his expressionistic *Camino Real*, while the second saw the triumphant success of his Pulitzer Prize-winning *Cat on a Hot Tin Roof*. The lengthiest gap, on the other hand, is the twenty-year period from 1958 to 1979, for which no journals seem to exist—although Williams suggests in one of his retrospective annotations that his life during those years was substantially "similar" to that recorded elsewhere.

In fact, the leitmotifs that will recur over and again in these journals are already well-established in the first several years: his insecurity and anxiety; his lack of confidence and sense of failure; his self-pity and self-absorption; his loneliness and restless wandering; his fear of death and of time's destruction of physical prowess and creative energy; his emotional problems and multiple physical ailments. He was prey to what he called, as early as 1943, his "blue devils" or "neuroses," a "Williams family trait . . . tak[ing] the form of interior storms that show remarkably little from the outside but which create a deep chasm between myself and all other people." Every day was undoubtedly a battle to keep going on; and yet write he did, virtually every single morning. In fact, "*En Avant!*" which first appears in entries for 1942, became his lifelong motto. The composite portrait that emerges is of an enormously conflicted and yet compelling human person, as complex as the best characters he created, with all the "mystery" and unknowability that he found essential marks of truth. Thus, Williams cautions his putative readers, "these notebooks despite their attempt at merciless candor about my life fall short, give very little, perhaps really distort unfavorably for I seem inclined to note only the seedier things." As Elia Kazan, the director of several of Williams's most lasting plays, warned Margaret Bradham Thornton, the independent scholar responsible for editing these *Notebooks*, "Williams was one of the most secret people he had ever known. 'Latch onto that word,' he instructed."

Two tensions that exerted an immeasurable impact on his development as an artist are his relationship with his sister Rose, with whom he shared an inordinately strong emotional attachment and who was ultimately diagnosed as suffering from dementia praecox and subjected to a prefrontal lobotomy, and his coming to terms with his own homosexuality. Williams, who felt enormous failure for not having been at home to prevent Rose's lobotomy, would immortalize her as the model for Laura in the autobiographical *Menagerie*. Still, that would not assuage a gnawing guilt—related both in the *Memoirs* and again here—over an incident when he experienced revulsion toward her and, in a moment of deliberate cruelty that he came to see as unforgivable, called her "disgusting." It is not just that her affliction is unfathomable, or that the string of "obscenities" she uttered during one of the family's visits to the sanitarium proved shocking, but that her mental condition makes him question the "mysterious" ways of God. Nevertheless, forty years later, in light of his commitment to always see that her financial needs were met, he praises her as "the living presence of truth and faith in my life . . . [who] defined a true nobility to me and gave to my life what I have known of grace."

The notebooks suggest that Williams's first consummated homosexual encounter occurred not in raffish New Orleans but on a trip to California in the summer of 1939, an event that apparently nauseated him as a violation of some essential "purity." Still, physical release is also liberating for him as a writer, something that he craves not only as a "diversion" but even more so because it is integral to and expressive of something essential to his nature as a human being. Nevertheless, the promiscuity involved in incessant cruising for sex partners as a surrogate for any strong family connection would continue to trouble him because of his residual Puritanism. He yearns, instead, for something that will be "clean" and lasting, not the transient and endless succession of one-night stands that seem sometimes to have an enervating effect upon his work. What he seeks can only be found when physical sex is linked to tenderness and love, "comfort" and affection; but then, that is no different from what characterizes mature heterosexual relationships in Williams's works, since it is only selfish sexuality that uses and abuses the other that Williams consistently denigrates and judges harshly.

Physical sexuality has the potentiality, then, for being not only transformative but even a kind of religious experience, as it was for D. H. Lawrence, one of the writers Williams most admired (along with Marcel Proust and Anton Chekhov). At the best of times, it is "as if a benign Providence, or shall we be frank and say God, had suddenly taken cognizance and pity of my long misery . . . and given me . . . a token of forgiveness." What he fears and condemns, both in his rejection of Rose and in self-centered acts of sex, is a kind of "calcification" of the heart that is the very opposite of the ethical code that adumbrates his plays: the requirement to go out non-judgmentally in kindness to all those other "tortured" people in need of compassion. What he valorizes most of all are decency, tolerance, and gentleness. As he writes in an entry from 1941 that presages the indelible curtain line of *A Streetcar Named Desire* (pr. 1947): "To you—whoever you are—when I am gone—Remember to be kind tonight to some lonely person—For me."

Those who approach the *Notebooks* hoping to find comments about specific works will generally be just as disappointed as those who read the *Memoirs* for that reason, for although the difficult process of composition is everywhere clear, there is little discussion of the plays themselves. As Williams wrote memorably in his *Memoirs*, in a passage that applies just as easily to the *Notebooks*: "Why do I resist writing about my plays? The truth is that my plays have been the most important element of my life for God knows how many years. But I feel the plays speak for themselves. And that my life hasn't and that it has been remarkable enough, in its continual contest with madness, to be worth setting upon paper." On the nature of his art in general, Williams reveals here that he early realized that he was a better playwright than poet, that writing drama required him to curb and control his lyrical impulse, and that he believes his works are most satisfying when they are most simple and direct. During the last twenty years of his life, oftentimes many critics were cruel not only in their dismissiveness of his more experimental works but also in their intensely personal attacks on Williams's choosing to continue to write—one even going so far as to suggest that it would have been better had he died in the late 1950's. To them his dignified rejoinder is: "Perhaps I was never meant to exist at all, but if I hadn't, a number of my created beings would have been denied their passionate existence."

To read just the pages reproducing Williams's journals means, however, learning only half the story, since that would be to ignore half of what appears in the published *Notebooks*. On the pages facing his entries, Thornton has provided close to 1,100 notes, identifying references to people, places, productions, and publications. These include thumbnail sketches of family members, friends, and companions, as well as of fellow authors (such as novelists Carson McCullers and Christopher Isherwood) and theatrical associates (including director Erwin Piscator, set designer Jo Mielziner, and actress Anna Magnani). Other annotations provide performance histories of plays; plot synopses of unpublished and unproduced works, many of which would later appear under other titles; and facsimiles (both holograph and typescript) of unpublished poems or passages from letters held in various scholarly archives.

Most usefully, Thornton traces the appearance of various abiding interests (including the influence of film), recurrent subjects (such as suicide), or thematic motifs ("the destructive impact of society on the sensitive, nonconformist individual") that infuse Williams's works; she inserts, as well, two dozen brief biographical and historical narratives that bridge the hiatuses in the journals themselves. Finally, she has searched out and selected the 200 facsimile pages and 350 photographs, including numerous set designs and more than a dozen of Williams's own paintings, that superbly illustrate the volume, ending with photos of the playwright's death mask and the crowd of admirers, mostly young, gathered outside New York's Hotel Elysee where he died. All in all, the book becomes not only a treasure trove for aficionados of Williams and the American theater and a sociocultural record of his life and times but also a meditation on the toll of success and celebrity and the inevitable tension between the public and private life of the artist.

*Thomas P. Adler*

## Review Sources

*Booklist* 103, no. 8 (December 15, 2006): 13.
*Georgia Review* 61, no. 2 (Summer, 2007): 422-427.
*Library Journal* 132, no. 2 (February 1, 2007): 73.
*London Review of Books* 29, no. 19 (October 4, 2007): 31-33.
*The New York Review of Books* 54, no. 20 (December 20, 2007): 38-44.
*The New York Times Book Review* 156 (March 4, 2007): 20.
*New Statesman* 136 (March 19, 2007): 56.
*Publishers Weekly* 254, no. 1 (January 1, 2007): 39.

# NOVELS IN THREE LINES

*Author:* Félix Fénéon (1861-1944)
*First published: Nouvelles en trois lignes,* 1997,
  in France
Translated from the French and with an introduction
  by Luc Sante
*Publisher:* New York Review Books (New York).
  208 pp. $14.00
*Type of work:* Current affairs, miscellaneous
*Time:* 1906
*Locale:* France and the Middle East

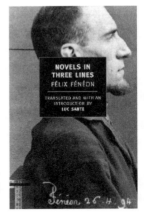

*A translation of 1,066 news items that were each con-
densed into three lines of text by the French anarchist and
literary figure*

*Novels in Three Lines* is a work that is all but impossible to characterize. Its translator notes that "the closest literary relative to Fénéon's three-line novellas may be
Charles Reznikoff's *Testimony: The United States (1885-1915), Recitative* (1965,
1968, 1978)," but, since Reznikoff's work is unlikely to be known by most readers,
the comparison conceals even more than it reveals. The story behind *Novels in Three
Lines* is this: For several months in 1906, Félix Fénéon (Arthur Rimbaud's editor,
former correspondent for the conservative newspaper *Le Figaro*, and anarchist sympathizer) wrote a series of brief entries for the liberal newspaper *Le Matin* under the
heading *Nouvelles en trois lignes*. The title of Fénéon's column was itself a play on
words that is difficult to convey in English. Since the term *nouvelles* applies to both
"news" and "novellas," Fénéon's column suggested that it was a series of either
"three-line news items" or "three-line novels," and the entries themselves reflected
qualities of each.

Each of Fénéon's columns would contain roughly twenty items, organized into
such categories as *banlieue parisienne* (events occurring in the area surrounding
Paris), *départements* (other French provinces), and *étranger* (foreign countries,
which to Fénéon almost always meant the Middle East). The author would take a few
news items that caught his eye, reduce them to no more than three lines of text, and
produce an extremely short but highly evocative story. Although written in prose,
Fénéon's entries possessed a highly poetic quality. Each entry is reminiscent of haiku,
the fragments of Sappho's lyric poems, or the epitaphs from Edgar Lee Masters's
*Spoon River Anthology* (1915). The result is equally a vivid picture of daily life in
1906 France and an exploration of what it is that makes a story compelling.

Fénéon was particularly interested in suicides, of which there were a surprising
large number during the months of his column. Hanging appears to have been the
suicides' method of choice in France of 1906, and the victims' motives included such
perennial causes of despair as rejection in love, business failure, and a desire to es-

cape debilitating illnesses. At times, however, Fénéon provides insight into more unusual aims for self-destruction, such as in the case of one man: "Widowed customs agent Ackermann, of Fort-Philippe, Nord, was to have been married today, but was found hanged over the tomb of his wife." This short narrative is typical of the entries that appear in *Novels in Three Lines*. With only a few words, Fénéon tells a complete story. The reader is able to visualize Ackermann, grieving (perhaps for many years) over the death of his wife, before finally hoping to make a new beginning. He agrees to marry again.

*Félix Fénéon was a minor figure in the avant-garde cultural circles of Paris during the early twentieth century. With interests in painting, fiction, and poetry, he translated into French the works of Jane Austen and James Joyce, edited several literary journals, reviewed trends in literature and painting, worked as a journalist, and sold paintings at the Bernheim-Jeune gallery.*

Perhaps he is even genuinely fond of his new fiancé, but all of this is not enough. On the day of the intended ceremony, Ackermann finds that he cannot go through with his plans. Unable to "betray" his deceased wife through this new marriage, he turns to the only option that he can find and hangs himself.

Many of Fénéon's entries are similar. Stories that, if told at any greater length, would cause a reader to skim them quickly and just as quickly forget them become memorable, almost archetypical in their nature. The actual people about whom Fénéon writes prove familiar to the reader—the grieving widower, the jilted lover, the young fool out on a careless spree, the inattentive parent—and the resulting stories condense to fifteen or twenty words an experience that somehow transcends its original setting. Fénéon is fond of the "pointed style" of the Roman poet Martial or the author O. Henry in which a detail revealed only at the very end causes the reader to reexamine everything that came before: "To ensure his place in heaven, Desjeunes of Plainfang, Vosges, had covered with holy pictures the bed where he killed himself with rum." Often Fénéon uses this type of ending merely to create a pleasant surprise. Nevertheless, at other times, such as in the case of the pious drunkard Desjeunes, the effect results in something far more profound. What is the reader to make of Desjeunes' unusual death? It is clear from the tone adopted throughout *Novels in Three Lines* that Fénéon (or perhaps his editor at *Le Matin*) was cynical about religion. Perhaps for this reason, Desjeunes is characterized as inconsistent at best, a genuine hypocrite at worst, who sought to redeem himself through mere tokens for defects that possibly spanned his entire life.

In other entries, Fénéon uses these surprise endings to suggest far more than he tells and to leave the reader imagining what may be the rest of the story: "At a ball in Saint-Symphorien, Isère, Mme Chausson, her lover, his parents, and his friends knifed to death M. Chausson." What, the reader is forced to wonder, could have caused so many different people to attack this single victim? Part of Fénéon's story is suggested by the pairing of Mme. Chausson with "her lover." Still, what caused M. Chausson's own parents and friends to unite against him so fatally? In the case of this story, the narrative impact is derived from unanswered questions, each of which the reader is entitled to answer as he or she wishes. The reader may envision M. Chausson as a modern-day Caesar, cut down on his own Ides of March, or as a real-life Ratchett, the victim who was stabbed by nearly everyone in Agatha Christie's *Murder on the Orient Express* (1934). Chausson may have been undeserving of his fate or he may have received his just comeuppance. In either case, it is in what Fénéon does *not* say that this story finds its power.

Several of Fénéon's stories have multiple layers and are capable of tragedy and comedy simultaneously: "Catherine Rosello of Toulon, mother of four, got out of the way of a freight train. She was then run over by a passenger train." The reader first experiences a sense of relief in Rosello's narrow escape, then dark humor as she dives out of the frying pan into the fire. The "punch line" comes as rapidly as the passenger train that seems to arrive out of nowhere, and yet, as one glances back at the passage, the words "mother of four," which are passed over almost without notice on a first reading, seem to stand out hauntingly from the passage. What at first seems humorous because Rosello is unknown to the reader assumes elements of tragedy in light of those words. Rosello's death, one realizes, has consequences, and it becomes all too easy to visualize its impact on the victim's young family. Despite its brevity, therefore, this entry and others like it develop a great deal of complexity.

It is also possible to view *Novels in Three Lines* as an exploration into the nature of what constitutes a satisfying narrative. Although Fénéon preferred to support the works of others rather than to publish on his own, he had excellent credentials as a man of letters. Fénéon edited Rimbaud's *Les Illuminations* (1886; *Illuminations*, 1932), encouraged the publication of Comte de Lautréamont's *Les Chants de Maldoror* (1868), translated Jane Austen's *Northanger Abbey* (1818), founded a bewildering array of literary journals, and published the first translation of James Joyce's fiction in France. He was a regular member of Stéphane Mallarmé's weekly salon and befriended several of the Symbolist poets. With a background such as this, *Novels in Three Lines* emerges as an experiment in minimalism. For instance, an accidental death can be retold with only a few words while still possessing all the elements of a complete narrative: "Some drinkers in Houilles were passing around a pistol they thought was unloaded. Lagrange pulled the trigger. He did not get up."

The structure that appears in the above example is repeated in many of Fénéon's entries, such as the following tale about a young man from a Parisian suburb: "Sigismond Martin, of Les Clayes, went to sleep in a field. His friends came to wake him up. They were unsuccessful; he was dead." In these two examples, the name of the deceased combined with the setting of the incident (Houilles, Les Clayes) gives the story an emotional weight that it would lack if it were merely about "a young man" from "some village." A bare minimum of background information (drinkers passing around a pistol, Sigismond Martin sleeping in a field) sets the stage for a misunderstanding—the drinkers thought the gun was unloaded; his friends thought Sigismond Martin was asleep—which is then followed by a single action (the pulling of the trigger, the inability of the group to rouse their friend) and a sudden dénouement.

Just as Fénéon's Symbolist colleagues were experimenting with concise phrasing that suggested multiple levels of meaning, and while the post-Impressionists who knew Fénéon were reducing images to a few essential shapes and colors, Fénéon's *Novels in Three Lines* was achieving a similar effect in prose. Fénéon drew his material from the strange events that occurred in the lives of ordinary people throughout 1906. He then stripped away everything that was not vital, leaving the reader with only a few core details capable of revealing everything that was really necessary.

Several repeated subjects suggest matters that were topical in Fénéon's day. For instance, about a dozen passages deal with the counterfeiting of coins, for instance, while roughly the same number involve a controversy over whether crucifixes should be allowed in public school classrooms. Usually, however, Fénéon introduces no thread that continues beyond a single three-line item. Someone appears, either does or suffers something unexpected, and then vanishes again, never to reappear. In several of Fénéon's entries, it is not the incident itself or the author's structure that is particularly interesting but an unusual turn of phrase that elevates the incident from the commonplace: "Prematurely jealous, J. Boulon, of Parc-Saint-Maur, pumped a revolver shot in the thigh of his fiancé, Germaine S." Here the words "prematurely jealous" cause the reader to study the entry. Perhaps, Fénéon appears to be saying, if Germaine had been Boulon's wife instead of his fiancé, this act of jealousy would have been less noteworthy. In other passages, Fénéon uses incongruity to achieve a similar effect: "Since Delorce left her, Cécile Ward had refused to take him back unless he married her. Finding this stipulation unacceptable, he stabbed her." "Finding this stipulation unacceptable" is language one more frequently associates with business negotiations than with affairs of the heart, particularly those that lead to violent assault. Nevertheless, by juxtaposing the two last clauses in this entry, Fénéon both surprises the reader and develops interest out of what may otherwise have been a merely tawdry and insignificant tale.

The entries included in this work were collected more than fifty years after Fénéon's death. Although *Novels in Three Lines* can be quickly read, it is a book that is best enjoyed when savored. Readers should remember that they would have encountered only a handful of entries in any one issue of *Le Matin* and resist the urge to read too many in a single sitting. Like short and evocative poems, Fénéon's three-line novels assume their deepest meanings only through reflection and close examination.

*Jeffrey L. Buller*

## Review Sources

*London Review of Books* 29, no. 19 (October 4, 2007): 9-11.
*Modern Painters*, July/August, 2007, p. 93.
*The New York Times Book Review* 156 (September 2, 2007): 21.
*Publishers Weekly* 254, no. 25 (June 18, 2007): 46.
*The Village Voice* 52, no. 49 (December 5, 2007): 44.

# NUREYEV
## The Life

*Author:* Julie Kavanagh (1952-    )
*Publisher:* Pantheon Books (New York). Illustrated.
    782 pp. $37.50
*Type of work:* Biography, fine arts
*Time:* 1938-1993
*Locale:* Russia, Paris, Denmark, London, and the United
    States

*An in-depth and probing portrayal of Rudolf Nureyev
as an exceptional ballet dancer, a star personality, an individual tormented by his otherness, and a volatile and
charismatic individual*

*Principal personages:*
RUDOLF NUREYEV, world-famous Russian ballet dancer
    and choreographer
HAMET NUREYEV, his father, an army man and Tartar
FARIDA NUREYEV, Rudolf's mother, who took him to ballet as a child
ALEXANDER IVANOVICH PUSHKIN, Nureyev's teacher and mentor
    in Leningrad
XENIA JOSIFOVNA JURGENSON PUSHKIN, Alexander's wife, friend,
    and lover of Nureyev
TAMARA ZAKRZHEVSKAYA, lifelong friend of Nureyev
TEJA KREMKE, East German student at the Vaganova School, friend
    and first male lover of Nureyev
CLARA SAINT, ballet enthusiast, instrumental in helping Nureyev defect
ERIK BRUHN, Danish dancer, the ideal dancer in Nureyev's opinion,
    and later his lover
GEORGE BALANCHINE, Russian choreographer working in the
    United States, revered by Nureyev
MARGOT FONTEYN, Royal Ballet prima ballerina assoluta, partner
    of Nureyev
NINETTE DE VALOIS, director of Royal Ballet
WALLACE POTTS, lover of Nureyev
CHARLES JUDE, protégé of Nureyev at Paris Opéra Ballet
DOUCE FRANÇOIS, friend who was obsessively in love with Nureyev

In *Nureyev: The Life*, Julie Kavanagh presents a detailed, factual account of
Rudolf Nureyev's life as a dancer, as an individual who was fascinated by all the arts
and ever eager to learn more about them, and as a man driven to experience as much
as he could during his life. The biography is supported by extensive and meticulous
research. Drawing on Nureyev's *An Autobiography*, published in 1962, and his personal letters and papers as well as interviews with his family members, Kavanagh

has provided a comprehensive coverage of
his childhood. This biography vividly portrays the poverty in which Nureyev lived as
achild and the hardships imposed upon the
family under the Soviet system. The biography also presents a considerable amount of
background information on his parents,
Hamet and Farida, as well as insights into the
Tartar culture in which Nureyev was reared.

Kavanagh's account of his arrival at the
Vaganova School in Leningrad and his years
of study there emphasize Nureyev's over-

~

*Julie Kavanagh is a journalist who has
worked as a dance editor for* The
Spectator. *She has also been an editor
for* Harpers & Queen, Vanity Fair, *and*
The New Yorker. *She received the
Dance Perspectives Foundation de la
Torre Bueno Prize for her biography*
Secret Muses: The Life of Frederick
Ashton *(1996).*

~

powering desire to dance and his determination to succeed regardless of his less-than-
ideal dancer's body and his rather late beginning of serious ballet training. Kavanagh
also fully develops the problems Nureyev faced as a result of his being different from
the other students and of his volatile and intensely sensitive nature. She portrays
Nureyev's insistence upon his own ideas about what dance should be and his individ-
ualism as a dancer even when he was a beginning student. He was never satisfied to
accept even a teacher's control of his dancing. Kavanagh's portrayal of his relationship with Alexander Ivanovich Pushkin and his wife, Xenia Josifovna Jurgenson
Pushkin, calls attention to how influential they were in his development both as a
dancer and as an individual.

Having obtained access to the KGB files regarding Nureyev's defection in 1961,
Kavanagh recounts the episode with a sensitivity to what it meant for Nureyev, for
his family and friends, and to Russia as a political entity. Although Nureyev was completely apolitical and wanted only the freedom to dance as he wished and to become
a star, the defection could be nothing other than a political embarrassment for the
country and a very difficult situation for his loved ones. Kavanagh emphasizes the
real and serious danger in which Nureyev placed himself but underscores his lack
of choices, as returning to Russia would have destroyed his career. Since he was unable to accept the state control that dominated every aspect of communist Russia,
Nureyev would not have been permitted to continue to dance with the Kirov Ballet
but would have been exiled to a provincial school. After his defection, he lived many
years with the ever-present fear of being either killed or seized by the KGB and
returned to Russia, where he would have been tried as a traitor.

Kavanagh includes myriad detailed descriptions of Nureyev's solo performances
in which he made changes to dances that had traditionally been performed in exactly
the same way since their creation. She also provides extensive descriptions of his
costumes and treats his interest in costuming and its importance for him as a dancer.
Concerned about his short legs, Nureyev was always very much aware of how a costume made him appear, and he used both color and design to lengthen the appearance
of his legs. Such passages provide further insight into why Nureyev needed to leave
Russia and to pursue his career in the West, where change and innovation were not
only welcomed but also encouraged.

Having studied ballet herself, Kavanagh includes informative discussions of the various schools of ballet and the techniques associated with them, especially the Vaganova and the Bournonville. She examines how these schools either conflicted with Nureyev's ideas about dance or complemented them. She repeatedly returns to Nureyev's obsession to transform the male ballet dancer from a mere support for the ballerina into a performer in his own right, equal to the ballerina he partnered. Nureyev incorporated certain ways ballerinas moved into his own dancing. He danced on the balls of his feet and used the emotive port de bras of female ballet dancers. Moreover, Kavanagh makes apparent Nureyev's extreme respect for and fascination with Erik Bruhn as the ideal male dancer and with George Balanchine as the most innovative of choreographers, as well as Nureyev's desire to emulate Vaslav Nijinsky. However, Kavanagh never loses sight of the fact that Nureyev never intended to be a replica of anyone but rather wished to learn from each dancer or choreographer the techniques and skills he admired and then to incorporate them into his own style.

Kavanagh gives a thorough, chronological presentation of Nureyev's work and performance after his defection. As she discusses his work with the various companies, she sensitively recreates the artistic and aesthetic tensions that he faced as he attempted to incorporate the styles and techniques of Western ballet into his own performance without totally rejecting his Russian traditions. Her discussion of how Nureyev and Margot Fonteyn, prima ballerina assoluta of the Royal Ballet, developed into the most renowned dance partnership of their time leads the reader to understand how dancers with different attributes and techniques can create roles together, acquiring new dimensions of performance from each other. With her controlled and concise way of dancing, Fonteyn brought about a measure of reserve and stability in Nureyev's dance while with his Russian bravura he released an intensity of emotion not seen in her before.

Nureyev's individualistic, temperamental, and egotistical characteristics dominate Kavanagh's portrait of the dancer. Nureyev appears as a disruptive force. He is always Nureyev the star, always insisting upon controlling the roles he dances and the costumes he wears. He is quick to anger and given to tantrums if he does not agree with how a role is being choreographed or how a dancer is portraying the role. With the Royal Ballet, he does not want to be simply one of the company but to remain Rudolf Nureyev who dances with the Royal Ballet. This inability to become one of the company delayed his dancing with Balanchine's company for a considerable time. His tenure as director of the Paris Opéra Ballet was fraught with discord with the administration as he insisted upon having his way. Kavanagh softens her portrayal with an emphasis on his charisma and enthusiasm for life.

Including many anecdotes in the biography, Kavanagh fully explores Nureyev as an individual as well as a dancer. She dwells on his Russian-Tartar heritage, which made him susceptible to melancholy and feelings of rejection. She touches upon the problems of communication that he always faced after his defection. He never lost his heavy Russian accent and often had difficulty understanding English. She also reveals how much he missed Russia and how he felt that only Russians could understand what it meant to be Russian. The longer he was away from his country, the more he wished to use classical Russian technique in the ballets he staged.

Kavanagh devotes a considerable amount of the book to Nureyev's sexual passion, the other driving force in his life. Kavanagh depicts Nureyev as endowed with a sensuality that was irresistibly attractive to both men and women. She recounts his many amorous attachments, both heterosexual and homosexual, including his first homosexual experience with Teja Kremke, his affair with Pushkin's wife (which was instigated by Xenia), his long love affair with Bruhn, his later love affair with Wallace Potts, and his attempted love affair with Charles Jude, as well as other sexual encounters and his tendency to cruise the homosexual sections of London and Paris.

The last chapters of the book deal with Nureyev's affliction with AIDS. The major themes of this section are his determination to continue to perform and to plan for the future and the devotion shown by a core of friends: Wallace Potts, Douce François, Charles Jude, Jeannette Herrmann, and his two sisters. For almost ten years, Nureyev still appeared on stage as a dancer, even returning to Leningrad to dance at the Kirov Theater. At the same time, he began to learn to conduct an orchestra in order to have a new career, since he was weakening as a dancer. Kavanagh devotes the final pages of her book to a description of Nureyev's funeral and internment in the Russian cemetery of Sainte-Geneviève-des-Bois.

Based on ten years of exhaustive research, *Nureyev: The Life* has been recognized as the definitive biography of Rudolf Nureyev. It has for the most part enjoyed a positive reception; however, there has been some objection to the amount of space devoted to Nureyev's sexual exploits as well as a certain dissatisfaction with Nureyev's portrayal as, for the most part, morose and difficult.

*Shawncey Webb*

## Review Sources

*The Advocate*, no. 994 (October 9, 2007): 57.
*Booklist* 104, no. 3 (October 1, 2007): 14.
*The New Republic* 237, no. 10 (November 19, 2007): 34-42.
*The New York Times Book Review* 157 (December 2, 2007): 34-36.
*The New Yorker* 83, no. 30 (October 8, 2007): 88-94.
*Publishers Weekly* 254, no. 32 (August 13, 2007): 58.
*San Francisco Chronicle*, October 14, 2007, p. M3.
*The Spectator* 305 (October 13, 2007): 50.
*The Washington Post*, November 11, 2007, p. BW03.

# OF A FEATHER
## A Brief History of American Birding

*Author:* Scott Weidensaul (1959-    )
*Publisher:* Harcourt (Orlando, Fla.). 358 pp. $25.00
*Type of work:* Environment, history of science, nature
*Time:* Prehistory to 2007
*Locale:* The United States

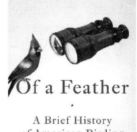

*Traces bird watching in America from the Native Americans' use and understanding of birds through the split of bird study into science (ornithology) and hobby (birding) to its reunification in the "citizen-scientist," the birder who contributes to scientific studies of birds*

*Principal personages:*
    JOHN JAMES AUDUBON, best-known early
        American illustrator and student of birds
    ALEXANDER WILSON, pioneer bird artist and student,
        often called the father of American ornithology
    MARK CATESBY, English naturalist who produced an early
        book describing and picturing American birds and other wildlife
    ROGER TORY PETERSON, American ornithologist who renovated the
        field guide, making it more attractive to and usable by laypersons
    DAVID SIBLEY, American ornithologist who took the field guide for
        birds to new heights of detail and precision

Scott Weidensaul seems to have two purposes in writing this book. The first, insinuated by the title *Of a Feather: A Brief History of American Birding*, is to outline the history of the burgeoning hobby of bird watching (birding). The second is to encourage bird watchers (birders) to go beyond their proclivity to count as many bird species as possible on each outing. He believes they should pay more attention to the natural history, behavior, and ecology of birds.

Expanding on the second purpose, Weidensaul explores the tensions that have existed between bird watchers and scientific students of birds (ornithologists). In the first chapter, he contrasts the two camps and suggests that no such tension was present in the early history of North American bird study, because each early student of North American birds was both birder and ornithologist. He describes the lives and work of Mark Catesby, Alexander Wilson, John James Audubon, and others as examples. At several points later in the book, he explores the development of different tensions between the two groups. Later still, he points out several ornithological endeavors that depend on nonscientists for much of their data and encourages birders to be involved in collecting those data, in a sense reuniting birder and ornithologist. Finally, he argues that birders and ornithologists need to be more proactive in bird protection and conservation.

His consideration of the origin and early development of the combined science and hobby is neatly done. After a very brief outline of the connections Native Americans had with birds, he considers the lives, contributions, and foibles of Catesby, Wilson, Audubon, and other ornithological pioneers, complete with the plagiarism of Wilson on Catesby, Audubon on Wilson, and Catesby on his predecessors. Weidensaul seems to excuse this malfeasance by pointing out that such "borrowing" was common in that day, but he does not let the plagiarists off the hook entirely. He points out that much of the borrowing was not acknowledged, a clear breach of morality, and he explains some of the subtle ways that the borrower changed his version, suggesting a conscious attempt to cover up the similarity and thus the plagiarism.

*Scott Weidensaul has written a number of popular books on natural history, including* Living on the Wind *(1999), which was a Pulitzer Prize finalist. He has also written for the* Philadelphia Inquirer *and other periodicals. He has a federal license for banding birds and, true to his own admonition, is an active birder, ornithologist, and conservationist.*

Weidensaul describes the methods of the early ornithologists in a chapter titled "Shotgun Ornithology": Find the organism, shoot the organism, prepare the organism for the museum, and study the prepared specimen. Catesby, Wilson, Audubon, and many others used that system. Later, however, these methods led to serious disagreement between ornithologists and birders. Few modern birders see the need for specimen collection. They would document the bird photographically or visually without collecting it, while some ornithologists still prefer to document species and their distributions with specimens.

In the "Shotgun" chapter and the following chapter, titled "Angry Ladies," Weidensaul traces the accomplishments of female ornithologists and birders. He introduces a few whose skill and determination carved out niches for them in the male-dominated field. He argues that women were the backbone of early conservation efforts, which opposed large-scale scientific collection and other activities detrimental to birds. Two examples of such female leadership involve the early history of the National Audubon Society, which was organized to protect birds from hunters, feather collectors, scientific collectors, and others who were slaughtering them at the time. Ironically, the society's namesake, Audubon, was a "shotgun ornithologist." The society was named for him because of his contribution to the knowledge of North American birds and his paintings, not for his collecting skills. Collection of specimens was (and still is) necessary to understand some aspects of ornithology. However, the combination of overenthusiastic collectors of birds and their eggs (often collecting more than necessary) and market hunters who killed birds for several uses, including feathers to decorate women's hats, was decimating bird populations. In 1886, George Bird Grinnell led an attempt to form an Audubon Society to protect birds. It failed in 1888. Beginning in 1896, Harriet Lawrence Hemenway and several other women renewed the effort, resulting in the Audubon Society's more permanent development.

The second example is from the 1930's. When the male leadership of the Audubon Society failed to press for the protection of the birds passing Hawk Mountain, Pennsylvania, women stepped in again. Local geography funnels migrating hawks past this point in the Appalachian Mountains, and hunters were shooting many of them as they passed. Richard Pough documented the slaughter photographically, but the Audubon Society responded sluggishly to the evidence. Rosalie Edge and her Emergency Conservation Committee (ECC) purchased Hawk Mountain and converted it into a hawk watching point instead of a killing field. It remains one of the best spots in North America to see migrating hawks.

Weidensaul uses another woman to introduce the growth in popularity of birding. Miss Jane Hathaway occasionally appeared as a nerdy bird watcher on *The Beverly Hillbillies* television show, a favorite of young Weidensaul. Although he recognized that the characterization was widespread opinion at one time, the birders he knew were not like Miss Hathaway. In contrast to the Hathaway model, he describes birding today as a widespread and rapidly growing hobby or sport. He goes so far as to declare it a mainstream activity, on the verge of cool.

He credits Roger Tory Peterson's field guide for the transformation from nerdy to cool and for generating widespread enthusiasm for bird watching. Peterson's field guide emphasized a few key characteristics that differentiated species from one another and that could be seen on the live bird in the field. In contrast, professional ornithologists often used a long list of minute details that could be seen only on a bird in the hand, often only on a dead bird in the hand. He painted pictures of each bird with arrows pointing to the key characteristics. He placed similar birds on the same page for easy comparison, rather than in an order entirely determined by evolutionary relationships. Incipient birders found the simplifications delightful. Several field guides preceded Peterson's and many followed his and are available today. Weidensaul describes some of them, exploring their strengths and shortcomings. *The Sibley Guide to Birds* (2000) gets the most attention. Admitting that it is quite large to be carried in the field, Weidensaul praises its thoroughness. To address the size problem, David Sibley has produced separate, smaller versions for the eastern and western sections of the continent. The original guide covered the whole of Canada and the United States.

Weidensaul spends the last part of the book encouraging birders to go beyond the focus on maximizing their species count as their ultimate birding goal. He documents their proclivity to do so by describing the history of bird identification contests such as the World Series of Birding, in which teams of birders compete to see who can find the most species in a given amount of time; the big day (or big year), in which a birder attempts to see as many species as possible in a day (or a year); and even the big sit, in which a birder counts the bird species that he or she sees or hears in a specified amount of time while sitting at a strategic point. Life lists, in which birders check off new birds as they see them for the first time, are another indicator that birders are too tied to the species count. He has no problem with any of these activities (he participates in them himself) except as they become end points in birders' efforts and thus interfere with other observations and activities. In his view, birding should go beyond counting, to include observing behavior, environmental associations, and other aspects of bird life.

To encourage birding beyond counting, Weidensaul suggests that birders become "citizen-scientists" and contribute data to ornithological studies. Opportunities to do so include Christmas bird counts, in which groups of birders fan out all over the country around Christmas day each year, counting the number of individual birds they see in each species they encounter; breeding bird surveys, in which specific routes with specific survey points are run each year and the number of individuals of each species encountered is reported; and breeding bird atlases, in which the species of birds reproducing in a given geographic subunit are determined and results from the subunits are put together to generate a pattern for an entire state. The first two activities are counting exercises and so might seem to feed into birders' tendency to count species only, but they also require the determination of the number of individuals in each species. The data are reported to a central location so that they can be used to monitor population changes through time, making it possible to suggest the species of birds that are declining so that action can be taken before they are so depleted that they are beyond help. The data are used in other studies as well. Breeding Bird Atlases demand that the birder record behavior related to breeding in order to determine where birds breed and in what numbers. These exercises take birders beyond their species-counting tendencies into the world of bird behavior and ecology, and in addition, generate data of use to the ornithological community.

The citizen-scientist idea is another source of tension between birders and ornithologists. Ornithologists (and more experienced birders) tend not to trust the less experienced birders' identifications and tend to question the validity of data collected by such citizen-scientists. On page 185, in the context of a similar argument, Weidensaul quotes Ludlow Griscom's answer to this concern. Admitting that there will be mistakes in the data if inexperienced participants are involved, he argues that the additional data (mostly correct) collected by the less experienced birders more than makes up for the errors. Without birders acting as citizen-scientists, none of the programs described in the preceding paragraph could be as extensive as they are.

Finally, Weidensaul urges birders and ornithologists to get involved with bird conservation. He criticizes them for not having conservation high on their agenda in the past. To support this accusation, he points out that, as a group, birders have been reluctant to pay fees for using wildlife areas to watch birds and to pay special taxes on the purchase of binoculars and other equipment related to birding. Theoretically, the money from these payments and taxes would go into the purchase and maintenance of natural areas with habitat for birds and other wildlife. He models these arguments on hunting and fishing, enterprises in which the participants are required to buy licenses for the right to hunt or fish and to pay special taxes on their equipment purchases.

The book fulfills its dual purpose. It presents an excellent outline of the history of birding and of field ornithology in North America, and it argues convincingly that birders should be more than listers, should produce useful data, and should work for, and help to pay for, bird conservation.

The book contains some errors. The most significant is probably on page 107, where the Santa Rita Mountains are placed north of Tucson, Arizona, when they are actually south of the city. In addition, abbreviations to be used later should have been introduced in parentheses with the first use of the term being abbreviated. For example, had the Emergency Conservation Committee (ECC) of Rosalie Edge been introduced as shown here, ECC would have been more easily recognized when it was used alone. The index is thorough, the notes and bibliography give extensive access to other works, and the illustrations complement the text. Reviews of the book have been very favorable.

*Carl W. Hoagstrom*

## Review Sources

*Booklist* 103, no. 22 (August 1, 2007): 18.
*Kirkus Reviews* 75, no. 15 (August 1, 2007): 781.
*Library Journal* 132, no. 13 (August 1, 2007): 115.
*The New York Times Book Review* 156 (September 9, 2007): 27.
*Publishers Weekly* 254, no. 27 (July 9, 2007): 44.
*Science News* 172, no. 10 (September 8, 2007): 159.

# ON CHESIL BEACH

*Author:* Ian McEwan (1948-    )
*Publisher:* Nan A. Talese/Doubleday (New York).
  208 pp. $22.00
*Type of work:* Novel
*Time:* 1962
*Locale:* England

A *young, sexually inexperienced British couple's wed-*
*ding night proves both upsetting and disappointing for*
*each, effectively ending their brief marriage*

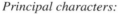

> Principal characters:
> FLORENCE PONTING, a young, upper-class
>   classical musician
> EDWARD MAYHEW, a young man whose
>   intellect and education have raised him
>   above his original social class
> GEOFFREY PONTING, Florence's father, a wealthy businessman
> VIOLET PONTING, Florence's mother, an Oxford don
> MARJORIE MAYHEW, Edward's brain-damaged mother
> HAROLD MATHER, Edward's friend

*On Chesil Beach* concerns the wedding night of a young British couple in 1962. As they dine together in their room in an unassuming hotel on the Dorset coast, they are both apprehensive about their first sexual experience but too polite and timid to share their feelings. Before their actual first encounter, which constitutes the heart of the novel, Ian McEwan supplies the reader with the background of both Florence Ponting and Edward Mayhew, including not only their personal situations but also the times in which they grew up.

Both born in 1940, Florence and Edward are the children of parents who endured economic depression and world war. They are well behaved and serious. Their careful upbringings have prevented them from anything in the way of sexual acquaintance; there is an almost stereotypical Victorian quality, in fact, to the inhibitions of Florence. Additionally, Florence and Edward come from very different social classes. Florence, a gifted classical musician, is the daughter of a woman who is not only an Oxford don but also a pioneer in what will prove to be a significant reformation of British cookery. Florence's father, a wealthy businessman, takes an interest in the arts. Edward, on the other hand, is the son of a schoolmaster; his mother Marjorie suffered brain damage in a railway accident involving some possible carelessness on the part of an upper-class businessman. While Florence is well-bred enough to be gracious about Edward's background, Edward finds Florence's father competitive and her mother's cool intelligence unsettling.

On a psychological level, there is a suggestion that Florence's problems with sexual intimacy may be a consequence of her mother Violet's reserved and undemonstra-

∼

*Ian McEwan is the author of two
collections of stories and ten previous
novels, including* Enduring Love
*(1997),* Amsterdam *(1998), for which
he won the Booker Prize,* Atonement
*(2001), and* Saturday *(2005).*

∼

tive nature, and although Florence forms a close bond with her father, this bond may also be responsible not only for her many intellectual and personal virtues but also for her severe sexual anxieties. Edward, on the other hand, is eager for his honeymoon night and is far more open to the sensual pleasures it promises. His problem is not with sexual inhibition but with anger; the reader learns that Edward is prone to moments of explosive violence. He finds in fighting a sense of freedom and release he experiences nowhere else in his regulated life; but as fulfilling as he finds street fighting, an incident involving the defense of one of his sensitive friends, Harold Mather, allows the reader to understand that his tendency to brawl is alienating him from the more civil side of English life. Sobered by the more self-controlled Mather's withdrawal from the friendship as a result of his violence, Edward is also tempered by his new status as a student of medieval history at the University of London. Anticipating a more genteel career as a historian, he finds that he is developing interests that are slowly raising and refining his cultural level in a way that would make him a fitting partner for someone like Florence.

Returning to the present moment at their honeymoon hotel, McEwan spends much time on the couple's awkward abandonment of their unappetizing meal and on their subsequent awkward attempts to consummate their marriage, which is depicted in an excruciatingly protracted sex scene that is at once horrific, comical, and sad. Far from achieving any real intimacy, Edward finds that his worst fears, of "arriving too soon," are realized, driving a squeamish and panicky Florence away and out into the night.

When Edward eventually follows her down to the long expanse of Chesil Beach, their escalating quarrel, ironically, becomes a time of intimacy greater than any they had previously experienced together. The reader has already learned that Edward is in fact in his element as a fighter, but as each gives vent to their disappointments with the other, their love for each other becomes more tenuous. Florence, who is not afraid to take the initiative when she sees fit, tries to save the day by offering him an unconventional marriage in which he will be free to have affairs, an offer she views as self-sacrificing, generous, and modern. An affronted Edward, however, explodes in righteous indignation at this attempt at negotiation, driving Florence from him. As Florence walks away on her own, Edward stands rigid with anger, watching her recede before his eyes, and although at the same time he senses that she would turn back to him if he simply called out to her, he is too proud and too furious to do so. This small decision—in which Florence turns from him and in which Edward fails to call back a woman who he knows is still in love with him—changes the course of each of their lives.

The novel, however, does not end with this dissolution of their union on Chesil Beach. Up until this point, in a fashion characteristic of McEwan, the perspective has moved deftly and frequently from Florence's to the differing Edward's and back again. The final section of the novel, however, is told exclusively from Edward's point of view. The reader does learn, however, that Florence was not only ahead of her time in her suggesting an "open marriage" but also, like her mother, ahead of her time in her ability to sustain a serious career in a profession largely associated with the opposite sex. Playing violin for a highly regarded string quartet that is praised for its skill, youthful passion, and intensity, Florence is singled out in a review that rapturously describes her musicianship as that of a woman in love with life itself. Although the reader never does return to Florence's perspective, McEwan here suggests that there was more to Florence than the reticent and intimidated bride on her honeymoon night.

Edward, on the other hand, who was always an advocate of jazz and rock music, has gone on to be an active part of London's freewheeling swinging sixties. He is delighted with the new freedoms of that era's sexual revolution and, most especially, with the era's happily sexually acquiescent women. He enjoys a childlike lightness and ease quite opposed to the adult seriousness of the years in which his tastes ran to women like Florence. Although he had thought to write history books, the ensuing decades saw him managing outdoor concerts and record shops, and, instead of marriage and family, his love life is composed of a number of far less earnest but essentially forgettable freewheeling romances. Edward's unmarried condition, however, also suggests that he never achieved what marriage represented to him, namely, a passage into maturity and adult responsibility.

Although Edward appears to have been pleased with the course his life took, at the age of sixty he begins to look back at his failed relationship with Florence with regret. Here, McEwan subtly shifts the reader's perceptions as he explores the rest of Edward's life. Even as Edward enjoyed greater comfort and personal freedom, he feels that the end of his relationship with Florence also saw the end of his ambition and his sense of serious purpose. Increasingly, he begins to blame himself for the failure of the marriage. Although he acknowledges that the sexual inhibitions and ignorance inculcated by the era in which they lived affected them both, he begins to feel that he did possess the resources of character necessary to work through the problems that ended up dividing them.

He applies to the incident on Chesil Beach a pet theory he had entertained back in the early 1960's, namely the "great man" theory of social change, which suggested that it was possible for an individual to rise to the occasion and change the course of his times by taking command of events. He begins to feel that had he tempered his own impatience, felt greater empathy for Florence, and rose to the occasion in a way that would befit a true leader, it would have been possible that their marriage—and all that the marriage would have represented—would have succeeded. That he did not take the initiative and did nothing to try to save his relationship with the woman he has come to remember as the rather magical girl with the violin haunts him as the moment in which he failed to answer the call to greatness. Furthermore, Edward's "great man" theory, which pointed not simply to personal change but to the redirection of national destiny, suggests that the blunders of Edward and Florence on one level represent the lost opportunities of England itself.

In addition to the historical setting of this novel, which took place just before the great social changes that ushered in a new era in British life, the physical setting of

Chesil Beach is another important aspect of this novel. Although an aspect of the honeymoon resort evokes a poky provinciality that is just slightly behind the times, the presence of the sea suggests something more enduring and eternal. The great, rolling sea can be said to mock the thwarted passions of the young couple, suggesting that they have managed to put themselves out of touch with a profound life force to which they are, ironically, in very close physical proximity, choosing instead to remain on the hard pebbles that are unique to this particular beach. The sea comes to represent a sexual mystery so remote from their daily lives as to be similar to a mystical experience; it is both exquisitely near and tragically far away from the young couple squabbling on the shore.

Additionally, Chesil Beach references McEwan's previous novel, *Saturday* (2005), which featured poet and critic Matthew Arnold's major Victorian poem "Dover Beach." There remains in this novel a faint echo of "Dover Beach," with its evocation of the sea's withdrawal as a metaphor for loss and vital absence. As Arnold's poem enjoined his two lovers to be true to one another in the face of the larger indifference of the universe, McEwan's *On Chesil Beach* suggests that the sundering of Florence and Edward is a failure to do just that and that their parting may have as much to do with the death of the heart as any sexual dysfunction.

The heartlessness of Edward on Chesil Beach informs both the novel's theme and narrative style: McEwan's own cool and fearless analysis of all that went wrong with this couple is what has led to this novel's evaluation as both a horror story and a comedy, each of which depend on a certain diminution of empathy. There is also in this novel the masterful narrative tension and surprising turns of plot that have contributed to McEwan's reputation as an author of literary thrillers. McEwan also is presenting a love story that is able to engage the reader empathically with Edward and Florence; his ability to evoke deep sympathy for his two characters as they struggle for intimacy is in the great tradition of the English novel's mission to educate the heart. Furthermore, the poetic way in which he juxtaposes his lost young couple against the great sea of life speaks not simply to issues that arose in one repressive era in recent times but to love problems that belong to the human condition and to all time.

*Margaret Boe Birns*

## Review Sources

*The Atlantic Monthly* 300, no. 1 (July/August, 2007): 134-138.
*Booklist* 104, no. 3 (October 1, 2007): 73-75.
*The Boston Globe*, June 3, 2007, p. C4.
*Los Angeles Times*, June 3, 2007, p. R2.
*The New York Review of Books* 54, no. 12 (July 19, 2007): 32-33.
*The New York Times Book Review* 156 (June 3, 2007): 1-13.
*St. Louis Post-Dispatch*, June 3, 2007, p. F9.
*The Seattle Times*, June 10, 2007, p. L8.
*The Washington Post*, June 3, 2007, p. BW15.
*Weekly Standard* 12, no. 46 (August 20, 2007): 39-40.

# OTHER COLORS
## Essays and a Story

*Author:* Orhan Pamuk (1952-    )
*First published: Öteki Renkler,* 1999, in Turkey
Translated from the Turkish by Maureen Freely
*Publisher:* Alfred A. Knopf (New York). 433 pp. $27.95
*Type of work:* Essays
*Time:* 1952 to the 2000's
*Locale:* Istanbul and Kars, Turkey; New York City;
   Stockholm

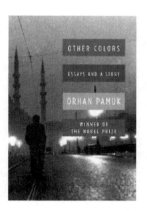

*A compilation of mostly short essays about Turkish cul-*
*ture that includes literary criticism, autobiography, and a*
*story by the winner of the 2006 Nobel Prize in Literature*

The opening line in Orhan Pamuk's preface to *Other Colors: Essays and a Story* states, "This is a book made of ideas, images, and fragments of life that have still not found their way into one of my novels." He says that the various pieces in the book are put together in a continuous narrative, but the book is not chronologically organized. It is divided into nine sections. The first one, called "Living and Worrying," contains sketches that Pamuk wrote between 1996 and 1999 for a magazine, *Öküz* (ox), devoted to politics and humor. The section begins with an essay that is essentially literary criticism or theory, "The Implied Author," that is also autobiographical. Pamuk says that for him literature is like medicine, and he needs a dose every day. It must be good literature—that is, dense and deep. About his own work he feels differently: He is happy if he gets a good half page after spending ten hours alone at his desk. He goes on to explain what he feels like when that does not happen and its effect on his family. What he most longs for is a kind of spiritual inspiration that he describes in his novel *Kar* (2002; *Snow,* 2004).

In his 2006 Nobel Prize speech, which concludes *Other Colors,* Pamuk repeats some of the aspects of novel writing and develops them further, but throughout his book he returns repeatedly to his experience as a writer or reader. In some respects, then, *Other Colors* resembles Philip Roth's *Reading Myself and Others* (1975), although it contains much besides Roth's kind of literary criticism. For example, the second essay in the book, "My Father," concerns Pamuk's experience the day his father died. Pamuk explains the importance of his father, an unpublished writer among other things, not only in this essay, but again in the Nobel Prize speech. The rest of the essays in the first section are much briefer sketches, some of them illustrated by the author, such as "When the Furniture Is Talking, How Can You Sleep" and "Giving Up Smoking." The first part also includes several sketches of his young daughter, Rüya, some of them humorous. Among the most compelling essays in this section are those that describe the earthquake that hit Istanbul on August 17, 1999, in which thirty thousand people died. The next essay

Orhan Pamuk, the most widely read
novelist in Turkey, is the author of
seven novels. His novel Benim Adim
Kirmizi *(1998;* My Name Is Red, *2001)*
won the 2003 International IMPAC
Dublin Literary Award, and in 2006 he
won the Nobel Prize in Literature.

describes the angst that the people of Istanbul experienced long afterward.

The second section, "Books and Reading," includes topics such as "How I Got Rid of Some of My Books," "The Pleasures of Reading," and "Nine Notes on Book Covers." What follow are essays of literary criticism that focus on various classics, beginning with the tales from *One Thousand and One Nights.* Pamuk's foreword to Laurence Sterne's *Tristram Shandy* (1759-1767) is an excellent piece of criticism, insisting on the patience necessary to read and grasp Sterne's novel. He concludes that the subject of that novel is the impossibility of ever getting to the point, hence the required patience on the part of the reader. Pamuk argues that novels are valuable insofar as they raise questions about the shape and nature of life. They offer a new way of understanding life, which, he contends, is exactly what *Tristram Shandy* does. Other essays in this section are on Victor Hugo, Vladimir Nabokov, Albert Camus, Salman Rushdie, and others, and three on Fyodor Dostoevski, whom Pamuk especially admires.

The next section in *Other Colors* is "Politics, Europe, and Other Problems of Being Oneself." Here one needs to recall that Pamuk was indicted in his native Turkey for speaking out, not in a novel but in an interview, about the Armenian genocide, which Turkish law forbids its citizens to criticize. In his essay "On Trial," Pamuk describes part of what he went through following the interview in February, 2005. Charges against him were eventually dropped, but he remains outspoken against certain aspects of his country's policies, especially regarding human rights abuses. Throughout many of the essays in this section and others, Pamuk also focuses on the contrast, if not the conflict, between Eastern and Western cultures, seeing himself as a Turk with a definite Western outlook. The problems of East and West are put into high relief in the essay "Family Meals and Politics on Religious Holidays." Opposition to the West among Muslims, Pamuk explains in "The Anger of the Damned," is motivated not by the religion of Islam or by the poverty that millions of Muslims experience daily, but by the "crushing humiliation" they feel caused by Western attitudes of superiority.

The fourth section, "My Books Are My Life," is aptly named, for Pamuk is a fully committed writer. The essays on his novels *Beyaz Kale* (1985; *The White Castle,* 1991), *Kara Kitap* (1990; *The Black Book,* 1994), *Yeni Hayat* (1992; *The New Life,* 1997), *Benim Adim Kirmizi* (1998; *My Name Is Red,* 2001), and *Snow* are extremely illuminating, essential reading for anyone interested in those books. Some of these essays derive from interviews he has given on them or are written retrospectively, as in the essay on *The Black Book,* looked at from the perspective of ten years later. The essays are highly personal and offer glimpses into the novelist's creative process and the problems he has encountered, as for example the difficulty in bringing *The Black Book* to a close, which took him almost five years to write. Pamuk confesses that it is his characters' uncertainties, sorrows, and silences that he relates to most closely, not their victories or acts of courage. Hence, he pays most attention to the moments of fragility in his books, comparing himself in this way to the miniature painters he has written about in *My Name Is Red*. The essay on *Snow* is made up of selections from Pamuk's notebooks written during many visits to Kars, the city in northeastern Turkey that is the locale for most of the story. Particularly interesting are the accounts of the Unity Teahouse and the police, who figure significantly in the novel.

"Pictures and Texts," the next section, begins with "Şirin's Surprise" and opposes a good story against theory. He admits that he has learned much from theory, has even been beguiled by it, but often feels the need to steer clear of it. The reason is that, however good and convincing the theory may be, it will always be someone else's theory; on the other hand, a good story that has affected a reader just as deeply becomes one's own. The difference between theory and a good story is the difference between the abstract and the concrete, and Pamuk proceeds to tell some very good stories. The first is one he tried to tell in *The Black Book* about a painting competition; the other derives from *One Thousand and One Nights* and tells of the love between Hüsrev and Şirin that is aroused through the use of portraits hanging on trees. Each story has been told over time with variations and raises important questions for the reader: For example, which is more effective, Hüsrev's picture or the man himself, the reality or the image?

Other essays in section five include "Murders by Unknown Assailants and Detective Novels," which claims that Turkey is the current leader in state-sponsored murder and other human rights abuses, and the very humorous "Entr'acte; or, Ah, Cleopatra!" which is subtitled "Going to See a Film in Istanbul." Films come late to Istanbul after their initial release because Turkish distributors are unable to meet Hollywood's prices for first-run showings, Pamuk says. This of course arouses all the more interest in some films, like *Cleopatra* (1963), starring Richard Burton and Elizabeth Taylor. The attraction for Pamuk, he admits, was not only to lose himself in illusion and become entranced by beautiful people in beautiful settings but also to come face-to-face with the West and to mimic various attitudes and gestures learned from such films. In "Why I Didn't Become an Architect," Pamuk explains why he dropped his studies in that field and decided to write instead. It was a question, he says, of being able to realize his dreams in ways that a Turkish architect could not at that time. "Bellini and the East" is another lively essay in this section, illustrated in the same manner as "Black Pen." The section concludes with a humorous essay on "Meaning," where the words on the page directly address the reader.

"Other Cities, Other Civilizations" contains two very vivid accounts of Pamuk's experience living in the United States, especially his time in New York City, where he was once mugged and had to deal with the police. It also includes his disappointment with cinnamon rolls and his encounter in a subway with someone he knew years earlier in Istanbul who had come to live abroad. Following this section is the *Paris Review* interview in which Pamuk again talks about his writing. He admits that over the years writing has not become easier for him but that he usually knows the whole story line of a novel in advance. Nevertheless, he sometimes gets blocked and moves from writing, say, chapter 5 to chapter 15, but he always waits to write the last chapter last. He is most happy, he says, when he is alone in a room and inventing. Here again he reminds one of another committed novelist, Philip Roth.

Before ending *Other Colors* with his Nobel Prize acceptance speech, Pamuk inserts a story, doubtless taken from life but fictionalized, called "To Look Out the Window." It is about a boy growing up in a middle-class Turkish family in Istanbul, visiting relatives, collecting picture cards, fighting with his older brother, and saying goodbye to his father, who goes off alone to Paris, leaving his family behind, just as Pamuk's own father did from time to time. The Nobel lecture, "My Father's Suitcase," is not only about the legacy his father left him (his writings) but also about being a writer at the present time, especially in Turkey. He repeats that to become a writer requires a full commitment: shutting oneself up in a room to escape crowds and company and all the rest of ordinary, mundane existence. One requires inspiration, but also hard work and patience. Writing, paradoxically, is not a lonely process, however; one has the company of words by those who came before—that is, tradition. Literature is, Pamuk insists, the most valuable hoard that humanity has gathered to help understand itself. Luckily, Pamuk's father had an extensive library that helped prepare the way for him. What a writer must do today, he insists, is to investigate people's basic fears—the fear of being left aside, of counting for nothing, and feelings of worthlessness. Here he speaks very much like the Istanbullu he is.

*Jay L. Halio*

## Review Sources

*Booklist* 104, no. 2 (September 15, 2007): 16.
*Kirkus Reviews* 75, no. 15 (August 1, 2007): 774.
*Library Journal* 132, no. 16 (September 15, 2007): 62.
*The New York Review of Books* 54, no. 17 (November 8, 2007): 4-8.
*The New York Times* 157 (October 5, 2007): E38.
*The New York Times Book Review* 157 (September 30, 2007): 16-17.

# OUT STEALING HORSES

*Author:* Per Petterson (1952-     )
*First published: Ut og stjæle hester,* 2003, in Norway
Translated from the Norwegian by Anne Born
*Publisher:* Graywolf Press (St. Paul, Minn.).
 258 pp. $22.00
*Type of work:* Novel
*Time:* The early twenty-first century and the 1940's
*Locale:* Norway's forests and countryside

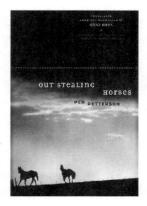

*In a poignant and personal novel, readers are allowed glimpses into the life of Trond Sander, as he reminisces about his childhood and family, and develop an under-standing of the life those experiences and relationships created*

*Principal characters:*
 TROND SANDER, the narrator, who tells the story from a
  sixty-seven-year-old and fifteen-year-old perspective
 LYRA, his dog and companion
 JON HAUG, his childhood friend
 LARS HAUG, Trond's neighbor and childhood friend, Jon's
  younger brother
 POKER, Lars's dog
 ODD HAUG, Jon's younger brother and Lars's twin, who
  dies during childhood
 BARKALD, local landowner from whom the boys steal horses
 FRANZ, a neighbor from Trond's youth
 ELLEN, Trond's daughter

 Per Petterson's *Out Stealing Horses* is a relaxing novel that takes the reader on a tour of the Norwegian countryside and forests throughout the eras, jumping between modern-day Norway and 1940's Norway just after the German occupation, following protagonist Trond Sander as he is forced to relive his past to understand his present and to accept his future.
 Three years after his wife died in a tragic car accident, Trond finds himself wid-owed and alone, living in a new house and environment. He has cashed out his retire-ment and moved to the remote countryside to avoid people, who he never cared for much, and spends the rest of his years living as he wishes with his dog, Lyra. Not knowing anyone, nor they him, Trond remarks how little communication is needed to form relationships in small communities where neighbors "know about my work-ing life, how old I am, that my wife died three years ago in an accident I only just sur-vived myself, that she was not my first wife, and that I have two grown-up children from an earlier marriage, and that they have children themselves." Trond accepts and

～

*Per Petterson's novels have received
much acclaim throughout Norway. He
has received the Norwegian
Booksellers' Prize, the Critics' Award
for Best Novel, and the* Independent
Foreign Fiction Prize. *In 2007,* Out
Stealing Horses *was awarded the
International IMPAC Dublin Literary
Award, the highest prize for a novel
published in English.*

～

enjoys his superficial relationship with his new community, offering them just enough information necessary for them to form their own understanding of him, knowing that "people like it when you tell them things, in suitable portions, in a modest, intimate tone, and they think they know you, but they do not, they know *about* you, for what they are let in on are facts, not feelings, not what your opinion is about anything at all, not how what has happened to you and the decisions you have made have turned you into who you are," and liking the fact that "what they do is they fill in with their own feelings and opinions and assumptions, and they compose a new life which has precious little to do with yours, and lets you off the hook."

Not having to make an effort to be accepted by the community and retaining his solitude seems to be working until Trond discovers that in his quest to remove himself from all aspects of his former life, he has moved next door to a ghost from his past. One evening, a neighbor wanders onto Trond's property while looking for his dog. Trond instantly recognizes the man as his childhood friend Lars Haug, stating, "Lars is Lars even though I saw him last when he was ten years old, and now he's past sixty, and if this had been something in a novel it would just have been irritating." Lars is a part of the past that Trond has worked a lifetime to repress. By pointing out the far-fetched coincidence that the protagonist should happen upon the person partially responsible for him wanting to escape society, Petterson gives the chance meeting realism and honesty, a twist of fate to which the reader is able to somehow relate, or at the very least, accept.

Unnerved by the unwelcome presence from his adolescence, Trond is thrown back to the summer of 1948, where he spends a summer working with his father on their timber farm in Norway's forests, while his mother and older sister remain at home in Oslo. He is woken one morning by fellow fifteen-year-old Jon Haug, who wakes him regularly to steal horses from their neighbor Barkald, the wealthiest landowner in the region, and take them for a joy ride, returning them unharmed. Their day begins as any other adventure, but after their ride, Trond witnesses a frightening side of Jon as he crushes a tiny bird's nest in his hands, destroying something helpless and precious and upsetting Trond without him fully grasping why. Trond returns home emotionally disturbed, soaked to the bone after a sudden rainstorm, and anxious to get away from his friend. As he dries by the fire, his father delivers the grave news that Lars, Jon's younger brother, shot and killed Odd, Lars's twin. The killing, of course, was an accident, but it had been perpetrated using Jon's air rifle, which he neglectfully left out loaded. Jon voluntarily left the family to live with relatives in Innbygda, never to see Trond again, and taking part of Trond's innocence with him. The incident causes an older Trond to reflect on "my friend Jon who one day just disappeared out of my life because one of his brothers had shot the other out of his life with a gun that he, Jon, had forgotten to unload. It was high summer then, he was his brothers' keeper, and in one instant everything was changed and destroyed."

The accidental killing, which is too much for anyone to comprehend, leaves fifteen-year-old Trond alone without his best friend to make sense of the unfathomable. Shortly after the killing, his father puts him on a train to Oslo, promising to follow shortly, but never making the return trip home. That summer, Trond would experience the death of a friend, and of his childhood, as he assumes the position of man of the house.

Trond had managed to live fifty years without having to revisit the tragedy that occurred during that summer, until he runs into his new neighbor Lars Haug, the very boy who had killed his twin brother by accident. The reunion, although not welcomed necessarily by either side, nor openly acknowledged between the two men (for the reader gets the feeling that Lars too has not made peace with the demons of his past), forces the adult Trond to return to the year when the innocence of his youth ended at the butt of an air rifle and the loss of a father. With age, life experience, and the clarity of time, Trond begins to reexamine other aspects of that summer and reevaluate his father and his actions with his adult perspective. He recognizes an inappropriate relationship his father had with Jon's mother and remembers revealing conversations he had with their neighbor Franz.

Petterson returns the reader once again to the boy's youth, displaying male pride, strength, and a sort of rite of passage, as Trond, his father, Jon's father, and Franz try to outdo one another as they work to get the logs downstream to Sweden. Trond at one point leaves the men and comforts Jon's attractive yet grieving mother by holding her innocently, yet a little too closely. The gesture does not go unnoticed by the working men. That evening, Trond and his father, battered and physically exhausted, have a conversation in which his father pronounces Trond a man, and then the two play like schoolboys as they ready for bed. The father, however, does not join Trond in the bedroom. Trond goes to look for his father and finds him in an intimate embrace with Jon's mother, understanding instantly that this is not the first time the two have been like this. Confused and upset about seeing this side of his father, Trond develops a friendship with Franz.

While young Trond believed his father was away working on their timber farm every summer, Franz informs Trond of his father's involvement with the Norwegian resistance under the Nazi occupation. Franz vividly describes his father's and Jon's mother's roles in smuggling people and documentation over the Swedish border with sometimes successful, sometimes heartbreaking results. Franz's revelations open up too many questions for a young mind to process, as Trond realizes he has no idea who his father is or where his allegiances lie. Confused and shaken by these revelations, Trond realizes that "life had shifted its weight from one point to another, from one leg to the other, like a silent giant in the vast shadows against the ridge, and I did not feel like the person I had been when this day began, and I did not even know if that was something to be sorry for." Before Trond has the opportunity to further question Franz, he is sent home to Oslo, never to see his father again.

Having given the reader just enough background from Trond's past to begin to see the layers that have made him the man he is presently, Petterson jumps back to the present as Trond prepares for the snowfall and settles into his newly chosen life. He is setting the table for dinner, for he is a widower but maintains his manners, when there is a knock at his door. His neighbor is found on the porch and is quickly invited in for dinner. Lars wastes no time in telling Trond that he knows who he is. Trond in turn admits that he too knows who Lars is, and the two men continue to eat their supper with the uncomfortable truth now behind them.

Lars turns out to be an invaluable friend and asset to Trond by helping him when his tree comes crashing down, to find a man to plow his driveway, and most importantly, to provide company at a distance, should it be needed. Lars also opens up many doors that were once closed, allowing Trond to make peace with his past so that he can put memories to rest and live the remainder of his life unburdened. Through their dinners together, Trond learns that Jon returned to the home that Lars had helped his mother maintain during Jon's absence and claimed the farm as his own without protest. Lars left the home that day and had never returned, nor had he ever spoken with his family members again. Out of politeness, Trond asks if Lars's mother or brother are still living, instead of asking his true question—whether they had been living with his absent father for all of these decades. The real question is never asked, and Lars never offers the information, leaving readers to arrive at their own conclusions. The two abandoned men are left to create new lives for themselves.

Petterson lulls the reader into a comforting serenity through his simple and honest descriptions of Norway's terrain and the tender yet disturbing memories of an innocent boy and an elderly man who mean no one any harm. Petterson's writing style is cinematic, painting vivid pictures and scene changes, while allowing the reader to develop an emotional bond with the characters. *Out Stealing Horses* is a relaxing and calming read whose occasionally cinematic simplicity is easily excused by the novel's unpretentious honesty and purity.

*Sara Vidar*

## Review Sources

*Booklist* 103, nos. 19/20 (June 1, 2007): 38.
*Chicago Tribune*, August 18, 2007, p. 10.
*Entertainment Weekly*, no. 936 (June 1, 2007): 71.
*Kirkus Reviews* 75, no. 9 (May 1, 2007): 415.
*Library Journal* 132, no. 9 (May 15, 2007): 84.
*The New York Review of Books* 54, no. 19 (December 6, 2007): 53-55.
*The New York Times Book Review* 156 (June 24, 2007): 1-13.
*The New Yorker* 83, no. 19 (July 9, 2007): 91.
*Publishers Weekly* 254, no. 15 (April 9, 2007): 32.

# THE OVERLOOK

*Author:* Michael Connelly (1956-    )
*Publisher:* Little, Brown (New York). 225 pp. $21.99
*Type of work:* Novel
*Time:* 2007
*Locale:* Los Angeles

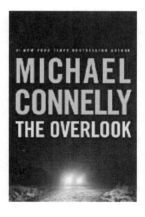

*Harry Bosch solves a complicated murder case despite interference from his colleagues and federal authorities*

Principal characters:
> HIERONYMUS "HARRY" BOSCH, a detective
> with the Los Angeles Police Department
> (LAPD)
> RACHEL WALLING, a special agent with the
> Tactical Intelligence Unit of the Federal
> Bureau of Investigation (FBI) and
> Bosch's former lover
> CLIFFORD MAXWELL, an FBI special agent and Walling's former partner
> JACK BRENNER, an FBI special agent and Walling's current partner
> DR. STANLEY KENT, a medical physicist who has been murdered
> ALICIA KENT, his widow
> IGNACIO "IGGY" FERRAS, a young detective with the LAPD and Bosch's
> current partner
> JESSE MITFORD, a young Canadian vagrant
> RAMIN SAMIR, a former professor at the University of California and
> a spokesman for Muslim causes
> CAPTAIN DON HADLEY, head of the LAPD's Office of
> Homeland Security

Veteran detective novelist Michael Connelly constructs two narratives in *The Overlook.* The first, overt narrative involves terrorists and the robbery of nuclear material that could be used in a terrorist attack. The other narrative underlies the first and involves what is by comparison an almost old-fashioned crime: a cold-blooded murder carried out for the sake of passion. The narratives run parallel to each other and unfold in little more than twelve hours.

*The Overlook* opens as Detective Hieronymus "Harry" Bosch receives a midnight call from his supervisor, Lieutenant Larry Gandle. It seems that a homicide victim has been discovered at an overlook above Mulholland Dam. At the moment, Bosch is a member of Homicide Special, a branch of the Robbery-Homicide Division of the Los Angeles Police Department (LAPD). Although the Hollywood Division would normally have handled the crime, Bosch's unit has been asked to take over the investigation, and Gandle has assigned the case to Bosch and his new partner, Ignacio "Iggy" Ferras.

After Bosch calls Ferras, he drives to the overlook, which is near his home, in his own car. There he discovers that the Hollywood detective waiting to hand over the

*Michael Connelly chose to become a writer after reading the works of Raymond Chandler in college. His novel* The Black Echo *(1992) won the Edgar Award for Best First Novel, and several of his subsequent novels have been named to annual "best books" lists compiled by* The New York Times *and the* Los Angeles Times.

case is his former partner, Jerry Edgar. The body appears to be that of Dr. Stanley Kent, discovered by a routine patrol investigating a car parked in a no parking zone. The body had been found lying face down in a clearing with two bullet wounds—apparently .22 caliber— in the back of the head, and the identification had been made through a wallet and a hospital identification tag on the body. As Bosch questions Edgar, it becomes clear that Edgar has done little to move the case forward.

A further complication arises when an agent of the Federal Bureau of Investigation (FBI) appears on the scene after Edgar leaves. To Bosch's consternation, the agent is Rachel Walling, his sometime lover. Walling explains that she too had been called out in the middle of the night, and she proceeds to confirm the identification. Kent's role as a medical physicist means that he has had access to the potentially deadly nuclear material cesium, and an initial search of his name by the LAPD on the National Crime Index Computer has alerted Walling's office. Suspicious of the FBI's involvement and of Walling's obvious reluctance to tell him more, Bosch tricks her into revealing the truth. She and her partner had interviewed Kent the previous year to warn him of his vulnerability to terrorists.

At Kent's house, Bosch and Walling find Kent's wife Alicia lying on the bed, stripped, gagged, and with her wrists and ankles tied together behind her back. When she is revived, she tells them that two men—one of them apparently Middle Eastern—forced their way into the house earlier in the evening. At this point, Walling's partner Jack Brenner arrives, and as the three listen to Alicia Kent's story they learn that the intruders have stolen her car and her husband's .22 caliber revolver. A check of her e-mail reveals that they had also sent her husband a photograph of her on the bed as a means of blackmailing him into stealing a quantity of cesium. It appears that he was executed after following the intruders' orders to bring the cesium to the overlook.

The first break in the case comes as Bosch learns in a phone call that Ferras has found a witness to the execution, Jesse Mitford. A young vagrant who has hitchhiked from Canada, Mitford had been sleeping in a deserted yard near the overlook and had seen and heard much of the murder. Afraid that the federal authorities will take Mitford under their control, Bosch checks him into a hotel under an alias but tells Brenner that he has let the young man go.

Ferras has been growing increasingly uncomfortable with his partner's methods, but when the two revisit the Kent residence at dawn, Bosch gives Ferras further cause for alarm. An officious FBI agent guarding the house refuses them entry, and, frustrated that he is being shut out from his own investigation, Bosch easily overpowers the agent—whose identification reveals that he is Clifford Maxwell—and handcuffs him. Bosch is puzzled by several seemingly unimportant details in the house, including a rectangular discoloration on the wall of the workout room where a poster or calendar might have hung, but does not know what to make of them. As the two detectives leave, Bosch tosses the keys to Maxwell's cuffs on the floor where the agent will have to crawl to retrieve them.

Another apparent break comes when Alicia Kent's car is located, parked in plain view in front of the house of Ramin Samir—for some time a "person of interest" to the LAPD. Samir is notorious for his noisy espousal of various anti-American causes, but, knowing that Samir's main interest is in self-aggrandizement, Bosch is immediately suspicious of a set-up. However, the location of the car is enough to send Captain Don Hadley, head of LAPD's Office of Homeland Security, into action with a paramilitary unit. Hadley's reputation for bungling has already earned him the sobriquet of "Captain Done Badly." Sure enough, Samir is shot and killed by Hadley's men, but no evidence of the stolen cesium is found in either the house or the car.

A deputy coroner provides Bosch with the most significant break in the case when he calls him with a tip. A patient named Digoberto Gonzalves has been admitted to a local hospital with acute radiation poisoning. When Bosch and Walling reach the hospital, the patient is unconscious, but a Toyota key recovered from his pocket leads Bosch to search the neighborhood where the man had been found. After cruising the parking lots in the area, Bosch and Walling find a dilapidated Toyota pickup and camper parked next to a large Dumpster. Inside the camper, Bosch finds an odd but incriminating assortment of materials: the portable lead container or "pig" that Kent would have used to transport the cesium, a rolled up poster of yoga positions, a .22 caliber revolver, and, ominously, several loose cesium capsules. However, it is the remaining trash and debris in the pickup that suggest the truth to Bosch—that Gonzalves had simply been scavenging in the early morning hours on trash-collection day. He had found the "pig" and the revolver in a Dumpster, and, not realizing the nature of his find, had poisoned himself.

At this point, the key elements of the case come together for Bosch, and as he explains them to Walling, the second, implicit narrative of *The Overlook* becomes apparent to the reader. Bosch had been troubled by the fact that Stanley Kent's murderers had spared his wife, and he realizes now that she has actually conspired in the murder. The recovered—and potentially incriminating—poster that had hung in the Kents' workout room pictured a yoga pose identical to the presumably painful position in which Bosch and Walling had found Alicia tied. The robbery of the cesium was a red herring. Whoever had worked with Alicia Kent had realized that in the current climate of suspicion, authorities would seize upon the robbery as the work of terrorists. The information Alicia had supplied about her alleged assailants, coupled with the presence of her car in front of Samir's house, would make the terrorist angle irresistible to credulous authorities. If Gonzalves had not found the cesium and the other evidence hours before trash was collected, it would all have disappeared into a landfill.

The final revelation comes as Bosch suggests to Walling that her partner Jack Brenner, who along with Walling had met Dr. Kent and his beautiful wife the previous year, would have been in a perfect position to work out the details of the crime. It is now Bosch's turn to be surprised as Walling explains that her partner that year had not been Brenner but Clifford Maxwell, the agent who had been so anxious to keep Bosch and Ferras away from the crime scene.

*The Overlook* now races to its conclusion as Bosch and Walling strive to capture Maxwell. However, the renegade agent shoots the one person who could implicate him, his lover Alicia, and then, as Bosch and Walling move in, himself.

*The Overlook* captures the underlying mood of paranoia and the concomitant mistrust of those of Middle Eastern origin that have gripped the United States since the terrorist attack on New York City on September 11, 2001. In addition, it illustrates how easily individuals and institutions can fall prey to such paranoia and mistrust while at the same time capitalizing on them. Last but not least, it highlights Connelly's ability to construct an ingenious plot from familiar and even hackneyed ingredients.

*The Overlook* was initially published in sixteen weekly installments in *The New York Times Magazine* in late 2006. In preparing it for book publication, Connelly expanded the work to twenty-two chapters and added a secondary story line. He also shifted the time from late 2006 to early 2007—essentially the period in which the book became available. Serialization before book publication was once common, and was practiced by such luminaries as nineteenth century English novelist Charles Dickens—one of whose books Jesse Mitford happens to be carrying in his backpack.

Despite Connelly's reference to Dickens, he works most obviously in a tradition of American crime fiction that stretches back to the middle decades of the twentieth century—a tradition created by Raymond Chandler (who also wrote memorably about Los Angeles) and Dashiell Hammett. He alludes indirectly to the former in many of his works, counting on astute readers to recognize the references. At the end of Chandler's masterpiece, *The Big Sleep* (1939), narrator Philip Marlowe wonders: "What did it matter where you lay once you were dead? In a dirty sump or in a marble tower on top of a high hill?" On the last page of *The Overlook*, Bosch allows himself a rare moment of introspection: "But Bosch thought that it didn't really matter if you died cornered in a butcher shop or on an overlook glimpsing the lights of heaven."

Unfortunately, such bravura moments are rare in *The Overlook*, which perhaps moves too quickly for its own good, nor does Connelly aspire to Hammett's lean, artfully honed style. On the next-to-last page of *The Overlook*, Connelly writes unimaginatively of Walling, "She looked at [Bosch] and smiled sort of sadly." For better or worse, Connelly's style resembles Harry Bosch himself: well meaning, fast moving, and a little tired.

Thanks to advances in telecommunications, however, Connelly has done his illustrious predecessors one better. He has written a final, twenty-third chapter distributed to subscribers to his electronic mailing list. Although it does not alter the sense of what has come before, it adds a sly fillip to the plot as well as a glimpse of Bosch and Walling setting off together on a tangentially related case. When *The Overlook* is reprinted in paperback, the chances are good that this chapter will find its way into it.

*Grove Koger*

**Review Sources**

*Booklist* 103, no. 15 (April 1, 2007): 5.
*Chicago Tribune*, June 18, 2007, p. 6.
*The Denver Post*, May 20, 2007, p. F13.
*Entertainment Weekly*, no. 935 (May 25, 2007): 87.
*Kirkus Reviews* 75, no. 8 (April 15, 2007): 354.
*Los Angeles Times*, May 20, 2007, p. R4.
*Publishers Weekly* 253, no. 14 (April 2, 2007): 40.
*St. Louis Post-Dispatch*, May 20, 2007, p. F9.
*Seattle Post-Intelligencer*, June 5, 2007, p. C1.

# PEELING THE ONION
## A Memoir

*Author:* Günter Grass (1927-    )
*First published: Beim Häuten der Zwiebel*, 2006, in Germany
Translated from the German by Michael Henry Heim
*Publisher:* Harcourt (New York). Illustrated.
  432 pp. $26.00
*Type of work:* Memoir
*Time:* 1927-1959
*Locale:* Danzig (now Gdańsk), Poland; Germany

*In this brilliant memoir, Grass tells the story of his life from his youthful exploits, his first love, and his military experiences up through the writing of his first novel and reveals his lifelong devotion to the power and beauty of art*

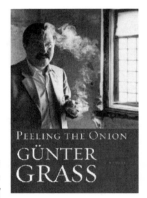

In August, 2006, Günter Grass aroused emotions across the literary world when he revealed in his memoir, *Beim Häuten der Zwiebel (Peeling the Onion)*, that he had been a member of the Waffen-SS as a teenager. Reaction to the news was swift, with many calling for him to hand back the Nobel Prize in Literature he received in 1999. Others were more supportive of Grass, pointing out that he had already paid the price of his youthful actions by living all these years with his guilt over having served in the SS. By the time the English translation appeared one year later, the controversy had died down considerably, but critics continued to raise questions about the nature of art and the artist's role in politics. Critics also raised questions about the nature of memoir, since Grass's book possesses a fictional quality, often alternating between a first-person telling of the story and a third-person narration of the story of a young man's life. More than any other quality, these shifting points of view raised serious questions about Grass's ability either to tell the truth about his past or to recall with any degree of clarity the events of his young life. Michael Henry Heim's elegant translation of Grass's memoir now allows English-language readers to see what all the fuss was about. Reading *Peeling the Onion* shows the controversy over Grass's involvement with the Waffen-SS to have been so much media puffery.

Many readers and critics have read Grass's first novel, *Die Blechtrommel* (1959; *The Tin Drum*, 1961), as an autobiography. In that story, young Oskar Matzerath decides to stop growing and talking when he reaches the age of three. Oskar is both attracted and repelled by the Nazi Party but eventually straps on a military drum and communicates by means of high-pitched screams and the beat of his drum. The novel captures not only the pervasive sense of German guilt over the loss of World War II but also the ambivalence that many Germans felt about Nazism and its programs to exterminate Jews. Like Oskar in the novel, Grass's childhood did come to an end with the beginning of the Nazi occupation of Danzig, and, like Oskar, Grass begins to ponder the meaning of these events and his involvement in them, but *The Tin Drum* is not autobiography. Grass writes *Peeling the Onion* in order that critics who mistake *The Tin Drum* for memoir cannot have this last word.

As the title indicates, Grass uses the metaphor of peeling an onion to write about the richly layered experiences of his life. As he slowly removes the dry, crackly skin of his present life, a moister layer appears, the removal of which reveals yet another moist layer ripe for the picking. If he were to chop the onion, it would produce tears, but his peeling produces a sober examination of the many layers of his life. However, *Peeling the Onion* resembles as well an impressionistic painting in which the uncovering of one layer on the canvas not only reveals another but also reveals how intricately the layers overlap. These are moments in the painting of a life, moments that touch all aspects of Grass's life and his readers.

*Novelist, poet, and artist Günter Grass is the author of numerous books, including* Die Blechtrommel *(1959;* The Tin Drum, *1961),* Katz und Maus *(1961;* Cat and Mouse, *1963),* Der Butt *(1977;* The Flounder, *1978),* Mein Jahrhundert *(1999;* My Century, *1999) and* Im Krebsgang *(2002;* Crabwalk, *2003). He was awarded the Nobel Prize in Literature in 1999.*

In *Peeling the Onion*, Grass does recall his involvement with the Waffen-SS. As a teenager, he became a part of this military operation, and he offers a quite stark portrait of life in the young Nazis. When he was ten, he joined a kind of young boy's cadet organization, the Jungvolk. He recalls that as a member of the Hitler Youth, he was a believer to the end. Part of the rank and file, Grass did not question the speeches of Adolf Hitler or Hermann Göring but took to heart the message that his fatherland was surrounded by and threatened by enemies. At fourteen, Grass participated as a volunteer in the Luftwaffe artillery, more as a diversion from his schoolwork than as a path to a military career. He recalls that he and his classmates spent long hours at their posts, scaring more rabbits than airplanes. However, Grass points out, he often spent these hours scribbling poems. By the age of sixteen, Grass had joined the Waffen-SS, and he spent his short-lived military career as a tank gunner.

Sent to the Eastern Front in the spring of 1945, Grass gets separated from his unit, is wounded, and eventually ends up in an American prisoner of war camp until the end of the war. At the camp, he continues to write, to draw sketches, and he plays dice with a fellow inmate named Joseph, whom Grass believes may have been Joseph Ratzinger, the man who was to become a famous conservative Catholic cardinal and then Pope Benedict XVI. While in the camp, Grass sees photographs from the concentration camps of the piles of corpses, the ovens, the starving and the starved, and the skeletal bodies of survivors from another world and cannot believe that Germans could have been responsible for such activities. These photographs send waves of shock and guilt through him. He also admits honestly and poignantly, though, that he never fired a shot while in the Waffen-SS and that the guilt and shame of his involvement have gnawed ceaselessly on him since then.

*Peeling the Onion* does not stop with his youthful military involvement. Grass recalls the tortures of his youthful life: his flirtations with religion, his lustful hunger for various young women, his consuming desire for art, and his earliest forays into the writing life. *Peeling the Onion* records Grass's life from his birth up until the publication of *The Tin Drum*.

In *Peeling the Onion*, Grass tells readers that hunger was his first teacher. Literally, after the war, he could not get enough to eat. Another hunger—the lustful desire of a young man for a young woman—soon began to compete with his physical hunger. The hunger that most motivated his life, though, was his hunger for art. As a young boy, he had collected coupons from cigarette boxes that reproduced classic works of art. He also read voraciously. Grass concedes that books have always been his gap in the fence, his entry into other worlds. In the late 1940's, he apprenticed himself to a tombstone maker in order to become a sculptor. During those years, he began writing poetry and discovered the way that words could satisfy this new hunger. Eventually, Grass marries his first wife, Anna. They move to Paris, where he joins a group of writers, including Paul Celan, and rattles away at his Olivetti typewriter on the pages that soon grow into *The Tin Drum*. From the writing of *The Tin Drum* until now, Grass has lived page to page and between book and book, his inner world still rich in characters.

His desire to be an artist emerged early in his youth. The collected albums of picture cards of great European masterpieces set him on his quest for art. Grass recalls that at the age of ten, he was able to distinguish right away Hans Baldung from Matthias Grünewald and Frans Hals from Rembrandt. When he was not leafing through these albums of paintings, he was curled with one of the books from his mother's bookshelves: Fyodor Dostoevski's *Besy* (1871-1872; *The Possessed*, 1913), Knut Hamsun's *Sult* (1890; *Hunger*, 1899), or Wilhelm Raabe's *Der Hungerpastor* (1864; *The Hunger-Pastor*, 1885) among them. Grass derived great pleasure from reading Vicki Baum's *Stud. Chem. Helene Willfüer* (1928; *Helene*, 1933), a book blacklisted by the Catholic Church because of its heroine's teenage pregnancy and her attempts to end it by abortion. Grass's uncle, Arthur, was a minor poet and novelist, and Grass one day discovered a suitcase full of Arthur's writings in the family's attic. Although the verses often glorify the fatherland or the great honor of the führer, Grass nevertheless recalls his fascination with the process of putting words on paper to form artistic works. Early in *Peeling the Onion*, Grass wonders what his own first scribblings would resemble, if they still existed. Would they reflect, like his uncle's verses, his unwavering faith in the fatherland and his ardor for Germany? Grass wrote a youthful first novel, now lost, and he wonders in his memoir whether it might have been marked by this same pride in country. Because of his early encounters with art and writing, Grass knew even as a teenager that he wanted to become a famous artist.

The final chapters of Grass's memoir chronicle his struggles to write and complete *The Tin Drum*. Since his hunger for art so consumed his life, he could not put down his pen to stop writing or put down his pencil to stop drawing sketches. He admits, however, that he experienced difficulty in finding a form that would adequately express his emotions and convey the weight of his own experience. He even evaded the attempt to capture on paper the stories that most engaged him and instead pursued writing characterized by wordplay. Grass's first exhibition of drawings and sculptures in November, 1955, in Stuttgart proved to be the event that broke open the vessel so that his words might pour forth. The memoir closes with Grass and Anna dancing until dawn at the Frankfurt Book Fair, celebrating the success of his novel.

*Peeling the Onion* offers readers a glimpse of the torturous, frustrating, consuming, and ultimately rewarding nature of the reading and writing life. In spite of the many obstacles that Grass encounters in his quest to become an artist, he succeeds famously to become a chronicler of postwar Germany and its attempts to come to terms with its past. Above all, though, Grass emerges from this memoir as a man whose heart continually questions the deeply seated morals and values of the time. Consequently, this book and his other works teach deep and abiding moral lessons about the nature of politics, the character of beauty, and the role of the artist in the world.

*Henry L. Carrigan, Jr.*

## Review Sources

*The Atlantic Monthly* 300, no. 3 (October, 2007): 139.
*Booklist* 103, no. 18 (May 15, 2007): 4.
*Harper's Magazine* 315 (July, 2007): 89.
*Kirkus Reviews* 75, no. 11 (June 1, 2007): 540.
*Library Journal* 132, no. 12 (July 1, 2007): 92-93.
*The Nation* 285, no. 5 (August 13, 2007): 25-28.
*The New York Review of Books* 54, no. 13 (August 16, 2007): 21-23.
*The New York Times Book Review* 156 (July 8, 2007): 1-10.
*Publishers Weekly* 254, no. 19 (May 7, 2007): 55.

# THE PENTAGON
## A History—The Untold Story of the Wartime Race to Build the Pentagon, and to Restore It Sixty Years Later

*Author:* Steve Vogel (1960-    )
*Publisher:* Random House (New York). 656 pp. $32.95
*Type of work:* History
*Time:* 1940 to the early 2000's
*Locale:* Washington, D.C.

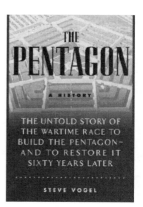

*Describes the political and engineering challenges that faced the people who built the Pentagon during the 1940's and the equally daunting challenges facing those tasked to rebuild the damaged structure after it was attacked on September 11, 2001*

*Principal personages:*

BREHON B. SOMERVELL, Army general who
    spearheaded plans to build the Pentagon
LESLIE R. GROVES, Army colonel who supervised Pentagon construction
FRANKLIN D. ROOSEVELT, president of the United States, 1933-1945
HENRY L. STIMSON, secretary of war under Roosevelt
JOHN MCSHAIN, builder whose firm constructed the Pentagon
G. EDWIN BERGSTROM, principal architect of the Pentagon
WALKER LEE EVEY, program manager for Pentagon renovations
    begun in 1997
ALLYN KILSHEIMER, construction supervisor for Pentagon
    rebuilding, 2001-2002

In 1940, as it stood on the brink of war with Germany and Japan, the United States government undertook one of the most colossal building projects in history: the construction of a new headquarters for the Department of War. Motivated by concerns that elements of the Army's various departments were scattered all over Washington, President Franklin D. Roosevelt allowed himself to be convinced that a giant new building would solve this important command-and-control problem. For the next three years, the unusual five-sided structure seemed to rise from the ground across the Potomac River from Washington, D.C., in northern Virginia. As its design became evident, people began referring to it as "the Pentagon building," and the name stuck.

When it was completed in 1943, the Pentagon was the largest office building in the world. Over the next sixty years, it would become the symbol of America's military might—so much so that when terrorists chose to attack the United States in 2001, it was one of four targets selected for destruction. Unlike the World Trade Center twin towers in New York City, however, the Pentagon withstood the devastating blow from the hijacked civilian jetliner flown directly into the structure. The resilience of the building's inhabitants, and of the government's efforts to rebuild it, quickly became a hallmark for the nation's response to the terrorist threat.

The story of the Pentagon's construction, and its role in American history since, is the subject of veteran military journalist Steve Vogel's detailed and engaging *The Pentagon: A History—The Untold Story of the Wartime Race to Build the Pentagon, and to Restore It Sixty Years Later.* Blending his skills as an interviewer and researcher with an exceptional ability to write clear, compelling prose, Vogel provides a detailed account of the genesis of what would become one of the most important edifices in the world. He explains how dozens of engineers and thousands of laborers transformed the swampy terrain along the banks of the Potomac into a solid foundation for a monumental building that would eventually house more than twenty-five thousand workers and the intricate network of roads and interchanges that would carry them to and from their jobs. He describes the construction methods employed to ensure that the building would serve not only as a safe and structurally sound home for the War Department but also later as a repository for government records—the ultimate purpose Roosevelt believed the Pentagon could serve when conflict with Germany and Japan ended and the nation could reduce its military to prewar levels. He details the architectural features that distinguish the building, noting how the final structure is a combination of the design of California architect G. Edwin Bergstrom, builder John McShain, who would go on to become one of the leading contractors in the nation's capital, and President Roosevelt, whose tinkering with the plans produced some of the most notable aspects of the Pentagon's final appearance.

*Steve Vogel is a military correspondent who has reported on operations in the Middle East and Africa. For his coverage of the U.S. involvement in Afghanistan he was nominated for the Pulitzer Prize in 2002.*

On the whole, however, Vogel's book is less about bricks and mortar (and concrete and dirt) than it is about people—the people who had the vision for the nation's largest building and the drive to get it built in the 1940's, and those who had the tenacity to rebuild sections of it destroyed by the terrorist attack of September 11, 2001. Insights into the personalities of men such as McShain, Bergstrom, and a number of others influential in getting the building approved, constructed, and opened provide the human touch that will appeal to a wider reading audience than those who might simply be interested in details of construction, architecture, and financing.

Dominating the pages of Vogel's narrative as he dominated the project to construct the Pentagon is Brehon B. Somervell, the audacious (some might say egomaniacal) Army officer who conceived the idea for the building and drove efforts to complete it. Somervell, a West Point graduate of 1914, had managed to see action during World War I but like most career officers had shifted from job to job for the next twenty years. By 1940, he had risen to the rank of lieutenant colonel and made a name for himself by cleaning up the corruption and inefficiency that had plagued the New York Public Works Administration. His efforts attracted the attention of officials in Washington, and Somervell was selected to oversee a massive buildup of military bases and facilities to serve the Army that Roosevelt and Secretary of War Henry L. Stimson knew would be needed when the United States finally entered the war against the Axis Powers.

Promoted to brigadier general, Somervell quickly realized that the Army needed a central command post. With typical bravado, he convinced Roosevelt and other key administration officials that such a facility was essential to the war effort. He assumed complete charge of the project, coercing politicians and military superiors to bow to what amounted to demands for a free hand in both design and construction. After selecting a site just east of Arlington National Cemetery, he set about assembling a team of architects, selecting a builder, and recruiting Army officers to work for him as day-to-day project managers. The key figure on this team was Colonel Leslie R. Groves, who, before he went on to head up the Manhattan Project that produced the world's first atomic weapon, was given the unenviable task of supervising construction of the Pentagon. Groves rode herd on the contractor, architect, and suppliers whose work had to be done on time, if not on budget.

As Vogel makes clear, the truly amazing aspect of the Pentagon's construction was not so much its vast scope but the speed with which construction proceeded. Somervell's grandiose plans for the building were sketched out over a weekend. He not only proposed to erect the largest building in Washington (more than five times the size of the Capitol) but also promised to do it in a year, with the first occupants moving in within six months. Although he did not keep to that schedule, he did deliver on his major promise: to construct a building large enough to house the essential members of the Army's leadership at this critical time in the nation's history. He rode roughshod over those who opposed him and dealt summarily with subordinates who did not share his sense of urgency. In fact, many soon found that Somervell (and Groves) would resort to anything—including subterfuge—to ensure that the project continued on schedule, even in the face of serious concerns expressed by some members of Congress that the building was fast becoming a poster child for fraud, waste, and abuse. That kind of scrutiny seemed to have little impact on Somervell's activities or his status within the War Department. By the time senior Army leadership moved into the Pentagon, Somervell had been promoted to lieutenant general and was serving as chief of services of supply, one of the three most important Army positions in Washington.

Of course, constructing a building as large as the Pentagon is hardly a one-man endeavor, and Vogel is careful to balance his account of high-level planning with stories of laborers who helped build the Pentagon and of the first workers who occupied the building even before construction was complete. Through the eyes of laborers, readers get a sense of both the immensity of the project and the sacrifices made to bring it to completion. These were the people who sweated in the broiling Washington summers or shivered in the freezing winters as they poured concrete forms or erected the Pentagon's superstructure. These were the bureaucrats who endured two-hour commutes over inadequate road systems and slogged through the muddy construction site to half-finished offices where they tried to get the Army's business accomplished in windowless offices inside a building where the air conditioning system did not work and the noise from bulldozers and pile drivers often drowned out conversation. Some of these people were African Americans who, as Vogel recounts with special poignancy, discovered they were welcome to work for the federal government but were still subjected to Virginia laws that demanded they use "separate but equal" facilities. One of the most stirring anecdotes in the book is Vogel's account of the group of courageous African Americans who refused to eat in the "colored only" cafeteria, insisting instead that they be served in the more luxurious dining area reserved for white patrons.

More than half of Vogel's book is devoted to an account of the Pentagon's construction. The brief middle section consists of a series of vignettes from the four decades between the end of the war and September 11, 2001. Included are stories of the reshaping of the structure to accommodate the newly created Department of Defense, a traumatic experience for Navy and Marine Corps leaders, who had to learn to live as equals with the Army and the newly created U.S. Air Force. Vogel also depicts the perilous days during the 1960's when the Pentagon became the target of antiwar protestors, describing the confusion that reigned among the highest military and civilian leaders who did not want to use force against American citizens exercising their rights of assembly and free speech but who could find no easy way to prevent violence—or bad press.

The final third of *The Pentagon* is an account of the heroism of the men and women who responded to the terrorist attack on the Pentagon in September, 2001. The stories of individuals who risked their lives to save others are related in some detail. Vogel's chief interest, however, is in explaining what happened to the structure, why it survived, and how it was rebuilt so quickly. The two men principally responsible for this near-miracle were Walker Lee Evey, the career government bureaucrat selected in the late 1990's to supervise much-needed renovations of the aging building, and Allyn Kilsheimer, a demolitions contractor hired by Evey within days after the attack who made it his personal mission to erase the scars on the Pentagon created by the attack. Evey's foresight in strengthening the building's interior structure—work already completed on the section that was hit by the plane—and Kilsheimer's almost maniacal drive to have the destroyed sections rebuilt within a year after the tragedy are described in a way that makes these men seem as heroic as the people who were caught in the building on September 11.

Throughout his narrative, Vogel employs a prose style that recreates the sense of urgency felt by the original builders in the 1940's and their successors in 2001-2002. His occasional digressions—such as his history lesson about the area in which the Pentagon was constructed (a seamy region known as Hell's Bottom), or about the infighting among the military services both before and after the Pentagon was constructed—enhance his narrative by providing a larger context in which to view the main story. As a result, *The Pentagon* offers readers a thorough and engaging account of the history of one of the nation's most important buildings.

*Laurence W. Mazzeno*

## Review Sources

*Booklist* 103, no. 18 (May 15, 2007): 8.
*The Economist* 383 (June 30, 2007): 93-94.
*Kirkus Reviews* 75, no. 9 (May 1, 2007): 439.
*The New York Times Book Review* 156 (June 10, 2007): 13.
*Publishers Weekly* 254, no. 18 (April 30, 2007): 150.
*The Washington Post*, June 17, 2007, p. BW03.

# THE PESTHOUSE

*Author:* Jim Crace (1946-      )
*Publisher:* Doubleday (New York). 255 pp. $24.95
*Type of work:* Novel
*Time:* An indeterminate future
*Locale:* Eastern America

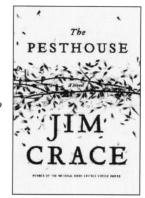

*Two strangers accidentally meet and begin a journey to embark on a voyage east to escape a ravaged America*

Principal characters:
 MARGARET, a thirty-one-year-old woman quarantined by her family because of an unnamed disease that is usually fatal
 FRANKLIN LOPEZ, a young man who has traveled from the Midwest seeking to escape America for Europe
 JACKSON LOPEZ, Franklin's brother, who leaves his younger sibling behind because of a wounded knee

Jim Crace is hardly a household name; however, his eight previous novels have received sterling reviews, and his reputation may be greater in America than in his native Great Britain. In each of his fictions, he defamiliarizes the familiar, creating worlds that parallel, but never duplicate, those most readers would recognize. His works span extraordinary historical ranges, from the pre-Bronze Age of *The Gift of Stones* (1988) to Christ's sojourn in the desert in *Quarantine* (1997) to his most recent novel, which imagines a future unthinkable to most Americans. His landscapes are frequently bizarre or unfamiliar, such as a seventh continent in *Continent* (1986), and he continually examines the implacable forces of nature, as in *Being Dead* (2000).

*The Pesthouse* partakes of all these features and more as it imagines a post-apocalyptic America some time in the future. The reader is never certain what exactly has happened, but the United States as a political and cultural entity is gone, replaced by a diseased landscape in which a few intrepid travelers trek eastward in hopes of boarding ships bound for Europe or beyond.

The novel begins nightmarishly, "Everybody died at night," and the air of mystery and foreboding is never entirely dispelled. Young Franklin Lopez and his brother, Jackson, have arrived in a burg called Ferrytown, hoping soon to make it to the ocean; however, Franklin has injured his knee and is left behind to allow his brother swift passage. During a torrential downpour, he laboriously climbs a hill outside town and takes refuge in an old shack, inhabited by Margaret, suffering from the "flux," some type of plague, and left for dead. During the night, toxic fumes from the nearby lake are stirred up, and the entire town expires, while Franklin slowly nurses Margaret back to health.

∽

*Jim Crace was born in 1946 in Hertfordshire, England. His first novel,* Continent *(1986), won the Whitbread First Novel of the Year Award, the David Higham Prize for Fiction, and* The Guardian *Fiction prize. Crace earned acclaim and awards with eight other novels—*The Gift of Stones *(1988),* Arcadia *(1991),* Signals of Distress *(1995),* Quarantine *(1997),* Being Dead *(2000),* The Devil's Larder *(2001),* Genesis *(2003), and* The Pesthouse.

∽

Franklin pushes Margaret and their few possessions miles in a handcart, until a band of marauders take him captive as a slave but shun Margaret because of her shorn head, a potent sign of her illness. Through a series of further peregrinations and misadventures, Margaret falls in with a fundamentalist sect known as the Finger Baptists, who live in an establishment they call the Ark, where metal is forbidden as an element of diabolical purposes. When the same marauders attack the fortification and kill the elders, Margaret escapes and inspires Franklin to do the same.

As they attempt to elude his captors, Franklin suddenly becomes homesick for his mother and the family farm and abruptly decides against embarkation in favor of a second odyssey back to his homestead. By now the couple are guardians of a little girl, Jackie, and although they are not lovers, it is clear that they have pledged their lives to each other. The novel ends on an entirely different note than its beginning, "Going westward, they would go free," and such a dire narrative suddenly seems almost sentimental.

One of the novel's most striking features is its vision of postapocalyptic America. This is a place with no electricity, machines, industry, money, employment, culture, books, learning. Few animals can be found anywhere, and crops have been almost entirely annihilated by some unexplained, meteorological disaster. Life is cheap and human relations are almost thoroughly exploitative or predatory. These are the new dark ages, or as Crace described it on his Web page, "The novel provides America not with a science fiction future but with something that it has always wanted and lacked—a medieval 'past,' an ancient European experience."

Disease is rampant; what they call the "Great Contagion" has claimed countless lives, and in the place of medicine superstition prevails. (Franklin and others believe a fever can be broken by tying a pigeon to the afflicted's feet.) Religion, or what passes for it, amounts to more superstition, as revealed by the Finger Baptists who disdain metal and bury any they find in large pits outside their compound. Their elders refrain from using their hands for labor, pleasure, or eating, to the point that they wither and become inoperable. Their destruction at the hands of the invaders suggests the relative ineffectuality of their beliefs and lifestyle.

By means of an episodic plot, Crace suggests that most human actions are chaotic and often purposeless. Characters wander ceaselessly, chasing rumors and half-formed dreams, and ultimately they are at home nowhere. America has devolved into a location of overwhelming failure and defeat, and rather than cast this vison in the stereotypes of rotting architecture and blasted surfaces, Crace constructs an alternate vison. America has become a vacuum. The landscape remains, but infertile and completely uninviting. Domiciles are intact but uninhabitable; sentimentality is a luxury few can afford. All are lost who journey here, and the impression is one of utter vacancy. Franklin's determination to turn back to his origins speaks to an overpowering need for orientation and positioning at a center. Suddenly, all their experience changes: "It was as if the country that had once been hostile to them was regretful for it and was now providing recompense—fewer dangers, warmer nights, softer going in a season that was opening up rather than closing down. It even decorated the way with early flowers."

This is hardly the America of early Puritan writing or that of Benjamin Franklin or Thomas Jefferson, all of whom emphasized abundance, fertility, and freedom. America's utopian promise has been replaced by a dystopian nightmare, and it is through his manipulations of the conventions of the dystopian novel that one can appreciate Crace's invention. The dystopian novel was primarily a twentieth century response to nineteenth century optimism. Novels such as Yevgeny Zamyatin's *My* (1927; *We*, 1924), Aldous Huxley's *Brave New World* (1932), George Orwell's *Nineteen Eighty-Four* (1949), and Anthony Burgess's *A Clockwork Orange* (1962) center on the idea of a monolithic, oppressive political state. Certain conventions remain fairly consistent: Individuality and originality are harshly controlled or punished; conformity becomes the highest virtue; and social mobility is impossible and social strata are inflexibly defined. Later in the century, economic and religious dystopias replaced political ones, as in Philip K. Dick's *Do Androids Dream of Electric Sheep?* (1968) and Margaret Atwood's *The Handmaid's Tale* (1985).

However, with *The Pesthouse* a new concern for a new century is evident. Most dystopian fictions begin with some explanation for the work's state of affairs; however, in *The Pesthouse* no such explanation ever appears. Indeed, there is a plague, but that alone cannot explain the lack of all social and political institutions and a complete loss of collective memory. Only some dire cataclysm, much larger than the one that decimates Ferrytown, could produce such monumental results. In this respect, Crace's novel stands in the company of Atwood's *Oryx and Crake* (2003) and Cormac McCarthy's *The Road* (2006). Thus, the book reminds readers of science fiction, the origin of most modern dystopian novels, while at the same time avoiding the usual sci-fi obsessions and clichés.

Unlike most science-fiction dystopias, which emphasize a soulless yet technologically advanced world, *The Pesthouse* is positively primitive. People are not overwhelmed by a sophisticated system; instead, this is a vision of lost humanity crudely destroying itself. Where most dystopias feature protagonists who boldly resist the dominant forces in their worlds, Franklin and Margaret are rather ineffectual. They do not so much oppose as evade or quietly assimilate themselves into the circumstances and forces they confront. Their ultimate decision to return west is not so much an escape as an embrace of hardship, although that embrace is motivated by a curious sense of hope and obligation. Franklin, in particular, knows how desperate that return will be, yet he yearns to make the attempt regardless.

Typically, dystopias arise out of a writer's attempt to link current situations to less desirable, and in some cases less predictable, results. In an interview with Suzi Feay of *The Independent*, Crace admits that the book began as a critique of American optimism and world domination: "[The book would] deal a blow to America at a time when I think it needs to have a blow dealt to it. It will take America from the top of the pile and put it at the bottom of the pile, politically and culturally. It will defer to Europe, instead of Europe having to defer to it. This is what I would do: I would reduce America in this work of fiction, and I would show it as an entirely failed nation." One way to read the novel, then, is to see it as the culmination of political hubris and technological rapaciousness. Here, in effect, is what happens when a nation has too much of everything and still grasps for more. However, the seemingly melodramatic ending reveals Crace's later attitude to his creation: "There's a moment when, if a book has any power of its own, it abandons you and takes over. And it became clear to me that what the book was doing was resisting the failure of America. It didn't want me to write this political novel that reflected my anger at America. It was too fond of the American dream, all those narratives we've been told of hope and getting your own acre. . . . The American dream doesn't always deliver, but there's something powerful about it."

Given the novel's dystopian features and Crace's comments, it is certainly inevitable that readers will be mindful of the American Dream. The notion of a civilized society that encourages the pursuit of happiness is radically called into question here. The fertile plains have dried up, there is no economic opportunity, Horatio Alger is long dead, there is certainly no wealth to be had for anyone, and the great belief in mobility and progress is found wanting. Some—the strong, able-bodied, or those endowed with booty—can journey east, but women, except for the few who are young and physically alluring, cannot book passage. Furthermore, the great dictum of heading west and finding fortune is inverted—everyone wants to travel east. In Crace's hands, America is no longer synonymous with opportunity.

Crace writes with a mesmerizing grace, a style that eschews verbal pyrotechnics yet delights at every turn. The narrator moves among pointed observations, clear descriptions of place and action, and arresting rhetorical questions ("how could anyone not know by now how mischievous the world could be?"). In all of his books, Crace reveals his fascination with natural history and natural processes to the point that he anthropomorphizes nature, yet never sentimentally. Instead, the inevitable workings of natural elements are given full play to the extent that they are characters integral to the text. Thus, the ocean becomes "one great weeping eye," illness is "a weak and passing visitor," and "death ususally expressed itself more forcibly."

Crace's imagination is remarkably fecund; he never writes the same book twice, and *The Pesthouse* is testament to the range of his vision and interests. He is at once an elegant stylist and incisive thinker, and when he experiments with genre fiction, as in this case with the dystopian novel, his creation is thoroughly his own and original. This novel will certainly not please ideologues and jingoists, but it is an important contribution to European assessments of the American experience.

*David W. Madden*

## Review Sources

*Kirkus Reviews* 75, no. 2 (January 15, 2007): 6.
*Library Journal* 132 (March 1, 2007): 69.
*New Criterion* 25, no. 9 (May, 2007): 33-37.
*New Statesman* 136 (March 5, 2007): 59.
*The New York Times* 156 (May 15, 2007): E9.
*The New York Times Book Review* 156 (April 29, 2007): 8.
*The New Yorker* 83, no. 10 (April 30, 2007): 84-85.
*Publishers Weekly* 254, no. 5 (January 29, 2007): 38.
*The Spectator* 305 (November 24, 2007): 49.
*The Washington Post*, May 13, 2007, p. BW05.

# POOR PEOPLE

*Author:* William T. Vollmann (1959-    )
*Publisher:* Ecco Press (New York). Illustrated.
  314 pp. $29.95
*Type of work:* Current affairs

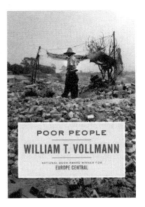

*Building on previous work from his seven-volume trea-*
*tise on violence, Vollmann turns his attention to poverty*
*throughout the world, interviewing people who seem poor*
*in order to learn about their circumstances and report*
*their views on poverty*

In *Poor People*, William T. Vollmann reports on poverty
with personal interviews from around the globe. Through
the use of local guides and interpreters, he asks randomly
selected individuals, and in some cases their family members, if they consider themselves poor and why some are poor and others rich. *Poor People* is therefore
Vollmann's report about those he interviewed. His narrative recounts their lives, the
conditions surrounding them, and their answers to his questions.

The responses to his questions range from a religious belief that the poor person is
paying for past sins from a previous life to the practical response that there is no work.
Vollmann offers his own perspectives and philosophies and compares poverty among
different countries. For example, in the United States, poverty to some might mean
not being able to afford cable television, while in Vietnam it might mean not being
able to have electricity. Poverty also seems to be subjective to the afflicted, as he
notes when he asked one young woman if she thought she was poor. Her reply, "I
think I am rich," provides an opportunity to reflect on what it means to be poor and
who makes the determination, society or the individual.

Building on this subjectivity, Vollmann delves deeper into the issue of poverty by
examining what it means to live a normal life. He wonders what living conditions
create normalcy and how that view of normalcy affects poverty. Is it normal to live in
a cardboard box or beg for money? Who decides? He also examines the effects and
consequences abject poverty has on the individuals he interviews. He notes how the
poor seem invisible and theorizes that perhaps the condition of poverty itself is what
makes them invisible. Is the invisibility due to a lack of money or is it because society,
or at least those with money, would like to pretend it does not exist? Do the affluent
tend to ignore the poor because they do not know how to help, or is it out of fear that
they could end up in a similar situation? For the poor women in Afghanistan, who are
required by the Taliban regime to wear a burka but forbidden to beg, the garment,
along with the government, comments Vollmann, makes them invisible.

In later chapters, Vollmann notes that in some instances poverty seems to offer
its victims a certain level of freedom that the more affluent do not have. For example, he observes that poor children typically are able to roam and play freely, while

experience with his daughter and even his own childhood memories offer no such recollection of being free to play with such wild abandon. He comments on some men in a tea shop leisurely enjoying the afternoon conversation, contrasted with his affluent neighbors who seem to be in a constant state of motion while rushing from one event to the next. Vollmann states that while the poor may lack monetary resources, they are rich in time.

*William T. Vollmann is an author of several novels, short stories, documentaries, and nonfiction critical analyses. His writings have won awards such as the National Book Award for his novel* Europe Central *(2005). His largest work to date is the seven-volume critique of violence* Rising Up and Rising Down *(2004), which was nominated for the National Book Critics Circle Award.*

Another consequence of poverty that Vollmann describes is a condition he refers to as accident-prone-ness. In this context, he is not writing about a tendency toward having accidents but the tendency to have detrimental consequences arise because of the conditions of poverty. An illness that might easily be cured with proper rest and appropriate medicine but instead is detrimental to the poor victim who can afford neither is an example of accident-prone-ness. The man who, in trying to resolve an arrest for violence, most likely due to poverty, ends up with more fines and a dead pet because of his lack of resources is another example. Vollmann also talks about crime as a condition of poverty, how a lack of resources seems to correspond with a loss of personal security, with more incidence of rape and murder. He devotes an entire chapter to the Snakeheads, Asian underground gangs primarily involved in human trafficking. His stories of the Snakeheads show how poverty breeds organized crime groups who prey on those seeking to escape their impoverished conditions. Vollmann also includes a chapter on pain, noting that lack of access to medical care for the poor results in missing teeth, visible sores, and premature aging. He explains that he did not include a section on hunger because it is a given when discussing poverty.

Vollmann goes on to offer more than just the commentaries from his interviews. In offering a broader perspective of poverty, he proposes that in some instances the poor hate the rich or may blame the rich for their present conditions. He also notes the expectation of the poor to be helped by the rich. There are times and circumstances where those with money, in turn, hate the poor because they may feel forced or pressured to give up their hard-earned resources. Vollmann shares his own experiences, noting that as a nonpoor person, he at times has felt inconvenienced by the presence of the homeless. There is also conflict that may be experienced by those who want to help but do not know how to effectively do so. Vollmann himself explains how he paid people for their interviews, noting at times his own desire to do more to help and knowing that simply throwing money at the people might alleviate hunger for a day but do nothing to alleviate their long-term impoverishment. He also touches on a fear of the poor by commenting on how intimidating it can be to interact with people who have nothing and who might be willing to resort to violence in order to ensure their own survival. He shares several personal stories to illustrate his own instances of fear and intimidation when interacting with people on the streets. He thus addresses many of the issues surrounding poverty by discussing how poverty affects everyone, rich and poor.

Vollmann shows in subsequent chapters how a desire for wealth and prosperity can create better conditions for some while creating more poverty for others. His chapters on the oil refining in Sarykamys, Kazakhstan, and the development in Nanning, China, illustrate that for those who are already living marginally, there are few choices for escaping. In these examples, it seems that Vollmann suggests that in some cases government is to blame for creating or continuing impoverished conditions. With Nanning, home owners were forced to sell their homes so that a larger road and newer housing units could be built. Their homes were demolished, and the payment they received from the government was not enough to afford the newer homes.

The story of Sarykamys highlights the problems that governments and big corporations can create in their pursuit of wealth. In this small corner of the world, the initial discovery of oil was viewed as economic salvation. Unfortunately, the necessity to refine sulfur out of the oil has created hazardous living conditions. In a footnote, Vollmann seems to indicate some notion from those he interviews, and perhaps his own bias, that governments should step in to prevent this type of abuse and to some extent that the affluent people of the world are to blame, because they demand the resource, causing the need to produce it, which in turn causes human ailments, further suffering, and more poverty. He does not directly place any blame with the corporation.

For whatever reasons, the mind-set of the townspeople in Sarykamys, who most likely live from one paycheck to the next, is one of acceptance of their conditions. Even more disturbing and perhaps more revealing of the problem is that many of the people from this town whom Vollmann attempted to interview would not talk with him out of fear of repercussions. He infers from his stories of Sarykamys and Nanning what happens when governments and corporations view people as somewhat disposable. He also highlights how poverty can create an unfortunate acceptance by those who lack the resources to fight or demand more equitable conditions. Ironically, the governments in both cases are, in theory, trying to create better conditions for the inhabitants.

*Poor People* has been well received, although commentaries on Vollmann himself seem contentious. Some have compared his work to another similar text on poverty written by James Agee, *Let Us Now Praise Famous Men* (1941). Even Vollmann himself mentions this work. Still, while similarities between the two works may seem obvious, *Poor People* offers a current global perspective on poverty. Vollmann also notes that his previous works have been criticized for being difficult to read; *Poor People*, however, is difficult to put down. While Vollmann does not himself offer any answers to the question of why some people are poor and others rich, his reporting of the matter provides groundwork for a better understanding of poverty and how it affects those afflicted. His comparison of the poor among various countries also shows both similarities and differences.

If Vollmann were a social scientist instead of a journalist, he might have attempted to conduct his interviews in a more systematic and controlled manner. In place of a scientific study on poverty, he offers a glimpse of poverty from many different angles. Along with his interviews and findings, he interjects his own experiences and suppositions. As he explains, he is not himself poor, nor has he ever experienced poverty. He also suggests that most of the people who will read *Poor People* will not be poor. Nevertheless, his snapshots of poverty, along with the deeply moving photographs of those he interviewed, provide a personal account of poverty from those who live it daily.

*Susan E. Thomas*

## Review Sources

*The Atlantic Monthly* 299, no. 3 (April, 2007): 116-117.
*Biography: An Interdisciplinary Quarterly* 30, no. 3 (Summer, 2007): 457.
*Booklist* 103, nos. 9/10 (January 1-15, 2007): 32.
*Esquire* 147, no. 3 (March, 2007): 86.
*Harper's Magazine* 314 (March, 2007): 81-82.
*Library Journal* 132, no. 4 (March 1, 2007): 98.
*New York* 40, no. 8 (March 5, 2007): 66.
*The New York Times Book Review* 156 (March 18, 2007): 11.
*Publishers Weekly* 254, no. 4 (January 22, 2007): 172.

# THE POST-BIRTHDAY WORLD

*Author:* Lionel Shriver (1957-    )
*Publisher:* HarperCollins (New York). 517 pp. $25.95
*Type of work:* Novel
*Time:* 1997-2003
*Locale:* London

*Children's book illustrator Irina McGovern's life branches into two concurrent time lines based on her decision whether or not to act upon her physical attraction to Ramsey Acton, a charismatic professional snooker player*

*Principal characters:*
IRINA MCGOVERN, an American children's
    book illustrator living in London
RAMSEY ACTON, a professional snooker player
LAWRENCE TRAINER, an American research fellow
    specializing in terrorism, Irina's live-in partner of several years
BETHANY ANDERS, Lawrence's coworker, with whom
    Lawrence has an affair in one time line
JUDE HARTFORD, a children's book writer and Ramsey's ex-wife
RAISA MCGOVERN, Irina's mother, a ballet dancer who resents that she
    had to give up performing when she became pregnant with Irina

In Lionel Shriver's *The Post-Birthday World*, Irina McGovern, a sensible and somewhat staid children's book illustrator, is fairly content with her equally rational boyfriend, Lawrence Trainer, with whom she has lived in London for several years. While Irina is slightly dismayed that Lawrence rarely kisses her and apparently has no desire to marry her, she genuinely believes herself fortunate for having found a stable, considerate man. One evening, however, Irina's world is turned upside down. Irina and Lawrence had made an almost accidental habit of celebrating the birthday of their casual friend, professional snooker player Ramsey Acton, with Ramsey and his wife, Jude. That couple's divorce, however, has taken Jude out of the picture, and Lawrence is away on a business trip, leaving Irina to entertain Ramsey on her own. At the end of the evening, Irina is startled to find that she is powerfully drawn to Ramsey, and she longs to kiss him. She senses that her decision to act on that impulse will have profound implications for her life. Further, she knows that if she does not kiss Ramsey she will always wonder what would have happened if she did.

The reader, however, is not left to wonder. At this point, the novel splits into alternating narratives marking the two very different paths that Irina's life takes. In one time line, Irina kisses Ramsey. They go no further than kissing that night, or on many subsequent meetings, because neither is comfortable with betraying Lawrence to that incontrovertible degree. Irina cannot get the prospect of sleeping with Ramsey out of her mind, however, and when Ramsey tells Irina that she must either leave Lawrence or stop seeing Ramsey, she follows her heart and leaves Lawrence. A few short months later, after a whirlwind tour of the professional snooker circuit, Irina marries Ramsey, setting forth on a more tumultuous relationship than she ever could have imagined.

In the other time line, Irina resists the impulse to kiss Ramsey, instead fleeing to the bathroom to compose herself. Then, because she does not see Ramsey often, she compartmentalizes the incident in her mind, taking it out occasionally to speculate what direction her life might have taken had she acted upon that impulse. Irina plods along, vaguely disturbed by Lawrence's increasing emotional distance, only to find out years later that Lawrence started an affair with a coworker not long after the fateful birthday with Ramsey.

*Lionel Shriver is an American novelist living in London. Her novel* We Need to Talk About Kevin *(2003) won the prestigious Orange Prize for Fiction in 2005, and she also won literature grants from the Northern Ireland Arts Council in 1993 and 1996. The Post-Birthday World* is her eighth novel.

While the idea of divergent outcomes based on a pivotal moment is not new, Shriver's deft handling of the alternate time lines makes this novel truly unique. For instance, certain conversations are repeated almost verbatim within the two narratives, but with different characters taking each part. In one life, when Irina takes Ramsey home to meet her family, she begs him not to pick a fight with her during the visit, knowing that any mention of her ex-partner Lawrence by her tactless mother is likely to set Ramsey off. In the other time line, Lawrence pleads with Irina not to pick a fight with her own mother during their Christmas visit. When the inevitable friction between mother and daughter occurs, the volatile Ramsey does indeed start an embarrassing fight with Irina yet fiercely defends his wife when his new mother-in-law criticizes her. Lawrence, on the other hand, would never humiliate Irina with such a jealous display, but neither does he support Irina in her family relationships, implicitly blaming Irina for not being able to get along with her mother.

The fact that Irina's possible lives differ so greatly depending on her choice of partner might lead some readers to infer that Shriver believes a woman's life depends more on the man she chooses than any other factor. This criticism is too simplistic, however, because the novel also examines the profound differences in the men's lives based on their relationships with Irina. For instance, the Lawrence that Irina ultimately leaves for Ramsey senses her pulling away during her months of indecision, such that he examines their relationship and tries to reestablish their emotional connection. For this Irina, it is too little and too late, but Lawrence nonetheless becomes a more thoughtful and emotionally available man because of Irina's influence. The Lawrence that Irina stays with, however, senses Irina's efforts to cling to him, and he responds by drawing back, ultimately seeking passion elsewhere instead of trying to reestablish it with Irina. Similarly, the Ramsey who marries Irina, distracted by their passion and his own jealousy, never wins the National Snooker Championship, an honor that has eluded him with several near-misses throughout his entire career, while the other Ramsey reconciles briefly with Jude and does win the championship, but he does not seem particularly happy.

Shriver draws clever parallels within this framework, in particular showing the effect of Irina's choices on her illustration work. The Irina who has married Ramsey at first neglects her work shamefully, because the jealous and childish Ramsey cannot bear to play in a snooker tournament without her at his side, and she is so addicted to her newfound passion that she loses interest in everything else. When Irina's sloppy work leads to a lost commission, however, she finally buckles down and writes her first children's book instead of merely illustrating the work of other authors. Her book tells the story of a young boy who must choose whether to pursue snooker against his parents' wishes or settle down to a more respectable career. The book is written and illustrated in one direction showing that the boy has become a snooker player, and it proceeds in the other direction showing his life as an astronaut. In both scenarios, the boy wonders what his life would have been like if he had made the other decision, concluding in both time lines that life is about compromises. Most important, Irina is able to infuse the illustrations with the long-dormant passion that Ramsey has awakened in her, and her previously obscure career takes a new turn when she is short-listed for a prestigious and financially lucrative Lewis Carroll award. Irina is shocked when she wins the award, ironically beating out Ramsey's ex-wife Jude for the same prize, but Ramsey ruins her triumph by creating a jealous scene at the awards ceremony to which Irina has invited her ex-partner Lawrence.

In the other time line, the Irina who has stayed with Lawrence also writes and illustrates her own book. She tells a story about a little boy who abandons his best friend for a new acquaintance but is attacked by such guilt and grief that he goes back to the first friend, who subsequently deserts him. Irina illustrates the story as with an Etch A Sketch toy, using computer graphic programs to do so. This book is also nominated for the Lewis Carroll award, but in this time line Irina loses the award to Jude, and one of the judges covertly whispers to Irina that while her illustrations were wonderful, they were somehow a bit too clinical. In spite of this, Irina is deliriously happy at the ceremony, because she realizes that Lawrence's shock that she did not win is evidence of his unwavering faith in her work.

Another effective technique that Shriver employs is to examine Irina's reaction to significant news events, such as the September 11, 2001, terrorist attacks. In one time line, Irina and Ramsey are having such a vehement, days-long argument over the awards ceremony that they are not even aware of the September 11 events until September 13. In the other time line, Irina and Lawrence are still in New York when the attacks occur, and Lawrence is much in demand by news networks seeking his expert commentary on the subject of terrorism. As happens often in the time line with Lawrence, Irina is humbly grateful for her life and somewhat ashamed about any dissatisfaction that she might feel. With Ramsey, however, her life is full of emotional ups and downs that often obscure what is happening in the outside world.

Though the beginning of the book moves slowly, and though Irina analyzes her feelings to a perhaps obsessive degree, Shriver successfully builds the narrative tension to a crescendo, such that the reader is anxious to find out what happens in each time line. Not long after the awards ceremony, Ramsey is diagnosed with terminal cancer in both time lines. In one, his wife Irina is shocked to find out that he has frittered away all of his substantial snooker earnings, yet she finds a certain strength within herself as she nurses him through his grueling cancer treatments. In the other time line, the Irina whom Lawrence has just deserted for his mistress finds herself turning back to Ramsey, but by this point he is in no condition to consummate the earlier passion upon which they had not acted. Instead, Irina is able to offer Ramsey the quiet companionship that he needs during this difficult time.

Ultimately, Shriver's genius is that she makes it difficult, if not impossible, for the reader to decide which choice and which life is better for Irina. With Ramsey, Irina discovers that she is capable of great passion in her life and her work. While she will always regret hurting Lawrence by leaving him, she believes that the incredible highlights of her too-short time with Ramsey before his death were worth the devastating low points. In the other time line, in the aftermath of Lawrence's devastating yet oddly gentle betrayal, Irina muses about what would have happened had she kissed Ramsey but believes that she maintained her integrity and therefore made the right decision. Ironically, while the predivergence Irina believed that she could not live without a man, each Irina ultimately ends up alone but learns in the process that she is capable of coping without a man after all.

Although the characters are fictional, Shriver has stated that the idea for *The Post-Birthday World* came from a real-life situation in which she had to decide whether to remain with her longtime partner or begin a new relationship with a man she had fallen in love with; she ultimately did the latter. Like Irina, Shriver found herself second-guessing her decision, which undoubtedly lends to the authenticity of Irina's doubts in both time lines. One can also draw parallels between Shriver's life and Irina's experiences as a nominee for an important literary award, which she wins in one time line and loses in the other. Shriver's seventh novel, *We Need to Talk About Kevin* (2003), won the prestigious 2005 Orange Prize for Fiction, which Shriver, like Irina, indicates was particularly gratifying after years of relative obscurity.

*Amy Sisson*

## Review Sources

*Booklist* 103, no. 11 (February 1, 2007): 33.
*Kirkus Reviews* 74, no. 23 (December 1, 2006): 1196.
*Library Journal* 132, no. 3 (February 15, 2007): 115.
*New Statesman* 136 (May 7, 2007): 72.
*The New York Times* 156 (March 9, 2007): E29-E34.
*The New York Times Book Review* 156 (March 18, 2007): 17.
*The New Yorker* 83, no. 6 (April 2, 2007): 79.
*People* 67, no. 11 (March 19, 2007): 49.
*Publishers Weekly* 253, no. 46 (November 20, 2006): 31-32.
*The Wall Street Journal* 249, no. 63 (March 17, 2007): P12.

# POWER, FAITH, AND FANTASY
## America in the Middle East, 1776 to the Present

*Author:* Michael B. Oren (1955-    )
*Publisher:* W. W. Norton (New York). 778 pp. $35.00
*Type of work:* History, current affairs
*Time:* 1776-2006
*Locale:* The United States and the Middle East

*An account of America's involvement in the Middle East from the earliest days of the republic to the Iraq War of the early twenty-first century*

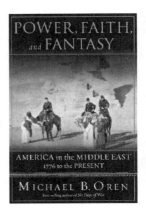

Principal personages:
JOHN LEDYARD, American explorer of the Middle East
WASHINGTON IRVING, American author
JAMES MADISON, U.S. president, 1809-1817
MARK TWAIN, American writer
WOODROW WILSON, U.S. president, 1913-1921
HARRY S. TRUMAN, U.S. president, 1945-1953
GEORGE H. W. BUSH, U.S. president, 1989-1993
BILL CLINTON, U.S. president, 1993-2001
GEORGE W. BUSH, U.S. president beginning in 2001

Michael B. Oren's *Power, Faith, and Fantasy: America in the Middle East, 1776 to the Present* describes American involvement in the Middle East that began at the time of the American Revolution. In his narrative, the author discusses the individuals and events that populate his historical canvas by interweaving the three themes of power, faith, and fantasy. The power is political, economic, and military, ranging from the wars waged against the pirates of Barbary in the early national era to the war against Iraq's Saddam Hussein in 2003. Faith pertains to Christianity. In the nineteenth century, many Protestants journeyed to the Middle East with the hope of converting the region's Muslim majority to Christianity. Few were converted, but the missionaries established schools and hospitals that had a lasting impact. More recently, with the emergence of Zionism and the later Nazi Holocaust, Palestine became the focus of many Jews. Last, the Middle East, with its religious roots, foreign cultures, and exotic landscapes, has proved to be an addictive fantasy for many Americans over the past two centuries.

*Power, Faith, and Fantasy* begins with John Ledyard, a New Hampshire frontiersman turned sailor who, after attempting to walk across all of Eurasia, journeyed to the Middle East in 1788, the first American to experience that region. He was not impressed with Egyptian society, then under Ottoman rule, nor even the Nile River, among whose sand dunes he died and was buried. The U.S. government's earliest encounters were occasioned by North Africa's Barbary pirates. Here, the concern was power, explicitly economic power and the right to trade. With no navy to protect the infant republic's merchant shipping, Americans were captured and held for ransom. Diplomacy and bribery were initially tried, with little effect. It was only in 1815 that the Barbary threat was eliminated after President James Madison sent warships against the pirates, but it was not the final end of North African seizure of Americans for ransom. In 1904, Ion Perdicaris, a businessman in Tangier and supposedly an American citizen, was taken hostage by a Berber chief, Mulai Ahmed el Raisuli. President Theodore Roosevelt's famous response was terse: "We want Perdicaris alive or Raisuli dead." Neighboring Morocco paid the ransom and Perdicaris was freed. The incident was later immortalized in the 1975 film *The Wind and the Lion*, and in typical Hollywood fashion history became fantasy, with the middle-aged Perdicaris played by Candice Bergen and Raisuli played by Sean Connery, a Scot.

*A native of New Jersey, Michael B. Oren immigrated to Israel, where he has served in both military and political capacities. The author of the award-winning* Six Days of War *(2002), he is a graduate of Princeton and Columbia Universities and has written extensively for numerous prestigious newspapers and magazines.*

While early nineteenth century presidents were creating a standing navy to confront the Barbary states, other Americans were discovering the Middle East as a place of fantasy and faith, where the women were lustful, the men brave warriors, and society corrupted by the false religion of Islam, a vision that resulted from the combined influence of the Bible and *One Thousand and One Nights*. Washington Irving's *A Chronicle of the Conquest of Granada* (1829) and *The Alhambra* (1832) presented a romanticized view of Spain under the Islamic Moors. After the Civil War, notable Americans, including Ulysses S. Grant and Mark Twain, discovered the region as tourists. One by-product of the United States' involvement in the Middle East was Frédéric-Auguste Bartholdi's iconic Statue of Liberty, originally intended to be placed adjacent to the Suez Canal and titled "Egypt Bringing Light to Asia." Because the bankrupt Egyptian government had no money for statues, it ended up in New York harbor. The Middle East as fantasy also occurred at the 1893 Chicago World's Fair, which included an Algerian Village, a Turkish Pavilion, a Moorish Palace, a Cairo Street, and the popular if controversial belly dancer Little Egypt. In the silent film *The Sheik* (1921), Rudolph Valentino's role as the title character sent female American hearts aflutter. Later, a more historical but still romanticized view of the Middle East was presented in 1962's *Lawrence of Arabia*, starring Peter O'Toole, which was based in part on the early reporting of Lowell Thomas, an American journalist.

With American missionaries, faith was often tinged with fantasy, including the belief that the Muslim Middle East could be converted to Christianity. Nevertheless, the

Protestant missionaries were at the forefront of American involvement in the region during most of the nineteenth century. The religious aim of converting Muslims as well as Jews and even Orthodox and Maronite Christians to Protestant Christianity was merged with the belief of America as a "city on a hill" with the obligation to create a new model of society for the world. For many Americans, one hope was to restore to the Jews their ancient land, and "restorationism" remained a major goal. The missionaries had little religious success, but they did establish schools and hospitals, and they fueled the interest of Americans at home.

In the 1880's, Zionism, with its vision of a Jewish homeland in Palestine, the biblical "Land of Israel," inspired many European Jews, although most American Jews were less enthusiastic. Some Protestant Americans supported Zionism as an extension of restorationism. Mark Twain was no Protestant enthusiast, but after becoming acquainted with Theodor Herzl, a leading Zionist, he gave his public support to the movement.

World War I was a watershed for Western civilization. Millions died, and ideals and beliefs collapsed, as did long-lived empires, including the Ottoman Empire. American relations with the Ottoman Empire had been generally positive, but the Armenian holocaust of 1914-1915 changed the hearts and minds of many. However, President Woodrow Wilson pursued a policy of noninvolvement in the affairs of the Old World until April, 1917, when the United States declared war against Germany, but not against the Ottoman Empire, a decision that ensured that America's influence on the region's postwar settlement would be minimal. The demise of the Ottoman Empire led to a restructuring of the Middle East. In 1917, Britain's Balfour Declaration gave assurances to Zionists that a Jewish homeland would be established in Ottoman Palestine. The existing Arabic Palestinian population, mostly Muslim, was ignored. By the early 1920's, an independent Turkey had come into existence, but much of the Arab world was divided into League of Nations' mandates, with France gaining Syria and Lebanon and Britain awarded Iraq and Palestine. The United States retreated into isolationism, and Wilson's hope for a democratic Middle East, with self-determination as the guiding principle, was not to be.

The story of modern Israel and its relations with its Arab neighbors plays a major role in *Power, Faith, and Fantasy*. In the early twentieth century, Zionism increased among American Jews as exemplified by Golda Mabovitz, a Milwaukee schoolteacher who moved to Palestine in 1921, known later as Golda Meir, an Israeli prime minister. There were also 100,000 Arabs in the United States in the early twentieth century, mostly Christians, and they were as opposed to an independent Israel as Middle Eastern Arabs were. During the interwar years, American policy toward Palestine was guarded neutrality. America's relationship with the Middle East became more complex because of demands for oil. In the 1920's, American oil companies were included in the consortium that gained oil rights in the British mandate of Iraq, and in the 1930's oil agreements were made with Saudi Arabia. The Americans and the Saudis were joined at the hip by oil, and, in spite of occasional differences, they have remained so to the present.

The military power of the United States returned to North Africa in 1942 in Operation Torch against the Axis Powers. Fantasy followed in the form of films such as *Ca-*

*sablanca* (1942) and *Ali Baba and the Forty Thieves* (1944). As a result of the Holocaust, support increased in the United States for an independent Israel, although President Franklin D. Roosevelt tried to walk a narrow line, given the increasing need for Middle Eastern oil, even meeting with Ibn Sa‘ūd, the Saudi monarch, who adamantly opposed any Jewish immigration to Palestine. After Britain was unable to quell the violence between Israelis and Palestinians, in 1947 the United Nations voted to partition Palestine into two independent states. The reaction in the Arab world was predictable, with war breaking out even before Israel's formal independence in May, 1948.

Since 1948, Cold War rivalry, the challenge of Arab nationalism, the more recent Islamic revival, and the ever-growing need for oil has found the United States increasingly involved in the region. In 1953, the Central Intelligence Agency (CIA) was instrumental in undermining Iran's prime minister, Mohammad Mossadegh. The British, French, and Israelis invaded Egypt after Gamal Abdel Nasser nationalized the Suez Canal; the Eisenhower administration forced the invaders to back down. For many Americans, the murky complexities of the Middle East were romantically simplified. In 1959's *Ben-Hur*, a Jewish prince comes together in alliance with an Arab sheikh. In the real world, American presidents' attempts to solve the Palestinian imbroglio met with little success, and war between the Israelis and Palestinians became the norm rather than the exception.

Fundamentalist Islam came to the attention of most Americans in 1979 with the overthrow of Mohammad Reza Shah Pahlavi and the establishment of the Islamic Republic under the Ayatollah Khomeini. In November of that year, sixty-six Americans were taken hostage by Iranian militants; fifty-two of the hostages were held for 444 days. In 1983, two truck bomb attacks in Lebanon killed more than 250 Americans. On December 21, 1988, Pan American Flight 103 was blown up over Lockerbie, Scotland, resulting in the deaths of 259 people onboard. Meanwhile, *Raiders of the Lost Ark* (1981) and Disney's *Aladdin* (1992) portrayed Hollywood's fantasies about the Middle East.

In the 1980's, during the Iran-Iraq War, the United States sided with Iraq. In the aftermath, Iraqi president Saddam Hussein invaded neighboring Kuwait. President George H. W. Bush responded, gaining U.N. approval, and with an alliance of more than thirty nations Operation Desert Storm quickly drove the Iraqis out of Kuwait. However, because of fears of Iran's strengthened role if Iraq was excessively weakened, Hussein was allowed to survive. In 1993, Islamic extremists attempted to destroy New York City's World Trade Center's twin towers, but casualties were minimal. During the 1990's, President Bill Clinton responded to Saddam Hussein's continuing threats by launching missiles against the regime, but with little effect. In 1998, the Islamic terrorist group al-Qaeda bombed American embassies in Kenya and Tanzania. The response to launch missiles against al-Qaeda training camps in Afghanistan had little result, as did Clinton's attempt to resolve the Israeli-Palestinian issue.

The death of almost three thousand innocent civilians at the World Trade Center on September 11, 2001, changed everything—and changed nothing. President George W.

Bush, whom Oren describes as a combination of previous American personalities involved in the Middle East—a warrior-diplomat and a warrior-evangelist—launched a "crusade" (an unfortunate term, given Muslim memories of the medieval Christian Crusades) against al-Qaeda and its Taliban allies in Afghanistan and, ironically, against some of the same forces that the United States had earlier supported when the Soviets invaded Afghanistan in 1979. Bush soon extended his crusade against Saddam Hussein and his "weapons of mass destruction" (WMD), and in March, 2003, the "coalition of the willing" (mainly the United States and Great Britain) invaded Iraq. No WMD were discovered, and, echoing Wilson's and America's earlier idealism, the justification for the invasion shifted from WMD to creating an American-style pluralist democracy in Iraq as a paradigm for the rest of the Middle East. The fantasy WMD were replaced by IEDs (improvised explosive devices), and the fantasy of a pluralist democracy became a wasteland of religious sectarianism.

*Power, Faith, and Fantasy* is well written, and in spite of its cast of thousands, the narrative is clear and its themes well developed. It could be argued that the author devotes too much space to the subject of Israel-Palestine, but the conflict between the Israelis and the Palestinians is a continuing cancer that affects the entire region.

*Eugene Larson*

## Review Sources

*American History* 42, no. 3 (August, 2007): 67-68.
*The Atlantic Monthly* 299, no. 1 (January/February, 2007): 148.
*Booklist* 103, no. 8 (December 15, 2006): 8.
*Commentary* 123, no. 1 (January, 2007): 53-57.
*Foreign Affairs* 86, no. 1 (January/February, 2007): 174-175.
*Kirkus Reviews* 74, no. 21 (November 1, 2006): 1116.
*Library Journal* 132, no. 1 (January 1, 2007): 124-125.
*National Review* 59, no. 1 (January 29, 2007): 44.
*The New York Times Book Review* 156 (January 28, 2007): 12.
*Publishers Weekly* 253, no. 46 (November 20, 2006): 52.

# PRIME GREEN
## Remembering the Sixties

*Author:* Robert Stone (1937-    )
*Publisher:* HarperCollins (New York). 229 pp. $25.95
*Type of work:* Memoir, literary history
*Time:* 1958-1972
*Locale:* The world's oceans, the United States, Paris, and
   London

*An evocation and assessment of a turbulent and fre-*
*quently misconstrued era in American history from the*
*personal perspective of one of the most admired and ac-*
*complished writers of that time*

PRIME GREEN:
REMEMBERING
THE SIXTIES
ROBERT STONE

*Principal personages:*
   ROBERT STONE, the author
   JANICE STONE, his wife, a paragon of patience
   KEN KESEY, a charismatic counterculture hero and great writer

Robert Stone's memoir of the 1960's, aptly named *Prime Green* to suggest the spirit of renewal and revitalization that defined the era for him, is designed as a corrective to the spate of recent volumes that demonize and denigrate the counterculture that Stone has recalled with a clear-eyed and candid depiction. Robert Greenfield's *Timothy Leary: An Experimental Life* (2006), for instance, is a study that is relatively accurate in terms of the factual information it offers but that misses the idealism and enthusiasm that were the crucial components of a vision of social reality that inspired a significant segment of those Americans born during or just after World War II. Like Stone, who was born in 1937 and raised in New York City by a single mother afflicted with a bipolar disorder, they took part in some of the most dynamic and disturbing events in American history, but the passage of time and the political agendas of some prominent commentators has resulted in a negative distortion of these moments. Stone's very readable book provides a necessary balance by recalling with what Richard Ford accurately identifies as "unnostalgic compassion and intelligence" what Ford designates "those tumultuous times."

Stone's highly acclaimed novels *A Hall of Mirrors* (1967), *Dog Soldiers* (1974), which won the National Book Award and was the basis for the film *Who'll Stop the Rain* (1978), *A Flag For Sunrise* (1981), and *Children of Light* (1986) are set in the 1960's and 1970's, as are the stories in his short-fiction collection *Bear and His Daughter* (1997). Stone followed what in retrospect seems like a classic American route toward his vocation. As he outlines in the inviting opening pages of *Prime Green*, he joined the Navy after graduating from high school, following in the tradition of Ishmael, who established a format for a young man yearning for the kind of experience that he might transform into literature. As Herman Melville's archetypal questor states, "Whenever it is a damp, drizzly November in my soul . . . I account it high time to get to sea as soon as I can." Among many others, Langston Hughes, Jack Kerouac, and Allen Ginsberg all embarked from a New York port, and Stone, already far in advance of most collegiate English majors in his familiarity with classical and contemporary literature, took to sea as both an avoidance of a specific, limiting job and in response to the call of faraway places. In a passage akin to the narrator's description of his first view of the East in Joseph Conrad's *Youth* (1902), Stone writes:

> In the Strait of Malacca, I saw the thousand little ringed lights of the fishing-pirate junks of the Malay sea people. Picking past their craft we heard their flutes and bells. It was a faraway ocean but was what I'd come for.
> Passing the Lipari Islands headed for Beirut we passed between Scylla and Charybdis. From the peak of Stromboli great rich salvos of flaming molten rock were tossed in the smoky air. The ocean smelled of the Malvasia grapes that grew on the slope.

Stone's evocation of his sojourn on the USS *Arneb*, "an ungainly naval transport ship with the lines of a tramp streamer," serves the essential function of introducing the narrative consciousness of the memorist, the mind through which the reader will experience the world and the voice that will make it vivid. Stone's skills as a writer of imaginative fiction are evident here, his descriptive powers engrossing, his sense of character compelling, and his ability to develop a supple but firm narrative structure that carries a kind of wandering expository thread skillfully constructed. As he relates his reactions to an endlessly varied seascape and the rituals of the Navy onboard, the captivating quirks of his personality emerge, as well as some of his core principles.

While the narrative is in the form of an ongoing present, it is apparent that the retrospect of a mature man is operative. When Stone observes that "history's narratives are being revised to suit our sorry times," his political perspective begins to take shape, and when he says that he admired the "Australian dimension" that "provided a sometimes prevailing good humor and a tolerant sense of absurdity," he is speaking for his own way of being.

The narrative turns toward the familiar "education of a young man" mode when Stone begins his first job as a very low-level employee of the *Daily News*, enrolls at New York University, and attends a few sessions at the Hagen-Berghof acting studio. Relatively down and out in the city, Stone is ecstatic about his freedom and the city's myriad possibilities, and, as he states summarizing the cultural turning that was beginning to gain momentum, "Rock and roll was coming. It would change everything." Interspersed among other observations are casual literary allusions, indicative of Stone's self-directed, eclectic course of reading and his ambitions. As his ship wallows amid icebergs, driven by a fierce wind in Antarctica, he hunkers below deck, staying "with Leopold Bloom as long as I could" in the copy of James Joyce's *Ulysses* (1922) he has from the Norfolk Library. He does not mention that it is newly published, but he relates that Kerouac's *On the Road* (1957) was "one of my other traveling books," and he tells how he had "amassed a small collection of magazine rejection slips" during his time in the Navy, encouraged by a handwritten note on the form from *The New Yorker* that advised, "Try us again."

To this point, the contents of *Prime Green* are essentially prologue. The heart of the book appears in an almost offhand fashion when Stone meets a classmate, Janice, who becomes his wife in a brief chapter that seems just as interested in Stone's attendance at the Seven Arts Gallery coffee shop where he heard Kerouac, Ginsberg, Gregory Corso, Ray Bremser, and Ted Joans—gods and lesser deities of the burgeoning Beat scene—read poetry.

He and Janice move to New Orleans in 1960 and start a life together that, contrary to many unions launched as the decade arrived, endures and evolves in ways that represent the trials and triumphs of Stone's life. Following a familiar path, Stone moves from one mundane job (encyclopedia salesman, actor in religious pageant) to another, the fascinations and temptations of the city partially compensating for the hardships of raising a family with hardly any money, while gradually realizing that the nature of his experiences were leading toward what he saw as "something like a novel." Troubled by a persistent sense "that authenticity, whatever it was, resided somewhere else," a kind of restlessness that also resulted in an inclination toward sexual adventure, he realized on a fundamental psychic level that his soul as a man and as an artist required an ultimate faithfulness to his craft and to Janice, resisting the immediate lure of various illicit pleasures. "I also knew at about that moment that I would never leave her, not ever, that this thing was forever," he recalls. What was not resistible, nor even considered improper, was the allure of the growing drug scene. Stone's entrance into the regions of psychic exploration and excess brought him into close proximity with some of the most prominent people of the entire epoch.

Casual use of marijuana was a common practice among the inhabitants of what Kerouac called the "subterranean" strata of society, easily available at jazz clubs, then ubiquitous among anyone associated with a bohemian subculture. At the same time, as Stone recounts with an insider's experience and a scholar's further investigative knowledge of a large phenomenon, the discovery of psychedelic substances led to a national craze that was responsible for a transformation in American society that has been summarized by the term "the Sixties." For Stone, whose descriptions of some of his mental excursions are terrifyingly beautiful, the perils were apparent, but the allure was sufficient to overcome reluctance. Part of the appeal was the attraction of the company he joined, and its hero/leader, Ken Kesey.

Kesey had already published *One Flew Over the Cuckoo's Nest* (1962) when Stone met him. His portrait of Kesey is a masterpiece of appreciative understanding, capturing the "transactional charisma" of an exceptionally gifted man who knew the power he had and tried to use it decently. Awed by Kesey's energy and insight, Stone sees him as a man "who personally embodied the winning side in every historical

~

*Robert Stone's first novel,* A Hall of Mirrors *(1967), won a William Faulkner Foundation award for best first novel, and* Dog Soldiers *(1974) won a National Book Award. His works* Damascus Gate *(1998), set in Palestine, and* Bay of Souls *(2003), located on a Caribbean island resembling Haiti, continue the imaginative realist concepts of his earlier volumes.*

~

struggle that had served to create the colossus that was nineteen sixties America: An Anglo-Saxon Protestant Western American White Male, an Olympic-caliber athlete with an advanced academic degree, he had inherited the progressive empowerment of centuries," while recognizing that there was also a Gatsby-like quality that could not be easily conveyed:

> His ability to offer other people a variety of satisfactions ranging from fun to transcendence was not especially verbal, which is why it remained independent of Kesey's fiction, and it was ineffable, impossible to describe exactly or to encapsulate in a quotation.

However, as Larry McMurtry tellingly observed about the deceptively named "Merry Pranksters" as a "floating court" for Kesey, "There were always a few good friends who were not of the court. Wendell Berry, Robert Stone, myself." Stone's presence on the bus, on which the Merry Pranksters careened across the country, enables him to catch the excitement, excess, stupidity, and damage that followed in Kesey's wake, his capsule images of people like Kerouac and Neal Cassady, "famous long ago" as Bob Dylan put it, revealing the sadness without deflating the enticement of that now legendary journey. Stone's time with Kesey as a fellow semi-outlaw when Kesey was hiding out in Mexico completely captures the psychic sense of romantic adventure and drugged-out, even dangerous, "drunken dumbshow" (as Ginsberg described it) that marked the moment.

At the same time, Stone was attending to the novel he had imagined in New Orleans. He got off the bus in the middle of the country, had some perilous encounters with heartland hostility while traveling east alone—an implied parallel with Kesey's wild ride—and carried his search for "authenticity" across the Atlantic to Paris and London, where his life shifted from a student's bottom view (Paris) to a privileged person's pleasures when *Hall of Mirrors* was published in the United Kingdom in 1968. When Paul Newman called to request permission to film the novel, with Stone as the screenwriter, in spite of his view of Hollywood as responsible for a significant portion of the rampant stupidity of American popular culture, Stone accepted immediately. His frustration and disappointment with the filmmaking process were predictable and probably inevitable, but he liked Newman immensely and saw him as a "considerate man, of grace and reserve. . . . The better I got to know him, the more I liked and respected him." In one of the most revealing expressions of his fundamental philosophy, Stone decries all dogmatic ideologies, insisting: "Ordinary decency, I thought, was about the best of which I, and again most people, were capable. And it was not so easy at that, not so ordinary."

Just when the urgency that has been driving the narrative seems to diminish slightly, its episodic elements perhaps undermining the imminence of revelation previously apparent, Stone juxtaposes the Moon landing with the Manson murders, bitterness overwhelming the fading vision of a corrupted hippie dream, his own life sinking toward a party where everyone—children included—is consumed by a desperate grasping for the nitrous oxide high that mingles blissful oblivion with greed-filled aggrandizement. Disgusted by his deterioration, Stone goes to Vietnam in an attempt to reconnect with the idealism that marked the start of the decade, to try to do something useful in "the heart of darkness."

The last section of the book, taut and trim, is evidence of the "authenticity" of Stone's account. Without overstating his expectations ("I was not over there to be Ernie Pyle or Richard Harding Davis"—noted war correspondents), the density of detail and the intensity of feeling that Stone brings to the narrative are a testament to the seriousness of his inquiry. His novel *Dog Soldiers*, not mentioned here, was built on the foundations of this experience. The final chapter, "Epilogue," is both an epitaph and epigraph for the era. As he says, recalling Walt Whitman's proclamation about the Civil War ("I was the man; I suffered; I was there"), "I knew a few things," and while he is as hard on himself and his peers as real wisdom demands, his envoi to an epoch reflects his ultimate judgement: "Measuring ourselves against the masters of the present, we regret nothing except our failure to prevail."

*Leon Lewis*

## Review Sources

*The American Spectator* 40, no. 4 (May, 2007): 68-71.
*Booklist* 103, no. 6 (November 15, 2006): 17-18.
*Commonweal* 134, no. 3 (February 9, 2007): 25-26.
*Kirkus Reviews* 74, no. 18 (September 15, 2006): 943.
*The New York Review of Books* 54, no. 2 (February 15, 2007): 36-38.
*The New York Times Book Review* 156 (January 7, 2007): 1-10.
*Publishers Weekly* 253, no. 40 (October 9, 2006): 45.
*The Wall Street Journal* 249, no. 5 (January 6, 2007): P12.

# RALPH ELLISON
## A Biography

*Author:* Arnold Rampersad (1941-    )
*Publisher:* Alfred A. Knopf (New York). 657 pp. $35.00
*Type of work:* Literary biography
*Time:* 1913-1994
*Locale:* Oklahoma, New York City, Europe

*A critically acclaimed biography of the author of* Invisible Man *(1952), the novel named as the most significant work of fiction by a twentieth century African American writer*

*Principal personages:*
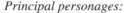
RALPH ELLISON, an African American
    author
IDA ELLISON BELL, his mother
LANGSTON HUGHES, an African American writer, a
    friend and supporter of Ellison's work
RICHARD WRIGHT, an African American novelist,
    Ellison's mentor early in his career
ROSE POINDEXTER, Ellison's first wife
IDA ESPEN GUGGENHEIMER, the patron who financially
    supported Ellison early in his career
FANNY McCONNELL ELLISON, his second wife
KENNETH BURKE, a literary critic whose modernist theories
    influenced Ellison's writing
STANLEY EDGAR HYMAN, the publisher who played a
    significant role in the publication of *Invisible Man*
JOHN F. CALLAHAN, the editor of *Juneteenth* (1999),
    published after Ellison's death

Ralph Ellison's novel *Invisible Man* was an immediate sensation in the literary world. White critics were enthusiastic, but black critics accused Ellison of unfairly stereotyping African Americans. Until the publication of *Invisible Man*, the leading black writers of the mid-twentieth century were Richard Wright, author of *Native Son* (1940), and poet Langston Hughes. While both Wright and Hughes mentored young Ellison and helped launch his writing career, Ellison eventually moved beyond their influence to discover his unique fictional voice. *Invisible Man*, employing myth, fantasy, and symbolism, was recognized as a breakthrough that changed the face of African American literature in the twentieth century.

Ellison and his wife Fanny saved the voluminous correspondence, journals, and notes that record the details of his life and placed them in the Library of Congress. Arnold Rampersad, author of biographies of Jackie Robinson and Langston Hughes and editor of several African American literary anthologies, made extensive use of the Ellisons' collected papers. He also conducted numerous interviews with Ellison's contemporaries. Rampersad's scholarly interpretation of this material has been frequently cited as the definitive treatment of Ellison's life and work.

The question that has intrigued Ellison's readers—why was he unable to complete the lengthy manuscript of his second novel?—is not Rampersad's main concern. He presents a portrait of a complex man, the foremost black intellectual of his generation, whose gentlemanly bearing and charm gave him entry into the exclusive world of white society. Ellison also drank heavily, behaved cruelly to his two wives, and ignored younger black writers who sought his support. Rampersad also offers keen critical insight into Ellison's creative process and the demons that plagued him as he struggled to write a second novel.

*Arnold Rampersad is Sara Hart Kimball Professor in the Humanities and a member of the Department of English at Stanford University. His books include biographies of Langston Hughes and Jackie Robinson, and he collaborated with Arthur Ashe on his memoir,* Days of Grace *(1993). Rampersad has published many articles in literary journals and is a member of the American Academy of Arts and Sciences.*

Ralph Waldo Ellison was born on March 1, 1913, in Oklahoma City, Oklahoma, to Ida and Lewis Ellison, whose ancestors had accepted the government's offer of one hundred acres in the Oklahoma Territory after the Civil War.

Ellison often expressed pride in his mixed Indian, white, and black heritage. This racial history of the territory profoundly influenced his lifelong view of America as a land of hope and opportunity. Ellison, named for the New England Transcendentalist Ralph Waldo Emerson, was initially embarrassed by his name but later acknowledged his debt to this distinguished heritage.

Lewis Ellison's death after an injury incurred while delivering ice was a disaster for Ida, three-year-old Ralph, and his younger brother Herbert. Dependent on the charity of friends and relatives, the family lived in abject poverty, humiliated and outcast by the respectable black community. Rampersad believes that Ellison, a proud and angry man throughout his life, never recovered from this childhood emotional damage. However, in later years, Ellison romanticized the experience of growing up on the Oklahoma frontier and returned several times—but only after he had become famous.

Young Ellison began work before he was twelve as a shoeshine boy and later as a waiter and as a drugstore clerk. He showed an early talent for music, excelling as a trumpet player and pianist, absorbing the jazz and blues of Oklahoma City dance halls. He enrolled as a music major at Tuskegee Institute, the conservative, all-black school founded by Booker T. Washington. These were unhappy years during which he constantly begged his mother for money for the barest essentials. Moreover, a dean of the school whom he trusted as a father figure made unwelcome sexual advances. However, it was a Tuskegee English professor who first inspired his interest in literature.

Ellison left Tuskegee without finishing his degree and moved to New York City in 1936. He supported himself as a server at the Harlem YMCA, and later as a clerk for a psychiatrist and a laboratory assistant at a paint company. At the YMCA, he met Langston Hughes, the generous poet who encouraged him to write. Both Hughes and Richard Wright, to whom Hughes introduced Ellison, were members of the Communist Party and wrote for socialist publications. Although Ellison was never a party member, he was initially in sympathy with socialist politics.

Ellison went to Ohio in 1937 after the death of his mother and was reunited with his younger brother Herbert. They spent several homeless months subsisting on their hunting skills. This hand-to-mouth existence, coupled with the discovery that an incompetent black doctor had caused his mother's death, reinforced his anger and cynicism. He returned to New York City, having begun to try his hand at writing fiction.

Sponsored by Wright, Ellison joined the New York Writers' Project, a program of the Depression-era Works Progress Administration (WPA). Here he researched African American history, material that would energize his novel. He disciplined himself to read extensively among classical novelists like Fyodor Dostoevski, as well as the modernists Ernest Hemingway and William Faulkner. The writings of French existentialist André Malraux inspired Ellison's search for an intellectual understanding of the relationship of the "Negro" (the term in common use at that time, and one he favored throughout his life) to the white American society. He supported himself by writing essays and book reviews for socialist publications and edited the short-lived *Negro Quarterly*. He served briefly as a cook in the merchant marine during World War II and married Rose Poindexter, a union that ended in 1945 after his affair with a white woman.

Rampersad traces in detail the genesis of the text of *Invisible Man*. Ellison was unsettled by Richard Wright's nonfiction book *Twelve Million Black Voices* (1941) and his novella "The Man Who Lived Underground" (1942). Under the influence of literary critics Stanley Edgar Hyman and Kenneth Burke, he was abandoning his communist leanings to explore modernist theories of mythology and symbolism. Two short stories, "Flying Home" (1943) and "King of the Bingo Game" (1944), attracted favorable critical attention.

In 1945, during a vacation in Vermont with Fanny McConnell Buford, who would become his second wife, he typed the words "I am an invisible man"—and his imagination took flight. He envisioned an epic masterpiece that would trace the history of the Negro in America. The invisible man of the title would, in Ellison's words, "move upward through Negro life, coming into contact with its various forms and personality types, will operate in the Negro middle class, in the left-wing movement and descend again into the disorganized atmosphere of the Harlem underworld." After years of struggle with the manuscript, Ellison published *Invisible Man* in 1952.

Crucial to the success of the novel, Rampersad believes, were Ellison's choice of the first-person narration and the surrealistic expression of chaos, as the black man tried to construct the meaning of his existence in an alien white society. His technique was experimental, juxtaposing comedy and tragedy, describing the wildly fantastic journey of the young protagonist toward self-fulfillment. Although certain plot incidents were based loosely on his experiences, the novel was not autobiographical. However, Rampersad interprets the isolation of the narrator in the epilogue as a sign of Ellison's increasing distance from the realities of the world of ordinary black people.

*Invisible Man* created an immediate sensation in the predominantly white literary world. Black critics, however, called it a betrayal of the race. Ellison's response was that his critics had neither the intelligence nor the sensitivity to understand his achievement. In 1953, *Invisible Man* won the National Book Award, winning over Ernest Hemingway's *The Old Man and the Sea* and John Steinbeck's *East of Eden*. In his acceptance speech, Ellison said: "The chief significance of *Invisible Man*" is "its experimental attitude and its attempt to return to the mood of personal moral responsibility for democracy which typified the best of our nineteenth-century fiction."

His success gave him entry into the white literary establishment and the homes of wealthy socialites, where he and Fanny, now married and greatly enjoying their celebrity, were usually the only black people present. He won a two-year fellowship to the American Academy of Arts and Letters in Rome. Back in America, Ellison formed friendships with noted writers, among them Saul Bellow, Robert Penn Warren, and John Cheever. However, in securing his place in the white world, Ellison was separating himself from African American culture, the roots of his creativity. Younger black writers looking to him for encouragement were ignored, even insulted. As he garnered honors and prestigious appointments with organizations such as the National Endowment for the Humanities and the National Endowment for the Arts, Ellison worked on his second novel. He accepted a series of university lecturing duties that allowed time for his creative work.

Despite his success, beneath Ellison's charming public persona lurked a different figure. He had frequent angry outbursts and drank heavily, becoming quarrelsome. He excused his affair with a white woman by blaming Fanny for their childlessness. It was rumored that he carried a knife and was dangerous. Invited to join exclusive organizations like the American Academy of Arts and Letters and the New York Century Club, he voted to keep out women and other African Americans.

During the Civil Rights movement of the 1960's, Ellison believed that as an artist he had no obligation to take an active role beyond some financial support for the National Association for the Advancement of Colored People (NAACP). He continued to ignore, and often insult, younger black writers, including James Baldwin. He publicly dismissed as inferior the work of Black Power activists such as Ishmael Reed and Amiri Baraka. Still, he was deeply hurt when students called him an "Uncle Tom." He began declining speaking engagements and academic appointments, claiming that he needed time for his second novel.

In 1964, Ellison published *Shadow and Act*, a collection of essays that Rampersad ranks among the best African American writing about race. His many honors included two Presidential Medals of Arts awarded by Presidents Lyndon B. Johnson

614

and Ronald Reagan. As African American literature gained acceptance in the academy, *Invisible Man* became an influential text. A second collection of essays, *Going to the Territory*, was published in 1986.

Ellison continued to gather honors and was in demand as a speaker for the rest of his life, but he never published a second novel. He died on April 16, 1994. The sprawling collection of episodes he had struggled for years to complete was edited and published as *Juneteenth* five years after his death.

Rampersad remains impartial in presenting this nearly overwhelming body of material. *Invisible Man* and the two collections of essays are, in his view, a monumental achievement. Ellison himself he describes as a liberal humanist, a lifelong believer in the possibilities of the American Dream and the conviction that the lives of black and white Americans must be inseparable. However, in cultivating his white relationships, he distanced himself from his roots in the African American culture whose strength and resiliency he revered.

The evidence preserved by Ellison and his wife Fanny reveals a troubled personality with a record of nasty, unpredictable, often cruel behavior. However, was he unfairly criticized for his failure to publish the long-awaited second novel? Perhaps. As this biography portrays him, Ellison was a perfectionist who had set his sights so high that to surpass the achievement of *Invisible Man* would have been impossible.

Rampersad concludes that, whatever Ellison's personal flaws, his many admirers believe that "no one who had written *Invisible Man* and so skillfully explicated the matter of race and American culture in his essays could ever be accounted a failure."

*Marjorie Podolsky*

## Review Sources

*American Scholar* 76, no. 2 (Spring, 2007): 121-126.
*Commentary* 124, no. 3 (October, 2007): 67-70.
*The Humanist* 67, no. 6 (November/December, 2007): 38-40.
*The Nation* 284, no. 21 (May 28, 2007): 11-18.
*The New Republic* 236, no. 18 (June 18, 2007): 48-51.
*The New York Review of Books* 54, no. 10 (June 14, 2007): 56-58.
*The New York Times Book Review* 156 (May 20, 2007): 18-19.
*Publishers Weekly* 254, no. 10 (March 5, 2007): 54.

# RAVEL

*Author:* Jean Echenoz (1947-      )
*First published:* 2005, in France
*Translated from the French by Linda Coverdale*
*Publisher:* The New Press (New York). 126 pp. $19.95
*Type of work:* Novel
*Time:* 1927-1937
*Locale:* France, the United States, and Canada

*A marvelously crafted yet carefully restrained picture*
*of the triumph and the increasing decline of the aging*
*composer Maurice Ravel during his final ten years of*
*travel and travail*

*Principal personage:*
MAURICE RAVEL (1875-1937), a famous French composer and pianist

Born of Basque and Swiss parents and raised in Paris, Maurice Ravel is perhaps one of the best-known musical innovators of the early twentieth century. His professional milieu was the emerging Impressionism in France, which served up a nouvelle cuisine of both visual and musical art. Ravel's contributions to this gastronomic abundance are well known.

In her novel *Ravel*, Jean Echenoz has selected several episodes from the composer's final ten years. The author's choices flesh out both the triumph and the tragedy of his life. The book is part cartoon, part tragedy, and is thoroughly readable. While the author is impeccably true to historical detail, he avoids the recitation of facts that constipate many nonfictional accounts of famous lives. The book is composed of nine rather brief vignettes, each illustrating a small slice of time in Ravel's life between 1927 and 1937. In 1927, Ravel has already achieved status as the darling of the international community. The selected ten years are illustrative of his success as well as his relentless but subtle disintegration. The book concludes with his final lingering illness and tragic death following brain surgery for a possible tumor.

In the first vignette, the reader is introduced to the famous composer in the nude, just as he steps from the bathtub. Given that the book begins at the zenith of Ravel's career, the detailed description of quotidian banality is somewhat quixotic. It is discomforting to be a voyeur at someone's daily routine. Later the reader appreciates this scene as a foreshadow of what is to come: Ravel's vulnerability, gradual decline in health, and eventually death.

The bath is part of Ravel's elaborate preparation for an extended victory tour of the United States. The very ordinariness of the scene provides a vivid contrast to Ravel's public presentation of himself, taken up later in the book. Echenoz describes in exquisite detail stray hairs in the tepid bubbles, the machinations of leaving the tub. ("Caution is advised, to avoid bumping one's crotch or risking a nasty fall.")

~

*Jean Echenoz published his first novel,* Le Méridien de Greenwich *(1979; the* Greenwich Meridian*), at thirty-two. He is the recipient of a number of literary prizes and resides in Paris.*

~

He prolongs the account of Ravel's extensive ritual of grooming. Every detail of personal toilet is described. The passage is reminiscent of the equally off-putting yet compelling description of John Updike's psoriasis in his reluctant memoir, *Self-Consciousness* (1989). However, there is a camera-like detachment to the account in *Ravel*. The description is devoid of emotion. Even though Ravel is presented as totally revealed in his nudity and in his personal rituals of daily life, the reader learns little of his inner life and thought. The shading and color must come later.

As the novel progresses, the composer's insecurity is uncovered bit by bit. Perhaps the novel illustrates that his vulnerability increases bit by bit. Ravel is meticulous about his dress and grooming, unwilling to enter the public eye with improper shoes or his pocket handkerchief not quite right. On his triumphant transoceanic trip to the United States—first class in a luxury liner—he brings a "squadron of suitcases" that include sixty shirts, twenty pairs of shoes, more than seventy ties, and twenty-five pairs of pajamas. Ravel at his prime is pictured as utterly preoccupied with his appearance. There is never a hair out of place nor an outfit less than perfectly congruent to the occasion. As he encounters his adoring public, he does so only in sartorial perfection—no stray hairs or tepid bubbles.

Sadly, there lingers a sense of loneliness and a lack of security about Ravel, even at the apex of his career. To some extent he is an anonymous passenger on the voyage to America. Time aboard ship lags: a swim in the pool, some parlor games, the endless changing of outfits to suit the prescribed events of luxury travel. Although Ravel is asked to give a small concert and to sign the special visitors' book that the captain brings to his cabin, the truth is that he is very much—forgive the double entendre— at sea. He wanders about the boat trying to kill time and to fill the seemingly endless days on the solitary and long Atlantic voyage. Even his first-class stateroom appears small. It "allots his body the precise range allowed by a hospital room—a vital but atrophied space with nothing to cling to but oneself."

The boat arrives in New York. Ravel is greeted by a gaggle of important people, representatives of various associations, and the press. Echenoz's take on the scene is that Ravel's preoccupation is not with the many who have come to greet him but rather with his dazzling wardrobe. Ravel shouts to friends on the dock, "Wait till you see . . . the splendid ties I brought with me!" Neckwear elegance notwithstanding, the grand tour of the United States is an abundant success. With barely a breath Ravel races, in nine exhausting pages, from coast to coast, giving concerts, attending receptions, and always selecting his wardrobe with care. He visits all the major cities of the time, as well as some of America's tourist attractions such as the Grand Canyon.

Perhaps this story is not so much about Ravel and his career as it is about the fragility of human life, even and maybe especially the life of someone famous and talented. Hints of what is to come are tucked neatly into the parsimonious accounts: a slip of memory here, an omission of a movement as he plays a concert there, the extensive medical treatments, and (always) the insomnia. Details of decline stain the pages with the foreboding of Ravel's degeneration and death. The triumphant trip to the United States, his first, will be also his last. It is a whirlwind tour from which Ravel draws energy. He is seemingly at the top of his game both in performance and in crowd adulation. Still, he often feels insecure and alone. Still, he cannot sleep.

The author constructs the nine sections in such a way that the length of the vignette indicates the inner perception of time by the composer. Echenoz spends one whole chapter getting Ravel from his bath to his boat. While the actual passage of time is brief in comparison to other parts of the story, the number of pages it occupies in the novel is large. He lavishes two rather long chapters on the sea voyage, mimicking the leisurely pace of luxury liner travel in more formal times as well as Ravel's boredom. With little to do, Ravel explores the ship, asks questions, swims, and reads. In contrast is the American tour itself, which lasts four months, and which the author dispatches very quickly. Ravel visits a long list of cities, performing and preening. His tour moves across the continent from New York, Boston, Cambridge, New Orleans, to the major West Coast cities of the United States and Canada. These frenetic four months are blown through in barely nine pages. The palpable sense of urgency and exhaustion is felt not only by Ravel but by the reader.

Upon Ravel's return home he is still "at sea." Without the structure of the tour and without the predictable flattery from his audiences, Ravel does not know quite how to behave. Plagued by inattention, insomnia, and boredom, he is not quite whole. He forgets to invite a close friend to a large party at his home. Echenoz's earlier hints at Ravel's worsening condition give way to stronger and stronger suggestions. There is no denying it. Ravel's ability to remember and to focus is degenerating. It is during this period that the controversial musical piece *Boléro* is composed.

A serious automobile accident seems to accelerate the progress of Ravel's decline. After his taxi is hit by a speeding car, he is incapacitated for three months. During this time, he appears acutely distracted and disinterested in his surroundings. Perhaps it is just a normal response to the accident. Perhaps it is more. None of the then state-of-the-art therapies seem to improve his condition. This event seems to mark the beginning of the end. The composer never returns to the level of function he enjoyed before the accident. The doctors conjecture that perhaps the decline is due to a tumor in the brain. They decide to operate. Ten days after the surgery, Maurice Ravel is dead.

The facts of Ravel's life have been documented elsewhere. Echenoz selects certain facts as a containing frame in order to paint a detailed canvas of his interpretation of Ravel's psychology. He pictures a man fastidious to a fault about his dress yet apparently lazy in the discipline it takes to be an accurate and excellent pianist. He is energized by the adulation of his audiences in his whirlwind tour of the United States, yet he quickly succumbs to apathy and insomnia when the crowds are gone. Here is a picture of a highly talented and successful artist as well as a fragile, vulnerable human being. Readers' detached observation of the man gives way to pity as Ravel unravels in front of them. His techniques for going to sleep, for example, appear merely pathetic.

Echenoz compresses the details of Ravel's final illness, which in reality lasted a prolonged four years. These years are telescoped into a tumbling-down-a-hill account given in the final two vignettes. Sleep becomes more and more elusive. The ability to remember details or even his very close friends slips through Ravel's increasingly inept fingers. At the piano, he is not the consummate performer that he was. Is it boredom that causes him to skip a movement or the ominous foreboding of a worsening dementia?

Unlike many books read in translation, *Ravel* does not leave the reader with the sense that he or she is missing something. The translation feels like a patent and faithful rendering of the original French. The text remains powerful and well crafted. In instances where the English-speaking reader may miss the allusions to persons or contexts, explanatory footnotes are given. The translation renders the French in beautiful English prose. It is no wonder that the translator is the recipient of awards for translation.

Overall, the book exudes a sober intimacy. The tepid water and stray hairs of the first chapter linger at the end, a tribute to the humanity and vulnerability of this larger-than-life composer. There is little wrong with the book except perhaps its inevitably somber tone.

*Dolores L. Christie*

## Review Sources

*Booklist* 103, nos. 19/20 (June 1, 2007): 41-42.
*Kirkus Reviews* 75, no. 6 (March 15, 2007): 243.
*Library Journal* 132, no. 12 (July 1, 2007): 74.
*The New York Times Book Review* 156 (August 19, 2007): 10.
*Publishers Weekly* 253, no. 14 (April 2, 2007): 36.
*Review of Contemporary Fiction* 26, no. 2 (Summer, 2006): 88.

# THE REAGAN DIARIES

*Author:* Ronald Reagan (1911-2004)
Edited by Douglas Brinkley
*Publisher:* HarperCollins (New York). 767 pp. $35.00
*Type of work:* Diary
*Time:* 1981-1989
*Locale:* Washington, D.C.; Santa Barbara, California;
Camp David, Maryland

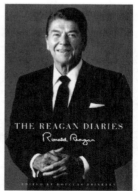

*The daily writings of President Ronald Reagan, skill-
fully edited by one of America's foremost historians*

*Principal personages:*
RONALD REAGAN (1911-2004), fortieth
president of the United States, 1981-1989
NANCY REAGAN (1921-    ), First Lady
TIP O'NEILL (1912-1994), Speaker of the U.S.
House of Representatives, 1977-1987

The presidency of Ronald Reagan is one of the most interesting of the twentieth century. It was a time of political and ideological realignment, as a new form of American conservatism came of age with Reagan's election. As the oldest elected U.S. president at sixty-nine, Reagan was often accused by the press of napping in cabinet meetings and working short days, and many people viewed him as not one of America's brightest or energetic chief executives. The appearance of *The Reagan Diaries*, edited by Douglas Brinkley, will put most of these misconceptions to rest. Brinkley, a professor of history at Rice University, is the author of *Tour of Duty: John Kerry and the Vietnam War* (2004) and *The Great Deluge: Hurricane Katrina, New Orleans, and the Mississippi Gulf Coast* (2006). He is the history commentator for CBS News and a contributing editor to *Vanity Fair.*

Only four other presidents—George Washington, John Quincy Adams, James K. Polk, and Rutherford B. Hayes—kept diaries on a consistent basis. Such access to a president's daily inner thoughts are therefore rare indeed. Reagan regretted that he had never kept a diary before becoming president. "The Sacramento years"—when he was governor of California—"flew by so quickly," he writes, but "we just did not seem to have time." From his first day as president, however, he was determined to write daily, which he did, except when he was in the hospital. Each night before retiring, Reagan would chronicle his day in longhand. Other twentieth century presidents, Harry S. Truman for example, left behind the official daily appointment books and then recounted their presidency in memoirs written after leaving office. Before Reagan, no president, even those who kept daily diaries, had ever revealed their daily activities so candidly and personally. Reagan wanted to leave a detailed daily record of his eight years in office not only for posterity but also so that he and Nancy could better remember their White House days after they left Washington.

〜

*Ronald Reagan achieved fame as a television and film actor before turning to politics, serving as governor of California from 1967 to 1975 and as U.S. president from 1981 to 1989. He was diagnosed with Alzheimer's disease in 1994 and died in 2004.*

〜

What quickly emerges from Reagan's writings is the grueling daily grind that comes with the nation's highest office. Endless meetings, speeches, luncheons, and ceremonies are all part of the job. Reagan took them all in stride. Apparently, the press was not aware of the tremendous amount of activities the president undertook during an average day: "The press keeps score on office hours but knows nothing about the never-ending desk and paperwork that usually goes on 'til lights out," he reflects. This was not a part-time president by any means.

Reagan's relationship with the press was cordial but often a source of annoyance. Regarding his visit to a Nazi military cemetery in Bitburg, Germany, in 1985, the president wrote that he could not understand why reporters continued to criticize him for what he viewed as honoring the war dead of both sides of a conflict that must never happen again. Despite the negative press, he stuck to his promise to West German chancellor Helmut Kohl to visit the cemetery. Eventually, the American people came around to Reagan's side. In another incident, the press tried to create a scandal over the so-called Jimmy Carter playbook. Sources claimed that Reagan's campaign staff had gained access to Democratic candidate Carter's strategy book for the 1980 campaign. Reagan wrote that he knew nothing about it. This denial, however, immediately started rumors of a cover-up. In frustration, he wrote that he hoped the whole matter would simply go away, which it soon did.

One feature that is very apparent throughout his writings is his deep love and affection for his wife, Nancy. She was his rock and the center of his life. He misses her greatly whenever she is away from him for any length of time. Days after he was shot by John Hinckley, Jr., on March 30, 1981, Reagan writes, "I opened my eyes to find Nancy there. I pray I'll never face a day when she isn't there." Interestingly, in spite of their extremely close relationship, he never seems to confide in her or seek her advice on government matters. His time with Nancy is relaxing time and family time, never business.

Throughout his presidency, Reagan found time to relax at his California ranch and at Camp David in the Maryland mountains. He loved horseback riding and farm work at his ranch—clearing brush, chopping wood, and repairing fences. At Camp David, swimming and movies were his diversion. As with most presidents, these times away from the White House were not true vacations. He maintained very close relations with his son and daughters, although his relationship with his adopted son Michael was stormy.

Reagan will probably be best remembered for his efforts to confront communism and the Soviet Union. His determination and steadfastness when dealing with Soviet leaders comes through forcefully throughout the diary. Facing down the Soviet military and maintaining U.S. military superiority was a top priority of his presidency and in his mind the road to a lasting peace in the world. Historians will long note Reagan's powerful "tear down this wall" speech at the Brandenburg Gate by the Berlin Wall on June 12, 1987. He mentions the speech in his diary but apparently was unaware of the lasting significance his words would have on history. "I addressed tens and tens of thousands of people—stretching as far as I could see. I got a tremendous reception— interrupted twenty-eight times by cheers." It would in fact become a defining moment in American-Soviet relations.

During his presidency, Reagan struggled with many problems on the international front. Grenada, Lebanon, Israel, Iran, Libya, Cuba, and Nicaragua were constant trouble spots. Reagan correctly predicted that the Middle East, and Iran in particular, would be a growing concern for the United States for years to come. His efforts to fight communism in Nicaragua led to the Iran-Contra affair, an attempt to funnel money to the anti-Sandinista rebels, or Contras, by illegally selling weapons to Iran. The diary shows that Reagan was kept in the dark about many of the dealings. He was concerned that the American people were now questioning his truthfulness about what he called "the Iran mess."

Reagan had long been planning to run for a second term in 1984. He knew that he was a popular president with the American people. His diary entries during the campaign contain not a hint of concern that he could lose the election. Proudly recording the outcome on election day, he writes: "Well 49 states, 59 percent of the vote and 525 electoral votes. . . . The press is trying to prove it wasn't a landslide or should I say mandate?"

An interesting insight into Reagan's personality is revealed through his numerous encounters with world leaders. He went to great lengths to ensure that visiting leaders were comfortable and made every effort to have them leave the United States not just as allies but as friends. Many times he would write how much he "liked" a particular leader and was certain he could count on him or her. Reagan's warm and friendly manner and his genuine sincerity served him well. He rarely has a mean word to say. One his favorite leaders was British prime minister Margaret Thatcher: "[She] is a tower of strength and a solid friend of the U.S."

In his dealings with Congress, Reagan used his enormous public support to keep the legislative branch in check. His main adversary was Congressman Tip O'Neill, Speaker of the House throughout the Reagan years. O'Neill clashed with the president on both domestic and foreign policy, arguing that Reagan favored the rich as well as large corporations at the expense of common people. Reagan frequently notes his frustration with O'Neill. He especially bristled when O'Neill would deliberately quote him out of context. Interestingly, there were many times when they could put their political differences aside.

It was certainly not the case that Reagan ignored or was insensitive to the personal struggles of ordinary Americans. There are anecdotes in which he would read about the plight of a family and quickly intervene with help. In one case, he saw a story on ABC News about a family in Los Angeles who were charged $6,000 back rent by the city for street lights and for years were never told they owed any money. Reagan personally called Frank Reynolds, the ABC News anchorman, to confirm the story. He then asked his Deputy Secretary of State Bill Clark to investigate. There are similar entries throughout the diary detailing the president's efforts to reach out to help. Also revealing is Reagan's forgiving of his would-be assassin, John Hinckley, Jr. "Getting shot hurts," Reagan wrote, and goes on to say that he could not ask for God's help while at the same time being filled with hatred for the man who shot him. "I began to pray for his soul," he writes, "and that he would find his way back to the fold."

Throughout his presidency, Reagan called hundreds of deceased servicemen's spouses and parents to offer condolences. He also frequently called the relatives of fallen Federal Bureau of Investigation agents and police officers. Reagan wrote that his most difficult phone calls were to the wives and husbands of the crew of the space shuttle *Challenger*, which exploded shortly after liftoff on January 28, 1986. "There is no way to describe our shock and horror," he writes. Reagan recounted that he was scheduled to give the state of the union address that night but decided to delay it for a week. Instead, he delivered a moving five-minute speech honoring the fallen astronauts. It would be one of his most memorable. He relates that every one of the astronauts' spouses urged the president to see that the space program continue.

Historian Douglas Brinkley has done a masterful job in editing and abridging the five volumes left behind by Reagan into a one-volume, eminently readable book. His selection of materials paints an in-depth picture of the daily pressures, triumphs, and disappointments faced by the president. Those who lived through the Reagan years will gain a new and deeper understanding of Reagan the person, as well as Reagan the president. They will also recall many of the events of their own lives—where they were and what they were doing as national and international events that Reagan writes about unfolded. For those too young to remember those eight years, this diary will provide a remarkable inside look into the daily activities of America's fortieth president.

*Raymond Frey*

### Review Sources

*The Economist* 384 (July 7, 2007): 81.
*The New York Times* 156 (June 17, 2007): 11.
*The New Yorker* 83, no. 14 (May 28, 2007): 72-76.
*Newsweek* 149, no. 23 (June 4, 2007): 13.
*Publishers Weekly* 253, no. 14 (April 2, 2007): 53.
*The Saturday Evening Post* 279, no. 5 (September/October, 2007): 20-22.
*The Spectator* 304 (July 14, 2007): 41.
*The Washington Post*, May 2, 2007, p. A1.

# THE REGENSBURG LECTURE

*Author:* James V. Schall (1928-    )
*Publisher:* St. Augustine's Press (South Bend, Ind.).
    174 pp. $20.00
*Type of work:* Religion, current affairs

*The complete text of Pope Benedict XVI's controversial lecture on Islam, faith, and reason, delivered in September, 2006, accompanied by Schall's commentary and exposition of the lecture*

The dust jacket of *The Regensburg Lecture* promotes the book with this teaser: "Pope Benedict XVI's Regensburg Lecture (included in this book) called for freedom of conscience in religious matters and a reasoned debate. Not everyone agreed." The importance of the pope's address, as the jacket implies, derives both from the content of the lecture and from the reaction to it. In the days following September 12, 2006, when the pope visited the University of Regensburg, Muslim protests occurred in Palestine, India, and Egypt, among other places, in reaction to what was perceived as anti-Islamist sentiments. In this book, James V. Schall, professor of government at Georgetown University, presents an exposition of the lecture. The pope's words themselves appear in an appendix, but that order distorts the true structure of the book. The lecture is central, and Schall clearly assumes his words are secondary to the pope's address.

The address itself is quite short, broken up into sixty-three numbered paragraphs. Because the pope was an academic, having been a professor at Regensburg from 1969 to 1977, his speech exhibits erudition, clarity, and orderliness. The thesis of the address is well defined: Any true religion must show itself to be compatible with reason because God's nature itself is reasonable. Following Thomas Aquinas, the pope argues that the Greek philosophical tradition needed to be complemented by the Judeo-Christian revelation of God and that neither can be viable apart from the other. It is important to see that the pope draws a distinction between modern rationality, which he likens to empiricism, and a broader sense of reason that derives from Plato and Aristotle. The pope worries that the mutually enriching conjunction of the best of Greek thought with the Christian message is weakening through a process he calls dehellenization.

The pope traces three historical stages of dehellenization: the influence of the Reformation, particularly Martin Luther; the rise of liberal theology in the late nineteenth century; and the pluralistic tendencies of the late twentieth and early twenty-first centuries. In each of these moments, certain individuals or groups within Christianity attempted to strip away metaphysics from religion, and in each case, both were devalued by the attempt.

However, the thesis of the address was, as Schall points out in his introduction, overshadowed by a single paragraph. In it, the pope cites a fourteenth century dia-

*James V. Schall teaches government at Georgetown University. He has written numerous books and articles for both scholarly and popular audiences. Many of his works, such as* Another Sort of Learning *(1988), focus on liberal education.*

logue in which a Byzantine emperor said about the Qur'ān—with what the pope calls "a brusqueness that we find unacceptable"—"Show me just what Mohammed brought that was new, and there you will find things only evil and inhuman, such as his command to spread by the sword the faith he preached." The pope uses this quote, along with a verse from the Qur'ān ("There is no compulsion in religion"), in order to examine Muslim theology. Is God, the pope wonders, free to act in a manner contrary to reason, and if so, is that the grounds for violence in Islam? For the pope, it is clear that since violence contradicts reason, it must also be contrary to the will of God. He pointedly wants to know whether Islam agrees with him.

In the aftermath of the lecture, many criticized the pope for intemperately fanning the flames of an already tense situation. His detractors argued that, if the pope himself found the emperor's language brusque, why use it at all? According to the pope's critics, he should have expunged this paragraph from the lecture and concentrated on his primary topic—the role of reason within religion. The question to ask about the speech is whether the medieval anti-Muslim quote was a misguided throwaway line or an integral part of the pope's argument.

Schall responds to this question by saying that it was absolutely essential that Pope Benedict bring up Islam. Schall begins by highlighting the significance of the university setting of the pope's lecture. For Schall, the pope's question of whether or not Islam condones violence, if the question is to be raised, ought to appear in a university setting. No question that honestly explores truth should be ruled out of bounds in a university discussion. Schall finds this accusation of the pope's rashness unpersuasive and says that the question, "Does the Qur'ān support religious violence?" must be posed. If nothing else, the question had the fortuitous consequence of drawing attention to an academic discourse that might otherwise have gone unnoticed. More important, the pope's provocation, along with the reaction in the Muslim world, demonstrates the absolute necessity of raising the question. Schall implies that a reticence to ask about the centrality of violence to Islam indicates an unwillingness to expose the root of terrorist acts done in the name of religion. It is a pertinent and reasonable query, as evidenced by the sporadic violent protests in the aftermath of the address, and the pope was right to urge Muslims to interrogate themselves about the centrality of violence in their theology.

According to Schall and the pope, the theological concept that most clearly separates Christianity from Islam is voluntarism. When monotheistic religions contemplate God's will, the question of God's freedom also arises. Voluntarism denotes the theological stance that God's freedom cannot be constrained; therefore, God can choose different actions and moralities at different points in history. In the most extreme case, voluntarism leads to notions of a "capricious God," to use the pope's words. Schall sees in Islam strong tendencies toward voluntarism, most heinously in the case of suicide bombers. These suicide bombers focus exclusively on the will of God, as if God were nothing more than will itself, and this myopic theology causes them to ignore God's connection to rationality and, more importantly, to humans. Voluntarism underlies suicide attacks because if God's will is supreme, no argument from reason or human compassion can ultimately matter. Against this view of God, Schall presents the Christian and Jewish conceptions of God, in which God's actions are consonant with reason. He argues that although some Christian thinkers have demonstrated voluntaristic tendencies, the pope is right to assert that, traditionally, reason is needed as a precursor to revelation. This is, in fact, the pope's primary theological claim in the address—that when John 1:1 says, "The word [*logos*] was God," it means that God abides by order and reasonability, both concepts intricately tied to the Greek understanding of *logos*.

The majority of the pope's lecture centers on history, and Schall devotes much of his book to historical analysis. The pope refers to a passage in Acts 16, in which the apostle Paul has a vision of a man from Macedonia pleading with him to come over from Asia. Paul's crossing of the Aegean into Macedonia signifies not only an important historical event in the spread of Christianity but also allegorically represents, according to the pope, the decisive and providential confluence of biblical faith and Greek rationality. Schall elaborates upon this bold thesis by pointing out the contributions Europe has made to world cultures. Because it has been based on both reason and revelation, Europe has been the shining global example of how society, at its best, could achieve vitality and peace. He even goes so far as to say that during the Crusades, the Europeans fought as defenders, not aggressors, and what they were defending was this bastion of reason and faith. Presently, since Christianity continues to decline in Europe, Schall wonders if it will lose its preeminence on the world stage, with a corresponding loss of the best hope for the world.

The historical investigation continues in Schall's exposition of the dangers of the dehellenization that the pope outlines in his lecture. All three of these waves led toward an unraveling of the synthesis of reason and revelation so central to Europe's identity. Schall's exposition of dehellenization finds two distinct dangers in the phenomenon: a devaluation of humanity and a philosophy of relativism. Greek rationality, when it became dehellenized, transformed into a scientific rationalism. Whereas reason for Aristotle or Plato or Paul explored the entirety of humanity's relationship to nature, now reason applies only to that which can be scientifically examined. This reason devoid of the influence of faith—a goal of the liberal theologian Adolf von Harnack, whom the pope often cites—severely constrains what it means to be human. Relativism follows in the train of dehellenization because modernity assumes that the Greek culture stands as only one among many, not the preeminent beacon of reason that the pope upholds. Schall intimates that this relativism vitiates any Western critique of Islam because once reason loses its foundational status, one cannot, for example, condemn a suicide bomber for acting irrationally.

The distrust of rationalism and relativism, in both the pope's lecture and in Schall's analysis, goes to the heart of the viewpoint expressed in each. These two men, both of whom are equally scholars and churchmen, see Truth as objective and universal. The Greeks expressed it best, and God revealed it most fully in Christianity, but that does not make Truth particular to those traditions. From their standpoint, both God and reason illumine humans about "what is" (a phrase used in particular by Schall) and therefore about universal matters. Until all humans, including Muslims, realize the universality of reasonable truth, civilization will continue to have the type of violent conflicts that have accompanied globalization.

This surety about Truth represents both the book's boldest and most controversial claim. The pope was both courageous and correct to question why and how the West and the so-called Muslim world have failed to interact. The analysis of the situation by both the pope and Schall, however, seems somewhat myopic. Perhaps the pope could not have addressed opposing viewpoints in the constraints he was given, but Schall certainly could have. He does not take seriously a number of trends in philosophy and theology that seriously question the pope's thesis. He ignores, for instance, defenders of moral relativism, some of whom come from the Catholic tradition. Neither does he refer to religious thinkers that strongly support dehellenization as a method to retrieve authentic Christianity.

Neither man claims that European Christianity alone exemplifies a closed system. In fact, both explicitly state that non-Western cultures—including Arab Islam—can teach Westerners new ways of understanding Truth. However, these men are perhaps too sanguine about the universality of their own understanding. In a postmodern world in which fragmentation is the norm rather than the exception, Pope Benedict and Schall envision a worldwide conversation whose ultimate outcome could be reasonable agreement. Their optimistic vision of a possible future characterized by reasoned dialogue looks backward nostalgically to a European Christianized culture that appears to be waning. The hopes and presuppositions of Pope Benedict and Schall may be too strongly linked to the past to reach fruition in the twenty-first century. The pope's address, however, correctly highlighted a need for a rapprochement between the Muslim world and the West through engaged dialogue. Even if it does not proceed in the direction he would like, the benefits of a dialogue are certainly pertinent in a global society.

*Kyle Keefer*

## Review Sources

*Booklist* 103, no. 12 (February 15, 2007): 18.
*Choice* 45, no. 2 (October, 2007): 300.

# THE RELIGION

*Author:* Tim Willocks (1957-    )
*First published:* 2006, in Great Britain
*Publisher:* Farrar, Straus and Giroux (New York).
  Illustrated. 618 pp. $26.00
*Type of work:* Novel
*Time:* Spring, 1540; 1565-1566
*Locale:* The Fagarus Mountains, Hungary; Malta;
  Messina, Sicily; Rome; Aquitaine, in France

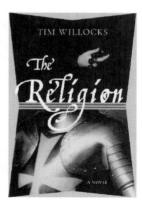

*The story of an adventurer whose search for the lost son
of a captivating noblewoman takes him to Malta, where he
finds himself fighting with the Christians against the Turks
besieging the island*

*Principal characters:*
  MATTIAS TANNHAUSER, a thirty-seven-year-old
    Saxon arms dealer, once a Muslim janissary
  CARLA LA PENAUTIER, a widowed French countess in her late twenties
  LUDOVICO LUDOVICI, a Dominican monk in his forties,
    a ruthless Inquisitor, once Carla's lover
  ORLANDU DI BORGO, Boccanera, the twelve-year-old
    illegitimate son of Carla and Ludovico
  AMPARO, a nineteen-year-old visionary whom Carla befriended
  ABBAS BIN MURAD, the kindly, cultured Turkish captain
    who reared Mattias as his son
  BORS OF CARLISLE, a Messina tavern-keeper, Mattias's
    business partner and friend
  JEAN PARISOT DE LA VALETTE, the seventy-one-year-old
    Grand Master of the Order of Saint John
  FRA OLIVER STARKEY, the sole Englishman in the Order of Saint John

Tim Willocks's first three novels were set in the American South during the late twentieth century. Though *The Religion* is similar to these earlier works in that it combines heroic deeds, graphic violence, and penetrating psychological analysis, unlike them it is a historical novel, epic in scope. *The Religion* is the first book in a projected series of three novels, the Tannhauser Trilogy, named for Mattias Tannhauser, who is introduced in *The Religion* and will be the epic hero of all three books.

Though the title of this novel is the specific term used by the Knights of Saint John on Malta to denote Christianity, in the minds of their Turkish enemies the only true "religion" is not Christianity, but Islam. Each group views the adherents of the other faith as heretics, destined to spend eternity in Hell. However, having lived both as a Muslim and as a Christian, Mattias Tannhauser knows that each side has both good and evil people. Thus, he is not committed to either religion. In fact, he loathes religious fanaticism, which he has seen used to justify horrific cruelty, and he distrusts all

*Tim Willocks, who for twenty years practiced psychiatry in London, published his first novel in 1991. His second,* Green River Rising *(1994), established his reputation as an impressive new author. Willocks also writes screenplays. He lives in Ireland.*

causes, religious or political, because in his experience they are merely means by which unscrupulous people seek wealth for themselves or power over others.

*The Religion* begins with a prologue, dated 1540, in which twelve-year-old Mattias has his first experience with religious fanatics. A band of Turks swoop down upon the Carpathian village where he lives and massacre all the members of his family except his blacksmith father, who is plying his trade elsewhere. Mattias himself is saved by the Turkish captain, Abbas bin Murad, the only humane person in the troop. It is later revealed that Abbas treated Mattias more like a son than a slave. The boy was trained as one of the select group of slaves called janissaries, and his heroism in the service of his sultan eventually earned him his freedom.

The narrative now moves ahead twenty-five years. "The World of Dreams," the first of the five main sections into which the novel is divided, begins on Sunday, May 13, 1565, in the office of the Grand Master of the Order of Saint John, the warrior monks based on Malta who refer to themselves as "the Religion." In planning his strategy for defending Malta against an imminent Turkish invasion, Grand Master of the Order Jean Parisot de La Valette has decided that the adventurer and arms dealer Mattias Tannhauser must be drawn to Malta, so that the Christian defenders of the island can make use of Mattias's intimate knowledge of the tactics and thought processes of his former captors. The English monk, Fra Oliver Starkey, is sent to Messina, Sicily, to entice Mattias to join the Christians on Malta. Since Mattias is known to have a weakness for women, La Valette suggests that Starkey use Carla La Penautier as an inducement; the countess has been begging the Grand Master for permission to come to Malta to search for her long-lost illegitimate son. As Starkey leaves the Grand Master's office, the merciless Ludovico Ludovici enters. Ludovico not only is the father of Carla's son, Orlandu, but also will become Mattias's archenemy and rival for Carla's love.

Eight days later, Mattias and Carla are on Malta, along with Mattias's friend, Bors of Carlisle, and Carla's protégée, Amparo. The homeless boy Orlandu has made his appearance, though he has not yet been identified as Carla's son. Moreover, Abbas bin Murad has appeared on the battlefield, determined to avenge the wrongs done to Muslim pilgrims and merchants over the last four decades.

Although Mattias intends to leave the island as soon as Carla locates her son, the chaotic conditions in the besieged city, along with the fact that she knows nothing about him except his age and parentage, makes the task of finding him more difficult than she anticipated. Throughout June, July, and August, Mattias and Bors take part in one bloody battle after another. From time to time, Mattias dons Turkish garb, slips off to the Muslim camp, and socializes with the soldiers there, picking up information that he relays to the Christians. At other times, he wanders through the Turkish market, trading for opium, which becomes one of his most useful tools. When he is with the Muslims, Mattias becomes once again the young man he once was; it seems as natural for him to invoke Allah as to breathe. Back with the Maltese, he will recite the Christian prayers he learned in his childhood. Mattias sees very little difference between the two creeds. What he does know is that in the heat of battle, the men on both sides are driven by their love of the god of war, not the god whose name they shout as they attack their opponents.

Mattias finds it just as impossible to commit to one woman as he does to one faith. While they are still in Messina, he strikes a bargain with Carla: If he goes with her to Malta and finds her son, she must promise to marry him, thus enabling him to rise into the ranks of the aristocracy, as he has long wished to do. The fact that Carla is young, beautiful, intelligent, and, as he later discovers, both kind-hearted and courageous makes the prospect even more appealing. On her part, Carla finds Mattias so attractive that, though she repels his initial advances, she almost immediately regrets having done so. Though thereafter she tries to encourage him, it is late in the novel before he succumbs. However, Mattias is also attracted to Amparo, who makes no secret of the fact that she has fallen desperately in love with him and, unlike Carla, is always available. Before battles and after battles, Mattias seeks out Amparo, and for a few moments they manage to forget the horrors around them.

Though Mattias is never long absent from the narrative, occasionally the author focuses on other characters, especially Ludovico. If the descriptions of battles in *The Religion* illustrate the human appetite for violence, the scenes in which Ludovico appears reveal human nature at its most cold-blooded. Ludovico's sins are those that are consigned to the lowest levels of Hell by the Italian poet Dante in his *La divina commedia* (c. 1320; *The Divine Comedy*, 1802): misuse of reason through deception, intrigue, and betrayal. Ludovico has a single goal: to become pope. From his beginnings as a monk, noted for his asceticism, he has risen steadily in the Church. Once he was named an Inquisitor, he could make a name for himself as a man who served God by stamping out heresies. Thus empowered, he could torture people at will, extract confessions of heresy, and burn them alive, thus gaining the respect—and the fear— of his colleagues and easy access to the most influential figures in the Church. Unlike many of the other characters in *The Religion*, such as Bors of Carlisle and even La Valette, Ludovico is not in love with war, though when he does find himself in battle he does enjoy the kill. Ludovico's only reason for joining the embattled forces on Malta is his ambition to become a member of the Order of Saint John, which would aid him in his papal ambitions.

Although reviewers praise Willocks for his skill in characterization, and though most readers would agree that his insight into characters as complex as Mattias, Carla, and even Starkey is almost flawless, the author seems less sure of himself where Ludovico is concerned, particularly near the end of the novel. Ludovico's attempt to make Mattias kill La Valette, thus removing an obstacle to the monk's plans, is quite in character. However, when throughout the book Ludovico has been motivated solely by his ambition, it is unlikely that he would become so besotted with Carla that he would rather marry her than become pope. His last-minute repentance also seems out of character; it is unlikely that a man who so misinterpreted the Christian message as to justify the most sadistic deeds would suddenly reverse his thought processes, even at the point of death.

At any rate, poetic justice prevails. Although Ludovico manages to block the planned escape and for a while has Mattias, Carla, and Amparo in his power, in the end Mattias kills Ludovico, and Mattias, not Ludovico, is made a Knight of the Order of Saint John, thus attaining the aristocratic rank for which he longed.

Most critics sum up *The Religion* as a gory but entertaining thriller, whose author is as skillful in his use of language as he is in characterization. However, the novel has more profound implications than may be evident at first reading. Willocks's basic theme is that the real difference between people is not their professed faith but their capacity for love. In the section titled "The Winnowing Winds," Mattias quotes Abbas's comparison of a winnowing wind, which separates wheat from chaff, to an event that separates the lovers of life, or the wheat, from the lovers of death, or the worthless chaff. Thus, though Abbas and Mattias are both warriors, they kill only because they must, not because they are infatuated with death-dealing.

This dichotomy between the lovers of life, who are capable of love, and the lovers of death, who are not, is related to another recurring theme in the novel: the father-son relationship. When Mattias sees Abbas again, he calls him "father," and though he knows that Mattias at least nominally is a Christian, Abbas treats him as a son. During the course of the novel, each of them saves the other's life. It is also significant that in the epilogue, which is titled "The Grace of God," Mattias has to seek out his real father and reestablish the ties between them before he can formalize his relationship with Carla. Even Ludovico has some feelings about fatherhood: His only selfless act comes when, finding that Orlandu is in peril, he goes to his son's rescue.

*The Religion* has been called the finest historical novel of the year. Certainly it has a broad appeal: a suspenseful plot, political intrigues, graphic battle scenes, and torrid sex. It also has characters of epic stature, just flawed enough to be appealing. Moreover, this brilliant re-creation of a major sixteenth century conflict has implications for the twenty-first century, not only because it shows two religions at war with each other but also because it suggests that the real meaning of life may not be found in dogmatic differences but in compassion and love.

*Rosemary M. Canfield Reisman*

**Review Sources**

*Booklist* 103, nos. 9/10 (January 1-15, 2007): 24.
*Kirkus Reviews* 75, no. 4 (February 15, 2007): 149.
*Library Journal* 132, no. 2 (February 1, 2007): 65.
*The New York Times Book Review* 156 (May 20, 2007): 19.
*Publishers Weekly* 254, no. 2 (January 8, 2007): 29.
*Times Literary Supplement*, August 11, 2006, p. 22.

# THE RELUCTANT FUNDAMENTALIST

*Author:* Mohsin Hamid (1971-    )
*Publisher:* Harcourt (Orlando, Fla.). 192 pp. $22.00
*Type of work:* Novel
*Time:* The early twenty-first century
*Locale:* Lahore, Pakistan; New York City;
Valparaíso, Chile

*A Pakistani man, torn between fundamentalist Islam
and America, relates his story to his American guest*

*Principal characters:*
CHANGEZ, Pakistani narrator torn between
Pakistan and the United States
ERICA, Changez's American girlfriend, who
is unable to get over her boyfriend
Chris's death
JIM, Changez's supportive mentor at Underwood Samson
JUAN BAUTISTA, Chilean businessman who helps Changez
see himself as a janissary
CHANGEZ'S GUEST, an American who is either a target or a killer

Mohsin Hamid's *The Reluctant Fundamentalist* is told from the first-person point
of view in the present, as a kind of prose dramatic monologue addressed to Changez's
unnamed guest at a restaurant in the Old Anarkali district of Lahore, Pakistan. With
first-person narration there is usually a problem with the reliability of the narrator,
and that is the case with this novel. As is the case with Robert Browning's dramatic
monologues, which are much shorter, the speaker not only tells his own story but also
gives his readers information that they must weigh and interpret. In effect, there are
two stories, the one Changez tells about why he became an Islamic fundamentalist
and the account of the interaction between Changez and his listener. Those two stories
are intertwined throughout the novel.

Changez's story begins with his trip to America, where his outstanding record at
Princeton University leads to his job with the Underwood Samson company, which
evaluates businesses. Before he joins the company, he and some other Princeton grad-
uates travel to Greece, where he falls in love with Erica, who is still recovering from
the death of her fiancé, Chris. Jealous of the time she devotes to Chuck and Mike,
Changez reveals his incipient anti-American feelings, feelings that deepen after 9/11.
He finds his American rivals to be "devoid of refinement," disrespectful of their elders, and insistent on having things their way. When Chuck mimics his mannerisms,
Changez states that his dream is to be the dictator of an Islamic republic with nuclear
capability; he suggests that it is only a joke, but later events indicate that it is not.
Erica, however, he considers above reproach, belonging more to the camp of the classy
actress Gwyneth Paltrow than to the camp of the vulgar pop star Britney Spears.

*Mohsin Hamid was born in Pakistan but was educated at Princeton and Harvard Universities before taking a position in New York City. Moth Smoke (2000), his first novel, won the Betty Trask Award, was a finalist for the PEN/Hemingway Award, and was named a Notable Book of the Year by The New York Times. His essays have appeared in The New York Times, Time, and The Independent. He lives in London.*

After Changez assumes his post with Underwood Samson, Erica's parents invite him to their home in the Hamptons, where he interprets Erica's father's comment, "You guys have got some serious problems with fundamentalism," as an expression of typical American condescension. While Changez becomes Erica's unofficial escort, she cannot forget Chris, and their "affair" is never really consummated. She drifts away from him and from life and finally is sent to a clinic, then disappears. Erica's mother gives him Erica's manuscript, but to his dismay he is not even a footnote in the book. What seemed so attainable is out of reach.

His business career follows a similar pattern. Jim, who interviews him for the job at Underwood Samson, sees his potential, notes that he is "hungry" (ambitious), and that like Jim, he is a "shark" and "outsider," a term that initially suggests that they both come from disadvantaged backgrounds. At Underwood Samson, efficiency is the god, and the training is "mental judo for business." Changez excels in this competitive environment, emerging first in the class and being assigned to work in the Philippines, where he does an outstanding job. The bombing of the World Trade Center's twin towers changes everything. He actually smiles at the 9/11 event, is "pleased at the slaughter of thousands of innocents," and relishes the notion that America has been "brought to her knees." Like other Muslims, he experiences some persecution: He is profiled at the airport, called a "fucking Arab" in the company parking lot, and encounters some prejudice at work. Nevertheless, he receives a good review and a bonus for his work.

He then returns to visit his family in Pakistan, where he discovers that he is seeing things through the eyes of a foreigner, an "entitled and unsympathetic American." The family home has not changed; he has changed. Even his parents sense that he is divided in his feelings about America. Partly as a result of what he begins to see as self-contempt, he begins to grow a beard, an act that only causes more apprehension when he returns to Underwood Samson. He asks himself "how it was that America was able to wreak such havoc in the world . . . with so few apparent consequences at home." Without a "stable core" and uncertain as to where he belongs, he is assigned to a job in Valparaíso, Chile, a city he compares to Lahore. Like Herman Melville's Bartleby, he stops working and goes into a kind of occupational coma. Juan Bautista, the owner of the firm he is evaluating, notices his state and tells him he is a janissary, a mercenary working for a foreign government. Looking at his life from a different perspective, he sees himself as a member of a suspect race and as an indentured servant. Changez returns to New York, where he meets with a disappointed Jim, who fires him. Changez has his regrets and wonders if he will miss "this city of possibility, with its magical vibrancy and sense of excitement." He returns to Lahore, becomes a university professor, becomes involved in politics, and even spends a night in jail for taking part in an anti-American demonstration.

Interspersed throughout Changez's story are his comments to his guest, who sits with his back against the restaurant wall and refuses to take off his jacket, which may contain a shoulder holster and gun. Changez describes his guest as inscrutable, with a "wary gaze" that seems to focus on the women in the marketplace. He is "ill at ease" as he glances constantly around him, and Changez wonders if he is "predator or prey." Since the guest is so suspicious, when the tea arrives, Changez switches the teacups in case the guest fears being drugged or poisoned. When the lights go out in the market, the guest leaps to his feet. From Changez's comments, the guest has reason to be apprehensive. Changez is curious about the nature of the guest's business and declares that "tonight . . . is a night of some *importance*." The waiter, described as "burly," is a bit intimidating and threatening, though the reader cannot tell if Changez is reassuring his guest or trying to make him more suspicious. As the evening wears on and the area becomes almost deserted, the tension increases, as does the ominous tenor of the comments Changez makes. He mentions that his guest is familiar with "the bloodiest of tasks" and declares that "such an America had to be stopped in the interests not only of the rest of humanity, but also in your own."

When Changez and the guest finally leave, the waiter follows them. Changez denies that the sound they hear is a pistol shot and notes that his guest seems ready to "bolt." The narrator even raises the possibility that he signaled the people following them. The situation is ambiguous: Changez admits he is paranoid and fears for his life because of his political activity, but his attempt to shake his guest's hand may be an attempt to detain him for the grim-faced waiter and his accomplices. One of his comments reflects the ambiguity: "You should not imagine that we Pakistanis are all potential terrorists, just as we should not imagine that you Americans are all undercover assassins." When Changez extends his hand, the guest reaches into his jacket and Changez sees the "glint of metal," which he adds enigmatically may be from a credit card holder. The indeterminate ending leaves readers with a host of unanswered questions: Who is the prey? Who is the predator? Is Changez attempting to ingratiate himself with the guest or is he trying to frighten him to forestall an assassination? What was the purpose of the meeting?

At the end of the novel, Changez is waiting, fearful that America might send an emissary to intimidate him or worse. He feels "rather like a Kurtz waiting for his Marlowe," an appropriate allusion to Joseph Conrad's *Heart of Darkness* (1902). Cultured, literary men, both Kurtz and Changez have "gone native" and turned to violence; Changez may, like Kurtz, be waiting for an emissary. As in *Apocalypse Now* (1979), Francis Ford Coppola's film adaptation of *Heart of Darkness*, *The Reluctant Fundamentalist* may indeed end in violence, but in Hamid's tale the reader is not sure who commits the violence, the American representing Western values or the Pakistani representing the East and the Other. Hamid's tale is told not by someone like Marlowe, but by someone like Kurtz.

*The Reluctant Fundamentalist* juxtaposes two cultures and has the protagonist adept at operating in both. America is the land of opportunity, riches, excitement, freedom, and "illiterate barbarians" as opposed to Pakistan, which is an older culture with traditional values. When speaking of bats, Changez remarks that they belong to "a dreamier world incompatible with the pollution and congestion of a modern metropolis." Changez resents the fact that people do not realize that his countrymen were creating magnificent literature and monuments while America was but a "collection of thirteen small colonies, gnawing away at the edge of a continent." He also resents the way America operates, using its financial power to impose its values on other peoples, including Iraq and Afghanistan.

Changez is, however, a "reluctant" fundamentalist, one who has to be forced by his experiences and by America's foreign policy (he is particularly upset by what he regards as America's pro-Indian policy) to turn against a country where he found so much success. He attained the American Dream so many immigrants desire, but then he rejected it. Essentially, his story is also the story of a Muslim world that also turned against the values and power it sought in America and the West. His story also accounts for why the twin towers were bombed, even though most Americans are more concerned with seeking revenge than in attempting to understand why the atrocity occurred. A reading of *The Reluctant Fundamentalist* provides some answers, even if they are not the ones Americans want to hear.

*Thomas L. Erskine*

## Review Sources

*Booklist* 103, nos. 9/10 (January 1-15, 2007): 50.
*Kirkus Reviews* 75, no. 1 (January 1, 2007): 6-7.
*London Review of Books* 29, no. 19 (October 4, 2007): 25-26.
*The New York Review of Books* 54, no. 15 (October 11, 2007): 22-24.
*The New York Times Book Review* 156 (April 22, 2007): 8.
*Publishers Weekly* 253, no. 49 (December 11, 2006): 42.
*School Library Journal* 53, no. 8 (August, 2007): 144.

# RETHINKING THIN
## The New Science of Weight Loss—
## and the Myths and Realities of Dieting

*Author:* Gina Kolata (1948-    )
*Publisher:* Farrar, Straus and Giroux (New York).
   257 pp. $24.00
*Type of work:* Medicine, psychology, science

*Billions of dollars are spent each year on the quest for thinness, while scientific evidence gained from repeated studies and data analysis indicates that all these dollars are being spent in vain*

Gina Kolata tackles one of the largest obsessions of Americans today—weight control. Her book, *Rethinking Thin: The New Science of Weight Loss—and the Myths and Realities of Dieting*, follows three distinct lines in alternating chapters. She takes readers through the history of dieting, touches on past and current university research on obesity, and follows a group of obese people participating in a two-year university study comparing the Atkins diet with a low-calorie diet. What she uncovers is fascinating, startling, and ultimately troubling.

Weight loss is big business, which should be no surprise to the reader. The surprise is that, essentially, most of what passes for accepted diet wisdom has been around for more than a century. Everything from eating less and exercising more to trendy diets such as the grapefruit diet have a long and unsuccessful history. Weight-loss programs and diet books eat up time and money, and yet more Americans than ever find themselves in the overweight or obese categories. For many who do manage to lose weight, sooner or later the weight comes back. Sometimes dieters gain even more pounds than they had before they started a diet program.

What is going on? According to "a report on obesity treatments by the National Academy of Sciences . . . the battle for weight control is never won, even after you lose weight. 'An obese individual faces a continuous lifelong struggle with no expectation that the struggle required will diminish with time.'" Still, the image of thinness portrayed as ideal in American society continues to be sought. Academic researchers warned that the belief that anyone can lose weight if they really try, the "blame-the-victim message," is "leading to a society in which prejudice against the overweight and obese has become the last remaining socially acceptable one."

Kolata sat in on the weekly support group meetings for the dieters in the Atkins versus low-calorie diet study. Four of the dieters talked with her at length over the course of the study, and she revisited the group at intervals of one, two, three, five, six, and ten months, and at two years (the end of the study). The average weight of the subjects was 216 pounds, and all had tried diet after diet, lost weight and regained it, and

*Gina Kolata writes on science topics for* The New York Times. *She is the author of five previous books, including* Sex in America: A Definitive Survey *(1994; with Robert T. Mitchell, John H. Gagnon, and Edward O. Laumann),* Flu: The Story of the Great Influenza Pandemic of 1918 and the Search for the Virus That Caused It *(1999), and* Ultimate Fitness: The Quest for Truth About Exercise and Health *(2003).*

hoped that being part of this study would make a difference this time.

For the researchers conducting the story, gathering information was the goal of the study. To their astonishment, no one had ever tried to compare diets in this way before. A discussion on their concerns about the then-wildly popular Atkins diet led them to see what evidence had been amassed so far. Their initial small study of 63 obese men and women revealed that, although both the Atkins and low-calorie diet participants lost and regained about the same weight, the Atkins dieters ended up with more HDL, the good type of cholesterol, and lower triglycerides, both of which reduce the risk of heart disease. This was not what the researchers expected to find, and so they set out to conduct a much larger study, using hundreds of subjects.

Going in to the study, the subjects did not know whether they would be assigned to the Atkins or low-calorie diet, but most of them fervently wished for Atkins. Probably because of its current popularity, they hoped that this diet, along with the monitoring and counseling, would help them reach their weight-loss goals. Unlike the researchers' purely academic interest, the subjects were deeply emotionally invested in the study, pinning all their hopes for success at last on this experiment. Randomized clinical trials such as this study did not allow them to choose which diet to follow; they were assigned one or the other.

During the first month, everyone lost weight. This was expected; most diets show at least preliminary losses. Three months into the study, the dieters have lost 10 percent of their body weight. The dieters are dismayed when the researchers tell them that they should be happy even if this is all that they lose. Their hopes are still high. At six months, the hopes are plummeting. Not only is weight loss stalling for some, but also weight is coming back. The desire to be thin has not diminished, but the dieters find their control over eating is slipping.

At ten months into the study, one of the dieters has reached his lowest weight, and he would begin to gain it all back. Everyone agrees that their control lasted only about six months. At the end of the two-year study, most of the dieters do not even show up. Despite not having reached their initial goals, all of the dieters, even those who did not come to the last meeting, agreed that they had had a useful experience. They now had more realistic expectations of the weight they could expect to lose.

Despite all the support and counseling, the lesson learned from the study is the same as all the previous studies: "No matter what the diet and no matter how hard they try, most people will not be able to lose a lot of weight and keep it off." Although overweight and obese persons can learn to control their eating, get regular exercise, and gauge portions and calories, they are facing a lifelong effort, and "true thinness is likely to elude them."

Kolata relates many historical attempts at weight loss. Even the ancient Greeks attempted weight loss, and the fact that gluttony was one of the seven deadly sins made fat frowned upon. The real change came in the nineteenth century, however. The poet Lord Byron popularized drinking vinegar as a way to lose weight, and he often lived on vinegar and water alone for days at a time. Despite warnings about this diet, it was popular both in America and Europe. In 1825, Jean Anthelme Brillat-Savarin wrote a best seller titled *Physiologie du goût* (*The Physiology of Taste*, 1949). In it, he related his loss of an eighteen-year-old woman he loved to the vinegar craze, and his observations of fat dinner companions eating potatoes, rice, and rich desserts led to his belief that eating only meat was key to healthy weight control. A London undertaker, William Banting, found relief from his obesity by giving up carbohydrates and sugars, and his last name became a synonym for dieting. The Reverend Sylvester Graham exhorted his followers to severely restrict their food intake, to eat simple foods, excluding beef and pork, and to drink only water. His followers were "the first Americans to keep close track of their own weight, and even to weigh their food." Next came Fletcherism, in which Horace Fletcher advocated chewing "every morsel of food until there is no more taste to be extracted from it." He thought that gobbling food caused overeating and thus obesity. Experiments followed in which Yale University athletes were instructed to eat only meat or become vegetarians for almost a year. The vegetarians turned out to be the strongest after testing, and so vegetarianism gained ascendancy. This fad did not last either.

When Kolata entered obesity research facilities to speak with the scientists first-hand, she learned of many studies that had not made their way out to the public, including the discovery of a substance named leptin, which helped control appetite and food consumption. Injections of leptin cured a young girl who could not stop eating and who was found to produce no leptin on her own. Unfortunately, the magic bullet again eluded scientists. Although the discovery of leptin led to the unraveling of the brain pathways that control appetite, simply injecting obese patients with leptin did not work, except in a few cases. Sometimes the problem was not leptin itself but was located somewhere else in the system.

Chapter 8, "The Fat Wars," relates an astounding discovery and a more astounding reaction against it. Katherine Flegal and David Williamson wrote a paper refuting the findings of another researcher, David Allison, in which he claimed that hundreds of thousands of Americans die every year solely from being overweight. Flegal and Williamson looked at the data Allison used and thought that he had not analyzed it correctly, but it took them some time before they could figure out how best to conduct the analysis. Using the federal National Health and Nutrition Examination Survey—in which the sample of Americans was more representative, and who had actually been weighed and measured rather than self-reporting their heights and weights—led to different conclusions. They found that, rather than overweight people having an increased risk of dying, they actually had a slightly lower risk than normal-weight people. Only the extreme ends of the scale of thin to obese persons had greater mortality risks.

They published their findings to a firestorm of professional and very public indignation. The critics who attacked their methods came from the obesity and research community, while statisticians uninvolved with obesity studies praised their work. Flegal and Williams were stunned at the level of hostility and backlash they received. Other studies held up to refute their findings all seemed to come from the Harvard University data that was not representative of the American population.

Such a reaction may be unheard of in professional circles, but the reason for it is not hard to figure out. There are research centers devoted to obesity research, and grant dollars flow in to support them. There are researchers whose only area of study is obesity. If being overweight is not a serious health and social problem, their reason for existence would be less pressing.

So many of the beliefs about dieting and being overweight have been held so long that people are reluctant to let go of them. Flegal and Williams' research abruptly challenged the status quo on weight and threatened with information that had been backed up by research and statistics, as well as commonly held opinions. Kolata speculates that now that smoking has been diminished as the number one killer, obesity has been targeted in its place, and over 40 percent of Americans believe obesity is equally bad.

Between research that reveals that even the simple "eat less; exercise more" regimen cannot help the overweight person and that all people have a genetic predisposition to being thin or fat, the notion that being fat is not such a horrible thing might relieve overweight Americans of the agony and guilt associated with their condition.

Kolata's writing flows easily, and she supports her reportage with numerous facts and citations, footnoted for further information. She approaches the subject with objectivity and wit. This book should be read by anyone who has ever looked in a mirror and thought they should lose a few pounds.

*Patricia Masserman*

**Review Sources**

*The Booklist* 103, no. 16 (April 15, 2007): 13.
*Entertainment Weekly*, no. 934 (May 18, 2007): 71.
*Kirkus Reviews* 75, no. 3 (February 1, 2007): 90.
*The New York Times Book Review* 156 (May 6, 2007): 22.
*People* 67, no. 18 (May 7, 2007): 55.
*Publishers Weekly* 254, no. 9 (February 26, 2007): 69.
*School Library Journal* 53, no. 10 (October, 2007): 188.

# RETURNING TO EARTH

*Author:* Jim Harrison (1937-    )
*Publisher:* Grove Press (New York). 272 pp. $24.00
*Type of work:* Novel
*Time:* 1995-1996
*Locale:* Mostly the Upper Peninsula of Michigan and
Ontario, Canada

*Donald, close to death at age forty-five, dictates his life
story to his wife so that family members will appreciate
their part-Native American heritage; after his death, the
people closest to him are forced to deal with the loss of an
important influence on their lives*

Principal characters:
DONALD, a man of mixed Native American and
Finnish ancestry who is dying of Lou Gehrig's disease
CYNTHIA, his wife and companion for nearly thirty years
HERALD, their son, a graduate student in California
CLARE, their daughter, who was especially close to her father
K, short for Kenneth, Clare's boyfriend who views Donald
as his substitute father
DAVID, Cynthia's eccentric brother, who spends winters in
Mexico and summers in northern Michigan
MR. BURKETT, Cynthia and David's father, an alcoholic
FLOWER, Donald's full-blooded Native American cousin
who knows many tribal folktales and legends

In Jim Harrison's *Returning to Earth*, Donald is very sick at an advanced stage of amyotrophic lateral sclerosis (ALS), commonly called Lou Gehrig's disease. He worked as a bricklayer for many years and was proud of his strength, but his body is giving out. His wife Cynthia must purée all of his food because swallowing has become very difficult. Sometimes his speech is almost impossible to understand. Worst of all is the excruciating pain of muscle seizures. As he describes it: "Back in high school when I ran track or played football you were likely to get a cramp. With this disease at times you are a cramp, your whole body seizes up so that even your mind seems inside a cramp. You're all cramp, pure and simple."

ALS is a cruel disease because of the pain. Cynthia has learned that there is no known cure and that the average survival time is only three years. Donald was embarrassed to go to a doctor when symptoms of muscle weakness first appeared, so he probably had the disease already for some time before it was diagnosed. Although he is only forty-five years old, he sees clearly that death is not far away. Donald has started dictating the story of his Native American and Finnish ancestry to his wife in order to preserve a family history for their two children and other relatives.

*Jim Harrison was born and raised in Michigan. He is the author of several works of fiction and poetry, as well as three books of nonfiction. He was awarded a Guggenheim Fellowship and received a grant from the National Endowment for the Arts.*

Donald's father, grandfather, and great-grandfather were all named Clarence. They mostly worked as laborers in mining, lumbering, and farming in northern Michigan and Minnesota. The first Clarence had lived with a Native American woman, which made their descendants part American Indian. Donald's mother was three-quarters Native American, so Donald inherited the characteristic appearance of dark skin, a large nose, and high cheek bones. Donald has a full-blooded Native American cousin named Flower, from whom he has heard some of the Native American legends about life and death, bears, ravens, natural medicines, and various tribal customs. Before Donald became ill, he had gone on a traditional vision quest. For three days, he lived in the woods without food, water, or shelter. He is reluctant to talk about his solitary experience, but he did say that he had a premonition of an early death when his parents (who were deceased) said to him in a vision, "Don't be afraid to come home, son."

Donald's father, Clarence, worked for a wealthy landowner named Mr. Burkett, who had a teenage daughter named Cynthia. Mr. Burkett liked young girls and once paid $100 to Cynthia's girlfriend to see her naked. Cynthia got so angry at her father that she hit him with a club. Donald met Cynthia when he came to work with his father to help dig the foundation for a building. Cynthia offered a glass of lemonade to Donald, which was the beginning of their romance. Mr. Burkett had another employee, a Mexican man with a twelve-year-old daughter named Vera. In a drunken fit, Mr. Burkett raped the young girl. She went back to Mexico with her father and later gave birth to a son. After this traumatic incident, Cynthia could not stand staying at home any longer, so she and Donald ran off and got married.

The story of Mr. Burkett is not finished yet. Donald tells about Cynthia's brother, David, who years later talked his alcoholic father into going to Mexico to look up Vera and her son. Instead of a reconciliation, a fight develops; Vera's son slices off Mr. Burkett's two hands with a machete and then sets him and David adrift in the Gulf of Mexico in a rowboat. David eventually dumps his father's body into the water. Donald's dramatic narrative skips quickly from one subject to another, so the story of Mr. Burkett is followed by memories of a fishing trip he took with his daughter, Clare. Donald tells stories as they occur to him, with no particular chronological connection. The fishing trip reminds him about a nature documentary that he saw on television, which leads into a sad story about a young fellow who was sent to prison for growing marijuana and now is confined with no access to the world of nature. Cynthia faithfully records Donald's stories as he tells them.

Donald has planned how he wants his life to end. He wants to be buried naked, not in a coffin (which explains the title of Harrison's book). He asks his doctor for medicine that can be used to induce death when he is ready, but the doctor refuses on the grounds that euthanasia is illegal. Donald has kept a quantity of pain pills that he received from a veterinarian when his dog was sick, and he figures that they will suffice.

He wants his grave to be on a hillside near the shore of Lake Superior on the Canadian side. As his seizures become more severe, Cynthia recognizes that the end is near and calls their two children home. Clare, who has always been close to her father, sits by his bed through a difficult night. Sensing his frustration with his sickness, she tells him, "Dad, I know what you are going to do and I can't say I blame you." Herald, after witnessing a convulsion by his father, is so upset that he says he is ready to suffocate him in order to stop the torture. The word "suicide" is never mentioned, but it has become clear to Donald's family that he has decided to end his pain.

Part 2 of Harrison's book is the story of a young man who goes by the name of K (short for Kenneth), with whom Donald has formed a close friendship. When K was quite young, his father had died in a motorcycle accident. K became part of Donald's extended family when David married K's mother. Donald became a surrogate father during K's teenage years and later helped him through a period of depression. K is a frequent visitor at Donald and Cynthia's house, where he becomes romantically involved with their daughter. Cynthia is thankful that K can take Donald on periodic trips, because he is strong enough to lift Donald into and out of the car.

K has a hard time finding his niche in society. His worldview is that life is chaotic, like "a ten-thousand-piece beige jigsaw puzzle." However, he is grateful to Donald as a mentor and a friend. In the plan for Donald to bring an end to his life, K and Herald are to dig the grave for him at the chosen location by Lake Superior. They will go through customs into Canada, pretending to go on a fishing trip. Following later in a second car will be Cynthia and Donald, together with Clare and David. Donald has chosen the summer solstice, June 21, when he wishes to return to the earth. K has obtained two hypodermics filled with Nembutal, which commonly is used to euthanize horses when they break a leg. Cynthia thought the hypodermics were necessary because Donald is no longer able to swallow pills. Everything proceeds according to the plan: Donald sits down at the edge of the grave that was dug for him, Herald gives him the injection, they lay Donald into the grave on a bed of cedar branches, and in a few minutes he is dead. The grave is refilled, tears are shed, and the family members return home.

Part 3 of Harrison's book is about David. David and Cynthia had received a substantial inheritance after their parents' death, so he does not have to work for a living. However, he feels the need to find some kind of meaningful occupation. One day, he saw a picture in a newspaper of some Mexicans who tried to cross the border into the United States but died of dehydration in the desert. David came up with the idea of an emergency travel kit to help these illegal immigrants make it across the border. He uses his inheritance money to buy thousands of kits, which he then takes to Mexican churches and community centers for distribution. He finds satisfaction in being personally involved in doing something to relieve suffering. Perhaps there is also a deeper psychological need for David to atone for his father's sin many years ago against the young Mexican girl Vera. The connection between David and Vera eventually is resolved in an unexpected way.

The last part of Harrison's book is titled "Cynthia." Several months have elapsed since Donald's death. Cynthia worries about Clare, who has gone to live in the woods with Flower. Clare is trying to learn Native American ways and thinks that maybe her departed father has become a bear. Cynthia gradually realizes that her daughter needs to grieve in her own way, while she has to get on with her own life without Donald.

A friend tries to help Cynthia by getting substitute teaching assignments for her. However, she decides that she would prefer to do individual tutoring, especially for students of Native American background who have difficulty adjusting to the white culture. Before Donald died, he had told his wife that after he was gone, she needed to find a new boyfriend. The boyfriend and the tutoring come together in the person of Vincent, a college student who needs help with English but who also becomes her ardent lover for a week-long "sexual extravaganza." As the first anniversary of Donald's death approaches, she reaches the decision to resume her teaching career, not in the white schools of Michigan but on an Indian reservation in Montana. Cynthia is ready to move on into the future.

The dominant personality in Harrison's book is Donald. He acts on his instincts with few regrets afterward. The stories he tells are about real people in specific situations. He has little interest in abstract ideas. In contrast to Donald, his son Herald thrives on mathematics but finds people confusing. His wife's brother, David, is an intellectual who does a lot of reading but has a hard time reaching a conclusion. Donald describes him as someone who "doesn't seem to have both oars in the water." Clare and K have an on-again, off-again love affair but seem unable to make a long-term commitment to each other. Cynthia is the one who has come the furthest in absorbing Donald's decisive lifestyle.

Harrison has created a memorable collection of diverse personalities, all in one family, for whom Donald has been a center of stability for their life journey.

*Hans G. Graetzer*

## Review Sources

*Booklist* 103, no. 4 (October 15, 2006): 5.
*Kirkus Reviews* 74, no. 20 (October 15, 2006): 1035.
*Los Angeles Times*, January 28, 2007, p. R2.
*The New York Times Book Review* 156 (February 11, 2007): 1-8.
*San Francisco Chronicle*, January 2, 2007, p. D2.

# RUN

*Author:* Ann Patchett (1963-     )
*Publisher:* HarperCollins (New York). 295 pp. $25.95
*Type of work:* Novel
*Time:* The early twenty-first century
*Locale:* Boston

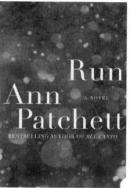

*This family saga tells the story of two adopted brothers whose birth mother suddenly reenters their lives through a car accident; the author portrays how bonds of love and affection develop in a family, whether its members are related by birth or by choice*

*Principal characters:*
> BERNARD DOYLE, a Boston politician and
>   lawyer whose wife had died of cancer,
>   leaving him to raise three sons
> SULLIVAN DOYLE, the oldest son, a rebellious
>   child after the death of his mother
> TIP DOYLE, an adopted African American son,
>   now a student at Harvard University
> TEDDY DOYLE, Tip's younger brother, who is
>   considering whether to enter the priesthood
> UNCLE SULLIVAN, an elderly priest, the brother of
>   Bernard Doyle's deceased wife
> TENNESSEE ALICE MOSER, the birth mother of Tip and Teddy
> KENYA MOSER, eleven-year-old daughter of Tennessee

Near the beginning of Ann Patchett's novel *Run*, Tip and Teddy Doyle, adopted sons of Bernard Doyle, are sitting with their father attending a lecture by civil rights activist Jesse Jackson on the campus of Harvard University. Doyle had named his sons after two well-known Massachusetts politicians, anticipating a career in politics for them. Both sons have come reluctantly to the lecture, out of a sense of obligation to their father. Tip had to interrupt his work at the Museum of Comparative Zoology, where he helps to maintain the large collection of fish. He is fascinated with ichthyology, but his father was disappointed for having "paid more than forty thousand dollars a year to one of the finest universities in the world to give his son the right to peer into glass jars at dead fish." Teddy has just come from seeing his Uncle Sullivan, a much-admired, elderly priest living in a nursing home. Uncle Sullivan is quite sick, and Teddy would have preferred to stay with him to deal with the many visitors who badger him with requests for intercessory prayers.

Tip is frustrated about the time he has to spend at the lecture. He needs to study for semester exams and to finish his work at the museum. When the lecture finally ends, the father makes a further demand on his time, asking him to attend a reception for Jesse Jackson, but Tip's resentment boils over into an emotional outburst: "I'm not

*Ann Patchett is the author of four earlier novels, including* Bel Canto *(2001), which sold more than a million copies and received the prestigious PEN/Faulkner Award. She has written for various publications, including* Harper's Magazine, The New York Times Magazine, The Atlantic Monthly, *and* The Washington Post. *She lives in Nashville, Tennessee.*

going to do this. . . . You don't care about the things I care about. I don't care about the things you care about." Distracted by his argument, Tip stumbles over the curb into the path of an oncoming car. At the last second, an African American woman standing nearby pushes Tip out of the way, taking the impact of the car herself. An ambulance is called to take the woman, who is in critical condition with multiple injuries, to a hospital. The woman's young daughter is left behind at the scene of the accident with the three men of the Doyle family.

Tip has a broken ankle from the accident and is about to be transported to the hospital in a police car with his brother and father. The girl is very upset to be separated from her mother and demands to be taken along. Teddy talks to her and tries to calm her down. She tells Teddy that her name is Kenya, "like the country," and her mother's name is Tennessee, "like the state." Teddy probes Kenya about getting in touch with her father or other relatives, but she insists that she wants to stay with them. Then she tells them "the one thing I'm never supposed to tell"—that the woman who saved Tip's life is actually Tip and Teddy's birth mother. Kenya's mother had taken an apartment in a housing development near the Doyles and had discreetly been watching her sons from a distance when they played outdoors and later when they went to school. Tennessee and Kenya had been sitting near the Doyles at the Jackson lecture and afterward were standing close by when the car collision was imminent. It is not just a chance coincidence that Tennessee was in the right place at the right time to save her son from serious injury.

The father is suspicious that Kenya's story may be a fabrication. A DNA test of Tennessee and his two sons would be needed to verify the maternity claim. Tip and Teddy are shocked to learn that they appear to have a younger sister. At the hospital, Tip gets a cast on his ankle and is released with crutches. Kenya's mother is in intensive care, scheduled for surgery the next morning. Exhausted, the Doyles take Kenya home with them. However, another surprise is waiting for the Doyles at home. The boys' older brother, Sullivan, who has been out of touch with the family for some two years, has come home unexpectedly.

Sullivan was a protective, older brother for Tip and Teddy when they were young children, but he became antagonistic toward his father after his mother died of cancer. He has been estranged from the family since causing a scandal some years ago. Most recently he had been living in Africa, delivering HIV medication to hospitals but making money on the side by selling some of it on the black market. When his illegal activity appeared to be on the verge of being discovered, he made a quick exit back to Boston. He arrives just in time to participate in the unfolding events.

When Sullivan is introduced to Kenya, he sees a clear resemblance to Tip and Teddy in her appearance. He is willing to accept the story of Kenya and her mother as genuine. While the others in the Doyle family go to sleep, Sullivan is restless with jet lag and decides to go to the hospital to see the black woman for himself. Tennessee is awaiting surgery, only half-conscious as a result of the pain medications, so Sullivan sits by her bedside. Gradually he is drawn to tell her a traumatic incident from his life. He tells Tennessee about the death of his girlfriend in college for which he had been responsible but had never before admitted to anyone. The scene is like a deathbed confession, but with the roles reversed. He finds great relief in finally being able to admit his guilt: "She had taken his burden for a moment, lifted the thing he had carried with him for so long he hadn't even understood that he was still holding it." Readers may find it difficult to accept the almost instantaneous bond of intimacy that develops between Sullivan and Tennessee. Nevertheless, the emotional confession is described by Patchett with compassion and great tenderness.

In the morning, Kenya wants to be taken to the hospital right away, but her mother is in surgery. It is an awkward time for the Doyles as they figure out what to do about Kenya. No one had any idea that Tip and Teddy had a sister or even if that story is to be believed. When Kenya mentions that she loves to go running, Tip volunteers to take her to the Harvard field house for some exercise after making a brief stop at the museum. Kenya is a precocious, delightful child who is fascinated by the thousands of jars filled with fish. As Tip gives her a tour of the collection, he is gratified to hear her express a genuine interest in his work, something that he never got from his brother or father. Later at the field house, Kenya runs with such speed and grace that she soon has an admiring audience of college students. Kenya is overjoyed to have an older brother who can give her entrance to a world where she could never have gone on her own. Tip and Kenya have bonded together in a special way.

After surgery, Tennessee is brought back to her hospital room under heavy sedation. She has a surrealistic vision of being visited there by her closest friend, a young woman who had died some years ago. The friend's name was Tennessee Alice Moser, and she had a baby daughter named Kenya. In grief after her friend's funeral, she decided to keep Kenya as her own child. To avoid the costly adoption process, she took her friend's name and moved to a different neighborhood in Boston. She took a different job using her new name and struggled to make ends meet as a single mother. She showered her love on Kenya, knowing that her own sons, Tip and Teddy, had a good home in which she had no role. She had told Kenya about giving up her sons for adoption and let her assume that they were her brothers. Tennessee dies at the hospital soon after surgery, without ever revealing to Kenya the story of her birth mother.

The final chapter of the novel is a celebration several years later. The Doyle family, now including Kenya, are all attending the graduation ceremony of Tip from medical school. Tip's classmates are talking about where they plan to go for an internship, but Tip has other plans. He has decided that his career will be in the scientific study of fish, no matter what expectations his father or other people may have for him. His medical training in physiology will help him in his chosen field. Kenya has been fully accepted into the Doyle family since the death of her mother. Her life has been transformed as she has moved from an environment of near poverty into the upper class. She is attending a private, Catholic high school, making a name for herself as an outstanding runner. She imagines that her mother somehow arranged for the car accident that enabled her to gain three brothers and a father.

Each character in Patchett's novel is portrayed as a unique, memorable personality. The father is a loving but controlling parent to his adopted sons, as shown by some tender incidents from their childhood. Tennessee's harsh life as a single parent is described sympathetically: working late hours for low pay, living in a low-cost housing development, watching out for the safety of her adopted daughter. Kenya is an obedient, loving, appreciative adolescent. Father Sullivan had been full of energy and confidence as a young priest, but his deteriorating health leads him to deeper questions about the effectiveness of prayer and the meaning of eternal life. Sullivan Doyle is the "black sheep" of the Doyle family, reinstated by the compassion he receives from the mother of his adopted brothers. Significant childhood experiences show how Teddy's close relationship with Uncle Sullivan and Tip's longtime fascination with fishes got started. Patchett skillfully uses conversations and events to round out the portraits of the people who make up this extended family.

Some of the coincidences in *Run* seem rather contrived. For example, just by chance Tennessee had been an employee at Father Sullivan's nursing home, so the characters already had a connection before the accident. Also, it seems far-fetched that Tennessee could so often observe Tip and Teddy from nearby without herself being noticed. Nevertheless, in this era of many dysfunctional families, it is refreshing to read a positive story of the bonding that can grow among family members, whether they are related by adoption or by birth.

*Hans G. Graetzer*

## Review Sources

*Booklist* 103, no. 21 (July 1, 2007): 31.
*The Christian Science Monitor*, October 9, 2007, p. 13.
*The Economist* 384 (September 15, 2007): 103.
*The New York Times Book Review* 157 (September 30, 2007): 7.
*The New Yorker* 83, no. 29 (October 1, 2007): 98-100.
*The Washington Post*, September 23, 2007, p. BW15.

# A RUSSIAN DIARY
## A Journalist's Final Account of Life, Corruption, and Death in Putin's Russia

*Author:* Anna Politkovskaya (1958-2006)
*Publisher:* Random House (New York). 400 pp. $25.95
*Type of work:* Current affairs
*Time:* The 1990's and early 2000's
*Locale:* Russia

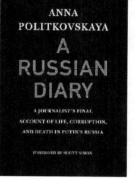

*A compelling account of recent Russian history, with special focus on terrorist activities in Chechnya and Russia and on political changes under Vladimir Putin*

*Principal personages:*
> ANNA POLITKOVSKAYA (1958-2006),
> Russian journalist whose insights frame
> the narrative
> VLADIMIR PUTIN (1952-     ), president of
> Russia beginning in 2000, whose efforts to
> consolidate and extend his political control
> over Russia dominate Politkovskaya's observations
> SHAMIL BASAYEV (1965-2006), Chechen terrorist,
> suspected of masterminding the *Nord-Ost* theater
> and Beslan school hostage crises
> RAMZAN KADYROV (1976-     ), an utterly ruthless
> and pro-Russian warlord who advises the Kremlin
> on matters of Chechen security
> GARRY KASPAROV (1963-     ), international chess
> champion turned politician

Celebrated internationally on its publication, *A Russian Diary* chronicles slightly more than two years worth of bald-faced political wrongdoing, deadening public apathy, and shockingly callous terrorism taking place in Russia under President Vladimir Putin. For certain audiences, the book offers much of value. For those readers with prior interest in or knowledge of recent Russian political history, the book offers a hard-nosed reporter's insightful anecdotes. For those with an interest in human rights or those who have read Anna Politkovskaya's other books—*A Dirty War: A Russian Reporter in Chechnya* (2003), *A Small Corner of Hell: Dispatches from Chechnya* (2003), or *Putin's Russia: Life in a Failing Democracy* (2004)—this work offers another glimpse into the dirty struggle of desperate men in troubled Chechnya. Those readers who are aware of the threats made against Politkovskaya and of her unsolved murder will appreciate her bravery in truth-telling whatever the cost. For those readers who are not in any of the above groups, however, most of *A Russian Diary* will seem slow moving and esoteric, if not bewildering.

*Called Russia's bravest journalist and the author of multiple books, Anna Politkovskaya won numerous awards for her accounts of life in Chechnya and Russia. While working on* A Russian Diary, *she was killed outside her apartment building in Moscow. The case remains unsolved.*

Born in 1958, Politkovskaya was a career journalist, cutting her teeth reporting news for *Izvestia*, the official newspaper of the Soviet government. During the glasnost period and the collapse of the Soviet Union, Politkovskaya covered news for *Novaya Gazeta*, a biweekly news digest. During the 1990's, she frequently found herself covering events in the First and Second Chechen Wars. Her specialty was covering the human side of major events, focusing on the impact of war, terrorist activities, and reprisals on the innocent men, women, and children who are made to suffer.

Most of the significant events in *A Russian Diary* relate in one way or another to two wars fought in Chechnya between Russian and Chechen forces. Both wars stemmed from Chechen nationalism after the collapse of the Soviet Union in the early 1990's. This desire for independence resulted in armed conflict between pro-Russian and separatist forces in Chechnya. A mountainous region, Chechnya was difficult for pro-Russian forces to pacify, and from 1994 to 1996 Chechen independence forces were able to wrest control of the region despite overwhelming Russian manpower. The cost of the war was enormous, and the new national government was unable to neutralize many warlords who dominated different regions. In 1999, the most powerful of these warlords began calling for the republic's transformation into a militantly Islamic state and arguing for the forcible transformation of predominantly Muslim neighboring states. One such warlord was Shamil Basayev, who led an unsuccessful incursion into Dagestan and who became the mastermind of various terrorist outrages in Russia, including the two events that bookend *A Russian Diary*.

For its part, the Russian government took a dim view of Chechen efforts to import Islamic revolution and invaded Chechnya in late 1999. It was the newly elected Vladimir Putin who became associated with the most destructive and heartless phases of this war; in particular, he wanted to limit Russian casualties by attacking Chechen towns with wave after wave of extremely lethal fuel-air bombs and enormous artillery attacks. As Russian forces advanced into the region, most civilians fled; those who remained were put into concentration camps. Although Russian troops seized the Chechen capital city of Grozny in early 2000, Chechen forces under warlords such as Basayev remained in existence, fighting small-scale combats against Russian and pro-Russian forces.

Besides encouraging the ill treatment of civilians, Putin's government made the stunning mistake of giving power to outrageously violent men such as Ramzan Kadyrov. One of the striking parts of *A Russian Diary*, in fact, consists of an interview with Kadyrov, a vain and stupid man. Politkovskaya recounts Kadyrov acknowledging his complicity in criminal acts against civilians and announcing his unrealistic plan to pacify Chechnya by fighting Basayev in single combat. As Politkovskaya points out, one of the worst aspects of Russia's policy in Chechnya was the support given to such men as Kadyrov. She considers it the hatching of "baby dragons," who must be continually fed lest they destroy everything. Under the control of baby dragons like Kadyrov, Chechnya becomes a land of endless terror, dominated by unending kidnappings, murders, rapes, and torture.

While this chaotic and violent region churns to the south, the rest of the country lies in apathetic somnolence, only occasionally shaken from slumber by terrorist actions. For example, *A Russian Diary* begins shortly after the conclusion of the *Nord-Ost* theater siege in October, 2002. At that time, a Moscow musical theater was taken over by Chechen terrorists who wanted Russian forces removed from Chechnya. The group took 800 hostages and threatened to blow them up should the terrorists' demands not be met. Over the course of three days, Russian security forces developed a plan to use knock-out gas to incapacitate the terrorists before storming the building. In the early morning hours of October 26, after hearing what sounded like gunfire inside the theater, Russian special forces pumped an opium-based gas into the building, opened a hole in a theater wall, and stormed inside, guns blazing. About two hours after storming the theater, the incident was over: Security forces had killed all the terrorists, shooting many at point-blank range. More than 110 hostages had died as well, most from the gas.

The incident points to a troubling conclusion for Politkovskaya: Either the security forces were slipshod in their tactics—hence demonstrating an official preference for ineptitude—or they intentionally chose a slow-acting gas, accepting that semiconscious terrorists would probably explode their bombs, thereby increasing the scale of the crime. A devious government could use the fear of such crimes to increase support for its policies, especially those aimed at defeating terrorism and ending the lingering conflict in Chechnya. The unfortunate conclusion reached by the author is that the government under Putin was both devious and inept. Its methods for maintaining political control are so obvious and so frequently illegal that only an apathetic or subdued population would countenance them.

As *A Russian Diary* continues, the narrative offers multiple examples of political malfeasance. One is the prosecution of Mikhail Khodorkovsky and the governing board of the Yukos Corporation. Formed during a period of privatization of government assets, Yukos was a petroleum giant—and its founders paid hefty bribes to national leaders. By 2002, however, it had become a new type of business in Russia; its board of directors were vowing to make the corporation transparent, with Western accounting practices and due diligence for its shareholders. As Politkovskaya observes, the determination to do business in a more honest way differentiated Khodorkovsky from Russia's new plutocrats who were living the high life while the rest of the country suffered shortages. When the bribes stopped flowing, the Russian government turned a vengeful eye on Yukos. Members of the governing board were found guilty of tax evasion, and Khodorkovsky was sent to Siberia even though the allegedly criminal actions were completely legal when undertaken.

As Politkovskaya describes, the Yukos prosecution demonstrates the end of an independent judiciary in Russia; the courts are another way for the government to silence opposition. The government gets away with this because there is literally no meaningful opposition. Indeed, *A Russian Diary* documents the difficulty of waging a presidential campaign against Putin. In the first place, Politkovskaya observes, one must have a viable candidate: Several of the opposition parties have to resort to running political nonentities or worse. Another legitimate candidate is apparently kidnapped, roughed up, flown into a country, and given memory-affecting drugs. Given this context, when one political party names its candidate, the man publicly announces his wish that Putin would win the election; oddly enough, the party continues to put him forward as a candidate.

To Politkovskaya, the fact that events like these provoke no outrage, no protest marches, no upsurge of support for outside candidates such as Garry Kasparov, the chess champion turned Putin critic, indicates the extent to which the average Russian is subdued. The average Russian, Politkovskaya observes, is content with little, expects the government to be brutal and callous, and feels uncomfortable with the notion that it is his or her duty to hold the government to account for its actions. Instead, she notes, the average Russian prefers living in a metaphorical bunker, ignoring everything that passes overhead.

The typical Russian feels this way, perhaps, because Putin's government is so ruthless in its control of the media. *A Russian Diary* documents the closing of independent television stations and newspapers. Their hard-hitting journalism is replaced by pablum. When he appeared on a television public affairs show, for instance, Putin was asked no hard questions regarding show trials, the lingering war in Chechnya, or meaningful reform; instead, members of the audience called him to ask about his plans for the puppies his pet dog recently had.

Toward the end of the book, Politkovskaya turns her attention to perhaps the most brutal of terrorist attacks in recent history, the Beslan school hostage crisis. The heinous attack was directed at children, some as young as five, and throughout the crisis children were made to suffer when their suffering could have been prevented. Early on September 1, 2004, on the first day of school, a group of thirty-four heavily armed men and women broke into a school in Beslan, a small town in North Ossetia, a region in Russia. Although some people managed to escape, more than 1,200 adults and children were herded into the school gymnasium. All the adult men (teachers as well as fathers who had taken their children to school) were selected from the crowd and shot. Within minutes, the terrorists began stringing high explosives around the perimeter of the gym and among the crowd of children. Using children as human shields, the terrorists called for all Russian troops to leave Chechnya or the children would be killed.

Despite intense negotiations over the next two days, the terrorists refused all compromises, including exchanging the children for adult hostages. As food and water ran low, the terrorists refused to feed the children or give them water. On September 3, in the early afternoon, several of the terrorists' bombs exploded, opening a section of the gym wall. In the chaos and confusion, many of the children tried to escape, and Russian security forces began storming the school; to compound the catastrophe, the walls of the gymnasium, weakened by the explosions, collapsed, and many were buried alive. As Russian special forces began clearing the school, an ugly event turned hideous: Small groups of terrorists held out in the school's cafeteria and basement, both groups using children as human shields. The final death toll amounted to more than 350, most of whom were only identifiable through DNA sampling; more than half of the victims were young children.

What goes unsaid during *A Russian Diary*, but perhaps should have been mentioned by the author, were the repeated threats against her and the attempts on her life. It would certainly be worthwhile to know that while documenting the political changes in Russia, Politkovskaya was followed by a group of men and women who took note of her comings and goings. It adds a dimension of immediacy and respect to know that on the flight to Beslan, Politkovskaya was poisoned. Certainly, she earned no small number of enemies in documenting the political corruption in Russia, the culture of bullying that dominated the army, and in interviewing the "baby dragons" of Chechnya. The goonish Kadyrov even staged a mock execution in front of Politkovskaya and has been implicated in her murder on October 7, 2006, when she was gunned down outside her apartment building in Moscow.

*Michael R. Meyers*

## Review Sources

*America* 197, no. 10 (October 8, 2007): 26-27.
*The Economist* 383 (April 7, 2007): 82.
*Foreign Affairs* 86, no. 5 (September/October, 2007): 177.
*Kirkus Reviews* 75, no. 9 (May 1, 2007): 436-436.
*New Statesman* 136 (April 16, 2007): 56.
*The New York Times Book Review* 156 (July 1, 2007): 7.
*Sunday Times*, April 1, 2007, p. 40.
*The Village Voice* 52, no. 49 (December 5, 2007): 42.

# THE SAVAGE DETECTIVES

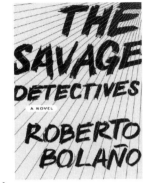

*Author:* Roberto Bolaño (1953-2003)
*First published: Los detectives salvajes,* 1998, in Spain
Translated from the Spanish by Natasha Wimmer
*Publisher:* Farrar, Straus and Giroux (New York).
  592 pp. $27.00
*Type of work:* Novel
*Time:* 1976-1996
*Locale:* Mexico City, Oaxaca, and Tlaxcala, Mexico;
  Madrid and Barcelona, Spain; Paris; Israel; Rome;
  Vienna; Los Angeles; Managua; Rwanda; Liberia;
  and the Sonoran Desert

*A multivoiced epic of two poets' search for the vanished*
*founder of visceral realism, and the consequences of their meeting, extending over*
*two decades and five continents*

  *Principal characters:*
    ARTURO BELANO, a visceral realist poet, based loosely on the writer
    ULISES LIMA, a visceral realist poet who joins Belano in the search for
      Cesárea Tinajero
    JUAN GARCÍA MADERO, a seventeen-year-old poet who narrates the first
      and third sections of the novel
    LUSCIOUS SKIN, a visceral realist poet
    LUPE, a Mexican prostitute who accompanies the poets on their search
    CESÁREA TINAJERO, the founder of the visceral realist school, who
      vanished in the Sonoran Desert some fifty years before the novel
      opens
    MARÍA FONT, a visceral realist poet and lover to García Madero
    ANGÉLICA FONT, Maria's sister and visceral realist poet
    QUIM FONT, father of the Font sisters and owner of the car driven by
      Belano and Lima

  In one of the great road stories of the twentieth century, Chilean-born writer
Roberto Bolaño traces the steps of his alter ego Arturo Belano and his friend Ulises
Lima as they search for the founder of the visceral realist school of poetry in the
Sonoran Desert, where she disappeared some fifty years earlier. *The Savage Detec-*
*tives* is not an easily read novel, but it rewards the persistent reader with its wit,
its playfulness, and, paradoxically, with its gravity. Bolaño's brilliance is evident
in the range of voices and breadth of character he creates.
  Bolaño's life offers much of the raw material from which the novel is crafted. Born
in Chile in 1953, he moved with his parents to Mexico in 1968. With the election
of leftist Salvador Allende in Chile in 1973, Bolaño returned to Chile, hoping to participate in a revolution. Shortly after his arrival, however, Augusto Pinochet over-
threw the Allende government, and Bolaño found himself in prison for several days.

He returned to Mexico City and began writing poetry, founding along with Mario Santiago a radical literary movement called infrarealism. These poets attempted to fully merge life with literature and to work against the current literary establishment. They would often show up at readings by other poets (including the great enemy of the fictional visceral realists, Octavio Paz) and disrupt the events, often by shouting or reading their own poems. Bolaño ultimately left Mexico, traveling around Europe and Africa before finally settling in Catalonia, near Barcelona. He married and had a son. After years of writing poetry, he understood that he could not support himself this way.

*Roberto Bolaño was born in Chile in 1953, moving to Mexico City with his family in 1968, and finally settling in Spain in the 1980's. The founder of the infrarealist school of poetry, he began writing fiction in the 1990's to immediate critical and popular acclaim. His work has won many major prizes and has been widely translated into English. Bolaño died in 2003.*

Thus, in the 1990's Bolaño began to write fiction. Critical and popular acclaim was immediate on the publication of his work, and in the ten years before his death while awaiting a liver transplant in 2003 he produced ten novels and three collections of short stories. It was with the publication of *Los detectives salvajes* in 1998, however, that he received the respect and fame reserved for writers such as Gabriel García Márquez and Carlos Fuentes. The year of this novel's publication, Bolaño won two major Spanish language literary awards, the Rómulo Gallegos Prize in Venezuela and the Herralde Prize in Spain. Natasha Wimmer's exceptionally well-received 2007 translation of *The Savage Detectives* made the novel widely accessible to English-speaking audiences around the world.

*The Savage Detectives* has a three-part structure. As narrator of the first section, Juan García Madero, a seventeen-year-old would-be poet and law school dropout, chronicles his introduction to the poetic group known as the visceral realists through a series of diary entries, beginning on November 2, 1975. García Madero's voice is charmingly naïve in its affected worldliness. Readers witness his initiation into both sex and drugs and discover that García Madero knows every word for every rhetorical and poetic device ever devised.

García Madero also offers readers their first glimpses of the peripatetic heroes of the story, poets Arturo Belano and Ulises Lima. These young men are the founders of the infrarealist movement and are thinly veiled stand-ins for Bolaño and his friend Mario Santiago. In a very funny scene, García Madero describes his poetry workshop, led by Professor Álamo, on the day that Belano and Lima crash it. In response to an attack on his critical system by the visceral realists, Álamo accuses them of being "cut-rate surrealists and fake Marxists." García Madero, along with a "skinny kid who always carried around a book by Lewis Carroll and never spoke," sides withBelano and Lima: "I decided to put in my two cents, and I accused Álamo of having no idea what a rispetto was; nobly, the visceral realists admitted that they didn't know either but my observation struck them as pertinent, and they said so; one of them asked how old I was, and I said I was seventeen and tried all over again to explain what a rispetto was."

By the end of the first section, García Madero not only has become a visceral realist but also has lost his virginity, hooked up with a prostitute called Lupe, and jumped
in a car with Lima, Belano, and Lupe as they race north out of Mexico City, running
away from Lupe's pimp Alberto, and racing toward their collective futures in the
Sonoran Desert. The tone of the story seems to change at this moment, toward some
darker, unknown, yet inevitable conclusion. In his last entry of the first part, García
Madero recalls:

> I realized that I always wanted to leave. I got in and before I could close the door Ulises
> stepped on the gas. I heard a shot or something that sounded like a shot. . . . I turned
> around and through the back window I saw a shadow in the middle of the street. All the
> sadness of the world was concentrated in that shadow, framed by the strict rectangle of
> the Impala's window.

The second part of *The Savage Detectives* abruptly leaves Belano, Lima, García
Madero, and Lupe driving north and turns to a series of first-person narratives of varying lengths, dated between 1976 and 1996. In all, there are over fifty narrators, including Belano's former lover, a mental patient, the "mother of Mexican poetry," fellow
visceral realist poets, a Mexican Jew, enemies, friends, intellectuals, and a variety
of other voices. In each case, the narrator speaks to some unknown interviewer about
his or her memory of Arturo Belano or Ulises Lima. Many of the same events are
recounted from a variety of perspectives; in other cases, a narrator speaks of his or her
relationship with Belano or Lima. What emerges from this collage of voices is a portrait of Belano, of Lima, and of the times.

With over fifty narrators, many of whom narrate more than one small section, it at
first seems difficult to keep track of the wide range of voices. However, once a reader
envisions himself or herself as a detective, a worker whose job is to piece together the
testimonies of a wildly divergent group of witnesses, the novel becomes irresistible.
Each new voice adds a new layer to what the reader understands about Belano and
Lima and about what must have happened to them in their drive north. Indeed, the
entire middle section of the book is a series of clues of what has happened to the
young characters who seemed so full of life (and so full of themselves) in the earlier
pages. The clues also point the reader to how the novel should be read. As narrator
Iñaki Echevarne says in a section dated 1994, "Everything that begins as a comedy
ends as tragedy." Or as narrator Felipe Müller says later, "Everything that begins as a
comedy ends as a comic monologue, but we aren't laughing anymore."

One of the most memorable voices is Auxilio Lacouture, an Uruguayan poet who
calls herself the "mother of Mexican poetry." This narrative provides a glimpse into
the university scene of the 1960's and her own role in the rebellions. She also indirectly warns readers about accepting any of the stories found in the book; her story
of remaining in the bathroom for fifteen days during the uprising has been co-opted
by other storytellers: "The legend spread on the winds of Mexico City and the winds
of '68, fusing with the stories of the dead and the survivors and now everybody knows
that a woman stayed at the university when its freedom was violated in that beautiful,
tragic year."

Another important narration is that of Ernesto García Grajales, in the penultimate scene of the middle section. He tells the reader, "In all humbleness, sir, I can say that I'm the only expert on the visceral realists in Mexico, and if pressed, the world. God willing, I plan to publish a book about them." Like the final moments of a movie that tell what happens to each of the characters in the years after the events of the movie, this small narration brings together all the characters of *The Savage Detectives*, telling who died, who lived, who still writes. Much of the information, however, contradicts what the rest of the book has asserted, even to the point of denying that García Madero was the name of the seventeen-year-old whose diary bookends the multivocal middle. The lesson here might be that it is the critics who always have the last word; or, just as likely, the vignette might be a cautionary tale about believing any narrator at all.

The third section of the book, called "The Sonora Desert," begins on page 527, nearly at the close of the novel. Suddenly, García Madero is back writing his diary, and readers are returned to January 1, 1976, chronologically just two months after the first page of the book. The four young characters are in Sonora, looking for Cesárea Tinajero and avoiding Alberto the pimp, who follows them with murderous rage.

While it has only been a short time since the quartet left Mexico City, it is clear that they are fraying. Living in the Impala half the time, driving from village to village, and always looking for the absent Cesárea takes its toll on the visceral realists. Their lives have now fully merged with the stories of their lives. The narrations that make up the middle section of the book, all of which occur chronologically after the ending section, now engender a sort of double vision in the reader, who now knows more than the characters themselves about their future. The picture of Belano and Lima as lost souls, endlessly traveling throughout the world, without ever finding peace or rest, now haunts the final section. In Sonora, the group finally finds Cesárea, and Alberto finds them. It is the consequence of these meetings that propels Belano and Lima into the future that the reader already knows awaits them.

*The Savage Detectives* is a masterful novel, a study on the nature of truth and storytelling. The language and the format work seamlessly in a work that is a strange combination of both amnesia and nostalgia. At once funny, satiric, sad, filled with hope, and filled with failure, *The Savage Detectives* captures the postmodern quest, a varied and endless attempt to piece together truth from shards of text.

*Diane Andrews Henningfeld*

## Review Sources

*Booklist* 103, nos. 9/10 (January 1-15, 2007): 47.
*Globe and Mail*, June 9, 2007, p. D10.
*Harper's Magazine* 314 (April, 2007): 99-106.
*Los Angeles Times*, April 8, 2007, p. R5.

*The New Republic* 236, no. 15 (May 7, 2007): 53-55.
*The New York Times* 156 (April 12, 2007): E6.
*The New York Times Book Review* 156 (April 15, 2007): 1-11.
*Pittsburgh Post-Gazette*, June 17, 2007, p. H5.
*Publishers Weekly* 253, no. 49 (December 11, 2007): 42.
*The Washington Post*, April 8, 2007, p. D1.

# SECOND DIASPORIST MANIFESTO
## (A New Kind of Long Poem in 615 Free Verses)

*Author:* R. B. Kitaj (1932-2007)
*Publisher:* Yale University Press (New Haven, Conn.).
   Illustrated. 160 pp. $26.00
*Type of work:* Essays
*Locale:* Los Angeles

*A famous modern figurative painter shares his strongly
felt impressions on the correspondences between literature
and art*

   R. B. Kitaj, who died in 2007 in Los Angeles, is one of
the most important American painters of the last half of the
twentieth century. Less well known in the United States
than in Britain, Kitaj was born in Cleveland, Ohio. After
studying at Cooper Union in New York City, where his earliest work resembled that
of abstract expressionists like Willem de Kooning, he enlisted in the U.S. Army. This
took him to Europe, where he remained after his army service; he continued his studies under the G.I. Bill in London, which became his home for the next thirty years.
He befriended the painters David Hockney, Frank Auerbach, and Lucien Freud, who
together with Kitaj constituted the London School, a sobriquet given to the group by
Kitaj himself in 1976. Their art gradually posed a formidable challenge to the
abstractionism that dominated modern art. Kitaj's brightly colored figurative paintings impressed critics and the public with his formidable drawing. With unusual
economy he could express a great range of emotions. A superb draftsman, his linear
control invited comparison with European masters like Giotto and Pablo Picasso. He
won many awards and honors, including appointment to the Royal Academy. He is
the only American painter, other than the famous James McNeill Whistler (1834-
1903), to receive that distinction, and "one of only a handful of American painters . . .
given a retrospective at the Metropolitan Museum of Art during his own lifetime."
   It is necessary to know at least the above about this artist in order to overcome
an initial skepticism and bemusement when confronted with the book under review,
his *Second Diasporist Manifesto (A New Kind of Long Poem in 615 Free Verses)*.
This volume follows the *First Diasporist Manifesto*, published in 1989. These
"manifestos" are fragmented, rhapsodic, repetitive, and, at first glance, superficially
intellectual. They allude to countless writers, thinkers, and artists of the modern age
but rarely rise above a curious nominalism. A thinker is merely cited, sometimes
quoted, and the quotation is often followed by a personal comment—whimsical, unpretentious, but rarely inductive or analytical. There is the suggestion of some kind of
dialectic, but it never rises to the surface.
   Almost any page taken at random in the *Second Diasporist Manifesto* will yield
passages like the following:

218 "I myself am a part of Nature." —*Einstein*
I myself am a part of Nature and it is in my Nature to paint Jewish pictures.
219 "My views are near to those of Spinoza." —*Einstein*
My views are near to those of Spinoza but closer still to Kafka, Einstein (essays) and
Cézanne plus Matisse and Munch, etc. And latterly, Mondrian, in a strange way (see
231).

As the reader comes under Kitaj's spell, the impression of aimlessness gives way
to a growing trust in the patterning of Kitaj's mind, the way he is trying to impose
order on the stream of his own thinking. The 615 entries seem to be journal or diary
notes that Kitaj has numbered. At times they seem sequential, but their principal connection is through cross-reference. That is where the numbers come in. There is
no pagination in this book. The reader must navigate by flipping back and forth and
following the numbers wherever they go. In the 1989 manifesto, the pages are numbered, and the entries are longer and resemble miniature essays. In this second manifesto, the entries are much shorter, often breathless, and the only reference points are
the numbers. One could argue that the painter Kitaj, as writer, is producing a kind of
verbal collage.

There are 613 *mitzvot* (commandments) to which every observant Jew must comply. To his own 613 observations, Kitaj adds two to give his manifesto the added clout
it needs to live up to the code of religious laws it imitates. One has to remember that
Jewish prohibition against "graven images" that represent the deity has tended to mitigate the importance of figurative art in Jewish culture. This is what makes Kitaj's
numbered entries "free verses." Their purpose is to vindicate Diasporism as an intrinsic artistic program necessary to ensure Jewish survival in the post-Holocaust world:

614 Rabbi Emil Fackenheim declared a famous 614th commandment: "The authentic
Jew of today is forbidden to hand Hitler yet another, posthumous victory." So be it!
Now, paint that!
615 As I make to die, here's my 615th: EASEL-PAINTINGS ARE NOT IDOLS, so,
JEWISH ART IS OK to do without consulting your Rabbi, so do it! It's good and uni-
versal!

What does Kitaj mean by "Diasporism"? In the manifesto of 1989, Kitaj proudly
announced that he had "Jew on the brain," a phrase he took from his friend, the celebrated novelist Philip Roth, who coined the phrase in *The Counterlife* (1986). Obsessed with the survival under stress that characterized the Jewish people ever since
their dispersion two thousand years ago, Kitaj became persuaded that the Diasporist
trauma at the core of his own ethnicity was a reliable metaphor or trope for the
"groundlessness" at the heart of much of modern art as a whole.

"You don't have to be a Jew to be a Diasporist," insisted Kitaj. Any artist caught
up in the "dramas of incertitude" that resonated throughout the modern world could
identify with his Diasporist credo. However, unlike earlier alienated generations of
modern writers and artists like W. H. Auden and T. S. Eliot, who felt themselves cut
off from traditional religious faith and who, in Eliot's case, reviled the marginal or
culturally alien person, Kitaj finds comrades-in-arms in all those exiled, reviled,

or persecuted: "The Diasporist (Jew, Arab, Homosexual, Gypsy, Asian, émigré from despotism, bad luck, etc.) is widely despised, disliked, mistrusted, sometimes tolerated, even taken up here and there and shown a nice life."

In the *Second Diasporist Manifesto*, Kitaj is no less inclusive. It is not only the socially or racially persecuted artist with whom he identifies but also great painters like Paul Cézanne and Henri Matisse, who were so innovative and boldly creative that they found themselves at the edges of convention without being victims of social or political hatred.

*R. B. Kitaj devoted himself to establishing the principles for a distinctively Jewish "easel painting" in the modern world. Elected to the American Academy of Arts and Letters and the Royal Academy, and awarded a Chevalier in the Order of Arts and Letters (Paris) and the Grand Prize for Painting (Gold Lion) at the Venice Biennale, he was also the target of vindictive critics in London.*

Similarly, the Jewish dimension in Kitaj's conception of Diasporist thinking takes on an increasingly theological and mystical character.

Partially because they were forced to the edges of the world by religious and racial persecution, the Jews evolved toward moments of intense visionary exploration. Kitaj alludes frequently to the writings of the great modern Jewish scholar of the Kabbala, Gershom Scholem, who made important connections between Jewish mysticism in the sixteenth and seventeenth centuries and the growth of a new spiritualized inwardness in Jewish belief.

It is here that Kitaj seems to break new ground in his own Diasporist vision. Cut off from traditional Talmudic study because of his sectarian upbringing and lack of Hebrew, Kitaj makes a daring leap and connects his talents as a figurative artist and painter, talents to which traditional Judaism pays little heed, to the visionary ideas of the Kabbala, ideas that to this day are still frowned on by many Jewish seminarians. A series of personal trials brought Kitaj to the point where the "diasporism" of his art took a sharp turn from solidarity with his Jewish identity and the marginality of the alienated artist to an existential embrace of what he called the "tragi-comic Jewish extreme":

> 28 DEVEKUT! This highest idea of the mystical life, this Communion with God, seems within my reach—the reach of a Jewish Art no less! . . . Devekut, essentially a private, ascetic communion in denial of the values of this world . . . is a value of contemplative, not of active, social life, says Scholem. I have been slowly withdrawing from the social world for many years anyway.

In 1994, the Tate Gallery in London mounted a Kitaj retrospective. The reviewers brutally attacked not only the paintings but also the literary texts that accompanied them. He was called a fake, a "Wandering Jew," whose art and ideas were foreign to British feeling and taste. Kitaj was not alone in thinking that the reviewers were driven by a combination of xenophobia and anti-Semitism.

Shortly after, his beloved wife, the artist Sandra Fisher, died at age forty-seven of a brain aneurysm. Convinced that the critics had caused her death, Kitaj decided to leave England and return to America, but before leaving he exhibited a painting at a summer exhibit of the Royal Academy in 1997 that took revenge on the critics he believed had killed his wife. The painting done in a lurid red shows Kitaj and Édouard Manet (the great French artist, also viciously attacked by critics) shooting an ugly monster who represents the art critic. This brilliant and hysterical painting was accompanied by a somewhat incoherent inscription: "The killer-critic assassinated by his widower, even."

Kitaj came to believe that his Sandra was Shekhina, the female aspect of God according to Kabbalistic teaching. After settling in Los Angeles with his son, Kitaj lived in semiseclusion but returned to his painting, relying on the memory of his wife for both spiritual sustenance and artistic inspiration:

> 28 . . . Sandra is therefore not only made in the image of God, but as Shekhina, she's the aspect of what is called God, to which I cleave (DEVEKUT) in painting her. (See 104.)
>
> 104 Trying to follow: Tract on Ecstasy by DOV BAER OF LUBAVITCH (1773-1827), contemporary of Goya. This Hasidic text is a rare understanding of mystical rapture and ecstasy says Scholem, who assigns an even higher stage than that to our old friend DEVEKUT (cleaving to God). I cleave to Sandra (as God) when I can if painting her sparks an ecstasy.

David Hockney, Kitaj's friend from their early days as art students in London, also settled in Los Angeles long before Kitaj's return to America. They remained close, and in the *Second Diasporist Manifesto* Kitaj recalls what Hockney, who is certainly one of the great artists of the later twentieth century, said to him at a crucial hour:

> 166 HOCKNEY TO KITAJ (in a letter during my Tate War): "How right you are to see wider perspectives in the spiritual history of your ancestors. One forgets that at one's peril."

Had Kitaj not made that commitment to his cultural and religious legacy, he would have been destroyed completely by the wrenching loss of his deeply beloved wife. One cannot help but reflect on great poets and painters of the past who turned to their heritage in order to sublimate a lost or unattained love. Dante and his Beatrice come to mind. William Blake, the great English painter and poet, like Kitaj also brought together painting and writing in a combined art form. Blake's many "emanations" are not substitutes for a lost love but rather are approximations of idealized visions for emotions and feelings that arose from his connubial life.

Finally, Kitaj's struggle in his manifestos to bring about a synthesis of what he read and thought with what he found himself wanting to paint proves that no matter how intuitive or spontaneous the creative act may be, it is no less imaginative for funneling its impulses through the ideas and thoughts of artists in all forms.

In entry 177, he notes the following: "The Talmud says that every passage in the Torah has 49 gates of purity and impurity. That saying is embedded among 49 stories of my life-in-art." The 49 gates include cities like London, Paris, New York, and Los Angeles. There are broad categories like Painting, Drawing, Books, and Study.

There are whimsical rubrics like Kids, Jews, Sex, Death, and Enemies. The bulk of the list consists of names of artists and writers, including Franz Kafka, Cézanne, Matisse, Giotto, Rembrandt, Edvard Munch, Piet Mondrian, Vincent van Gogh, Scholem, and Edgar Degas.

Readers of the *Second Diasporist Manifesto* are treated to some fifty illustrations of Kitaj's paintings. These include portraits of Aharon Appelfeld, the prominent Israeli writer, Gertrude Stein nude, Peter Lorre, Kafka, and several haunting studies of his wife Sandra. There are self-portraits and a famous study of a man sitting in a railway compartment titled simply, *The Jew*.

*Peter Brier*

# THE SECRET SERVANT

*Author:* Daniel Silva (1960-     )
*Publisher:* G. P. Putnam's Sons (New York)
    385 pp. $25.95
*Type of work:* Novel
*Time:* The early twenty-first century
*Locale:* Amsterdam; Israel; England; France; Germany;
    Cyprus; Cairo; Zurich; Copenhagen; Colorado;
    Langley, Virginia; Washington, D.C.

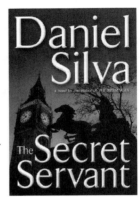

*Israeli spy Gabriel Allon tries to rescue the daughter of
the American ambassador to the United Kingdom after she
is kidnapped by terrorists*

Principal characters:
    GABRIEL ALLON, an art restorer and Israeli intelligence agent
    UZI NAVOT, an Israeli spy
    ARI SHAMRON, an Israeli spy
    IBRAHIM FAWAZ, an Egyptian exile in Amsterdam
    ISHAQ FAWAZ, his son
    ROBERT CARLYLE HALTON, American ambassador
        to the United Kingdom
    DR. ELIZABETH HALTON, his daughter, a physician
    SOLOMON ROSNER, a sociology professor at the University
        of Amsterdam
    SAMIR AL-MASRI, an Egyptian terrorist in Amsterdam
    DR. YUSUF RAMADAN, a history professor at the American
        University in Cairo
    SHEIKH ABDULLAH ABDUL-RAZZAQ, an Islamic fundamentalist
        held by the Americans
    SHEIKH TAYYIB ABDUL-RAZZAQ, his brother
    CHIARA ZOLLI, an Israeli spy and Allon's fiancé
    SARAH BANCROFT, a CIA agent trained by Allon

After many years as a journalist, Daniel Silva launched his highly successful career as an espionage novelist with *The Unlikely Spy* (1997), a World War II thriller. Beginning with *The Kill Artist* (2000), Silva has created one of the most popular spy series ever. After three novels focusing on the legacy of the Holocaust, the Gabriel Allon books have shifted their concern to international terrorism.

In *The Messenger* (2006), the middle-aged art restorer turned reluctant spy and assassin tackled a billionaire Saudi suspected of financing al-Qaeda. With *The Secret Servant*, Allon, "the legendary but wayward son of Israeli intelligence," has to deal not only with terrorism but also with increasing pressure to take charge of Israeli intelligence. Allon does not want to be the boss, seeing his true calling as a restorer of paintings by Italian old masters, and longs to retire to Italy. Israeli intelligence

considers art restoration a good cover, not an
occupation for a serious man.

Silva uses Allon's other calling as more
than a plot device. While art restoration figures less in *The Secret Servant* than in any of
the previous books, it is constantly lurking in
the background, an indication of the spy's divided nature. By extension Silva uses Allon's
cover to suggest something universal about
people's impulses both to the contemplative
life and a more chaotic one, the thin line between being a destroyer or a protector.

The events of *The Secret Servant* are set in
motion by Solomon Rosner, a sociologist
who operates the Center for European Security Studies at the University of Amsterdam
and produces reports on the rise of militant Islam within the Netherlands' borders. Professor Rosner, whose grandparents were sent to
Auschwitz, has warned in his latest book of

∽

*After graduating from San Francisco
State University, Daniel Silva was a
reporter for United Press International
from 1984 to 1988. He was then an
executive producer of* Crossfire *and
several other programs at CNN until he
left in 1997 to concentrate on writing.*
The Secret Servant *is his tenth thriller.*

∽

the efforts to turn the country into a Muslim-dominated state, a view widely attacked
by the Dutch press. Though Silva was once a journalist and his wife, Jamie Gangel, is
a National Broadcasting Company (NBC) reporter, he presents the news media negatively several times in *The Secret Servant*. Of an NBC reporter, someone tells the president of the United States, "I'm not sure she has a pulse, let alone a sense of patriotism."

Rosner is murdered, in circumstances recalling the 2004 killing of Dutch filmmaker
Theo van Gogh, and Allon is summoned by Uzi Navot, chief of Israeli intelligence's
special operations unit, to Amsterdam to clean out the professor's files so that no
link with his secret employers can be found. If Rosner's activities are revealed,
Dutch Jews will be at great risk. Allon's task is all the more difficult because he has
been banned by European intelligence services for violent acts detailed in the previous novels.

In Amsterdam, Allon is approached by Ibrahim Fawaz, an Egyptian exile who supplied Rosner with information about Muslim activities. From Ibrahim, Allon learns
about Samir al-Masri, an Egyptian who has come to Amsterdam to foment violence.
Ibrahim's information sends Allon to London, "the epicenter of European Islamic
extremism." He alerts British authorities to a potential threat but is too late to prevent
Samir from kidnapping Dr. Elizabeth Halton, the physician daughter of American
ambassador Robert Carlyle Halton, during an attack killing three hundred people.

As the goddaughter of the president of the United States and a vocal supporter of
his war in Iraq, Dr. Halton is more than just another political hostage. If Sheikh
Abdullah Abdul-Razzaq, a fundamentalist political prisoner, is not released in a
week, she will be killed. This demand is merely a ploy, however, by Sheikh Tayyib
Abdul-Razzaq, the prisoner's brother, who wants to start a revolution in Egypt.

The rest of *The Secret Servant* involves the effort to find out who is behind the kidnapping and where Dr. Halton is being held, as Allon unravels the complex motivations of the group called the Sword of Allah and the part played by the mysterious figure known as the Sphinx. Because the Sphinx always seeks revenge against those who arrest or kill his men, Allon is at the top of his hit list. The human side of the dilemma becomes clearer when the situation pits Ibrahim against his son, Ishaq, and when Allon is torn over having to endanger the innocent to achieve his objective.

The Allon of *The Secret Servant* differs a bit from his previous incarnations. In the novel's first paragraph, Silva has him declare that Rosner is more valuable dead than alive, a comment others see as "uncharacteristically callous." The earlier Allon would also never say, "Where are they taking her, you motherfucker! Tell me before I blow your head off!" The darker, angrier Allon suggests Silva has grown more pessimistic about any effective means of dealing with terrorism. Allon explains why killing is the only recourse: "We have to kill the monsters before they kill us. . . . The killing has to take place in the shadows, where no one can see it. We have to hunt them down ruthlessly. We have to terrorize *them*."

Even more than in his previous novels, Silva sounds a warning about the increasing dangers posed by Islam. Silva explains the concept of *takfir*, which originated in Egypt in the 1970's and gives Muslims the right to kill anyone at any time as long as such acts advance their cause. According to *takfir*, democracy violates the laws of God; therefore, democracies and Muslims living in democracies are the enemies of Islam.

*The Secret Servant* opens with an epigraph from historian Bernard Lewis: "On present demographic trends, by the end of the twenty-first century at the latest, Europe will be Muslim." Silva concisely delineates how the United Kingdom has foolishly opened itself to terrorist threats by accommodating known extremists, assuming that they would limit their actions to other Arabs. He is hardly a keep-Europe-pure extremist, just a realist pointing out potential threats, nor is he saying that all Arabs are terrorists. The acts depicted in *The Secret Servant* are the unfortunate result of the excesses of the Hosnī Mubārak regime in Egypt.

The predicament painted by Silva is complicated. The young Muslims in the Netherlands suffer high unemployment and are angry about how they are treated. Then, religious leaders paid by Saudi Arabia stir up their hatred for the West. Silva's terrorists are not cardboard villains but thinking, feeling individuals caught up in a situation out of their control.

Ibrahim tells Allon that despite living in Holland for twenty-five years and becoming a citizen, he will always be an outsider. A professor in Egypt who came to Amsterdam seeking more opportunities for his son, Ibrahim has had to work as a laborer and has always been seen as a temporary resident. He eloquently explains the frustrations of such aliens and their families. Allon realizes that by being not quite Arab and not quite European, the children of immigrants are "lost in the land of strangers." "When we are wronged," explains Ibrahim, "we *must* seek revenge. It is in our culture, our bloodstream. Each time you kill or torture one of us, you are creating an extended family of enemies that is honor bound to take retribution." By striving for a balanced view of a complicated situation, Silva tries to raise his fiction above the level of the standard thriller.

Some reviewers, however, painted Silva's views of the terrorism threat as extreme. In the *Los Angeles Times Book Review*, Richard Schickel accused Silva of overstating the danger of Islamic terrorism to sell books and of presenting the Central Intelligence Agency (CIA) as a more efficient organization than press reports make it appear to be. Warren Bass, a member of the 9/11 Commission, attacked Silva in *The Washington Post* for having a humorless political agenda and making a crude simplification of the issues. Molly Nixon, in *The Jerusalem Post*, saw Silva's characters as mere mouthpieces for opinions more suitable to editorial pages. Too often Silva writes like a journalist rather than an artist, spelling out what needs only to be suggested.

*The Secret Servant* is full of insight into how intelligence services work. The United States appoints politicians and party functionaries, instead of intelligence professionals, as head of the CIA, and the Israelis traditionally give the job to a general. Yet while Ari Shamron, Allon's mentor, is not officially in charge, he actually runs the operation and is less directly influenced by political pressures. Silva also explains the *sayanim*, the bankers, doctors, hoteliers, and others around the world without whose assistance Israeli intelligence could not operate.

Silva explains how the methods of dealing with radicals differed among Egyptian presidents, how Anwar el-Sadat's leniency led to the spread of fundamentalism abroad, and how the torturing of political prisoners under Mubārak worsened the situation further. The terrorists see Mubārak as "an apostate thug . . . who grew rich while the Egyptian people slipped deeper into poverty and despair with each passing day." The Americans have the paradoxical dilemma of keeping Mubārak in power to prevent radicals from taking over Egypt, yet by doing so foster terrorism.

The novel's title comes from Navot's insistence that Allon is "a secret servant of the State of Israel, and you have no right to leave the fighting to others." Allon is deluding himself in thinking he can retire to Italy, because Europe will be the "next battleground." *The Secret Servant* has a darker, more pessimistic tone than previous Allon novels. The fight for Jewish survival has turned into a war without end against terrorism, involving not just Israel but the entire world.

*The Secret Servant* offers many detailed character studies. With just a few details, Silva is able to create complex, believable characters. The most vivid of these is Dr. Yusuf Ramadan, professor of Near Eastern history at the American University in Cairo and head of the Institute of Islamic Studies in Paris. A world-renowned intellectual and a frequent presence on French television, Ramadan succeeds as a villain because he is so adept at hiding his true motivations.

Silva is occasionally guilty of bad writing: "350 acres in size." Late in the novel, Silva gives a full identification of Ramadan as if he has not been mentioned before. Calling the main villain the Sphinx may also strike some as a bit hokey. Sarah Bancroft, a protagonist in *The Messenger*, is unnecessarily brought back as a CIA agent who does little. Having special operations plan Allon's wedding to Chiara Zolli, a fellow agent, creates a jarring shift in tone.

Some may complain that not enough is at stake in *The Secret Servant*, that the kidnapping of a single American, no matter how noble she may be, is not enough around which to build an intricate plot. Nevertheless, the Halton abduction is merely a device to explore larger issues. As a work of entertainment, *The Secret Servant* is much more of a procedural than its predecessors but is still well written, engrossing, and often fascinating.

*Michael Adams*

## Review Sources

*Booklist* 103, no. 18 (May 15, 2007): 5.
*The Jerusalem Post*, September 21, 2007, p. 29.
*Library Journal* 132, no. 9 (May 15, 2007): 84.
*Los Angeles Times*, July 29, 2007, p. R8.
*Publishers Weekly* 254, no. 21 (May 21, 2007): 32.
*The Washington Post*, August 20, 2007, p. C3.

# THE SHADOW CATCHER

*Author:* Marianne Wiggins (1947-    )
*Publisher:* Simon & Schuster (New York). Illustrated.
    323 pp. $25.00
*Type of work:* Novel
*Time:* 2007 and 1868-1952
*Locale:* Hollywood; Las Vegas; St. Paul, Minnesota;
    Seattle and the Puget Sound area of Washington; Ohio

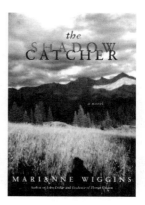

*This dual narrative twines the character Wiggins's trip
to investigate the illness of a man professing to be her father with the story of photographer Edward Curtis's life,
marriage, training, and work documenting Native Americans by taking their photos in tribal dress and settings in
the early twentieth century*

*Principal characters:*
    MARIANNE WIGGINS, a contemporary screenwriter working on the
        text for a biographical film based on a novel she has written about
        Edward Curtis's life and work; her father has been dead thirty years
        at novel's beginning
    CLARA, a young woman from Minnesota, orphaned and
        destitute after her parents' deaths, who marries Edward Curtis
    HERCULES, Clara's younger brother
    ELLEN CURTIS, wife of Johnson Curtis and Clara's mother's best friend,
        who takes Clara and Hercules in after their parents' demise
    EDWARD,
    RAPHAEL,
    ASAHEL, and
    EVA CURTIS, children of Ellen and Johnson
    HAROLD,
    FLORENCE,
    BETH, and
    KATHERINE CURTIS, children of Edward and Clara Curtis
    MR. LESTER SHADOW, a Navajo who delivers Curtis Edwards
        to the hospital
    CURTIS EDWARDS, the true identity of the man who claimed
        to be John F. Wiggins, Marianne's father
    COLONEL CURTIS EDWARDS, JR., Air Force colonel, the son
        of Curtis Edwards

    By using her name as the name of *The Shadow Catcher*'s main character, Marianne
Wiggins immediately signals a unique approach to storytelling. Her strategy calls into
question a basic maxim for reading novels: Never assume the narrator's voice or the
main character in a novel can be equated with the author. She then goes on to write a

∾

*Marianne Wiggins is the author of
eight novels and two collections of
short stories. Her novel* John Dollar
*(1989) won the Janet Heidinger Kafka
Prize for the best novel written by an
American woman.* Evidence of Things
Unseen *(2003), a novel about
photography, the Tennessee Valley
Authority's creation, and the
development of the atomic bomb, was
nominated for a National Book Award
in 2003 and for a Pulitzer Prize in
2004.*

∾

book where the equation "writer equals character or narrator" makes no difference whatsoever.

The thin slice of character Wiggins's life the novel unveils does not make for much cross-referencing with the writer Wiggins's life, except as it shows the actual writer's interest in photography developing as a discipline and art form from the nineteenth century on. Her experience being married to Salman Rushdie and sharing years of his life in hiding when he was declared an enemy of Islam by Iranian religious leader Ayatollah Khomeini does not surface directly in the novel. The radical nature of the Islamic threat to their lives and their seclusion echo in the unexpected avalanche that orphans Clara and her brother Hercules, suddenly severing ties with all they know. It is a stretch to force similarities beyond an emphasis on loss, uses of memory, and an interest in photography; no easy correspondences between Wiggins and her character come to mind. Instead, the book braids the contemporary story of character Marianne Wiggins, novelist-screenwriter, with the fascinating life of Edward Curtis, photographer, entrepreneur, husband, and opportunist subject to wanderlust and infatuated with his own ambition.

The novel begins with a cleverly sardonic commentary on driving in Los Angeles. At a meeting with prospective producers, screenwriter Wiggins lays out Curtis's life, her fascination then disenchantment with him, and the unwinding of his marriage as he photographed Native Americans while employed by J. P. Morgan. She resists the fixation with Curtis as a wandering artist cowboy that the Hollywood producers want to create because it will not capture the truth of his life. It is too simple. The real story that captured her, she tells her agent, is that all four of Curtis's adult children are buried beside him despite his desertion of them for most of their childhoods. She wrote to discover what made them crave the closeness in death they never achieved in life. The author of *The Shadow Catcher* narrates the lives of Los Angeles writer Marianne Wiggins and photographer Edward Curtis, both complicated by mysterious disappearances.

Following the meeting, Wiggins receives a phone call informing her that her father is seriously ill in a Las Vegas hospital. The preposterous claim unsettles the writer, whose father had died some thirty years earlier. After contacting her sister to talk things over, she decides to investigate the situation. The reader knows she will be heading to Nevada in her car, the modern equivalent of Huck Finn's lighting out for the territory.

With the turn of a page the reader is in the Washington Territory with Clara and Hercules. The long chapter is not technically a flashback, because it is woven around Clara's memories of the Curtis family mingled with her family's life in St. Paul and descriptions of her present situation, being a charity case in the Curtis household. The reader learns about her loving home and casually elegant parents, whose indulgent and cultured approach to life introduced music, art, and people who loved them into their children's lives. The reader also learns that Clara attends a nursing academy, expecting to pursue a career.

On a Christmas shopping trip after a snowfall, her parents are tragically killed in an avalanche of snow that falls from a building while Clara and her brother are inside selecting a gift. Their disappearance alters life forever, and the siblings find that they are bankrupt. The only person Clara can imagine helping them is Ellen Curtis, her mother's longtime friend, a woman inept at managing her own affairs and whom Clara's parents had aided in the past. Still struggling with the shock, the sister and brother find themselves in a spartan island frontier camp where the Curtis family hangs onto existence through exhausting hard work and sheer nerve. Edward enters the novel as the wandering son of a now dead, wandering father. His mysterious comings and goings, accepted by his family, seem odd and unexplainable to Clara, who feels isolated from civilization and the prospect of finding a school for Hercules. Eventually the section becomes the story of how Edward Curtis and Clara discover their attraction for one another. Clara relishes love because she witnessed her parents' mutually nurturing marriage.

Clara offers Edward education and a wider lens on the world, and he offers her the chance for love. She discovers his passion for photography and capturing figures. They have a sexual relationship while he recuperates from an injury, and afterward he leaves abruptly. She knows then that he will always leave, that he will be a distant and demanding lover and companion. Before she can act on her resolve to leave to find work in Seattle, he returns and claims her. She takes the offer of love, giving in to the fatal vulnerability to Edward that will shape her life.

The first half of the book contains imagery and commentary about the shadows of life, the landscape, and the past as well as the West as a mythic landscape. From age twelve to age twenty, Edward Curtis wandered with and cared for his itinerant father. The burden of that lost youth and the resentment against authority affected his orientation toward meeting desires and facing responsibilities for life. It influenced his ambitions and relationships with the pressure of restlessness and the need to flee. Clara's need for vital stimulation and intelligent work drove her away from the farm where fundamental religion and rough work seemed a death sentence. Shaped by her past, she wants the humane and enlightened life she believes she can build with Edward.

The events of Clara and Edward's involvement segue into the contemporary writer's road trip to Las Vegas. Wiggins's plan for the book lends itself to layered treatment of the past and present. By using Curtis as a character who abandons his family and creates the illusion of Indian tribes photographed in their nineteenth century grandeur, the living Marianne Wiggins gives herself the perfect vehicle for linking her character's past with Curtis's and the nation's. The wandering writer passes magnificent landscapes as she muses over Edward Curtis's trajectory in place and life. Her thoughts about the Native Americans who once controlled the land the highway traverses lead to a collage-like interlude about American character, exploitation, and personal loneliness. The reader senses that the three have a deep connection that lies beneath the surface of current existence. As the Marianne Wiggins character lights out for the territory the reader learns about the childhood she left behind, the journeys her family made, and what they meant.

In her travel chapter, Marianne Wiggins experiences the wide open West in a rush. "When you stand there in a place as immense as our own continental west with not another creature in your sight for miles and miles and miles around, you realize you are standing in the jaws of your existence. That the journey you make through time— where you light out to—is the only meaning you can claim." She keeps recalling Curtis's journey through various parts of the West as she heads to Las Vegas. Thus, even when he and Clara are not part of the novel's action, they enliven Wiggins's thoughts about what it means to be a single soul, an American, a person in search of meaning and connection in the American West. This technique folds the past into the present. It reminds readers that history, personal and national, coalesce in the present moments of lives—sometimes as echoes of one another, sometimes with the past enriching the experience of a place with the deeper drama of what happened to other Americans there as the nation came into being.

The reader learns that the writer's father "lit out" on a regular basis, sometimes just for a few hours, and that it was essential to "how he thought and lived." On one of his trips he disappeared, and his family never knew where, how, or why. Wiggins's road trip to Las Vegas is a journey to someone who may unlock the deepest secret of her past.

Arriving in Las Vegas, she is confounded by discovering an African American man lying in an ICU ward. He had her father's name, driver's license, and some information about her family to substantiate his identity. The Navajo man who brought him to the hospital is aptly named Mr. Lester Shadow, making his appearance a convenient fit after the many musings about displacement of Native American tribes and history that readers have been privy to during the trip. His father, called Owns His Shadow, had died after a long life that included attending Carlisle Indian School and scouting sites for the photographer Edward Curtis. A handmade Navajo bracelet that Lester Shadow has brings the connection to light, and he and Marianne Wiggins determine to go to the sick man's residence the next day to try to contact a next of kin. While there, they find the patient's true identity, Curtis Edwards, stamped on the cover of an old Bible.

The final chapters of the book detail the disintegration of Clara's and Edward's marriage caused by his repeated absences and the flamboyant style that took him into the White House and the homes of men as powerful as J. P. Morgan. The tragedy of Clara's children deserting her when she divorced their always-absent but romantically charged father led to her suicide in a boat on Puget Sound after she heard of her brother's drowning in Colorado. Her children refused to believe she had the nerve to do this, but they did not know of her plans to join her brother or the shock his accidental death gave Clara.

Marianne Wiggins and Lester Shadow uncover the truth of her father's disappearance; Curtis Edwards had come upon the hanging body of Wiggins's father in

Shenandoah National Park. Being an African American reporting a white man's death in the 1950's, he did what he thought safest—stole his identity, reported the death, and eventually left his family to start a new life out West.

The novel triangulates loss via three missing fathers. Wiggins, the living writer, also weaves together the fate of Native Americans at the hands of the government, the pressure of racial intolerance, and the randomness of tragedy that can catapult lives like Clara's and Hercules', or anyone's, into a crisis that starts a chain of events from which they cannot recover despite intelligence and determined effort.

As the character, Marianne Wiggins burns Lester Shadow's medicine leaves as she tells readers: "I watch the smoke braid into the tree [above Edward Curtis's and his children's graves], . . . and I think about . . . the way one life touches another, our lives and all the lives of others a long continuous thread—a train—of independent yet contiguous actions." Thus, the book ends on a note that gathers reader, writer, and characters into the flow of ideas and beauty that create life and the possibility of meaning. By placing herself in the novel as a character, Marianne Wiggins erases the distance between artist, subject, and beholder. She fabricates the past to behold, performing with language the trick Edward Curtis did with photos.

*Karen L. Arnold*

## Review Sources

*Booklist* 103, no. 17 (May 1, 2007): 75.
*Kirkus Reviews* 75, no. 8 (April 15, 2007): 363.
*Library Journal* 132, no. 8 (May 1, 2007): 77.
*The New York Times Book Review* 156 (July 1, 2007): 11.
*Publishers Weekly* 254, no. 16 (April 16, 2007): 29.
*The Washington Post*, June 3, 2007, p. BW05.

# SHADOW OF THE SILK ROAD

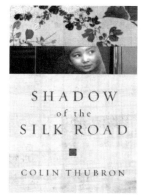

*Author:* Colin Thubron (1939-    )
*First published:* 2006, in Great Britain
*Publisher:* HarperCollins (New York). 363 pp. $25.95
*Type of work:* Travel
*Time:* The 2000's
*Locale:* China, Central Asia, Afghanistan, Iran, and
    Kurdish Turkey

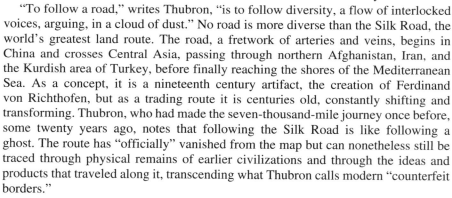

*Thubron describes an eight-month journey along the fabled Silk Road, from China to Antioch in Turkey*

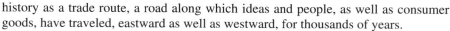

Modern Central Asia is a continent in political upheaval. In *Shadow of the Silk Road*, Colin Thubron sets this in the context of the Silk Road's ancient and tumultuous history as a trade route, a road along which ideas and people, as well as consumer goods, have traveled, eastward as well as westward, for thousands of years.

"To follow a road," writes Thubron, "is to follow diversity, a flow of interlocked voices, arguing, in a cloud of dust." No road is more diverse than the Silk Road, the world's greatest land route. The road, a fretwork of arteries and veins, begins in China and crosses Central Asia, passing through northern Afghanistan, Iran, and the Kurdish area of Turkey, before finally reaching the shores of the Mediterranean Sea. As a concept, it is a nineteenth century artifact, the creation of Ferdinand von Richthofen, but as a trading route it is centuries old, constantly shifting and transforming. Thubron, who had made the seven-thousand-mile journey once before, some twenty years ago, notes that following the Silk Road is like following a ghost. The route has "officially" vanished from the map but can nonetheless still be traced through physical remains of earlier civilizations and through the ideas and products that traveled along it, transcending what Thubron calls modern "counterfeit borders."

The effect of these counterfeit borders preoccupy Thubron throughout his journey, not only in practical terms of having to deal with border officials, who very often do not understand the visas and permissions he is showing them, but also because of how they shape the lives of the people he meets. Borders have placed artificial constraints upon them, turning land into nations and states, often in ways that do not reflect their lived experience. Standing in Xian in China's Shaanxi province, where the Silk Road is said to begin (or end), Thubron reflects on the movement of peoples and ideas up and down the length of its route, and how they have shaped world civilization.

Thubron is struck by the pace of change since he last visited this area of China. There are parts of the cities he no longer recognizes, and he comments on the way in which they seem to have embraced the "unmediated West" in terms of architectural style and consumer demands. Visiting friends, he is struck by how eager they are, how necessary it has become, to "forget" Mao Zedong's Cultural Revolution. Those who remember it forget to protect themselves from its memories, while the young have no point of reference with which to remember it. Thubron visits old friends who welcome the transformation, but with caution, and encounters many people who remain scarred by their experiences.

This sense of needing to forget seems to haunt Thubron as he sets out on his journey. Aware of how history is being reconstructed around him, providing a seamless narrative of Chinese supremacy, Thubron seems to be determined to dig as deep as he can into the ancient history of the Silk Road, showing how, before the borders became hardened, before the Yellow Emperor defined the nature of Chinese civilization, the area the maps now call China was a shifting landscape of peoples and allegiances.

*Colin Thubron's travel books include* Among the Russians *(1983),* Behind the Wall: A Journey Through China *(1987),* The Lost Heart of Asia *(1994), and* In Siberia *(1999). He has won the Hawthornden Prize and the Thomas Cook Travel Book Award. His novels include* A Cruel Madness *(1984), winner of the PEN/Macmillan Silver Pen Award;* Falling *(1989);* Turning Back the Sun *(1991); and* Distance *(1996). His most recent novel is* To the Last City *(2002).*

While the Silk Road was once the route by which silk, paper, printing, and gunpowder made their way west into Europe, now it is a route along which the deadly SARS virus, which breaks out in Central Asia during Thubron's journey, is equally capable of traveling. During the first part of his journey, Thubron is constantly beset by officials solicitous of his health; he is detained in a quarantine hospital for several days before being released and allowed to go on his way. It is an early indication of the official belief in the power of boundaries and how fragile that reliance actually is.

As Thubron shows, the Silk Road was always a counter to boundaries. As easily as trade goods made their way westward, so did ideas and peoples from the west make their way eastward. Thubron traces the remains of a small group of Nestorian Christians who settled in Shaanxi province in 781 and remained there for sixty years. Centuries later, European missionaries found people who still made the sign of the cross over their food, without knowing why. Later, he examines a story about the descendants of Roman soldiers, imprisoned by the Huns and made into mercenaries, who settled in a Chinese village; he meets people who are taller than is usual and who have reddish hair. It is, Thubron acknowledges, a good story, but the Silk Road has generated centuries of "genetic confusion," and these mysterious people could be descended from any number of other races. Buddhism traveled from India into China, and Muslim travelers brought their beliefs with them.

As Thubron finds, the modern Chinese authorities are deeply uncomfortable with the idea that their ancestors may have come from the west. The mummified bodies of the Tocharian people, buried in the Taklamakan Desert, provide only one more example of a truth the Chinese try to avoid. Despite the fact that their own stories of national foundation are as much a myth as anything else that Thubron encounters on the way, they cling firmly to the belief that the Yellow Emperor founded Chinese civilization and that there was nothing before. Even now they seem to be as intent on stamping their own identity on the region, no matter what the cost might be to others. As Thubron travels eastward, he meets many groups who are struggling to maintain their own identity in the face of Chinese influence, their predicament summed up by a Uighur man who has taken Kazakh nationality, feeling his own country is occupied, and a young Tibetan Buddhist monk whose brother has already fled to India, where he also wants to go.

As Thubron leaves China and crosses into Kyrgyzstan, there is a sense that he is moving into a place where borders mean less than they did just a few miles down the road. Thubron has already wondered whether the Great Wall of China was really intended to keep the Chinese people in rather than to repel invaders. Here he describes himself as being in a place where "the maps in people's minds dissolve," and yet politics intervenes once again. Kyrgyzstan, having rid itself of Soviet rulers, unexpectedly settled for a liberal democracy, only to find that its leader, struggling to deal with endemic corruption within the government and an ongoing failure to solve the country's crippling poverty, transformed himself into a dictator, allying himself with the region's great mythological story cycle, of the hero, Manas, in order to justify his actions.

As he travels westward, it might seem that Thubron moves away from myth and into history as he moves into regions that have shrugged off Soviet rule and reverted to older ways of defining themselves. Here people are grouped by tribal membership and by religious belief as much as they are governed by national boundaries. The influence of Islam, noticeable even at the Chinese borders, becomes ever stronger, and the story of Tamerlane is as potent today as it ever was. Thubron meets people who identify with this fourteenth century Turkic hero as strongly as if he had died only yesterday. His supposed burial site is still a place of pilgrimage.

As always, Thubron is on the lookout for the odd, the unusual, the sites off the beaten track, but there is a sense that as he travels west, the Silk Route is becoming more crowded, the ancient being overwhelmed by the modern. He has to search harder for the traces of long-forgotten travelers, but now and then he finds them. In a remote valley, a hundred miles from Tehran, where a group of builders is working on a new hospital in what was once the heartland of the Assassins, Thubron comes across evidence of the Mongols, led by the grandson of Genghis Khan, who wiped out the followers of Rukn-ad-din, the last of the Assassins' Grand Masters. Scrambling up the cliff face, he finds himself in caves whose ceilings are blackened by Mongol fires. Alas, without a torch, Thubron can explore no further.

As Thubron continues his journey toward the Mediterranean, modern history begins to come to the fore once again. In Afghanistan, he talks with survivors of the Taliban's rule, and as he moves west toward Iran, the Iraq War comes into sharper focus. In Tabriz, he meets female students at an English-language college. They talk frankly about their experience of living in post-Khomeini Iran. They are angry with the situation, hungry for change, and unafraid to express their views to Thubron, while doubtful that they could expect change for the better. This contrasts sharply with Thubron's experience earlier in his journey, at the eastern end of the Silk Road, where old friends felt their lives had, for the most part, improved in some measure.

Even the unsettled and discontented people on China's borders felt that they could eventually change their lives.

Thubron finally makes his way to Turkey and to Antioch, the end of the Silk Road. Antioch is an intruder, he suggests, "a Hellenistic island in a Semitic sea," a latecomer in the East, but dazzled by the silks from China, which passed through it on their way to Rome. Here, at the end of his journey, Thubron reflects on the ways in which borders have become muddled, in his notes and in his memories, but also on the ground. Official boundaries rarely reflect the true natures of the peoples they supposedly enclose, and Thubron imagines "different, ghostly maps laid over the political ones: maps of fractured races and identities." His conversations with the people he has met have shown that their allegiances often lie in unexpected places, in the past as well as in the present. No matter what the official boundaries may say, for Thubron it is clear that the Silk Route continues to exert its mysterious influence on the regions through which it passes.

*Maureen Kincaid Speller*

**Review Sources**

*America* 197, no. 12 (October 22, 2007): 25-27.
*The Economist* 380 (September 30, 2006): 93.
*Kirkus Reviews* 75, no. 10 (May 15, 2007): 492.
*New Statesman* 135 (September 25, 2006): 78-79.
*The New York Review of Books* 54, no. 20 (December 20, 2007): 18-24.
*The New York Times Book Review* 156 (July 15, 2007): 1-10.
*The Times Literary Supplement*, November 17, 2006, p. 9.

# SHORTCOMINGS

*Author:* Adrian Tomine (1974-    )
*Publisher:* Drawn & Quarterly (Montreal). Illustrated.
    108 pp. $19.95
*Type of work:* Novel
*Time:* The early twenty-first century
*Locale:* San Francisco Bay Area and New York City

*In his first full-length graphic novel, the prolific Tomine combines gritty realism and subtle humor to create a memorable, sometimes painful exploration of Asian American identity*

Principal characters:

> BEN TANAKA, a thirty-year-old manager of a movie theater
> MIKO HAYASHI, his thirty-one-year-old live-in girlfriend, a film student
> ALICE KIM, a twenty-nine-year-old graduate student at Mills College, Ben's best friend
> AUTUMN PHELPS, a twenty-two-year-old performance artist and clerk at Ben's theater
> SASHA LENZ, a twenty-eight-year-old graduate student at Mills College
> MEREDITH LEE, a thirty-two-year-old professor at New York University

Long regarded as the illegitimate offspring of literary fiction, the comic-book story and graphic novel have come into their own during the last generation. Gifted illustrators like Robert Crumb and Art Spiegelman have provided visual counterparts to stories of their own and of writers like Harvey Pekar (*American Splendor*, 1986) and Paul Auster (*City of Glass*, 1985). Although there has been great interest in fantasy fiction like the Sandman stories of Neil Gaiman, published in ten separate volumes after having appeared in seventy-five comic-book numbers, much of the best fiction has approached the dirty realism of serious fiction writers like Raymond Carver and Richard Ford.

Meanwhile, thanks in part to the success of Japanese animated cartoons, known as Japanimation, or anime, American readers have eagerly bought up translated books of Japanese cartoons, or manga. The edgy illustrated stories of Yoshihiro Tatsumi have found cult following among young cartoonists like Adrian Tomine, who has introduced translations of two collections and has hand-lettered the English text. Tatsumi coined the term *gekiga* (literally "dramatic pictures") for the realistic cartooning that he pioneered in the 1960's. In some ways, it seems preferable to "graphic novel," a term coined in the late 1970's for the illustrated fiction of Will Eisner and scorned by many actual practitioners for its connotations of "graphic sexuality" or "graphic violence."

Tomine gained recognition in the 1990's with a series of the semiautobiographical tales that he first self-published at the age of sixteen and then produced for the Tower Records story magazine *Pulse*. By the time he was a college student, at the University of California, Berkeley, his *Optic Nerve* comic books were being published by Drawn & Quarterly, a leading firm in the new genre. Before he turned thirty, in 2004, his stories from these comics were being reissued in book form. Tomine has told interviewers at *New York* and other publications that early acclaim as an artist of great promise made him feel pressure to fulfill the promise. With the release of *Shortcomings*, it should be clear

*A fourth-generation Japanese American, Adrian Tomine self-published his* Optic Nerve *comics at the age of sixteen. At twenty, he was hired to produce them as a regular series for* Drawn & Quarterly. *Early stories have appeared in* Thirty-two Stories: The Complete Optic Nerve Mini-Comics *(1998), more recent ones as* Summer Blonde *(2002), and still others in* Scrapbook: Uncollected Work, 1990-2004 *(2004). He is a regular contributor to* The New Yorker.

that he has done that but has also taken on new challenges as he has moved into the longer format.

A graphic novel in three chapters, *Shortcomings* tells the story of Ben Tanaka, a disaffected young man with a liberal arts education and a dead-end job managing an independent movie theater in Berkeley. Ben has a girlfriend, the active and attractive Miko Hayashi, with whom he shares an apartment. He has a single friend, the lesbian graduate student Alice Kim, whom he has known since their freshman year in college. He also has a large collection of DVDs, including a stash of lesbian porn videos. As he enters his thirties, he is overdue for some serious self-reflection.

At first glance, the book's opening could not be less promising—the tear-jerking finale of an immigrant story that pulls all the stops and uses all the clichés. The six panels on the first page look like scenes from a bad movie at an ethnic-identity festival, and that is exactly what they turn out to be. On the second page, the film ends to general applause but for one dissatisfied moviegoer. Ben complains to Miko that he wishes people would concentrate on telling a good story rather than making a statement about race. The remark seems insensitive under the circumstances, for she was one of the festival's chief organizers. It says something about Ben, who is ambivalent about their relationship. It also says something about the author-illustrator. Tomine wants to tell a good story first of all, and only then to say something about the issues that haunt his characters.

After two years together, Ben and Miko seem like an old married couple. They argue over little things. He would rather stay up and watch videos than follow her to bed. When she discovers his stash of porn videos, she is hurt—not because he is looking at other women, but because all the women are white and she is Asian. When she is offered an internship at an Asian film institute in New York City, she decides that they are ready for some time off from each other.

With Miko gone, Ben begins the serious self-reflection that he so badly needs. In conversations with the irrepressible Alice, usually at a restaurant, he obsesses on various stereotypes of race and gender. The book's title refers not only to the inadequacy of his own reasoning but also to fears that Asian men do not measure up sexually to their Caucasian counterparts. The book's cardbook cover, which Tomine designed, has a ruler running across the bottom edge and reaching from the back cover across the spine to the front.

Having failed with two blonds, the outrageous Autumn Phelps and the sexually ambivalent Sasha Lenz, Ben follows Alice to New York, hoping to rekindle his relationship with Miko. When he finds her in the company of a tall white male who is learning Japanese, he cracks. In a telling conversation with Alice and her new lover, Meredith Lee, he rants about his disgust at the sight of Asian women with white men. Asked how he feels about seeing Asian men with white women, he says, "Good for him! Good for both of them!" At this point, Meredith, a college professor of mixed ancestry, asks: "Is your attraction to white women a sublimated form of assimilation?" When she goes on to warn that it is risky "making moral generalizations based on your own wounded ego," he can only sigh.

The story ends with Ben literally up in the air, flying back to the San Francisco Bay Area, where he may or may not have a future. One expects a sequel, and indeed *The New York Times* has reported that Tomine's publisher signed a three-book deal with the British firm of Faber & Faber, of which this is the first. Tomine is to some extent a breakthrough artist; like Spiegelman before him, he is among the first comic-book artists to find a serious following among the literati. With its telling insights and clever dialogue—not all so highbrow as Meredith's—the book is a good starting point for story lovers who have never read a graphic novel. It will still find a ready audience with the genre's connoisseurs.

Over the last fifteen years, Tomine has developed a minimalist style of black-and-white illustration. It is often cinematic, but in the retrained fashion of Ingmar Bergman rather than the epic manner of George Lucas. Each page of this novel is a grid with six to nine frames, which give it the look of a photo album. There are no thought bubbles, no stage directions, no indications of time or place other than what appears in the drawings and in the characters' words, and relatively few sound effects. Tomine has set the characters in real places, including record stores and restaurants that will be familiar to readers in New York City and the San Francisco Bay Area. Juan's Place in Berkeley becomes Jose's Place, where Ben connects with Sasha; the Park Slope in Brooklyn becomes the Hunan Delight, where Meredith makes her telling observations about Ben. Whether drawing from memory or from real life, Tomine gives just enough detail in the illustration that the feeling is absolutely true to life. Similarly, small details in the face or gestures of a character suggest a wide range of action and emotion.

For Ben, the emotions range from sadness to anger, and the signs are apparent. Physically nondescript, he is usually seen with stooped shoulders and frown lines on his face and an apathetic manner. He looks as though he is trying to fit in with others, wearing contact lenses and reasonably fashionable clothes, but he gives every sign of insecurity. At five feet, eight inches, he stands on a level with his white dates, several inches above his Asian girlfriend, but several inches below her non-Asian friend

Leon, of whom he becomes irrationally jealous. In her two years of living with Ben, Miko has learned how to push all his buttons, and she admits that she sometimes does so just to get some sort of response. That response usually leads to fits of anger. She knows that he has bought the whole American Dream of the young and beautiful blond and that he has simply settled for her. She is right; the reader can see his eyes wander after a passing blond, but he takes even the slightest suggestion that he has an ideal "type" as a personal attack, often reducing the discussion to witty absurdities while resisting any possible change. It is in such scenes that the artwork proves especially helpful. It reduces the text to pure dialogue, providing all necessary descriptions and transitions. It also enhances the dialogue, suggesting what the speakers are feeling at any given point in the discussion. Without this context, the dialogue might sometimes sound like the transcript of a group therapy session, focusing on the "relentless negativity" that Miko correctly observes in Ben. With the illustrations, Ben's partial breakthrough, his occasional moments of self-awareness, seem far more poignant.

*Shortcomings* appeared to generally favorable reviews. In England, the *New Statesman* called it a book that asks to be read and reread, noting that Miko's early actions and expressions invite reinterpretation. The *Los Angeles Times* called it a playful treatment of race by a careful draftsman who has no axes to grind. *Entertainment Weekly* said it was as true to life as any work of prose fiction. *The New York Times Book Review* called Tomine's work "meticulously observed," with a "Philip Roth vibe." The main complaint about the story is that, far from overdramatizing his characters, Tomine has made them unpleasant, lacking friends for good reason. *The Chicago Sun-Times* wondered how anyone could have been attracted to Ben. A reviewer for *Paste* compared reading their story to watching a car crash for one hundred pages. Along similar lines, the reviewer for *Bust* remarked that Tomine's fiction loses some of its bite and sad charm when extended to the book length.

Tomine's fans—many of them Gen Xers who have grown up with him and his characters—will recognize the dilemmas that his viewpoint character gets himself into. Asian American readers may find even more, particularly in the very occasional scraps of Korean and Japanese dialogue. One need not be Asian, however, or male or thirtysomething to enjoy *Shortcomings*. Tomine's accomplishment is to tell a story that people will want to read and that also happens to concern topics of race, gender, and sexual orientation.

*Thomas Willard*

## Review Sources

*Booklist* 104, no. 3 (October 1, 2007): 43.
*Bust* 47 (October/November, 2007): 105-106.
*The Chicago Sun-Times*, October 21, 2007, p. B8.
*Entertainment Weekly*, no. 958 (October 12, 2007): 79.
*Kirkus Reviews* 75, no. 12 (June 15, 2007): 12.
*Los Angeles Times*, September 2, 2007, p. R5.
*New Statesman* 137 (September 10, 2007): 56-57.
*The New York Times Book Review* 157 (November 11, 2007): 7.
*Publishers Weekly* 254, no. 30 (July 30, 2007): 34-36.

# THE SLAVE SHIP
## A Human History

*Author:* Marcus Rediker (1951-    )
*Publisher:* Viking Press (New York). 434 pp. $27.95
*Type of work:* History
*Time:* 1700-1807
*Locale:* West Africa, Atlantic Ocean, various Caribbean
islands, England, and the United States

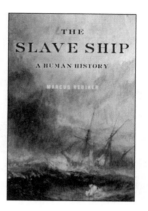

*A well-researched study that describes the physical
structure of slave ships that transported slaves from West
Africa to the New World during the eighteenth century*

*Principal personages:*
THOMAS CLARKSON, a British author who
wrote against the slave trade
EDWARD KIMBER, a captain of slave ships
who was infamous for his cruelty
JOHN NEWTON, a captain of slave ships who later became an opponent
of the slave trade and wrote the famous hymn "Amazing Grace"
WILLIAM WILBERFORCE, a member of the British parliament who
worked to abolish the slave trade in the British Empire

*The Slave Ship: A Human History* is a historical study of the incredible human suffering and terror experienced by slaves who were transported from West Africa to the New World on British slave ships between 1700 and 1807, the year that the British parliament approved the Act for the Abolition of the Slave Trade. Marcus Rediker, a professor of history at the University of Pittsburgh, undertook extensive archival research in British libraries and record offices, and he based this thorough study on original documents and on important but little-known eighteenth century books on the slave trade. The solidity of his research and his fifty-two pages of footnotes demonstrate clearly his scholarly expertise in this human tragedy that caused so much avoidable suffering in Africa, on numerous Caribbean islands, and in the United States. He wisely decided to limit his investigation to the British involvement in the slave trade over just one century. His choice of the eighteenth century also makes sense because it has been estimated that almost half of the total slaves transported from Africa to the New World endured this trip in the bottom of slave ships during that century. Had Rediker also chosen to examine participation in the slave trade by France, the Netherlands, Portugal, and Spain, this book would have been three or four times longer.

Rediker explains clearly that England relied greatly on the slave trade for its immense wealth and political influence in the eighteenth century. The infamous slave trade was part of the triangular trade. English merchants shipped finished goods from England for sale in West Africa or to be traded with African chiefs for slaves. Rediker

∼

*Marcus Rediker is a professor of history and head of the History Department at the University of Pittsburgh. The Slave Ship is his fifth book on the slave trade and on maritime history.*

∼

points out that most black Africans who were transported to the New World as slaves had been kidnapped by other black African leaders and tribes and then sold or traded to captains of English slave ships. This may come as news to many readers who may not have realized that black Africans had sold other black women, men, and children into slavery.

Rediker describes how slave ship captains and members of their crew worked through intermediaries or directly with African leaders to get slaves. He also relates how captured Africans were taken on small boats from which they were taken in chains onto slave ships, where they were kept chained on the lower deck. Rediker illustrates the horrendous conditions that the slaves endured by reproducing a 1787 drawing of the slave ship *Brooks*. The ship was built in 1781; its lower deck was designed to accommodate 294 slaves. Each slave occupied a space comparable to the that which a coffin would occupy. Each adult man was allocated a space six feet long and fifteen inches wide, while adult women, boys, and girls had even less space. The height of the prison area was just five feet, and there were no toilet facilities for the slaves. Those slaves who died during the "Middle Passage" were simply thrown overboard, where their bodies were eaten by ravenous sharks.

Rediker explains that captains of slave ships attempted to justify such cruelty by claiming that the slaves had to be chained in order to prevent uprisings and to protect the crew from attacks. He argues persuasively that the physical and psychological mistreatment of slaves was part of organized terror designed to transform free human beings into subservient prisoners whom the captains planned to sell to plantation owners in the New World. Other forms of physical and psychological terror were experienced by slaves when they were dragged from the lower deck to the main deck. Slaves were then ordered to "exercise" in chains; those who resisted were whipped or captains threatened to throw them overboard. Other captains went even further. A captain named Edward Kimber ordered adult and adolescent women to "dance" naked before the crew in order to bring lascivious pleasure to the sadistic captain and crew. When one modest fifteen-year-old girl refused to "dance" in front of Kimber, he ordered his crew to flog her to death. Upon his return to England, Kimber was-indicted for the murder of this slave, but an English jury had no problem acquitting him because of its racist belief that killing an adolescent black slave did not constitute murder. This outrageous acquittal made it clear to slave ship captains that they could act with impunity. No English jury was willing to endanger the wealth that the slave trade brought to England. The captains had personal financial motivation to transport as many slaves as possible because they received a commission for each slave sold in the New World.

The living conditions on the lower deck of slave ships may have been much worse than the illustration of the slave ship *Brooks* would have readers believe. There may well have been even less space on slave ships for each slave than the dimensions described above. It is not at all surprising that a very large number of slaves died from infectious diseases and dysentery. Rediker notes that it is impossible to determine how many slaves died on English slave ships during the eighteenth century because slaves who did not survive the trip across the Middle Passage were simply thrown overboard. Records were not kept for dead slaves. It is reasonable to assume, however, that the fatality rate was very high.

The third part of the triangular trade was also very profitable for England. After selling slaves to plantation owners, slave ship captains purchased raw materials and brought them back to England. By a cruel irony, the lower decks of slave ships were fully cleaned after the removal of slaves. Slave ship captains were more concerned with keeping raw materials clean and dry than with the health of the human beings whom they had enchained.

In this book, Rediker writes frequently of his scholarly interest in economic history. He explains that a desire to increase profits motivated all the actions of slave ship captains and their masters back in England. Allowing more space per slave in the lower decks would have reduced profits, as it would have permitted the sale of fewer slaves in the New World. Relying on less sadistic methods of control than chains, whips, and psychological terror would have required hiring more crew members, and the wealthy slave ship owners in Liverpool and Bristol, then the two major English ports for slave ships, did not want to spend any more money than was absolutely necessary to transport the slaves.

Rediker does an excellent not just in describing the crass economic motivation for the English participation in the slave trade throughout the eighteenth century but also in explaining how English Protestant leaders struggled for almost two decades to persuade Parliament to abolish the slave trade. With the 2007 film *Amazing Grace*, the general public became acquainted with the key involvement of William Wilberforce (1759-1833) in persuading Parliament to approve the Act for the Abolition of the Slave Trade. The very title of the film reminds viewers of the famous Protestant hymn composed in 1772 by the Anglican clergyman and former slave ship captain John Newton (1725-1807). Although the film illustrates effectively how Wilberforce's religious beliefs convinced him that Christian moral values were totally incompatible with the existence of the slave trade, this otherwise admirable film underestimates the lengthy efforts that had preceded William Wilberforce's successful efforts in 1807.

Rediker explains that it took many years of repeated efforts by a number of people to change British attitudes toward the slave trade so that the British public slowly began to pressure its members of Parliament to abolish the slave trade. Opponents of the slave trade realized that they needed to shock the public by presenting viscerally powerful images and arguments. Slave ship owners in Bristol and Liverpool had no intention of cooperating with these opponents. An Anglican lay member named Thomas Clarkson (1760-1846), who had written against the slave trade while he was studying at Cambridge University, decided in the late 1780's that he wanted to tell the British public what actually happened on a slave ship. Although slave ship owners ordered their captains not to answer any questions from Clarkson, this did not prevent him from acquiring firsthand information on the reality of human suffering during the Middle Passage. Clarkson went to pubs frequented by former crew members of slave ships, who told him that slaves were chained under horrendous conditions on the lower decks of slave ships and were frequently whipped by sadistic slave ship captains.

Clarkson described bluntly the psychological and physical torture experienced by slaves during the Middle Passage. In addition to his verbal arguments, he reproduced in a 1787 pamphlet, first printed in Plymouth, England, and frequently reissued in book form, a drawing of the lower deck of the slave ship *Brooks*. Clarkson wanted his readers to conclude that the slave trade was nothing more than the systematic torture and murder of human beings. Newton, a highly respected Anglican priest, wrote a treatise titled *Thoughts upon the African Slave Trade* (1788), in which he wrote of his previous work as a slave ship captain. He spoke of the mistreatment that he had inflicted on slaves before his religious conversion and his eventual repentance for the sins that he had committed. His readers came to associate his hymn "Amazing Grace" with the grace that he had received during his religious conversion experience.

On their own, Clarkson and Newton could not have succeeded in persuading the British parliament to abolish the slave trade, but they successfully convinced their fellow Anglican William Wilberforce, who was also a member of Parliament, to put forth their arguments in the House of Commons. The abolishment of the slave trade required the cooperation of numerous religious and political leaders in England. Marcus Rediker has done an excellent job of describing both the very real horrors of the slave trade and its abolition.

*Edmund J. Campion*

## Review Sources

*Booklist* 104, no. 2 (September 15, 2007): 9-10.
*Kirkus Reviews* 75, no. 15 (August 1, 2007): 776-777.
*Library Journal* 132, no. 15 (September 15, 2007): 72.
*The New York Times Book Review* 157 (October 21, 2007): 15.
*Publishers Weekly* 254, no. 30 (July 30, 2007): 67.
*The Wall Street Journal* 250, no. 86 (October 11, 2007): D8.

# THE SNORING BIRD
## My Family's Journey Through a Century of Biology

*Author:* Bernd Heinrich (1940-    )
*Publisher:* HarperCollins (New York). Illustrated.
 461 pp. $29.95
*Type of work:* Autobiography, biography, natural history,
 science
*Time:* 1896-2006
*Locale:* Maine, Poland, and Germany

 *Heinrich recounts his father's life and scientific career,
and his own, with emphasis on their interactions with each
other and with the events and biology of their times*

*Principal personages:*
> GERD HEINRICH, self-taught expert on a
>  group of parasitic wasps
> BERND HEINRICH, Gerd's son, a conventionally
>  trained zoologist and author of the book
> ERWIN STRESEMAN, German ornithologist and
>  Gerd's colleague, mentor, and friend
> HILDEGARDE BURUVNA (MAMUSHA), Gerd's field
>  assistant and third wife, and Bernd's mother
> ANNELIESE MACHATCHEK, Gerd's field assistant and second wife

The central theme of *The Snoring Bird* is the relationship between a father, Gerd Heinrich, and his son, Bernd, as seen and recorded by the son. The younger Heinrich explores the philosophy of science and a number of biological principles in the context of this relationship and the comparison of the two men's scientific careers. He touches on the two world wars from a German perspective—his father fought on that side in both wars. He considers the Cold War, Vietnam, and the impact of all those international events on his family and their biological endeavors.

Bernd Heinrich gathered much of the information about his father from letters his father wrote to, and received from, colleagues and friends, especially Erwin Streseman, a German scientist who was his father's mentor for much of his career. Heinrich found many of the letters to his father stored in the family's barn and stained with pigeon waste. To flesh out his father's career, he also used the books and scientific papers his father wrote and his own interactions with his father, including stories that his father told when he and his sister were young.

Heinrich describes his father, whom he calls Papa throughout the book, as a single-minded, self-taught scientist whose life centered around a group of parasitic wasps, the ichneumon wasps. With the assistance of family members and friends, he collected wasps from all over the world and wrote scientific papers on their characteristics, relationships, and natural history. He worked as a biological collector, and wherever

~

*Bernd Heinrich is a University of Vermont emeritus professor of biology. He has written a number of popular books, most about nature, several of them best sellers. He is also author of a large number of scientific papers, some published in premier journals such as Science.*

~

he went he collected and preserved ichneumon wasps as well as the specimens he was paid to collect, primarily mammals and birds. His wives, Anneliese Machatchek and Hildegarde Buruvna (Mamusha, Bernd's mother), and Anneliese's sister, Liselotte Machatchek, were frequent members of his field crew. Anneliese participated even after he divorced her so he could marry Hildegarde. He drew Bernd into the effort in hopes that his son would take up the research on the ichneumon wasps and continue his work.

Bernd did take up a career in biology and natural history, but he worked with sphinx moths, bees, and ravens, not ichneumon wasps. Unlike his father, he obtained an undergraduate degree, a master's degree, and a Ph.D.; he embraced a new biological philosophy and methodology that paid less attention to collections of whole animals and leaned more on behavioral, physiological, and molecular methods. He was employed as a faculty member at universities and published papers in the most prestigious scientific journals. Such accomplishments were difficult for his father to achieve; some eluded him entirely, at least in part because he did not have the appropriate degrees and because his methods were those of a previous generation.

Heinrich describes his father's participation in both world wars as a member of the German military, including a number of brushes with death. Later, when Bernd decided to volunteer for the Vietnam War, his father advised against it and based his advice on the contrast between his own enthusiastic loyalty to Germany in World War I and his lack of enthusiasm for Hitler's leadership in World War II. He suggested that, from his German perspective, Vietnam was more like World War II. The younger Heinrich volunteered anyway but was rejected because of a bad back. He eventually came to agree with his father that the Vietnam War was a mistake.

At the end of World War II, the Heinrich family immigrated to the United States. The story of their journey and life on a farm in Maine is an example of the immigration experience of a number of Europeans at the time. The consideration of his family's interaction with these and other historic events enriches both the narrative and the reader's appreciation for the events themselves.

Heinrich compares his father's attachment to Borowke, his estate in Poland until it was confiscated by the Soviet communists at the end of World War II, with his own attachment to two properties of his youth: Germany's Hahnheide forest, where the family stayed for several years after World War II, and the property he grew up on in Maine, were Bernd's Borowke. He considers each man's love of nature and of discovery to be rooted in those attachments.

Heinrich describes his father's collecting trips as great adventures full of hardships, close calls, and outstanding success. An example, from which the title of the book is derived, is his Indonesian collecting trip. A bird, a type of rail with a call that sounds like a snore, was the primary target for the trip. After two years of collecting and with thousands of specimens collected, the elder Heinrich was packing to return to Germany without the snoring bird, despite many diligent searches. The team planned to return to Indonesia to search more locations after they spent some time at home. However, because World War II was imminent, they realized that they would be unable to return in the near future. The disappointment over the missing rail was deepened in the light of this realization. On a whim, just a few days before departing for Europe, Gerd grabbed his bush knife and shotgun and went looking for specimens. He collected the snoring rail on this impromptu outing, putting the final touch on an exceptionally successful collecting trip. He wrote about the Indonesian trip in a book using the German for "snoring bird" as the title, and the younger Heinrich borrowed that title for the book reviewed here.

The senior Heinrich led many other collecting trips, including trips to Bulgaria, Persia, Burma, Mexico, Africa, and different locations in the United States. Everywhere he went, he collected species for his sponsors and ichneumon wasps for his own collection. However, he was seldom included as an author of the papers describing his finds—those were left to the people with degrees. He was just a paid collector. That bothered him, as did the difficult time he always had getting financial support for his trips and other scientific efforts. Gerd's disappointments bothered Bernd as well, although he contributed to them once. He refused to help his father apply for funding to analyze an ichneumon collection from Russia. Before asking Bernd for help, Gerd submitted a grant proposal asking for one thousand dollars. It was rejected, and Bernd felt that the resubmission was unlikely to be successful and that his father would blame him for the failure, stressing the relationship even more than did his refusal to help.

Important aspects of the history and philosophy of biology are explored in the context of the father-son relationship. One example involves their contrasting research methods. The father's focus was on collecting as many specimens from as many locations as he could and studying the specimens to learn about their distribution, diversity, and other characteristics. The methodology was modeled after that of Alfred Russel Wallace, Henry Walter Bates, and other giants of nineteenth century biology and exploration. In the twentieth century, however, it was considered old-fashioned, descriptive science and not very informative. In contrast, the twentieth century biologist worked by proposing theories and then testing them. That was the modern way to do science. Ironically, in the nineteenth century, Wallace was criticized for spending too much time "theorizing" when he should have been collecting. Bernd embraced the modern philosophy and methods, but in summarizing his view of the argument he gives credit to the old ways as natural first steps in the progress of science, important background for the new biological methods. He also describes theories proposed and tested by his father. They were neither as formal nor as rigorously crafted as the new biologists prescribed, or as the tests applied by the younger Heinrich in his own work, but his father was not blindly collecting specimens with no thought given to theory.

Heinrich discusses some of the biological questions of the time as well; many of them still puzzle biologists today. One example is the latitudinal gradient in species diversity, in which the total number of species increases toward the equator and decreases toward the poles. He considers only two of the many hypotheses that have been proposed to explain the latitudinal species diversity gradient. One of these assumes that the tropical zones were unaffected by glacial advances and retreats during the Ice Age and hypothesizes that stability through time resulted in widespread, long-lasting habitats in the tropics. This stability allowed time for the evolution of more species than in the more variable temperate and polar latitudes, which were alternately impacted by cold, moist conditions and advancing glaciers and then by warmer, drier conditions as the glaciers melted.

The second hypothesis suggests the opposite—that the glacial cycles did affect the tropics. In the tropics, dry periods occurred when the glaciers advanced, and moist habitats existed only in scattered patches, leading to isolation of the plants and animals in those habitat patches. Isolation led to a new species evolving in each patch. When the glaciers retreated and climatic conditions turned moist, those habitat patches expanded and fused, forming a widespread habitat throughout which the new species spread. With the next glacial advance, populations of these species were isolated in the scattered habitat patches, driving the evolution of more new species. Repetition of these events generated the high species diversity of the tropics. Collections the Heinrichs made on an African trip were designed to provide evidence to help settle this question. These and other scientific problems, presented in the context of Heinrich family history, add substance to the book.

*The Snoring Bird* is particularly interesting for the diversity of topics integrated with its play on the universal theme of parent-offspring tensions. Bernd comments often on his Papa's disinterest in things important to him, but it is clear that their time together was special to him. He took a year off from his undergraduate studies to help his father with a collecting trip in Africa. He hesitated to interrupt his college career, but in retrospect he was glad he went because it was his father's last big collecting trip. It does seem that the father did little to support the son's interests while the son was frequently involved in supporting the father's. Though troubled by his father's inability to fulfill all his ambitions as a scientist and hurt by his father's inattention to things important to him, Bernd expresses the conviction that his father lived a full and successful life and that he (Bernd) derived much of value from his association with his father.

The book contains a few minor errors. "Mammalogist" is misspelled as "mammologist" on page 99. On page 250, "could not to publish" should have been either "not to publish" or "could not publish." "Streseman" is sometimes rendered "Stresseman." A parenthetical statement at the bottom of page 305 reads as if the most recent glacial advance started twenty thousand years ago, which was actually the beginning of the last glacial retreat. On the whole, however, the book is well edited. Unfortunately, there is no index. The "Notes and References" help to make up for the missing bibliography. The numerous illustrations, which include maps, drawings, and photographs, are very helpful. Reviews of the book have been enthusiastic.

*Carl W. Hoagstrom*

## Review Sources

*Biography: An Interdisciplinary Quarterly* 30, no. 3 (Summer, 2007): 427.
*Globe and Mail*, June 2, 2007, p. D6.
*Library Journal* 132, no. 9 (May 15, 2007): 113.
*Los Angeles Times*, May 13, 2007, p. R6.
*The New York Times Book Review* 156 (June 24, 2007): 24.
*Science News* 172, no. 8 (August 25, 2007): 127.
*Scientific American* 297, no. 2 (August, 2007): 100.

# SNOW PART

*Author:* Paul Celan (1920-1970)
*First published: Schneepart*, 1971, in Germany
Translated from the German and with an introduction by
 Ian Fairley
*Publisher:* Sheep Meadow Press (Riverdale-on-Hudson,
 New York). 198 pp. $14.00 paperback
*Type of work:* Poetry

  *Tormented Holocaust survivor Celan's last poems, in-
cluding his unpublished ones, are ably translated*

  Paul Celan is a strange and magical poet—a Jew who
survived the Holocaust and yet did not; a writer who could
use at least seven languages but could write poetry in only one, German, the language
of the death camps. He was born Paul Antschel in 1920 in Romania and grew up
speaking German and Romanian. His parents died (his father from typhus, his mother
by shooting) in work camps in the Ukraine. He himself was forced to work in labor
camps between 1942 and 1944, but survived. Survivor guilt is one of his recurring
themes. When the war was over, after some moving around he relocated in Paris. He
was attempting to distance himself from German society, yet he taught German literature in France. He even changed his name, first to Ancel, and eventually to Celan, an
anagram of Ancel that sounded more French.

  He is perhaps best known for his widely anthologized poem "Todesfuge" ("Death
Fugue"), which tells of the horrors of the Holocaust with eerie rhythms and repetitions,
suggesting his personal losses as well as evoking the entire machinery of destruction.
In "Todesfuge," translated into many languages, "Golden-haired Margarete" contrasts with "ashen-haired Shulamith"—the Aryan ideal woman and the canceled Jewish woman, associated with his mother. The "black milk of sunrise" that the "we"
drink in the poem and the miasma of ashes that accompanies his lines re-create the
nightmare landscape of the camps. There are numerous references to smoke and ashes
throughout Celan's poem, to the extent that the poems seem to bathe the reader in the
ashes of his destroyed people.

  In Paris, Celan married the artist Gisele de Lestrange, but the poet was never able
to get away from the torment of the Holocaust and his fortuitous survival in the labor
camp. The wonder and delight he experienced through his son Eric appears in some of
the work in *Snow Part*, but these emotions were not enough to outweigh his past. He
committed suicide by drowning himself in the Seine in 1970, after leaving in his diary
the comment, "Depart Paul."

  Celan's poems are haunted and haunting. Language, death, and silence are their
subjects. Celan's earlier poems are fairly direct, but as he got older and kept on struggling with his ghosts and the German language, the poems became knotted, enclosed in
themselves. It was as if he and the language were engaged in a struggle to the death. He

invented words, putting together combinations that can barely be translated because of the multiple meanings of his neologisms, and the poems became so dense as to be almost impenetrable. Still, the sense of total loss and absolute despair are the same in *Snow Part* as in the first poems. There is no escape for Celan, and there is none for the reader.

*Snow Part* contains Celan's last work and is very difficult indeed. The first five sections of the book comprise "Snow Part," poems written during and around the poet's breakdown in 1967. The last section, "Other Poems," includes some unpublished work. Celan's concentrated intensity communicates even when the poems resist paraphrase or explication. Each poem appears in German with a facing translation. The introduction is

*Paul Celan published or authorized seven collections of his poetry:* Mohn und Gedächtnis *(1952),* Von Schwelle zu Schwelle *(1955),* Sprachgitter *(1959;* Speech-Grille, *1971),* Die Niemandsrose *(1963),* Atemwende *(1967;* Breathturn, *1995),* Fadensonnen *(1968;* Threadsuns, *2000), and* Lichtzwang *(1970;* Lightduress, *2005); he did not authorize the publication of* Schneepart, *which appeared in 1971, after his death. He was awarded both the Bremen Literature Prize and the George Büchner Prize, Germany's most prestigious literary award.*

very helpful, as the translator, Ian Fairley, explains some of the historical events referred to in the poems that may not be in the reader's frame of reference and provides some basic principles of his translation; also, Fairley places the writing of these poems in the context of Celan's life. The conclusion, a brief biography of Celan, is useful as well as interesting and sends the reader to full biographies of this tragic figure.

Most of the poems in this collection are short, some only a few lines; Celan has left behind him the expansiveness of "Todesfuge." The themes and subjects are much the same as in his earlier poems. However, the casual reader would not want to enter Celan's work by this gate—these poems are too compressed, too interior for those who have not followed his other work. They do have a few new directions; they include, for instance, the poems to his son Eric, which seem somewhat more positive than the others yet are freighted by the sorrow that comes with the knowledge of vulnerability. Nevertheless, the poems proclaim the miracle that his son should have come into existence.

Most of these poems pit the struggle to articulate horror against silence and death. The poems are terse, brief, elliptical. Usually the lines are short, often containing only a few syllables. An example is this complete poem:

> TO SPEAK with blind alleys
> about what's facing,
> about its
> expatriate
> sense—:
>
> to chew this
> bread, with
> writing teeth.

The Celan conflict is encapsulated in these few lines. How is it possible to express the absolute annihilation visited on his people by the Holocaust? Only through a writing that is like consumption, like self-consumption. The black milk of "Todesfuge" becomes the dark communion, the bad bread. The original poem contains the invented word *Schreibzähnen*, which Fairley translates correctly as "writing teeth." However, there are perhaps additional implications that are found only in the one-word description—the suggestion that writing teeth are a real property, that in fact the only way to face the horror is to chew over it and make it into poetry. This bad bread is the only nourishment available; chewing it with "writing teeth" is the poet's obsession and duty. Moreover, the creation of poetry becomes a physical event, a kind of drive or instinct that gives the poet his sole reason for staying alive.

Social philosopher Theodor Adorno initially claimed that there could be no poetry written after Auschwitz, but he too was caught by Celan's enigmatic poetry of pain. By 1966, Adorno had modified his position to say, "Perennial suffering has as much right to expression as the tortured have to scream, hence it may have been wrong to say that no poem could be written after Auschwitz." At first believing that attempting to describe the Holocaust resulted in aestheticising it, Adorno was led to believe, partly through his experience of Celan's work, that the experience of total horror could be, and maybe needed to be, represented. In a sense, though, Celan agreed with Adorno's initial position and saw the writing of such poetry as a deathly struggle with a central silence. The more constricted and knotted the poems are, the closer the poet comes to this silence.

In this collection, there are only a few poems that are longer than half a page. In addition to their brevity, they are notable for their extreme precision about abstract things, their lack of colors or tones except for dark and light, the heaviness of each syllable. The longest poem here is probably "What Knits," which carries its spare lines to a second page. It begins: "What knits/ at this voice?" The voice approaches silence, seems to attempt to charm it with words, to disarm it. It has a ritual feel to it that may suggest Sylvia Plath's attempts at exorcising the ghost of her dead father. "Tumuli, tumuli," Celan's poem calls, "you/ hill out of there, alive,/ come/ into the kiss." The German makes the noun *Hügel* (hill) into a verb, *hügelst*—an appropriation not easily represented in English, a language without such precise conjugations. "What Knits" is a kind of poem rare in Celan—a work in which positives seem to outweigh negatives. The "you" of the poem is webbed by worms, known by beetles, yet the "great globe" gives "safe passage." If, as in Plath's poem "Daddy," the exorcism does not seem successful, this may be because we are reading the poem into the poet's life and death.

The unidentified "you" is a presence throughout this work, the shifting "you" standing for the self, the other, the silence, death, God. Its secondary effect is to pull the reader into the poem as an ear, as the listening silence. The poems suggest a wrestling with religion—an attempt to call forth an answer from the great silence, to find a word that is the Word, that makes sense of the nightmare. The dark mysticism of Celan's work contributes to its power. Reading Celan's work from beginning to end shows a drawing close to the silence that is also the listening, but there is no answer from the silence as Celan edges closer and closer to it in his last work.

The translator's introduction shows well some of the issues involved in the representation in English of this German work. The translation itself occasionally seems too hard or harsh—the German words assigned specific meanings when their implications are wider. For instance, Fairley translates *Gelausch* as "auricle"—a specific, physical part of the ear, but the invented word suggests the hearing, the listening-space, not necessarily the ear or any part of the ear. There are a few other cases in which the translation seems to close off the poem in ways the poet may not have intended. There are some resonances that do not translate—multiple meanings that exist only in German and that cause a translator to choose among them. Also, the translator occasionally invents words when Celan has not, or chooses odd synonyms: He translates *Geduld*, which is something like patience or endurance, as "thole," which is accurate but is an uncommon word that may not be in most readers' vocabulary. Such linguistic comparisons will bother only those who scrutinize the originals. By and large, the translation does carry most of the vibrations of Celan's cryptic, enclosed work.

Paul Celan's work is of course widely known, and many would answer only his name when asked for the names of Holocaust poets. Yet Celan's work is only beginning to be fully explored by scholars and critics. This collection will help to fill in the gaps and define the trajectory of his thought, as will the collection of his letters recently released. *Snow Part* will be an essential component of his final oeuvre, showing the last effort to penetrate silence with language, to pass through horror into peace.

*Janet McCann*

**Review Source**

*Library Journal* 132, no. 12 (July 1, 2007): 95-96.

# SOMETHING IN THE AIR
## Radio, Rock, and the Revolution That Shaped a Generation

*Author:* Marc Fisher (1958-    )
*Publisher:* Random House (New York). 374 pp. $27.95
*Type of work:* History
*Time:* 1949 to the early twenty-first century
*Locale:* The United States

*A scholarly yet readable account of changes that took place within America's broadcast industry as rock-and-roll music came of age*

> *Principal personages:*
> TODD STORZ, the developer of the Top 40 formula
> HAL JACKSON, an African American deejay
> ALAN FREED, a Cleveland deejay who played rhythm and blues
> JEAN SHEPHERD, a radio talk-show pioneer
> BOB FASS, a politically oriented FM host
> TOM DONAHUE, a San Francisco deejay
> PAUL SIDNEY, a Long Island radio personality

Hunter S. Thompson once wrote, "The radio business is a cruel and shallow money trench, a long plastic hallway where thieves and pimps run free, and good men die like dogs. There's also a negative side." One of many appealing things about *Something in the Air: Radio, Rock, and the Revolution That Shaped a Generation* is that the author, while conceding Thompson's points about the medium's cash nexus, is a true fan who appreciates its potential, albeit rarely achieved, for greatness. As an adolescent, he listened to raconteur extraordinaire Jean Shepherd on a cream-colored transistor hidden under a pillow and in college hosted his own all-night show. Like the late David Halberstam, who died in an auto accident in 2007, Fisher proves himself to be an esteemed journalist, an excellent historian, and, at times, an insightful participant-observer. Based on a hundred interviews and extensive secondary research, his book contains "not a bit of dead air" (to quote from a *Publishers Weekly* review) and is a welcome supplement to Erik Barnouw's three-volume *A History of Broadcasting in the United States* (1966-1970).

In a dozen chapters about broadcast innovators, Fisher captures the vicissitudes of a nearly century-old industry adapting to technological change and defying periodic predictions of its impending demise. "As it ages," Fisher writes, "radio absorbs the new, co-opts the rebellious, and reinvents itself every step of the way." Big consoles quickly became affordable during the Jazz Age (a model costing $34.95 appeared in the 1927 Sears catalog). During the 1940's, sets commonly appeared in kitchens and bedrooms. In 1949, however, a *Life* magazine article wondered, "Is

Radio Doomed?" News, live drama, variety hours, game shows, situation comedies, soap operas, and other staples seemed better fitted for television. As ratings plummeted, Jack Benny, Lucille Ball, Ed Sullivan, Sid Caesar, and other celebrities jumped ship, including former deejays Mike Wallace, Dave Garroway, Hugh Downs, Bill Cullen, and Soupy Sales. Even Arthur Godfrey, "Mr. Morning Radio," telecast his show. No longer the family entertainment center, radio morphed into sundry niches, including the Top 40 format. The objective: to capture and retain a devoted following.

In 1949, Todd Storz, with help from his family, purchased KOWH in Omaha, Nebraska, for $75,000; at the time, local ads

*A columnist for* The Washington Post *whose Sunday column "The Listener" covers contemporary radio, Marc Fisher has an online chat program, Potomac Confidential, and a blog titled Raw Fisher. He is the author of* After the Wall: Germany, the Germans, and the Burdens of History *(1995).*

sold, as the saying went, for "a dollar a holler." Observing waitresses putting dimes in jukeboxes to hear their favorite tunes even though they had been playing all day, Storz believed repetition to be the key to success. As one station manager told a skeptical deejay, "About the time you don't like a record, Mama's just beginning to learn to hum it. About the time you can't stand it, Mama's beginning to learn the words. About the time you're ready to shoot yourself if you hear it one more time, it's hitting the Top Ten." Within two years, KOWH's market share jumped from 4 to 45 percent. Storz sought out flamboyant personalities and had them mix in news, local doings, weather, traffic, jingles, call-in contests, offbeat sound effects, and stunts (including treasure hunts that caused maximum consternation from law-enforcement authorities). In short order he acquired half a dozen stations from Minneapolis to Miami. We all learned from Storz, one protégé admitted.

Trailing behind Top 40 for market share were stations playing jazz, show tunes, classical compositions, big band standards, and so-called race records. Only the latter flourished, thanks to the growing popularity of rhythm and blues, which gave birth to rock and roll. White deejays Hunter Hancock in Los Angeles and Alan Freed in Cleveland attracted fans of all stripes, and before long African Americans such as Hal Jackson in New York and Dr. Hepcat (Lavada Hurst) in Austin carved out careers— Dr. Hepcat with a line of patter resembling rap. When Memphis executive Bert Ferguson hired a black host, he received bomb threats, but with 40 percent of the city's population African American in 1948, WDAI's format clicked and spawned imitators in Birmingham and Atlanta (home to the first black-owned station). Memphis residents could dig Brother Theo Wade at dawn ("Get up outta that bed, children") and Rufus Thomas at dusk ("I'm young, I'm loose, I'm full of juice. I got the goose, so what's the use?"). Bluesman B. B. King even had a show of his own.

With the advent of rock and roll, Top 40 became more youth-oriented. Deejays such as New York City's Cousin Bruce Morrow were pied pipers to a special subculture that liked the lingo and frenetic pace. Critics predicted that sponsors would balk at shows appealing mainly to teen angst and complained that the fare was poisoning young minds and promoting sexual license and race mixing. Of course, Top 40 charts also included ballads ("Davy Crockett" was number one in 1955), novelty songs ("The Purple People Eater" topped the charts in 1958), slow standards (The Platters scored with "Twilight Time" and "Smoke Gets in your Eyes," among others), and throwbacks like the Jimmy Dorsey Orchestra's "So Rare" (number two in 1957). Rock-and-roll bashers persuaded Congress to investigate the degree to which deejays receied money for plugging records—a practice not illegal at the time. How else, they charged, to account for such trashy music flooding the airways? The investigation led to the payola scandal, which ruined some pioneers, including Alan Freed.

While pop music dominated the AM dial, an eccentric genius named Jean Shepherd invented what came to be known as talk radio. Twice fired for persistently digressing from the music, he migrated to WOR in New York, where he held forth nightly for four and a half hours. Intermittently spinning jazz records between acerbic monologues, Shepherd's tales of festering youth had a universal appeal, as did his irreverence toward sponsors and management functionaries. His eventual successor, Long John Nebel, attracted night owls interested in UFOs, health nostrums, and conspiracy theories of all kinds.

During the 1960's, FM came into its own. The Federal Communications Commission (FCC) forced stations to stop simulcasting AM shows, and automobile manufacturers wired their vehicles for FM. Carrying on Shepherd's legacy in Los Angeles was John Leonard with *Nightsounds*, while New Yorker Bob Fass hosted *Radio Unnameable* on WBAI. Blatantly political, as befitting the 1960's, Fass provided a forum for Bob Dylan and lesser folk artists, as well as counterculture activists such as yippie prankster Abbie Hoffman. The scent of marijuana ever-present, *Radio Unnameable* was, in Fisher's words, "an art piece, created anew each night, an improvised mélange of sound—live music, recorded speeches, random phone calls, eyewitness reports from war zones and urban conflicts, recitations of poetry and prose, solicitations for political causes eternal and evanescent, advertisements for illegal drugs, experiments with noise and beauty and silence."

In 1969, Thunderclap Newman's hit single "Something in the Air" captured the existing antiestablishment mood in England and America. While political revolution remained a fanciful pipe dream, technology continuously revolutionized radio in ways that fostered variety and creativity. Album sales had surpassed singles, giving rise to alternative programming targeting baby boomers. Fed up with Top 40 blandness, Tom Donahue had quit KYA in San Francisco to promote concerts before taking a job with struggling FM station KMPX. Spinning cuts from acid rock albums, Donahue was attuned to the burgeoning psychedelic scene. Head shop advertisements were acceptable, but spots for gasoline, cigarettes, fast food, alcohol, or branches of the armed services verboten. Larry Miller signed off with the quip: "May each and every one of you find a little pot at the end of your rainbow." In 1971, the FCC attempted to ban songs that glorified drugs, but Donahue refused to trim his sails. When KMPX's owner tried to stamp out illegal drug use at the station, Donahue organized the "Great Hippie Strike" before bolting to KSAN.

Eventually, market researchers such as Lee Abrams at WMYQ in Miami drained much of the eccentricity and joy out of album-oriented rock programs, but noteworthy college stations such as Buffalo's WBFO kept the faith. Launching a "superstars" format with the slogan "More music! Less talk!" Abrams had focus groups "scientifically" select cuts based on seven-second snippets from the Eagles, Fleetwood Mac, the Rolling Stones, and other familiar favorites. The premise, according to Fisher, was that listeners could not get enough of the songs they loved nor stand even one spin of those they loathed. Abrams resuscitated one New York station by switching from Spanish-language programs to disco, while in Chicago he boosted the ratings of WLUP ("The Loop") by making it antidisco (shock jock Steve Dahl's Disco Demolition Night at Comiskey Park became legendary).

Whereas Top 40 had been, in theory, "everybody's music," by the late 1970's listeners could choose from a menu that included progressive rock, hard rock, oldies, disco, country, all talk, and soul. To some, the variety signified progress; to others, ghettoization. Soul stations, usually white-owned, more than held their own, especially on AM. After *The Washington Post* donated WHUR to the historically black Howard University, for three years the station featured a smorgasbord of avant-garde music, culture, and politics. The highlight was *360 Degrees of Black Experience*, a three-hour news block during evening drive time. Eventually, eager to attract black middle-class listeners, the station went mainstream, cutting *360 Degrees* down to an hour, and then ten minutes. The ratings-driven station manager filled the seven-to-midnight slot with *Quiet Storm*, emphasizing love songs targeted for women. Cathy Hughes, who had guided WHUR through its early days and was not about to cop out, purchased rival WOL and, adopting a talk format, started hosting a prime-time slot.

During the 1980's, more and more stations were switching from Top 40 to all talk. For one thing, the FCC no longer enforced the fairness doctrine, and satellite technology made syndication inexpensive. The result was standardization in various guises, including sports talk, a genre ignored by the author. Chauvinist Tom Leykis in Los Angeles was master of the double entendre, while Rush Limbaugh rose to stardom in Sacramento mixing reactionary politics with showbiz flair. Howard Stern pushed the envelope of indecency more than most and was fired from one station after speculating about the Statue of Liberty's masturbation technique. Hoping to attract men, the emphasis, to quote Fisher, was on "piercingly partisan politics and relentless raunch." More edifying was National Public Radio, which commenced in 1970, but after a period of experimentation sacrificed diversity for homogeneity, thanks in part to consultant David Giovannoni, who believed that a program with a minimal audience was not providing a public service. A few public radio stations, such as KCRW at Santa Monica College, remained experimental, but most listeners favored network staples (*Morning Edition, All Things Considered, A Prairie Home Companion*). Also hurting local coverage was consolidation by corporations such as Clear Channel Communications (infamous for barring the Dixie Chicks from its airwaves and staging prowar rallies in 2003). In Minot, North Dakota, for instance, Clear Channel bought all six stations. In 2002, a train derailed, causing a toxic ammonia spill. The one full-time news staffer was unavailable, so Minot stations were no help in providing coverage.

Despite all that is wrong with the contemporary scene, Fisher remains upbeat. Satellite radio, for instance, offers subscribers variety (zydeco, bluegrass) not normally found elsewhere. Lee Abrams, of all people, upset over research techniques gone haywire, became programming chief for XM Satellite Radio in 1998 and told his deejays: "If you sound like FM, you're fired." The Internet spawned Web radio (no license necessary) and creative "podcasts" ready for downloading. Low-power FM has enabled small markets to provide local coverage despite efforts by religious zealots to monopolize the territory. For decades, eccentric Long Islander Paul Sidney has delivered old-fashioned radio to his community, doing 250 remote broadcasts a year and holding forth on a Main Street public bench gauging the public pulse. In a moving tribute to Sidney and others like him, Fisher concludes: "For a society to work, Edmund Burke said, its people must recognize what it is they have in common. Those bonds can be big concepts such as liberty and democracy, but they can also be small things, single voices that remind us of who we are and what we care about."

*James B. Lane*

## Review Sources

*Booklist* 103, no. 8 (December 15, 2006): 8.
*Kirkus Reviews* 74, no. 21 (November 1, 2006): 1110.
*Library Journal* 132, no. 1 (January 1, 2007): 111.
*The New York Times Book Review* 156 (January 28, 2007): 11.
*Publishers Weekly* 253, no. 47 (November 27, 2006): 44.
*Wired* 15, no. 1 (January, 2007): 76.

# SOULS OF THE LABADIE TRACT

*Author:* Susan Howe (1937-    )
*Publisher:* New Directions (New York). 127 pp. $16.95
*Type of work:* Poetry

Susan Howe

Souls of the Labadie Tract

*Howe explores historical episodes, including the foundation and dissolution of the Labadist utopian community (1684-1722) in Maryland, through the lens of her experimental poetry, employing both verbal and visual elements*

A significant problem facing experimental writers is that of reputation. Once identified as such, the writer suffers from the reaction that "experimental," to many readers, is nearly synonymous with "inaccessible" or "incomprehensible." This especially holds true in poetry. Many general readers feel reluctant to open a book of poems, of any sort. Having it described as experimental only makes their reluctance the greater. Susan Howe certainly ranks among the most prominent poets of an avowedly experimental nature in the United States. In her new collection, *Souls of the Labadie Tract*, she adopts a strategy that seems designed to mitigate this reaction to her work.

Rather than asking the reader to dive into the poems without explanation, a common practice among experimental writers, Howe opens the book with several prose pieces. Even esoteric poetry, Howe essentially acknowledges, can acquire more lucidity when original source materials are unveiled. Her poems are of an esoteric nature, to be sure, yet the reader of these prose pieces can move forward into the poetry with more assurance than would be the case had Howe offered no helpful context or explanation.

In a book whose contents page lists only six items, half are prose. Two selections have identical titles: "*Errand.*" Another is titled "Personal Narrative." In addition, the collection's title poem, "Souls of the Labadie Tract," opens with two pages of prose. Each prose section focuses on some area of personal fascination for Howe, always relating to New England history. Journeys of various kinds also figure in these accounts. The first "*Errand,*" for instance, discusses horseback rides taken by Jonathan Edwards (1703-1758) during his ministry in Northampton, Massachusetts. One particular habit seizes Howe's attention: "As an idea occurred to him, he pinned a small piece of paper on his clothing. . . . I love to imagine this gaunt and solitary traveler covered in scraps, riding through the woods and fields of Massachusetts and Connecticut." The second "*Errand*" discusses, among other matters, walks taken by American poet Wallace Stevens (1879-1955), including his daily two-mile walk from home to office, when he, too, would jot thoughts on scraps of paper. In its dictionary sense, the word "errand" refers to a short journey, often relating to the delivery of a message—a meaning making the word a most fitting choice for title, in these two instances.

~

*Susan Howe graduated from the Boston Museum School of Fine Arts in 1961 with a degree in painting. In her art, she employed techniques of visual quotation and collage, as she would in her later poems. She held the Samuel P. Capen Chair for Poetry and Humanities at the State University of New York at Buffalo and was the Bain-Swiggett Professor of Poetry at Princeton University before her retirement in 2007.*

~

The name of the longest of these prose works, "Personal Narrative," takes on resonance because of the subject of the first "*Errand.*" In an essay of his own, written around 1743, Jonathan Edwards described his life in terms of his Puritan Christian awakening, and he titled it "Personal Narrative" as well. Edwards's account progressively moved through the stages of his life, beginning with childhood. In contrast, Howe's account begins at a moment in her adult life, when she was "a poet with no academic affiliation" in the 1970's and early 1980's and living near New Haven, Connecticut. While reading a narrative written by a seventeenth century Massachusetts minister and militia member, the Reverend Hope Atherton, Howe experienced a moment of awakening of her own: "I vividly remember the sense of energy and change that came over me one midwinter morning when, as the book lay open in sunshine on my work table, I discovered in Hope Atherton's wandering story the authority of a prior life for my own writing voice," Howe writes.

Howe's "Personal Narrative" describes her research in Yale University's Sterling Library and her encounters with the past. Although these encounters took place within a library, the historical literature with which she engages is not of a tamed and wall-constrained nature but rather wild and natural. She cites the beginnings of Henry David Thoreau's 1862 essay "Walking" and describes how Thoreau saw his walks out of Concord, Massachusetts, into the "impervious and shaking swamps" as a journey into a sacred place. Thoreau's example helps give Howe words to discuss her own journey. She employs little of the diction or expansive approach of Thoreau, however, presenting her thoughts in a manner distinctively hers. Both the thoughts and the means of their expression reveal her intentions and desires as a writer. "I wished to speak a word for libraries as places of freedom and wildness," she writes in "Personal Narrative." "Often walking alone in the stacks, surrounded by raw material paper afterlife, my spirits were shaken by the great ingathering of titles and languages. This may suggest vampirism because while I like to think I write for the dead, I also take my life as a poet from their lips, their vocalisms, their breath." This "library nature" reappears in the poems within this collection, and so does a contrasting nature—that of the world of society, commerce, and even the arts—which appears in recurring images and accounts relating to threads, cloth, and garments.

As important as "Personal Narrative" is, "Souls of the Labadie Tract" is undoubtedly the book's central work. Ambitious in its experimental methods, it yields meaning to the reader by several means, beginning with introductory notes on Labadist history. The Labadists were members of a utopian sect who followed the teachings of French Quietist Jean de Labadie. Quietism was a contemplative, mysti-

cal movement within the Catholic Church. The Labadie Tract of the title is an actual section of land, 3,750 acres in size, near where Maryland, Pennsylvania, and Delaware meet. The Labadists established their community in 1684. It was dissolved in
1722.

This prose introduction, placing the Labadists in a specific range of years and in
specific geographic location, is paired with another introductory item on its own
page: a single line by Wallace Stevens. This gesture of contrast, between prose exposition and poetic line, seems to indicate that the historical precision of the Labadist
subject of the poem is to be presented through methods influenced by Stevens, whose
emphasis on the evocative and musical potential of words could at times diminish and
even eliminate semantic clarity and precision. "Souls of the Labadie Tract" itself is
presented in a striking manner. On each page are one or two stanzas of five to eight
lines total, set in a small block at the center of the paper. They are small rectangles of
words framed by open space—visually echoing the note-covered scraps of paper of
Edwards and Stevens.

The poem displays a certain narrative movement based on the story of the Labadist
community. The initial joy of the Labadists in the community's formation is expressed, in part, with ample musical reference. In the following, as in other stanzas,
music appears allied to clothing:

> I'll borrow chapel voices
> Song and dance of treble
> bass for remembrance Stilt-
> Walker Plate-Spinner air
> piebaldly dressed heart's
> content embroidered note
> Distant diapason delight

The opening and middle sections of the poem suggest aspects of the Labadist community and its "Millennial hopes." The sections appear to have several speakers, with
the voice at times seeming to be the poet, at other times the historical Labadist figures,
who are rising from that "library nature" of the printed and written word. At times
the voices seem in conversation with one another: "There it is there it is—you/
want the great wicked city/ Oh I wouldn't I wouldn't." Lines toward the poem's end
point toward difficulties, perhaps even crisis, faced by the community as it comes
to an end.

The poem does present distinct obstacles to the reader's understanding. Howe iso-
lates sentences and sentence fragments from narrative context, a method that inevitably leads to loss of meaning. Some lines, moreover, include deliberately archaic
elements, presumably drawn from the historic texts themselves. Her technique of
sometimes slicing apart words (for instance, the name "Alciato" in one section
becomes "Alciat" in the next) also serves to sever meaning from the text. In the
following section, several of these difficulties appear:

To swim for sake of rhyme
for meter faint letter slield
in pencil after subscribeth

Shorthand on it because of
streights all glue for strife

In this example, the words "subscribeth" and "streights" suggest historical texts, in the former case by its archaic conjugation, in the latter by its spelling. The word "slield" may be an archaic term not preserved in dictionaries, or a word that has suffered truncation of some sort at Howe's hand. Whatever the case, if it bears meaning, it does so only for those privileged to know Howe's intentions; thus, it presents another obstacle to extracting meaning from the lines.

Use of such a word as "slield" may give notice to the reader that something besides reading-for-meaning is being offered by these stanzas—even though a *reader* is obviously the one being addressed. In other words, the word may serve to direct the reader to approach the page as *viewer*, with the verbal-graphic element being preeminent, or as *listener*, in which case the verbal music is being emphasized. The use of techniques that distance the reader from the page may be taken as evidence of a sort of elitism on Howe's part. Alternately, it may be accepted as simply part of her method: Combining the verbal color of words and names with their graphic appearance is part of her technique.

That the graphic appearance of a text is of importance to Howe is stressed in several places in *Souls of the Labadie Tract*, not only in the obviously careful presentation of the poems but also in explicit terms, as in her statement, "Font-voices summon a reader into visible earshot," found in "Personal Narrative." Her reference in the title poem to "black letter," for instance, probably refers to the common but archaic font and lettering style, not to either blackness or the alphabet.

The closing poem of the volume, a paean to a piece of a garment, is dominated by its visual exploration of dissected, shaped, and graphically rearranged text fragments. Titled "Fragment of the Wedding Dress of Sarah Pierpont Edwards," it begins with an image: a black-and-white reproduction of the square piece of cloth. The wedding-dress fragment provides an ideal focus for Howe's attention. It not only resembles one of the squared pieces of paper on which Jonathan Edwards and Wallace Stevens jotted notes while riding or walking but also is a piece of cloth, literally a fragment, that is preserved not in a textile museum but—much more appropriately—in a rare-book library.

In "Personal Narrative," Howe states that "Hope Atherton is lost in the great world of nature." By offering the reader this fragment of a dress, Howe expresses much the same sentiment of another historical figure, the wife of Jonathan Edwards. The textual fragments used to create collage-like masses of words, which are in essence the stanzas of the poem, presented one per page across thirteen pages, are mostly literally unreadable, having been so chopped, truncated, effaced, and distorted that the sense to be taken from them is almost purely visual in nature. The penultimate page presents an exception, being three sentences and presented in a simple, sans serif font, with the first sentence again referring to a garment: "We are all clothed with fleece of sheep I keep saying as if I were singing as these words do."

Relating words, poems, and ideas to thread, cloth, and clothing seems an essential focus—perhaps even the "errand" of the poem, and of the book. In that initial prose description of Edwards, Howe's own jagged poetic vision erupts in stark, startling statement: "Words give clothing to hide our nakedness."

*Mark Rich*

## Review Source

*Publishers Weekly* 254, no. 46 (November 19, 2007): 40.

# SPOOK COUNTRY

*Author:* William Gibson (1948-    )
*Publisher:* G. P. Putnam's Sons (New York).
   371 pp. $25.95
*Type of work:* Novel
*Time:* February, 2006
*Locale:* Hollywood; New York City; Washington, D.C.;
   Vancouver, British Columbia

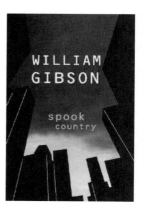

   *The second book in a trilogy started with* Pattern Recognition *in 2003, bringing a science-fiction sensibility to bear on the contemporary world*

Principal characters:
> HOLLIS HENRY, a former member of a rock
>    band, now defunct, trying out a new
>    career in journalism
> HUBERTUS BIGEND, a Belgian magnate with far-flung interests
> TITO, a young man in an extended Cuban Chinese family,
>    based in New York City, who operates outside the law
> MILGRIM, a slacker, trained as a Russian translator, shanghaied
>    for a covert operation
> BROWN, his captor, a Blackwater-style "contractor" employed by
>    shadowy U.S. government elements, who has Tito under surveillance
> THE OLD MAN, Brown's antagonist, a retired U.S. national security
>    specialist who is on a personal crusade against the direction the
>    country has taken

   William Gibson's imagination seems to work naturally in threes. His first novel, *Neuromancer* (1984), the book that made him famous, turned out to be the first installment in a trilogy that also included *Count Zero* (1986) and *Mona Lisa Overdrive* (1988). This was science fiction—Gibson was hailed as the virtuoso of "cyberpunk"—but already he was being read by people who did not hang out in that genre. With his second trilogy, comprising *Virtual Light* (1993), *Idoru* (1996), and *All Tomorrow's Parties* (1999), Gibson moved much nearer to the present—*Virtual Light* is set in 2005—and with *Pattern Recognition* (2003) and *Spook Country* he has dropped the conventions of science fiction altogether while maintaining the sensibility that gave us the word "cyberspace" ("the consensual hallucination that was the matrix," as he wrote in *Neuromancer*).
   *Spook Country* interweaves three narrative lines with three protagonists. First among equals is Hollis Henry, formerly of the Curfew, a rock band that flourished in the early 1990's, disbanded, and still enjoys a cult following. Her post-Curfew investments having gone sour, Hollis—who has done a little writing—has taken an assignment with a magazine start-up, *Node*, described as a European *Wired*. She is supposed to write about "locative art"—a species of virtual reality that would allow a person

who had donned a "helmet" to see an image "tagged" to a specific place by the artist, such as a re-creation of actor River Phoenix lying dead on the sidewalk on Sunset Boulevard, overdosed. Take the helmet off and the sidewalk is empty. The assignment brings Hollis to Hollywood.

The second strand centers on Tito, a Cuban Chinese man in his early twenties with a complicated family history. His grandfather was involved in the founding of Fidel Castro's intelligence service after the revolution in Cuba and worked closely with the Russians when they came. (He spent some time in the Soviet Union himself and received extensive training there, as did Tito's beloved aunt, Juana; Tito himself speaks Russian as well as Spanish.) Tito's father also worked in Cuban intelligence. After he was killed, when Tito was still a boy, the grandfather put family welfare above his commitment to the cause (unlike most of the family and indeed unlike most Cubans, he remained a true believer in communism), bringing the rather improbable clan to New York, where they employ a mixture of tradecraft and Santería to pursue various enterprises outside the law.

*Born in Virginia, William Gibson immigrated to Canada in 1968. His first novel, the best-selling* Neuromancer *(1984), swept the major science-fiction prizes and introduced the world to "cyberspace," a term he had coined in a 1981 short story. In addition to his many books, he has written for magazines such as* Wired, *and he contributed two scripts to the television series* The X-Files.

The third strand involves Milgrim, a slacker—probably in his early forties—who has worked in the past as a Russian translator but has fallen on hard times. Addicted to tranquilizers and barely scraping by, he is easy prey for Brown, a nasty fellow who kidnaps Milgrim because he needs someone with a knowledge of Russian to translate intercepted text messages in Volapuk. (The original Volapuk was an artificial language akin to Esperanto, but in this context it refers to the use of roman letters as equivalent to Cyrillic characters, so that a Russian speaker can send a message without a Cyrillic keyboard; it can function as a code of sorts.)

The novel consists of a series of short chapters, eighty-four in total, shifting among these three lines of the narrative, with Hollis the most prominent but the other two strongly represented, not merely secondary characters. Also, as the book progresses, the connections linking the three become clearer and increasingly intricate. All three plotlines converge in the tale of a mysterious shipping container, which ultimately turns out to contain $100 million in cash. The money was siphoned from the nearly $12 billion in Iraqi funds—primarily oil revenue, held by the Federal Reserve under a U.N. mandate—sent by the United States to Iraq between March, 2003, and June, 2004, intended to aid in the reconstruction of the country but much of it subsequently unaccounted for.

Whoever planned this heist—and that is never specified, beyond the clear implication that some government functionaries, "no one you would have heard of," were involved—has had unexpected difficulty finding a place to launder the cash. Moreover, they have learned that someone else is trying to track the container in its passage on the seas. Brown is employed by these shadowy conspirators as a "contractor," and he has Tito under surveillance because Tito is acting as a courier for information concerning the shipping container.

Hollis, meanwhile, stumbles on the story in what seems entirely an accident in the course of her research on locative art, but she does not begin to understand what she has discovered until she meets Hubertus Bigend, a fabulously wealthy and secretive Belgian magnate who is the money behind *Node*. Indeed, as they talk, and it becomes clear how much he knows about Hollis, she begins to wonder if she was hired for this assignment specifically because he believes that through her he will learn more about the container and the machinations surrounding it. (It is the knowledge—the "intelligence"—that interests him.)

In the climax of the action, Hollis, Tito, Milgrim (brought by Brown), and Bigend are all drawn to Vancouver, British Columbia, where the container finally comes to port. There—and again by an accident that is not quite an accident—Hollis meets an enigmatic figure described as "the old man," whom the reader has met earlier in conjunction with Tito. The old man is a retired specialist in national security who, Hollis is told, went off the edge after September 11, 2001. He hates the direction the country has taken since then—the abuse of law, the torture, the corruption—and he has responded by calling on old friends in the trade to help him in a quixotic personal crusade.

In this respect, *Spook Country* resembles a wide variety of novels published in the shadow of the war in Iraq and the "war on terror," in which a plot of byzantine complexity leads in the end to the White House or somewhere in that neighborhood, and where the heart of darkness often reveals an embrace between shadowy government conspirators and Evangelical Christians. Examples include Michael Chabon's *The Yiddish Policemen's Union* (2007) and Peter Abrahams's *Nerve Damage* (2007). As for *Spook Country*, the money from the shipping container is supposed to end up at a megachurch in Idaho—"with its own television station . . . with an adjacent gated community." That $100 million has to be laundered somewhere.

This trope hardly begins to encompass what Gibson is up to in the novel, which has to be read in conjunction with *Pattern Recognition*. The title of that novel introduces what seems to be the overarching concern of the trilogy in the making. Human beings are inveterate pattern recognizers. The protagonist of *Pattern Recognition*, Cayce Pollard, makes her living doing just that. She is a "coolhunter," anticipating trends in style and fashion and consumption: "What I do is pattern recognition. I try to recognize a pattern before anyone else does."

Cayce remembers her father, Win Pollard, a security consultant, warning against "apophenia," the "perception of connections and meaningfulness in unrelated things." Gibson has frequently zeroed in on what he regards as instances of this human weakness, and he does so again in *Spook Country*—as when, for example, a character says that the effectiveness of terrorism depends on the same human flaw that permits people to imagine that they will win the lottery. In both *Pattern Recognition* and *Spook Country*, this vigilance against "an illusion of meaningfulness, faulty pattern recognition," is balanced by an awareness of an opposite error: a stubborn refusal to acknowledge patterns, connections, meanings—perhaps because they violate preconceptions.

In both novels, the odd word "steganography" turns up at a crucial juncture. Steganography is a way of transmitting a message by hiding it in a larger message. Such a "carrier" message does not appear to be hiding anything. It could be—as in *Spook Country*—a digital music file, in which the secret message has been very thinly spread (and perhaps encrypted to boot). Reading a novel in some ways resembles reading a "stego file" with an alert eye for the hidden message (and a healthy respect for the power of apophenia to seduce the mind).

In *Pattern Recognition*, Win Pollard—who was in the vicinity of the World Trade Center on September 11, 2001—is missing and presumed dead, though on several occasions he seems to be speaking to Cayce. She recalls putting posters of him up after the attacks, hoping someone will recognize him: "Win, deeply and perhaps professionally camera-shy, had left remarkably few full-face images, and the best she'd been able to do had been one that her friends had sometimes mistaken for the younger William S. Burroughs." In *Spook Country*, meeting the nameless "old man," Hollis thinks "he looked a little like William Burroughs, minus the bohemian substrate (or perhaps the methadone)." Are Win Pollard and the old man one and the same, or is this merely a coincidence? Gibson makes us think about the way in which we seek patterns, recognize them, evaluate them, find meaning in them.

Gibson is also a superb observer of the everyday. Hollis may be speaking for him when she thinks about the appeal of writing: "She had always, she'd reluctantly come to know, wanted to write. . . . She was fascinated by how things worked in the world, and why people did them." Gibson seems to share that fascination, and he looks at all manner of things with the gaze of a visitor to a distant world. Hollywood, New York, Washington, D.C., Vancouver: All are at once familiar and passing strange, via the virtual reality of ink on a page.

*John Wilson*

### Review Sources

*Booklist* 104, no. 7 (December 1, 2007): 66.
*Entertainment Weekly*, no. 947 (August 10, 2007): 72.
*Kirkus Reviews* 75, no. 11 (June 1, 2007): 521.
*Library Journal* 132, no. 20 (December 15, 2007): 166.
*The New York Times Book Review* 156 (August 26, 2007): 12.
*The New Yorker* 83, no. 20 (July 23, 2007): 79.
*Publishers Weekly* 254, no. 25 (June 18, 2007): 35.
*Time* 170, no. 7 (August 13, 2007): 67.

# STANLEY
## The Impossible Life of Africa's Greatest Explorer

*Author:* Tim Jeal (1945-    )
*Publisher:* Yale University Press (New Haven, Conn.).
   608 pp. $38
*Type of work:* Biography
*Time:* 1841-1904
*Locale:* Denbigh, Wales; Liverpool; New Orleans; Ten-
   nessee (Battle of Shiloh); Colorado; Turkey; Greece;
   Spain; London; Africa (Ethiopia, Zanzibar, East Af-
   rica, the Congo Free State, the Sudan); Brussels

*This biography of Henry Morton Stanley presents new*
*information on the discoverer of David Livingstone and*
*emphasizes his role as an explorer; though marred by*
*excessive defensiveness about Stanley, the book raises im-*
*portant issues about European colonialism*

*Principal personages:*
   HENRY MORTON STANLEY, born JOHN ROWLANDS, an explorer
   ELIZABETH PARRY, his mother
   HENRY HOPE STANLEY, his supposed adoptive father
   DAVID LIVINGSTONE, an African explorer
   JAMES GORDON BENNETT, JR., the publisher of the *New York Herald*
   TIPPU TIP, an Arab slave trader
   LEOPOLD II, the king of Belgium
   EMIN PASHA, the governor of southern Sudan
   KATIE GOUGH ROBERTS, Stanley's fiancé
   ALICE PIKE, Stanley's fiancé
   DOROTHY TENNANT STANLEY, Stanley's wife

The most startling thing about *Stanley: The Impossible Life of Africa's Greatest Explorer*, a new biography of Henry Morton Stanley, is Tim Jeal's claim that Stanley's famous greeting never happened. Jeal argues that Stanley never said, "Dr. Livingstone, I presume," when he found David Livingstone in the African wild. For those with only a passing knowledge of African exploration, this will come as a shock. The only thing most people know about Stanley is that he was an American journalist sent out to find Livingstone and that he uttered his famous line on finding him. According to Jeal, most of that is untrue. Stanley was not an American; in fact, his real name was not Stanley. He was not primarily a journalist; at least in later life, he abandoned journalism for exploration. The famous line was an invention, albeit by Stanley himself when writing about the incident and in press interviews. More-over, Jeal recounts that Livingstone, the renowned explorer and missionary, was not actually lost when Stanley found him.

This is revisionism with a vengeance, and perhaps not all of it is to be believed. On the issue of the famous line, for instance, Jeal's argument is mainly based on the absence of evidence (a page torn from Stanley's diary and a lack of any confirmatory statement from Livingstone) rather than on positive new information. In the end, the truth about Stanley, as Jeal demonstrates, is that he became inextricably associated with the famous line, even mocked for it, which is ironic if he indeed never spoke it and only invented it because he thought it made him sound like the proper English gentleman he wished he were.

*Tim Jeal is the author of two previous biographies,* Livingstone *(1973) and* Baden-Powell *(1989). He has also published a memoir,* Swimming with My Father *(2004), and numerous novels, including* Cushing's Crusade *(1974), which won the John Llewellyn Rhys Prize.*

According to Jeal, Stanley's life was full of such ironies. He not only was mocked for saying something he only pretended he said but also was savagely criticized for doing things he only pretended to have done. Throughout his life, Stanley told lies to create a better impression of himself, lies that came back to haunt him. Most notably, he exaggerated the number of Africans he killed in order to appear strong. As a result, he was reviled for being callously cruel and in the end was denied a burial spot beside Livingstone in Westminster Abbey.

All this is not to say that Jeal criticizes Stanley for telling lies. Throughout this very sympathetic biography, Jeal is at pains to defend Stanley at every turn, to justify his actions, even his lies and his killings, or at least to excuse them and understand them, in an attempt to have readers pity Stanley and to admire the way he overcame his difficult background and became a "Homeric" hero. In this way, Jeal sets himself at odds with both the debunking fashion in biography writing, in which biographers set out to condemn their subjects, and the current views on Stanley, colonialism, and African history. This aspect of his revisionism is in fact far more significant than his attempt to discredit the "Dr. Livingstone, I presume" story. Jeal sets himself against the proponents of "postcolonial guilt" and attempts to justify nineteenth century European colonialism in Africa.

Jeal begins by tracing Stanley's origins as an illegitimate child named John Rowlands in Wales. Sent from relative to relative and eventually ending up in a workhouse, the young Stanley had a hard time of it, especially in Jeal's version of events. Frank McLynn, an earlier biographer, downplays the suffering, but Jeal plays it up. McLynn, writing in the late 1980's and early 1990's, adopted the debunking tone, painting Stanley as cruel, even sadomasochistic, and also latently homosexual. Jeal's aim throughout is to refute McLynn and portray a humane, compassionate, fully heterosexual Stanley.

Escaping from the workhouse, Stanley went first to Liverpool and then to the United States, landing in New Orleans, where he changed his name. Jeal did not discover the name change; in fact, it was included in Stanley's own autobiography, published after his death. However, one of Jeal's new claims is that Stanley's account of how he came by his new name is false. Stanley was not adopted by a rich merchant by the name of Henry Stanley who bestowed his name on the penniless refugee. Instead, young John Rowlands simply appropriated the original Henry Stanley's name in order to create a more impressive life story for himself. Again, Jeal is understanding, summoning popular psychology to the defense of his subject by saying, "Young people who lie usually do so because they feel bad about themselves and need to enhance their self-esteem."

Jeal also defends Stanley's desertions during the American Civil War, his threatening a U.S. Army officer with a gun after the war, and his violent attack on a Turk in an early exploration effort in the Middle East. Jeal either accepts Stanley's version of events (he was acting in self-defense in Turkey) or calls his actions "not unforgivable." Jeal's book is very much the case for the defense, which mars it as much as a prosecutorial approach would. In the end, posterity cares little whether Stanley was a good or bad man; no doubt he was a mixture of the two. The real reason to write or read a biography about him is to understand his achievements.

Jeal certainly thinks Stanley had achievements, primarily as an explorer. Again, this will surprise those who have heard that Stanley was a journalist sent by the publisher of the *New York Herald* to find Livingstone. Jeal questions that story too, suggesting that the impetus for the mission came not from the publisher but from Stanley himself, who became obsessed with Africa and Livingstone.

Jeal also suggests that Livingstone was not lost at all, just as on a later mission, Emin Pasha, whom Stanley was supposedly going to rescue in the Sudan, did not really need rescuing. In the first instance, and perhaps in the second, the motivation was not that Livingstone was lost or that Emin Pasha was endangered but rather that Stanley himself sought to perform a great deed and make a name for himself. In fact, Stanley was worried that someone else would find Livingstone first and thus deprive him of the glory. Still, Livingstone, who was ill and short of supplies, was glad to see him, and the public was thrilled; it was a journalistic coup to find the famous explorer, a coup that Jeal does not make as much of as he might have, perhaps because he wants to portray Stanley as an explorer in his own right, not just as the discoverer of one.

This biography makes a case for Stanley's achievements as an explorer. On a second expedition into Africa, he helped establish the sources of the Nile and became the first person to map the whole length of the Congo River. He also mapped various African lakes and established the first settlement at what became first Léopoldville and later Kinshasa. The latter work he did in the employ of the notorious King Leopold II of Belgium, who established the so-called Congo Free State, the site of numerous atrocities perhaps best known through Joseph Conrad's novella *Heart of Darkness* (1899). Jeal argues that Stanley became associated with the atrocities even though he left the Congo region before most of them occurred. As for the other atrocities, they were mostly committed by his subordinates. Jeal spends a great deal of time going over the accusations against Stanley, in effect describing events twice over: when they actually happened, and when controversy erupted over them. This analysis adds unnecessarily to the length of the book, as does the tedious recounting of Stanley's marches through the wilderness.

Whereas, according to Jeal, Richard Hall's *Stanley: An Adventurer Explored* (1974) skimped on the details of Stanley's exploration, Jeal's biography certainly does not do that. He repeatedly describes the swampy terrain; men struck down by dysentery, malaria, or smallpox; men starving, being attacked by natives, attacking the natives, surviving rains and cataracts, trading with the natives, negotiating with them, fighting among themselves, and so on. The effect is probably the opposite of what Jeal intends. Instead of highlighting Stanley's achievements, the writing drowns them in a mass of detail. Hall's shorter, brisker book may give a better sense of the achievement, and it does so without resorting to debunking Stanley or defending him; he presents the record and lets readers judge for themselves.

Hall also presents a clear discussion of the confused issue of the date of Stanley's birth (January 28, 1841, it appears). Jeal does not even mention Stanley's birthday, except in a late footnote, oddly beginning his story when Stanley was five years old. However, Jeal has made some discoveries, for instance about how Stanley acquired his name and about the "Dr. Livingstone, I presume" incident, and most of all he raises the important issue of how we are to look on European colonialism in Africa.

Almost in passing, Jeal mentions that Stanley's dispatches from Africa helped lead to the abolition of slavery in Zanzibar. He might have elaborated more on this; in general, he gives short shrift to Stanley's writings, but it would be interesting to learn more about what Stanley said, what his ideas were, and whether he had an over-arching philosophy. However, there is enough here to give pause to the reader with a limited knowledge of African history. Stanley was both a supporter of European colonialism and an opponent of slavery. Readers might think this contradictory, but they will learn from Jeal's account that in East Africa at this time slavery was the province of Arab slave traders, and it was the Europeans who put an end to it.

Stanley thought that opening Africa to modern, European commerce and civilization was a noble cause, and Jeal seems to agree with him. He notes of course the terrible atrocities that occurred under colonial rule, notably in Leopold's Congo, but his point seems to be that these were aberrations or perhaps unfortunately inevitable.

Jeal's somewhat contradictory accompanying point is that Stanley did not commit atrocities on the scale of others and was against Leopold's exploitive approach, at least once he understood it for what it was. That is, Jeal argues that others were more guilty than Stanley, but he also says that European guilt in general has been overstated and that in some respects the European entry into Africa was a good thing.

A biography is probably not the place to discuss the merits and demerits of colonialism, but if Jeal's book can inspire a new look at what is now so easily condemned and dismissed, it will perhaps have done something useful.

*Sheldon Goldfarb*

## Review Sources

*The Economist* 382 (March 17, 2007): 90-91.
*The Guardian*, March 24, 2007, p. 10.
*History Today* 57, no. 4 (April, 2007): 63-64.
*London Review of Books* 29, no. 7 (April 5, 2007): 9-10.
*The New York Review of Books* 54, no. 19 (December 6, 2007): 47-49.
*The New York Times Book Review* 157 (September 30, 2007): 1-11.
*The Observer*, April 1, 2007, p. 27.
*Sunday Telegraph*, March 18, 2007, p. 38.
*Sunday Times*, March 18, 2007, p. 39.

# THE STILLBORN GOD
## Religion, Politics, and the Modern West

*Author:* Mark Lilla (1956-      )
*Publisher:* Alfred A. Knopf (New York). 334 pp. $26.00
*Type of work:* History, religion

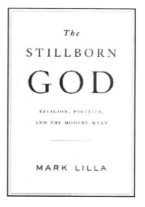

*An intellectual history of the separation of politics from religion during the early modern period of Western civilization and of efforts to bring the two together again*

Principal personages:

THOMAS HOBBES (1588-1679), English
    political and social philosopher known
    for his pessimistic view of human nature
JOHN LOCKE (1632-1704), English
    philosopher known as an early empiricist
JEAN-JACQUES ROUSSEAU (1712-1778),
    French political philosopher who saw human beings
    as fundamentally good but corrupted by contemporary society
IMMANUEL KANT (1724-1804), German thinker who argued
    that the human mind imposes a basic framework of understanding
    on the world
GEORG WILHELM FRIEDRICH HEGEL (1770-1831), the most influential
    German philosopher of the late eighteenth and early nineteenth
    centuries who saw human life in terms of a progressive movement
    of history
HERMANN COHEN (1842-1918), German Jewish thinker who argued
    that Judaism was consistent with a modern German state
KARL BARTH (1886-1968), one of the most influential Protestant
    theologians of the twentieth century
FRANZ ROSENZWEIG (1886-1929), early twentieth century German
    Jewish thinker
FRIEDRICH GOGARTEN (1887-1967), theologian and collaborator of
    Karl Barth who became an advocate of the pro-Nazi German
    Christians for a time
ERNST BLOCH (1885-1977), utopian German Marxist author

Most Americans and Europeans today accept the idea that religion and politics should occupy distinct places in public life and the related idea that people who follow different religions can be citizens of the same national state. There are still some debates about the relationship between these two, concerning religious displays in governmental spaces or the acceptability of encouraging expressions of faith in state-run schools, but these debates are based on variations in shared assumptions. In *The Stillborn God: Religion, Politics, and the Modern West*, Mark Lilla argues that these assumptions about the distinction between theology and politics are not necessary products of increasing rationality or of modernization. Instead, tensions within the

*Mark Lilla is professor of humanities at Columbia University. He writes about the history of ideas, focusing on how religion and politics have been influenced by the Enlightenment. His work* The Reckless Mind: Intellectuals in Politics *(2001) attracted attention for its critical examination of the attraction of modern intellectuals to extremist ideologies.* The Stillborn God *is based on the Carlyle lectures that Lilla delivered at Oxford University in 2003.*

Christian tradition created a Western reaction against political theology.

Political theology, according to Lilla, involves thinking and talking about political authority as based on the divine. Christian political theology inherited tensions at the core of Christian beliefs about the world. The central article of Christianity, that God became man through Christ, set up questions about God's nature and about the divine relationship to the world. In the Trinity, God is threefold, but one of the three parts is a transcendent deity and one of the parts is a human in the world. Is the world therefore good because God made it and came into it, or is it bad because it requires divine grace? The question of working in the world or rejecting the world therefore recurs throughout the history of Christian theology, as does the question of the nature of the Trinity. Christ came into the world apart from the Father, according to Christian beliefs, but he departed to a heavenly realm and is expected to return to Earth again at some point in the future, at which point both worlds will be reunited. Christians are continually in the position of living in this world but looking to another world, and expecting that this world will be ended. In addition, Christianity was historically an otherworldly religion that became the faith of a worldly empire. Struggles between religious and political authorities and disagreement about the true nature of the Christian state were therefore not only results of the development of competing institutions but also consequences of an unresolved problem at the heart of the faith.

The difficulty of drawing a clear line for the descent of authority from God to humanity could and did lead to violent conflict. By the sixteenth century, the religious wars had become so violent that they were tearing Europe apart. Lilla finds in Thomas Hobbes, author of the social and political treatise *Levianthan* (1651), the beginning of an answer to the religious crisis of Christendom. According to Lilla, Hobbes changed the nature of the political discourse about religion. Instead of asking what kind of worldly order should be derived from the divine order, Hobbes asked why human beings seek religious belief. He shifted the focus from God to humanity. Lilla makes a helpful contribution to our understanding of Hobbes by maintaining that the early modern author's account of religion was essentially the same as his account of political order. Hobbes famously argued that governmental authority is based on fear. The struggle of all individuals for their own ends creates an insecurity that can be resolved only by handing over power to a sovereign. Similarly, though, Lilla points out that Hobbes also based his religious psychology on fear. Fear of the power of nature leads to belief in God (the religious version of raising up a sovereign), and fear of God then leads to obedience to some set of religious precepts and to efforts to impose religious precepts on others. Hobbes, in Lilla's view, was the author of what

Lilla calls the "Great Separation," since Hobbes showed the way for talking about both politics and religion in naturalistic terms, in place of considering nature and politics from the perspective of theology. Even those, such as philosopher John Locke, who disagreed with the view of the nature of humanity presented by Hobbes tended to follow Hobbes in focusing on human experience rather than on divine order.

After Hobbes forced faith and authority apart, Jean-Jacques Rousseau and Immanuel Kant brought them back together, but in a manner that had been fundamentally changed. Rousseau, like Hobbes, explained religion by asking why people believe, instead of explaining human institutions in terms of the sacred. However, Rousseau placed the origin of religion in the moral feelings of people and believed that similar moral feelings could guide social life. Lilla places particular importance on Rousseau's story in the book *Emile* (1762) of the Savoyard Vicar, who found the answer to his own religious doubts by looking to his own sentiments. Kant took a darker view of human nature than Rousseau did, but he maintained that religion was necessary to direct human beings toward the ethical life. For Kant, belief in God and in immortality was necessary in order for a rational human being to avoid despair and pursue the highest good in life. Therefore, any rational human should believe. Both Rousseau and Kant followed the basic reorientation toward the human prescribed by Hobbes by psychologizing religious life.

Georg Wilhelm Friedrich Hegel continued the human-centered reintroduction of religion into political life. Again, however, he relied not on revelation but on the role of belief in human life. Hegel conceived of religion as the historical expression of the progress of human awareness and portrayed Protestantism as the last religious stage in this progress, so that faith became an expression of a citizenship. Under Hegel's inspiration, German thinkers of the nineteenth century created a liberal Protestantism that served the order of the day. German Jewish theologians such as Hermann Cohen attempted to bring Judaism into the liberal fold by demonstrating that Jewish beliefs had also progressed over time and served the same civic goals as Protestantism. English and American discourses about politics tended to follow directly from Hobbes by considering government solely in terms of social interactions and competing interests. German discourses, directed by the liberal Protestant heritage from Hegel, considered how religion was part of the evolution of the modern state. Neither followed the old political-theology line of deriving government from divine revelation.

In Lilla's view, Hegel and his successors had brought religion into the service of the state and progress. Following World War I, though, religious thinkers staged a revolt against this type of statist progressivism in faith. Lilla points out the Christian theologian Karl Barth and the Jewish thinker Franz Rosenzweig as two German authors who inspired the reaction against the Hegelian strand of religious thinking. Barth emphasized God's radical otherness from the world and was distinctly antipolitical in his early writings. Rosenzweig saw in Judaism an impulse toward messianic utopianism that maintained the Jews outside politics and the state. Both of them emphasized a need to break dramatically with the things of the present and to look beyond the current organization of society and government toward an ultimate, otherworldly reality. Lilla characterizes these two as gnostics, using a term from early Christian history for those who reject the material world in favor of a radically separate spiritual realm.

While neither Barth nor Rosenzweig advocated extreme politics, Lilla maintains that their celebration of a dramatic break with the present led to the reintroduction of religion into politics through the messianic political religions of Nazism and Communism. Lilla connects the dramatic, millennial version of religious feeling expressed by Barth, for example, to the assumption of power by the Nazi messiah Adolf Hitler in 1933. Lilla points out that Friedrich Gogarten, a friend and close collaborator of Barth, was led by a rejection of modern liberalism and an advocacy of a new dispensation in religion to support the pro-Nazi German Christian movement. On the Left, the German Jewish thinker Ernst Bloch became almost literally a worshiper of Communism, believing that this ideology would bring about an end-time utopia.

Lilla concludes that Hobbes was right about the need for the Great Separation, even if the English philosopher was wrong about finding the origins of belief in fear. The examples of Gogarten and Bloch are cautionary about the dangers that can result from introducing the sacred into civic life. Lilla sees a rebirth of political theology in our own times. He maintains that long centuries of assuming the secular nature of politics in the English and American traditions have bred a complacency, so that those within these traditions lack the vocabulary for talking about the psychological complexities of religion in social life.

*The Stillborn God* provides a fascinating, well-written inquiry into the role of religion in modern political life. It gives fresh accounts of the thinking of some of the major authors on this topic. Lilla manages to give new views of even such foundational and widely recognized writers as Hobbes. One of his valuable contributions is to explain aspects of some of the most difficult theorists, such as Hegel. With the apparent increasing influence of religion on political life in many countries today, the questions of how the two have been connected historically and should be connected take on critical importance.

The book does have its limitations. One of those is the tendency to approach religious modernity purely in terms of the history of ideas. Lilla accounts for historical developments at the level of intellectual activity alone, as if human experience were the product of disembodied theories. Reading him, one would think that Hobbes just thought up the separation of religion from politics and the anthropocentric view of faith and government and that his thinking led to widespread change throughout Western society. This ignores the part played by urbanization, the centralization of nation-states and the consequent rise of secular bureaucracies, the growing economic complexity that promoted social pluralism, and the flourishing of print media in creating both multiplicities of beliefs and governments that had to accept those multiplicities. Hobbes, Rousseau, Kant, and Hegel were arguably expressing the currents of their times, not creating those currents, as Lilla indicates.

This question about whether the intellectuals Lilla discusses created or simply expressed the worldviews of their times raises the broader problem of causation that runs throughout the book. If Hobbes did cause the Great Separation, as Lilla seems to imply, just how did he do this? Were most of the citizens and politicians who spoke and thought in secular terms directly inspired by their readings of *Leviathan*? More recently, what contribution did the theology of Karl Barth really make to the rise of Adolf Hitler?

*The Stillborn God* provokes more questions than it answers. Still, it is an engaging, valuable piece of intellectual history that will appeal to a broad range of readers.

*Carl L. Bankston III*

## Review Sources

*Commentary* 124, no. 4 (November, 2007): 60-65.
*Commonweal* 134, no. 18 (October 26, 2007): 32-34.
*The Humanist* 68, no. 1 (January/February, 2008): 45-46.
*The New York Times Book Review* 156 (September 16, 2007): 9.
*Publishers Weekly* 254, no. 27 (July 9, 2007): 49-50.
*Weekly Standard* 13, no. 14 (December 17, 2007): 39-42.

# THE SUICIDAL PLANET
## How to Prevent Global Climate Catastrophe

*Author:* Mayer Hillman (1931-     ), with Tina Fawcett
  and Sudhir Chella Rajan (1961-     )
*Publisher:* St. Martin's Press (New York).
  296 pp. $23.95
*Type of work:* Environment

*Hillman argues that drastic, rapid measures must be taken immediately to reduce greenhouse gases in order to save humans and other species from the pernicious effects of global warming, and he and his colleagues recommend a practicable, albeit civilization-altering, program*

Granted its basic assumption about global warming, *The Suicidal Planet: How to Prevent Global Climate Catastrophe* offers a rational model policy to reduce the use of fossil fuels in order to prevent environmental catastrophe. Writing a sober, earnest appeal to action, the authors, Mayer Hillman, Tina Fawcett, and Sudhir Chella Rajan, all environmental scientists, carefully avoid sensationalism while explaining the nature of the problem and its likely consequences. Nevertheless, their message is alarming. Humanity, collectively, faces a uniquely perilous threat during this century. Likewise, their remedy is alarming to all those, the vast majority of people, who want life to go on more or less as before, except better. That remedy is a new attitude toward energy consumption known as "contraction and convergence," and it would entail a fundamental reordering of culture, at least in those industrialized societies that produce most of the harmful pollution.

The book's tone is cautiously optimistic, yet its arguments seem ill-suited to changing the attitudes of those who now most enjoy the benefits from fossil-fuel usage. *The Suicidal Planet* is, unfortunately, like a medicine that, while sure to effect a cure, is so unpalatable that the patient prefers the disease, however much pain it is sure to cause eventually. That is to say, the authors hope that their readers will respond rationally, responsibly, and unselfishly when for many people in developed countries, the United States above all, insouciant waste is the very basis of their present well-being.

The authors develop their basic assumption about the environment's health in the first of the book's three sections, "The Problem." It is an assumption well supported by recent research: Waste carbon produced by burning fossil fuels, such as petroleum and coal, creates atmospheric carbon dioxide that prevents heat from venting into outer space (the greenhouse effect), thereby warming the atmosphere. So far, the global average temperature has risen a little over 1.1 degrees Fahrenheit during the last two centuries, two-thirds of that rise occurring since 1970. That seemingly modest amount comes mostly as the result of a human-caused increase of carbon dioxide

from 280 parts per million (ppm) before the
Industrial Revolution to about 380 ppm during the first decade of the twenty-first century. Should there be another degree of temperature increase, the authors warn, changes
to climate will occur that may render much
of the globe uninhabitable for thousands of
years. The book summarizes the likely consequences, all of which are familiar from accounts in the news media and in films: rising
sea levels and displacement of coastal populations; more powerful and destructive extreme weather events, such as hurricanes
and tornadoes; altered precipitation patterns,
leaving some now-fertile areas parched by
long-lasting drought; widespread economic
devastation; spread of diseases and pests out
of the tropics; and a wholesale loss of plant
and animal species.

∼
*Trained as an architect and city
planner, Mayer Hillman holds a
doctorate from the University of
Edinburgh. He is a senior fellow
emeritus at London's Policy Studies
Institute.*
*Tina Fawcett holds a doctorate in
household energy use from University
College London and is a senior
researcher at the Environmental
Change Institute at Oxford University.*
*Sudhir Chella Rajan heads the
Global Politics and Institutions
Program at Tellus Institute in Boston.
He has a doctorate in environmental
science and engineering from the
University of California, Los Angeles.*
∼

Because greenhouse gases are accumulat-
ing at a swiftly accelerating pace, 2 degrees Fahrenheit of global warming is likely to
come soon, perhaps by 2020. If readers accept that this constitutes a "tipping point"
that will trigger rapid, irreversible climate change, then the authors' subsequent recommendations are cogent and urgent. Therein lies a problem, however. Unacknowl-
edged in their succinct, lucid explanations, the question of a tipping point, or at what
temperature it may come, remains in some dispute. While scientists overwhelmingly
agree that danger lies near and is potentially lethal, prognostications differ, albeit not
by much. Really, it should not matter whether the point of no return comes after a rise
of 2 degrees Fahrenheit or 4 degrees, within twenty years or fifty nears. It should matter no more to a sane person than the question of whether to slow a speeding car before
entering a blind curve just because the exact sharpness of the curve is not yet apparent.
However, the credibility of the science does matter. It matters because whenever experts disagree, however slightly, or even appear to disagree when they do not, that
"controversy" is seized upon to defend the status quo until "there is better science" (to
paraphrase one prominent American mentality). To continue the analogy, it would
be as if the speeding car's driver decides not to reduce speed, despite all traffic signs,
until after entering the curve, when its shape becomes completely visible. That is suicidal.

The authors are well aware of the nuisance of politicized science. Most unfortunately, their references to scientific consensus, environmental ethics, social justice,
and crusading politicians like former vice president Al Gore do little to attract the
attention of those people who do not want to pay attention and do not think that they
have to yet. The authors do much better in exposing the rationalizations that encourage a comfortable complacency among the people who do nevertheless accept that a

problem exists: that climate change will be ephemeral; that advances in technology will solve the problem; that there is nothing that can be done about it; or that climate change actually may be beneficial, providing only that one lives in the right area.

Those readers who are willing to acknowledge the book's cogency then are confronted with a somber assessment in the second major section, "Current Strategies." Those measures now being undertaken to reduce dependency on fossil fuels and to mitigate their environmental impact are all insufficient to stave off catastrophe. One by one the authors explain why these measures have either only modest effect, no real net effect, or an unintended deleterious effect. The measures include renewable energy sources, such as wind and solar power; nuclear energy; innovations, such as hydrogen as fuel, electric motors, or fuel cells; energy efficiency in general; and carbon sequestration (removing carbon dioxide from the atmosphere and pumping it underground). Here the authors explain tellingly and fault even "green" political action organizations for promoting measures that are little more than wishful thinking. They show that even if all current methods that are being promoted were used to their greatest projected capability, only 12 percent of the needed reduction could occur by 2020 and only one-third by 2050. Do not depend on these measures, the authors insist. They also insist that individual action alone, however well-intentioned and wisely implemented, will fall short. Nor do the authors countenance the belief, advanced by President George W. Bush, that a free market economy and economic growth will supply a solution. Business as it is currently practiced exacerbates the problem.

Their remedy to carbon dioxide accumulation is austere. They delineate it in the book's third section, "The Solution." To avoid catastrophe, carbon dioxide levels must be stabilized at no higher than 450 ppm sometime between 2020 and 2050, only 70 ppm more than the level as of 2007. To achieve this a staggering 80 percent decrease in worldwide fossil fuel consumption is essential, starting at once. It would indeed, as they write, "require a fundamental reevaluation of the character and quality of our life." In nations long accustomed to high levels of consumption, like the United States, much would change. Gone, for instance, would be cars powered solely by gasoline engines and most air travel, drastically altering one of the nation's most prized freedoms, mobility. Moreover, since these are primary transportation modes for tourism and since tourism accounts for 11 percent of the global economy, the consequences of just these two types of reduction would be dire. When one considers the effects on goods and services even if cleaner transportation eventually becomes available, as well as dependency on coal-fired power plants for electricity, it is clear that the authors do not understate the challenge.

They never claim their proposed solution will be easy, only possible and drastically needed. However disruptive and complicated in execution, contraction and convergence is simple in concept. Contraction is the reduction of carbon dioxide emissions to a safe level by a given date; convergence means an equitable per capita share of the burden of reduction. Two problems are evident at once. The first lies in the phrase "safe level," which almost surely will be controversial. Second is their contention that emissions policy must be mandatory, enforced by governments, and strictly adhered to everywhere in the world all the time. Wealthy, industrialized, high-consumption countries would have to sacrifice much more than low-consumption countries. To make the idea more attractive, the authors recommend that a "cap-and-trade" system of some sort be instituted. Wealthy countries, to mitigate the impact on their styles of life, could buy carbon emissions rights, as tradable credits, from low-emissions countries that do not use up their "cap" allotment. (European countries began a version of this system in 2005.) The same might be feasible at an individual user level, such as a person or corporation. Even despite incentives, however, a binding international agreement would be difficult to negotiate. The history of past environmental treaties, such as the Kyoto Protocol, does not encourage optimism for a speedy outcome.

*The Suicidal Planet* treads lightly over many practical issues integral to any global agreement. How would contraction be enforced internationally and locally? What body would set the value of emissions credits? How would cheaters, exploiters, and gougers be dealt with? What of war, disasters like Hurricane Katrina, or social collapse? Obviously a short book such as this one cannot provide specific recommendations to answer every possible worry, and this one is concerned with a general conception, not formulated policies. Nevertheless, it seldom even nods at such large potential problems, and that is unnerving. How can a fundamental reevaluation of quality of life occur in the face of these concerns, not to mention the ongoing conflicts that obsess humanity's many factions, and how can it be done in time to be practicable?

It is true, as the authors claim, that climate change is not taken seriously enough by most people or by most governments, and the urgency of the problem makes it tempting to ask more of a book like *The Suicidal Planet* than it is designed to deliver. While reading, one cheers for the authors' thoughtfulness and sense of justice but wishes for greater guidance and gusto. To avoid sensationalism and to be plain and clear, the book reads like a PowerPoint presentation, complete with bulleted main points, much repetition, and commercial prose. While there are a few helpful charts to help readers comprehend the occasional statistics, the authors make few concrete gestures to reader engagement. Their attempt to be sobering is altogether too sober to engage enthusiasm.

Enthusiasm will become important. If contraction and convergence, or any worthwhile policy, is to be implemented in time, popular sentiment will force it. The authors rightly call on government action, not individual volunteerism, and that requires political leadership. Putting the right leaders—provided they can even be found—in power will in turn require electorates focused on global warming as the central issue of the next half century. Wisdom, lasting commitment, and global unity: That is asking a lot. Of course, the alternative is to do nothing or too little. Then humanity will have to adapt to climate change, which will surely cost far, far more in wealth, peace, and life.

*Roger Smith*

## Review Sources

*Booklist* 103, no. 11 (February 1, 2007): 9-10.
*Future Survey* 29, no. 7 (July, 2007): 4-5.
*Publishers Weekly* 254, no. 6 (February 5, 2007): 49-50.

# SUNDAY
## A History of the First Day from Babylonia to the Super Bowl

*Author:* Craig Harline
*Publisher:* Doubleday (New York). 450 pp. $26.00
*Type of work:* History

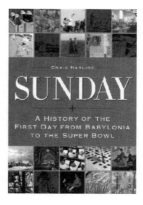

*A lively account of the rise and development of a day that
has been both dreaded and beloved, focusing especially on
England, Holland, France, Belgium, and the United States
and showing that the way Sunday has evolved in these settings says much about what is unique to them*

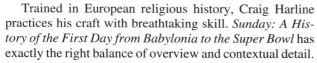

Trained in European religious history, Craig Harline
practices his craft with breathtaking skill. *Sunday: A History of the First Day from Babylonia to the Super Bowl* has
exactly the right balance of overview and contextual detail.
Intriguing "close-ups" offer the reader tangy characters and vivid situations, breaking
up denser explanatory and technical material into more appropriable units. Both specialized and general audiences are bound to profit from this fine work.

Harline's first chapter, "Prologue: Sunday Ascendant," helps one understand how
Sunday came into Western culture, becoming both a blessing and a problem. While
the ancient world employed diverse calendars and schemes (many of them lunar-
based) for determining weeks, the modern system comes from the Hellenistic Greeks
and Judaism by way of Rome. In pre-Christian, Ptolemaic Alexandria, astronomers
fixed the distance from Earth of the seven known planets. Saturn was the furthest
away; then came Jupiter, Mars, the Sun, Venus, Mercury, and the Moon—these
names, of course, are Anglicized versions of the Latin variants. Each of these heavenly bodies exerted its particular influence on the earth and became associated not
only with days of the week but particular hours within that week. Curiously, their
distances did not correlate with a planet's place in the scheme of days. Rather, "Saturn
Day was the first day, Sun Day the second, then Moon Day, Mars Day (Tuesday),
Mercury Day (Wednesday), Jupiter Day (Thursday), and Venus Day (Friday)."
Significantly, at this point no day enjoyed a privileged status.

In 587 B.C.E., the Babylonians conquered the Jewish kingdom and carried many of
its inhabitants into exile. According to Harline, one cannot determine whether the
Babylonian fascination with the number seven influenced the pattern of the Jewish
week or a preexistent Jewish scheme influenced the mental habits of the captors.
In any case, by the second century C.E. Jews and their rigorous Sabbatarian practices
had exerted tremendous influence on surrounding cultures. Christianity only deepened this influence, though for a variety of reasons the followers of Jesus of Nazareth
moved the special day to the first day of the Roman week—which had earlier become
Sunday instead of Saturday. One reason for this change was the increasing prestige
of Sunday in pagan religion—especially the cult of the Invincible Sun, favored by a

~

*Craig Harline is the author of* A Bishop's Tale *(2000),* The Burdens of Sister Margaret *(2000), and* Miracles at the Jesus Oak *(2003). He is a professor of history at Brigham Young University.*

~

succession of emperors, and Mithraism, the influential religion of the Roman soldiers, which honored Sunday with special rituals and rest.

Constantine's proclamation in 321 declaring Sunday as the official holy day for Roman citizens may have been made to benefit the huge number of Christians now under his rule. "More likely, Constantine, like many Roman aristocrats of the time, was simply trying to find common ground for his mixed pagan and Christian subjects, especially his soldiers," observes Harline. Herein resides one of the great problems of Sunday, however. By setting aside a day for a general cessation of normal activities, a society doubtlessly benefits most people and thereby elicits greater loyalty, but how should "cessation" be handled? Inevitably a tension is established between those who "understand the true meaning" of Sunday—"it is the Lord's Day"—and those who follow other (or no) traditions.

How the meaning of Sunday gets worked out in the European West is the subject of Harline's six major chapters. Behind his account is a vast literature, but he eschews point-by-point documentation, providing instead fifty-three pages of bibliographical notes at the end of the book. He also uses several focusing devices to give narrative power to the book—discussing a typical Sunday in a particular village, drawing on personal journals, memoirs, short stories, novels, and even film. The result is a satisfyingly detailed work that still manages to sustain several conversations about scholarly disputes and interpretive problems.

Chapter 2, "Sunday Middle-Aged," is set in a fictional village in the south of England around the year 1300. Following a renowned essay by the historian H. S. Bennett, Harline traces out the events of a single Sunday in June from the standpoint of "houselings" or common villagers. While medieval theologians stressed with utmost clarity the need for Sundays to be worshipful and restful, the realities of agricultural life meant that plenty of work still had to be done before Mass. Haying and harvest season pressed peasants into Sabbath labor, much of it for the lord of the manor of which the village was a part. As the lord's word carried more weight than that of the priest, such work met with little criticism. Moreover, poor vicars usually led village churches, and they too had to labor in barns and fields. However, attendance at Mass was a paramount duty and, as Harline presents it, a singularly meaningful one because of the miracle that occurred at Eucharist.

Also, by this period, substantial Norman (Romanesque) churches were available to most villagers, who rejoiced in their beauty and learned from their sculptures, murals, and decorated rood screens. After Mass, the best meal of the week waited at home, with afternoon and evening bringing the festal character of the day to full expression. Meeting in the churchyard and at taverns, the houselings drank, gossiped, sang, danced, played games, wagered, and held competitions and fairs. Naturally, "depravity" or "concupiscence" might beckon at such times. Harline points out that the official Christian prohibition of sex on the Sabbath had spread to other days too—

Wednesdays, Fridays, Saturdays, all of Advent and Lent, and numerous other days and seasons. "This left fewer than one hundred days in the year for licit sexual relations—as long as the woman was not lactating or menstruating, of course, which were also proscribed days," he explains, adding dryly: "How many Christian villagers kept to such a schedule is unknown."

"Sunday Reformed," Harline's third chapter, develops a complex and surprising picture of the Sabbath in The Hague in 1624. Recalling that the rigorous Pilgrims sojourned in Holland before sailing for the New World, Americans might assume that the Protestant Reformation had triumphed there, but while the followers of Martin Luther, John Calvin, Huldrych Zwingli, and others transformed many of the churches in the Low Countries, the old "permissive" Catholic culture remained a vital force. Further, having fought a war of independence against militantly Catholic Spain, the Dutch Republic refused to install a regime of religious conformity. Thus, the Puritan Separatists' emigration was motivated by the perceived laxity of their fellow non-Catholics.

In any case, Luther and Calvin disagreed on the meaning and significance of the Sabbath, with Luther taking the position that, just as all vocations could be occasions for serving God, so too were all days of the week holy. Therefore, the Sabbath had no intrinsic significance. Calvin upheld the Sabbath as a "perpetual" institution, "established at Creation for all peoples and times." Calvin advocated a "moderate" Sabbath, and this view was echoed in The Hague by Dutch Reformed preachers. Drawing on diary materials, Harline shows how such moderation looked by following widower and schoolteacher David Beck on a typical Sunday. Beck indeed attends two long Sunday services, replete with biblical- and creedal-centered preaching, but he also gets in plenty of walking, visiting, eating, and drinking, relishing the opportunities for Sunday pleasure offered by one of Europe's richest cities.

"Sunday à la Mode," the book's second-longest chapter, begins with a summary of the opening scene of Louis Morin's humorous *Parisian Sunday: Notes of a Decadent* (1898). This work is the perfect vehicle for Harline's exploration of the "Continental Sunday," long celebrated by painters like Georges Seurat, Pierre-Auguste Renoir, and Édouard Manet. The aristocratic protagonist and his lady, "Pompon," decide that their lives have become boring. What better way to gain new amusement than to stay in Paris for the year and make every Sunday an exploration of the legendary *dimanche*? They would even turn their adventures into a book. There would be more than enough material to sustain their "research," for Paris's population had exploded after 1800. After 1830, church and state were separate; thus, blue laws did not exist. Also, while the urban working class outnumbered the bourgeoisie in France, the latter dominated cultural and political life. Both classes needed their Sunday outings, and renowned institutions had developed to make that possible. Morin's "decadents" therefore sample a cornucopia of delights: promenading on the city's wide boulevards, listening to singers at a café-concert, dancing at the Moulin Rouge on Montmartre, attending horse races—and even the occasional Mass. Throughout, they remain fastidious and snobbish observers, reflecting their breeding and status. In the end, however, they concede that "the people's Sundays were not necessarily more vulgar . . . than 'our own.'"

As Harline makes clear in his concluding "A Word After," the country whose Sundays most agree with him occur in Belgium. This gives special poignancy to Chapter 5, "Sunday Obscured," set in that country "on the last Sunday before the Great War." Relying on the Flemish writer Ernest Claes, Harline limns a lovely portrait of the old Catholic Sunday in this nation of villages. Attendance at Mass and afternoon catechism, dove racing, marvelous food, brass bands, cafés, singing, storytelling, and amenable drinking—these were some of the ingredients of a day looked forward to by most citizens. With the war, everything changed. Belgium was mostly occupied and experienced the full horror of trench warfare. The Hun-like Germans who have long dominated American imagery about this period do not show up in Harline's account. Like everyone else, they seem more victims of the elaborate plans of distant generals and new battlefield technologies. Belgian priests in the occupied territories conducted services for German Catholic soldiers. As they rested behind the lines, Bavarians "often worshipped alongside the Belgian locals at Sunday Mass, where they made a big impression." Still, warfare did not cease on the Sabbath. Thus, for most Belgians, the fighting became nightmarish in its totality. Days blended into other days so that many simply lost track of the calendar. Church bells could not sound, and in any case, many churches were damaged or in ruins.

In "Sunday Still," Harline resumes a narrative begun in his treatment of the Dutch Reformed Sunday in Holland. While proponents of a moderate Sunday prevailed there, many clergy advocated "the English Sabbath." Even before the Reformation, the English had become quite strict about Sunday observance. The publication of Nicholas Bownd's *The Doctrine of the Sabbath* in 1595 strengthened this tendency. Here Sunday becomes the specific choice of Christ as the day of celebration for a redeemed humanity. It is to be entirely devoted to worship and therefore include no work—and no play. If hailstorms threatened a harvest, the farmer should simply wait it out. Harline depicts Sundays in London in the 1920's and 1930's, a time of transition when the influential Lord's Day Observation Society (LDOS; founded in 1831) had to cope with such novelties as cinema, golf, soccer, and "the weekend." The shortening of the workweek throughout Europe meant the LDOS could claim that, as recreation now took place on Saturday, Sundays could again become truly restful, including "merely reading, light walking, music, contemplation of nature, and time with family and friends." If that seemed restrictive, Englishmen could look northward to Scotland to find the strictest Sundays in the Western world.

The English preference for a quiet Sunday remained, if considerably modified by novel opportunities for amusement. Harline compares a working-class Sunday with that of the middle class, finding much overlap. Both included church and Sunday school, although at different times of the day. Working-class men were drawn to the pubs. Middle-class homes generally set out an elegant tea, and families might sing hymns around the piano afterward. The afternoon "lie-down" was a national institution, giving real meaning to the phrase "a sleepy English Sunday." Reading was exceptionally important, with surveys showing that a quarter of the adult population read three or more Sunday papers. Founded in 1922, the commercial-free British Broadcasting Corporation (BBC) gained an enormous following, despite its rather stultifying Sunday programming. As elsewhere, the English debated the relative value of particular recreations. Particularly favored were gardening, cycling, park visiting, and walking and hiking. While English professional football (soccer) was not played on Sunday, amateur teams abounded, and the same was true of cricket. As in medieval times, the pubs beckoned, but in deference to Sunday their hours were shorter, and there was a greater attempt to accommodate the entire family.

"Sunday All Mixed Up" is how Harline titles his treatment of the United States in the 1950's. In some ways, the topic is too vast for a book surveying two thousand years of cultural history. Readers might be better advised to consult Alexis Mc-Crossen's fine *Holy Day, Holiday: The American Sunday* (2002), to which Harline often refers. To do so, however, would mean missing several interesting arguments. First, for Harline, the United States is unique in the way it has come to blend business, play, and religious observance. By the 1950's, the vaunted service economy had already emerged, and it required Sunday to be profitable. Americans started to regard shopping as a form of recreation, ultimately feeling little anguish about visiting a supermarket after church. What about the people who therefore have to work on Sundays? The economic abundance that characterized this period allowed almost everyone to have two days off a week—if not the same days. The commercialization of the Sabbath might appear to represent yet more secularization, but Harline is impressed by the fact that "while at the founding of the republic not even two in ten Americans belonged to churches, by 1956 six in ten did." The 1950's were, of course, a high tide in religiosity. America therefore developed a "hybrid Sunday"—where "holy day," "holiday," and "sales day" became melded.

Second, the 1950's saw the rise of television and professional football. Harline shows that this combination brought to the surface certain questionable cultural tendencies. Foreign visitors often comment on the brutality of this sport, thus raising the question of how football could have escaped condemnation by the church. Like so many other Sunday activities, football therefore had to become became "sacralized," he argues. Amos Alonzo Stagg and Vince Lombardi figured importantly in this development. Trained by Jesuits at Fordham University, Lombardi brought religious fervor to the game. At Green Bay, in an intensely Catholic part of Wisconsin, Lombardi cultivated local priests and nuns, went to Mass before every game, and insisted that "football and religion were interchangeable in their promotions of sacrifice, discipline, obedience, and more." Ironically, this view of the sport also appealed to players and coaches from the Protestant South. It made for a potent combination, as the growth of the Fellowship of Christian Athletes (founded in 1955) shows.

Craig Harline is a practicing Mormon and as a youth in Southern California kept a rather strict Sabbath. He is thus aware of the extraordinary perversions that the American Sunday is capable of. At its furthest extreme, this day becomes an expression of an essentially pagan American civil religion—described well by sociologist Will Herberg in 1955. Now, "Super Bowl Sunday" culminates its ritual season—having become an ultrapatriotic event wherein America celebrates its achievements, remembers its fallen, revels in its consumptive lifestyle, and calls upon its no-particular God. Whether that deity has any relation to the Lord of the Sabbath is a question worth much discussion.

*Leslie E. Gerber*

## Review Sources

*Booklist* 103, no. 13 (March 1, 2007): 43.
*Library Journal* 132, no. 7 (April 15, 2007): 102.
*The New York Times Book Review* 156 (August 26, 2007): 17.
*Publishers Weekly* 254, no. 7 (February 12, 2007): 83.
*U.S. Catholic* 72, no. 7 (July, 2007): 49.
*Washington Monthly* 39, no. 5 (May, 2007): 70-72.
*The Wilson Quarterly* 31, no. 2 (Spring, 2007): 96-97.

# THE TEMPTATION OF THE IMPOSSIBLE
## Victor Hugo and *Les Misérables*

*Author:* Mario Vargas Llosa (1936-      )
*First published: La tentación de lo imposible:*
  *Victor Hugo y "Los Miserables,"* 2004, in Spain
Translated from the Spanish by John King
*Publisher:* Princeton University Press (Princeton, N.J.).
  196 pp. $24.95
*Type of work:* Literary criticism

*Vargas Llosa explores Hugo's endeavor to write a novel*
*enveloping a complete fictional world and by so doing to*
*change the real world*

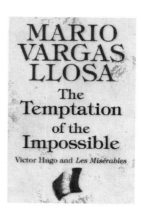

MARIO
VARGAS
LLOSA
The
Temptation
of the
Impossible
Victor Hugo and *Les Misérables*

Mario Vargas Llosa states that Victor Hugo attempted
two impossible goals in *Les Misérables* (1862). Hugo set
about creating a complete fictional world that contained its own fictional reality independent of the real world. Moreover, he wanted to effect positive change in the real
world. In a brief introduction to *The Temptation of the Impossible*, Vargas Llosa looks
at Hugo the man and Hugo the creative novelist. Then he analyzes *Les Misérables*
in terms of the novel's various components in order of importance: narrator, setting,
characters, and language. Finally, he examines Hugo's intention for the novel.

In the introduction, Vargas Llosa describes his experience reading *Les Misérables*
as a student at the boarding school of Leoncio Prado Military Academy. He affirms
that the novel made his life better, as the novel's fictional world gave him refuge from
the boring, dreary reality of his own life, yet he admits that it also made reality even
more colorless. He then turns to the questions of who Victor Hugo was and what he
believed about literature and himself.

Vargas Llosa profiles Victor Hugo as a man of immense talent, energy, and appetite for life. He discusses Hugo's knowledge of Spanish, his capacity for sexual
activity, his enormous literary output, and his social concerns, particularly his desire
for reform of the justice and prison systems and opposition to the death penalty. He reminds the reader of Hugo's great popularity during the nineteenth century. He was
admired as a poet, dramatist, and novelist, as well as a political leader and social
reformer.

Hugo believed in the power of literature to make the world a better place by improving human beings and by making God known to them. Vargas Llosa proposes
that Hugo envisioned *Les Misérables* as a religious tract and actually had come to
consider himself as more than a novelist. Hugo was excessively concerned with the
afterlife and held séances resulting in what he believed to be communication with the
dead. In Vargas Llosa's opinion, Hugo wished to fulfill the role of a seer who revealed
the truth of life after death. His novel was intended to go beyond the redemption of
humankind to the forgiveness of Satan.

∽

*Mario Vargas Llosa is a Peruvian novelist, essayist, and literary critic. His first novel was* La ciudad y los perros *(1962;* The Time of the Hero, *1966). He won the Rómulo Gallegos International Novel Prize for* La casa verde *(1965;* The Green House, *1968) and the National Book Critics Circle Award for* Making Waves *(1996).*

∽

In chapter 1, "The Divine Stenographer," Vargas Llosa introduces the narrator as the most important character and the real hero of the novel. This narrator is endowed with omniscience, exuberance, and omnipotence, and while he does not actually participate in the story, he is always present. He switches from first-person to third-person narrative as he wishes. He attempts to convince the reader that he is Victor Hugo. Of course, the narrator is a fiction, a creation of Hugo's mind; he is not the author but rather the first character that the author must create. Vargas Llosa points out that the way in which an author handles the narrator is one of the major distinctions between the classical novel and the modern novel. With its ever-present narrator, authoritarian and judgmental, *Les Misérables* is a great classical novel.

Vargas Llosa also emphasizes that it is through the narrator's monologues that Hugo lengthened his novel in the 1862 version. The narrator digresses for chapters on various subjects, such as the sewers of Paris when Jean Valjean carries the wounded Marius through them. According to Vargas Llosa, this is an essential part of the fictional reality of the novel. The fictive society is obsessed with wordiness. It is not only the narrator who is given to monologue but also the characters.

The chapter concludes with a refutation of the idea that the novel is a children's book. Vargas Llosa believes that it is precisely the visible, controlling narrator who refuses to let the reader participate in the novel that has caused the work to be seen in this fashion. He stresses that the nineteenth century reader did not view it this way.

Next in importance to the novel's creation is its setting, which includes not only the places and time period but also the controlling force of the events and of the characters' lives. In chapter 2, "The Dark Vein of Destiny," Vargas Llosa looks at how Hugo uses chance and coincidence to regulate the lives of the characters and to move the plot forward. Hugo uses three important scenes to connect and bring together the various stories within the novel: the ambush at the Gorbeau tenement, the barricade at La Chanvrerie, and the Paris sewers. Vargas Llosa refers to these scenes as "active craters," emphasizing that these incidents are fraught with danger and death for the characters. In each scene, characters whose fictional realities to that point appeared to be separate are suddenly inescapably intertwined. Their interactions affect each others' lives from there forward. In this way, Vargas Llosa states, Hugo creates a tension and emotional flow that not only reaches forward to future happenings in the novel but also reaches back to past episodes. Thus, destiny controls the fictional reality and carries the characters along to their unavoidable fate.

In chapter 3, "Touchy Monsters," Vargas Llosa considers the nature of Hugo's characters. The main characters are, as the chapter title implies, monsters in that they are superior beings governed exclusively by either good or evil. Each character behaves in an extreme and unusual fashion. They are archetypes of the saint, the hero, the villain, the just man, the fanatic. Vargas Llosa points out that nineteenth century readers saw them as real people possessed of extraordinary humanity. Such characters represent what the nineteenth century readers, imbued with Romanticism, believed they were or wanted to be. For instance, M. Bienvenu, the priest of Digne, is the saint who is responsible for the conversion of Jean Valjean from a criminal to a good man; Jean Valjean represents the just man; Javert, who never wavers from following the law, is the fanatic. In contrast to these super characters, Marius, whom Vargas Llosa calls a character without qualities, is the most realistic one in the novel. His actions are not predictable. He does not fit the Manichaean scheme of characters who populate the novel.

Marius is like the monsters, however, in his lack of sexual desire. Vargas Llosa suggests that Hugo, out of a nostalgia for his own chaste youth and of rejection of the carnal desire that filled his adult life, has created a fictional world in which chastity is the ultimate virtue. Contrary to the example of his own life, he portrays the characters in *Les Misérables* as endowed with physical and moral strength and health as a result of their asexuality. Jean Valjean loves duty that leads him to God; Javert loves the law and justice. The young revolutionary Enjolras loves his country. They have no lovers, no wives, no mistresses.

Among the myriad characters in the novel, Vargas Llosa identifies Gavroche, the street urchin who lives in the Elephant of the Bastille, as one of Hugo's most memorable characters. Unruly and marginal, he is reminiscent of the picaresque heroes of Golden Age Spanish literature, yet he lacks their callous attitude toward life. Gavroche is kind, witty, good, and courageous. Vargas Llosa feels that his death is one of the most tragic events in the novel.

Hugo also populates his novel with what Vargas Llosa refers to as collective characters. The bohemians, the seamstresses, the revolutionary students of the ABC (until they are at La Chanvrerie), the Patron-Minette gang, and the nuns of Petit Picpus have no real individuality. They serve to provide a backdrop for the main characters.

In chapter 4, "The Great Theater of the World," Vargas Llosa discusses the theatricality of the novel. In regard to the control exercised over the characters, he compares the novel to the allegorical religious plays of Calderón de la Barca. The characters are actors who follow a script prepared by the narrator. In the tradition of the popular farces, the characters of *Les Misérables* constantly change names, take on disguises, and play roles. The language of the novel is made theatrical both by Hugo's choice of excessive, colorful adjectives and by the characters' and the narrator's penchant for monologue and soliloquy. The settings—extraordinary, sinister, and totally unexpected—are also theatrical. The Paris sewers, which represent Hell, are the most theatrical of these. For Vargas Llosa, the life presented in the novel is a fiction, and the theatricality with which it is presented extends beyond the fictive life of the novel to suggest that all earthly life is a fiction and that reality exists only in the afterlife.

In chapter 5, "Rich, Poor, Leisured, Idle, and Marginal," and chapter 6, "Civilized Barbarians," Vargas Llosa discusses the social issues addressed in the novel. He reviews the criticism that Hugo received from his contemporaries for lack of realism and for exaggeration in his depiction of poverty, ignorance, and working conditions. Vargas Llosa then reiterates that the world in the novel is fictive. While Hugo wished to remedy social injustice, the novel was not intended to be a mirror of the actual situation in France. In addition, Vargas Llosa emphasizes that Hugo's politics changed many times during the writing of the novel, resulting in certain contradictions in the sociopolitical aspects of the work.

Furthermore, Vargas Llosa states that both history and fate control the fiction of the novel. What fate controls is unchangeable and must be accepted. On the other hand, history controls social injustice, which can be changed. Among the issues of social injustice, Hugo was obsessed with the injustice of the law, the penal system, and the death penalty, which he consistently opposed during his entire life. According to Vargas Llosa, these are the great social issues of *Les Misérables*.

In chapter 7, "From Heaven Above," Vargas Llosa discusses the importance of the"Philosophical Preface" that Hugo intended to add to the novel for understanding the meaning and purpose of the work. In view of the preface, he states that the novel cannot be understood as a work of social criticism. It is rather a religious tract with a godlike narrator who can leave nothing out. The story must be total. In Vargas Llosa's view, Hugo is recounting the battle between good and evil and reaffirming humanity's redemption and the triumph of good.

In his final chapter, Vargas Llosa returns to the idea of the "temptation of the impossible." Using Alphonse de Lamartine's severe criticism of the novel as a starting point, he proposes that all great fiction convinces the reader that its fictive world is reality. *Les Misérables* convinces the reader, whom it takes on a journey to find the impossible.

Vargas Llosa's book is a significant addition to the criticism of *Les Misérables* and of Hugo as a novelist. Vargas Llosa makes Hugo accessible to the reader as an author who was not fettered by the time period in which he wrote. He also presents valuable insights into the genre of fiction and what "reality" means in a fictional work. Since Vargas Llosa is himself a highly respected novelist, his book has been particularly welcomed by critics in the field.

*Shawncey Webb*

**Review Sources**

*Booklist* 103, no. 17 (May 1, 2007): 64.
*Library Journal* 132, no. 8 (May 1, 2007): 81.
*Los Angeles Times*, May 13, 2007, p. R7.
*The New York Review of Books* 54, no. 11 (June 28, 2007): 52-54.
*The Times Literary Supplement*, October 5, 2007, pp. 12-13.

# TEN DAYS IN THE HILLS

*Author:* Jane Smiley (1949-   )
*Publisher:* Alfred A. Knopf (New York). 449 pp. $26.00
*Type of work:* Novel
*Time:* March 24, 2003-April 2, 2003
*Locale:* Hollywood Hills, California

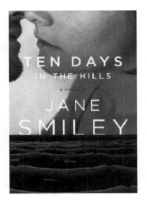

*In her latest novel, Pulitzer Prize-winning author Smiley uses Giovanni Boccaccio's* Decameron *(1349-1351) as a template for her tale of ten days in the Hollywood Hills, where ten characters try to make sense of things during the conflict in Iraq*

Principal characters:

NATHAN "MAX" MAXWELL, an aging
    director whose home in Hollywood
    becomes the staging area where ten interrelated persons converge
ELENA SIGMUND, Max's girlfriend of several months,
    who takes the Iraq War personally
STONEY WHIPPLE, Max's current agent and longtime
    but surreptitious lover to his daughter
ISABEL MAXWELL, Max's twenty-three-year-old daughter
CHARLIE MANNHEIM, Max's friend since childhood,
    who has a conservative voice in the household discussions
SIMON SIGMUND, Elena's son, who is known for his
    good looks and anything-goes attitude
ZOE CUNNINGHAM, Max's former wife, Isabel's mother,
    and famous actress and singer
PAUL SCHMIDT, Zoe's latest in a series of men who serve
    as her companion
DELPHINE CUNNINGHAM, Zoe's mother, a Jamaican
    immigrant who continues to live near Max
CASSIE MARSHALL, Delphine's best friend, who lives
    next door to Max and runs an art gallery in town
MIKE, a Russian millionaire who wants Max to write and direct a movie

Beginning *Ten Days in the Hills* with an epigraph from Giovanni Boccaccio's *Decameron: O, Prencipe Galeotto* (1349-1351; *The Decameron*, 1620), a collection of one hundred stories told by ten persons escaping the plague at a queen's villa in the countryside around Florence, Italy, Jane Smiley encourages her readers to make comparisons between her novel and the earlier medieval text. Like *The Decameron*, Smiley's text includes ten people who are brought together and end up telling stories. In *Ten Days in the Hills*, however, the convening of friends and relatives of Nathan "Max" Maxwell occurs rather arbitrarily one morning at his home in the Hollywood Hills. Though he and his new girlfriend Elena Sigmund are expecting a visit from Max's boyhood friend Charlie Mannheim, they soon find that Max's

*Jane Smiley has published several works of fiction and nonfiction, including the memoir* A Year at the Races *(2004) and a biography of Charles Dickens. Her novel* A Thousand Acres *(1991) won the Pulitzer Prize and was made into a film. She was inducted into the American Academy of Arts and Letters in 2001. In 2006, she received the PEN USA Lifetime Achievement Award for Literature.*

daughter, Isabel; Elena's son, Simon; Max's former wife, Zoe Cunningham; Zoe's current lover, Paul Schmidt; Max's agent, Stoney Whipple; and Max's former mother-in-law's best friend, Cassie Marshall, all show up for breakfast one morning. Fortunately, his former mother-in-law Delphine Cunningham lives in a guest house on the premises and has helped welcome the guests. The group members make themselves at home in Max's house for a few days, then, at Stoney's urging, they eventually retreat to an even more luxurious home owned by a mysterious Russian known only as Mike, who wants Max to write and direct a movie about fifteenth century Cossacks in the Ukraine.

Though *The Decameron* features a contrived situation in that the ten Italian visitors are required to tell stories on assigned subjects such as love and death, Smiley's characters are not obliged by their host to entertain with a tale. Given their close proximity and talkative natures, however, each member of the group finds it impossible to keep quiet. At the beginning of the novel, each day seems to be tied directly to an individual character, and the consciousness of that character serves as a filtering agent for the action of that day. Thus, while readers learn particular details about that person, they are also exposed to the multitude of stories told by others in the presence of that person. For example, day one opens with Max and Elena in bed, but Max notes the subtleties of the room and the woman, meets the guests, and relays important character information to Elena. Throughout the first part of the novel, Smiley loosely follows this pattern, giving many of the main characters specific focus, but by the time the characters move to Mike's house for the final four days, the narration becomes more omniscient and fragmentary, allowing stories and storytellers to alternate narratives quickly without a clear focus on one character.

In both Max's and Mike's houses, characters divide themselves into different sleeping arrangements: Known couples such as Elena and Max share a bedroom, and others sleep alone or with another character, unbeknownst to the rest of the house. Isabel, for example, has been having a sexual relationship with Stoney, who is fifteen years her senior, since she was a teenager. During the ten days chronicled in the novel, he spends every night in her bedroom, though others in the house are not aware of this arrangement until the two purposefully choose a room together at Mike's house. Because of the intimacy of the bedroom scenes, the characters often reveal private stories when they are with a partner. These stories relay personal philosophies, child-hood dramas, hopes, dreams, and fears. Later, the group meets for meals and a movie in the evening, thus opening the possibilities for more embedded stories within the larger narrative. In these larger gatherings, Elena argues against the Iraq War, Cassie recounts unusual events she has heard from others, and the group generally discusses broader topics.

When the group moves to Mike's house, however, the novel moves more quickly, generally relying on bedroom scenes to reveal what is happening inside the house and the minds of its inhabitants. Because much of the action and conversation in the later fourth of the book occurs in bedrooms, these vignettes are often more eroticized. In keeping with Boccaccio's focus in *The Decameron* on both the bawdy and the roman-tic, *Ten Days in the Hills* demonstrates a wide spectrum of intimate relationships—from Max and Elena's tender lovemaking to Simon Sigmund's ménage à trois with two of Mike's house staff.

Because the novel is set during the first few days of the Iraq War, *Ten Days in the Hills* uses this conflict and other political, environmental, and cultural issues of the time period as pivotal centers for many of the tales. Both Elena and Isabel are deeply troubled by the war and what they feel is a sense of impending doom, a dramatic downturn in America's position in the world. Elena in particular feels threatened by the events and obsessively talks about her position. Though the other characters do not necessarily share Elena and Isabel's convictions—particularly Max's friend Charlie, who repeatedly argues with those who speak negatively of America's mili-tary position—they all begin to enjoy a sense of isolation away from the concerns of the world, first in Max's house, and then even more so in Mike's house, where there are no televisions or newspapers. Just as the visitors to the queen's villa in *The Decameron* flee Florence, Italy, to escape the plague, so too do the ten characters in this novel flee Hollywood to escape the war. This not-so-subtle comparison allows Smiley to indict political policies in the larger frame of the novel, as well as within in-dividual characters' political diatribes.

This political thread, however, is only one of many that make up the tapestry of the novel. Another of Smiley's overarching themes that is highlighted by the Holly-wood setting and many of the characters' direct involvement with the movie industry is the importance of stories and storytelling to the self and the group. At the beginning of the novel, Max decides he wants to make a movie with the dialogue-rich structure of Louis Malle's *My Dinner with Andre* (1981). He wants to title his movie "My Lovemaking with Elena" and feature not the pornographic aspects of such an enter-prise but rather the dialogue between the two lovers, a concept that his agent Stoney says "has every single thing that American audiences hate and despise—fornication, old people, current events, and conversation." This kind of storytelling contrasts sharply with Mike's idea of remaking the epic *Taras Bulba*, a 1962 film starring Yul Brynner and Tony Curtis and adapted from the 1842 novel by Nikolai Gogol. This multilayered epic depicts the Cossacks facing a variety of sixteenth century oppo-nents, yet Mike urges Max to let the movie give voice to each group's story, each perspective of the struggle.

These two kinds of film methods illustrate the way Smiley uses stories and story-telling in the novel. The intimate stories become critical in developing relationships in the cases of Elena and Max and of Stoney and Isabel, and in devastating relationships in the case of Paul and Zoe. When the intimate groups gather, everyone benefits from telling stories in that each person's perspective can be honored within the larger framework of the topical or familial issue. When the characters tell their stories, the others in the group begin to understand their situations. For example, Max does not want to make Mike's film until he hears Mike's account of the movie's importance. Thus, in the context of the novel, stories build consensus, develop intimacy, convince, and entertain.

One could also argue that Stoney's original indictment of Max's movie about Elena has some validity as a criticism of Smiley's text. One has to care about the characters and their stories in order to care about what those characters have to say. Max illustrates this principle to some degree when he describes problems he might have while making a movie: "Even when I try to make it as compelling as possible, I know they are stories and the audience knows they are stories and the actors know they are stories. The thing about a story is that if affects you if you want it to, but you can take it or leave it." Each person in *Ten Days in the Hills* has his or her own story and wants to be understood. Isabel, for example, wants desperately to bond with her mother. On the other hand, Zoe wants Isabel to understand where she comes from and why she cannot be anyone but herself. Stoney wants to live up to his father's ideals. Paul wants to reach a path to enlightenment.

Unless others recognize the value of these individual stories, no one will feel compelled to care about the narrative. As Charlie Mannheim puts it, "My own story is very big to me—the marriage and the kids, and the house we built, and the separation, and now my cholesterol levels and how far I can run on the beach and getting my supplement business going, but coming out here puts it in perspective and makes me know it's just a story. You know, eight million stories in the naked city." Just as the individual story can seem so important to the self, stories have to be larger than the self to spark others' interest. By creating so many stories embedded within stories, all encased in the larger frame narrative, Smiley risks losing an audience that wants to focus on an individual character's development and an overarching plot that can bring the disparities of the fragmented group together. Characters in the novel are often underdeveloped. Though another character suggests that Cassie Marshall and Delphine Cunningham may be lovers, their background and motivations for their behavior are largely unexplored. Because so much of the text relies on dialogue, many of the more important plot shifts in the text seem too sudden because of a lack of exposition. Despite these issues, *Ten Days in the Hills* has a kind of fairy-tale-like quality, offering the characters respite from a real-world conflict, just as Smiley's novel and its attendant stories offer its readers an entertaining fictional world.

*Rebecca Hendrick Flannagan*

## Review Sources

*Booklist* 103, no. 8 (December 15, 2006): 5.
*Books & Culture* 13, no. 2 (March/April, 2007): 40.
*Entertainment Weekly*, no. 921 (February 16, 2007): 80.
*Kirkus Reviews* 74, no. 24 (December 15, 2006): 1241-1242.
*Library Journal* 132, no. 3 (February 15, 2007): 115.
*New Statesman* 136 (March 12, 2007): 59.
*The New York Review of Books* 54, no. 7 (April 26, 2007): 29-30.
*Publishers Weekly* 253, no. 48 (December 4, 2006): 33.
*Time* 169, no. 8 (February 19, 2007): 66.
*The Times Literary Supplement*, March 2, 2007, p. 23.

# THINKING IN CIRCLES
## An Essay on Ring Composition

*Author:* Mary Douglas (1921-2007)
*Publisher:* Yale University Press (New Haven, Conn.).
169 pp. $28.00
*Type of work:* Anthropology, literary criticism

*A distinguished anthropologist explains a technique of composition widely used in oral societies but little understood in the modern print culture*

In 1905, Dwight Terry established an annual lectureship at Yale University. Under the terms of his bequest, the lectures were to explore the relations of science and religion or, in Terry's words, to build "the truths of science and philosophy into the structure of a broadened and purified religion." The lectures were to be given by "men eminent in their respective departments," and for the first fifty years all the eminent thinkers (including such giants as the American educator John Dewey and the Swiss psychologist Carl Jung) were men. The British novelist and suffragist Rebecca West became the first woman to lecture in the series, in 1955, and she was followed by the American anthropologist Margaret Mead in 1957. After that, nearly a half century elapsed before another woman was invited to deliver the famed Terry Lectures.

Mary Douglas gave four lectures in October, 2003, under the general title "Writing in Circles: Ring Composition as a Creative Stimulus." At age eighty-two, she was looping back to subjects she had worked on at the outset of her career and was consciously bringing her work full circle. Since completing a three-part study of the Old Testament's Pentateuch, or Torah, she had been giving lectures on what she claimed to be the organizational principle that held the five books of Moses together: the principle of ring composition. She offered a summation in the first of her Terry Lectures, "How to Recognize a Ring Composition."

The term "ring composition" was coined in 1948 by W. A. A. van Otterlo, a Dutch scholar working on the Homeric epics. Throughout the previous century, classicists had broken down the *Iliad* and *Odyssey* into smaller poems, suggesting that they derived from a vast oral tradition. Van Otterlo asked how the fragments were stitched together and suggested that the basic principle was the "ring": a circular pattern based on repetition and balance. In a simple frame, a narrative might have an introduction that somehow anticipated the central event and a conclusion that harkened back to the introduction. In a full-scale ring composition, there would be a careful balance of elements.

To explain the ring composition, it helps to use a visual illustration. Douglas provides fifteen figures, eight tables, and three editorial boxes. In lieu of a visual aid, one might use the analogy of a clock face. If the narrative begins and ends at 12:00, the action has its turning point at 6:00. In a simple tale, the closing action may have certain parallels to the opening action. Cinderella must return home, and the prince must come to find her. However, in a ring composition there is a quite exact set of correspondences, so that the events of 7:00, 8:00, and 9:00 echo those of 5:00, 4:00, and 3:00, respectively. There may even be a ring within the ring, so that the events of 7:00 and 8:00 are echoed, respectively, in those of 11:00 and 10:00.

~

*Mary Douglas established her reputation as an interpreter of cultural patterns with* Purity and Danger *(1966), for which she earned the Rivers Medal. She turned her attention to the Old Testament while teaching religious studies at Princeton and Northwestern Universities and pointed out new patterns in three books, the last of which won the Bernal Prize. She was made a dame of the British Empire in 2006.*

~

Presented in this clockwork analogy (which is not Douglas's), the ring composition seems a highly unlikely proposition. In fact, however, the ring is a type of a rhetorical figure known as chiasmus (from the Greek letter *Chi*, which is written χ), the inverted relationship of two parallel phrases. A good example of chiasmus is the famous sentence from John F. Kennedy's inaugural address: "Ask not what your country can do for you—ask what you can do for your country." Chiasmus can happen on the level of the letter, notably in a palindrome like "Able was I ere I saw Elba." It can also occur at the level of the image or event in a story. Thus, in the story of the binding of Isaac, in Genesis 22, the 6:00 turn is the angel's call to Abraham, just after the pious father has raised his knife against his own son. The angel instructs Abraham to substitute a ram for the human sacrifice. The burning of the animal sacrifice at 9:00 echoes the gathering of wood for the sacrificial fire at 3:00, and the whole chapter forms a perfect ring. All of this may seem a mere curiosity until one comes to the age-old question of Abraham's sanity in preparing to kill his beloved son—or God's in demanding the sacrifice. Douglas suggests that readers who recognize the ring composition will see that Isaac's life is never seriously at risk, only Abraham's faith, and that the happy outcome is predicted from the beginning.

Having identified the salient features of a ring composition, Douglas turns to the book of Numbers, widely considered a grab bag of Old Testament narratives and laws. She suggests that it is in fact a carefully constructed ring, a case she first made in her 2001 book *In the Wilderness*. She suggests further that Numbers was written for an audience with established patterns of thinking, patterns that show up in the narratives and laws.

In 2003, Douglas followed the lectures on ring composition and the book of Numbers with observations about the difficulty facing scholars from a linear print culture and speculations about the reasons that humans have thought in circles. In preparing the lectures for publication, she has added material from two other series of lectures that she gave, in London and Edinburgh, so that the published "essay" has eleven numbered sections. Moreover, she has turned the original project into a full-scale ring composition.

Lest any linear reader miss this feature, or feat, the contents page of *Thinking in Circles* is followed by a diagram showing "contents in a ring": the eleven numbered sections in a circular pattern where the section on "How to Construct and Recognize a Ring" is directly across from another on "How to Complete a Ring." This is very clever, of course, but it serves the larger purpose of showing that the ring is not an esoteric device available only to the initiated but a feature of human thought. It also reinforces her suggestion—never quite an assertion—that writers in societies from India to Israel have consciously created rings to give their creations shape. Western cultures today tend to think negatively about "circular reasoning," and there is a gentle, self-effacing humor in Douglas's title. Nonetheless, Douglas offers reasons to rethink our cultural prejudices.

One way to recognize a ring composition, says Douglas, is to look for a repeating element. In the story of Abraham and Isaac, there is the repeated answer to God's call: "Here I am." Douglas uses as her own recurring motif a statement by the Russian linguist Roman Jakobson. Commenting on the use of parallelism in language, Jakobson said that it occurred with remarkable frequency and served to give the parallel lines "both clear uniformity and great diversity." He added that it was so universal as to be based, most probably, on the functioning of the human brain. Douglas mentions this observation in the first section of her essay, returns to it at the turning point (6:00 in the clock analogy), and devotes the final section to reflection on "Jakobson's conundrum": "that writing in parallels comes to everyone naturally—but we do not understand why we are slow to recognize it." She explains this conundrum by "resorting to cultural theory," which has been an important aspect of anthropology for the last generation. In doing so, she comes back to her own intellectual beginnings.

As a doctoral student in the 1940's, Douglas did her fieldwork in what was then the Belgian Congo. While studying traditional African religions, she wanted to understand why different groups feared different risks. After writing an ethnographic study of the Lele peoples, she developed a full-scale theory, which she termed the "cultural theory of risk." In the now-classic *Purity and Danger* (1966), she argued that societies generate "cultural biases" in order to create cohesion. Some biases allow more individual choice; others demand more group solidarity. She found parallels between Western systems like the taboos in the Old Testament and non-Western ones like those she had studied in the field, thus beginning a process of pattern-seeking that would mark the rest of her career.

Douglas suggests that the ring composition served the needs of more hierarchical societies, where it was important for members to recognize boundaries, and that the very concept is difficult for members of a postmodern culture that distrusts clear-cut categories. In a footnote, she observes that anthropologists have now published more than seven hundred books and articles on what they commonly call Cultural Theory (uppercase). She is too modest to note that most of these are footnotes to her own work. Her original audience at Yale would have known this, however, and readers of this deceptively simple essay should keep it in mind.

In a circular story, there is both a journey out (1:00-5:00 on the clock face) and a return home (7:00-11:00). In the ring story, there is a parallel between events in the journeys out and home. In order to meet the rules of a ring composition as she has identified them, Douglas creates a parallel discussion of the *Iliad* toward the end of the essay to reinforce the discussion of the book of Numbers near the beginning. In the biblical work; she has found a recurring movement from law to narrative, which serves to organize the book; in Homer's epic, she finds alternating stories of night and day that, while fragmentary in themselves, are arranged in such a way as to create the unity in diversity that critics have long cherished in works of literary art.

In a circular story, there is also a turning point (at 6:00), at which one is furthest from the beginning but still affected by it. Douglas finds her turning point in modern literature. She takes as her test case Laurence Sterne's wildly digressive novel *Tristram Shandy* (1759-1767), but she also discusses works of detective fiction like the Poirot novels of Agatha Christie. Her findings are perceptive, even ingenious, but admittedly inconclusive. There would seem to be no modern ring compositions in modern literature, and one has to wonder if she has deliberately avoided or simply overlooked such carefully organized works as Thomas Mann's *Der Zauberberg* (1924; *The Magic Mountain*, 1927) and indeed such highly symmetrical plots as William Shakespeare's *The Tempest* (pr. 1611). Although well aware that poets of Shakespeare's day were attracted to circular structures found in works of antiquity, such as Virgil's *Aeneid* (c. 29-19 B.C.E.), she is most interested to see whether a ring structure can be found in works as apparently disorganized as the book of Numbers. It would be difficult to find a work as apparently random as *Tristram Shandy*, or an analysis of Sterne's plot as orderly as Douglas's.

In the first major review of this book, Edward Rothstein of *The New York Times* admired Douglas's ability to spot patterns but found her book more suggestive than conclusive. He recognized that audiences always look for meaning and order, whether they are attending a concert, an art opening, or a poetry reading. He wondered whether perception of the symmetries in the ancient epics does not amount to a sort of rite, engaged in by a limited community.

Mary Douglas died a few weeks after the book's publication. At eighty-six, she had outlived her husband of fifty years, the anthropologist James Douglas, and had completed all her projected research. Among the glowing obituaries, *The Guardian*'s pointed out that this final essay is a summation, continuing her long-running effort to apply discoveries from non-Western civilizations to her own cultural milieu.

*Thomas Willard*

## Review Sources

*Choice* 45, no. 2 (October, 2007): 277.
*The Guardian*, May 18, 2007, p. 44.
*The New York Times* 156 (March 26, 2007): E1-E6.

# THOMAS HARDY

*Author:* Claire Tomalin (1933-     )
*First published:* 2006, in Great Britain
*Publisher:* Penguin Press (New York). 512 pp. $35.00
*Type of work:* Literary biography
*Time:* 1840-1928
*Locale:* England

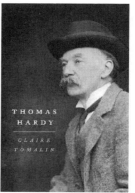

*Tomalin examines the life of the renowned writer who began his career as a novelist at the end of the Victorian era but became one of the leading Modern poets*

Principal personages:
    THOMAS HARDY, novelist and poet
    JEMIMA HARDY, his mother
    EMMA GIFFORD HARDY, his first wife
    FLORENCE DUGDALE HARDY, his second wife
    FLORENCE HENNIKER, socialite and friend of Hardy
    EDMUND GOSSE, editor and friend of Hardy

For the 1912 centennial of the birth of Charles Dickens, the editors of *Bookman* sent out a questionnaire to hundreds of writers asking them to explain how Dickens had influenced their work. Quite a few wrote extensively about the impact of the most celebrated Victorian novelist on their work. George Bernard Shaw, by then recognized as the foremost English dramatist of the time, went so far as to claim that Dickens was influential in ways not even imagined by his Victorian contemporaries in revising attitudes toward society. The response submitted by Thomas Hardy was hardly so effusive. In his laconic two-line reply, he said he supposed he was influenced in some way by Dickens—he suspected everyone was—but he was unable to say how or why.

That comment speaks volumes not only about Hardy's attitude toward Dickens but also about his own approach to novel writing. By his own admission, he cared little for the fiction he turned out over nearly three decades. He wrote novels, he often said, as a way to earn a living so he could practice the craft for which he had a deep and abiding love: poetry. Although by the end of the century he was among the country's most successful novelists, according to legend (a legend Hardy endorsed), when public opinion turned against him after the publication of *Jude the Obscure* in 1895 he turned his back on fiction and devoted the rest of his life—another three decades—exclusively to writing verse.

That story and many others are retold in Claire Tomalin's well-written and engaging *Thomas Hardy*, a biography that humanizes the man whose private life was often a well-guarded secret from his contemporaries. The facts of that life contain no spectacular secrets. Born in 1840 of working-class parents, Hardy was apprenticed as an architect at age fifteen and took up novel writing before he was thirty. He fell in love with and married Emma Gifford, a woman above his social station, at nearly the same time. Encouraged by friends, such as the editor and writer Edmund Gosse, he spent three decades cranking out stories in which he tried to explain something about people's passions, while constantly battling censors who were unwilling to let him speak freely lest he bring a blush to the cheek of some young unwed maid by alluding to anything that might remotely suggest there was a sexual side to human relationships. While he was battling to

*Claire Tomalin, a graduate of Cambridge University, is a veteran journalist and biographer who has published a dozen books, including studies of Jane Austen, Mary Wollstonecraft, and Katherine Mansfield. Her biography* Samuel Pepys: The Unequalled Self *(2002) was the Whitbread Book of the Year.*

become more open about sexuality in his fiction, he was undergoing a gradual estrangement from his wife, who eventually moved into the attic of the country home Hardy had built with the profits from his novels. In the 1890's, he flirted seriously with an attractive socialite named Florence Henniker, but nothing came of the affair. In 1905, he began a relationship with a much younger woman, Florence Dugdale, whom he married shortly after Emma Hardy died in 1912. He lived until 1928—long enough to be hailed as one of the foremost writers England ever produced.

These events have been told before—in fact, in greater detail than Tomalin provides. Hardy himself completed a two-volume autobiography—*The Early Life of Hardy* (1928) and *The Later Years of Thomas Hardy* (1930), together as *The Life of Thomas Hardy* (1962)—that was published after his death, with his second wife listed as author in order to give the story a facade of objectivity. Several scholars have taken up the story during the twentieth century, and lengthy accounts by Robert Giddings and Michael Millgate are just two of a rather imposing group of biographical studies that attempt to get at the man behind the work. Additionally, just before Tomalin's book appeared, Picador Press and Yale University Press issued *Thomas Hardy: The Guarded Life* (2006) by Ralph Pite, professor at the University of Cardiff and an accomplished poet in his own right. One might have wondered, then, if there would be anything left for another biographer to say.

Tomalin proves that, indeed, there is. Without resorting to outlandish speculation, and often restating information provided by other sources, Tomalin nevertheless manages to create a portrait of the writer that is sympathetic, well developed, and filled with details that bring Hardy to life for her readers. Throughout the narrative, she contrasts Hardy's rather well-ordered, conservative lifestyle with those of the characters he creates. It must have been surprising to his friends and relatives to discover that the man who rose from very modest roots to become a diligent if not inspired architect could have boiling inside him the passions that emerge in his fiction. Certainly Hardy the man would never have thought to defy convention in the ways his heroes and heroines do. Tomalin does provide clues to Hardy's inner discontent, though, especially his fondness for the poetry of Percy Bysshe Shelley and other Romantics. Unfortunately, the age into which he was born did not permit Hardy the freedom to explore the possibilities of self-expression that his Romantic heroes enjoyed. By the time he reached adulthood, the conventions of behavior and expression that characterized the Victorians had reached their zenith.

The tug-of-war in Hardy's personality is the central subject of Tomalin's story. Urged by his mother to advance beyond the limits of the class into which he was born, Hardy struggled to become a writer in a period when frank discussion of many forms of human relationships were strictly taboo. Worse for him, the rather limited opportunities he had to interact with women left him unfulfilled, and his experiences in marriage were not entirely satisfactory. Much of that frustration emerges in his fiction, and Tomalin's brief commentaries on individual novels hint at the biographical genesis of much of Hardy's fiction. While she acknowledges Hardy's oft-stated dismissal of his novel writing, Tomalin takes pains to point out how carefully Hardy crafted his work, often preparing different versions for serial publication and hardcover release, and working incessantly to revise novels in second and subsequent editions. While she never states it directly, Tomalin is clearly convinced Hardy was much more devoted to the craft of fiction than he wished to let on. She is forthright in her admiration of his ability, claiming novels such as *The Return of the Native* (1878), *The Mayor of Casterbridge* (1886), *Tess of the D'Urbervilles* (1891), and *Jude the Obscure* are masterpieces, but she is also willing to concede that works like *The Hand of Ethelberta* (1875-1876) and *A Laodicean* (1880-1881) are failures. She concludes that the story of Hardy abandoning fiction because he received bad reviews is half right, but a bit disingenuous. By 1897, Hardy had become wealthy enough not to have to work at all, so he turned his attention to what he truly loved, writing verse.

If Tomalin is competent in her handling of Hardy's life as a novelist, she is truly impressive in her analysis of his work as a poet. In fact, she finds much evidence about Hardy's character in his verse. For example, much of what is known of Hardy's first marriage comes from information in *The Life of Thomas Hardy*—a book Florence Hardy altered to present her predecessor in the worst possible light. Compounding the problem is that Hardy led a very private life. He entertained few friends at his home, and although he spent some time in London mingling with the social elites once his novels brought him notoriety, he was not a regular among the set whose lives would have been the subject for gossip spread in private correspondence. To compensate for a relative dearth of reliable information, Tomalin looks to the poetry Hardy wrote during his lifetime, but especially in the two years following Emma's death, to fill in the gaps. Because much of Hardy's poetry has an autobiographical basis, her task is not as difficult or as unscholarly as might be imagined. Always careful not to draw conclusions too freely, Tomalin is still able to explain as well as anyone has why Hardy fell in love with the rather spinsterish, educated sister-in-law of the parson at St. Juliot's Church in the far reaches of the countryside, and what kept the couple together through three decades during which any real sense of passion completely disappeared from the relationship. Tomalin does not subscribe to the theory that Emma Gifford went mad. Instead, she ascribes her unusual behavior quirks—including her decision to move to the attic at Max Gate and spend most of her time there—to mere eccentricity. What concerns Tomalin is not so much why Emma behaved as she did but rather what effect the estrangement had on Hardy.

Tomalin quotes extensively from the poetry, including entire poems or long segments that demonstrate not only how Hardy intertwined his personal feelings with larger social themes but also how carefully he constructed his verses. The rather spare, understated quality of the poems may surprise some, since his favorite poet was helley and since both he and his wife enjoyed reading the work of their older contemporaries Alfred, Lord Tennyson and Robert Browning. The outpouring of excessive emotion that one finds in Shelley and Tennyson, or the complicated patterns of versification and language structure characteristic of Browning, are notably absent from Hardy's work. There is, as Tomalin points out repeatedly, a distinctly modern cast to the verse. Although she clearly admires Hardy's poetry, even Tomalin has difficulty making a case for *The Dynasts* (pb. 1903, 1906, 1908, 1910; pr. 1914), Hardy's philosophical epic. This is no surprise, however, seeing that the work has not attracted a large readership even among scholars.

Tomalin has read widely about both Hardy and the period in which he lived; her extensive (though not exhaustive) bibliography attests to her care in researching both the man and his times. That research is carefully woven into a seamless narrative designed to engage the reader's interest in her subject. As a consequence, there emerges from the pages of *Thomas Hardy* a well-rounded portrait of a man who thought deeply about human relationships and spent considerable time and energy attempting to communicate his insight through his fiction and verse. One might quibble over some of the rather brief summaries of the novels, or wonder why Tomalin did not delve deeper into certain aspects of Hardy's character or his relationships with publishers or other literary figures who crossed his path. For Tomalin to have done so, however, would have required her to write a considerably longer book—something twenty-first century readers may have balked at picking off the shelf. What Tomalin presents seems just right: As a biography designed for her own contemporaries, *Thomas Hardy* is a first-rate piece of scholarship that reveals the character of one of the late nineteenth century's most enigmatic literary figures.

*Laurence W. Mazzeno*

## Review Sources

*Booklist* 103, no. 6 (November 15, 2006): 17.
*The Economist* 381 (November 11, 2006): 96.
*Kirkus Reviews* 74, no. 21 (November 1, 2006): 1119.
*Library Journal* 131, no. 19 (November 15, 2006): 72.
*London Review of Books* 29, no. 1 (January 4, 2007): 25-29.
*The New Republic* 236, nos. 8/9 (February 19, 2007): 29-33.
*The New York Times Review of Books* 54, no. 3 (March 1, 2007): 21-24.
*Publishers Weekly* 253, no. 48 (December 4, 2006): 47.
*The Spectator* 302 (October 21, 2006): 46-48.
*The Washington Post*, January 21, 2007, p. BW15.

# A THOUSAND SPLENDID SUNS

*Author:* Khaled Hosseini (1965-    )
*Publisher:* Riverhead Books (New York). 370 pp. $25.95
*Type of work:* Novel
*Time:* 1964-April, 2003
*Locale:* Kabul and Herāt, Afghanistan; Murree, Pakistan

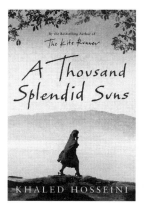

*The second novel by this Afghan American author recounts the woes of two very different Afghan women in their homeland during a time of violent political upheaval, bloody civil war, and foreign invasions by Soviet as well as U.S. and NATO troops*

Principal characters:
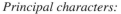
> MARIAM, illegitimate daughter of a wealthy
>   man from Herāt
> LAILA, daughter of a middle-class family in Kabul
> RASHEED, brutal shoemaker husband to Mariam and Laila in Kabul
> NANA, Mariam's unwed, epileptic mother
> JALIL, Mariam's wealthy father, living in Herāt
> HAKIM (BABI), Laila's gentle, uxorious father, a teacher in Kabul
> FARIBA (MAMMY), Laila's high-strung mother
> TARIQ, Laila's childhood playmate and lover in later life

Khaled Hosseini's first novel, *The Kite Runner* (2003), was also the first novel by an Afghan American writer, and it became a runaway success. It remained for more than two years on American best-seller lists, sold 8 million copies worldwide, and was made into a film, released in December, 2007. When Hosseini revisited Afghanistan after its publication, he had been living in political asylum in California for almost twenty years. On that visit, as he wandered his bombed-out boyhood haunts in Kabul and conversed with its war-scarred people, he felt impelled to tell an Afghan story different from *The Kite Runner*'s. That book had been about men—fathers and sons, male friendship, male treachery. Hosseini now felt drawn to tell a contemporaneous story about Afghanistan's women. The brilliant result is *A Thousand Splendid Suns*, a novel about two women protagonists, Mariam and Laila. The trajectory of their lives forms the double plot of the book, and although the narrative is in the third person, the point of view itself shifts to that of the character whose plotline is being developed. One is reminded of Leo Tolstoy's management of the double plot in *Anna Karenina* (1875-1877).

Indeed, the two women's narrative points of view structure the novel with intricately wrought symmetry. Part 1 is told entirely through Mariam's point of view, part 2 wholly through Laila's. In part 3, however, the viewpoint alternates between the women with each chapter. Then, just as Mariam's part 1 begins the novel, the concluding part 4 of the novel is told through Laila's point of view.

*A Thousand Splendid Suns* can also be read as a female bildungsroman, and the growth of these two girls into maturity, marriage, and maternity aptly illustrates the travail of Afghani women. Hosseini's two women are strategic contrasts physically, socially, and psychologically. Socially, Mariam is from the rural lower class; Laila, the urban middle class. Psychologically, Mariam is accustomed to humiliation; Laila, to consideration. Physically, Mariam's features are "unshapely," "flat," "unmemorable," "coarse," while Laila is a green-eyed blond beauty.

*Khaled Hosseini was born in Kabul in 1965. His family took political asylum in the United States in 1980 following the Soviet invasion. Hosseini earned a medical degree in 1993 and practiced medicine in Northern California, rising early in the morning to write his first novel,* The Kite Runner *(2003). In 2006, he became an envoy to the United Nations High Commissioner for Refugees (UNHCR).*

Their common fate is to become co-wives of the same misogynistic, brutal man. As Hosseini spins out their fate, their sharp individual differences only serve to demonstrate the breadth of commonalty among Muslim women in Afghani society during the drastic political upheavals of the 1970's to 2003— a king deposed, a communist coup, a Soviet invasion, a civil war, a faith-based Taliban dictatorship, an invasion by American and North Atlantic Treaty Organization (NATO) forces.

In Mariam, Hosseini presents a being at the lowest link of the Afghan social chain. She is poor, female, and illegitimate. She lives in a shack (*kolba*) beyond the pale of Herāt, itself a city on the border with Iran, far from the center, Kabul. Clearly Hosseini locates Mariam on the periphery of society. Mariam's mother, Nana, is an unmarriageable epileptic. She works as a maid until impregnated by her wealthy employer, Jalil. It is rather unaccountable that Jalil, proprietor of the town's cinema, owner of a Mercedes, husband to three wives, and father to nine children, would dally with the unlovely Nana. To assuage his Muslim conscience, Jalil sets up Mariam and Nana in their shack, provides for Qurʾānic instruction from Mullah Faizullah (the sanest and most positive influence in Mariam's young life), and visits her every week, regaling Mariam with stories of what her life might be if she were legitimate. Mariam idolizes Jalil. For her fifteenth birthday, Mariam asks Jalil to take her to his cinema to see *Pinocchio* (1940) and eat ice cream with her siblings. She is in fact asking for legitimation and distancing herself from her mother. Jalil sighs ambiguously.

Nana pleads with Mariam not to go, or she (Nana) may suffer a mortal epileptic fit. When Jalil does not appear at the appointed hour, Mariam, in a rare act of self-assertion and initiative, makes her way to his home. Refused admission, she stubbornly spends the night at its gates. The next day, Jalil's chauffeur forcibly escorts her back to her shack. There she is confronted with the grisly spectacle of her hanged mother.

This defining trauma, then, teaches Mariam that to assert oneself, to dare, to take the initiative is to suffer pain, cause hurt to others, and precipitate tragedy. Better to bear and forbear. Hosseini thus prepares the psyche of this character for the almost incredible burden of abuse and suffering that she has to bear in her marriage.

Hardly a week after this traumatic experience, the fifteen-year-old Mariam is hurried into an arranged marriage with a forty-five-year-old shoemaker and widower from Kabul named Rasheed. He is smelly, "thick-bellied," "broad-shouldered," and "heavy-footed," with nails the color of "the inside of a rotting apple." In Kabul, after a 650-kilometer bus journey, Mariam is made to don a head-to-toe burka (Hosseini reportedly tried one out himself to experience its confinement—and odd comfort), and Rasheed exercises his connubial rites painfully and lovelessly. When Mariam conceives, Rasheed is joyful in anticipation of replacing his dead son, who had drowned because of Rasheed's drunken negligence, but when Mariam has the first of several miscarriages, Rasheed turns cold and brutal. Once, when Mariam's rice is not to his liking, he stuffs her mouth with pebbles and makes her chew until two molars break.

Growing up in Mariam's Kabuli neighborhood is Laila, nineteen years her junior, born on the date of the communist coup in 1978. She is the apple of her loving father's eye. Laila's is a close-knit, middle-class, monogamous Muslim family with three children. Laila's father, Hakim (Babi), is a mild-mannered man who was proposed to by his wife, Fariba (Mammy), his childhood playmate—and who is now the family's decision maker. Babi is a university-educated teacher who was reeducated by the communists into a bread factory laborer, but he bears no grudges, only becoming more of a ditherer. However, he firmly believes in education for women as well as men and wants Laila, her school's star pupil, to continue her schooling even though her teacher is a blatant communist sympathizer. It is notable that although Babi is but a cameo character, Hosseini has admirably conceived him as a foil to Jalil (who is weak like Babi, but selfish) and to Rasheed (who is far from weak, and also selfish).

Mammy is more forceful than her husband, but she is moody (perhaps even bipolar)— sometimes partying euphorically, sometimes taking to bed for weeks on end. She blesses her sons' joining the mujahideen to fight the Soviet occupation, but she predictably spirals into deep depression when they become martyrs.

There are moments of brightness in Laila's life. One such occurs when Babi takes her on an outing to marvel at the giant Buddhas of Bamiyan—but all the world knows with dramatic irony that this moment of brightness will soon be extinguished permanently when the Taliban destroy the statues in 2001. Another source of brightness is her friendship with Tariq, a neighborhood boy who has lost a leg to a land mine; it is a friendship that blossoms into love. After the mujahideen defeat the Soviet troops in 1989, however, civil war breaks out between the victorious factions, turning Kabul into a battleground. Tariq's family leaves to seek refuge in Pakistan, but not before Tariq and Laila have consummated their love. Ironically, when Mammy finally emerges from her depression and decides to leave also, a shell hits their home, leaving Laila the lone survivor.

Part 3 of the novel opens with Mariam discovering Laila amid the rubble of her home and nursing her back to health. To Mariam's and the reader's dismay, Rasheed, now in his sixties, has his eye on Laila as a marriage prospect. A traveler from Pakistan comes with an eyewitness account of Tariq's death. (Later it is revealed that Rasheed had suborned him into concocting this story.) Laila is heartbroken and destitute, and suspects that she is carrying Tariq's child, so when Rasheed proposes, Laila reluctantly accepts—causing Mariam great pain. Hosseini skillfully and credibly develops the relationship between these two co-wives, one feeling resentful, the other feeling like a usurper, but both constrained to coexist under the tyrannical regimen of a brutal husband. Their enmity turns toward amity after Laila's daughter, Aziza, is born, and Mariam's frustrated maternal nature comes to the fore. They bond as they share household chores, then personal grooming, then their most intimate secrets. Fearing for Aziza's safety should Rasheed discover her paternity, the women plot an escape to Pakistan, but they are detained at the bus depot (women unaccompanied by male relatives are suspect), Rasheed is informed, and he thrashes them mercilessly.

Some time after this, Laila realizes that she is again pregnant. She almost aborts herself but desists, giving birth to a boy on whom Rasheed dotes. Meanwhile, the fundamentalist Taliban has taken over from the fractious warlords, making life even more restrictive for the women. Events take a dramatic, even a melodramatic, turn after Rasheed confronts Laila with his suspicions about Aziza and forces her into an orphanage. Then Tariq suddenly returns from Pakistan.

Hosseini's concatenation of the concluding action is as violent and bloody as that of a Renaissance revenge tragedy when the women are forced to rise up against their common oppressor. In part 4 of the novel, Hosseini attempts to provide a coda of calm for the survivors, albeit in the fragile unquiet of post-9/11 Afghanistan.

*A Thousand Splendid Suns*, then, is indeed a splendid successor to *The Kite Runner*. Though some may carp at the melodramatic quality of some of Hosseini's episodes, his protagonists are flesh-and-blood women who are wrenchingly sympathetic, and their plight of living on the front line of political, fundamentalist, and domestic terror may be closer to home than many Western readers would like to think. Besides, Hosseini's prose is clear and unpretentious, his narrative urgent and compelling. He has written another page-turner.

*C. L. Chua*

## Review Sources

*Booklist* 104, no. 5 (November 1, 2007): 74.
*The Economist* 383 (May 26, 2007): 99.
*Entertainment Weekly*, nos. 971/972 (December 28, 2007): 83.
*Financial Times*, June 9, 2007, p. 36.
*The New York Times* 156 (May 29, 2007): E1-E8.
*The New York Times Book Review* 156 (June 3, 2007): 58.
*Publishers Weekly* 254, no. 9 (February 26, 2007): 52-53.
*The Spectator* 304 (June 2, 2007): 42.
*The Times Literary Supplement*, June 1, 2007, p. 23.

# TIME AND MATERIALS
## Poems, 1997-2005

*Author:* Robert Hass (1941-      )
*Publisher:* Ecco Press (New York). 88 pp. $22.95
*Type of work:* Poetry

*In this long-awaited, Pulitzer Prize-winning collection
of poetry from a celebrated California poet, Hass explores
the subjects of art, nature, and social issues*

Robert Hass ranks high among America's academic poets, winning admirers for his transparent language, the verbal music of his lines, and his earnest political sensibility. His work wins admirers even among those who care little for the trappings of academia or the intellectual gamesmanship that preoccupies many university writers. This places him among the few who are able to straddle the divide splitting contemporary American poetry.

Poets of the academy stand in opposition to those of everyday life, in an uneasy relationship whose roots may be traced back two hundred years. In the early 1800's, the division noticeably widened between the writers of New England and those of the rest of the young United States. While many New England writers aspired to fit into the British and European tradition, those elsewhere, notably in the South, dreamed of producing an indigenous American literature.

The European-leaning writers tended to lead lives of relative ease; New England's European-style institutions of higher learning, such as Yale and Harvard Universities, in aiding the spread of colleges across the Old West, planted the seed for Americans' continuing association between comfortably placed university poets and an academic milieu that seems removed from everyday American life.

Long associated with the University of California, Hass has built his substantial reputation with works in the traditional mold. Through his translations, especially those cotranslated with Polish poet Czesław Miłosz, he has conspicuously emphasized a connection to the European example. In his own poems, moreover, his concerns take a decidedly academic turn. His objects of contemplation are often exterior, formal, and aesthetic—and frequently European. In this new collection, for instance, notes about the poverty-stricken life of German philosopher Friedrich Nietzsche provide subject matter for the lyric "A Supple Wreath of Myrtle." Similarly, contemplation of a painting by Dutch artist Jan Vermeer gives rise to the long poem "Art and Life." The volume also includes translations and imitations of works by Roman poet Horace, Swedish poet Tomas Tranströmer, and Hass's longtime literary friend and cotranslator, Miłosz.

This is not to say Hass avoids American subjects, or subjects taken from the other side of the "town-gown" divide. Words by American poet John Ashbery provide the initial impetus for the long poem "I Am Your Waiter Tonight and My Name is

Dmitri"—even if Russian author Fyodor Dostoevski takes an equally important role as literary stimulus as the meditative poem goes on. In a like manner, a quotation from American poet Richard Eberhardt opens the strongly political work "A Poem," concerned with the impact of American military actions overseas, from the Vietnam War to the present day.

*Robert Hass is a professor at the University of California, Berkeley. U.S. poet laureate from 1995 to 1997, Hass is a MacArthur Fellow and two-time winner of the National Book Critics Circle Award. His translations from the works of Czesław Miłosz have appeared in seven volumes.* Time and Materials *was awarded the National Book Award.*

The poet most frequently mentioned in *Time and Materials*, moreover, is the one typically considered the most American of all: Walt Whitman—a telling choice, given that Whitman's work stood in stark opposition to the work of the intellectuals of his day. Even a poem initially concerned with an intimate moment between lovers can transform into a meditation upon Whitman—as occurs in the short lyric "Futures in Lilacs," in which Hass visualizes the nineteenth century poet studying etchings in the Library of Congress. The striking irony is that Whitman, the poet of experience, has become for Hass an object of academic knowledge—even though he puts this knowledge to poetic use.

The emphasis Hass places in his poems upon knowledge neither dampens the verbal music of his lines nor derails the essential artistic aim of his poems. In the previously mentioned "Art and Life," he establishes his initial focus upon the Dutch painting almost conversationally: "You know that milkmaid in Vermeer?" Subsequent lines vividly establish the poet's impressions of the painting. A string of associations then leads to a moment of more personal immediacy, when the poet finds himself contemplating the people around him in the museum cafeteria and considering the curious act of painting restoration. Surrounded by suggestive facts and elusive notions, he concludes: "Something stays this way we cannot have,/ Comes alive because we cannot have it."

Ironically, it is at his most personal, and least academic, that Hass's words take on a heavier, less musical tone. Examples may be found in "Three Dawn Songs in Summer" or "The Distribution of Happiness," both short lyrics. In both cases the verses make no reference outside the moment described. They are poems of immersion in experience, free of the trappings of knowledge that so heavily decorate others. Still, the melodic ease of those other poems seems less easily achieved in these more purely experiential works—as may be seen in this, the entire first section, or song, from "Three Dawn Songs in Summer":

> The first long shadows in the fields
> Are like mortal difficulty.
> The first birdsong is not like that at all.

The conception is powerful. The introduction of the notion of "mortal difficulty" is effective as a means of transforming the reader's idea of those "first long shadows." The subsequent progression of ideas also operates successfully, for, to the reader's mind, that opening sense of struggle, suggested by sight of the shadows, is followed by a contrasting suggestion of ease, as heard in the rising birdsong. The phrasing, however, has a flatness akin to that of an equation. The linking-verb structure of the first two lines, "Are like," is reemphasized by an opposite echo, "is not like," in the third—an echo that then ends in mundane statement. That song of the bird "is not like that at all," it asserts. The language falls short of displaying the balanced and melodious verbal sense evident in Hass's countless lines not concerned with direct experience but rather with indirect experience, and with knowledge.

Hass seems to have some awareness of this distance being crossed, from his direct experiences to the expression of those experiences on the page. In the short poem "The Problem of Describing Trees," he begins with two lines reflecting experience ("The aspen glitters in the wind/ And that delights us.") followed by lines that render the opening images into scientific terms:

> The leaf flutters, turning,
> Because that motion in the heat of August
> Protects its cells from drying out. Likewise the leaf
> Of the cottonwood.

How strange it is, for the reader of poetry, to find that word "likewise" serving no poetic function, but only to indicate botanical similarity. That something has gone awry in the progress of the poem, in terms of traditional poetic effect, seems directly affirmed by the single-line fourth stanza: "It is good sometimes for poetry to disenchant us." As if in proof, the poem then ends with a dulled and deadened echo of the opening lines: "The aspen doing something in the wind."

Among the liveliest works in *Time and Materials* are those in which the rational connection loosens its firm hold on Hass's pen—as in "A Swarm of Dawns, a Flock of Restless Noons." In this stanzaic poem, thoughts succeed one another with seeming recklessness, pushed along by means of verbal association and the accidental conjoining of thoughts. The associations are engendered at least in part by the poet's alert reactions to the words being brought into play—as occurs with "haywire" in the following lines:

> while I sliced a nectarine for Moroccan salad
>
> And the seven league boots of your private grief. Maybe
> The syntax is a little haywire there. Left to itself,
>
> Wire must act like Paul Klee with a pencil. *Hay*
> Is the Old English word for *strike*. You strike down
>
> Grass, I guess, when it is moan. Mown. The field mice
> Devastated the monastery garden. Maybe because it was summer

Even in this gently wandering and inventive poem, fraught with the trappings of knowledge but also enlivened by flashes of radiant imagery, some sense of the troubles suggested in "The Problem of Describing Trees" recurs, in speaking of the character of "the elderly redactor": "He has no imagination, and field mice have gnawed away/ His source text for their nesting."

Similar to the struggle between experience and knowledge in the poems of *Time and Materials* is the conflict between poetic truth and political awareness. The balance, or imbalance, is explicit in "Winged and Acid Dark," a poem that skirts around a moment of violence between a man and a woman, apparently during the waning days of World War II. Interposed in the middle of the poem—and in the middle of the action—is reference to Japanese poet Matsuo Bashō, with his advice concerning the writing of poetry, "to avoid sensational materials":

> If the horror of the world were the truth of the world,
> he said, there would be no one to say it
> and no one to say it to.

The poem's narrative then returns to where it left off—a return that serves to emphasize that the poem's weight has shifted toward "the horror of the world."

Poetic attention to the political comes to the foreground in several poems in *Time and Materials*. In the longer poem "Bush's War," Hass pursues a string of associations that aim to "Set the facts out in an orderly way." Where they lead is toward enumerations of death and destruction:

> Firebombing of Tokyo, a hundred thousand
> In a night. Flash forward: forty-five
> Thousand Polish officers slaughtered
> By the Russian army in the Katyn Woods,
> The work of half a day. Flash forward:
> Two million Russian prisoners of war
> Murdered by the German army . . .

More striking in its enumeration of war horrors is the shorter poem "On Visiting the DMZ at Panmunjom: A Haibun," with its opening line, "The human imagination does not do very well with large numbers." In the next twenty-four lines, Hass aggressively emphasizes those same large numbers: "Five hundred thousand Chinese soldiers died in battle, or of/ disease. A million South Koreans died, four-fifths of them civilians./ One million, one hundred thousand North Koreans." He breaks the litany with lines addressed to the reader: "The terms are/ inexact and thinking about them can make you sleepy." The poem as a whole, which mixes the enumeration of horrors with both commentary and snippets of experience, ends on a note returning to, or perhaps establishing for the first time during the poem, an actually poetic vision:

> The flurry of white between the guard towers
> —river mist? a wedding party?
> is cattle egrets nesting in the willows.

Even when invoking uncomfortable political realities, the poems of Hass are, above all, expressions of a self comfortable with its place and position in the world.

They are poems that rise easily and pleasantly from the page and into the reader's eye, ear, and mind. Only a dull ear would fail to respond to their music, which rings as truly in Hass's translations from other poets as they do in his original evocations of the natural and social worlds surrounding him. If these lines have an overriding quality, it might be pinpointed as that of appreciation. Hass seems appreciative: of happenings, surroundings, and memories. Rare is the bewailing moan, the strident regret, the angry raising of voice. Even in his political moments the voice continues sounding reasonable, intelligent, and even satisfied. While the satisfaction expressed never quite descends into self-satisfaction, it also never quite ascends to joy—which may suggest why Whitman, whose works spanned both passionate self-absorption and unfettered joy, so fascinates this important American poet of our own time.

*Mark Rich*

## Review Sources

*Booklist* 104, no. 4 (October 15, 2007): 21.
*The New York Times Book Review* 157 (October 7, 2007): 11.
*The New Yorker* 83, no. 36 (November 19, 2007): 92-96.
*Publishers Weekly* 254, no. 30 (July 30, 2007): 57.
*San Francisco Chronicle*, November 11, 2007, p. M3.
*The Seattle Times*, November 18, 2007, p. J9.
*The Washington Post*, October 7, 2007, p. BW11.

# THE TIN ROOF BLOWDOWN

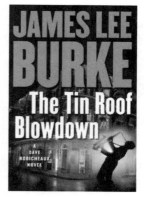

*Author:* James Lee Burke (1936-    )
*Publisher:* Simon & Schuster (New York).
   373 pp. $26.00
*Type of work:* Novel
*Time:* 2005
*Locale:* New Orleans and Iberia Parish, Louisiana

*In his sixteenth Dave Robicheaux novel, Burke weaves*
*a New Orleans tale of death and destruction wrought by*
*small-time criminals with the horror of Hurricane Katrina*
*and its aftermath*

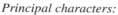

Principal characters:
   DAVE ROBICHEAUX, New Iberia police
      detective
   CLETE PURCELL, bounty hunter and Dave's best friend
   MOLLY ROBICHEAUX, ex-nun and Dave's wife
   ALAFAIR ROBICHEAUX, Dave's adopted daughter
   FATHER JUDE LEBLANC, junkie priest from New Orleans
   BERTRAND MELANCON, small-time criminal
   EDDY MELANCON, Bertrand's brother
   COURTNEY DEGRAVELLE, Clete's love interest
   OTIS BAYLOR, New Orleans insurance adjuster
   THELMA BAYLOR, Otis's daughter
   MELANIE BAYLOR, Otis's wife
   SIDNEY KOVICK, mobster who owns a flower shop
   RONALD BLEDSOE, psychopathic private eye
   HELEN SOILEAU, New Iberia sheriff

   James Lee Burke's sixteenth novel in the Dave Robicheaux series opens as Hurricane Katrina churns its way through the Gulf of Mexico, homing in on its target of New Orleans. In *The Tin Roof Blowdown*, New Iberia police detective Dave Robicheaux finds himself in the heart of the Hurricane Katrina disaster when his department is temporarily assigned to rescue and response duty in the Big Easy. Burke once again assembles a large cast of characters whose lives inevitably collide, causing chaos and death.
   The story of Father Jude LeBlanc sets the novel in motion. A priest who has prostate cancer and is addicted to drugs, Jude serves the poorest and most desperate people in New Orleans, residents of the Ninth Ward. His greatest fear is that the shaking of his hands will cause him to drop the chalice during communion. Father Jude decides to stay with his parishioners in spite of repeated warnings that everyone should leave; the poorest of the poor have nowhere to go and no way to leave. When he finds himself trapped in a church attic full of people about to drown in the rising water, he heroically breaks out a window, finds a boat, and tries to help his flock escape. It is at this

∼

*James Lee Burke has written more than two dozen novels, sixteen of which feature Cajun detective Dave Robicheaux. The winner of two Edgar Awards for crime fiction, Burke lives with his wife, Pearl, in New Iberia, Louisiana, and Missoula, Montana.*

∼

moment, however, that he encounters four young thugs. He does not give up his boat without a struggle; however, he sustains a blow to the head and presumably drowns.

The boat thieves, Andre Rochon, a kid named Kevin, and the Melancon brothers, Bertrand and Eddy, next appear as looters in a wealthy white neighborhood. They ply the flooded streets, looking for a darkened house to rob and destroy. Their troubles begin when they enter the house of Sidney Kovick and in their rampage find wads of money behind the walls. They also find a sack of diamonds. After destroying the interior of the house and stealing everything they can carry, they return to the boat, only to find themselves out of gas. Bertrand finds fuel in a carriage house belonging to Otis Baylor, an insurance adjuster, who has chosen to ride out the storm at his home along with his wife Melanie and daughter Thelma. The Baylor family can clearly see the looters with light provided by their larger generators, and, in a twist of fate, Thelma recognizes Eddy and Bertrand as the two men who raped her months earlier, after her senior prom. With their boat refueled, the young men cannot believe their good luck. They have more money than they have ever seen. Their luck immediately turns sour, however, when Eddy flicks a cigarette lighter, giving someone from the Baylor household a target. Gunshots ensue, killing Kevin immediately and simultaneously turning Eddy into a quadriplegic.

Bertrand Melancon's troubles are only beginning. He does not realize that the diamonds he has stolen are blood diamonds and that flower shop owner Sidney Kovick is also a ruthless gangster, someone who is rumored to have cut up a neighbor with a chain saw in his basement. Even worse, Kovick has double-crossed other villains to obtain the stones, placing Bertrand in double jeopardy. Ironically, Kovick is a greater threat to Bertrand than the police. As a New Orleans policeman tells Bertrand, "Hey, kid. If you stole anything from Sidney Kovick, mail it to him COD from Alaska, then buy a gun and shoot yourself. With luck, he won't find your grave."

Burke's portrayal of Bertrand Melancon is masterful. Bertrand is a serial rapist, a thief, and the murderer of a priest, the kind of lowlife that Burke uses to populate his books and for whom Dave generally can find little sympathy. Nonetheless, there is some moral ambiguity in Bertrand's creation. Burke allows him to be penitent for his actions; Bertrand attempts to write a letter of apology to Thelma and her family for the crime he perpetrated on her. He believes that if he gives the family the blood diamonds that somehow he will be redeemed. He is a dreamer, trying to fantasize his way out of the terrible mess that is his life. He is a sick man, suffering from bleeding ulcers that will kill him even if Kovick's goons do not find him. Last, he is a failure, never able to achieve what he sets out to do. It is not that Burke (or Dave) forgives him for the series of events he sets in motion; there is, however, some recognition of the circumstances that would lead a young person to such a terrible place. As Dave says at the end of the book, "I didn't like Bertrand Melancon or, better said, I didn't like the world he represented. But as I have to remind myself daily, many of the people I deal with did not get to choose the world in which they were born. . . . Bertrand was able to perform a couple of noble deeds before he disappeared. That's more than we can expect from most men who started off life as he did."

There are other bad guys trolling New Orleans whose stories fit into the ever-tightening plot line of *The Tin Roof Blowdown*. Private detective Ronald Bledsoe, with his smashed-in face and sadistic nature, undertakes a series of increasingly aggressive actions against Dave's daughter Alafair in response to humiliation he has suffered at her hands. Dave's response is predictable: "I didn't want revenge against Ronald Bledsoe. I wanted to kill him. I wanted to do it close up, with a .45, one loaded with 230-grain brass-jacketed hollow-points. . . . I wanted to smell the good, clean, head-reeling odor of burnt gunpowder and feel the jackhammer recoil of the steel frame in my wrist. I wanted to see Ronald Bledsoe translated into wallpaper."

Several familiar minor characters also make cameo appearances. Helen Soileau, Dave's former partner and now the sheriff of New Iberia, leads her department's efforts in New Orleans. Likewise, Federal Bureau of Investigation (FBI) agent Betsy Mossbacher comes through with some crucial information for Dave. Their roles are small, however, overshadowed by the power of Hurricane Katrina.

Clete Purcell, Dave's best friend, is present as well. As a jail bondsman, he has been tracking Andre Rochon. Once again, Clete falls in love, only to be destroyed when Courtney Degravelle, the woman he loves, is kidnapped, tortured, and murdered in connection with the missing blood diamonds. In addition, Alafair Robicheaux, now an adult and budding young novelist, demonstrates her courage under fire.

There is no doubt about the hero of the novel, however. Dave Robicheaux's stature has grown over the years since his first incarnation in *The Neon Rain* (1987), and his presence in *The Tin Roof Blowdown* is quietly controlled. Longtime readers of the Dave Robicheaux series will once again encounter Dave's struggles with his alcoholism and morality, his problems with his hapless friend Clete, and his love for his daughter and wife. Nevertheless, while this is familiar territory, never has Burke handled a story or a character so lyrically. Dave's demons, while still present, are quelled in the face of the larger tragedy of the Katrina disaster, and his humanity is never more evident than in his response to the poor people displaced and damaged by the water and politics.

While the human characters of *The Tin Roof Blowdown* are well drawn and alternately tragic and amusing, it is in the characterization of Katrina that Burke is at his very best. The enormity of the Katrina experience for Burke was hinted at in his last Dave Robicheaux book, *Pegasus Descending* (2006); his description in that novel of riding out Hurricane Audrey (1957) on an oil platform in the Gulf of Mexico was excruciating in its poetry and verisimilitude. It is therefore not surprising that Burke chose for his next novel to focus on the experience of Hurricane Katrina. Burke spelled out his views on Katrina and the disgrace of the national response in an op-ed piece he wrote for the *Los Angeles Times* shortly after the event. Many of these views are also shared by his main character, Dave.

In the opening chapter, Burke has Dave revisit his worst nightmares, the killing fields of the Vietnam War. In poetic language, he re-creates the crash of a helicopter carrying wounded, and the agony of the men as they die "incrementally—by flying shrapnel and bullets, by liquid flame on their skin, and by drowning in a river." To calm himself back to sleep, he says, he tells himself that this terrible killing of innocents is in the past and that he will not have to experience it again, nor will he have to witness "the betrayal and abandonment of our countrymen when they need us the most." The last paragraph, however, reveals Dave's (and Burke's) judgment on Katrina: "But that was before Katrina. That was before a storm with greater impact than the bomb blast that struck Hiroshima peeled the face of southern Louisiana. That was before one of the most beautiful cities in the Western Hemisphere was killed three times, and not just by the forces of nature."

Both the beauty of Burke's language and the bitterness he feels are nowhere more clear than in the epilogue. Dave, as is his habit, is wrapping up the events of the novel, trying to make sense of the long and twisted tale that he has just told readers. "New Orleans was a song that went under the waves. Sometimes in my dreams I see a city beneath the sea. . . . Perhaps the city has found its permanence inside its own demise, like Atlantis, trapped forever under the waves. . . . But the reality is otherwise. Category 5 hurricanes don't take prisoners and the sow that eats its farrow doesn't surrender self-interest in the cause of mercy."

*The Tin Roof Blowdown* is filled with many such moments; it is likely that this novel will be remembered as much for the immediacy and potency of Burke's writing about Katrina as it will be for its tightly constructed plot. In either case, the novel is Burke's best in several years, and perhaps the best he has ever written. Readers will find themselves haunted by Burke's images long after turning the final page.

*Diane Andrews Henningfeld*

## Review Sources

*The Boston Globe*, August 13, 2007, p. C5.
*Entertainment Weekly*, no. 944 (July 20, 2007): 78.
*Kirkus Reviews* 75, no. 12 (June 15, 2007): 568.
*Library Journal* 132, no. 12 (July 1, 2007): 72.
*The New York Times* 156 (July 23, 2007): B1-B7.
*Publishers Weekly* 254, no. 21 (May 21, 2007): 32.
*USA Today*, August 2, 2007, p. D1.
*The Washington Post*, July 23, 2007, p. C3.

# TOUCH AND GO
## A Memoir

*Author:* Studs Terkel (1912-    )
*Publisher:* New Press (New York). 288 pp. $24.95
*Type of work:* Memoir
*Time:* 1912-2007
*Locale:* Chicago

*Terkel looks back on the astonishing ninety-five years of his life*

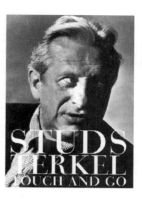

Principal personages:
 LOUIS "STUDS" TERKEL, writer, activist,
  and Chicago radio and television
  personality
 ANNIE FINKEL TERKEL, his mother
 IDA GOLDBERG TERKEL, his wife from 1939 to her death in 1999
 SAM TERKEL, his father, a Polish immigrant and a tailor

Although he has enjoyed successful careers as a radio and televison host, a soap opera actor, a playwright, and an activist, Louis "Studs" Terkel is best known as a compiler of oral histories. With the aid of a tape recorder and a keen ear for narrative, Terkel has interviewed scores of common and uncommon folk and stitched together seamless first-person accounts in their own voices for best-selling books, including *Working: People Talk About What They Do All Day and How They Feel About What They Do* (1974) and *Race: How Blacks and Whites Think and Feel About the American Obsession* (1992). In what he has declared to be his last book, *Touch and Go: A Memoir*, Terkel has attempted an approximation of the method that enabled him to capture the memories and voices of hundreds of others, interweaving excerpts from earlier works with new material dictated over the phone to longtime friend, assistant, and amanuensis Sydney Lewis, herself an accomplished compiler of oral history.

Alert and curious, Terkel has been witness to many of the most significant events in the past century. As he often retells it, he was born only two weeks after the sinking of the *Titanic*, "Make of it what you will." One of his earliest memories is of sitting on his father's shoulders in New York City, where the family lived until he was two or three, watching an Armistice parade pass by. He listened to parts of the "Scopes Monkey Trial" and the arguments of attorneys Clarence Darrow and William Jennings Bryan over the radio. He served in the Works Progress Administration's Federal Writers' Project during the Great Depression, did desk duty in the Air Force in World War II, organized unions, knew the singers and activists Mahalia Jackson and Pete Seeger, and was blacklisted during the Joseph McCarthy anticommunism era. He was a pioneer actor and broadcaster in the early days of radio and television. Through more than a dozen books, he has helped common Americans tell their own

∽

*Studs Terkel is the author of more than a dozen books, many of them, including* Division Street: America *(1967) and the Pulitzer Prize-winning* The Good War *(1984), based on oral histories of average Americans. Terkel was also a Chicago radio host for almost fifty years. In 1999, he was awarded the presidential National Humanities Medal.*

∽

stories about what it was like to live through the Depression, the Great War, and the country's struggles to find new ways to deal with work, with race, and with faith.

For Terkel, so closely associated with Chicago, life began in 1912 in New York City, where his parents Sam and Annie, Eastern European Jewish immigrants, worked hard to support a growing family that eventually included four sons. Sam Terkel, who ran a tailoring business, was an admirer of the socialist labor leader Eugene V. Debs (1855-1926), instilling in his sons a respect for unions and for "Gene's style of speech, easy as well as fervent." In 1920, the family moved to Chicago, where Terkel made his home for the rest of his life. His mother ran the Wells-Grand Hotel, a rooming house, for ten years, and Terkel loved to argue with the tenants hanging out in the lobby. These conversations, and the almost daily chance to hear radical speakers (some rational, some not) declaiming from soapboxes at Washington "Bughouse" Square, taught Terkel to listen well. "Perhaps none of it made any sense," he writes, "save one kind: sense of life." He graduated from the University of Chicago with a law degree in 1934 and worked in Chicago radio and television into the twenty-first century, parlaying his skills as a speaker and a listener into a career.

In one of the book's first extended history lessons, Terkel interrupts the narrative of his family's move to introduce Jane Addams (1860-1935), founder of Hull House in Chicago and the first American woman to win the Nobel Peace Prize. Decades later, Terkel remembers, he interviewed a woman named Jessie Binford, who lived in Hull House from 1906 until the mid-1960's, shortly before her death. Binford spent the last years of her life fighting, unsuccessfully, against plans to raze the settlement to provide space for the growing University of Illinois. In the story of Hull House and its eventual relocation, Terkel finds the central tension that informs his love for the city of Chicago: the compassionate and brave activists who work for the common good, and the mercenary, corrupt aldermen and other politicians who throw hurdles in their way. Both groups emerge in Terkel's tales as the main characters in the drama that shapes the city he loves.

Terkel's career has really been two careers, with largely different audiences. Terkel the writer has kept to the background, and those who know him primarily through his oral histories—a large readership—may stop to realize that they know very little about the man whose name appears on the covers of his books. Clearly, the man who would choose to write about how average people feel about their jobs, or how the American Dream has failed as many as it has helped, or how race shapes the way neighbors live together is a man with a strong social conscience and an affinity for the voiceless. Still, his aim in books like *Coming of Age: The Story of Our Century by Those Who've Lived It* (1995) is to help others tell their stories, not to comment or sermonize, although he too experienced many of the things his subjects describe. As he explains, his goal when interviewing is to not to put himself center stage, but to "recreate in my mind exactly what it was like to be with that person, to get as much as possible of what was in that person's mind at that particular moment."

Terkel did not write his first book of oral history, *Division Street: America* (1967), until he was fifty-five years old. Before that, he had established himself as a public figure whose personality, character, and opinions—his physical and his metaphorical voices—were in no way concealed. In retracing that parallel life, *Touch and Go* will be a revelation to many readers outside Chicago. Terkel's first job after earning his law degree was in Washington, D.C., where he worked in a civil service job for the Federal Emergency Relief Administration (FERA), and where he performed in the Washington Civic Theater Group's production of Sinclair Lewis's *It Can't Happen Here* (1935), a cautionary tale of fascism in America. By this time, Terkel had already drawn the attention of the Federal Bureau of Investigation (FBI) because of his radical politics, a fact Terkel learned decades later when he obtained copies of his FBI files.

Returning to Chicago after a year in Washington, Terkel attended plays frequently and soon became an actor with the Workers' Theater, a labor theater group that performed in small theaters and "at picket lines and soup kitchens." His gravelly voice led to work as a gangster in soap operas on Chicago radio stations—his first opportunity to earn real money. Piecing together an income to help support himself and his wife, Ida, he also worked as a writer with the Works Progress Administration (WPA) Radio Division and later as a commentator with his own radio show. Ida, a social worker, had also worked for FERA, and with Terkel's influence she too joined the Workers' Theater, by then renamed the Chicago Repertory Company.

Terkel continued to combine his passions for theater, leftist politics, and the new media of radio and television. For a time, he was a sportscaster on station WBBM, and later a disc jockey on WENR on a show he called *The Wax Museum*, after the wax record albums he played. Terkel notes that in the 1940's he was able to play good music of many types on a single show, "not just jazz, but *all* kinds: classical, folk, blues, opera." From 1949 to 1951, he hosted a nationally popular television show, *Studs' Place*, combining musical performances and short plays, and from 1952 to 1997 he hosted *The Studs Terkel Program* on WFMT radio, a one-hour weekday program on which he interviewed Chicagoans about a wide range of topics. During all these years in Chicago media, he supported progressive causes, including the labor movement and the Civil Rights movement, and gave activists a voice by reading their work, playing their music, or interviewing them. He was unable to work on television for a time after being blacklisted by the House Committee on Un-American Activities, but he retained his loyal fans and ultimately was recognized with city, state, and national awards for his courage and insight. This very public side of Terkel's career, and the dozens of fascinating figures he encountered over the years, is the focus of this book.

*Touch and Go* is Terkel's second memoir. His first, *Talking to Myself: A Memoir of My Times* (1977), is a more straightforward memoir, more linear and deliberate.

In it, as in *Touch and Go*, Terkel's emphasis is not on himself but on the quirky and influential people he has encountered. In *Touch and Go*, however, he also reveals welcome details about his family, and the style is conversational and meandering, the wandering reminiscences of an old sage nearing the end of his career. When he does mention his own accomplishments, he is self-deprecating, as when he reveals that he has never learned to drive a car or use a computer, and that he is even rather helpless when it comes to the machine with which he is most identified, the tape recorder.

Terkel's erudition is evident on every page. His own nickname, "Studs," was taken from the fictional Studs Lonigan, the protagonist in three novels by James T. Farrell. (Terkel took the name when he was acting in a play with two other actors also named Louis.) The title of this memoir, *Touch and Go*, is from Dylan Thomas's radio play *Under Milk Wood* (pr. 1953), and Terkel reprints the appropriate quatrain as the book's epigraph. In the first three paragraphs after his prologue, Terkel mentions Natacha Rambova, Rudolph Valentino, Pola Negri, Frida Kahlo, Diego Rivera, Theda Bara, Flannery O'Connor, and the Cincinnati pitcher Eppa Jeptha Rixey, with only the barest hints for those who cannot identify the names. Occasionally through the book he will make an unattributed allusion to Edgar Allan Poe or a popular song. It seems that he has read everything, seen everything, met everyone, and forgotten nothing.

This makes some passages difficult to get through. A reader whose attention drifts away for a second is apt to miss an important but tiny detail that reveals the meaning or the importance of an anecdote, and sometimes even careful attention is not enough: Keeping an encyclopedia handy for reference is both necessary and rewarding. For the countless readers who have come to know Terkel only through his books of oral history—those unlucky enough to have missed the opportunity to hear the author in his countless radio and television appearances—this book is the closest they will come to hearing Terkel the raconteur in his own voice. The Terkel they will meet in this memoir is charming, irascible, radical, insightful, and brave—a true American treasure.

*Cynthia A. Bily*

## Review Sources

*Harper's Magazine* 315 (November, 2007): 81-82.
*Kirkus Reviews* 75, no. 17 (September 1, 2007): 915-916.
*Library Journal* 132, no. 20 (December 15, 2007): 129-130.
*Los Angeles Times*, October 28, 2007, p. R3.
*The New York Times Book Review* 157 (December 9, 2007): 17.
*Publishers Weekly* 254, no. 34 (August 27, 2007): 70.

# TOUSSAINT LOUVERTURE
## A Biography

*Author:* Madison Smartt Bell (1957-    )
*Publisher:* Pantheon Books (New York). 333 pp. $27.00
*Type of work:* Biography
*Time:* Primarily 1791-1803
*Locale:* The French colony of Saint Domingue (now
   Haiti)

*A scholarly and balanced account of Toussaint-Louverture's life, with an emphasis on his struggle against slavery and for Haitian autonomy*

Principal personages:
   TOUSSAINT-LOUVERTURE (FRANÇOIS
      DOMINIQUE TOUSSAINT BRÉDA; 1743-
      1803), dominant leader of the Haitian
      revolution
   JEAN-JACQUES DESSALINES (c. 1758-1806), black
      general and first emperor of Haiti
   HENRY CHRISTOPHE (1767-1820), black general and
      later president of the state of Haiti
   NAPOLEON BONAPARTE (1769-1821), French first
      consul, r. 1799-1804, and emperor, r. 1804-1814
   CHARLES-VICTOR-EMMANUEL LECLERC (1772-1802),
      French general and Napoleon's brother-in-law
   LÉGER-FÉLICITÉ SONTHONAX (1763-1813), member of
      the French commission to Haiti
   ANDRÉ RIGAUD (1761-1811), leading mulatto general
      who opposed Louverture in 1799

The introductory chapter of Madison Smartt Bell's biography describes the culture and economic conditions in the French colony of Saint Domingue during the late eighteenth century. Although contemporary Haiti is commonly characterized as the poorest country of the Western Hemisphere, Saint Domingue was for many years the richest European colony in all of the Americas. The large sugar and coffee plantations enriched both the landowners and the French nation as a whole. Unfortunately, this prosperity was built upon slave labor, with conditions that were "extraordinarily severe." Although the Black Code of 1685 set minimum conditions, Bell writes that they were "more often honored in the breach than in the observance." Flogging was common, and amputation of an arm or a leg was sometimes the punishment for attempted escape.

The colony was composed of three ethnic groups: about 500,000 slaves of African ancestry, 40,000 white Europeans, and 30,000 mostly free "mulattos" of mixed African-European ancestry, commonly called *gens de couleur* (colored persons). The

*Madison Smartt Bell is a professor of English at Goucher College and the author of twelve novels, including an acclaimed trilogy about the Haitian revolution. One volume of the trilogy,* All Souls' Rising *(1995), was a finalist for the National Book Award.*

Europeans were divided into two groups: the wealthy, conservative property owners, called *grands blancs*, who usually opposed the French Revolution, and persons of limited economic resources, called *petits blancs*, who tended to support the Revolution. Although the official religion of the colony was Catholicism, a large percentage of the African-ancestry population combined the official religion with a variety of traditional animistic beliefs and practices called Voodoo. Practitioners of this syncretism believed that the spirits (*lwa* or *zanj*) of the dead remained nearby and were capable of having contact with living persons, often with the aid of hypnotic chanting and drumming.

As the most prominent leader of the only successful slave revolution in recorded history, Toussaint-Louverture was a person of great historical significance. The grandson of an African chieftain, he was born a slave on the large Bréda Plantation in 1743. He never showed an inclination to rebel until about the age of fifty. As a young man, in fact, he fully cooperated with his owner, distinguishing himself as a dependable supervisor of the other slaves. He also demonstrated an unusual ability to work with domestic animals. After gaining his freedom about 1774, he acquired considerable wealth in land and slaves, an unusual accomplishment for a former slave. He fathered at least eleven children (eight out of wedlock). Because so little information has been preserved about the first fifty years of his life, Bell writes that he "walked so very softly that he left next to no visible tracks at all."

There is no evidence that Louverture expressed any opposition to the institution of slavery before 1791, when large numbers of slaves rebelled in the northern plain. That year, he joined a band of rebel slaves led by George Biassou, but he opposed widespread bloodshed and even helped his former master's family to escape. By 1793, he was a recognized leader when he wrote in the Camp Turel Proclamation: "I have undertaken vengeance. I want Liberty and Equality to reign in Saint Domingue. I am working to make that happen." This proclamation is the earliest surviving record that he had changed his last name from Bréda to Louverture (which means "opening," frequently misspelled "L'Ouverture"). The reasons for his name change are unclear. Some historians have written that the new name was based on a gap between his two front teeth, while others believe that it referred to his ability to find openings for surprise military attacks. Without definitely rejecting such suggestions, Bell suggests that the name was probably a reference to a Voodoo spirit named Legba, the spirit of the gates and crossroads, a spirit believed to open the gateway between the living and the dead.

From the beginning, the revolt was complicated by the fact that the three ethnic groups were attacking each other, even murdering women and infants, in a violent orgy that Bell characterizes as a "three-way genocidal race war." In addition, rival groups of angry slaves frequently fought with one another. It is not known how many people died in the mass slaughter, but certainly they numbered in the thousands. Louverture recognized that violence was an inherent part of warfare, but unlike his associate, Jean-Jacques Dessalines, he was reluctant to order the mass slaughter of persons because of their race or economic class.

The government of the French Revolution, despite the announced principles of "liberty, equality, and brotherhood," was very hesitant to end slavery in the colonies. It was not until May, 1791, the third year of the revolution, that the French National Assembly passed a law recognizing some civil rights for the free *gens de couleur*, and it was not until the next year that the assembly decreed full civil rights to all free persons in the colonies, including blacks. In 1793, Léger-Félicité Sonthonax, chief representative for France in Saint Domingue, took the initiative in proclaiming the end of slavery in the colony, and the French Convention finally voted to abolish slavery in 1794.

Louverture's constantly changing goals, alliances, and enemies can be rather confusing. Initially he called for the restoration of the French monarchy, and when France and Spain went to war in 1793, he fought on the side of the Spanish. After France decreed an end to slavery, however, he switched sides and played a major role in driving Spanish and British troops out of Saint Domingue. He then was victorious over General André Rigaud's largely mulatto army in an ugly civil war, called the War of Knives (1799-1800). In this effort, Louverture had the support of American president John Adams, who hoped to promote the movement toward Haitian independence in order to weaken France. By 1801, Louverture was governor-general of the colony as well as the de facto ruler of the entire island. Bell writes that he managed the colony in a way that would "prove to the whole European world that slavery was not necessary to the success of the plantation economy." However, Bell also notes that he established a labor regime based on "raw authoritarianism," in which former slaves took charge and coerced other former slaves to work as hard as they had in the days of slavery.

Bell observes that historians, novelists, and politicians "have constructed whatever Toussaint Louverture they require," usually presenting him as either an idealistic martyr for the cause of freedom or as a savage, fanatical tyrant. Bell's account makes it clear that he conformed to neither of these stereotypes and that his complex personality and belief system contained many inconsistencies. While he denounced the cruelty of slavery, his oversight of free agricultural workers was tyrannical and oppressive. He wrote in 1793: "We receive everyone with humanity, and brotherhood, even our most Cruel enemies, and we pardon them wholeheartedly." Still, Bell believes that some of Dessalines's bloody atrocities were committed either with his tacit approval or under his secret orders. He was also inconsistent in the area of sexual morality, expressing views that were strict to the point of "prudery," forbidding his soldiers to practice extramarital relations, and insisting that women in his presence dress modestly. When he traveled, however, his residence was a "bachelor's paradise," with numerous liaisons with women from all three ethnic groups.

In 1801, Louverture was at the pinnacle of his power when he convened an assembly to formulate a constitution. Within a few months, he announced a constitution that contained progressive features; it prohibited slavery, forbade distinctions according to color, and promised equal protection of the law. On the other hand, the document named Louverture as the governor of the colony "for the rest of his glorious life" and even recognized his right to name a successor. Of greater consequence was its proclamation of a semiautonomous status for Saint Domingue, a provision that infuriated Napoleon Bonaparte, who was determined to consolidate and expand France's empire and at the same time to restore slavery. Napoleon therefore commissioned his brother-in-law, General Charles-Victor-Emmanuel Leclerc, to the island with a large army. Although Louverture's soldiers were badly outnumbered with inadequate weapons, their determination and guerrilla tactics prevented the French from winning the quick and decisive military victory they needed in order to prevail. Even more, the French experienced deadly outbreaks of malaria and yellow fever, which eventually resulted in the death of some fifty thousand of the eighty thousand French troops who had been sent to put down the black rebellion.

Before the French were forced to withdraw, however, Louverture uncharacteristically walked into a trap that Leclerc had prepared. Following his arrest, he declared: "In overthrowing me, you have only cut down the trunk of the tree of liberty of the Blacks in Saint Domingue: it will spring back from the roots, for they are numerous and deep." He was shipped to the Jura Mountains of France, where he was held in a cold medieval castle, the Fort de Joux, without adequate nutrition or medical care. In vain, he protested to Napoleon that he had been imprisoned without any due process. He died of pneumonia in 1803, and his body was thrown into an unmarked grave. When Napoleon was later exiled, he acknowledged that he had made a terrible mistake in not cooperating with Louverture and the other black generals of the colony. If this had happened, Bell speculates that Louverture's army of thirty thousand might have spread the abolition of slavery throughout the Caribbean region and perhaps even into Louisiana.

While such a crusade was highly unlikely, there were many long-term consequences of Louverture's revolution. The abolition of slavery in Saint Domingue represented the first massive achievement of its kind in the New World. Often an inspiration to opponents of slavery, the mention of Saint Domingue evoked terror and alarm among slaveholders in the Southern states. The revolution also made it possible for Haiti in 1804 to become the first independent country in Latin America. The catastrophic failure of the French intervention, moreover, convinced Napoleon of the impracticality of restoring a French empire in North America, which motivated him to sell Louisiana to the United States. Unfortunately, Louverture failed to establish a workable constitutional system, and thus he is arguably in part responsible for Haiti's subsequent experience with tyrannical and unstable government. Nevertheless, given the colony's social divisions, widespread poverty, and lack of constitutional traditions, it is unlikely that a wiser and more democratic leader would have been able to establish a secure foundation for anything approaching a stable democracy.

In writing this biography, Bell has utilized both primary and secondary sources. Louverture left a large collection of correspondence and other documents, most of which has never been translated from French into English. A few of the letters were written in his own hand in the Haitian Creole patois, but most were dictated by him to secretaries who often edited the ideas and translated them into standard French. Although the vast majority of Bell's reference notes refer to published works, he made some limited use of the French National Archives, and he managed to discover a few unknown sources in private hands, in particular those belonging to a man named Gérard Barthélemy. In addition to the rich French writings about Louverture and the revolution, Bell also took advantage of several important English-language works, including those of Laurent Debois, Gordon Brown, Carolyn Fick, and David Geggus.

Bell's account of Louverture is the first serious biography to appear in the English language in more than half a century. A balanced work of historical synthesis, its purpose is not to present information that is particularly original, although it does contain numerous facts and insights not readily available to English readers. A few of his interpretations are questionable, as when he suggests that the *grands blancs* helped to stir up the black insurrection with the idea that it would frighten the *petits blancs* into submission. Readers unfamiliar with Haitian history should be forewarned that the book's large number of military leaders and other persons can be confusing, and Bell does not always identify them when first mentioned. Taken as a whole, nevertheless, the biography is a pleasure to read, and it will likely become recognized as the standard work on Louverture in the English language.

*Thomas Tandy Lewis*

## Review Sources

*Biography: An Interdisciplinary Quarterly* 30, no. 3 (Summer, 2007): 433-434.
*Booklist* 103, no. 11 (February 1, 2007): 21.
*The Nation* 284, no. 15 (April 16, 2007): 32-34.
*The New Republic* 237, no. 5 (September 10, 2007): 41-47.
*The New York Review of Books* 54, no. 9 (May 31, 2007): 54-58.
*The New York Times Book Review* 156 (February 25, 2005): 7.
*The New Yorker* 83, no. 3 (March 12, 2007): 85.
*Publishers Weekly* 253, no. 44 (November 6, 2006): 50.
*The Times Literary Supplement*, March 16, 2007, p. 4.
*The Wall Street Journal* 249, no. 15 (January 19, 2007): W4.

# A TRANQUIL STAR
## Unpublished Stories

*Author:* Primo Levi (1919-1987)
Translated from the Italian by Ann Goldstein and
  Alessandra Bastagli
*Publisher:* W. W. Norton (New York). 164 pp. $21.95
*Type of work:* Short fiction

*Light, darkness, and shadows permeate this collection
of stories, echoing the Holocaust and exploring the beauty
and ugliness of which humans are capable*

Divided into early and late works written between 1949
and 1986, the seventeen short stories assembled in Primo
Levi's *A Tranquil Star*, originally published in Italian magazines and books, are here collected and translated into
English for the first time. Though Levi is known primarily for his testamentary works
written as witness to the Holocaust and its aftermath, these short stories are not
overtly or nominally Holocaust-themed, although shadows and echoes of Auschwitz
eerily reverberate throughout them. Most literary critics have appreciated *A Tranquil
Star*'s varied themes and images that inform and are informed by Levi's stunning,
major works. While a few critics have viewed these valedictory stories as tainted
by Levi's probable suicide, most have seen them as praiseworthy reflections of
his broad imagination, deep conscience, and brilliant literary talent.

About some of his stories, Levi wrote, "all interpretations are true . . . a story must
be ambiguous." Levi's multilayered writings, filled with images of good and evil, are
"painted" either in chiaroscuro (the juxtaposition or overlapping of light, dark, and
shadow) or in darkness alone; both "shadings" are used naturalistically, ironically,
or ambiguously and as incisive and insightful commentary on human behavior and
experience.

Light and dark exist literally and metaphorically in "The Death of Marinese," the
earliest of the stories and redolent of Levi's experience as a freedom fighter in 1943
(during which he was sent by the Nazis to the Auschwitz death camp). Marinese and
another Italian partisan are captured under a gray sky on a snowy, icy road. Light
and dark are in conflict too, for while he contemplates his imminent death by the
Germans, Marinese finds himself in virtual darkness, "submerged in a long, narrow
tunnel . . . like the light that penetrates closed eyelids." When he notices a grenade
attached to the belt of one of the Nazis, Marinese's light, "gentle soul" bursts into an
upsurge of shame and rage, "dark and primeval," and he detonates the grenade, killing
four Nazis and himself. Clearly, light and dark overlap here, for Marinese does kill
the Nazis, but at the cost of his own life.

In "Knall," the dichotomy between light and dark is not literal but rather a schism
between tone and meaning. The narrator's light, informal tone masks the dark, ugly

∾

*An industrial chemist who bore witness to the Holocaust, Primo Levi wrote short fiction, poetry, and essays, as well as* Se questo è un uomo *(1947; If This Is a Man, 1959);* La tregua *(1963; The Reawakening, 1965), covering his repatriation to Italy; and* I sommersi e i salvati *(1986; The Drowned and the Saved, 1988), dealing with the emotional legacy of Auschwitz.*

∾

reality that a knall is a weapon that kills quickly and efficiently, leaving no mess. The narrator casually describes this German-sounding "handy device" as unique, clever, and neat, the perfect tool for quiet, up-close mass murder that "does not spill blood." It is a tool to activate that need of humans, "acute or chronic, to kill their neighbor or themselves." The ambiguous tension between the detached tone and very dark topic evokes the shadows of Auschwitz, where Nazis used the insecticide Zyklon B to commit genocide "neatly," without messy bullets or blood.

"One Night" begins in the gray half-light at dusk and continues until dawn, although daylight reveals a more sinister darkness. With echoes of the chugging deportation trains containing their "cargo" of Jews en route to the death camps, a train stops in a dark forest. From the woods come swarms of men and women who dismantle the train and destroy the rails. This potentially hopeful story ends in shocking darkness, however, for after tearing apart the train and tracks, the people turn on each other and themselves. The story echoes loudly the diabolical way in which the Nazis in the camps forced Jewish Kapos to torture other Jewish prisoners so as to blur the line between the innocent Jews and the nefarious Nazis.

In "The Magic Paint," an industrial chemist in a paint factory (Levi's own profession for many years) creates a Teflon-type paint that, when applied to oneself, allows one to experience great fortune, protected from all harm. However, its protective qualities vanish in water. It is almost as if the "magic paint" of the good life experienced by deportees before Auschwitz was cruelly washed away by the obligatory shower that preceded their slow death in the camp.

Metaphoric darkness takes the shape of bleak, absurdist bureaucracy in "Fra Diavolo on the Po," in which Levi writes about his first notice to report for induction into the Italian military. When he reports as scheduled, he is screamed at, called a deserter by "a giant in a Fascist uniform," and sent away. Like the 1935 Nuremberg Laws in Germany that stripped Jews of their rights and citizenship, Fascist laws in Italy prohibited Jews from carrying guns, and Levi, after enlisting on his own, was therefore thrown out of the Italian military. Insane darkness culminates when, after his survival from Auschwitz and his eventual repatriation to Italy, he is ordered, despite his obvious physical weakness, to appear for a military preinduction physical, during which the doctor scolds him for having no written documentation of his time at the concentration camp, other than the tattoo of 174517 on his arm. The story is reminiscent of those surviving offspring who were refused release of their murdered parents' money by Swiss banks because they lacked their parents' death certificates.

In "Bureau of Vital Statistics," another absurdist story with an unstated Holocaust link, Arrigo's job in this government agency is to add a cause of death to index cards printed with a person's name and date of death. Bureaucrats like Arrigo "were all sheep . . . and no one dared protest and no one took the job seriously" because they were insulated from death itself. Arrigo is a prototype of the Nazi bureaucrats of the Aktion T-4 eugenics program, through which, by 1941, some seventy thousand mentally retarded, deformed, and disabled people, "undesirables" termed "life unworthy of life," were placed in state-run institutions and then murdered. The Nazis covered their crimes by reporting to the victims' families such bogus causes of death as pneumonia or influenza.

In the science-fiction story "The Molecule's Defiance," a frustrated industrial chemist creates a batch of synthetic resin that turns inexplicably bad, with dire implications. It is as if nature itself has gone berserk, rebelling against humanity at the molecular level as a "monster molecule" evolves from this tainted chemical soup, "a yellow mass full of lumps and nodules." The chemist calls this "deformed but gigantic" molecule an "obscene message and symbol . . . of other ugly things . . . that obscure our future . . . of unseemly death over life." It is clear that Levi experienced the penultimate, darkly "obscene message" in the sadistic brutality—"the derisiveness of soul-less things"—in Auschwitz.

"The Sorcerers," a story based on a real South American tribe, is the darkest human answer to "The Molecule's Defiance." Two ethnographers study the dialect and culture of the primitive Sirionó people in the rain forests of Bolivia, who once had the knowledge to light fires and make canoes but now have regressed to the point that their only skill is carving bows for hunting. Levi concludes, "not in every place and not in every era is humanity destined to advance." As a victim of the Holocaust, he is justifiably suspicious about the human desire and capacity for progress. For Levi, civilized society is frozen in place or is backsliding.

A story suffused with light, but dark around the edges, is the ambiguous "In the Park," in which famous authors and literary characters inhabit an alternative universe. Writers like François Villon and François Rabelais coexist with such characters as Moll Flanders, Holden Caulfield, and Leopold Bloom. In this well-lit literary heaven, the spectacular sunsets "often . . . last from early afternoon until night," yet the light-filled sky turns the "color of lead" when characters from the World War I-era antiwar novel *Im Westen nichts Neues* (1929; *All Quiet on the Western Front*) are spied. With chilling, foreboding darkness, Levi writes, "Who knows how many of them would . . . take up arms again twenty years later, and lose either their skin or their soul."

How can one tell the tortured, untellable tale at all? No language exists to encapsulate, let alone approximate, the inexpressible darkness of the Holocaust. "It's clear that something in our lexicon isn't working," avers the narrator in the last story in the collection, "A Tranquil Star." We are also severely limited in our comprehension of human motivation: "We understand only—and approximately—the how, not why." For Levi, the Holocaust was not an anomaly but a horrific yet unsurprising example of the human capacity for evil.

Clearly, for Levi, the human instincts to create and transcend will always war with and be overshadowed by powerful instincts for violence and destruction. The triumph of survival, transcending the unendurable (as Levi did at Auschwitz), is at the heart of the initiation story "Bear Meat." Bathed in a dusklike half-light, the narrator experiences great danger and fear while mountain climbing, only to discover "at the first ghostly light" that the ultimate human achievement is "being your own master . . . to feel strong," to transcend.

Levi paints destructive human instincts in unrelenting darkness. In "Gladiators," a reticent young man under "a shadow of reluctance" is persuaded by his girlfriend to attend a Friday night's weekly gladiatorial spectacle. The gladiators use cars and forklifts to destroy their opponents, accompanied by spectators' cheers. As the rage of sadistic and senseless destruction darkens, the young man and woman depart early and go home separately, both feeling revulsion and guilt at the insanity they have witnessed and that their presence helped make possible. Shadowy half-light has become full darkness.

In between light and darkness, "The Fugitive" is bathed in ambiguous shadow as Levi explores the human capacity to create beauty, however elusive and temporary. Pasquale composes the most beautiful poem ever written. His success is thrown into dark shadows, however, when the poem mysteriously disappears. He tries in vain to find or re-create it, but the poem is irretrievably gone, a victim of human transience: "To compose a poem that is worth reading and remembering is a gift of destiny."

Human-created beauty is always elusive, but Levi's varied and provocative, light and dark short stories of *A Tranquil Star* are his posthumous "gift of destiny" to the world. As in some of Levi's stories, the question of whether the human race is presently at the shadowy half-light of dawn or dusk remains ambiguous. By exploring the human need to create, which wars with the propensity to destroy—coequal parts of our destiny—Levi uses light, shadow, and darkness to create in each story "a fable that awakens echoes and in which each of us can perceive distant reflections of himself and of the human race."

*Howard A. Kerner*

## Review Sources

*The Guardian*, May 5, 2007, p. 17.
*Kirkus Reviews* 75, no. 5 (March 1, 2007): 189.
*London Review of Books* 29, no. 11 (June 7, 2007): 35-36.
*Los Angeles Times*, April 22, 2007, p. 5.
*The New York Review of Books* 54, no. 12 (July 19, 2007): 51-52.
*The New York Times Book Review* 156 (May 27, 2007): 14-15.
*The Spectator* 303 (May 5, 2007): 59.
*The Times Literary Supplement*, July 13, 2007, p. 17.
*The Washington Post*, July 1, 2007, p. BW06.

# TRAVELS WITH HERODOTUS

*Author:* Ryszard Kapuściński (1932-2007)
*First published: Podróżez Herodotem,* 2004, in Poland
Translated from the Polish by Klara Glowczewska
*Publisher:* Alfred A. Knopf (New York). 275 pp. $25.00
*Type of work:* Essays, travel, memoir
*Time:* 1950-1980
*Locale:* Poland, India, China, Egypt, Sudan, Belgian
Congo, Iran, Ethiopia, Tanzania, Algeria, Senegal,
Greece, and Turkey

*A journalist parallels his early travels to Asia and Africa as a foreign correspondent to the life and times of Herodotus, an ancient Greek historian*

Principal personages:
RYSZARD KAPUŚCIŃSKI (1932-2007), a Polish journalist
HERODOTUS (c. 484-c. 425 B.C.E.), Greek writer, commonly
called "the father of history"

As one of the twentieth century's most notable journalists, Ryszard Kapuściński often brought a personal element into his writing, especially in his essay collections *Wojna futbolowa* (1979; *The Soccer War,* 1990), *Imperium* (1993; English translation, 1994), and *Heban* (1998; *The Shadow of the Sun,* 2001). In *Travels with Herodotus,* his final book of essays, he reveals more about his life and approach to writing than in any of his previous works.

In *Travels with Herodotus,* Kapuściński returns to his origins as a foreign correspondent, describing many of his early assignments, as well as his devotion to *Historiai Herodotou* (c. 424 B.C.E.; *The History,* 1709; also translated *The Histories*) by Herodotus, a work Kapuściński carried along on his journeys to cover coups, wars, and revolutions in places few other writers would go. For Kapuściński, Herodotus—with his love of travel, his appreciation of a good story, his fascination for the unusual, and his broad understanding of disparate civilizations—was both a literary companion and role model. The writings of Herodotus reinforced the Polish journalist's reportorial instincts, helping Kapuściński become a writer who combined informed journalism, multicultural knowledge, vivid prose, and surreal imagery to create true literature. At the time of his death, Kapuściński's books had been translated into twenty-eight languages, and critics favorably compared his work to the wide-ranging novels of Joseph Conrad and the Magical Realist writings of Gabriel García Márquez.

The opening essay of *Travels with Herodotus,* "Crossing the Border," establishes the book's central motifs—Kapuściński's desire to encounter the world and his admiration for the ancient Greek historian. With this essay, Kapuściński also begins the book's parallel structure, with events in Herodotus's history echoing Kapuściński's experiences. For example, Kapuściński explains that a scholar named Seweryn Hammer translated Herodotus in the mid-1940's, yet the Polish government kept *The Histories* off the shelves until 1955, after Joseph Stalin had died and the Soviet bloc could breathe easier. Kapuściński intertwines this discussion of Communist censorship with Herodotus's description of King Thrasybulus's advice to Periander, the tyrant of Corinth, on how to keep one's kingdom under absolute control by killing off all the outstanding subjects, thereby creating a mediocre populous that

~

*Polish author Ryszard Kapuściński was born in 1932 and became a journalist in 1955. For the next forty years, he traveled extensively in Africa, Latin America, and Asia, writing a number of world-renowned books, including* Jeszcze dzień życia *(1976;* Another Day of Life, *1986) and* Szachinszach *(1982;* Shah of Shahs, *1985). He died in 2007.*

~

would be easier to rule. In this passage, Kapuściński comparatively links Stalin to Periander, a technique he used in *Cesarz* (1978; *The Emperor*, 1983), a portrait of Ethiopia's King Haile Selassie I, which Poles read as an allegory criticizing Soviet totalitarianism.

In "Crossing the Border," Kapuściński recounts landing his first job in 1955 with *Sztandar Młodych* (*The Banner of Youth*), a newspaper based in Warsaw. When on assignment in the Polish countryside, he occasionally goes near the borders, and he becomes obsessed with the desire to cross national boundaries. Finally, summoning his courage, he asks his editor if he could be sent abroad. She assigns him to India, a country he knows nothing about. Before he leaves, she gives him a copy of Herodotus's *The Histories* to accompany him. Thus, the pattern of the book's essays is set—Kapuściński travels to exotic and often dangerous places he knows little about, and Herodotus helps him to survive these journeys and to thrive as a top-shelf foreign correspondent.

However, what Kapuściński calls his "first encounter with otherness" is not very successful. As he travels across India, he finds its complex tapestry of ethnicities, religions, gods, castes, landscapes, and histories overwhelming. Its vastness and mystery humble him, and he realizes the need extensively to prepare when entering an alien culture. Also in India, Kapuściński discovers the need for a lingua franca to get around in the world. In this, he envies Herodotus, whose native Greek was widely spoken in the fifth century B.C.E. As a citizen of the twentieth century, Kapuściński must learn English, which he begins to do by crawling word by word through Ernest Hemingway's *For Whom the Bell Tolls* (1940). It is also on his assignment to India that Kapuściński experiences his first serious problem in crossing borders. On his return flight to Poland, he is detained in Kabul for not having a visa. Dressed for the tropics, Kapuściński must spend a frozen night camped out on the runway with only a wan fire and a guard's overcoat to keep him warm.

Next, Kapuściński travels to China, a largely unsatisfying voyage since he is always in the presence of his guide and keeper, Comrade Li, and except for some brief trips to the Great Wall and Shanghai, he remains largely in his hotel room. With a lot of time to wile away, Kapuściński reads the works of Mao Zedong, Confucius, and Laozi. Kapuściński finds much to consider in the two sixth century B.C.E. Chinese sages, with Confucius calling for social engagement and an adherence to form, and Laozi for a departure from social structures and an embracing of nature and spontaneity. Despite these differences, Kapuściński notes that they both promote humility, as did their contemporary philosophers in India and Greece.

Abruptly, the Chinese authorities send Kapuściński home, and he returns to Warsaw, where he leaves *The Banner of Youth* to join the Polish Press Agency. In the essay "Memory Along the Roadways of the World," Kapuściński describes reading Herodotus late at night when the agency's offices are empty. With this essay, the parallels between Kapuściński and Herodotus go beyond experience to include motivations, beliefs, and methods as well. Herodotus writes that his purpose in writing *The Histories* is "to prevent the traces of human events from being erased by time." Kapuściński's enthusiasm for this statement makes it clear that this is also his motivation for writing. Just as there is an allegorical correspondence between Haile Selassie and all autocrats in *The Emperor*, so too is there a connection between Herodotus and Kapuściński in *Travels with Herodotus*, so that when Kapuściński describes Herodotus's characteristics as a writer and historian, he is essentially revealing his own literary and reportorial approaches and precepts.

In the next essay, "The Happiness and Unhappiness of Croesus," Kapuściński begins an extended digression through *The Histories*, describing the defeat of Croesus, king of Lydia, by Cyrus the Great, king of Persia. In turn, Cyrus meets his nemesis in Queen Tomyris of the Massagetae, who defeats the invading Persians in a bloody encounter that devastates both armies and leaves Cyrus dead on the field of battle. Kapuściński sees in these battles the epic conflict between East and West, Asia and Europe, that continues into the twenty-first century. After Cyrus's violent end, Kapuściński explores Herodotus's fascination for Africa, especially Egypt. Herodotus proposes that the Greek gods originated in Egypt, and Kapuściński argues that this belief supports the concept that European culture derived from Egypt, and that Africa is the cradle of the West.

Like Herodotus, Kapuściński felt a deep fascination for Africa, and he made the first of many journeys there in 1960. The Polish journalist finds Africa to be a kaleidoscope of joys and terrors, wonders and horrors. In Cairo, he is robbed in a minaret of an abandoned mosque. In the Sudan, he smokes hashish with two strangers from the desert in a Land Rover and later joins them at a Louis Armstrong concert in Khartoum. The Congo he finds in a state of bloody anarchy, as it transforms from a Belgian colony into an independent nation (present-day Democratic Republic of the Congo). Describing a stateless land infested with gangs of former policemen preying on bands of refugees, Kapuściński writes, "One could see clearly how dangerous freedom is in the absence of hierarchy and order—or, rather, anarchy in the absence of ethics." He makes his way across hazardous stretches of Ethiopia's outback with a driver who knows only two phrases in English—"problem" and "no problem." When he goes to Algeria, he witnesses the overthrow of its first president, Ahmed Ben Bella, precipitating the struggle between a modern Islam open to contemporary ideas and a fundamentalist Islam that turns inward, toward the past. In his most hopeful note, Kapuściński describes the first World Festival of Black Art held in Senegal in 1963, with its masked dancers, impromptu street theater, and exhibits of sculpture ancient and modern.

As a narrative counterpoint to his African journeys, Kapuściński weaves together his recollections of that continent with Herodotus's accounts of Persia's wars. After recovering from the defeat by the Massagetae, and subduing an internal revolt by the Babylonians, the Persians, under the leadership of King Darius the Great, turn on the Scythians, who occupied what is today southern Russia. With modern-style guerrilla tactics, the Scythians, whose warriors scalp their foes and drink their blood, force Darius to withdraw from their lands. The Scythian victory inspires the Ionians to revolt, and though they fail to break from Persia, the aid the Ionians receive from Athens leads Xerxes I, son of Darius, to invade Greece and wreak revenge.

Now the stage is set for the great conflict between Persia and Greece, a conflict that for Kapuściński epitomizes the struggle of East and West. Darius sets off with an army that may have numbered in the hundreds of thousands. All of his vast realms, stretching from the eastern shores of the Mediterranean to India, gave troops to the effort. He builds a bridge across the Hellespont made from connected ships, and his horde pours unchallenged into Europe, crossing Thrace, Macedonia, and Thessaly. Then, Xerxes' army encounters a small Greek force at Thermopylae, a narrow strait of land between the Aegean Sea and the mountains. The Greek force, massively outnumbered, nevertheless slaughters a great portion of Xerxes' men, and may have ultimately won the battle if it were not for treachery. Despite overwhelming odds in its favor, Xerxes' fleet also loses at the Battle of Salamis. Xerxes, in despair at seeing his incredibly massive armies defeated by a comparative handful of Greek soldiers, retreats to his palace at Persepolis, where he will devote his remaining fifteen years to his harem.

By alternating between Herodotus's *The Histories* and his own African and Asian encounters, Kapuściński emphasizes the universality of human experience across time and space. The full range of human reactions—from bravery to cowardice, kindness to cruelty—along with a breathtaking array of cultural paradigms, have been present for thousands upon thousands of years. At the same time, Kapuściński explores the eternal verities of a writer's craft, especially the writer of travel literature, which have not changed since the days of Herodotus, who traversed the known world to gather stories, witness events, and see new places and peoples. As authors, Kapuściński and Herodotus share much—a passion for journeying, a desire to understand the world, a strong narrative instinct, an attention to detail, an eye for the unusual, and an ability to penetrate the causes of violence.

Most important, Kapuściński, like Herodotus, expresses a compassion for humanity, along with a desire to share its grief and its joys, and to celebrate its nearly infinite variations. In the essay "Herodotus's Discovery," Kapuściński describes Herodotus's most important insight about humanity and its multitude of cultures: "That there are many worlds. And that each is different. Each is important. And that one must learn about them, because these other worlds, these other cultures, are mirrors in which we can see ourselves better—for we cannot define our own identity until having confronted that of others, as comparison." As shown by *Travels with Herodotus*, one could say the same for Ryszard Kapuściński.

*John Nizalowski*

## Review Sources

*The Atlanta Journal-Constitution*, June 17, 2007, p. 5L.
*Booklist* 103, nos. 19/20 (June 1, 2007): 31.
*Kirkus Reviews* 75, no. 7 (April 1, 2007): 316-317.
*Los Angeles Times*, June 10, 2007, p. R8.
*The Nation* 285, no. 9 (October 1, 2007): 25-32.
*The New York Times Book Review* 156 (June 10, 2007): 18-19.
*The Spectator* 304 (July 14, 2007): 39.
*The Wall Street Journal* 249, no. 134 (June 9, 2007): P8.
*The Washington Post*, June 24, 2007, p. BW08.

# TREE OF SMOKE

*Author:* Denis Johnson (1949-    )
*Publisher:* Farrar, Straus and Giroux (New York).
  614 pp. $27.00
*Type of work:* Novel
*Time:* 1963-1983
*Locale:* Vietnam, Malaysia, Japan, Arizona, the Philippines, and Hawaii

*An ambitious novel that chronicles a CIA intelligence operation gone awry during the Vietnam War*

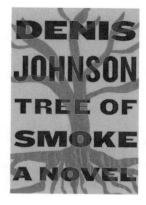

*Principal characters:*
  WILLIAM "SKIP" SANDS, CIA agent for
    psychological operations, first in the
    Philippines, and then in Vietnam
  COLONEL FRANCIS X. SANDS, mythical war hero
    who initiates the Tree of Smoke intelligence operation
  FATHER THOMAS CARIGNAN, a Catholic priest who
    lives in a small town in the Philippines
  KATHY JONES, Canadian missionary and Skip's love interest
  BILL HOUSTON, Navy seaman from Phoenix, Arizona
  JAMES HOUSTON, Bill's younger brother, who joins the
    Army at age seventeen
  NGUYEN HAO, a Vietnamese businessman who attempts to help the CIA
  SERGEANT JIMMY STORM, one of Colonel Sands's colleagues
  TRUNG THAN, a Viet Cong double agent
  TERRY CRODELLE, Regional Security officer who investigates
    Skip Sands's undercover activities
  CADWALLADER, a one-legged G.I. who goes boating with James

Mostly known for his collection of short stories *Jesus' Son* (1992), author and journalist Denis Johnson writes well of drug addicts, drifters, and delinquents struggling to keep themselves from jail or complete destitution, yet he also looks for the visionary potential of such deprivations. With *Tree of Smoke*, his first full-length novel in nine years, Johnson blends together multiple story lines of the Vietnam War and leaves it up to the reader to make connections between them. The main strand concerns the misadventures of a deluded young American Central Intelligence Agency (CIA) agent. As Johnson ironically associates him with Graham Greene's *The Quiet American* (1955), William "Skip" Sands believes in his country's stated goal of fighting communism by taking on the Viet Cong, and he looks to his uncle Colonel Francis X. Sands to guide him to a successful mission gathering intelligence. Tangentially, Bill and James Houston from Phoenix, Arizona, join the military to escape their working-class existence and their mother's fundamentalism. Skip's erstwhile love interest, Kathy Jones, turns to Calvinism to help explain her missionary

~

*Author and journalist Denis Johnson has written several novels, one book of reportage, three collections of poetry, and one influential short-story sequence,* Jesus' Son *(1992).* Tree of Smoke *won the National Book Award for 2007.*

~

experiences working for the International Children's Relief Effort. By moving yearly from the Kennedy assassination (1963) through the Tet Offensive (1968) and the evacuation of Saigon (1975), Johnson depicts an increasingly deranged war until the final coda in 1983 when a disillusioned Skip is executed for gun-running in Malaysia. Throughout the novel, whatever narratives Americans bring to the war, they are inevitably undermined by the surreal realities on the ground.

The novel consistently depicts the heavy psychological and environmental toll of the conflict. Johnson begins with an emblematic scene in which eighteen-year-old recruit Bill Houston absentmindedly shoots a monkey in the jungle of Grande Island in the Philippines. In a kind of parody of the Ernest Hemingway manly ideal, Houston initially seeks wild boar, but when he kills the monkey, he picks it up to find it crying as it dies in his hands, so he weeps in turn at what he has done. This scene is the first of many in which Americans learn of their destructive potential in foreign lands. Johnson then cuts to a later scene in 1967 where Bill meets his just-enlisted brother James at a Peanut Bar in Yokohama, Japan. They get drunk together and eventually admit that they never liked each other. Bill spills his beer on a Japanese woman and then tells her "I came across this ocean and died. They might as well bring back my bones. I'm all different." The rest of the first half of the novel goes on to explain how Bill reached this state.

To help show how the madness of the war got started, Johnson introduces the reader to the Colonel Francis X. Sands, a deliberately mythological character with strong echoes of Colonel Kurtz in Francis Ford's Coppola's *Apocalypse Now* (1979). The colonel conveys an old-fashioned assurance and masculinity because of his background that includes playing football for coach Knute Rockne at Notre Dame and barely surviving as a Japanese prisoner of war in Burma in 1941. After he has his cousin work in the Philippines for awhile, Colonel Sands moves Skip to the South Vietnamese countryside to the home of a former French doctor so that he can help organize data for the "Tree of Smoke" project. Since Skip had dreams of being more of a James Bond than a clerk drearily collating files away from all of the action, he comes to resent his uncle's directives even as he continues to believe in the myth of his macho prowess. As the colonel claims, "War is ninety percent myth anyway, isn't it? In order to prosecute our own wars we raise them to the level of human sacrifice, don't we, and constantly invoke our God. It's got to be about something bigger than dying, or we'd all turn deserter." The colonel also has plans of mapping the Cu Chi tunnels, which proves another myth-laden maze that they never really explore. Instead of gaining an understanding of the war, the CIA agents entangle themselves in their own labyrinth.

Johnson finds multiple ways to represent what one soldier calls the "Disneyland on acid" random nature of the war. The colonel's psychological operation, titled "Tree of Smoke," works as an evocative symbol both of a biblical portents of the apocalypse, the mushroom cloud of the atomic bomb, and of the heedless American poisoning of the Vietnamese countryside. At one point, the colonel brings in a generator to show a film about John F. Kennedy to some Vietnamese villagers. No Vietnamese arrive, naturally, but the colonel still solipsistically watches it himself as the generator spreads smoke pollution through the local countryside, thereby alerting the Viet Cong of the American presence. Repeatedly, the intelligence community seems more concerned about reinforcing their own myths than in actively understanding the country in which they are at war. To try to get a sense of the large picture of the operations, the colonel repeats a quote from St. Paul: "There is one God, and many administrations." The biblical passage at least acknowledges the disjointed nature of an American campaign on a foreign country that operates under different laws, but no one has fully foreseen the violent corruption of the soldiers. Some worry about creating bad karma, but once the Tet Offensive begins and American soldiers start to die in larger quantities, all of the nobler aims tend to disappear. As one G.I. discovers, "You realize this is a war zone and everybody here lives in it. You don't care whether these people live or die tomorrow, you don't care whether you yourself live or die tomorrow, you kick the children aside, you do the women, you shoot the animals."

In the midst of the general drift into "the cutting edge of reality itself," right "where it turns into a dream," some characters try to retain some perspective of the war. Canadian Kathy Jones works for the International Children's Relief Effort and other charitable organizations, so she sees the effects of the war on the young and the poor. She also loses her husband, Timothy, in the jungles of the Philippines, so, in despair, she strikes up a relationship with Skip Sands as she meditates on John Calvin's bleak theological writings. After they separate, Skip receives letters from her proclaiming that all of the earth is a hell and everyone is damned. Since Skip likes to retain his patriotic cheerfulness, at least at first, he neglects their correspondence, but later, once he is imprisoned, he repents of his callous treatment of her. Once Skip faces execution for running guns in Malaysia, he finally writes her back and professes his love for her. By letting her have the last scene in the novel, Johnson shows how Jones's righteous outrage had validity all along.

In terms of structure, *Tree of Smoke* reads like a free association of scenes depicting the points of view of a bewildering array of characters, but they are arranged mostly sequentially from 1963 through 1970, and Johnson finds ways to have elements reappear in different contexts throughout the novel. For instance, the opening scene involving the dead monkey finds its echo later during the year of the monkey and again when Kathy Jones visits a Biomedical Centre that lost many monkeys in a military attack. A long trip by foot across the Philippine countryside early in the novel finds its parallel late in the novel when Sergeant Jimmy Storm works his way across Vietnam to the Thai border in search of the colonel or his burial remains. Johnson places the Tet Offensive, a major cross-country uprising of the Viet Cong, near the exact center of the novel so that the rest of the narrative can play out both the expectations of and the aftereffects of the violence.

In the midst of the fighting, Johnson sketches the extremes of joy and grief of the soldiers. For the Houston brothers, the attacks are exhilarating at first, clearing out the everydayness of military routine. As Kathy realizes, "The war hadn't been only and exclusively terrible. It had delivered a sense, at first dreadful, eventually intoxicating, that something wild, magical, stunning might come from the next moment." However, when soldiers they know are killed or badly wounded, the American soldiers respond by torturing a captured Viet Cong man by gouging out his eyes. Fed up with their cruelty, the colonel finally shoots the prisoner to put him out of his torment. Soon after, James goes to visit his sergeant, Harmon, who has sustained paralyzing injuries across his intestines and spine, and weeps when he sees him. Then James goes AWOL for awhile, eventually spending time with a one-legged man named Cadwallader who likes to play with his nine-millimeter pistol and make cryptic remarks like "We all die. . . . I'll die high" and "You can't just paint everything with your mind to make it look like it makes sense." Scenes like these show how a lackadaisical, seedy encounter between two AWOL soldiers suits a novel about Vietnam so well. Without military direction, they both become momentarily humanized by their camaraderie. Whimsically, James and Cadwallader head out on a small boat until the latter cries out metafictionally, "We're lost at sea! . . . My head is *swimming* from the *symbolism* of it."

Though James and his kind know that they are at sea, the higher officials in the CIA take much longer to figure out the misguided nature of their intelligence operations. Skip gets befuddled as he tries to sift his way through his uncle's files, which prove as labyrinthine as the tunnels they are supposed to be mapping. As the colonel increasingly comes under suspicion, Regional Security officers send out men to investigate Skip, so he finds himself abruptly at odds with his superiors, eluding capture and dropping out of the agency altogether. His actions make sense, because there is never any indication in the CIA that real data is being applied in any practical way. As portions of an essay that the colonel wrote for the journal *Studies in Intelligence* come to light, the reader learns how data can be used to serve as "justification for political policy" and then corrupted still further: "The final step is to create fictions and serve them to our policy-makers in order to control the direction of government." This last impulse, to make up narratives, calls to mind the evidence used to start the Iraq War, and even though Johnson never explicitly brings up more recent American foreign policy decisions, the novel invites the reader to tease out correspondences between the idealistic beginnings and the unforeseen destructive effects of both wars.

By writing *Tree of Smoke*, Johnson gives shape to the war even as it retains its bewildering and chaotic feel. Before his execution, Skip concludes his impressions of his misspent career by claiming, "This Asian war . . . failed to give away any romances outside of hellish myths," but Johnson also acknowledges the war's excitement and the way it can unleash new mysteries to ponder.

*Roy C. Flannagan*

## Review Sources

*Booklist* 103, no. 22 (August 1, 2007): 8.
*Esquire* 148, no. 3 (September, 2007): 80.
*Harper's Magazine* 315 (October, 2007): 110-118.
*Library Journal* 132, no. 13 (August 1, 2007): 69-70.
*New Criterion* 26, no. 3 (November, 2007): 86-87.
*The New York Times* 156 (August 31, 2007): E25-E28.
*The New York Times Book Review* 156 (September 2, 2007): 1-8.
*Publishers Weekly* 247, no. 26 (June 25, 2007): 30.

# THE TRIUMPH OF THE THRILLER
## How Cops, Crooks, and Cannibals Captured Popular Fiction

*Author:* Patrick Anderson (1936-      )
*Publisher:* Random House (New York). 272 pp. $24.95
*Type of work:* Literary criticism
*Time:* 1840's to the early twenty-first century
*Locale:* Primarily various regions of the United States

*A breezy overview of contemporary thriller writers by an engaging thriller novelist and book reviewer that is nevertheless weak on the history of the genre and provides no guide to other studies*

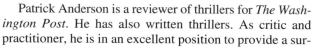

Patrick Anderson is a reviewer of thrillers for *The Washington Post*. He has also written thrillers. As critic and practitioner, he is in an excellent position to provide a survey of the best work in the genre. He is not much interested in judging his contemporaries—although he does chide popular authors who have become too formulaic—such as James Patterson (machining plots of violence and gore), John Grisham (who forsakes the grittiness of his early work), and Tom Clancy (too mechanical and lacking in character development).

Anderson's main concern is to highlight the best-written thrillers and to account for their dominance of the best seller lists, especially in the last three decades. His argument is not simply that thrillers are, on the average, better written and more widely read than ever before. Rather, he believes that the genre at its best has become a part of mainstream American fiction. Though he cites important English writers, he clearly suggests that the most important development of the thriller has occurred in the United States. Indeed, he believes it is time to consider certain thriller writers as just great writers deserving of the elite literary awards that have been reserved for so-called mainstream fiction. His main candidates for honors are Elmore Leonard, George Pelecanos, and Michael Connelly.

Anderson's definition of the thriller is quite elastic. It encompasses writers as various as Wilkie Collins and Mickey Spillane. Indeed, Anderson is short on definitions and explorations of what precisely the thriller is. Although it has emerged as a dominant category in contemporary fiction, he still seems to regard the thriller as a subgenre evolving out of the mystery story as pioneered by Edgar Allan Poe, Sir Arthur Conan Doyle, and Agatha Christie. It seems quite a stretch to trace contemporary thrillers to these writers rather than, say, the eighteenth century gothic novel or an early crime novel such as William Godwin's *Caleb Williams* (1794).

Rather than evolve a theory of the thriller or ground his definition of the genre in carefully chosen works that comprise its history, Anderson prefers to describe what thriller writers do while taking a rather ahistorical view of literature. Thus, Poe, for example, is faulted for drawing out the story in "The Mystery of Marie Roget" (1842), as if he should be judged by the lean and mean prose of more recent thriller writers such as Elmore Leonard, one of Anderson's touchstones. Even a classic writer like Raymond Chandler gets a drubbing when compared to later novelists such as James Ellroy.

Part 1 of *The Triumph of the Thriller* is divided into four chapters, the first introducing Anderson's brief for the superiority of the contemporary thriller, the second presenting a swift and rather superficial examination

*Patrick Anderson, who for several years has written a weekly book review for* The Washington Post, *is the author of nine novels and three previous books of nonfiction. He served as a speechwriter in the John F. Kennedy and Bill Clinton administrations and in Jimmy Carter's 1976 presidential campaign.*

of Poe, Doyle, and Christie, the third presenting their hard-boiled, tough-guy counterparts created by Dashiell Hammett, James M. Cain, and Chandler, and the fourth presenting the postwar grouping of Spillane, Ross Macdonald, Ed McBain, John D. MacDonald, and Charles Willeford. Willeford, known mainly by devotees of the genre, has been rediscovered—much to Anderson's pleasure. Willeford's 1955 novel, *Pick-Up*, is included in the Library of America's collection *Crime Novels: American Noir of the 1950's* (1997). Originally published in cheap paperback editions, his novels now seem destined to surpass the reputation of Ross Macdonald, whose Freudianism, Anderson suggests, has become dated. John D. MacDonald's Travis McGee, on the other hand, seems timeless to the critic, a detective who has become the epitome of a certain male confidence that Anderson admires.

In part 2, chapter 5, Anderson claims that the year 1981 represents a "tipping point" in the history of the thriller. Mainstream writers like Truman Capote and Norman Mailer were employing the true crime reportage in *In Cold Blood* (1966) and *The Executioner's Song* (1979) that had earlier been the province of genre writers. James Dickey produced the "quintessential literary thriller" in *Deliverance* (1970). Soon a new generation of writers like Scott Turow, Connelly, and Pelecanos were combining their serious interests in literature with the format of the thriller. In effect, the thriller was reborn in this cross-fertilization between mainstream and genre fiction.

While Anderson's argument has merit, its force is dissipated in chapters 6, 7, 8, and 9 as he conducts surveys and provides plot summaries—exposing Clancy's "literary offenses" in a takeoff of Mark Twain classic essay on James Fenimore Cooper's literary offenses, and grouping such disparate writers as Sue Grafton, Sara Paretsky, and Patricia Highsmith under the unilluminating rubric "Dangerous Women." Grafton and Paretsky are very polished genre writers, but Anderson does not seem to recognize that they are in a lower class of achievement than Highsmith's sophisticated and daringly amoral books. Certainly Turow and John Lescroart have brought honed literary sensibilities in legal thrillers, whereas Grisham has merely used the law to titillate, but in the absence of a unified argument the chapters in part 2 read like patched-together book reviews and guides to good reading.

Chapter 9, "Spy Masters," perhaps because the subject matter of novels by Charles McCarry, Robert Littell, Daniel Silva, and Alan Furst is the same, seems more coherent than other chapters in part 2. These authors write with a literary elegance that rivals the best of John le Carré. Chapter 10, however, is Anderson at his worst, presenting a potpourri of "Literary Thrillers, Killer Clowns, Barroom Poets, Drunken Detectives, Time Travel, and Related Curiosities." Anderson seems to forget his own argument—that thrillers should be considered "literary" the same way other mainstream books are. If so, what is it that unites them as a form of literature different from earlier thrillers? It is a question Anderson never pauses to ask, let alone explore with any care.

Anderson redeems his argument in part 3, "Four Modern Masters," which provides a persuasive brief for Thomas Harris, Dennis Lehane, Pelecanos, and Connelly. Harris, best known for his Hannibal Lecter series, is perhaps the most strikingly original because he constantly overturns the expectations inherent in genre fiction. Lecter, for example, shifts from villain to hero, putting the reader in the uncomfortable position of identifying with a serial killer. Not only has Harris raised the level of violence in the contemporary thriller to unprecedented heights (Anderson has his qualms about this), he also has influenced a legion of new writers that Anderson features for a page or so each. Although Barry Eisler, the author of the John Rain series, a provocative and sympathetic study of a professional assassin, is not yet in the same league as these writers, it is odd that Anderson does not mention him here or in other chapters devoted to novels that are breaking the conventional patterns of the thriller.

Part 4 looks suspiciously like a series of chapters in which Anderson crams his enthusiasms for a miscellaneous grouping of writers, including a chapter on "Brits," and another on the pitfalls of creating series characters who do not develop from one novel to the next. In this regard, he might have written more about John Lescroart, who has devised a subtle series of novels featuring a homicide detective, Abe Glitsky, and Dismas Hardy, a defense attorney. Both men become extraordinarily complex characters in novels that test their friendship and their convictions as they deal with crimes that expand and challenge their views of the world.

On the other hand, Anderson does full justice to Connelly's Harry Bosch novels, presenting a paragraph of analysis that is one of the critic's best:

> The tormented wild man of the early novels has been replaced by the avenging angle, a kind of saint. We see now that the series has an arc; the Bosch novels have become a classic story of rebirth and redemption. At the end of *The Closers*, Harry vows "to carry on the mission . . . always to speak for the dead." His vow is a dramatic reminder of how far the crime novel has come. In the drawing-room mysteries of the early twentieth century, no one really cared about the corpse on page one. It was a formality, the starting point of the puzzle that would allow author and detective to demonstrate their brilliance. That's no longer true in modern crime fiction, and nowhere is it less true than in the Bosch novels.

This passage, unfortunately, is rarely equaled elsewhere. It is a pity that in a book that seeks to extol the thriller's literary qualities Anderson's own style is often shoddy. The flabbiness of his prose is especially evident in his use of clichés such as "the mind boggles" and "all things being equal, reality is the place for a novelist to be." A long quotation is given no introduction other than "I want to quote at length." Anderson writes about his guilt over having become a "middle brow," forsaking the modernist literature he was taught to revere. Sadly, his own style seldom achieves the kind of distinction he claims for the best thriller writers.

It is a puzzle as to why Anderson has not made his book more useful. There is no index or bibliography, no acknowledgment of other important reviewers and critics who are also treating the thriller as an important literary genre. Otto Penzler, for example, writes a weekly column for *The New York Sun*, drawing on his vast experience as a critic and publisher of mystery fiction, but Anderson gives no hint that his views are in fact gaining considerable currency in the work of other reviewers. This failure to provide sources for further study suggests a certain lack of rigor. Even a work written not mainly for critics but for a lay audience ought to respect certain basic requirements of literary criticism.

Despite these drawbacks, *The Triumph of the Thriller* is an indispensable guide to the contemporary thriller. It is hard to believe that any critic has read more of what is valuable in this genre. Anderson's enthusiasm for the genre is infectious. He provides, as well, a list of his favorite novels. Certainly Anderson has to be consulted for anyone beginning a study of the thriller, and his book should appeal to fans of the genre who want to make sure they have not missed any gems. In the main, Anderson is a generous critic, and even where he finds fault—as in his discussion of Tom Clancy's novels—he also finds strengths in which he wishes the author would build. A less mean-spirited work of literary criticism would be hard to find.

*Carl Rollyson*

## Review Sources

*Booklist* 103, nos. 9/10 (January 1-15, 2007): 40.
*Kirkus Reviews* 74, no. 24 (December 15, 2006): 1249-1250.
*Library Journal* 131, no. 20 (December 1, 2006): 124.
*The New York Times Book Review* 156 (February 18, 2007): 12.
*Publishers Weekly* 253, no. 45 (November 13, 2006): 42.
*The Wall Street Journal* 249, no. 34 (February 10, 2007): P8.

# TWENTY-EIGHT ARTISTS AND TWO SAINTS

*Author:* Joan Acocella (1945-    )
*Publisher:* Pantheon Books (New York). 524 pp. $30.00
*Type of work:* Essays, fine arts, literary criticism
*Time:* 1900-2006
*Locale:* New York City, London, and Paris

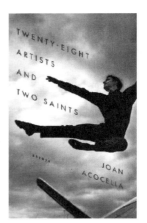

*A collection of essays that are representative of Aco-
cella's literary, dance, and art criticism originally published primarily in* The New Yorker *and* The New York
Review of Books

The thirty-one essays in *Twenty-eight Artists and Two
Saints* fall into several categories that bring together Joan
Acocella's interests and expertise in literature and liter-
ary criticism, dance and dance criticism, psychology, and
women's studies. Eighteen of the essays are on literature. They are primarily about
literary figures of the twentieth century, both well known, such as Saul Bellow, Philip
Roth, Simone de Beauvoir, and Susan Sontag, and less known, such as Italo Svevo,
Stefan Sweig, and Marguerite Yourcenar. One of the essays in this group is about
Andrea de Jorio, a nineteenth century Neapolitan priest, who wrote a study of the
meaning of hand gestures used by natives of Naples. The other essay in this literary
group, the only essay that does not focus on a particular person, is titled "Blocked,"
about writer's block.

Another group of nine essays is about dance. Most of these essays are "portraits"
of dancers and choreographers in ballet, Broadway dance, and modern dance. They
include Vaslav Nijinsky, Frederick Ashton, Suzanne Farrell, Mikhail Baryshnikov,
Jerome Robbins, Martha Graham, Bob Fosse, and Twyla Tharp. There is also an
essay on Lincoln Kirstein, who was responsible for bringing George Balanchine to
the United States and was the founder and manager of the New York City Ballet. An
additional essay related to dance is on Lucia Joyce, the daughter of James Joyce who,
before her descent into insanity, tried to be a modern dancer.

Of the three remaining essays, one is on the sculptor Louise Bourgeois. The other
two are about "saints," Mary Magdalene and Joan of Arc. Both of these essays are
more about the cultural reception of these saintly females in the twentieth century.
The springboard for the essay on Mary Magdalene is the popular interest in her cult
arising from the 2003 novel by Dan Brown, *The Da Vinci Code.* The essay on Joan of
Arc focuses on the way her story was treated in films of the twentieth century.

In such a diverse group of talented people working with various forms of artistic
expression, the question arises about whether any themes recur that in some way
serve to unify this collection of essays. Acocella addresses this point in her introduction. The theme that she chooses is "difficulty, hardship." By this she does not
mean the artists' background in trauma and its attendant psychological difficulties

but rather "the pain that came *with* the art-making, interfering with it, and how the artist dealt with this." She points out that many brilliant artists and writers have not had the inner strength, tenacity, and courage to persevere in the face of the many difficulties, rejections, and disappointments that are inherent in the artistic process and in remaining true to an artistic vision and purpose. Acocella wants to examine the "ego strength" that makes it possible for an artist to rise above the obstacles to creating and practicing his or her particular art.

*Critic Joan Acocella has published books on psychology, such as* Abnormal Psychology: Current Perspectives *(1977), and on literature, including* Willa Cather and the Politics of Criticism *(2000). She is well known for her writings on dance history and criticism, which include a study of the modern dancer Mark Morris and an edition of the diary of Vaslav Nijinsky. She covers dance and books for* The New Yorker.

In reading these essays, several problems emerge with Acocella's thesis about the ego strength of successful artists. One difficulty is that a number of the essays demonstrate just the opposite, the fact that many artists lack this personal quality. The first essay on Lucia Joyce, for example, shows how the burdens of being the child of a famous writer limited her own artistic inclinations in dance. Joyce became so mentally ill that she ended up being institutionalized. The case of the dancer Nijinsky differs in the specific aspects of his life story, but the result was the same. Nijinsky had a phenomenal but very short career as a dancer before psychosis overtook him. The essay on writer's block is filled with writers who never were able to realize their creative potential.

Another problem with the ego strength thesis is that Acocella never really analyzes what it is and especially how it operates in the case of the more successful artists and writers. When the artists do overcome obstacles, the key seems to be turning inward to draw on themselves. Acocella says of Baryshnikov, who survived the suicide of his mother when he was twelve years old and dealt with the creative restrictions placed on him by the policies of the former Soviet Union by defecting to the West, "Homelessness turned him inward, gave him to himself. Then dance, the substitute home, turned him outward, gave him to us."

In addition, the price of ego strength in many instances is paid in the cost of the artists' health and especially in their relationships and the treatment of others. Alcoholism is rampant through many of these profiles. Graham and Tharp, both modern dancers and choreographers, and Fosse, a Broadway dancer and choreographer, are examples. Fosse drove himself to death, collapsing on a street with his second heart attack at age sixty. Many of these artists can be cruel to those who support them in various ways or who want to learn from them. Acocella reports that at Sunday salons mainly for younger artists held by Bourgeois, "people have been known to exit . . . in tears, but if you can take it the dynamics are interesting." Numerous marriages and divorces are commonplace. The children inevitably suffer. Penelope Fitzgerald, the British writer, admits some of the toll on children in a roundabout way. When Acocella asked Fitzgerald if Fitzgerald's children were like the children in her novels who are "outspoken, tough-minded, frighteningly precocious," Fitzgerald replied affirmatively saying: "I think if your mother isn't very grown-up you have to be very grown-up yourself."

Another problem is that although Acocella states in the introduction that she is not interested in the "unhappy-childhood theory" and its cousin, "that art was born of neurosis," almost all of her essays present glaring examples of the effects of trauma on the artists and therefore on their art. Some of the trauma comes from the tremendous dislocation and horror of war. Her essay on Primo Levi, a Holocaust survivor, focuses on how this inhuman experience affected the course of his life and his writing. None of the subjects of the essays had anything close to a normal childhood with secure attachment to parents or caregivers. Tharp's father threw a hatchet at her mother. Sontag was only briefly told of her father's death in China and then endured life on the move with her mother's series of boyfriends and eventually her stepfather. Sontag has called her childhood "a long prison sentence." Sybille Bedford's father was sixty years older than her mother. Much of her childhood was spent in the chaos of her mother's numerous liaisons and finally in trying to deal with her mother's addiction to morphine. Yourcenar's mother died when she was born. Her nursemaid would take her to "houses of assignation." Yourcenar's first sexual encounter was with a woman when Yourcenar was eleven years old. Baryshnikov's mother hanged herself when he was twelve.

One of the most striking cases is Bourgeois. The third daughter in a family of French artisans who restored tapestries, Bourgeois was dominated by her father. "She hated him, and she loved him like crazy." One of the many traumas that she suffered as a child included the betrayal of her English governess, who became her father's mistress. Acocella's essay states that Bourgeois has had "crushing anxiety attacks" that have occurred four times a day "for as long as she can remember." Her sculptures bear titles such as *The Destruction of the Father*. Her photo that accompanies this essay shows her holding one of her famous sculptures, a disembodied penis. Fear and anger are the key themes of her work. She has written that her art "is a form of therapy, a way of preventing herself from going out and killing someone, or herself."

Trauma of this magnitude is serious, and even when not immediately obvious it leaves deep wounds and scars. Recent trauma work that incorporates insights from neuroscience demonstrates the profound effects of trauma, loss, and attachment patterns on the brain and therefore on the mind. Rather than dismissing such profound trauma as simply an "unhappy childhood," it would be more compelling if Acocella had provided a more thoughtful view of how trauma interacts with ego strength to find expression in various art and literary forms.

It may, however, be somewhat artificial to try to impose unifying themes on a group of essays that were written separately and published in several journals over a period of about fourteen years between 1992 and 2006. Indeed, one value of this collection is that it brings together these essays in a format that makes them accessible to more readers. As Acocella says in her introduction about her choices: "I thought I was simply choosing the pieces that I liked best, and wanted to send out into the world again."

Looking at the essays from this perspective, taking each one individually and savoring the insights that it has to offer, readers will recognize that this collection is filled with ideas, information, and viewpoints that enhance their understanding of both the artists and the various works of literature, dance, and art. Two of the essays that are most interesting are not really about personalities at all. The essay titled "The Neapolitan Finger" discusses a recent edition of a book on hand gestures of the Neapolitans published in 1832 by de Jorio. This essay not only explains some of the fine art of these gestures and the nuances of their meaning but also brings out some of the intriguing aspects of gesture as a nonverbal form of communication. The essay "The Saintly Sinner" presents an excellent overview of recent "reception history" of Mary Magdalene and especially her recent revival in the study of primitive Christianity as well as in feminist Bible scholarship. Acocella's essay enlivens this body of scholarly material and makes the intriguing questions about Mary Magdalene's place in the history of Christianity accessible to readers.

The essays on dance are especially illuminating. In various ways, Acocella's writing examines the inner processes of dance in ways that help the reader to "see" and understand what dance is all about. The essay on Farrell is more about her transformation from a principal dancer with the New York City Ballet to a teacher and head of her own ballet company. Farrell talks about the importance of space in dance and the relationship between that space and the music. "'There's sound in movement,' . . . and space in sound. The dancer's job is to show—or make—the relation between the two." Several of the essays touch on the opposition of order and disorder in dance. With classical ballet there is a sense "that experience has order, that life can be understood." The dances by Tharp are often about that precarious balance between order and disorder.

This collection of essays presents many ideas to explore. They raise issues about the relationship of the creative personality and the work, about permanence and preservation of artistic creations, especially with dance, and about how artists challenge established boundaries and conventions. The variety of topics and perspectives makes this collection a valuable resource.

*Karen Gould*

## Review Sources

*Dance Magazine* 81, no. 8 (August, 2007): 54.
*Kirkus Reviews* 74, no. 24 (December 15, 2006): 1249.
*The New York Review of Books* 54, no. 4 (March 15, 2007): 31-33.
*The New York Times Book Review* 156 (February 18, 2007): 13.
*Publishers Weekly* 254, no. 2 (January 8, 2007): 47-48.

# TWO HISTORIES OF ENGLAND

*Authors:* Jane Austen (1775-1817); Charles
  Dickens (1812-1870)
*First published:* Jane Austen's *The History of England*,
  wr. 1791, in Great Britain; Charles Dickens's
  *A Child's History of England*, 1851-1853, in Great
  Britain; together as *The History of England*, 2006,
  in Great Britain
Introduction by David Starkey
*Publisher:* Ecco Press/HarperCollins (New York).
  157 pp. $16.95
*Type of work:* History
*Time:* 1399-1649
*Locale:* Mainly England, but also Scotland, Ireland,
  and briefly France

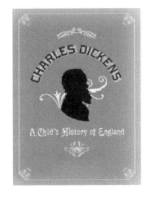

*Sixteen-year-old Austen's highly subjective tongue-in-cheek history of England
from Henry IV to Charles I parodies subjective eighteenth century histories for
young ladies, while Dickens's lively, dramatic children's tale of England from Elizabeth I to the death of Charles I provides personal insights into how England acquired
democratic freedoms*

*Principal personages:*
  CHARLES I (1600-1649), king of England, r. 1625-1649, whom Austen
    defends as an amiable Stuart but whom Dickens attacks as a master
    deceiver, committed to the absolute right of kings to wage wars, tax
    citizens, and plunder their nation as they please and to the idea that a
    king can do no wrong
  ELIZABETH I (1533-1603), queen of England, r. 1558-1603, whom
    Austen finds wicked and mischievous, surrounded by bad ministers,
    but whom Dickens sees as a crafty monarch
  JAMES I (1566-1625), king of Scotland (as James VI), r. 1567-1625,
    and king of England, r. 1603-1625, whom Austen says she cannot
    help liking despite his faults, but whom Dickens loathes and despises,
    calling him by the nickname a favorite chose, "his Sowship"
  MARY, QUEEN OF SCOTS (1542-1587), queen of Scotland, r. 1542-1567,
    ill-fated and sorely abused by Elizabeth I, and a noble-minded
    heroine steadfast in her faith, asserted Austen, but a murderous
    schemer, the center of plots against the throne, according to Dickens
  OLIVER CROMWELL (1599-1658), English military and political leader
    who was a necessary counter to Charles I, says Dickens, one who
    nearly lost his life early in the English Civil War
  ROBERT DEVEREUX (1565-1601), second earl of Essex, the hero of
    Austen's comic narrator, noble and gallant, but unfortunate,
    tormented, and executed by the scheming Elizabeth, who used him
    in her power plays, says Dickens

SIR FRANCIS DRAKE (c. 1540-1596), English navigator whose glory will
be outshone, asserts young Austen, by her eldest sister's husband;
Dickens focuses on his plundering Spanish vessels

SIR WALTER RALEGH (c. 1552-1618), English writer and explorer who
flourished under Elizabeth but of whom Austen has nothing good to
say because he was the enemy of her hero, Lord Essex; Dickens
praises Ralegh for finishing off the Spanish fleet at Cadiz

The title *Two Histories of England* invites comparison of these very different
works, neither of which fits the modern idea of approaching history with distance, objectivity, and cultural context. Though they share the same purported subject matter,
the history of England, and a similar premodern assumption that history is by nature
subjective, an anecdotal account to defend personal values and biases, they diverge
greatly in highly interesting and diverting ways that David Starkey's insightful introductory remarks push readers to discover for themselves. Starkey observes that
both Jane Austen and Charles Dickens came
from Hampshire. While Austen enjoyed the
security of a clerical family's middle-class
respectability, Dickens enjoyed the pleasures
of rural life until apprenticed in a London
boot-blacking factory near the strand when
his father went to debtors' prison. The two
histories reflect this difference in class experience, politics, and values. Both writers developed a keen eye for satire, with Austen
focusing on the society amid which she spent
her entire life, but with Dickens exploring the
full range of society from top to bottom. Both
were buried in Westminster Abbey, a tribute
to their accomplishments as satiric novelists.

*Jane Austen wrote six novels:* Sense
and Sensibility *(1811),* Pride and
Prejudice *(1813),* Mansfield Park
*(1814),* Emma *(1815),* Northanger
Abbey *(1818), and* Persuasion *(1818);
she never completed* The Watsons
*(1871) and* Sanditon *(1925). Charles
Dickens wrote far more, including*
Pickwick Papers *(1836-1837),* Oliver
Twist *(1837-1839),* Nicholas Nickleby
*(1838-1839),* The Old Curiosity Shop
*(1840-1841),* A Christmas Carol
*(1843),* David Copperfield *(1849-
1850),* Bleak House *(1852-1853),* Hard
Times *(1854),* A Tale of Two Cities
*(1859), and* Great Expectations *(1860-
1861).*

Austen's *The History of England: From the
Reign of Henry the Fourth to the Death of
Charles the First*, a thirty-four-page manuscript containing her sister Cassandra's thirteen watercolor miniatures of the monarchs
discussed, was a precocious adolescent's idea
of how to provide her family with evening
entertainment. It was not intended for publication, and, in fact, remained unpublished
until 1922, 131 years after its completion.
Dickens's *A Child's History of England* is a
solid work published over a three-year period
and containing thirty-eight chapters, of which
only three are excerpted here ("England Under

Elizabeth," "England Under James the First," and "England Under Charles the First"). The work was a product of his maturity, its goal being the education of English school-children. In fact, it became a popular educational tool, a history textbook that Starkey says was used well into the twentieth century, declining in popularity only after World War II as the concept of how one retells history changed, and not disappearing totally from the English classroom until the 1950's.

Austen intended her history to be read aloud, archly and dramatically, for the amusement of her household. She assumes their knowledge of the sentimental excesses and the contrived moral lessons of the "histories" provided young eighteenth century ladies; she parodies these, calling herself a "partial, prejudiced, and ignorant Historian" and intentionally muddling facts and forcefully asserting ill-supported biases. Her chosen stance is that of a Yorkist, contemptuous of all Lancastrians, enamored of Charles I, and most disdainful of Elizabeth I. She asserts her partiality to Roman Catholics but regretfully confesses that under James I the English Catholics failed to behave "like Gentlemen" toward Protestants, and were, in fact, quite "uncivil." Her Henry IV ascends the throne "much to his own satisfaction," then retires to Pomfret Castle, "where he happened to be murdered," while his son Henry V thrashed Sir William Gascoigne as a prince but gave up doing so as king, though he had Lord Cobham "burnt alive," though she forgets why.

She dismisses Henry VI as Lancastrian and warns readers that she intends to vent her "Spleen" and show her "Hatred" to anyone whose principles vary from her own. Since Richard III was of York, she asserts his high respectability and counters rumors about his killing his nephews with rumors about Henry VII, whom she labels "as great a Villain as ever lived." She gives Henry VIII short shrift since it would be unfair to her readers to assume that they know less about this famous personality than she. She asserts Anna Bullen's (Anne Boleyn's) innocence and declares that Henry's dissolution of religious houses was probably intended to improve the English landscape, asserting, "Otherwise why should a Man who was of no Religion himself be at so much trouble to abolish one which had for Ages been established in the Kingdom." Her duke of Northumberland performed his trust to protect Edward VI so well that "the King died and the Kingdom was left to [the Duke's] daughter in law the Lady Jane Grey." At the end of her text, Austen, tongue-in-cheek, asserts that her principal reason for undertaking this history was special pleading: to prove Mary Queen of Scots innocent and to abuse Elizabeth (though she fears she has fallen short in that part of her plan, she proclaims). Thus, Austen employs her facetious narrative "I" to mock the partisanship, hyperbole, and clichéd sentimentality of historical biographies.

Dickens's history is to some degree the type of history Austen mocked, with significant names capitalized, historical figures, battles, conspiracies catalogued chronologically, villains and heroes described colorfully, and prejudices and personal theories asserted firmly. Dickens is quite negative about Scotland, which he describes as a half-savage country of sullen people and small miserable horses where murder and rioting were common and where rigid Protestant reformers destroyed much of value. He condemns Puritans as "uncomfortable people," who found it "meritorious" to wear hideous attire, "talk through their noses," and denounce "harmless enjoyments." He balances this image with a description of the horrific Massacre of St. Bartholomew, in which Catholics killed ten thousand Protestants in Paris and fifty thousand throughout France, and then had a commemoratory medal struck. Dickens expresses a practicality and a moral sensibility of which Austen would probably have approved (the Victorians certainly did).

Dickens explores history in far greater depth than does Austen, for his goals are quite different. He seeks to make history accessible to young people in clear, plain language. He also seeks to bring it to life with vivid details and memorable anecdotes that will stick in children's minds for a lifetime—for example, the image of Mary Queen of Scots' small dog cowering with fear under her dress during her execution, of Elizabeth I's red-wigged ladies-in-waiting appealing to her vanity, or of Archbishop William Laud's predilection for slicing off the ears and slitting the nostrils of recalcitrant Roundheads. Furthermore, Dickens seeks to counter some of the biased, unrealistic images of historical figures who were much admired, like the popularizing of Henry V as a fun-loving, spirited young Hal or the defense of Henry VIII's destruction of the monasteries as a determined effort to free England from papal plots. Thus, for all his positive statements about Elizabeth I, who was greeted with great enthusiasm after the atrocities committed during Mary's reign and who fostered letters, learning, and exploration during her reign, he seeks middle ground, showing her as cunning, manipulative, hot-tempered, and obsessed with her public image (particularly the image of Maiden Queen, which Dickens finds contrived and trite). This attempt at balance includes his observation that decent people with good motives swelled the ranks of both Cavaliers and Roundheads.

Ultimately, Dickens's goal is sectarian: He wants his youthful readers to understand that sometimes the best of monarchs infringed on the rights of citizens and got away with doing so because of their popularity, while sometimes the worst of monarchs brought about major improvements in the rights of citizens as a public reaction against the atrocities and outrages they inflicted upon ordinary people. He is particularly concerned for ordinary citizens, whose lives the historical strengthening of Parliament improved, and he admonishes his young readers not ever to trust monarchs, whom he repeatedly describes as wily, devious, two-faced, and self-centered. Among his moral lessons is an admonition against torture, as he describes what happened on the rack, and observes that anyone would confess to any absurdity to end such terrible pain. He designates Sir Philip Sidney a perfect example of nobility and humanity, for when wounded to death himself, he gave his badly needed water to a suffering, wounded foot soldier. Dickens attacks James I as the worst monarch ever, calling him "cunning, covetous, wasteful, idle, drunken, greedy, dirty, cowardly, a great swearer, and the most conceited man on earth"—and that is only the beginning of his diatribe, as he points to James's open fawning and slobbering over male favorites, his disdain for Parliament, his unifying Catholics and Puritans in conspiracies against him, and his transformation of decent citizens into servile, corrupt, lying hypocrites. Charles I's life may have been cut short, but Dickens asserts that his despotic twelve-year reign was more than long enough.

Intriguingly, Austen's satiric history makes readers appreciate Dickens's highly personalized history.

*Gina Macdonald*

## Review Sources

*Publishers Weekly* 254, no. 32 (August 13, 2007): 58.
*The Indianapolis Star*, November 11, 2007, p. D2.

# TWO LIVES
## Gertrude and Alice

*Author:* Janet Malcolm (1934-    )
*Publisher:* Yale University Press (New Haven, Conn.).
Illustrated. 229 pp. $25.00
*Type of work:* Literary biography, literary criticism

*Three essays, originally published in* The New Yorker, *explore Gertrude Stein and Alice B. Toklas's relationship, works, and lives*

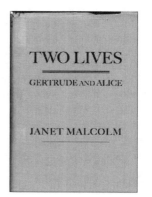

Principal personages:
  GERTRUDE STEIN, the expatriate American
    writer
  ALICE B. TOKLAS, her companion
  BERNARD FAY, a French professor, official,
    translator, and Nazi collaborator who was their protector in occupied
    France during World War II
  EDWARD M. BURNS,
  ULLA E. DYDO, and
  WILLIAM RICE, Stein scholars
  LEON KATZ, a Stein scholar who conducted extensive interviews
    with Toklas about Stein's unpublished notebooks

American culture has always shown a particular fondness for eccentrics and icono-clasts, inventors and innovators. Although most of Gertrude Stein's writing is so experimental that it is impenetrable to all but a few devotees, her name and image are familiar to many people who have never read her work because she was all of these things and more. She is known for a few phrases—"A rose is a rose is a rose," "Pigeons on the grass alas"—that, like Jackson Pollock's drip paintings, seem to epit-omize the popular idea of avant-garde modern art as a confidence game built on praise of work that any child could do. She is recognized through iconic images in photo-graphs and a famous portrait by Pablo Picasso that present her as a kind of massive American Buddha. She is associated with tales of the expatriate "lost generation" of the 1920's and remembered for the salon she hosted in Paris at 27 Rue de Fleurus where friends such as Picasso, Henri Matisse, and Ernest Hemingway were frequent guests. She is even recalled by some of the disappearing generation of World War II veterans as somehow a part of the American liberation of France. Over the past forty years, she has also become a leading member of the feminist and lesbian pantheons of neglected women artists.

Criticism and scholarship—including biographies such as James R. Mellow's *Charmed Circle: Gertrude Stein and Company* (1974); memoirs, beginning with W. G. Rogers's *When This You See Remember Me: Gertrude Stein in Person* (1948); and critical studies, from Edmund Wilson's influential chapter on Stein in his pioneering

∽

*Janet Malcolm first gained fame with* Psychoanalysis: The Impossible Profession *(1981). A regular contributor to* The New Yorker *and* The New York Review of Books*, her best-known books also include* In the Freud Archives *(1984),* The Journalist and the Murderer *(1990), and* The Silent Woman: Sylvia Plath and Ted Hughes *(1994).*

∽

study, *Axel's Castle* (1931), to Richard Bridgman's indispensable *Gertrude Stein in Pieces* (1970)—long ago went beyond these popular images to seriously examine her life, her work, and her importance to the history of American modernism. In 1998, she was officially canonized in two volumes of the Library of America series.

Since the publication of *In the Freud Archives* (1984), Janet Malcolm has combined journalism, psychological analysis, and skepticism about the nature of biography in fascinating and elegantly written examinations of psychoanalysis, journalism, and the arts. In *Two Lives: Gertrude and Alice*, the third in a series focused on writers that also includes *The Silent Woman: Sylvia Plath and Ted Hughes* (1994) and *Reading Chekhov: A Critical Journey* (2001), she sets out to reconsider Gertrude Stein. The book consists of three related essays that, like much of Malcolm's work, first appeared in *The New Yorker*. Although the book's three chapters have been described by reviewers as treating Stein's and Alice B. Toklas's experiences during the war, the composition of *The Making of Americans* (1925), and Toklas's years "staying on alone," they are, in fact, far more meandering and fragmented than this clear division suggests.

Malcolm does not really have much to add to the critical and biographical scholarship that already exists, but her work is not intended for scholars. Instead, she draws on previous scholarship to present the general reader with a study of the character, writing, and relationship of her two principals. Perhaps surprisingly, the most impressive part of *Two Lives* is its attentive and provocative readings of Stein's work and artistic evolution rather than its biographical elements or journalistic discoveries.

Beginning with her initial observation that Stein wrote "stories, novels, and poems that are like no stories, novels, and poems ever written but seem to be saturated with some sort of elixir of originality," when she is talking about Stein's writing itself Malcolm is consistently at her most original and engaging. In *Three Lives*, Stein's collection of stories written in 1909 that inspired her own title, she says for example, "Stein is still writing in regular, if singular English, but by 1912 she had started producing work in a language of her own, one that uses English words but in no other way resembles English as it is known." Malcolm precisely captures the appeal of *The Autobiography of Alice B. Toklas* (1933), Stein's only commercially successful book, when she notes that Stein's "playful egomania pervades" it, "as does the optimism that gives the story of her life the character of a fairy tale."

The highlight of Malcolm's analysis of Stein's writing is her discussion—in the first half of the second essay and in other passages throughout the book—of what caused Stein's style to change between 1905 and 1912. The underlying question is how the unhappy, insecure, directionless young woman who began her life as an expatriate in Paris in 1903 in the shadow of her older brother Leo came to think of herself as a literary genius by 1912. Malcolm's answer lies in her examination of the making of *The Making of Americans*, completed in 1911, and the beginning of her lifelong relationship with Alice B. Toklas in 1907.

Like James Joyce's *Finnegans Wake* (1939) or Ezra Pound's *Cantos* (1930-1969), *The Making of Americans* is consistently alluded to as a modern classic but seldom actually read, even by scholars. In fact, its 925 pages of densely packed and sparsely punctuated text are pretty much unreadable by anyone except confirmed Steinophiles like the professors Malcolm consults in the course of her research.

Malcolm decided to join the small group of the book's readers, but only, she comically explains, after she took out a kitchen knife and cut the massive Dalkey Press volume into six easily portable sections—thereby "unwittingly [making] a physical fact of its stylistic and thematic inchoateness." What she found in these pages is both a fascinating autobiography and "a text of magisterial disorder," "something so monstrously peculiar that although it is possible to finish, it is impossible to sum up."

It is, she discovers, a "dark, death-ridden work," but after Stein completes it "this atmosphere lifts, and never again descends on her" writing. It is also an antinovel that seems to turn into "a kind of nervous breakdown," whose main subject is the author's inability to write it. In fact, "the jolts and lurches of her engagement with writing are the book's plot," and words—rather than the family she initially sets out to write a nineteenth century novel about—are its real characters. ("Stein's vocabulary is small and monotonous," Malcolm writes, in an observation that most readers of Stein's work have made. "When she uses a new word," she then adds in an insight that is very much her own, and characteristically astute, "it is like the entrance of a new character.") Since Stein cannot invent characters, this novel that is not a novel consists of "a kind of literal translation of what is going on in her mind" each day as she sits down to write.

Stein wrote in longhand and dropped the pages on the floor next to her desk as she finished them. As she wrote page after page, she constantly wondered whether anyone would ever actually read what she was writing, and wrote about that. "Bear it in your mind my reader," she says near the beginning of *The Making of Americans*, "but truly I never feel it that there ever can be for me any such creature." Then, apparently just in time, Alice B. Toklas entered her life. Toklas not only read but liked what Stein was writing, finding it "more exciting than anything had ever been," and she soon began to pick up the scraps of paper and type them out every day. As Malcolm describes it, "the transformation of dirty scraps of paper into clean pages of typescript was surely a pivotal event in the life of the work, which might well have floundered on Stein's anxiety about the maddening complexity of what she had undertaken." Instead, "Toklas's belief in Stein's genius, made manifest by the growing pile of typed pages, emboldened Stein in her excruciating endeavor."

The impact of Toklas's love, admiration, and support suffuses the extraordinary passage from *The Making of Americans* from which Malcolm drew the title of the second of her essays when it appeared in *The New Yorker*: "Someone Says Yes to It." "It is a very strange feeling," Stein writes, when you like something that is a dirty thing and no one can really like that thing or you write a book and while you write it you are ashamed for every one must think you a silly or a crazy one and yet you write it and you are ashamed, you know you will be laughed at or pitied by every one and you have a queer feeling and you are not very certain and you go on writing. Then some one says yes to it, to something you are liking, or doing or making and then never again can you have completely such a feeling of being afraid and ashamed that you had then when you were writing or liking the thing and not any one had said yes about the thing.

Unfortunately, not all of *Two Lives* demonstrates either the originality or the finesse of its discussion of *The Making of Americans*. "Biography is the medium through which the remaining secrets of the famous dead are taken from them and dumped out in full view of the world," Malcolm wrote in *The Silent Woman* in words that describe her own biographical approach here. "The biographer at work, indeed, is like the professional burglar, breaking into a house, rifling through certain drawers that he has good reason to think contain the jewelry and money, and triumphantly bearing his loot away." The reader and the biographer collude and tiptoe "down the corridor together, to stand in front of the bedroom door and try to peep through the keyhole." Too much of this book is devoted to such investigations and sinks into a kind of celebrity gossip, complete with its characteristically exaggerated tone of revelation. "Why did Toklas omit any mention of her and Stein's Jewishness (never mind lesbianism)?" Malcolm disingenuously wonders out loud on the book's fourth page, when she is well aware that the times make the answer obvious. "Has the book dropped from the reader's hand?" she melodramatically asks after reporting that some men found Stein sexually attractive.

*Two Lives* is also marred at times by writing that is surprising from an author who is usually so eloquent. "Every writer who lingers over Stein's sentences is apt to feel a little stab of shame over the heedless predictability of his own," Malcolm points out. Ironically, just such heedlessness weakens parts of *Two Lives*. There are too many clichés—characters "pull their punches," "toil in different parts of the Stein vineyard," bring back "trophies of great worth." There is too much slang—characters face a "scary moment of decision" and "bad-mouthings," are "sucking-up" or "ripped off." There is also too much awkwardness—revisions are "clear disimprovements," the handful of scholars who have actually read all of *The Making of Americans* are "non-shirkers," Leon Katz is "the winkler-out of Toklas's secrets," and an episode demonstrates Stein's "ultra-importance."

If Janet Malcolm's biography and writing are sometimes disappointing this time—like the quality of the reproduction of most of the book's photographs—*Two Lives* is still well worth reading by anyone who is interested in Stein for the truly original observations, insightful readings, and acutely expressed insights scattered within it.

*Bernard F. Rodgers, Jr.*

## Review Sources

*The Boston Globe*, October 14, 2007, p. E4.
*The Chicago Sun-Times*, October 14, 2007, p. B11.
*The Chicago Tribune*, October 6, 2007, p. 3.
*London Review of Books* 29, no. 24 (December 13, 2007): 10-16.
*The New York Review of Books* 54, no. 16 (October 25, 2007): 4-8.
*The New York Times Book Review* 157 (September 23, 2007): 7.
*Newsweek* 150, no. 19 (November 5, 2007): 62.
*The Times Literary Supplement*, January 4, 2008, pp. 7-8.
*The Washington Post*, September 30, 2007, p. BW09.

# UNCOMMON ARRANGEMENTS
## Seven Portraits of Married Life in London Literary Circles, 1910-1939

*Author:* Katie Roiphe (1968-　　)
*Publisher:* Dial Press (New York). 344 pp. $26.00
*Type of work:* Literary biography, women's issues
*Time:* 1910-1939
*Locale:* London

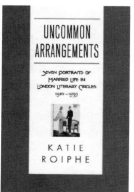

*Roiphe examines seven couples in literary London in the opening decades of the twentieth century and reveals the difficulties they had in trying to redefine marriage for modern times*

*Principal personages:*
H. G. WELLS, the world-famous novelist
JANE WELLS, his wife
REBECCA WEST, a young writer and
　feminist who became Wells's lover
ANTHONY WEST, the son of Wells and West
　who suffered a troubled childhood
KATHERINE MANSFIELD, the short-story writer
JOHN MIDDLETON MURRY, her husband, an editor and critic
ELIZABETH VON ARNIM, author of *The Enchanted April* (1922),
　among many books
FRANK RUSSELL, her overbearing husband
VANESSA BELL, an artist, the sister of
VIRGINIA WOOLF, the novelist and essayist
CLIVE BELL, Vanessa's husband, an art and literary critic
DUNCAN GRANT, a painter and one of Vanessa's many lovers
OTTOLINE MORRELL, a literary hostess and magnet for many men
PHILIP MORRELL, her husband, who maintained affairs of his own
RADCLYFFE HALL, the author of *The Well of Loneliness* (1928)
UNA TROUBRIDGE, her partner for eighteen years
EVGUENIA SOULINE, a nurse and Hall's lover for half of that time
GEORGE GORDON CATLIN, a professor and politician
VERA BRITTAIN, his wife, a successful writer
WINIFRED HOLTBY, a writer who completed their extended family

Ottoline Morrell was the most famous literary hostess in England before and during World War I. Her "Thursdays" at her house on Bedford Square in London were matched only by the weekends at Garsington, the country estate where Ottoline and her husband, Philip, entertained some of the most famous artists and writers of the day, including W. B. Yeats, Charlie Chaplin, and T. S. Eliot. D. H. Lawrence parodied Ottoline in the character Hermione in his novel *Women in Love* (1920), and Aldous Huxley did the same in his novel *Crome Yellow* (1921). She had an affair with a gardener at Garsington in 1920 (which may have influenced Lawrence's 1928

*Lady Chatterley's Lover*), and another, longer affair with the brilliant philosopher Bertrand Russell, author of *Principia Mathematica* (1910-1913). Her husband was not idle: He propositioned the novelist Virginia Woolf, among others, and in March of 1917 announced to his wife that he had not one but two pregnant mistresses on his busy hands.

*Katie Roiphe has written* The Morning After: Sex, Fear, and Feminism *(1994),* Last Night in Paradise: Sex and Morals at the Century's End *(1997), and the novel* Still She Haunts Me *(2001), as well as articles in* The New York Times, Esquire, Harper's Magazine, *and other journals. She lives in New York and teaches in the Cultural Reporting and Criticism Program at New York University.*

The story of the Morrells is just one of seven fascinating narratives Katie Roiphe weaves together in *Uncommon Arrangements: Seven Portraits of Married Life in London Literary Circles, 1910-1939*. Her focus is less the scandals and the sexual adventures of these couples—and the triangles of various sizes and configurations they all maintained—than their attempts to forge something new, marriage based on equality, freedom, and honesty. This period was one of incredible social instability. The Great War decimated a generation of British men at the same time that it propelled women into new roles and a new consciousness of the power they possessed, as in both the pacifist and the feminist movements of the time. The period also saw immense artistic experimentation and production. The major modernist artists—Pablo Picasso, James Joyce, among many others—were at work in this period redefining the very substance and structure of literature and art. Lovers were trying to shed outdated Victorian mores at the same time that writers were discarding inherited forms, in order to carve out something new, for literature as well as for human interaction.

Roiphe focuses on seven famous "families" in England in this intense period, from before World War I until just before World War II. She chooses writers and artists, plus one literary hostess, and uses their letters, diaries, and memoirs to reveal what they thought, wrote, and said about marriage and married life. This may have been the most writerly generation on record, for psychologists like Sigmund Freud and Havelock Ellis had taught them the importance of feelings, especially sexual feelings, and their expression. They wrote voluminously about their feelings and about their relationships. Roiphe mines this library (her selected bibliography is a dozen pages long) and comes up with revealing glimpses of some of the most creative artists the twentieth century would see, people who were trying to figure out intimate relations in imaginative ways. Every chapter begins with a crisis in a marriage and shows whether it was resolved or not, and, in the process, Roiphe shows how successful these people were at forging something new in human relations.

H. G. Wells, for example, was the author of popular scientific romances (*The Time Machine*, 1895, *The War of the Worlds*, 1898) and in 1914 was settled into a comfortable country house in Essex with his open-minded wife, Jane, who had tolerated the series of sexual liaisons he carried on, when his current mistress, the writer and feminist Rebecca West, one hundred miles away, was giving birth to their son, Anthony. Roiphe spends her first chapter describing how these people managed their decade-long ménage à trois. West was a feminist and, like Wells, believed that not acting on one's sexual attractions was hypocritical, but Roiphe concludes that, in spite of their radical ideas, West and Wells fell into a life of traditional marital hypocrisy anyway. In the end, she feels, they succumbed to fairly outmoded, Victorian notions of marriage. Wells remained in his family and maintained his string of sexual affairs, and West married banker Harry Andrews in 1929 and went on to write *Black Lamb and Grey Falcon: A Journey Through Yugoslavia* in 1941, among other works, and to be featured on the cover of *Time* magazine in 1948 as the world's single most famous woman writer. Their son Anthony would go on to write a bitter account of his childhood.

Roiphe's remaining portraits are equally intriguing. The short-story writer Katherine Mansfield—who would write "Bliss," "The Daughters of the Late Colonel," and "The Garden Party," among other famous stories—married the editor and critic John Middleton Murry, but their marriage seemed almost childish, and they spent much time apart. In her battle with tuberculosis and early death, when Murry was unable to stand by her, it was her intimate friend Ida Baker who would nurse her. Ironically, editors would consider her one of the experts on "Modern Love," but her own marriage appears both restless and irresponsible. Elizabeth von Arnim was another famous writer, the author of the instant sensation and best seller *Elizabeth and her German Garden* (1898). Her feminist novels urged women to abandon their domestic responsibilities for greater freedom and travel, but she ended up marrying a controlling tyrant, Frank Russell. In the end, in what sounds like the plot of a Evelyn Waugh comic novel, she had to flee the marriage to California but still ended up in court, fighting a suit by her husband that she stole his possessions—including his tennis balls. The overlapping ironies in Roiphe's narratives are rich and recurring: Von Arnim was herself at one point a mistress of H. G. Wells, and her cousin, Katherine Mansfield, had early envied her "what she saw as the ease and lightness of her life— Elizabeth had somehow managed to live a full domestic life with children and husbands, *and* achieve literary success."

Roiphe's centerpiece in these seven portraits is her chapter on Vanessa Bell, her husband Clive, and her fellow painter Duncan Grant, and their complex emotional arrangements. This triangle was close to the center of the Bloomsbury Group, that famed artistic and intellectual circle of friends that included Vanessa's sister, the novelist Virginia Woolf; the social critic Lytton Strachey; and the economist John Maynard Keynes, among others. Vanessa and Clive felt themselves "part of a sudden, liberating break from the last remnants of Victorian propriety," and in 1918 Vanessa was living with him in an open marriage that included her current lover, Duncan Grant, and *his* lover David Garnett. Her former lover, the art critic Roger Fry, called their arrangement, in apparent seriousness, "an almost ideal family based as it is on adultery and mutual forbearance. . . . It really is rather a triumph of reasonableness over the conventions." Vanessa managed to maintain this complicated emotional family for some time, through the death of her son Julian in the Spanish Civil War in 1937, and even the marriage of her daughter Angelica (by Grant) to David Garnett in 1942.

The ménage of Una Troubridge, Radclyffe Hall, and Evguenia Souline appears rather traditional by contrast. Hall and Troubridge were together for nearly two decades, which included the obscenity trial over Hall's *The Well of Loneliness* (1928)—"the first serious chronicle of a lesbian's life to appear in print," and a novel advertised as "the most controversial book of the century." Troubridge maintained her firm support of Hall's career, even during the period when Hall drew her new love Evguenia into what the French called their "trio Lesbienne," but Troubridge had the last word when Hall fell sick. She nursed Hall through a long illness until her death and cut Evguenia out of the will. Likewise, there was the triangle of professor George Gordon Catlin; his wife, the writer Vera Brittain, author of the best-selling 1934 *The Testament of Youth* (an autobiographical account of the war years that brought back both the physical and psychological violence); and the friend who supported her through much of her adulthood, the novelist Winifred Holtby, author of the popular novel *South Riding* (1936). In their case, a ménage in which they were physically if not emotionally separated from each other seems to have worked best, and this final chapter is certainly less impassioned than Roiphe's earlier accounts.

In her postscript, Roiphe returns to the questions she sketched out in her introduction, "Marriage à la Mode"—"How does one accommodate the need for settled life with the eternal desire for freshness?" and "why do people drift apart? Why do they stay together?"—and concludes that these seven couples "were torn as we are torn: between tradition and innovation, between freedom and settled life, between feminist equality and reassuring, old-fashioned roles." Roiphe's study is valuable for what it tells modern readers about the abiding institution of marriage, its strengths and inherent pitfalls. As she shows, "those tattered, sentimental, Victorian images of marriage that they were so eager to cast off proved more stubbornly entrenched than they would have thought possible," and, in spite of their progressive ideas, some of these writers "were at the same time constantly reproducing traditional structures of female dependence." Like other examples of a new literary form of writing biography—and Roiphe credits Phyllis Rose's *Parallel Lives: Five Victorian Marriages* (1983) among other recent works—her study is lateral rather than chronological, linking together like (and unlike) entities so that their juxtapositions often reveal something startlingly new. Her writing is itself fresh and inviting, and the stories she relates make literary history come alive again.

*David Peck*

## Review Sources

*Booklist* 103, nos. 9/10 (June 1, 2007): 28.
*The Christian Science Monitor*, July 10, 2007, p. 13.
*The Gazette*, August 18, 2007, p. J5.
*International Herald Tribune*, June 23, 2007, p. 15.
*Kirkus Reviews* 75, no. 8 (April 15, 2007): 378-379.

*Los Angeles Times*, June 25, 2007, p. E4.
*The New York Times* 156 (July 24, 2007): E7.
*The New York Times Book Review* 156 (June 24, 2007): 11.
*People* 68, no. 6 (August 6, 2007): 46.
*The Wall Street Journal* 250, no. 5 (July 7, 2007): P9.

# THE UNNATURAL HISTORY OF THE SEA

*Author:* Callum Roberts (1963-    )
*Publisher:* Island Press/Shearwater Books
(Washington, D.C.). 436 pp. $28.00
*Type of work:* Environment, natural history, science
*Time:* The eleventh century to the early twenty-first century
*Locale:* The oceans of the world

*By examining the thousand-year history of fishing and hunting of marine life, the author shows how increasingly sophisticated technologies have facilitated depleting once superabundant oceans of more than 90 percent of their fish and mammals, but marine reserves offer a hope for resurrecting these vanished ecosystems*

In 1968, biologist Garrett Hardin provided a name for a phenomenon that, for centuries, had plagued humankind and its interaction with the environment. Wherever such common-property renewable resources as lands, lakes, and forests existed, humans overused them to the point of total exhaustion or degradation. Hardin called this overuse of free-access resources "the tragedy of the commons," and a principal theme of Callum Roberts's *The Unnatural History of the Sea* is that ocean resources, as limited as those of land, have also been appallingly squandered. Because humans occupy a water planet, with more than 90 percent of its surface covered by water, those who have plied their livelihood on the seas developed a conviction that its riches were inexhaustible. For five years, Roberts collected a wide variety of evidence from the writings of explorers, travelers, and fishers as well as from books and articles by scientists to convince general readers that the oceans of today are dangerously empty compared to the plenitude of the past.

Although most of his book depicts in heartrending detail how human greed and lack of foresight have resulted in the extirpation of a significant portion of the world's sea life, Roberts nevertheless insists that his purpose is not to spread the word of the sea's demise but to galvanize fishers and ordinary people to transform their relationship to marine life in ways through which the lost abundance of the oceans may be recovered. Because of a long-standing and deeply held conviction by fishers and scientists of the inexhaustible bounty of the seas, Roberts traces how this belief developed and how unfettered commercialization has revealed its falsity. In part 1, "Explorers and Exploiters in the Age of Plenty," Roberts argues that marine life began to disappear along European shores as early as the Middle Ages, when fishermen shifted from dwindling freshwater varieties to such saltwater species as herring, cod, and haddock. Overfishing along England's coast led to serious declines in catches, forcing fishermen to seek these species along the coasts of other countries.

*Callum Roberts is a marine conservation biologist at the University of York. He has been awarded a Pew Fellowship in Marine Conservation (2000) and a Hardy Fellowship in Conservation Biology at Harvard University (2001). He has also served on a U.S. National Research Council Committee on Marine Protected Areas.*

The commercialization of ocean fishing and hunting accelerated after the European discovery of the New World. Fishermen from several countries then began withdrawing gigantic numbers of cod from the coastal waters of New England and Canada. During the seventeenth and eighteenth centuries, thousands of ships so overfished these waters that cod sizes and numbers were driven to deleteriously low levels. In the eighteenth century, on the west coast of North America, Russian hunters drastically reduced the numbers of sea otters, seals, and sea cows. In Caribbean waters, where millions of sea turtles once existed, most species are now on the endangered list.

Roberts calls whaling "the first global industry," and from the eighteenth to the twentieth century whales were hunted and killed in ever greater numbers as sailing ships evolved into large, steam-powered vessels. Onboard factory ships, thousands of workers processed whale oil that, during the nineteenth century, lit European and American homes and streets. As whale numbers diminished in the North Atlantic, whalers discovered "hot spots" in the South Atlantic and Pacific Oceans. Even in these new locations, whales were soon overhunted to the point of commercial and actual extinction. Cetologists have estimated that, before whaling, 360 million fin whales and 240 million humpbacks existed, but, by the end of the twentieth century these numbers had declined to 56,000 fin whales and 9,000 humpbacks. Because of extinctions of several other species, an international ban on all whaling was instituted in the 1980's, though such countries as Japan, Norway, and Iceland defied the ban. Roberts tells analogous stories about walrus, otter, and seal hunting in which millions of animals were slaughtered to meet the demand for skins and ivory. In 1911, the first international environmental treaty was signed in an attempt to save the pelagic seal, but harp seal hunting continues in Newfoundland, despite annual protests.

New technologies contributed to the decline of not only sea mammals but also such fish as the herring, once called "the lord of fishes." In the spring, off the coasts of Great Britain and Holland, schools of herring were caught in drifting gill nets. Even more destructive to fish numbers was modern beam trawling, which, in the nineteenth century, revolutionized commercial fishing. When steamships used steam engines to draw beamed bag nets across seabeds, huge numbers of fish were caught, and with the mid-century technique of ice preservation, millions of Europeans and Americans could purchase inexpensive fresh fish. When some fishermen complained that trawling was destroying their livelihood, a British commission studied the problem. Despite the expertise of such distinguished scientists as Thomas Henry Huxley, the commissioners overwhelmingly rejected the fishermen's contention of dramatic fish declines. Instead, when, at the end of the nineteenth century, the Sea Fisheries Act became law, sea trawlers felt encouraged to expand their operations. Roberts claims that sea trawling has destroyed most habitats of the world's seabed, annihilating webs of life that had existed for millions of years.

Roberts devotes the second part of his book to the "Modern Era of Industrial Fishing." From the end of the nineteenth to the start of the twenty-first century, fishing and hunting methods became so productive that neither the extinctions of many species nor the collapse of many industries was able to halt the overexploitation of the sea. Even such a sensitive environmentalist as Rachel Carson praised diversification as the industry's solution to overfishing. When haddock numbers plummeted, cusk, a deepwater cod, served as a substitute. Furthermore, commercial fishing and hunting were interrupted by the two world wars, during which some species were able to increase their numbers. Nevertheless, in the 1950's and 1960's declining catches, particularly in coastal areas, became the rule rather than the exception. Bluefin tuna had become so depleted that, in Japan, a single fish sold for $100,000. Some countries extended their coastal zones to twelve, then fifty nautical miles, and in 1973, at a United Nations conference on the law of the sea, more than a hundred nations agreed to the creation of a two-hundred-mile "Exclusive Economic Zone." However, these and other regulations did little to stop overfishing. For example, they could not prevent the collapse of cod fisheries during the final decades of the twentieth century.

Through several case studies of Chesapeake Bay, coral reefs, and the Sea of Cortez, Roberts demonstrates how a variety of marine ecosystems experienced their own "tragedy of the commons." When English colonists settled around the shores of Chesapeake Bay, its waters were teeming with life, but during the nineteenth century oyster fisheries kept expanding until numbers inevitably declined, resulting in an "oyster war" between police and pirate fishers during which several lives were lost. It was not until 1967 that concerned citizens and scientists formed a foundation to study the bay's problems and seek solutions. Similarly, coral reefs around the world were once habitats for many varieties of sea life, but by the 1970's most reefs had lost their largest and most valuable species, and many had become "ghost reefs," nearly empty of any flora and fauna. The Sea of Cortez was once a favorite destination for sportsmen from around the world, including the writer Zane Grey, but dams along the Colorado River reduced the flow of freshwater into the Gulf of California, precipitating a massive loss of spawning areas and a consequent decline of many game species. Examples could be multiplied, but the conclusion remains the same: Today's oceans are much less diverse and productive than the oceans before commercial fishing.

In the third and shortest part of his book, Roberts analyzes possible futures for the world's oceans. In one scenario, he considers what would happen if past trends continue. With faster boats, larger nets, and more sophisticated fish-detecting devices, fishers will be able to catch the remaining creatures of rapidly declining populations. In the end, this will mean that, with the fish of most species gone, humans will be reduced to consuming jellyfish. On the other hand, humans are capable of developing new ways of managing ocean fish and mammals. Roberts admits that, in the past, marine management has been an ineffectual competition between fishers and regulators in which the fishers have usually been able to discover ways around regulations. Roberts's suggestions are to decrease fishing and increase marine reserves. These reserves, such as the recently created Northwest Hawaiian Islands National Monument, will help fish to live longer and produce more offspring, which will then spread beyond the reserves to replenish the seas.

Since most of Roberts's book has depicted fishers, scientists, and citizens behaving myopically or selfishly, some critics have found his optimism Pollyannaish, but he defends his optimism by arguing that commercial fishers, conservationists, and citizens have vested interests in resurrecting ocean habitats and life. Other critics have called attention to his ignoring global warming in his book, and note that since oceans have been absorbing mammoth amounts of carbon dioxide since the Industrial Revolution, the acidity of seawater has also been increasing, posing yet another danger to sea life. Roberts has responded to this criticism by pointing out that the consequences of increased acidity are still unknown, whereas the consequences of overfishing are very well known. He encourages fishing industries to curtail their catches, governments to establish more reserves, and citizens to purchase seafoods that have been sustainably produced. In short, his book is an eloquent plea for all people on Earth to work together to save the seas, because it is in the best interest of all life—fish, mammalian, and human—that this important task be accomplished.

*Robert J. Paradowski*

## Review Sources

*Audubon* 109, no. 5 (September/October, 2007): 108.
*Booklist* 103, no. 22 (August 1, 2007): 30.
*Chicago Tribune*, October 17, 2007, p. 7.
*Issues in Science and Technology* 24, no. 1 (Fall, 2007): 91-95.
*Library Journal* 132, no. 12 (July 1, 2007): 116.
*Publishers Weekly* 254, no. 23 (June 4, 2007): 44.
*Science News* 172, no. 9 (September 1, 2007): 143.
*The Washington Post*, July 29, 2007, p. BW15.

# THE UTILITY OF FORCE
## The Art of War in the Modern World

*Author:* Rupert Smith (1943-    )
*First published:* 2005, in Great Britain
*Publisher:* Alfred A. Knopf (New York). 430 pp. $30.00
*Type of work:* Current affairs

*A British general argues that the era of conventional interstate industrial war is over and that the world has entered a period in which wars will be limited, long, and fought among the people*

General Rupert Smith's *The Utility of Force* is a compelling analysis of war in the present era. Smith begins boldly; his first sentence declares, "War no longer exists." By this he does not mean that international law and institutions have rendered state-sanctioned violence obsolete. Smith is much too hardheaded for that. Forty years of service in the British army, including stints commanding British troops in Operation Desert Storm and Northern Ireland, and U.N. forces in Bosnia, immunized him from any sort of illusions about humanity's nature or institutions. What Smith means is that the type of military operations that most people associate with war—main-force engagements between formally constituted armies, leading to a victory and subsequent peace settlement—no longer have utility in a world where conflict is characterized by ethnic cleansing and terrorism. War has changed, and Smith believes that most people, including political and military leaders, have failed to notice the new reality. The consequences, in Iraq and elsewhere, have been deadly.

Smith's work is a theoretical treatise firmly grounded in experience. Though the book is not a memoir, Smith illustrates many of his points with examples drawn from his long career as a soldier. He also devotes much of his book to historical analysis, to provide context for his thesis that war as it was once known is dead. *The Utility of Force* in many ways echoes the writings of a man Smith quotes respectfully and often, Carl von Clausewitz, the Prussian military theorist whose writings prefigured the rise of mass, industrial war in the nineteenth and twentieth centuries. Like Smith, Clausewitz was a professional soldier. He observed the dramatic changes that came over war in the Napoleonic era. No longer was war a limited struggle fought for limited aims by monarchs employing limited, and hence expensive, mercenary armies. War became instead a struggle of nations, with the rise and fall of dynasties at stake. As a result of what he saw, Clausewitz voiced the great insight that war is an extension of politics. War could no longer be waged in a strategic vacuum. A military operation had to be both an expression and fulfillment of a political aim. Thus, a military had to be attuned to and in constant communication with its government. Further, Clausewitz believed that this government, even the absolute monarchy that he himself served,

~

*General Sir Rupert Smith is one of Britain's most distinguished soldiers. He commanded the U.K. Armored Division in the Gulf War and U.N. forces in Bosnia in 1995. He was general officer commanding in Northern Ireland from 1996 to 1998 and served as deputy supreme allied commander of NATO from 1999 to 2001. He retired in 2001.*

~

had in an increasingly democratic age to be sensitive to the will of the people. The days were gone when people were disinterested bystanders to their monarchs' wars. Kings now had to turn to their people for men and money. For Clausewitz, only the effective coordination of this trinity of military, government, and people could lead to victory.

Smith sees himself playing a role similar to that of Clausewitz. He is describing a revolution in warfare and reminding his readers of the connection between politics and warfare, but the nature of this politics is different. The balance between the military, government, and people has changed since the great wars of the twentieth century. His message is that people must accommodate themselves to an era in which battle no longer brings decision.

The modern era of war began with the wars of the French Revolution and Napoleon. Smith calls this interstate industrial war. The armies of the French Revolution, inherited by Napoleon, were armies of the people, citizen soldiers, fighting for the new political ideal of the nation. What these armies at first lacked in training and discipline they more than made up for in numbers and ideological enthusiasm. Reorganizing this force, Napoleon created a redoubtable military machine that dominated Europe for a decade and a half. He made and unmade kings and brought a terrifying new decisiveness to warfare. Great battles like Austerlitz and Waterloo ended wars with stunning finality. Napoleon's brand of war bred up a reaction among his enemies. In Spain, Germany, and Russia, nationalism spurred resistance. In Prussia, initial defeat inspired military reforms that led to the creation of a general staff, an elite corps of officers whose mission it was to plan intensively for war, developing a common doctrine that could be communicated to an entire army. This was the nursery of Clausewitz's ideas on warfare. By the end of the Napoleonic period, war had become a massive enterprise, drawing on the resources of both state and people. The foundations had been laid for total war.

Technological changes accelerated both civilian and military life in the nineteenth century. The telegraph made communication almost instantaneous. The railroad revolutionized transportation, making it possible to shift great numbers of people rapidly over great distances. The American Civil War saw the first application of these new technologies to war. This conflict also saw the introduction of all-metal warships and new and more deadly firearms and artillery. True to form for industrial war, the Civil War ended only when the resistance of the South had been crushed both militarily and politically. Although some Europeans studied the lessons of the Civil War, it was the comparable exploits of the Prussians that brought home the new military reality wrought by technology. The Prussian general staff, led by its brilliant chief Helmuth von Moltke, mastered the art of railroad mobilization. In three short, sharp wars, the Prussian army swiftly concentrated and defeated less nimble and organized foes.

The world wars saw the fulfillment of interstate industrial war. In August, 1914, the European Great Powers believed that the war that they were embarking on would be brief, decided by a few decisive battles, but the mass armies and new technologies that they had inherited this time thwarted their goal. The tremendous firepower now available drove the armies underground for shelter. For more than four years, the contending powers struggled for a way to break the deadlock of the trenches. The tremendous demands for men and munitions entailed by this form of war compelled states to mobilize the economic and social life of their nations. Total war was born. World War II saw offensive power restored by a marriage of tanks and airpower. The German Blitzkrieg harnessed these technologies with devastating results. However, the new tactics did not shorten the war. Once again, whole populations were harnessed to the war effort. The logic of total war was carried to a grim, if logical, conclusion when civilians became acceptable military targets. Strategic bombing gutted city after city. Civilians overwhelmingly paid the price when the United States ended the war by dropping atomic bombs on Hiroshima and Nagasaki.

Smith believes that the employment of these weapons, the products of a massive scientific and engineering effort, simultaneously marked the culmination and the passing of interstate industrial war. Once the atomic bomb was dropped, all the great militaries of the world, with their fleets of ships, tanks, and planes, suddenly lost their ability to achieve decisive results. Conventional weaponry was naked before the nuclear threat. Smith argues that the sudden advent of the Cold War helped mask this new reality, as the alliance systems that grew up around the United States and the Soviet Union began a confrontation that would last for almost fifty years. Great militaries endured; those of the two superpowers proliferated, but as bargaining chips in a nuclear standoff that inexorably led to the strategy of mutually assured destruction. Major conflicts abounded in the shadow of the Cold War. Some, like the Korean and Vietnam Wars, were enormously costly and destructive. Invariably, Cold War restraints kept them from being waged to a decisive end. Even the spectacular victories of the Israelis in the Middle East resulted in the frustrations of the intifadas, and borders that are still unsettled.

The end of the Cold War left the superpowers and their allies heavily armed for a war that they never had to fight. Many in the 1990's hoped for a peace dividend that would enable governments to cut back drastically on funding. Many governments did so, but peace did not come. Instead, the post-Cold War world saw the outbreak of a number of brutal wars that shocked world opinion and stretched dangerously depleted military resources. Smith writes that these wars revealed the hitherto obscured new paradigm for postatomic conflict. Wars are now fought among the people. Decision cannot come from military means alone. Many of these conflicts are fought against or between guerrilla groups sheltering within a civilian population. In such struggles, the armor and airpower amassed for industrial war have no utility because a traditional military victory is impossible to achieve. Militaries must now fight for a political settlement. They must wage an essentially psychological struggle for the hearts and minds of the people, even at the cost of sacrificing conventional military advantages. They also must do so while endeavoring to protect as much as humanly possible the increasingly expensive and limited forces at their disposal. Smith's vision of war among the people will disturb both the supporters and critics of contemporary wars. He scoffs at the notion that traditionally organized militaries can be effective instruments of nation building, but he argues that national interests will have to be defended, even though the consequent struggles will inevitably be long and ugly, something especially painful for impatient democracies.

Smith illustrates his points about the new face of war by drawing on his experiences on a variety of fronts in the 1990's. In 1991, he commanded the British armored division in Operation Desert Storm. Already the British were taking advantage of the end of the Cold War to draw down their forces. Smith learned that, because of the high maintenance required by desert conditions, he controlled virtually all the tank engines of the British army. Had he lost them all, British armor would have been immobilized for the foreseeable future. He did not lose them, but he notes that the glittering battlefield success of Desert Storm merely set in motion more years of confrontation and conflict.

In 1995, Smith was appointed to command the United Nations Protection Force (UNPROFOR) in Bosnia. This was a motley collection of battalion-sized units that were supposed to protect the civilian population during the murderous Bosnian civil war. Because of political confusion over the mission of UNPROFOR and the determination of the sponsoring nations that no casualties be incurred, the U.N. peacekeepers soon became as much hostages as the people they were supposedly protecting. U.N. troops ended up standing helplessly by as Bosnian Serbs massacred seven thousand Muslim men in Srebrenica. Only after the world learned of this outrage, and the United States decided to act, did Smith get authority to strike back at the Serbs. A formal peace treaty would be signed at Dayton, but outside troops remained as peacekeepers in the region into the early twenty-first century.

As commander of British forces in Northern Ireland from 1996 to 1998, Smith had to respond to the Irish Republican Army (IRA) with the most minimal force possible to avoid derailing a delicate peace process. Finally, as deputy supreme allied commander in the North Atlantic Treaty Organization (NATO), Smith helped oversee an armed intervention in Kosovo that was confined to air strikes because of a fear of risking allied casualties. Once again, the campaign proved a success, but European peacekeepers remained still on the ground in Kosovo.

Smith never enjoyed a Napoleonic triumph during his career as a commander. Arches of victory will not be erected in wars among the people. Smith had to work within rigid constraints set by governmental policy and scarce resources. None of his wars achieved decisive results; the political disputes that inspired them remain unresolved. Smith does not despair at this. The world has entered a period where limited and long-lasting conflicts will be the norm. Smith's sage advice is to learn to live with and manage this new reality.

*Daniel P. Murphy*

## Review Sources

*Booklist* 103, no. 11 (February 1, 2007): 10-11.
*The Economist* 377 (December 24, 2005): 117-118.
*Foreign Affairs* 85, no. 2 (March/April, 2006): 193.
*Harper's Magazine* 314 (June, 2007): 83-87.
*Journal of Strategic Studies* 29, no. 6 (December, 2006): 1151-1170.
*Library Journal* 132, no. 3 (February 15, 2007): 133.
*New Statesman* 134 (November 14, 2005): 55.
*The New York Times Book Review* 156 (February 4, 2007): 14-15.
*The Times Literary Supplement*, December 16, 2005, pp. 3-6.
*The Wilson Quarterly* 31, no. 2 (Spring, 2007): 86-88.

# VACCINE
## The Controversial Story of Medicine's Greatest Lifesaver

*Author:* Arthur Allen (1959-     )
*Publisher:* W. W. Norton (New York). 523 pp. $27.95
*Type of work:* History of science, medicine, science
*Time:* 1721-2006
*Locale:* The United States

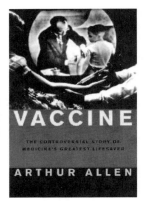

*An account of the development and use of vaccination as a means to control disease; political, industrial, and medical controversies associated with vaccination have all played their respective roles in the subject*

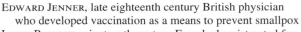

*Principal personages:*
COTTON MATHER, eighteenth century
    Massachusetts minister who was
    instrumental in introducing smallpox
    variolation to America
EDWARD JENNER, late eighteenth century British physician
    who developed vaccination as a means to prevent smallpox
LOUIS PASTEUR, nineteenth century French chemist noted for
    development of the first anthrax and rabies vaccines
ALMROTH WRIGHT, late nineteenth century British physician who
    developed a typhoid vaccine, one of the first such measures used
    for widespread immunization in the military
JOSEPH MCFARLAND, American bacteriologist who, by demonstrating
    the role of smallpox vaccines in an outbreak of tetanus, produced an
    awareness of possible dangers inherent in vaccine "quality control"
JONAS SALK, mid-twentieth century American physician who developed
    the first effective poliovirus vaccine using killed virus
ALBERT SABIN, American physician and Salk antagonist who developed
    an oral poliovirus vaccine which replaced that developed by Salk
BARBARA LOE FISHER, Virginia parent who, following the diagnosis
    of "mental regression" in her son, became a significant figure in
    the movement to associate vaccination with autism and other side
    effects in children
DAN BURTON, Indiana congressman who was one of the most powerful
    supporters of the lobby arguing the danger of vaccination

An item of trivia noted by another reviewer of *Vaccine* created an immediate interest in the subject addressed by Arthur Allen. Like many parents, I had a child whose favorite plaything at one time was an old Raggedy Ann doll. As described by Allen, Raggedy Ann originated as a rag doll created by New York City illustrator Johnny Gruelle, made for his daughter who became fatally ill following a smallpox vaccination. Indeed, *Vaccine* is filled with items for the trivia buff, ranging from the origin of the medical phrase "guinea pig" (George Bernard Shaw) to the method of delivering fresh smallpox vaccine to city residents—"cattle drives" consisting of infected animals.

Allen begins his story with the history of the earliest use of inoculation—the term "vaccination" was not yet applied—in a widespread manner to immunize a population. Human civilization is ripe with epidemic disease, and smallpox certainly ranks among the most-feared diseases. Its reputation was de-

∽
*Arthur Allen is a former foreign correspondent for the Associated Press and has been a frequent contributor to major newspapers and popular magazines such as* The New York Times Magazine, The New Republic, *and* The Atlantic Monthly.
∽

served. Two forms of the disease have long been known: *Variola major* and a less virulent *Variola minor*. The molecular basis for the difference is still not understood, but those infected with the more virulent form, if they survived—and 20-30 percent did not during most outbreaks—frequently suffered lifelong scarring. Helplessness in facing a smallpox epidemic began to change in the early eighteenth century, the result in large part of observations on the part of Lady Mary Montagu, wife of the British ambassador to the Ottoman Empire. Herself once a victim of the disease, Lady Montagu became aware of the process of variolation, a medical procedure in which material from a drying pock was inoculated under the skin of a patient. When the procedure worked, the patient suffered only a mild illness but became immune to the disease. Sometimes the procedure failed, and the patient actually developed smallpox.

Variolation made its way to America, where in Boston two unlikely allies began the widespread use of the procedure: the Reverend Cotton Mather of Boston, who despite his deserved reputation as an intolerant minister, was surprisingly literate, even liberal, in the ways of science, and Zabdiel Boylston, a physician in the city. Overcoming opposition within the Church as well as the medical establishment of the day, the two men were instrumental in evolution of the idea that disease was not a punishment for sin but rather a challenge that could be overcome. Allen concludes this first section with the discovery and application by Edward Jenner, that material prepared from lesions of a similar disease, cowpox, was a safer measure than variolation for immunization against smallpox. The very word "vaccination" is a testament to the procedure, being derived from *vacca*, Latin for "cow."

Even as the disease began to recede in the early twentieth century, the direct result of the widespread use of vaccination, controversies began to appear. Indeed, a significant portion of *Vaccine* deals with the arguments, pro and con, associated with vaccination against childhood disease in general. Some arguments were of course political: Should the state have the power to force vaccination on its citizenry? The author describes how in Philadelphia in 1903, patrol wagons carrying both physicians and police would suddenly appear at job sites, where mass inoculation of immigrant workers would take place. Even the first Raggedy Ann doll was made by the father of a child who died shortly after receiving forced inoculation at school. (The actual cause of death was unclear. Health authorities argued a heart defect was the reason.) Eventually the decision was made by the Supreme Court: The individual was indeed a free man and could not be forced to undergo vaccination on that basis. However, if public health was the factor at risk, the Court ruled that vaccination could be made compulsory.

The issue was more than political. Allen provides numerous examples of the tragic results from vaccine poorly made, of nonexistent quality control, and even contamination by bacteria of vaccine stocks. Controversies over vaccination represent a running theme throughout the book, and contamination, either inadvertent or through neglect, is a common factor. Many of the most tragic examples are associated with smallpox vaccination; it is no surprise that the antivaccine movement came to the forefront during these first years of the twentieth century. All that was needed by the movement was funding, and with Philadelphia-area oil baron John Pitcairn, the movement found its backing. When the Anti-Vaccination League of Pennsylvania failed in its efforts in Pennsylvania state courts as well as attempts at legislation, it went national, eventually joining together a conglomeration of vaccine opponents, homeopaths, and the occasional charlatan. While the movement eventually came to naught, it played a key factor in forcing health departments to provide better oversight for vaccine production and vaccination policies.

Smallpox was certainly not the only target for modern medicine, and *Vaccine* moves into the history behind the fight against rabies, though never a major problem in terms of actual numbers, and diphtheria, which was a major killer of children. It was through the effort to control diphtheria that Herman Biggs, chief medical officer for New York City, and his associate, William Park, director of the city's Bureau of Laboratories, developed not only a swab test for detection of the diphtheria bacillus but also the large-scale manufacturing of an effective antitoxin. Unfortunately, since guinea pigs were one of the few nonhuman animals in which the antitoxin could be tested, thousands of the furry creatures were killed in the process. It was in the extension to human experimentation that writer George Bernard Shaw coined the epithet, human "guinea pigs."

What worked for diphtheria would seemingly work against other diseases. As noted by the author, typhoid fever was long a bane of marching armies, as well as the civilians in their paths. Spread through poor disposal of sewage, typhoid could decimate an army. (As a side note, many of the early laboratory tests developed to monitor the presence of *Escherichia coli* in drinking water were actually using the organism as a surrogate marker for sewage contamination, *E. coli* being significantly more easily detected than the typhoid bacillus.) The first typhoid vaccine was developed by British physician Sir Almroth Wright—called "Almost Right" behind his back—and tested on British soldiers during the Boer War around 1898. It "almost worked," but side effects were often so severe that it never found widespread use; better sanitation was the answer for typhoid, as events later proved.

As described in *Vaccine*, the soldier frequently made the ideal "guinea pig": trained to take orders, the soldier too frequently suffered from the carelessness in vaccine production. Yellow fever vaccine was a prime example. Millions of doses were provided, but by 1942 it became increasingly clear that something in its production was wrong. Tens of thousands of soldiers were being hospitalized with jaundice.

Eventually it was discovered that certain lots of vaccine had been contaminated with what later was known as hepatitis B virus, the result of the addition of contaminated human serum as a stabilizing agent.

Much of this was forgotten in the most important medical triumph of the mid-twentieth century: the development of an effective vaccine to prevent polio. Poliomyelitis was largely a twentieth century disease. Ironically, epidemics occurred only after public health measures had reduced the exposure of young children to the virus while still possessing a measure of protection from maternal antibodies. Versions of a killed vaccine had been developed in the 1930's, one by William Park, but they had proven worse than useless: Children had received live virus, and several died. A number of timely discoveries came together in the late 1940's, including the ability to grow the virus in cell cultures instead of animals, and providing a means to monitor immunity. The first effective, and largely safe, polio vaccine was developed by Jonas Salk in the early 1950's. When the results of the field trial were released in April, 1955, Salk became a household name. Shortly afterward, an attenuated vaccine was developed and tested by Albert Sabin. While controversies surrounded both vaccines—largely based on which was safer or provided better long-term immunity—the result was that polio ceased to be a public health problem.

The issue of vaccine safety covers most of the second half of *Vaccine* and could easily represent a book unto itself. As noted above, arguments over safety were never far from the surface. With the elimination of most childhood killers—the result of a combination of factors ranging from proper public health practices to herd immunity, the inability of disease to spread if a proportion of the public is immune—parents developed concerns about whether the sheer number of vaccines, booster shots, and so forth could overload the immune system. Of particular concern was the DPT or DTP (diphtheria, tetanus, pertussis) vaccine series. While there had been some suggestion that medical problems such as autism or "mental regression" might have been associated with DTP shots, the issue came before the general public in a television documentary, *DPT: Vaccine Roulette*, which aired in April, 1982. The prevailing images in the show were those of babies showing evidence of brain damage, convulsions, and even death. The implication was that such tragedies were the result of the DTP vaccine. The show provided the impetus for a national movement against vaccination in general, and DTP specifically. Barbara Loe Fisher, an Alexandria, Virginia, mother whose son had allegedly exhibited brain damage after a shot, became one of the more strident voices for the antivaccine movement. Congressman Dan Burton of Indiana, with a grandson later diagnosed with autism, provided one of numerous political faces to the controversy.

Was vaccination potentially harmful, in particular the DTP immunization? Certainly there was gist for the vaccination opponents: the 1976 swine flu debacle, which ultimately forced the government to pay out some $100 million to persons who allegedly developed neurological illnesses as a result; the use of thimerosal, a mercury-containing organic material sometimes used as a preservative in some vaccines; and the "explosion" in the number of children diagnosed with autism. At some point, it hardly mattered whether "defects" appeared in children who were never exposed to thimerosal or whether the increase in autism was as much the result of a changing definition and subsequent governmental funding as a possible cause associated with vaccination. Much of the public thought so, and often juries did as well. The cost of litigation drove many pharmaceutical companies out of the vaccine business, and diseases such as whooping cough and even polio showed a resurgence. Regulation, while necessary, has almost reached the point of overkill, as exemplified by the shutting of an entire Merck, Sharpe and Dohme factory—the name itself an example of "merger mania"—by an inspector on a filling line, endangering the country's supply of MMR (measles, mumps, rubella) vaccine. Is there a solution? The author both begins and ends *Vaccine* with the same example: the fear of biological terrorism as the driving point for immunization against—something.

*Richard Adler*

## Review Sources

*Booklist* 103, no. 6 (November 15, 2006): 12-14.
*Kirkus Reviews* 74, no. 19 (October 1, 2006): 997.
*The Lancet* 369 (April 28, 2007): 1421-1422.
*Library Journal* 131, no. 19 (November 15, 2006): 87.
*Nature* 448 (July 12, 2007): 137.
*The New England Journal of Medicine* 357, no. 6 (August 9, 2007): 628.
*The New York Times Book Review* 156 (February 4, 2007): 12.
*Publishers Weekly* 253, no. 40 (October 9, 2006): 46.
*The Wall Street Journal* 249, no. 26 (February 1, 2007): D6.
*The Washington Post*, February 11, 2007, p. BW06.

# VARIETIES OF DISTURBANCE

*Author:* Lydia Davis (1947-      )
*Publisher:* Farrar, Straus and Giroux (New York). 219
   pp. $13.00
*Type of work:* Short fiction
*Time:* The twentieth century

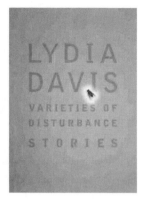

   *A brilliant, opaque writer's seventh collection, a gathering of fifty-seven stories that range from one-sentence jolts of recognition to forty-page faux case studies*

   Lydia Davis has built a reputation for explicating the inner territory of daily life with the stylistic approaches of minimalism and postmodernism. Irony, dispassionate observation, interior monologue, and elliptical analysis are among the tools she brings to the predicaments and concerns of ordinary people. Often nameless, they are characterized largely by their preoccupations and quirks. Davis admits that her stories never paint a fair or a complete picture of a situation; their material comes from life, but she makes it "safely fictional" by turning one mood, or one afternoon's events, into something strong enough to stand by itself.

   Throughout adulthood, Davis has pursued a parallel career as a translator of French literature. Her translating credits include works as disparate as those of social observer Alexis de Tocqueville and scientist Marie Curie, as well as those of more purely literary writers. Her aim in translation appears to be shared by the central character of the present volume's "The Walk," who is also a translator: "accuracy and faithfulness to the style of the original." This granted, a primary virtue of the translator becomes invisibility. This quality carries over into Davis's original work in a curious way: The line between authorial voice, narrator's voice, and character voice is either blurred or invisible.

   Time and place in most of her stories is left deliberately vague also, yet the characters do seem frozen in a sort of mid-twentieth century time warp. The two long "case study" stories actually establish a partial setting that frames the book. The hospitalized boy of "We Miss You," sends a reply to his teacher dated "Feb 20 1951." Helen and Vi of the health study grew up, respectively, in Connecticut and Virginia, and their long lives span most of the twentieth century. However, the prevailing outlook of other stories' narrators reflect a similar, circumscribed worldview that predates many commonplaces of the era after approximately 1975. Typewriters are common, but computers are unknown; tuberculosis is treated by long stays in a sanitarium; HoJos and gas stations are frequent highway features. It is difficult to tell whether this subliminal "dating" effect stems from the author's fascination with a recently bygone era or whether it is simply an artifact of the stories having been written at an earlier time (those previous-publication credits that cite a date range from 1989 to 2006). However, this feature lends the collection a certain old-fashioned

~

*Even before her 1970 graduation from Barnard College, Lydia Davis published a translation of French poetry. Subsequently, she has drawn acclaim for both her translations and short fiction, with several story reprints appearing in the Pushcart Prize anthologies. She has won many awards, including a prestigious MacArthur Fellowship in 2003.*

~

resonance, which may jar readers drawn by its more avant-garde "flash fiction" formats.

The title story originally appeared in *A Little Magazine* and was reprinted in the not-so-little *Harper's Magazine* of April, 1993. It deals with the implications of a white lie told by the narrator's mother to discourage her son (the narrator's brother) from coming to help out while she convalesces from a hospital stay. The lie itself is of little moment, and the real reason for inventing it was to avoid "disturbing"—perhaps angering—her husband, but it becomes the source of a whole array of further "disturbances." These spiral around the family constellation in a dizzy display of hurt feelings and self-justification. Although the specifics are left vague, the narrative uncannily resembles those flaps-over-nothing that flare up in so many families. Critic Thad Ziolkowski has praised its "sestinalike effect," which he characterizes as "High Analytical Vertigo." In less rarefied terms, it could as easily be called "The Woman Who Thinks Too Much." Indeed, the daughter-narrator may be the only one giving more than a passing thought to "the disturbances." In either case, the story is a unique example of attempted domestic logic.

"How She Could Not Drive" starts out as a catalog of circumstances that prevent a nameless, presumably neurotic woman from being able to drive. The hypnotic effect of the run-on listing segues into a surrealistic scene where the reader realizes that she is indeed driving, possibly vision-impaired, and battered by the onrushing montage that the night casts onto her path. Precise details give way to evocative images: "the massive airship of motel lights floating across the highway." A rare flash of vicarious experience, of being able to live for a moment in the driver's skin and mind, results.

Three short pieces are concerned with death. "How Shall I Mourn Them" approaches it sideways, as a numbered list of the eccentricities that survivors adopt. "Burning Family Members" juxtaposes two deaths, both of which raise quietly horrifying moral questions. One reviewer believes that "'They' burned her thousands of miles away from here" refers to the Iraq War. It is possible; the references are opaque enough to support several different meanings. "Grammar Questions" is an indirect, but more understandable, cry from the heart. The narrator, presumably his daughter, is on deathwatch at her father's bedside, trying desperately to distract herself from what is happening. Her way involves worrying about how to speak of his selfhood when he is dead. The story is one of Davis's understated masterpieces, offering absolute emotional truth on a serious subject.

"The Walk" is among the few Lydia Davis stories that takes place in a defined location—in this case, Oxford, England. It tells of a translator (female) and a critic (male) who linger there the evening after a conference closes. Both are stranded until morning. They dine together, chat about their work and opinions, then decide to stroll through the quiet, twilight-shadowed streets. The story is notable for its sets of opposites. The first paragraph opposes the grandeur of a great university town to the shabbiness of their lodgings. Later, there is the clash of their differing opinions on the translator's art, and the woman's simultaneous pleasure at the critic's charm and resentment of his disapproval of her work. After the walk, she sits quietly in her quarters, letting images from the walk fill her mind. With these, she tries to convince herself that she is not disappointed by the conference. Throughout the story, there is an unspoken hint that the evening might include a romantic encounter. Of course, the two people being the people they are, it does not happen. The material about the translator's craft reflects Davis's other intellectual pursuit. Even academics may be surprised to learn that there are people who make their living as translation critics.

"Helen and Vi: A Study in Health and Vitality" is the collection's longest story. It examines the life trajectories of two elderly women. Vi, an African American, was brought up along with her siblings by her grandparents in rural Virginia. Helen, a Swedish American, grew up on a dairy farm in Connecticut. Their work experiences, living conditions, recreation, religious practices, and health are all described in the plain, objective prose of a case study. The two women have much in common. The narrator attributes their long lives to their sensible diets and active habits, along with an outgoing quality hard to quantify—they are genuinely interested in other people. Despite the story's flat tone, its subjects "come alive" more fully than any of the volume's other characters. They are also the only characters shown acting as members of an ongoing community. Perhaps the two facts are connected.

The vagaries of fourth-grade writing skills are displayed in "We Miss You: A Study of Get-Well Letters from a Class of Fourth Graders." The story is purportedly a study of letters rediscovered, sixty years later, and analyzed, in order to draw some conclusions about the children's daily lives and the ways their minds worked. After some background information about the boy Stephen's accident and the school's neighborhood, twenty-seven letters are given an exacting content analysis. Paper quality, penmanship, the form and content of sentences, and the varying way "miss you" sentiments are expressed are all described and quantified. The style is plodding and humorless. The bulk of the "study" resembles an academic article written under publish-or-perish pressures and submitted to a second-rate education journal. Davis seems to have written the story in a bout of secret amusement, perhaps as a tongue-in-cheek parody of a colleague's work. Only at the very end, in a long passage evoking the childhood pleasures of sledding and moviegoing in the darker shadows of the hospital, does the author speculate on the children's "other life" or their emotions. An addendum paragraph gives a sort of closure, with its update of Stephen being out of the hospital and recovered.

If gentle parody is the subtext of "We Miss You," the snarky tone of "Mrs. D and Her Maids" hints at a darker message. The collection's third long piece, it chronicles the many maids who have worked for the D family, and their deficiencies. Mrs. D needs a maid to relieve her of household and child-care duties so she can do her other work as a writer. She readily sells the stories she writes to "ladies' magazines." What she needs is uninterrupted time to work on them. The narrator makes a point of her pride at selling her stories, subtly contrasting it with some other, finer motive that Mrs. D lacks.

However, the parade of maids cuts into her attention to writing. Some maids are so conscientious that they never get caught up with their work. One maid strews diapers all over the bathroom. Another is great with the baby but unpredictable about showing up. Many maids "don't work out." Mrs. D is fated to have more than a hundred maids in her lifetime. The storyteller's suppressed rage sometimes seems directed at Mrs. D, for her assuming that she is entitled to have a maid. At other times it appears to be directed at the system, where some women are professors' wives with private incomes, and others, for lack of other life choices, have to go into domestic service. If, as the level of detail about Mrs. D's fashion sense and writing routine seems to confirm, the story is about Lydia Davis's mother, another layer of speculation emerges. In any case, the story reflects a simpler era, when potential maids were plentiful and could be hired for $20 a week.

"Cape Cod Diary," near the end of the book, is a refreshing blast of sea air after the morose self-examination of some of the other stories. The narrator is taking a solitary August vacation, but she ignores her internal states to concentrate on the sensory treats of beach, harbor, village, and stormy weather. Some snippets could adorn a travel brochure. Other passages document her occasional ventures into the social realm by attending parties or wandering into a church service. She still works during vacation, translating the work of a French historian, but despite some snags in this project, she maintains her bemused attitude of well-being. The reader glimpses a different Lydia Davis in this story, one not so haunted by the existential discomfort shown by many of her narrators. "Cape Cod Diary" may make even casual readers want to try more of Davis's works—it is that accessible.

This volume's fifty-odd stories show surprising diversity of form and style. They have in common an almost total concentration on domestic life, the world of words, and the small disturbances of head and heart. Within these boundaries the author creates little story gems, shot through with a unique bolt of perception.

*Emily Alward*

### Review Sources

*Booklist* 103, no. 17 (May 1, 2003): 71.
*Kirkus Reviews* 75, no. 6 (March 15, 2007): 242.
*Library Journal* 132, no. 7 (April 15, 2007): 80.
*New York* 40, no. 19 (May 28, 2007): 81.
*The New York Times Book Review* 156 (May 27, 2007): 25.
*Publishers Weekly* 254, no. 8 (February 19, 2007): 146.

# VICTORY OF THE WEST
## The Great Christian-Muslim Clash at the Battle of Lepanto

*Author:* Niccolò Capponi
*Publisher:* Da Capo Press (New York). Illustrated.
  412 pp. $27.50
*Type of work:* History
*Time:* 1571
*Locale:* The Mediterranean Sea

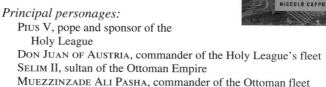

*Capponi presents a meticulously researched and brilliantly written account of the Battle of Lepanto, which saved the West from domination by the Ottoman Turkish Empire*

*Principal personages:*
> PIUS V, pope and sponsor of the
>   Holy League
> DON JUAN OF AUSTRIA, commander of the Holy League's fleet
> SELIM II, sultan of the Ottoman Empire
> MUEZZINZADE ALI PASHA, commander of the Ottoman fleet

The naval engagement fought near Lepanto (Návpaktos), Greece, in 1571 was a military rarity; it was a genuinely decisive battle. It marked a turning point in the long war between Islam and Christianity in the Mediterranean region. Up to this point, the triumphant jihad of the Ottoman Turkish sultans had carried all before them. After Lepanto, the tide would begin to turn. Though the Turks remained a formidable threat to Christian Europe, and as late as 1683 would be besieging Vienna, their empire slipped into a long decline. The power of the West grew rapidly as its fractious inhabitants embraced the Renaissance and Scientific Revolution. These intellectual revolutions laid the foundations of a global dominance that would last for four centuries. Indeed, it was the Europeans' employment of new technologies that made possible the great victory of Lepanto.

Niccolò Capponi, a distinguished Italian historian of the Renaissance, is well aware of the modern resonance of a history of this famous clash between the West and Islam. He makes a gentle allusion to the multicultural orthodoxies of present times in his preface. His title, *Victory of the West: The Great Christian-Muslim Clash at the Battle of Lepanto*, is a rebuke to such moral equivalence, but Capponi goes no farther than that. His work is a history, not a commentary on current events. What he gives his readers is an epic story of conflict and heroism. Capponi brings a novelistic flair for the dramatic to his work. This is a tale of men and their struggles, not a dry analysis of impersonal and hence inscrutable forces. Capponi reminds readers that the future of a civilization can hinge on the wisdom and courage of a very few people.

Context is all-important in history. Capponi devotes the first third of his book to describing the dangerous Mediterranean world of the sixteenth century. The great

*Niccolò Capponi is a distinguished Italian historian of the Renaissance. He is curator of the Capponi Archive. He lives in Florence, Italy.*

destabilizing power of the day was the aggressively militaristic Ottoman Turkish Empire. For centuries, the waning force of the ancient Byzantine Empire had held the Turks at bay, acting as a shield for medieval Europe. However, in 1453 the Turks breached the walls of Constantinople; the last Byzantine emperor died fighting. Soon the Turks were probing deep into the Balkans. Other Ottoman armies took control of Egypt and much of North Africa. Muslim corsairs harassed shipping and raided the exposed coastline of southern Europe for slaves. Under the great Sultan Süleyman the Magnificent, the Ottoman Empire reached the pinnacle of its glory. Süleyman hammered the Christians. He captured Rhodes from the crusading Knights of Saint John in 1522. Four years later, he invaded Hungary and killed the Hungarian king and most of his army at the Battle of Mohács. Süleyman ruled an empire that stretched from Hungary to Algiers. Europe was being encircled. Ottoman armies were within marching distance of its heart. Fortunately for the Europeans, wars with the Persians and internal disturbances kept Süleyman from concentrating all his forces on the west.

Ottoman expansionism was driven by a combination of religious zeal and economic necessity. The Turkish sultans arrogated to themselves the role of commanders of the faithful, associated with the traditional Islamic caliphate. By waging jihad against the infidel, they legitimized their claims to be the champions of Islam. The sultans also had pressing practical reasons to take lands from the Christians. Although elite units like the janissaries garnered the most attention from European observers, the bulk of the Turkish army was made up of horsemen who served the sultan in exchange for land. The feudal foundation of Ottoman military force constrained sultans to acquire new land with which to reward and maintain their troops. Thus, in the empire's heyday, ideological and financial imperatives kept the Ottoman military machine in perpetual motion.

In the face of the Ottoman juggernaut, Europe was divided politically and religiously. These differences kept the Europeans from uniting and effectively resisting the Ottomans. The kings of France battled first the Habsburgs of the Holy Roman Empire, then the Habsburgs of Spain. The French were even willing to ally with the Turks at the expense of their hereditary enemy. When the wars with France subsided, Philip II of Spain showed more interest in battling Protestant rebels in the Netherlands than Muslim enemies in the Mediterranean. Italy paid the price for being weak and became a prize in the rivalry between greater powers. Foreign armies beset the peninsula. In 1527, a Habsburg army sacked Rome itself. Religious hatreds born of the Reformation envenomed many of these wars. The history of the sixteenth century was darkened by the atrocities perpetrated by Catholics and Protestants upon each other.

A few Westerners kept up the fight against the Ottomans. The Knights of Saint John retained their old crusading fervor. In 1565, an Ottoman army besieged their new base at Malta. After a heroic defense, the knights broke the siege, inflicting grievous losses on the Turks. Also on the front line was the mercantile republic of Venice.

The Venetians would have preferred to trade with the Turks; Constantinople histori-cally had been a major entrepôt for their traders. Unfortunately, the sultans coveted Venetian outposts in the Aegean. In 1570, Sultan Selim II launched an assault on Cyprus, a Venetian possession that he believed posed a strategic threat to Ottoman shipping lanes. He assembled a massive fleet and army to take the island. Once Cyprus fell, he intended to push his conquests west. The Venetians resisted fiercely but were hard-pressed in an unequal combat. The threat to Cyprus and the prospect of a Turkish onslaught in the Mediterranean attracted the attention of the chanceller-ies of Europe, but councils were divided. Few had the stomach to challenge so dan-gerous a foe. The Venetians became the most vociferous Western advocates of taking the offensive against the Ottomans. They could not afford the deadly illusion of appeasement.

The Venetians found a formidable ally in Pope Pius V. An exemplary pontiff of the Counter-Reformation, Pius V was a saintly man, determined to root out the abuses that had divided the Church. He recognized that the reforms promulgated at the Coun-cil of Trent would mean nothing if the crescent rather than the cross flew over Rome. The pope threw himself into organizing a coalition to launch a counter-attack against the Turks. The pope's fervor, combined with the obvious danger posed by the Ottoman offensive, finally overcame diplomatic doubts. He became the ani-mating spirit of the Holy League, founded on May 25, 1571, composed of Spain, Venice, and a number of Italian states. This was a fragile alliance, with the participat-ing powers riven by deep-seated suspicions and conflicting goals. It would hold to-gether just long enough to justify the labors of Pius V.

The allies of the Holy League began gathering ships to relieve Cyprus. Because Spain was the leading Christian power, Philip II's illegitimate half-brother, Don Juan of Austria, was given command of the fleet. Don Juan was a dashing young man, imbued with chivalric ideals; he would prove to be a capable soldier. Unfortunately, it took time to equip and organize his forces. In the meantime, the Ottomans, alerted to the creation of the Holy League, responded vigorously. They gathered another large fleet and pressed the conquest of Cyprus. Stronghold after stronghold fell, amid scenes of carnage that shocked Europe. Last to surrender was the town of Famagusta. The defenders were massacred after their capitulation; the governor was tortured and then skinned alive. The savagery of these atrocities hardened the resolve of the Chris-tians. The Venetians vowed revenge.

Capponi provides his readers with a detailed description of the naval forces that clashed at Lepanto. The standard warship was the galley, a shallow draft, oar-driven ship that had dominated Mediterranean waters since antiquity. The galleys of the six-teenth century were equipped with cannon and complements of soldiers to engage in hand-to-hand fighting when the ships closed with an enemy. The Turks were famous for their skill with the sword and bow. The Christians countered this by providing their soldiers more body armor and firearms. The Christian ships also carried more artillery. Although outnumbered in ships at Lepanto, the Christian fleet had twice as many guns. The Venetians brought with them six galleasses. These were large mer-chant vessels converted into portable batteries. A typical galley might only carry three guns. A galleass could support more than ten times as many. The greater stability of the galleass allowed cannon to be fired in every direction, giving it deadly firepower in a sea fight.

The fleet of the Holy League reached the eastern Mediterranean in early October. It numbered around 240 ships. Facing it was an Ottoman fleet of 300 ships under Muezzinzade Ali Pasha. On October 7, the two fleets encountered each other off the Curzolaris islands on the Ionian coast of Greece. Muezzinzade Ali was confident of victory. The Ottoman fleet had dominated these seas for years. He knew that the Holy League was a fragile coalition. He was, however, concerned that the many Christian slaves rowing in the Turkish galleys might rebel; confident of acquiring many new slaves that day, he promised his Christian rowers their freedom. Despite this promise, during the battle many rose up anyway to aid their coreligionists.

Don Juan deployed his fleet into line. Ahead of his main force he placed the six Venetian galleasses. Muezzinzade Ali was puzzled by the exposed position of what looked like six transports. Reassured by prisoners that they possessed few guns, and anyway contemptuous of the Venetians after their many defeats, Muezzinzade Ali ordered his fleet to attack in the traditional crescent formation, expecting to encircle and overwhelm the Christians through force of numbers. The Ottoman fleet was a formidable sight as it advanced to the accompaniment of drums and horns. Muezzinzade Ali's galley flew a great banner on which the name of Allah was embroidered 29,800 times. When the Turkish armada came within range, the batteries on the galleasses opened up with devastating effect. The surviving Ottoman galleys increased speed to try to escape the Venetian's galling fire. Their formation was thrown into disorder. Despite this, the Turkish ships drove into the Christian line. What followed was a fierce melee. Capponi brilliantly evokes the close-quarters brutality of the fight. Here Miguel de Cervantes, the future author of *El ingenioso hidalgo don Quixote de la Mancha* (1605, 1615; *Don Quixote de la Mancha*, 1612-1620) had his left hand shattered by a Turkish bullet. Don Juan was in the thick of the fight and received a wound from a dagger. Muezzinzade Ali was killed, and his severed head was raised on a pike. In the end, Christian firepower proved decisive. The Ottoman fleet was shattered. Ninety Turkish galleys were sunk and 130 captured. 35,000 Turks were killed, wounded, or captured. Between 12,000 and 15,000 Christian slaves were liberated. The price of victory was steep; 7,650 Christians were killed and 7,800 were wounded.

On the afternoon of October 7, Pius V was talking to a group of officials. Suddenly the pope went to a window and looked out for a time. He turned back to the others and declared ecstatically: "It is no time for business. Let us go and thank God, for this very moment our fleet has defeated the Turks." The victory at Lepanto was worthy of the pope's miraculous vision. In the short run, the Ottomans would rebuild their fleet, and the Holy League would fall apart amid mutual recriminations. Nevertheless, the pope's joy was justified. Europe had been saved. The technological superiority displayed at Lepanto would grow only greater over the years. For good and ill, Europe's destiny would be its own to decide.

*Daniel P. Murphy*

## Review Sources

*Booklist* 103, no. 14 (March 15, 2007): 17.
*Journal of Military History* 72, no. 1 (January, 2008): 223-224.
*Kirkus Reviews* 75, no. 3 (February 1, 2007): 75.
*Military History* 24, no. 5 (July/August, 2007): 70-72.
*New Criterion* 25, no. 10 (June, 2007): 75-79.
*Publishers Weekly* 254, no. 9 (February 26, 2007): 76.

# THE WATER CURE

*Author:* Percival Everett (1956-    )
*Publisher:* Graywolf Press (St. Paul, Minn.).
    216 pp. $22.00
*Type of work:* Novel
*Time:* The early twenty-first century
*Locale:* Taos, New Mexico, and Southern California

*One man's exploration of sanity, rationality, humanity, and justice as he transforms himself from victim to assailant after he captures the monster that brutally murdered his eleven-year-old daughter*

*Principal characters:*
> ISHMAEL KIDDER, narrator, author,
>     and father of murdered Lane
> LANE, Ishmael and Charlotte's eleven-year-old daughter,
>     who is abducted from her mother's front yard
> CHARLOTTE, Ishmael's ex-wife and Lane's mother
> CHARLEY, Charlotte's boyfriend
> REGGIE, Lane's murderer and Ishmael's captive
> SALLY LOVELY, Ishmael's agent, who attempts to save
>     not only his writing career but also Ishmael himself
> ESTELLE GILLIAM, Ishmael's pseudonym
> BUCKY PAZ, Taos sheriff

In a nonlinear novel that asks what circumstances could push a law-abiding citizen to become a criminal captor and torturer, Percival Everett's *The Water Cure* explores one father's quest to avenge his daughter's murder and to bring sanity into his suddenly insane life. Ishmael Kidder's eleven-year-old daughter Lane's body is discovered in a park by two schoolboys after she had been missing for two days. One minute Lane was standing on her mother's lawn playing with her bike, and the next minute she vanished from her parents' lives forever. The totality and the quickness of the act, as well as the fact that no one saw anything, causes a grieving father to contemplate: "And so a longstanding philosophical question was answered for me: if your child screams in the forest and there is no one around to hear, does she make a sound? It turns out she does not."

Lane's premature and brutal death elicits unquenchable desires for revenge. Lane's rapist and murderer is apprehended, but he is released after questioning and later captured by Ishmael, who follows him out of the police station. The capture allows Ishmael to have his revenge, to which he confesses, "I am guilty not because of my actions, to which I freely admit, but for my accession, admission, confession that I executed these actions with not only deliberation and premeditation but with zeal and paroxysm and purpose, above all else purpose, that I clearly articulate without apology or qualification." So opens *The Water Cure*, setting the pace for a thrilling

and hypercerebral novel that explores uncon-
ditional love and hate, motivations for revenge, human thought processes, and the fundamental factors that determine one's actions
and communication.

The protagonist's life has changed against
his will, both through the death of his daughter and through the capture of her assailant,
whom Ishmael refers to as Reggie or W. Ishmael no longer defines himself by the life he
created for himself and his family but rather
by determining the fate of the prisoner in his
basement. Although he wishes that the man
tied to a board in his house meant nothing to
him, he reluctantly admits, "You are also,
sadly, importantly, necessarily . . . the existential proof of the sincerity of my so-called
convictions, among other things. I believe it
is true, and this might be one of the ills of
our culture, that no judge among us really has
the courage of his convictions." As Ishmael
slowly tortures Reggie mentally and physically, Ishmael changes from victim to perpe-
trator and transforms Reggie as well: "You

*Percival Everett has written more than
twenty novels and poetry collections.
He has received the PEN Center USA
Award for Fiction, the Academy Award
in literature from the American
Academy of Arts and Letters, and the
Hurston/Wright Legacy Award for
Fiction. He published his first novel,
Suder (1983), while pursuing his
M.F.A. at Brown University. Everett is
a distinguished professor of English at
the University of Southern California.*

were the sinner, but now you are the punished, someone new altogether. The question
is, are you the same man?" The question can also be posed to Ishmael himself,
although the reader might ask if there is any man left in Ishmael at all.

Ishmael, in fact, has lost all sense of self, for his former self died with his daughter.
He lives alone in Taos, New Mexico, after divorcing his wife, Charlotte. He trusts no
one, to the extent of bringing his own food to restaurants. Ishmael supports himself
through the publication of romance novels under the pseudonym of Estelle Gilliam,
further removing Ishmael from reality, but knows that "I simply am of course who
I am, Ishmael Kidder, but I am better known as Estelle Gilliam, the romance novelist." His agent, Sally Lovely, the closest semblance of a friend he has, visits Ishmael
to review his writing (which has ceased) and to check on his well-being. She hears
noises emanating from the basement that Ishmael passes off as the normal sounds old
houses make. Satisfied, but still concerned for him, Sally leaves, and Ishmael is once
again alone.

Of course, Ishmael is far from lonely. In addition to Estelle, his alter ego, and his
captive in the basement, Ishmael has marijuana-induced conversations throughout
the book with historical figures such as Benjamin Franklin, Socrates, Aristotle, and
Samuel Beckett. Through these conversations, Everett sheds light on the motivating
factors and beliefs that Ishmael relies upon to justify his actions, be they religious,
cultural, moral, or legal. In one such conversation with Benjamin Franklin, Franklin

asks Ishmael if he intends to kill his victim, and if so, does he approve of cruel and un-usual punishment, to which Ishmael replies, "I suppose I'd have to know first what is not *cruel* and what is *usual*. If *not* cruel is *kind*, then is it in fact punishment? And it seems to me that *kind* punishment sounds a bit *unusual*," giving the reader insight into the logic of the protagonist and the wordsmith talents of Everett.

At times, Everett reveals a tender, human side to Ishmael in between his bouts with insanity and his moments of torture. It is the tenderness and introspection of his char-acter, the relentless torture Ishmael lives under, that is revealed when he laments, "Daily, I slice away at my love for my daughter, at my guilt for surviving, at my re-solve for revenge and slice away at merely myself, and it remains painfully obvious that I'm all still here, always big enough to be cut a million more times. And so, no matter how small I become I remain infinitely, miserably, painfully, laughably, eter-nally, and interminably large." The passage reminds the reader what horrific events have shaped the protagonist, having lived through something no one should ever have to face. He remarks that survivors, no matter what they have endured, always have to battle to survive, and feel the guilt of doing so. Survivors must work to make it through every day while "the dead are still dead. No matter who lives or dies, the dead remain dead. That is all the dead have to do, all that is required of them, to stay that way." Ishmael learned of life through his daughter's death even though "she had been too young to truly imagine death, too young to have understood enough of life to cherish it, but old enough to have taught me to do so." Throughout *The Water Cure*, Everett cryptically shares Ishmael's revelations on life, what defines a person, and what motivates his or her actions.

Everett displays Ishmael's mental anguish and grief not only through his thoughts and speech but also through the very letters and type he employs. In an E. E. Cum-mings fashion, Everett plays with words, their meanings, and their physical structure, misspelling them, repeating certain letters, spelling words phonetically, and finally deconstructing language down to its basic elements and turning it into random strings of characters. The grammar and syntax cause confusion and frustrate the reader at times as the chapters become increasingly difficult, and at times impossible, to deci-pher. As this linguistic confusion grows, Ishmael's insanity also increases, allowing the reader to experience his mental breakdown through a schizophrenic writing style. Everett jumps from one chapter (consisting of a few paragraphs) describing memories of Lane, to another chapter that describes the torture being inflicted on her murderer, to another chapter in which Ishmael is within a philosophical debate with Aristotle, to another chapter where Everett spells all words phonetically, making it difficult for the reader to decipher the intended meaning at times, to another chapter in which Everett literally strikes random keys with no hope of construing any words or meaning what-soever. The constant jumping from style to style is hard on the reader and at times takes away from the overall cohesiveness of the novel.

In the few moments of clarity sprinkled throughout the novel, Everett expresses his discontent with the George W. Bush administration as the narrator openly exam-ines the administration and its influence on American culture and society, claiming that the United States has become an amoral, unquestioning, and bloodthirsty, revenge-driven country. Everett uses Ishmael, a law-abiding citizen turned torturer, as a symbol of what American society as a whole has devolved into and how the world sees this society. Ishmael takes the method of torture he inflicts upon his prisoner from one of the torture methods the Central Intelligence Agency condoned at Guantánamo Bay, Cuba—the water cure, or waterboarding.

> The practice of waterboarding was once referred to as the water cure. The subject is bound (as in *tied up* not *headed for*) in my case with duct tape . . . to a board . . . with his head positioned lower in elevation than his feet, taped up tight so that he cannot move and then a rag . . . is tied tightly over his face, and then water is slowly poured onto the cloth. The subject, I prefer the term *victim*, has trouble breathing and becomes fearful . . . that he will drown, that he will die of asphyxiation.

Ishmael justifies his torture by claiming to be patriotic, claiming that Americans have all become war-loving, pain-inducing, and vengeful for personal reasons or no reason at all. Everett takes a bold and controversial position, as Ishmael questions the difference between his child's murderer and a United States soldier, "Not a popular thing to say, but they are trained killers. Just because they are our young men doesn't make them good young men, not down to a man, not every single man. After all, they have chosen to carry guns."

While Everett makes extremely insightful glimpses into grammar and linguistics—as well as into the effect the Bush administration has had on the American psyche and international image—the lack of structure within certain passages, and the attacks toward, and disregard of, the reader, at times detracts from the novel on the whole. Everett sums up his novel when he writes,

> The words on these pages are not the story. The words on these pages are not this story. The words on these pages are the words on these pages, not more, not less, simply the words on these pages, one after the another, one at the beginning and one at the end, bearing possibly some but probably no relation to each other, but they can, if you desire to find a connection, need to, or if it irresistibly, axiomatically, ineluctably reveals itself to you.

Everett places a tremendous responsibility on readers not only to comprehend but also to construct the story themselves. Basic foundations and clues are laid down, but the reader must construe the story, its past and future, from an almost nonexistent plot.

*Sara Vidar*

## Review Sources

*Booklist* 104, no. 1 (September 1, 2007): 57.
*Kirkus Reviews* 75, no. 14 (July 15, 2007): 683.
*Library Journal* 132, no. 16 (October 1, 2007): 58-59.
*Los Angeles Times*, September 16, 2007, p. R6.
*San Francisco Chronicle*, September 16, 2007, p. M1.
*The Washington Post*, August 26, 2007, p. BW04.

# THE WELSH GIRL

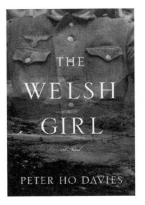

*Author:* Peter Ho Davies (1966-     )
*Publisher:* Houghton Mifflin (New York). 338 pp.
    $24.00
*Type of work:* Novel
*Time:* The final months of World War II, 1944-1945,
    notably D day
*Locale:* Mostly Cilgwyn, a village in North Wales

*A first novel by Davies chronicling the wartime conver-*
*gence of three young people: a sheep farmer's seventeen-*
*year-old daughter who must live a devastating lie, a Ger-*
*man POW who falls in love with her, and an Anglicized*
*German Jew, an interrogator assigned to break through*
*Rudolf Hess*

*Principal characters:*
    ESTHER EVANS, the seventeen-year-old girl of the title,
        a part-time barmaid who longs for a larger world
    ARTHUR EVANS, Esther's fiercely nationalistic father,
        a sheep farmer, opposed to the war
    KARSTEN SIMMERING, a guilt-ridden, eighteen-year-old
        German POW perilously involved with Esther
    ROTHERAM, a half-Jewish German who works as British
        interrogator of Rudolf Hess and Karsten
    RHYS ROBERTS, Esther's childhood friend; Cilgwyn's only war casualty
    JIM, an intelligent, young evacuee for whom Esther is caretaker
    RUDOLF HESS, a real-life former deputy to Adolf Hitler who fled
        Germany in 1941, landing in Scotland, perhaps in a botched
        attempt to negotiate peace with Britain; held in a Welsh safe house
        and interrogated by Rotheram in the novel's prologue and epilogue

    A good case could be made for regarding World War II as anchored to temporal
chronology, and yet, by the larger-than-life emergence of its leaders and campaigns,
the war resists boundaries. The archive is inexhaustible, the tide of Holocaust memory alone, oceanic. In astonishing ways, such cataclysmic events change not only history but also the geography of individual minds.
    As World War II recedes in time and its survivors dwindle, patriotic movies like
*The Longest Day* (1962) and *They Were Expendable* (1945) seek to keep alive Tom
Brokaw's "Greatest Generation," reminding viewers and readers how hallowed—and
halo-ed—the "good war" was compared to any since. The novelists who chronicled
that war—such as Norman Mailer, Irwin Shaw, and James Jones—left a distinguished legacy. In recent years, several novelists not alive in the 1940's are reviving,
reinventing, and (most crucially of all) rescuing World War II from the overlay of history. Peter Ho Davies is one such writer. *The Welsh Girl* is his first novel. Davies,

born in Wales of a Welsh father and a Malaysian Chinese mother some two decades after the war, is not interested in the conflict itself. Although he sets *The Welsh Girl* in the region of North Wales called Snowdonia during the time of the Allied landings in Normandy and employs military artifacts and at least one historical figure from the war, he is much more concerned with the split between local and national identities, between personal history and history itself as it plays out on the world stage.

∽

*Peter Ho Davies, hailed as one of* Granta*'s "Best of Young British Novelists," is the author of two award-winning short-story collections:* The Ugliest House in the World *(1997) won the* John Llewellyn Rhys Prize *and the* PEN/Macmillan Award *in Britain, and* Equal Love *(2000) was a* New York Times *Notable Book. Davies lives in Ann Arbor, Michigan, where he teaches in the graduate program in creative writing at the University of Michigan.*

∽

For his debut novel, Davies utilizes a convention of stories from Geoffrey Chaucer's *The Canterbury Tales* (1387-1400) to Sebastian Brant's *Das Narren Schyff* (1494; *Ship of Fools*) and Terence Rattigan's *Separate Tables* (pr. 1954)—a fixed arena in which persons who would not ordinarily meet can be gathered together: an ocean liner, an inn, or, as here, a prison camp. The author chose Cilgwyn, a hamlet in North Wales—not only because young evacuees from London, for safety's sake, have been interned there but also because the town has lately been filled with sappers, English soldiers who are building a mysterious new camp against the hillside. Germans who surrendered during the invasion will be imprisoned there. Esther Evans, the seventeen-year-old title character, lives on a farm with her father, Arthur. He, in common with most of the townspeople, is passionately opposed to "Churchill's war." He looks no further than his sheep for a guiding philosophy—*cynefin*, a Welsh term embracing his flock's unerring sense of where they belong, their home turf. It is a word for which, he boasts to the recalcitrant Esther, the empire-building British have no equivalent. "But how do the new-born know?" she asks her father after her mother's early passing. "The males teach each other," he replies. Esther knows the wethers (males) are sold for meat each year. Whatever was passed down—however *cynefin* was preserved—she knows it had to be from mother to daughter.

*Cynefin* becomes Davies's dominant metaphor. This is not so dramatic until the second half when the other two young protagonists—Karsten Simmering, an eighteen-year-old German prisoner of war (POW), and Rotheram, a half-Jewish German émigré, now a bilingual captain of British intelligence, cross paths in Cilgwyn. The three young people are forever trying to fathom where they belong. Esther is not content to sit out—or, more accurately, since she is a barmaid—to stand out the war and life. She inclines to a young soldier wearing the uniform her father hates. Karsten is guilt-ridden because he, the only English-speaking soldier in his outfit, was spokesman for its surrender. Accused of cowardice by his fellow prisoners, he had given up to save the life of a terrified underage boy in his unit.

Rotheram, the most shadowy of the three, is difficult to formulate. He will occupy center stage before either of the others, in a prologue whose main goal may be to connect the reader with World War II via one of its unsolved mysteries, the strange odyssey of a henchman of Adolf Hitler named Rudolf Hess, who in 1941 landed a plane in Scotland in what may have been a botched try to negotiate peace. Readers find him late in the war confined in a Welsh safe house, being interrogated by Rotheram in hopes of learning whether the ex-Nazi is fit to stand trial with Hermann Göring, Heinrich Himmler, and others at Nuremberg.

Esther is a part-time barmaid at the Quarryman's Arms, one of the two pubs in her small, proud, nationalist village. As much as her father and his cronies deplore the English army, Esther does not care. If she cannot see the world, she will settle for the world coming to her. She secretly steps out with a handsome sapper named Colin, who rapes her. She becomes pregnant, and Colin leaves when he and his buddies have built the POW camp. At this point, Karsten enters the story. As Esther guards her secret, even from her father, as long as she can, Karsten endures an enforced indolence that gives him too much time to mull over the unheroic surrender. Karsten finds some inner peace in memories of his innocent Bavarian childhood; in the construction of toy airplanes and ships in bottles for the local youths who come to the camp gates every night to jeer; and in the arms of Esther—a sublime experience for both. He can forget the French whore he bedded during a leave in Paris, his erotic dreams often coalescing into the face of his mother. Esther will invent a relationship with Rhys Roberts, a boy she knew who has become the village's only war casualty. Only her confidant-lover Karsten knows who the father is.

The romance between Karsten and Esther is predictable from the moment they lay eyes on each other through the prison-camp fence. That it takes Davies half the novel to affirm a foregone conclusion may doom the book with some of the same readers who gave up on another extraordinary World War II novel, Michael Ondaatje's *The English Patient* (1992), but adored the Oscar-winning film version.

As the novel's chapters alternate between Esther and Karsten, the barbed wire that separates the prisoner inside the camp from the woman inside her tyrannical father's home becomes, as one reviewer puts it, "metaphor-thin." Of course, Karsten escapes, and the two come face to face. After hiding out in Esther's father's barn for a few days, eating food she prepares for him, Karsten decides to give himself up and is returned to camp. While the two have been lovers, Esther's emotions are mixed, but, with a baby on the way, she is mostly relieved.

What are readers to make of Hess, who was spared at Nuremberg and whom, fictively, Davies exploits as both a "reference" character and as a buffer for his interrogator's—for Rotheram's—conflicted sense of his Jewish side? The reader first encounters him in a private, smoke-filled room, hounded by British intelligence officers, being forced to watch footage of himself ranting at a Nazi rally. Among the group is Rotheram, who studies Hess's blank face in the light refracted from the film screen for a giveaway sign of complicity in the so-called final solution.

Writing in London's *New Statesman*, Sebastian Harcombe cogently finds the Hess-Rotheram prologue "an appropriate entrée into a novel whose focus is unstintingly microscopic, whose prevailing preoccupation is the way in which obligations to family, community and country shape one's sense of identity, honour, destiny, and personal purpose." It is through Rotheram, in the book's twenty-three-page epilogue, that the reader learns the fate of all the characters, including Esther's baby. It would not be appropriate to disclose their postwar fortunes except to say they are good. The reader even follows Hess to his cell in West Berlin's Spandau Prison, where he hanged himself in 1987 at age ninety-three, a puzzle to the end.

*Richard Hauer Costa*

## Review Sources

*Booklist* 103, no. 6 (November 15, 2006): 6.
*The Boston Globe*, February 11, 2007, p. E4.
*The Daily Telegraph*, May 26, 2007, p. 26.
*The Guardian*, May 5, 2007, p. 16.
*London Review of Books* 29, no. 10 (May 24, 2007): 25.
*Los Angeles Times*, February 11, 2007, p. R9.
*The New York Times Book Review* 156 (February 18, 2007): 10.
*Newsday*, February 11, 2007, p. C30.
*Publishers Weekly* 253, no. 42 (October 23, 2006): 27-28.

# WHAT HATH GOD WROUGHT
## The Transformation of America, 1815-1848

*Author:* Daniel Walker Howe (1937-    )
*Publisher:* Oxford University Press (New York).
  904 pp. $35.00
*Type of work:* History
*Time:* 1815-1848
*Locale:* The United States

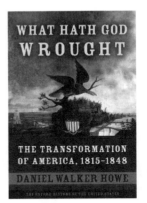

*A comprehensive narrative account of the United States from the end of the War of 1812 until the end of the Mexican War, with a good balance among political, military, cultural, technological, and economic components*

When Samuel F. B. Morse demonstrated his invention of an electric telegraph in 1844, his famous message, "What hath God wrought," expressed the attitude, quite common at the time, that divine providence was responsible for the nation's territorial expansion as well as its technological and scientific developments. When later transcribing the message, Morse added a question mark, which unintentionally changed the affirmation of a providential faith into a question about whether the United States was a divine blessing to humanity. Daniel Walker Howe explains that he uses Morse's statement without out punctuation in his book's title because he "seeks both to affirm and to question the value of what Americans of that period did." While emphasizing the theme of economic and social progress, he also recognizes that "American history between 1815 and 1848 certainly had its dark side: poverty, demagogy, disregard for legal restraints, the perpetuation and expansion of slavery, the dispossession of the Native Americans, and the waging of aggressive war against Mexico."

*What Hath God Wrought* is the most recent addition to the prestigious series The Oxford History of the United States and winner of the 2008 Pulitzer Prize in history. Another historian, Charles Sellers, had earlier been commissioned to write the book for the period, but Sellers's work, which was published in 1991 under the title *The Market Revolution: Jacksonian America, 1815-1846*, was rejected by the late C. Vann Woodward, the series editor at the time, reportedly because of its lack of balance and controversial point of view. According to Sellers, the United States during this period changed profoundly from an agrarian to a capitalistic society, which benefited a small capitalistic class to the detriment of the working-class majority. Rejecting Sellers's influential "market revolution" thesis, Howe concludes that the weight of historical evidence shows that an active market economy already existed in the eighteenth century. He further argues that the early nineteenth century was first and foremost a period of technological revolutions in communications, transportation, manufacturing, and farming, just as most contemporaries recognized at the time.

Sellers and Howe have fundamentally different views about the developing capitalism of the period. Whereas the former emphasizes its costs and inequalities, Howe tends to focus on its benefits and efficiencies. Sellers holds that the majority of Americans living in the agrarian society of the preceding century were happier and better off than those living in the more modern, urbane society of the nineteenth century. In contrast, Howe sees evidence of real progress and improving conditions—a glass that was at least half full.

*Daniel Walker Howe is professor of history emeritus at both Oxford University and the University of California, Los Angeles. His previous books include* Unitarian Conscious: Harvard Moral Philosophy, 1805-1861 *(1970),* The Political Culture of the American Whigs *(1984), and* Making the American Self: Jonathan Edwards to Abraham Lincoln *(1997).*

As a result of the Industrial Revolution, commodities became cheaper and more accessible to the average person. A mattress that sold for fifty dollars in 1815, for instance, was selling for five dollars thirty years later. Although uncertain about whether the disparity between the rich and the poor increased during these decades, he writes that if inequality did grow, it was likely caused primarily by the arrival of large numbers of poor immigrants. Acknowledging that workers resented the inequality that existed, he finds that the small scale of antebellum manufacturing permitted many opportunities for social mobility and "thus blurred the line between capitalist and working classes."

Looking upon technological innovations as the motor force behind most historical changes, Howe discusses the efforts and accomplishments of many innovators, including Eli Whitney's interchangeable parts, Cyrus McCormick's reaper, John Deere's steel plough, and Peter Cooper's improved locomotive. Howe's treatment of the communications and transportation revolutions goes far beyond the information to be found in most historical syntheses. The building of turnpikes was of considerable significance, even though they were slow, undependable, and often called "shun-pikes" because of the ease of avoiding the tollbooths. Steamboats provided a dependable way of traveling against the current on powerful rivers like the Mississippi, although they were quite dangerous, with forty-two exploding boilers killing 273 people between 1825 and 1830. The completion of the Erie Canal in 1825 allowed New York to become the "Empire State," with the number of ships in New York harbor growing at least 500 percent from 1820 to 1850. Railroads, beginning with the B & O Railroad in 1828, had an even greater impact. By end of 1830, there were 450 locomotives and 3,200 miles of track, twice the number as in Europe. Ten years later, the United States had 7,500 miles of track. Before railroads, it took Henry Clay three weeks to travel from Kentucky to Washington, D.C., whereas he could make the trip in four days by 1846. Howe writes: "If the railroads did not initiate the industrial revolution, they certainly speeded it up."

Despite the numerous technological and social changes of the period, Howe observes that living standards remained quite low. As in previous centuries, it was difficult to earn a living wage, and agriculture continued to be the sources of livelihood for the vast majority of Americans. Howe summarizes: "Life in America in

1815 was dirty, smelly, laborious, and uncomfortable. People spent most of their waking hours working, with scant opportunity for the development of individual talents and interests unrelated to farming."

Many historians have focused on the extent to which representative democracy, particularly the right to vote, was expanded during the period. Howe argues that this thesis has been greatly exaggerated. The great majority of white males in most states (outside of South Carolina) had already been granted the legal right to vote before 1815. While it is true that the popular vote tripled in size from 1824 to 1828, this was primarily because of heightened public interest and organized efforts to turn out the voters. Howe concedes, nevertheless, that many states were still in the process of removing the few remaining property qualifications and that the period saw a new development, "the emergence of mass political parties offering rival programs for the electorate to choose." Increasingly, the majority of Americans perceived their country as a democracy that offered an example for the rest of the world.

Howe does not hesitate to express moral judgments about particular individuals and their deeds. When discussing President Andrew Jackson, he is particularly critical of Jackson's strong support for slavery and his policy of coercing the "five civilized tribes" to move west of the Mississippi River. Rather than referring to Jackson as the candidate of the "common man," he suggests that Jackson is more accurately called the candidate of the white man. Despite being a lawyer, moreover, Jackson "did not manifest a general respect for the authority of the law when it got in the way of the policies he chose to pursue." However, in contrast to some left-wing historians, Howe does not automatically make an unfavorable analysis of all "dead white males." He believes that John Quincy Adams, for instance, was a man of integrity and noble principles, even writing that Adams's "intellectual ability and courage were above reproach, and his wisdom in perceiving the national interest has stood the test of time."

Since many of Howe's previous publications have been devoted to the field of intellectual history, it is not surprising that *What Hath God Wrought* contains a wealth of material about the beliefs, ideas, and publications of the period. Chapter 5, titled "Awakenings of Religion," deals with the revival that is commonly called the Second Great Awakening, with in-depth discussions of emotional preachers like Charles G. Finney and theologians like Nathaniel William Taylor. Chapter 8, "Pursuing the Millennium," provides fascinating information about utopian projects, both religious and secular, including William Miller's prediction of the world's end, Robert Owen's brand of socialism in Indiana, Joseph Smith's establishment of Mormonism, and John H. Noyes's founding of a free-love community. Chapter 16, "American Renaissance," is an excellent account of literary and philosophical giants, such as Ralph Waldo Emerson, Henry David Thoreau, Nathaniel Hawthorne, and Henry Wadsworth Longfellow.

Taking a critical perspective of westward expansion under the doctrine of manifest destiny, Howe does not hesitate to utilize the label of "imperialism," and he asserts that the movement "derived from the domination and exploitation of the North Amer-

ican continent by the white people of the United States and their government."
The emergence of an American empire did not occur spontaneously, but "like all
empires, the American one required conscious deliberation and energetic government
action to bring it into being." Despite his critical stance, Howe maintains as much
objectivity as possible in attempting to tell what happened. It would be difficult to
find more interesting accounts of the Lone Star Revolution in Texas, James K.
Polk's strategies, and the Mexican War. Other notable topics in Howe's richly
textured book include Jackson's victory of New Orleans in 1815, the Missouri Com-
promise, the "Bank War" between Jackson and Henry Clay, the emergence of the
Whig and Republican Parties, the Supreme Court under John Marshall's leadership,
and the challenges of Irish immigrants. Rather than making a dichotomy between
social history and the study of elites, Howe holds that the transformation of America
was the result of the decisions and actions of both the common people and their leaders. He observes: "History is made both from the bottom up and from the top
down, and historians must take account of both in telling their stories."

*What Hath God Wrought* concludes with a discussion of the exceptionally large
number of revolutionary events that occurred in 1848. Conservatives and liberals
reacted differently to the democratic and nationalist uprising taking place in Europe
that year. Howe goes into great detail about the frustrating work of American diplomat Nicholas Trist in negotiating the Treaty of Guadalupe Hidalgo, which ended
the war with Mexico. Just after John Quincy Adams voted against expressions of
appreciation for the generals who fought the war, he lost consciousness and expired.
Within a few months of the discovery of gold in California, people began streaming
into the area hoping to make their fortunes, thereby making it almost impossible
for California to become a slave state. The election of 1848 was the first time that
all the states in the country chose their electors on the same day. Still, the year's
most momentous revolution for the future was the holding of the world's first feminist convention in Seneca Falls, New York, which resulted in the influential Declaration of Sentiments, asserting that men and women were created equally.

As a work of synthesis, Howe's historical sources appropriately consist almost
entirely of published works. His copious footnotes make it clear that he has been reading and thinking about the period for many years. He utilizes his impressive knowledge of modern scholarship to describe and explain the trends and developments
that were establishing a distinctive national identity during this age of transformation.
The book concludes with a twenty-page bibliography essay that includes succinct
commentary about the immense body of historical writings available for further
study.

Even though *What Hath God Wrought* is filled with stimulating interpretations,
Howe's primary goal is to present a balanced narrative of the events, controversies,
ideas, and achievements of the period. He writes that his book "tells a story; it
does not argue a thesis." Unlike some contemporary historians, he clearly appreciates
the value of narration, and he is a skillful storyteller who knows how to choose
relevant anecdotes and revealing quotations. Both general readers and professional
historians can benefit from this large book of nine hundred pages. It can be read

with pleasure from cover to cover, and it also provides an excellent reference for looking up concise but rather detailed historical information that cannot be found in standard textbooks and encyclopedias.

*Thomas Tandy Lewis*

## Review Sources

*The Atlantic Monthly* 300, no. 5 (December, 2007): 114-115.
*Library Journal* 132, no. 8 (November 1, 2007): 83.
*The New Yorker* 83, no. 33 (October 29, 2007): 88-92.
*Publishers Weekly* 254, no. 25 (June 18, 2007): 45.

# WHAT THE DEAD KNOW

*Author:* Laura Lippman (1959-    )
*Publisher:* William Morrow (New York). 376 pp. $24.95
*Type of work:* Novel
*Time:* The early twenty-first century
*Locale:* Baltimore

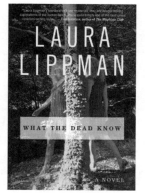

*Thirty years after two adolescent sisters mysteriously disappeared from a Baltimore mall, a woman stopped by police following a hit-and-run accident on the Baltimore Beltway claims to be one of them*

*Principal characters:*
HEATHER BETHANY, a fortysomething
woman
SUNNY BETHANY, her older sister
KEVIN INFANTE, a Baltimore police officer
NANCY PORTER, Infante's coworker
KAY SULLIVAN, a social worker
GLORIA BUSTAMANTE, a high-powered defense attorney
CHET WILLOUGHBY, the original police detective assigned
to the Bethany sisters' case
DAVE BETHANY, the girls' father
MIRIAM TOLES BETHANY, the girls' mother
SERGEANT LENHARDT, Infante's superior
STAN DUNHAM, a former Baltimore police officer and the
girls' alleged abductor
TONY DUNHAM, Stan's son
PENELOPE JACKSON, the owner of the car Heather was
driving at the time of the accident

The first of Laura Lippman's some dozen novels to make *The New York Times* best seller list, *What the Dead Know* is an intriguing mystery centered on the disappearance thirty years earlier of two sisters from a Baltimore mall. Sunny and Heather Bethany, aged fifteen and eleven, took the city bus on March 29, 1975, to Security Square Mall, where they were going to shop for a few hours, then be picked up by their father, Dave—except that they were never seen again.

The novel starts in the present day, as a woman driving a car on the Baltimore Beltway hits an oil patch on the road and causes another car to lose control. As the woman attempts to leave the scene, she is stopped by a police officer. He questions her, but she is injured and apparently disoriented. The car she is driving is registered to a Penelope Jackson of South Carolina, but the woman denies being Penelope. She eventually blurts out that she is one of the Bethany girls—and so the story begins.

The author swerves back and forth between past and present, feeding the reader details—but Lippman chooses what to tell, and when. The woman claims to be the younger sister, Heather, who was within a week of her twelfth birthday when she disappeared, but she has no identification and admits that she has assumed many names over the last three decades. She will not provide the one she currently uses, as she has finally achieved a stable career and does not want to endanger it. Because of the possibility that she may be one of the missing girls in a case that was never solved, she avoids jail and instead is placed in the care of a social worker, Kay Sullivan. Kay introduces her to a high-powered defense attorney, Gloria Bustamante, who agrees to take her case.

~

*Laura Lippman worked as a newspaper reporter for twenty years and has won numerous major mystery awards, including the Gumshoe Award for Best Novel for* To the Power of Three *(2005), the Anthony and Barry Awards for* Every Secret Thing *(2003), and the Nero Wolfe Award for* The Sugar House *(2000).*

~

The mystery woman is hesitant to talk, however, only giving out bits and pieces of information over the next few days, most of which lead nowhere. She claims that a former Baltimore police officer named Stan Dunham abducted the girls from the mall and that he killed Sunny but kept Heather in his Pennsylvania home, sexually abusing her until she turned eighteen. At that point, she says, he put her on a bus and sent her away. Since then, she has roamed from one place to the next, assuming new names and new identities along the way.

Stan Dunham is now senile and living in a nursing home. His wife is dead, as is his only son, Tony. Their house is gone, sold to developers, and so is Sunny's grave, which Heather claims was on the property. In addition, the girls' father, Dave, is dead, and their mother, Miriam, has left the country. Penelope Jackson, owner of the car involved in the accident and who, as it turns out, had been living with Tony Dunham, has disappeared. Hence, police officer Kevin Infante keeps running up against brick walls in his investigation. Even the original investigating officer, Chet Willoughby, now retired, is unable to shed any additional light. Instead, he shoots down Infante's hope of finally resolving the woman's identity with DNA testing when the girls' mother is located in Mexico: Chet reveals that he had removed a vital piece of information from the case files years ago in deference to Dave—that the girls were, in fact, adopted.

Lippman has done a masterful job of telling this story. Her omniscient narrator takes the reader inside the minds of the characters as well as into the past. As Heather slowly yields information, what she says has the ring of truth, yet there are moments that raise red flags for Infante—and the reader. Lippman drops hints suggesting that not all is as straightforward as it seems: Early on, the woman admits to herself that the tricky part of being Heather was "not knowing what she should know but remembering what she *wouldn't* know." When the police ask whether she saw anyone she knew at the mall that day, Heather says no. The police know that Sunny's music teacher was playing the organ at the mall's music store that day, and he claimed he saw her watch him perform. In addition, he claimed that a man grabbed Heather from behind and spoke to her angrily, but upon seeing her face, appeared to realize he had made a mistake and subsequently left. Heather makes no mention of any of this. Also, Heather had had a large sum of money saved that was gone from her room when the police searched it, yet when asked what she had taken to the mall, the woman says only a small amount of cash. She did, however, describe Heather's purse, found empty in the parking lot after the abduction, to perfection.

After starting off in the present day, the author cuts back to the day of the girls' disappearance, depicting a very ordinary morning with their dad making pancakes for breakfast and singing along to the songs on the radio. Sunny's petulance at having to take Heather with her to the mall that day seems true to form. Heather both adores her older sister and drives her crazy by following her around, sneaking into her room, and reading her diary—a fairly common sisterly dynamic. Sunny feels put upon by her father's insistence that she take Heather with her that day—and the reader sees their interaction as they take the bus together. The seemingly innocent events of that day at the mall, as fed to the reader in flashback, turn out to hold the secret to the girls' disappearance.

Lippman has established herself as a mystery writer over the last ten years with her series of Tess Monaghan books—Tess being a former newspaper reporter turned private detective. Lippman herself was a reporter for *The Baltimore Sun* for twelve years. She alludes in the narrative to several real-life child abduction cases and even mentions in an author's note that this story was inspired by the real abduction of two teenage sisters from Wheaton Plaza in 1975, although any resemblance to that case ends there. *What the Dead Know* is one of the author's several stand-alone mysteries, although several of its secondary characters have appeared before in her other novels, such as Kevin Infante, Sergeant Lenhardt, Nancy Porter, and Gloria Bustamante.

Throughout the novel, the author strings the reader along just as Heather does the police. The reader instinctively dislikes the protagonist from the moment she causes the accident and drives away. She cannot (or will not) produce identification; she weasels her way out of jail time, finagles herself into the private home of a kindly social worker, then sneaks onto the social worker's computer. She deceives the well-meaning officials who are all trying to help her. Still, the reader is intrigued by her at the same time. She obviously has been abused, her concern for the child she injured in the accident seems genuine, and she appears to be honestly afraid of something or someone. She plays the victim well, but she is also conniving and devious.

The reader constantly questions what this woman stands to gain by claiming to be Heather Bethany. Her family has disintegrated; there is no money, no property. She may be simply trying to avoid facing charges in the hit-and-run accident, yet she knows so much about the 1975 case. She provides so much detail about the day of the girls' disappearance: how Sunny tried to lose her at the mall, bought a ticket for *Escape to Witch Mountain* but snuck into the R-rated *Chinatown* instead, and then refused to buy Heather the Karmelcorn she promised when Heather spoils the day by sneaking into *Chinatown* after Sunny. Her claim to be Heather seems genuine, yet she also seems to give an inordinate amount of thought to playing the part.

The reader does not question Heather's allusion to sexual abuse by her captor—after all, what other reason could there be to kidnap two young girls from a middle-class family with no ransom possible? The story Heather spins rings true to the reader's ear, yet the man accused was a beloved former Baltimore police officer. Although Infante did not know Stan Dunham personally, he knew of him and his standing in the community. Other questions also arise, such as, where has the woman been these past thirty years, and what has she been doing? The author provides a few intriguing tidbits, in flashback. One such insight is that the woman claiming to be Heather worked for a while under the name of Barb as technical support for a newspaper but was fired after an amusing scene in which she pours a Diet Pepsi over the head of a persnickety reporter. Lippman's years of newspaper work add verisimilitude to scenes such as this one.

The reader will identify with Infante's skepticism. He distrusts Heather from the moment he meets her, and she makes no effort to win him over. Social worker Kay Sullivan plays good cop to Infante's bad cop: She takes Heather's word at face value, believing her implicitly. The two characters provide a nice counterbalance. Another contrasting pair is the girls' parents, Dave and Miriam, shown in flashback scenes at the time of the girls' disappearance, one year later, and then in 1983 and again in 1989. They each deal with their grief very differently: Dave is dogged in his insistence that they must never give up the search for the girls, while Miriam yields to the probability that the girls are gone forever. Dave is frustrated by Miriam's lack of faith, whereas Miriam realizes that she needs to let go in order to move on with her life. Sadly, Dave hangs himself in despair a decade after the girls' disappearance. Much the way the character claiming to be Heather has done, Miriam changes her name (reverts to her maiden name) and relocates several times in her attempt to distance herself from the tragedy.

Fortunately, the author does a masterful job of pulling all these seemingly disparate pieces of information together into a satisfying whole. As the reader comes to learn, every detail and event that the author supplies is important and key to solving the mystery. The answer, when it finally comes, is simple and logical. *What the Dead Know* is the type of book readers will want to read twice: once to find out the ending, and then again, more slowly, to see how Lippman managed to hoodwink the reader.

*C. K. Breckenridge*

## Review Sources

*Booklist* 103, no. 13 (March 1, 2007): 68-69.
*Library Journal* 132, no. 5 (March 15, 2007): 61.
*The New York Times* 156 (April 5, 2007): E9.
*Publishers Weekly* 254, no. 4 (January 22, 2007): 156.
*School Library Journal* 53, no. 5 (May, 2007): 174.
*The Times Literary Supplement*, June 8, 2007, p. 23.

# WHEN A CROCODILE EATS THE SUN
## A Memoir of Africa

*Author:* Peter Godwin (1957-    )
*Publisher:* Little, Brown (New York). 341 pp. $24.99
*Type of work:* Memoir
*Time:* 1996-2004
*Locale:* Zimbabwe

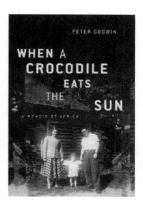

*A poignant memoir of the African-born author's return visits to Zimbabwe, where he strove to protect the welfare of his aging parents in the midst of deteriorating political and economic conditions; while looking after his parents, he made a startling discovery about the true origins of his father that moved him to see his own life from a radically new perspective*

*Principal personages:*
PETER GODWIN (1957-    ), the author, a freelance writer
  who was born and raised in what is now Zimbabwe
GEORGE GODWIN (1924-2004), his father, a retired engineer
  who immigrated to Africa from England after World War II
HELEN GODWIN (c. 1923-    ), his English mother, a retired
  medical doctor who practiced in Zimbabwe for nearly fifty years
GEORGINA GODWIN, his younger sister, a radio broadcaster
  who resettled in England
ROBERT MUGABE (1924-    ), the aging president of Zimbabwe,
  who came to power in 1980

This remarkable book defies simplistic categorization. On its surface, it is a narrative account of an African-born white man's return visits to his African homeland between 1996 and 2004. The author, journalist Peter Godwin, is a keen observer and compelling writer who has an extraordinary ability to convey powerful emotions without resorting to sentimentality. He is that paragon of the journalist, a true reporter who observes almost everything, writes so that his readers see with his eyes, and allows his readers to find their own emotional responses.

*When a Crocodile Eats the Sun* tells several stories, each of which is powerful in its own way. On one level, the book is a straightforward memoir of Godwin's many return trips to look after his retired parents in Zimbabwe. As a travel account, the book is full of interest, with details of the complications of getting in and out of that troubled country and fascinating anecdotes about the rigors of everyday survival inside Zimbabwe. On another level, the book is a sober journalistic account of the descent of one of Africa's most promising countries into poverty and repression under President Robert Mugabe, the nation's only head of government since independence in 1980. Zimbabwe's awful decline is one of the most important and ominous developments in

~

*Born and raised in Southern Rhodesia (now Zimbabwe), Peter Godwin relocated to England and began traveling the world as a foreign correspondent and documentary filmmaker. He later became an adjunct professor at Columbia University's School of International and Public Affairs.* His other books include Rhodesians Never Die: The Impact of War and Political Change on White Rhodesia, 1970-1980 *(1993; with Ian Hancock and)* Mukiwa: A White Boy in Africa *(1996).*

~

recent African history, and Godwin's book is a valuable firsthand document of that decline. There is, however, still more to *When a Crocodile Eats the Sun*, and that is the author's moving voyage of rediscovering his father, who kept secret his true origins throughout most of his life. After Godwin learned his father's secret, he had to reevaluate his views about his own African background and about white settlers in Africa generally.

Having been born and raised in Zimbabwe, Peter Godwin knows the country intimately and has a deep affection for it that shines through his objective and almost entirely unsentimental prose. During the eight years and approximately ten return trips that his narrative covers, Zimbabwe fell ever deeper into a steep economic decline. That country had been one of Africa's most prosperous and self-sufficient nations at the time of its independence in 1980. However, by the mid-1990's, it had reached the bottom of world scales in virtually every economic and quality-of-life index, becoming what Godwin calls "undisputed leader of the comparative economic decline," with "the world's fastest shrinking economy." By 1996, when Godwin paid the first return visit described in *When a Crocodile Eats the Sun*, Zimbabwe's once strong agricultural industry was nearly ruined; basic goods, such as food and fuel, were becoming increasingly difficult to obtain; modern health services were disappearing; and the population's life-expectancy rates—particularly among black Africans—were dropping to among the lowest in the world. Meanwhile, hyperinflation was making the national currency nearly worthless, and, as Godwin points out, the country's foreign reserves were so low that it could not even pay to have new currency printed abroad. These and other factors were causing commerce to regress into barter trade.

In some ways, Zimbabwe's precipitous economic decline resembles those of Weimar Germany during the early 1920's and post-World War II Hungary, when hyperinflation nearly destroyed those countries' economies. However, two things make Zimbabwe's case different from those of the European nations. First is the fact that much of Zimbabwe's decline is attributable to the systematic dismantling of the national economic structure by Mugabe's government, which almost seems intent on self-destruction. The second difference is that Zimbabwe lacks the kind of solidly entrenched infrastructure needed for recovery after Mugabe's regime is gone.

This is a tragedy of a large order. Before its independence, Zimbabwe had the most diversified economy, most fully developed infrastructure, and most productive agricultural system of any tropical African nation. This was true despite the fact that the nation made its transition to independence almost directly from a devastating civil war and a decade of living under international economic sanctions that had severely restricted external trade. Indeed, sanctions had actually helped make the country more self-sufficient than it would have been otherwise by forcing it to produce goods it could not import. However, the industrial base built up before independence was created and managed by white settlers—the very people whom Mugabe's government has targeted for removal. At independence, the population of Zimbabwe included about 220,000 white settlers, most of whom were at least second-generation residents of the country. These people controlled the overwhelming bulk of the modern economy—from factories and mechanized farms to banks and retail stores. Moreover, they also accounted for disproportionate numbers of high-level government bureaucrats, engineers, physicians, and other professionals. By the mid-1990's, the settler population had dwindled to about half its preindependence level and was significantly shrinking every year. Not surprisingly, the flight of this segment of the population left gaping holes in the economic infrastructure and health services that could not be readily filled by educated black Africans. Indeed, many of Zimbabwe's most highly educated Africans were fleeing the country to escape political repression.

*When a Crocodile Eats the Sun* is a revealing firsthand account of Zimbabwe's frightening decline. In each chapter in which Godwin describes another return to the country, it is evident that things are worse than they were during his previous visit. Many of his chapters are taken up with moving stories about ousters of the Godwin family's friends and neighbors from their farms, along with descriptions of his growing concern for his parents' security, the increasingly desperate condition of unemployed Africans, the runaway prices of ordinary goods, the scarcity of desperately needed medications, the rising crime rates, and the increasingly intense political atmosphere. Although much of Godwin's attention is focused on his parents and their settler friends, his book is not merely an account of the woes of white Africans. Godwin also devotes a great deal of space to the problems of Zimbabwe's black citizens, whose material losses may not be as great as those of their white compatriots, but whose suffering is far worse. Many of his most moving passages are about the hardships of black Africans.

Although Godwin provides chilling details of Zimbabwe's decline, what has gone wrong with the country and who is responsible are not his primary concerns. In this book and in his other writings, Godwin always remains an extraordinarily objective observer. It is impossible for him not to be appalled by the conditions he observes in the country he so clearly loves, but *When a Crocodile Eats the Sun* wastes few words expressing dismay or objections. The book is better seen as a personal exploration of the effects of Zimbabwe's deterioration on its citizens, particularly his own parents, who steadfastly refused to consider leaving the country.

Godwin's parents had come to Southern Rhodesia from Great Britain after World War II. His father, George, was an engineer with diverse skills, and his mother, Helen, was a medical doctor. One need not look far to understand why people with their professional skills immigrated to Africa when they did. Britain's settler colonies in Africa attracted thousands of immigrants after World War II. Slow to recover from the war, Britain was to many of its people a cold, dreary, and dank place with an uncertain economic future. Its rapidly developing overseas colonies had much to offer

British subjects worn out by their homeland's climate and postwar hardships. They offered sunshine, exotic scenery, and higher standards of living that invariably included cheap servants. Among Britain's settler colonies, Southern Rhodesia was the crown jewel. It attracted more immigrants than any other territory in Africa, except its much larger southern neighbor, the independent Union of South Africa. Although Southern Rhodesia lay entirely within the tropics, its eastern mountains and high central plateau gave much of it a comparatively salubrious climate. That advantage, along with abundant and fertile agricultural land, rich mineral resources, spectacular scenery, and a settler-friendly colonial regime, made Southern Rhodesia unusually appealing to settlers throughout the early to mid-twentieth century.

George Godwin initially went to Nyasaland (now Malawi) but soon relocated to Southern Rhodesia, where he was joined by Helen. There he held a series of important posts in public works departments, and Helen had a long career in medicine, working mostly among black Africans. When the Godwins arrived in the colony, its white population was small, but its members enjoyed an unusual degree of autonomy from the imperial government. Since 1923, when Britain had taken formal administrative control of Southern Rhodesia away from the chartered company that had created the colony three decades earlier, the settlers had been virtually self-governing, despite their small numbers. After World War II, they aspired to lead Southern Rhodesia to independence under white rule. To achieve that goal, they needed to increase their own numbers and encouraged more European immigration.

Of the three children born to the Godwins in Southern Rhodesia, Peter was the second. He was born in 1957—the same year in which Britain's Gold Coast in West Africa became the first black African colony to win its independence, as Ghana. It would be nearly a quarter century more until Southern Rhodesia followed suit, but other major changes would happen there during the intervening years.

At the moment Peter Godwin was born, Southern Rhodesia was part of the Central African Federation, which loosely united it with its northern neighbors, Northern Rhodesia and Nyasaland. Britain had created the federation at the urging of the Southern Rhodesian government in the hope of accelerating the development of all three colonies. However, the African populations of the other territories refused to acquiesce to the domination of Southern Rhodesia's white settlers and opted to go their own ways. Not long after the federation collapsed in 1963, Northern Rhodesia became independent as Zambia and Nyasaland as Malawi. Britain balked at granting independence to Southern Rhodesia, however, without guarantees that its African peoples would have an equal voice in its future government. That was something that the white settlers were not prepared to concede in the colony that by then they were calling simply Rhodesia.

Under Prime Minister Ian Smith, the settler government declared Rhodesia unilaterally independent in late 1965. Peter Godwin was not quite eight years old at that moment. Through the next fifteen years of his life, he would grow up in a political anomaly: a white-ruled state in the midst of a black continent with a vast African majority of its own. Moreover, it was a state that claimed to be independent but which no other state in the world recognized. As African nationalism developed within Rhodesia, the political dynamics changed. While Britain and the rest of the world pressured Rhodesia to renounce its independence and give full voting rights to all its peoples, the country's own nationalist movement turned to violent resistance. By the mid-1970's, the country was immersed in a full-scale civil war that was unresolved until the Rhodesian regime conceded defeat, and Britain formally recognized Zimbabwe's independence in 1980. Robert Mugabe, one of the primary leaders of the nationalist movement, has ruled the country ever since. Faced with growing pressure from former freedom fighters for material improvements in their lives, he has tried to satisfy their demands by redistributing the businesses and farms of the long-resented white settlers, awarding the cream of the seized properties to favored henchmen. While these distribution schemes have benefited some Africans, they have also had the pernicious effect of lowering productivity and raising unemployment among vastly larger numbers of people.

Godwin grew up in the midst of the tumultuous changes leading up to the civil war, in which he served as a reluctant member of the government's army—an experience that he calls being on the wrong side of the war. However, that interesting period of his life is not his subject of his present book. He tells the story of his youthful years in his earlier work, *Mukiwa: A White Boy in Africa* (1996), a powerfully evocative memoir that makes an apt companion volume to *When a Crocodile Eats the Sun*. Indeed, anyone intending to read the latter book would do well to read *Mukiwa* first. One of the most interesting questions raised in *When a Crocodile Eats the Sun* is why Godwin's parents so adamantly resisted suggestions that they leave Zimbabwe, despite the fact that the comfortable life they had built for themselves was steadily eroding away. Their closest friends were leaving or dying off, their income was shriveling to next to nothing in the face of hyperinflation, their physical security was diminishing, their political rights were constricting, and all these changes were gradually transforming them into prisoners within their own home. Remarkably, through all these negative developments, they seem to express no bitterness or rancor.

A first key to understanding Godwin's parents can be found in *Mukiwa*, which recalls their rewarding, earlier life in Africa. A second, more poignant key can be found within *When a Crocodile Eats the Sun*, in which Godwin recounts his startling discovery that his father was not, as he had always believed, an Englishman. His father was, in fact, a Polish Jew originally named Goldfarb who happened to be studying in England when World War II began. He never returned to his homeland; after serving in the British military during the war and completing his education, he married an Englishwoman, changed his name, and shed his Jewish identity—a transformation made easier by the loss of his mother and sister in the Holocaust and his relocation to Southern Africa. When his son finally asked him why he had concealed his Jewish identity for so long, he answered,

> "Why? . . . for my children. For you. So that you could be safe. So that what happened to them," he nods toward the photo of his mother and his sister, "would never happen to you. Because it will never really go away, this thing. It goes underground for a generation or two, but always reemerges."

The younger Godwin uses the middle chapters of *When a Crocodile Eats the Sun* to recall his reactions to the news of his Jewish heritage and to explore his father's early history. He does not dwell on the subject of his Jewishness, but the revelation also changed his thinking about his own place in Africa as a white man. Parallels between the condition of Jews in Europe during the 1930's and that of white settlers in Africa seven decades later are too obvious to require overt comment. Godwin's father had been driven from his original homeland because of his ethnic identity; he was clearly unwilling to let that happen a second time. It was thus entirely appropriate that he died in Zimbabwe and not in yet another alien land.

*R. Kent Rasmussen*

## Review Sources

*Booklist* 103, no. 16 (April 15, 2007): 20.
*Kirkus Reviews* 75, no. 3 (February 1, 2007): 89.
*The New York Review of Books* 54, no. 20 (December 20, 2007): 30-36.
*The New York Times Book Review* 156 (June 17, 2007): 21.
*Newsweek* 149, no. 23 (June 4, 2007): 69.
*People* 67, no. 17 (April 30, 2007): 51.
*The Times Literary Supplement*, April 6, 2007, p. 29.
*Washington Monthly* 39, no. 7 (July/August, 2007): 54-55.

# THE WHISPERERS
## Private Life in Stalin's Russia

*Author:* Orlando Figes (1959-     )
*Publisher:* Metropolitan Books/Henry Holt (New York).
   740 pp. $35.00
*Type of work:* History
*Time:* 1917 to the early twenty-first century
*Locale:* Russia and the Soviet Union

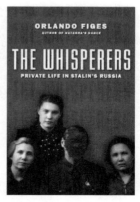

*An account of the private lives of ordinary Russians that focuses on the totalitarian Soviet Union from the Revolution of 1917 until Joseph Stalin's death in 1953*

   *Principal personages:*
   JOSEPH STALIN, Soviet dictator, 1928-1953
   KONSTANTIN SIMONOV, Soviet writer
   ZHENIA LASKINA, Konstantin's first wife
   ALEKSEI SIMONOV, their son
   VALENTINA SEROVA, actress, second wife of Konstantin

In *The Whisperers*, Orlando Figes, author of the prize-winning *A People's Tragedy: The Russian Revolution, 1891-1924* (1996) and *Natasha's Dance: A Cultural History of Russia* (2002), explores the private lives of mostly ordinary Russians from the 1917 Bolshevik Revolution to the death of Joseph Stalin in 1953, and beyond. Many studies of Soviet Russia focus on the Communist Party leadership, or they examine particular groups within Soviet society who were, for example, victims of the regime, such as the kulaks or the supposedly wealthier peasants, or those incarcerated in the tentacles of the gulag prison system. Figes attempts to concentrate on specific individuals and their families who were caught up in the Soviet utopian dream, or nightmare, tracing what he calls "the moral sphere" of families through several generations.

   Approximately twenty-five million Russians were repressed in the quarter century after 1928, when Stalin came to power in the Soviet Union. Many were executed, others sent to the gulag, others to "special settlements" to be worked as slave labor, and still others were deported to far corners of the Soviet empire. Figes claims that one person for every 1.5 families was subjected to such repression. However, it was not only those officially repressed who were affected; other family members were affected by the stigma attached to the "guilty" and were forced to hide their familial connections by creating fictional backgrounds and by hiding family histories from their children and grandchildren. Even after being released from confinement, former inmates were often unable to restore the wholeness of their families; parents and children as well as wives and husbands remained estranged for decades, often until their deaths.

~

*Before accepting a chair in history at London University's Birkbeck College, Orlando Figes was a lecturer at Cambridge. His book* A People's Tragedy *(1996), about the Russian Revolution, was awarded the Wolfson History Prize, the W. H. Smith Literary Award, and the* Los Angeles Times Book Prize. *He also writes for* The New York Review of Books *and other publications.*

~

One consequence was the resulting conformity by Soviet citizens to the regime's demands. Fear was one cause. Most Russians knew someone—a family member, a friend, an acquaintance—who had been arrested, and even ordinary citizens kept a suitcase packed under the assumption that at any time they could be arrested. Also, in totalitarian states like Stalin's Soviet Union, Nazi Germany, and the People's Republic of China during the Cultural Revolution, the entire society was conditioned to give unquestioning allegiance to the state as represented by its leader. How deep the conditioning went varied, and individuals might conform outwardly but not inwardly. To survive in that environment, where most Russians lived in close proximity, sharing communal kitchens, common living areas, and thin wall partitions, whispering among family members and between friends was necessary for survival.

No work that encompasses several decades and millions of people can be exhaustive, and *The Whisperers* only samples a small fraction of the total Soviet population. Reluctant to rely on the memoirs of Russia's intelligentsia, in part because dissident intellectuals do not fully represent the ordinary Russian, the author relied on contemporary diaries and letters and particularly on oral testimony. The recipient of several monetary grants, Figes employed experts who interviewed numerous Russians, usually more than once, on their personal experiences and their family memories. He then chose what he considered to be a cross section of Russian society.

*The Whisperers* begins in the period of the 1917 Bolshevik Revolution and the costly civil war that followed. Vladimir Ilich Lenin died in 1924, with Stalin emerging as the new leader by 1928. The Bolsheviks demanded the abolition of private life for the collective good, which necessitated the destruction of the bourgeoisie family structure, including affection between parents and children. New collective values were to be inculcated by public schools and youth organizations such as the pioneers and the Komsomol, whose young members were encouraged to denounce their parents. To be excluded because of family background, as were the kulaks, could bring intense shame to a child. Some families tried to maintain their older beliefs, as in religion, and conformed outwardly, but parents kept their traditional beliefs private even from their children, who were encouraged to adopt the ideology and practices of the Soviet state.

If the model for repression and the practice of whispering began in the 1920's, it became more extensive by the 1930's, with Stalin's Five-Year Plan for rapid industrial development and the transformation of Soviet agriculture into giant, collective farms. The poorest peasants were supposedly equivalent to the urban proletariat, while the richer peasants, or kulaks, were its class enemies. The term "kulak" was imprecise and subject to abuse. The kulaks were generally the harder-working and most productive members of the community, and collectivization led to extensive famine. Under the slogan of "liquidation of the kulaks as a class," at least ten million kulaks were displaced. Many were tortured, many imprisoned in "special settlements" or forced labor camps, and millions died. The new collectives were failures, ruining Soviet agriculture for generations. Those who survived became "whisperers," inventing new identities and thus leading double lives, always fearful of being discovered. There was a retreat from the rigors of the Five-Year Plan in 1932. Consumer goods were emphasized, but the beneficiaries were mainly the expanding number of Soviet bureaucrats who were replacing the old Bolshevik cadres. For most there continued to be shortages of consumer goods, and living space was at a premium, with a dozen people inhabiting two or three rooms. For almost everyone, party members and non-members alike, it was whispering as usual.

Fearful about losing control to elements in the Communist Party, in 1937 Stalin instituted a purge that brought about the arrest and imprisonment of at least 1.3 million people, about half of whom were subsequently executed. Probably one-fifth of all office workers officially informed on their colleagues. Many informers were opportunists and feared being arrested, but others fervently believed in the purge campaign, having unquestioning faith in Stalin. One who did was Konstantin Simonov, an aspiring writer in the late 1930's and the central personage among the many hundreds who populate *The Whisperers.* Many turned their backs on friends and relatives who were arrested, refusing even to mention their names in the confines of their own family. Children were taken away, given new names, and sent to Dickensian-type orphanages, while others survived on the streets.

Born in 1915, Simonov's mother was of aristocratic descent, and his father was a general in the czarist army during World War I who later fled to Poland. His mother refused to leave the motherland, and later married another military officer, the son of a railroad worker. Because of his problematic background, Simonov pursued a vocational education in order to appear to be a member of the proletariat, but this move was not just an attempt to hide his old identity: Like many others, Simonov was an enthusiastic supporter of the Soviet dream. When his stepfather was arrested, Simonov assumed it was just a mistake, and he remained an ardent Stalinist even as his aunts were sent into internal exile, with one eventually executed and another dying in a labor camp. In the mid-1930's, he turned to writing, composing a series of poems glorifying Soviet accomplishments, and was admitted to the state's Gorky Literary Institute. In 1939, he married Zhenia Laskina, a daughter of Samuil Laskin, a nonreligious Soviet Jew who supported the revolution because of the increased opportunities it supposedly gave the Jewish community. Zhenia gave birth to a son, Aleksei.

As the threat of war loomed in the late 1930's, Stalin agreed to a nonaggression pact with Nazi Germany, an agreement that was a great shock to fervent antifascist Stalinists like Simonov. When the Nazis invaded the Soviet Union in 1941, the Soviet armies suffered disastrous defeats, in large part due to Stalin's purges. However, Stalin was still the Soviet icon; his decisions were unchallenged, and when he stressed Russian patriotism rather than Soviet ideology, the Russian people rallied to their country. Simonov's marriage to Zhenia failed, and in 1943 he married a film actress, Valentina Serova. By then, Simonov was a major literary figure, largely because of the fame of his poem "Wait for Me," a work that captured the spirit and sacrifice of wartime. Written for Valentina, it was a personal love poem, far from the Socialist Realism demanded by the party, but "Wait for Me" was used by the government in boosting morale. Simonov received the Stalin Prize in 1942 and 1943, becoming a rich member of the ruling elite and a lieutenant colonel in the Soviet army. Patriotism united the Russians, but the victory over Germany came at great cost: Twenty-six million Russians lost their lives, of which two-thirds were civilians, and during the war more than a million citizens were shot, imprisoned, or served in penal work battalions.

Stalin refused to reform the Soviet system. Victorious generals were written out of the historical record, potential opponents were imprisoned and executed, and economic reconstruction relied on forced labor: By 1949, there were 2.4 million people in the gulag. A new elite of engineers and managers emerged, less ideological than the old Bolsheviks, and there were new educational opportunities, but most still hid their nonproletariat backgrounds. In 1946, during the early Cold War, Simonov visited the United States, where he was something of a celebrity because of his writings. He became a high official in the Soviet Writers' Union, reaping material rewards, but he had to serve the state in propaganda activities, during which writers and composers had their works repressed or censored. An anti-Jewish campaign was launched after the founding of Israel, a campaign Simonov reluctantly supported. The Laskins, the family of Simonov's first wife, had one of their other daughters sentenced to twenty-five years at hard labor. Even Simonov, the loyal Stalinist, was accused of being a Jew. He survived, but Stalin did not, dying of a stroke in March, 1953.

Most Soviet citizens, including Simonov and members of the Laskin family, were shocked and depressed by the dictator's death, not knowing what might follow. In the gulag there was more joy, and often uprisings when prisoners were not immediately released. In the two years after Stalin's death, only four percent of the prisoners were freed, but many of those who were allowed to leave the camps were often unable to overcome the psychological and physical damage that they had endured, and family relationships never healed. In spite of all that they had experienced, there were those who continued to believe in the correctness of the Stalinist regime's actions.

It was not until 1956 that Simonov began to reject his Stalinist past. He was shocked by Nikita S. Khrushchev's denunciation of Stalin in that year, a turning point in Soviet history. Even then, as editor of the journal *Novy mir*, he refused to publish Boris Pasternak's *Doktor Zhivago* (1957). A few began to question the Soviet structure, but most remained cautious and cowed. Simonov divorced Valentina in 1956, marrying Larisa Zhadova, an art historian. After adjusting to Stalin's death, he reunited with his son, but Aleksei was quicker to embrace the dissident reform movement than Simonov, who more easily adapted to the conservative policies of Leonid Brezhnev than to the Khrushchev era of mild reform. World War II had been the defining event in his life, and history was passing him by. He spent the last decade of his life—he died in 1979—collecting memoirs, diaries, and letters from the war, increasingly regretting his complicity in Stalin's rule. His literary reputation declined with the demise of the Soviet Union.

Figes notes that myth and memory were intertwined in post-Stalin Russia. Much was repressed by both the victims and the victimizers. Memoirs appeared, often masking, consciously or not, the reality of experiences. There was even nostalgia for Stalin after the fall of the Soviet Union that coexisted with a fear that the time of whispers might again return. *The Whisperers* is a groundbreaking work, with its reliance on oral history, portraying as it does the costs of totalitarianism on ordinary people. It also implicitly suggests that authoritarianism in Russia might not have permanently ended with the collapse of the Soviet Union.

*Eugene Larson*

## Review Sources

*The Atlantic Monthly* 300, no. 5 (December, 2007): 115.
*Booklist* 104, no. 3 (October 1, 2007): 10.
*The Economist* 385 (October 20, 2007): 115-116.
*Foreign Affairs* 86, no. 6 (November/December, 2007): 197.
*Kirkus Reviews* 75, no. 16 (August 15, 2007): 836.
*New Statesman* 137 (December 10, 2007): 54.
*The New York Times Book Review* 157 (November 25, 2007): 26.
*Publishers Weekly* 254, no. 29 (July 23, 2007): 53.

856

# WHITE WALLS
## Collected Stories

*Author:* Tatyana Tolstaya (1951-   )
Translated from the Russian by Jamey Gambrell
  and Antonina W. Bouis
*Publisher:* New York Review Books (New York).
  404 pp. $16.95
*Type of work*: Short fiction
*Time:* The Soviet era
*Locale:* The Soviet Union

*A collection of twenty-four stories, including all those
from the author's first two books, as well as previously
uncollected stories*

It is impossible to ignore the family heritage that
Tatyana Tolstaya's name evokes. She is the granddaughter of the Soviet writer
Alexei Tolstoy, who wrote historical novels about Peter the Great and Ivan the Terrible in the 1930's and 1940's, and the great-grandniece of the even more famous author of *Voyna i mir* (1865-1869; *War and Peace*, 1886), Leo Tolstoy. However, as
many of the best of her stories indicate, her true literary ancestors are Anton Chekhov
and Ivan Bunin, for her tales are tightly built explorations of the disillusionments of
little people, not the expansive socialist realism of her grandfather, nor the epic history of her great-granduncle. There are few references in her short fiction either to the
nobility of the pre-Soviet era or to the political upheavals that have occurred in the
Soviet Union since the revolution. For the most part, she avoids the lengthy political rhetoric common to earlier Soviet writers, insisting that she is glad Mikhail
Gorbachev does not seem to care about literature and therefore has no desire to control it; she says she asks no more from a political leader. Her one political conflict has
not been with the Russian government but with the Moscow Writers' Union, which
refused to admit her, even after the success of her first book, because she dared to criticize one of the union's most beloved authors. She has since been admitted and has
called the controversy an awful joke.

Tolstaya was born in Leningrad (now St. Petersburg) in 1951 and earned a degree
in classics at Leningrad State University, after which she worked for several years at a
Moscow publishing firm. She began publishing her own stories in the mid-1980's in
literary magazines. An English translation of her first collection, *On the Golden
Porch*, was published in 1989 to great acclaim. The original Russia edition, *Na
zolotom kryl'tse sideli*, published in 1987, sold out immediately in Moscow book-
stores. An English translation of her second collection, *Sleepwalker in a Fog*, appeared in 1992. Her first novel, *Kys* (2001; *The Slynx*), was published in English
translation in 2002.

The tone of most of Tolstaya's stories is established by the opening tale in *White Walls*, "Loves Me, Loves Me Not," in which a child tells how she hates her governess, preferring instead her beloved Nanny. Told from the little girl's point of view, the story mixes fantasy and reality, as a child, who is learning how frightening and hostile the world can be, would be most apt to do.

*Tatyana Tolstaya's first collection of short stories established her as one of the leading Russian writers of the Mikhail Gorbachev era. She taught at several U.S. universities during the late 1980's and 1990's and has hosted a Russian cultural interview television show.*

The lushly lyrical "Okkervil River" ultimately undercuts the romanticism of an aging bachelor named Simeonov, who listens to old records of love songs by a singer named Vera Vasilevna. The story ends predictably, but nonetheless pathetically, with his discovery that she has turned into a vulgarian, white, huge, and rouged, paid court to by other aging suitors. Simeonov tries to console himself by insisting that the Vera Vasilevna he has loved must have died and been eaten by this horrible old woman. He continues to escape his dreary life by losing himself in the divine voice of his dream woman.

Similarly in "The Circle," Vassily Mikhailovich, a man of sixty, for whom fur coats get heavy and stairs get steep, longs for a six-winged seraph or some other feathery creature to come and carry him away from his drab and loveless life. Like Simeonov in "Okkervil River," he too dreams of another woman whom he has transformed in his imagination, a woman named Isolde, who he hopes can bring him out of the cramped little pencil case called the universe, a woman who can shatter the ordinary world like an eggshell. However, what he ultimately discovers is a horrible-looking, wrinkled old hag, blowing beer foam on her cloth boots. Like many of Tolstaya's characters, Vassily Mikhailovich is a victim of the relentlessness of time and the sadness of missed chances and misplaced romantic fantasies.

In "Peters," a librarian fantasizes about all the lovely young women he will impress once he learns the German language, but when he overhears a woman call him a wimp and a sissy, he feels he has been run over by a trolley and sticks his head in an oven, only to discover that the gas has been off all day because of repairs. Seeing life as a chain of dreams and a charlatan's store, he furiously considers killing the women who have tricked, seduced, and abandoned him, thus revenging all the fat and tongue-tied men who are locked in dark closets and never invited to the party. Accidentally, as if in passing, he marries a cold, hard woman with big feet and, finally, wanting nothing and regretting nothing, he looks out his window and smiles gratefully at treacherous, mocking, meaningless, and ultimately marvelous, life.

The same disillusionment occurs to young boys in Tolstaya's stories. In "Date with a Bird," young Petya, spending the summer in the country, fantasizes about a neighbor woman named Tamila, a beautiful teller of fabulous stories with a magical name who lives on a blue glass mountain with impenetrable walls. He dreams that when he grows up, he will marry her and lock his hated Uncle Borya in a high tower. However, as might be expected in a Tolstaya story, the dream ends when he finds his uncle in bed with his beloved Tamila. As usual in Tolstaya's stories about children, "Date with a Bird" combines fairy-tale motifs with gritty reality in an indissoluble way.

Tolstaya's women are not immune to hopeless fantasies either. In "Sweet Shura," Alexandra Ernestovna, now in her nineties, having survived three husbands, wonders still if she had not made a mistake sixty years before in staying with one of her husbands and leaving her lover standing on a train platform. The narrator of the story ponders about the passing of time, how the invisible layer of years get thicker, and thinks there must be a door somewhere way back there on that fateful day when Alexandra decided not to leave. The narrator holds on to the futile hope that even though everything must have been shut up, a crack in some old house was missed and that if one pulls back the floorboards in the attic one will find a passage to the past.

The stories included in *White Walls* from Tolstaya's second collection, *Sleepwalker in a Fog*, focus on some of the same defeated dreamers as in her first. However, her mistaken sense that she must expand her stories to short novel length, complete with numerous extraneous details and clever asides, results in a weaker group of stories overall. Tolstaya's first collection was so well received because of her stories' tight lyrical structure and folktale sense of universality. In this second collection, she tries to show she can sustain her fiction over a longer span, but with limited success. The title story is an obvious example. "Sleepwalker in a Fog," appropriately titled for Tolstaya's typical character, begins with the kind of hopeless fantasist that she drew with such poignant success in her first book. Denisov, who is at the midpoint of his life, begins to think he should make some contribution; he tries inventing things, but nothing gets invented; he tries writing poems, but they refuse to be written. He finally begins writing a treatise on the impossibility of the existence of the continent of Australia, for it seems so utterly improbable to him, and he hopes by proving the country's nonexistence he can find his own path to immortality. The character Denisov is a clever invention, typical of a figure out of Nikolai Gogol or Vladimir Nabokov, certainly suitable for a brief exploration of absurdity and the grotesque, but Tolstaya belabors his silly fantasies of making a name for himself for more than forty pages until the reader grows quite tired of the satiric fun she makes of him.

In the longest story in the collection, "Limpopo," which runs to sixty pages, Tolstaya turns more completely to comic satire, moving even closer to the discursive novel form. The rambling tale focuses on Judy, a young, black African woman who comes to the Soviet Union to study veterinary medicine and falls in love with an intellectual and idealistic young poet named Lyonechka, a union opposed by the poet's Uncle Zhenya. However, when Zhenya, who is appointed to a diplomatic post in an African country, is torn apart by a wild animal, other relatives hope that Judy and Lyonechka will have a child who will become a new Alexander Pushkin. The story ends with the narrator, largely responsible for the comic tone of the overlong tale, who takes Uncle Zhenya's widow to the grave of Pushkin. Aunt Zina whispers that if the couple had made a little more effort, the new Pushkin would have been born, but the narrator tells her they had better leave before the police chase them off.

Tolstaya is more effective when she returns to the shorter and tighter structure of her earlier stories in which the life of one of her typically misguided and under-appreciated dreamers is created by poignant poetry. "Most Beloved" shows how brilliantly Tolstaya writes when she sticks to the lyrical short story form that she does best. The story centers on Zhenechka, a governess who has spent her entire life teaching Russian grammar to young children, but time, the constant enemy of so many of Tolstaya's characters, passes, and she finds herself more and more alone, ignored by both her relatives and the students she has so lovingly instructed. The narrator describes her as a woman of honesty, simplicity, and truth but acknowledges that she has a mouth not made for kissing, a woman with a soul like a smooth, straight pipe, with no dead ends or secret places.

Nina, a doctor in the story "The Poet and the Muse," is convinced that as she nears the age of thirty-five she needs a wild, true love, an animal passion. During an epidemic of Japanese flu, she meets and cares for a frail young poet named Grishunya, whom she later marries and decides to transform into a successful man of the real world. She throws out the poems she thinks are not decent for a married man to write and urges him to write things that will make it possible for him to publish a book, hounding him until he dies.

The few uncollected stories included in *White Walls* also return to the tightly compressed structure and lyrical style of Tolstaya's earlier works. The title story is a lyrical piece about a summer house owned by a family, who in 1997 decide to scrape off all the old wallpaper and repaper it. They find layers of old newspapers charting the history of Soviet life since the revolution, ripping off layers of time until they get down to the naked boards. They then replace it all with plain, white wallpaper with no pattern, nothing superfluous, just welcoming, white walls. Thus, metaphorically, they remove the last traces of the previous owner that had covered the walls for half a century, accepting the fact that his history is no longer needed in the new bleached and disinfected world in which they live.

*Charles E. May*


## Review Sources

*Kirkus Reviews* 75, no. 2 (January 15, 2007): 49.
*Library Journal* 132, no. 7 (April 15, 2007): 80.
*Publishers Weekly* 254, no. 6 (February 5, 2007): 39.

# WHY KEROUAC MATTERS
## The Lessons of *On the Road* (They're Not What You Think)

*Author:* John Leland (1959-    )
*Publisher:* Viking Press (New York). 205 pp. $23.95
*Type of work:* Literary history, literary criticism,
    literary biography

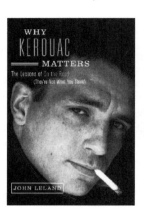

*Leland presents a compelling argument for the endur-*
*ing value of Jack Kerouac's novel as a guide to growing up*
*and leading a responsible life*

> *Principal personages:*
> JACK KEROUAC (1922-1969), the author of
>     *On the Road* (1957)
> NEAL CASSADY (1926-1968), his friend and
>     road companion

John Leland's *Why Kerouac Matters* is an attempt to come to terms with the legacy of Jack Kerouac on the fiftieth anniversary of the publication of his masterpiece *On the Road*. This is a necessary task. While Kerouac's place is firmly ensconced in the American popular imagination as the leading figure of the Beat generation, his literary reputation is much less certain. His books are far more often taught as cultural or historical documents than as works of art.

Leland believes that Kerouac's work needs to be taken seriously. He wants to challenge the popularly held notion that *On the Road* (1957) is an ode to escapism, with its two protagonists prolonging their adolescence in a wild search for kicks. Instead, Leland argues that Kerouac's most famous novel is a story about growing up, a quest for a meaningful, responsible life. To do this, Leland provides an insightful rereading of *On the Road*. Each chapter of his book is a meditation on a lesson to be drawn from the novel. Along the way, he examines Kerouac's life, his famous friendships with Neal Cassady, Allen Ginsberg, and William S. Burroughs, and the origins of the legendary Beat movement. The effect of this is to distinguish the flesh-and-blood Kerouac from the hipster image that he came increasingly to resent. Kerouac in Leland's pages is a writer far more complex and interesting than the icon he came to be.

Jack Kerouac was born in 1922 to working-class French Canadian parents. His family was devoutly Roman Catholic, and a mystical religiosity would color all of Kerouac's writings. Athletics gave him a ticket out of his hometown of Lowell, Massachusetts. He won a football scholarship to Columbia University, but an injury sidelined his career on the gridiron. Then came the war, and service in the merchant marine. Back at Columbia, Kerouac met Allen Ginsberg and William S. Burroughs. Together they became the core of a group of literary friends alienated from Middle American values and eager to explore new artistic forms. Kerouac began work on his first novel, *The Town and the City*, an autobiographical work that was published in

1950. In 1946, Kerouac met Neal Cassady, a young drifter from Colorado with an insatiable appetite for life. Together they embarked on a series of road trips across the United States and down to Mexico City. Cassady was a con man and a thief, but his irrepressible energy and unmediated awe at the wonder of

∽
*John Leland writes for* The New York Times *and lives in New York City. He is the author of* Hip: The History (2004).
∽

life made him an example and inspiration for Kerouac. Given the name Dean Moriarty, he became the emotional center of *On the Road*.

The myth of the origins of *On the Road* is that in April, 1951, Kerouac sat down, swallowed some Benzedrine, and in three weeks typed out the novel. Kerouac did hammer out a draft of the novel in a frenzied burst of writing, fueled by coffee, not amphetamines. This, however, was the culmination of years of pondering and experimenting with drafts of a picaresque tale of two friends traveling the country. Kerouac first began to work on what became *On the Road* in 1948; he spent the next three years searching for the right characters and the right voice for his novel. It was a letter from Cassady that finally crystallized for Kerouac the qualities that he wanted to capture: Cassady's breathless, rapturous embrace of experience, expressed in prose that had the immediacy of stream of consciousness yet an evocative descriptive power that captured the sad beauty of life.

Kerouac hammered out his book onto sheets of tracing paper that he taped together into a great roll. It was this unwieldy manuscript that he carried to his publisher Robert Giroux of Harcourt Brace. Giroux read and rejected the book. Giroux's refusal of the novel devastated Kerouac. He believed his novel was the best writing that he had done, better than anything that he had seen published that year. After a short period of demoralization, Kerouac began rewriting the book in an even more unconventional form that eventually became *Visions of Cody*. For the next six years, Kerouac wrote more books that nobody wanted to publish. By the time a revised version of *On the Road* was finally published in 1957, Kerouac had been living with it for nine years. He was a thirty-five-year-old writer, with one other published book to his credit, who lived with his mother. Success had not come easily to him. When it arrived, seemingly overnight, he would not know how to deal with sudden celebrity.

Leland observes that the long gestation of *On the Road* left Kerouac disoriented when he was discovered by an inquisitive media. The book was a product of the immediate postwar years, the America of Harry S. Truman, a world before interstate highways, rock and roll, and the pervasive influence of television. The drivers bureaus, small-town diners, and hobo customs that he described had been consigned to obsolescence by streamlined roadways dominated by sleek, tail-finned automobiles, Howard Johnsons, and new fast-food outlets. *On the Road* was already a period piece when it was published. Kerouac was never comfortable appearing on television to promote his book. He was disgusted when the media labeled him "the King of the Beats" and tried to make him into a lonely voice of a new lost generation. He did not understand or have any sympathy with the facile marketing that merged "beat" and "Sputnik" to create a new subculture of "beatniks," goateed, bongo-playing, beret-topped hep cats that were soon parodied by Bob Denver's character of Maynard G. Krebs on the situational comedy *The Many Loves of Dobie Gillis*. The mass media won in its appropriation of Jack Kerouac. The man disappeared behind a myth. Kerouac became an icon of cool. *On the Road* became a talismanic accessory for wannabe rebels.

Leland wants to rescue Kerouac and his novel from the hype. He does this by exploring themes in the book that have long been hiding in plain sight, obscured by the effervescent energy of the story. At the center of the book is a friendship. Sal Paradise, Kerouac's fictionalization of himself, meets Dean Moriarty/Cassady, and the pair set out on what become journeys of discovery. They are seeking many things. It is Leland's conviction that many of the answers that they find are fundamentally traditional.

In the original scroll version of *On the Road*, Kerouac has Sal Paradise declare: "I believed in a good home, in sane and sound living, in good food, good times, work, faith and hope. I have always believed in these things. It was with some amazement that I realized I was one of the few people in the world who really believed in these things without going around making a dull middle-class philosophy out of it." This passage was dropped from the published book. For Leland, this credo reflects the real Kerouac. It is notable that most of the wild times in *On the Road* are associated with Moriarty/Cassady. Kerouac's alter ego is much more subdued and reflective. While hardly a paragon of bourgeois rectitude, willingly going along with the mad antics of his friend, Sal Paradise consistently yearns for something more stable and enduring in his life. Kerouac was highly critical of the glossy, consumerist culture that emerged following the war, and he worried about the parlous nature of life in the shadow of the atomic bomb. What he never did was reject the hard-working, religious world that he had known in his youth. In the novel, Sal Paradise always ends up returning to the home of his aunt, just as in reality Kerouac lived for years with his mother. In some ways, the paradoxical message of *On the Road* is that you can go home again.

The novel can be read as a quest to capture an idealized domesticity. An unfulfilled mission of Sal and Dean is to find Dean's long-lost father, who has become an alcoholic hobo. Over and again, they try to create families for themselves. Dean does this literally with his marriages, even becoming a father. Sal, in an extended passage of the novel, settles down with a Mexican American woman named Terry and her son. He works picking cotton and enjoys for a time the sensation of being a breadwinner for his improvised family. Sal and Dean see each other as brothers. Inside various cars, and with various companions, they form a sort of family on wheels. The tragedy for Kerouac, as for Cassady, was that they could not live up to their ideal. In the book, Dean routinely abandons his wives and children. Sal leaves Terry and her son behind. Dean and Sal even betray each other. Dean ditches Sal while he is sick in Mexico City. Sal ultimately turns his back on Dean on a cold street in New York City. Despite this, Kerouac ends the novel with Sal meeting his second wife. He does not record that the marriage broke up some months later. Kerouac's hope of settling down becomes a triumphant dream in the final pages of *On the Road*. Sal gives up the road for the love of a good woman. The fact that it was not true does not sully the aspiration.

In his own way, Kerouac was deeply religious. Raised a Catholic, he flirted with Buddhism, and ended up an idiosyncratic Catholic mystic. A religious sensibility permeates *On the Road*. It is often overlooked by people more interested in the partying and driving. In what would become a famous photograph of Kerouac and members of the San Francisco Beat literary renaissance, he wore a crucifix conspicuously outside his shirt. When the photograph was reproduced widely after he became famous, the crucifix was routinely airbrushed out. Such an open display of religious feeling did not fit with the media's conception of "the King of the Beats." In the novel, Kerouac repeatedly resorts to religious imagery. Sal sees God in the sky and in the faces of Mexican peasants. He comes to regard Dean as a kind of mad saint, a "HOLY GOOF," a figure having the same effect on his circle as Fyodor Dostoevski's "idiot." Sal and Dean agree that there is no reason to doubt the existence of God. Part of the intoxication the characters experience on their journeys is a result of their openness to the beauty and miraculousness of Creation. Kerouac and Cassady shared a Roman Catholic vocabulary and ethos that enabled them to easily communicate their spiritual insights. Their view of the world, and that of *On the Road*, is essentially sacramental. The cross-country quests were a form of worship.

Leland believes that in grappling with such themes, Kerouac was endeavoring to embrace, not escape, adulthood. He sees *On the Road* as a bildungsroman, a coming-of-age story. Profoundly traditional at heart, always his mother's son, Kerouac wanted to have what the media image-makers made it seem that he wanted to escape. He failed to achieve his dream. This and the grotesque misrepresentations by the media ate away at him. He drank himself to death at the age of forty-seven. In his last years, he was back with his mother and a caretaker wife, grumbling about hippies and praising conservative commentator William F. Buckley. He had long since left behind the counterculture that acclaimed him as an inspiration.

Leland's *Why Kerouac Matters* reminds readers that Jack Kerouac was much more than a rebel poet. He addressed fundamental issues in a way that can continue to speak long after most books published in his day have grown dated and stale. Leland's book is a fitting tribute to a writer whom he admires deeply.

*Daniel P. Murphy*

## Review Sources

*Booklist* 103, no. 22 (August 1, 2007): 25.
*Kirkus Reviews* 75, no. 12 (June 15, 2007): 593.
*Library Journal* 132, no. 13 (August 1, 2007): 87-88.
*National Review* 59, no. 17 (September 24, 2007): 59-60.
*The New York Times Book Review* 156 (August 19, 2007): 13.
*Publishers Weekly* 254, no. 25 (June 18, 2007): 46.
*USA Today*, August 21, 2007, p. D1.

# THE WORLD WITHOUT US

*Author:* Alan Weisman (1947-    )
*Publisher:* Thomas Dunne Books (New York).
   336 pp. $24.95
*Type of work:* Environment, natural history, science,
   sociology

*Weisman imagines an Earth from which all people sud-*
*denly vanish and traces what might then happen to the*
*homes, factories, and farms left abandoned, as well as the*
*natural world as it begins to regenerate and reshape itself*
*for post-human existence*

   In 2005, journalist Alan Weisman published in *Dis-*
*cover* magazine an article titled "Earth Without People," in
which he speculated on what might happen to the structures supporting human civilization if the humans who built and maintain them were suddenly to vanish. In researching the article, however, he discovered there was far more material than he
could use—enough, in fact, for a whole book, and so he began work on *The World*
*Without Us*. In the book's brief introduction, he addresses and dismisses the nagging
issue of how such a human disappearance might occur. Among the means he suggests are "a *Homo sapiens*-specific virus—natural or diabolically nano-engineered,"
"some misanthropic evil wizard," or even that "Jesus . . . or space aliens rapture us
away, either to our heavenly glory or to a zoo somewhere across the galaxy." His
point, of course, is that, though people may be troubled by the specter of the sudden
departure of their entire species, in the end, the means by which people might vanish
from the planet makes no difference to the elaborate thought experiment that follows.
What matters is merely that readers of the book accept its initial premise: Humans
are here one day and gone the next.
   Weisman is deeply fascinated by the natural world, and it is there that *The World*
*Without Us* begins, in Poland and Belarus's Białowieża Puszcza, the last old-growth
primeval forest in Europe. Only a tiny fragment remains of this forest, which once
swathed large sections of the continent, and Weisman ponders the question of to what
degree, given sufficient time without human interference—say, five hundred years—
the old forest might return. In a later chapter, the author asks a similar question about
the potential for reforestation in Africa, were the agricultural lands that now fragment
the continent left untended for a few generations. Despite the tantalizing suggestion
of these chapters, however, this is not a book that dwells on those portions of the
planet still relatively untouched by human endeavor, nor does it suggest that a post-
human world would closely resemble the prehuman one. Rather, the majority of the
book takes a hard look at those parts of Earth people now inhabit, stripped suddenly of
them. Much of what it reveals, therefore, revolves around what would become of human artifacts, from plastic bags to skyscrapers.

Perhaps the single artifact that carries the most emotional weight for people is their houses, so Weisman briefly explains how relatively quickly all the houses on the planet would dissolve were it not for the constant maintenance their owners bestow upon them. From here, he moves on to the single most discussed chapter in the book, in which he describes the process by which nature—albeit a nature changed by now-absent humanity— would reclaim New York City. Weisman chooses New York for his focus because, as

～

*Journalist Alan Weisman's articles have appeared in many of America's leading magazines and have been heard on public radio. His previous books include* An Echo in My Blood *(1999),* Gaviotas: A Village to Reinvent the World *(1998), and* La Frontera: The United States Border with Mexico *(1986).*

～

he writes, its "sheer titanic presence . . . resists efforts to picture it wasting away," but wasting away is precisely what is described, beginning with the flooding of subway tunnels that would relatively quickly undermine the foundations of roads and buildings above, even while cycles of freezing and thawing, unmitigated by human-made heat sources, would weaken these structures still further. Meanwhile, as centuries of toxins slowly flushed out of the soil, native plants would return in some numbers, but probably not sufficient to hold their own against an invasion of exotic plant species escaping from gardens and parks. Coyotes and bears would be among the original fauna able to return and take up residence in a disintegrating Manhattan. Interestingly, rats and roaches, which seem to so many city dwellers the most hearty of species, would not fare so well. As Weisman points out, it is people's refuse and central heating that allow these creatures to thrive now; soon after humankind's departure, their numbers would plummet to the brink of extinction in New York's harsh climate.

Leaving the city behind, later chapters of the book look to other evidence of human habitation, some of which would evaporate more readily than others, but none of which would fail to leave behind evidence of humanity's onetime dominion over the landscape. The human-cleared land of farms would, for the most part, be gradually replaced by the forests, grasslands, or swamps that were themselves tamed to make way for human agriculture. In intensively farmed areas, though, this reabsorption would be slowed considerably by decades' worth of residue from agrochemicals. Even more problematic for an Earth recovering from the shock of human habitation would be the remnants of the petrochemical and nuclear industries. Indeed, both petroleum processing plants and nuclear weapons and power facilities require the presence of human monitors to keep their toxins contained. When lack of monitoring and maintenance eventually led to the collapse of these structures, the resulting explosions and leaks could leave behind highly contaminated zones that would remain nearly free of life for hundreds or even thousands of years.

One of the more chilling chapters in *The World Without Us* examines a phenomenon of relatively recent vintage: humanity's ever-increasing reliance on plastics. It is sobering to read Weisman's enumeration of the myriad ways modern humans employ this substance unheard of until the middle of the twentieth century, from containers to furniture to a cosmetic ingredient. The problem with plastics, though, is not their

ubiquity but their longevity. Most plastics do not break down into component chemi-
cals that can then be reabsorbed by nature. They simply break apart into smaller and
smaller pieces of plastic, which become toxins and choking hazards for smaller and
smaller creatures on land or, more often, in the ocean, where most of the plastic that
humans lose or throw away eventually ends up. The substance has not been around
long enough for anyone to know when it might genuinely degrade, but the best scientific guesses assume hundreds or thousands of years. A world without people, then,
would be drowning in waste plastics for a long while, even those watery parts of the
world where humans have never lived.

In addition to examining the detritus of human societies, Weisman also devotes
chapters to topics whose connection to humanity is less immediately evident. He
devotes many pages, for instance, to a discussion of the evolution of large animals in
Africa, which, he posits, remain abundant because they evolved alongside humans
and developed strategies for either avoidance of or coexistence with them. A similar
variety of large animals—both herbivores and predators—existed in North America
at one time, but the extinction of many of them coincides rather neatly with the arrival
of humans on this continent, suggesting habitat destruction and hunting played a hand
in their demise.

While these discussions seem to be less about a world after human habitation than
before it, Weisman does return to his principle theme. He stresses that even if humans
were gone, much of the earth would not return to its prehuman state, in part because
people have killed off so many of the creatures (such as the North American
megafauna) that were crucial to maintaining the ecosystem before humans arrived. A
whole chapter of *The World Without Us* is devoted to birds and the surprising variety
of ways in which they are killed, from habitat loss to hunting, from high-tension
power lines to predation by pet cats. Though extinction is a phenomenon that long
predates humanity, people have contributed to the rapid loss of many species, particularly of large animals and birds. Of course, once gone, these animals would remain
gone, even in a world without people.

Though people do not inhabit the book's imaginary world, they inhabit its pages in
the form of the passionate scientists, ecologists, and others who serve as Weisman's
guides to his imagined human-free world to come. It is their stories—their passions,
worries, and sometimes disagreements with one another—that animate *The World
Without Us* and create much of its appeal and readability. The book is also brimming
with fascinating facts and accidental case studies that keep readers turning pages.
Weisman explains how the Demilitarized Zone between North and South Korea, a
swath of land bound by barbed wire and heavy armaments, has been gradually returning to nature since the end of the Korean War in 1953. He also visits Varosha, Cyprus,
a town suddenly abandoned during civil strife in 1974, and describes its state of decay
after more than thirty years without human caretaking. Parts of the book are written in
a purely speculative, subjunctive mood, with plenty of words like "might" and "perhaps" reminding the reader of the provisional and exploratory nature of Weisman's
project. In many places, however, the author writes in simple present tense. In the
chapter on New York, for instance, he writes that after a few years "pipes burst all

over town, the freeze-thaw cycle moves indoors, and things start to seriously deterio-
rate." There is undeniable power in that straightforward language suggesting not a
possibility but a reality.

Though Weisman seems to begin by taking on the scientist's role of the dispassionate observer, meaning only to inquire into an important question, his objectivity is
short-lived. Fairly early in *The World Without Us*, another agenda begins to emerge in
tandem with the stated one. Between frequent asides about climate change and laments about the residue of manufacturing and a disposable society, it becomes clear
that the author wishes to alert his readers to what he sees as the negative impact the
human species has on the planet it inhabits. The book, in fact, ends with the hopeful
suggestion that a smaller human population might have a less devastating effect, followed by a proposal—sure to be unwelcome in some quarters—that women voluntarily restrict themselves to bearing one child each, thus bringing the population down
to perhaps a quarter of its current total in a matter of a few generations. Such social
and political analysis is certainly tangential to the original intent Weisman declares
for his book. Still, for those who either agree with the author or are willing to read past
his occasional rallying cries, as well as to buy into the rather unusual premise of the
book as a whole, *The World Without Us* amply rewards reading, both as a source of
information and as stimulating food for thought.

*Janet E. Gardner*


## Review Sources

*America* 197, no. 16 (November 19, 2007): 23-24.
*The Humanist* 67, no. 5 (September/October, 2007): 46.
*Library Journal* 132, no. 15 (September 15, 2007): 99.
*Mother Jones* 32, no. 4 (July/August, 2007): 76-77.
*Nature* 448 (July 12, 2007): 135-136.
*New Statesman* 137 (October 1, 2007): 53-54.
*The New York Times Book Review* 156 (September 2, 2007): 12.
*The New Yorker* 83, no. 23 (August 13, 2007): 85-86.
*Publishers Weekly* 254, no. 20 (May 14, 2007): 43.
*Science News* 172, no. 6 (August 11, 2007): 95.

# A WORLDLY COUNTRY
## New Poems

*Author:* John Ashbery (1927-      )
*Publisher:* Ecco Press (New York). 76 pp. $23.95
*Type of work:* Poetry

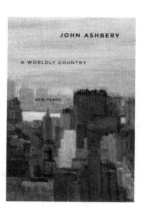

*The twenty-sixth collection by a prolific and preeminent American poet*

The fifty-eight lyric poems in John Ashbery's *A Worldly Country* are consistent with his twenty-five earlier volumes of verse. Written when he was almost eighty years old, the poems continue to focus on the limits of language and the difficulty of expressing meaning, but the poems also concern aging and impending death. They progress not logically but by associative leaps that are almost impossible for readers to follow. Mixed with arcane language and philosophical ideas are chatty asides, interruptions ("Wait!"), and flippant comments.

Time is the subject of "A Worldly Country," the title poem of the volume. At the end of the poem, "the time we turn around in/ soon becomes the shoal our pathetic skiff will run aground in." The skiff, not a ship, is life fated to run aground, to fail to reach its goal; and it is time, the repetition of events, that destroys life and meaning. Earlier in the poem the speaker states, "In short all hell broke loose that wide afternoon," but "By evening all was calm again." The afternoon is "wide" because it is long-lasting and replete with negative images like "insane clocks," "the sullen mockery of Tweety Bird," and "the scent of manure." The images are not powerful but banal and pathetic, and those of the evening are equally trivial and pedestrian. Nevertheless, the circle continues, for tomorrow produces "the great ungluing," when things are not destroyed, but merely fall apart. As the speaker gazes at the "quiet rubble," he wonders "What had happened, and why?" The "rebelliousness" and "hellishness" was replaced by peace, but that peace is far from pleasant and life-affirming; it is more like quietude, inertia, and stagnancy. It is "worldly" in the worst sense of that word; the speaker's world is more likely to end with a "whimper" than a "bang."

In "Old-Style Plentiful," the speaker describes lost love from the perspective of several years. "It's so long ago/ now, yet some of it makes sense, like/ why were we screwing around in the first place?" Now only some of it makes sense, and the speaker is uncertain about why the affair ever happened. Regardless of the lack of connection between the past and the present, "something" matters, even though there were many indications that the relationship was far from perfect. The flood of time obliterates where they sat, and the breeze and the light ignore the "unkindness" and pretend that "it was all going to be OK some day." Of course, it never was "OK," and only being "drunk on love" enabled them to ignore the problems. The last line, "That sure was some summer," is vintage Ashbery, an enigmatic comment more suggestive of ennui than wistfulness.

Unlike John Donne's romantic poem of the same name, Ashbery's "The Ecstasy" provides a cynical view of a relationship. During the winter, the speaker and his mate go skiing, but their vision of the future is incomplete; they see just to the "margin" but no more. His statement, "I want out now" comes as an abrupt switch in mood, which he goes on to explain in detail as having traveled in this country (or relationship) too long. He desires "a little sweetness" to balance his "hunger" for the winter when "friendships come unknotted/ like tie-dyed scarves." Then there is another switch to describe their attendance at a boring reception; then another switch, the revelation that when he went out the next morning on some pretext, he stayed away for twenty years. Asked if he had forgotten something when he returned, he said

*John Ashbery has published twenty-six volumes of verse in addition to a novel, literary criticism, and art criticism. His* Self-Portrait in a Convex Mirror *(1975) won the Pulitzer Prize, the National Book Award, and the National Book Critics Circle Award. Ashbery is a member of the American Academy of Arts and Letters and the American Academy of Arts and Sciences.*

"no, only the milk." If this were not uncaring enough, he adds, "Which was the truth," reiterating not only his distance but also his unwillingness to soften the blow.

"Forwarded" involves another leave-taking. The "consequences" (an even more negative word than "result") of his having fallen in love with her include "bright lights, lit sea,/ buttered roofs, dandelion breath," largely positive descriptors, albeit a bit unusual. The speaker states, however, that "Next year let's live in harm's way," suggesting a more daring, less conventional relationship; but this relationship will be "under the big top," a circus reference that implies repetitive performances and negates the idea of "harm's way." The antithetical "blue" (blues) and sun will "find us" there. The concluding comparison is to the "growl of a friendly dog" that retreats ("shivers itself/ out of here"). The italicized conclusion, *Never heard . . . anymore,* suggests indeed that the relationship has been "forwarded."

"Ukase" features another leave-taking, this time from the country. The poem begins with language ("thesaurus," "word-rabbits") in an upbeat way, but as dusk approaches "it was time to mold the analytical/ to the time-sensitive," to admit that they had survived something that had happened during the summer. In his farewell to the farm, the speaker abruptly switches gears ("What a chump! Excuse me . . . ") and describes what has gone before as "afterthoughts." He admits that he is digressing, perhaps because he is unwilling to pursue what happened, and speaks of being able to "finesse" everything through language as the couple is "incurably, undeniably aging." That comment is undercut by a qualifier ("only I can't tell what that feels like"), which is followed by "Not when, but if"—as if the aging were not part of the picture. Then the speaker writes, "But we'll know it before it happens—we'll/ recognize us from the way we look at each other,/ not from any urgent movement forward/ or anything like that." They will see in each other the aging process, but not as a result of any dramatic change in them or their situation. As with the other poems, "Ukase" changes directions and lacks dynamic images and action.

Many of Ashbery's poems deal not only with language but also with the writing of poetry. "For Now" is concerned with "who does the illuminating?" After discussing how a writer would deal with "the victimhood of all those years," the speaker declares, "We brought something else—/ some enlightenment," though the claims for that illumination are modest: "the meaning of dreams" and "how hotel rooms/ can become the meaningful space one has always lived in." While explaining dreams is important, the second aim is ridiculous at best, and the speaker's admission that the enlightenment is "only a shred," "a fragment of life/ no one else seemed interested in" denies the importance of the insights. "Seemed" might suggest that there were some people interested in the speaker's enlightened poetic offerings, but clearly the speaker realizes that his work cannot "be carried away," cannot be applied to one's life, or, even more devastating, cannot be carried away in the sense that it cannot be deciphered. It belongs, like "décor" or "dance," art forms whose meaning is determined by the individual spectator or reader.

"One of His Nature Poems" is more about poetry than nature. The speaker's "Painted truths" and "unvarnished arabesques" refer to his poetry, which is certainly not "lively" or "straightforward and cool." The "purity" he seeks is paradoxically in the "room of lost steps," false starts, unfinished endings, and confusing associative leaps. Then the speaker pulls in an old adage: "Everything has a silver lining." To get to that silver lining the reader must engage in "turning it over," interpreting it, and then "scrubbing some sense into it," attempting to find the essence of what Ashbery wrote. The "last few spectators" (readers) will give up after dealing with the "rude wind, mud, and chaos" of Ashbery's poetry. They will be "literate for a day but otherdirected." This poem suggests that Ashbery is well aware of the problems his poetry poses for his readers but may also delight in their problems.

Ashbery's poems contain many images of water (often floods that obliterate), shoals (designed for people to run aground on), time (usually running out), and the cinema. "To Be Affronted," one of the early poems in the volume, contains a reference to "a movie that is the same/ as someone's life, same length, same ratings." The speaker asks the "you" (in this case the reader) to imagine playing the "second lead," which is "more important than the principals'." The question becomes, "How do you judge when it's more than/ half over?" Again, the focus is on time and aging: Everything is happening "too late," and things are "running out" before certainty about the "wizard" and "charlatan" can be established. "Now I'm not so sure," the last line of the poem, could apply to many of Ashbery's poems.

"Yes, 'Señor' Fluffy," on the other hand, is a rarity in this volume; it is an amusing poem about attending a thriller. It is replete with references to "reaction-shots" and "credits," describes the silly yet dense plot, and puts the speaker in the situation of being labeled as the killer. "Pavane pour Helen Twelvetrees" also contains cinematic references such as "starlets," "process shot," "casting call," and "rushes," but in this poem God, who will also write the sequel, is the director. Reading a huge volume, He admits that "that one might have turned out/ differently, if I'd been paying attention." An inattentive God, a plot (the Fall of Man?), and a casting call that might produce a different ending—these are the ingredients for an interesting opening night, but at the last minute God suggests that they not attend the premiere, perhaps the only performance of this alternative plot, before the world returns to "the chain of living and dying,/ pleasing and ornery." In "The Recipe," which has an introductory quotation from the 1942 film *The Palm Beach Story*, the speaker compares his relationship with his lover to two actors who are "on the wrong set,/ at the wrong time, even as the cameras rolled." The tone is lighthearted as the speaker says that he can be anything she wants, can play any role she desires, and will make the wedding arrangements.

Near the end of *A Worldly Country*, Ashbery begins "Objection Sustained" with a comparison between a French king and himself: "I/ know and do not know what it is I am./ Suffering aimlessly, pointlessly,/ I think I'm on the spot right now." The quotation unfortunately seems an apt description of some of the poems because there are so many abrupt shifts in subject, so many qualifiers, and so many enigmatic comments that the poems resist easy or even thorough readings. That said, his images, his themes, and his less-than-thoroughly articulated views make for interesting, challenging reading, and some of the lines remain with the reader. As one critic noted, there is in the poems a "restlessness to express something that won't quite come out."

*Thomas L. Erskine*

## Review Sources

*American Book Review* 29, no. 1 (November/December, 2007): 19-20.
*Booklist* 103, no. 12 (February 15, 2007): 25.
*Library Journal* 132, no. 12 (July 1, 2007): 96.
*New Criterion* 25, no. 10 (June, 2007): 61-68.
*The New York Review of Books* 54, no. 5 (March 29, 2007): 20-22.
*Publishers Weekly* 253, no. 50 (December 18, 2006): 43.
*World Literature Today* 81, no. 6 (November, 2007): 68-69.

# THE WORLDS OF LINCOLN KIRSTEIN

*Author:* Martin Duberman (1930-    )
*Publisher:* Pantheon Books (New York). Illustrated.
     792 pp. $37.50
*Type of work:* Biography
*Time:* 1907-1996
*Locale:* New York City

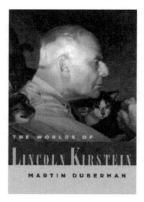

*Duberman's monumental biography reveals for the first time the fascinating public and private worlds of the brilliant man responsible for bringing George Balanchine to America, for helping to create the Museum of Modern Art and Lincoln Center, and for founding the New York City Ballet*

          *Principal personage:*
          LINCOLN KIRSTEIN (1907-1996), American writer and patron of the arts

Anyone who has ever attended one of the spectacular performances of the New York City Ballet at Lincoln Center in New York, viewed an exhibit at the Museum of Modern Art (MoMA), or performed research on dance at the New York Public Library owes a tremendous debt to Lincoln Kirstein. In the same way, anyone who has read Ezra Pound, T. S. Eliot, R. P. Blackmur, or W. H. Auden owes a debt to Kirstein. Kirstein gained his greatest fame from his commitment to ballet—the art he most cherished and the art to whose beauty and splendor he capitulated at the age of ten—and he is most often remembered as the man who brought the choreographer George Balanchine (Georgi Balanchivadze) to America. Thanks in large part to his family fortune—his father owned the Boston-based department store Filene's—and to his own generosity and commitment to fostering and preserving the arts in society, Kirstein helped create Lincoln Center and City Center in New York City, as well as founding the School of American Ballet and the New York City Ballet.

As an undergraduate at Harvard University, Kirstein started the famous literary magazine *Hound and Horn*, publishing writers like Pound and Eliot, Stephen Spender, William Carlos Williams, Wallace Stevens, and Edmund Wilson, and carrying the early photographs of Walker Evans (who later gained fame for his photographs of southern sharecroppers in his and James Agee's *Let Us Now Praise Famous Men*, 1941). He also founded the Harvard Society for Contemporary Art, largely viewed as the precursor of MoMA in New York City. Because of his devotion to dance, he founded *Dance Index*, the major scholarly journal of dance in America. Consumed by his passion for the arts and his desire to make them an integral part of modern society, Kirstein worked frenetically and tirelessly in his efforts to accomplish this.

Duberman, whose previous biographies of James Russell Lowell and Paul Robeson and whose study of the Black Mountain poets have intimately captured their subjects, here splendidly captures Kirstein's energy, his majestic writings, and his often tortured personal life. Drawing primarily on Kirstein's own diaries, journals, letters, and books, as well as interviews with Kirstein's friends and colleagues, Duberman provides not only a magisterial biography of Kirstein but also a

∼

*Martin Duberman is distinguished professor emeritus of history at the City University of New York. He is the prize-winning author of numerous books, including* Paul Robeson *(1989),* James Russell Lowell *(1966), and* Black Mountain: An Exploration in Community *(1972).*

∼

first-rate cultural history of mid-twentieth century New York. Duberman's biography probes Kirstein's ambivalence toward his Judaism, his homosexuality, and his family, thereby creating a portrait of a man whose private life and public lives often overlapped but whose energies were directed to the greater good of the community. As Duberman points out, Kirstein's frenetic pace caught up with him later in life when his bipolar disorder resulted in mental breakdowns, for which he underwent electric shock.

Lincoln Kirstein was the second of two children born to Louis and Rose Stern of Rochester, New York. His parents named him after Louis's idol, Abraham Lincoln. When Lincoln's older sister, Mina, (who was ten when Lincoln was born) first saw her baby brother, she proclaimed that he looked like a lobster; when Lincoln's younger brother, George, was born two and a half years after Lincoln, Lincoln tried to bash his newborn brother's head in with a tin of talcum powder. Lincoln almost died as a result of a botched circumcision, leaving him with both physical and psychological scars. When he was twelve, he tried to hack off the scar tissue on his groin with his mother's scissors.

As a preteen, Kirstein discovered music and began writing verse. Every day after school, he went to the YMCA, where there would be a short religious service. He disliked the impassionate and reedy music of his temple, but at the YWCA he discovered how passionately music could be sung when the ringing voices of the children were accompanied by the majestic chords of the grand piano. He developed a love for the symphony and the theater and at age twelve went to his first ballet, *The Dance of the Hours*, from Amilcare Ponchielli's *La Gioconda*. Although that performance left him unmoved, he was swept off his feet the following year by Anna Pavlova's wonderful performances, attending them five nights in a row and discovering in ballet the consuming passion of his life. Sometime earlier, Kirstein had begun to keep a drawing book—which revealed the significance of visual imagery in his life—and when he was twelve, he began to keep a diary. Kirstein's early passion for the arts developed into a lifelong devotion to the development of major artistic institutions and organizations.

In 1927, Kirstein entered Harvard University and quickly became involved in efforts to introduce the literary avant-garde and modernism to the campus. At Harvard, Kirstein also discovered his homosexuality and engaged in relationships with classmates as well as one-night stands (a trait that was to follow him throughout his life). At the same time, however, Kirstein could not classify himself as a "fairy," a term then used to describe homosexuals, because he was also attracted to women and often dreamed of lying on a beach filled with girls waiting for him to fondle them. Kirstein's greatest accomplishment at Harvard was the founding of *Hound and Horn*. Kirstein, along with his classmate Varian Fry (who became the first literary editor at *The New Republic*), hoped to secure a place on the board of Harvard's literary magazine, the *Advocate*. Rejected by the *Advocate*, the two began their own small magazine, determined to introduce some of the best new American writers in its pages. Through the financial support of his father, and with the intellectual support of the poet and essayist R. P. Blackmur, the magazine began to flourish and gained significant recognition. James Agee published his first piece in the magazine, and writers as diverse as Allen Tate, Katherine Anne Porter (whose story "Flowering Judas" was published there), Kenneth Burke, and William Carlos Williams published their work in the magazine. In his junior year at Harvard, Kirstein helped create the Harvard Society for Contemporary Art, a forerunner of MoMA, where he would become an adviser before he turned twenty-three.

Once he left Harvard, Kirstein launched into the life of patron of the arts in great earnest. Until he inherited his father's money, Kirstein himself never had the financial means to support his various passions. As late as 1948, the New York City Ballet was running more than $47,000 under budget, and Kirstein's mother wrote a check to make up the deficit. Even so, his charmed life had thrust him into monied circles, and he developed a genius for raising funds to support various artistic endeavors. Among Kirstein's many triumphs were bringing George Balanchine to America and establishing a great national ballet company built on the model of the Russian ballet. In 1929, Sergei Diaghilev died, and his company, the Ballets Russes, split into several competing companies. One of the smaller ones, Les Ballets 1933, featured Balanchine as choreographer, and Kirstein, an admirer of Diaghilev, quickly became an admirer of the young Balanchine. Kirstein valued the classicism of Balanchine's ballets; when the two met at a party in the summer, Balanchine told Kirstein that he would like to go to America. Kirstein arranged for the choreographer to make the trip, though Balanchine insisted that Kirstein include return fare in the event he did not like America. Although the School of American Ballet opened in 1934—where students performed Balanchine's first American-made piece, *Serenade*—the New York City Ballet did not make its debut until 1948, after years of financial wrangling and periods of Balanchine's bouts of illness. Not until 1954, with the success of Balanchine's *The Nutcracker*, would the New York City Ballet gain secure financial footing.

Duberman's exhaustive biography also provides glimpses of Kirstein's personal life. In 1941, Kirstein married Fidelma Cadmus, the sister of the artist Paul Cadmus. Neither set of parents seemed to approve of the union, so the marriage took place at city hall. In spite of his marriage, Kirstein continued to have affairs with both men and women. Kirstein had an ongoing romance with the dancer José Martinez, and he spent many nights in male bordellos, sailors' hangouts, and gay baths. Kirstein never tried to hide his sexual liaisons from Fidelma, but in the early years of their marriage she apparently seemed to be too enamored of the art world (she had learned some of this world from her brother's exploits) to be too exhausted or shattered by Kirstein's exploits. However, she did truly love Kirstein—ironically, her name means "faithful soul"—and as the years progressed her husband's affairs were harder and harder to bear. She retreated to the kitchen to prepare elaborate meals or she would involve herself in packing and unpacking for their trips. On a trip to Japan in 1961, though, exhausted by his sexual activities and his leaving her to search for yet another sexual escapade, she had a nervous breakdown and had to be taken back at once to New York. She eventually retreated to a country house in Connecticut where she could enjoy the outdoors and taking care of her animals.

In the later years of his life, Kirstein was not involved in starting up new ventures, but he remained as involved as ever in the arts through his writings. He did participate in the march on Selma, Alabama, in 1965. He wrote an elegy for Balanchine, "A Ballet Master's Belief," that was published in 1984, a year after Balanchine's death. Between 1987 and 1994, he published five books: *The Poems of Lincoln Kirstein* (1987), *Memorial to a Marriage* (1989), *Puss in Boots* (1992), *Tchelitchev* (1994), and *Mosaic* (1994), a memoir up through 1933. He also published a beautifully illustrated book, *Nijinsky Dancing* (1975), a paean to the Russian dancer.

In 1995, Kirstein developed a series of debilitating physical problems: phlebitis, bedsores, and an enlarged prostrate for which he had surgery. He died, likely of heart failure, on January 5, 1996.

Duberman's spectacular book provides insights into the man who almost single-handedly established ballet in America. This richly layered book chronicles the genius, the financial power, and the tenacious commitment to the arts that drove Kirstein's life and work. Duberman pulls no punches in describing Kirstein's shortcomings, though Duberman clearly demonstrates that his sometimes unlikeable traits were often overshadowed by his generosity and his warmth. Duberman's epic biography matches the epic story of this American genius.

*Henry L. Carrigan, Jr.*

## Review Sources

*Booklist* 103, no. 16 (April 15, 2007): 14.
*Chicago Tribune*, April 15, 2007, p. 4.
*Dance Magazine* 81, no. 10 (October, 2007): 76-77.
*The Nation* 285, no. 2 (July 9, 2007): 28-34.
*The New Republic* 236, no. 15 (May 7, 2007): 39-45.
*The New York Review of Books* 54, no. 10 (June 14, 2007): 8-12.
*The New York Times Book Review* 156 (April 29, 2007): 9.
*The New Yorker* 83, no. 8 (April 16, 2007): 142-152.
*Publishers Weekly* 254, no. 9 (February 26, 2007): 71-72.

# THE YEARS OF EXTERMINATION
## Nazi Germany and the Jews, 1939-1945

*Author:* Saul Friedländer (1932-    )
*Publisher:* HarperCollins (New York). 870 pp. $39.95
*Type of work:* History

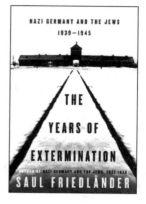

*A multifaceted account that includes analysis as lucid as it is complex, the second volume of Friedländer's history of the Holocaust covers the years of World War II and achieves distinction by continuing the author's insightful integration of narratives about the German perpetrators and their Jewish victims*

The first volume of Saul Friedländer's two-part history of the Holocaust, Nazi Germany's genocide against the Jewish people, concentrated on what he called "the years of persecution," the period from 1933 to 1939. Analyzing Adolf Hitler's consolidation of power and its increasingly disastrous but not yet fully murderous impact on German and Austrian Jews, Friedländer advanced his thesis that a "redemptive anti-Semitism" characterized Nazi ideology. He also showed that sound historical investigation of the Holocaust depends on integrating the experiences of the German perpetrators, their Jewish victims, and many other groups and individuals who were also involved in that catastrophe.

Friedländer's emphasis on "redemptive anti-Semitism" clashed with so-called functionalist interpretations of the Holocaust, which contended that Nazi Germany was not necessarily a genocidal regime from the beginning but evolved toward its "final solution" when other options for solving the Nazis' "Jewish question" proved unworkable. Friedländer disagreed, contending that Nazism early on harbored potentially genocidal intentions. Hitler and his followers saw "the Jew" as the worst threat to civilization. The world's redemption required the elimination of that menace.

This analysis did not mean, however, that Nazi leadership in the 1930's already had a blueprint for mass murder, let alone specific designs for killing centers such as Treblinka and Auschwitz. Friedländer maintained that the decisions to commit mass murder, the attention to detail needed to implement them, did evolve over time, eventually involving persons and places scattered far and wide in the Holocaust's vast continental scope. Nevertheless, as Friedländer shows in *The Years of Extermination*, his Pulitzer Prize-winning account of the wartime period from 1939 to 1945, Nazi Germany's fervent, indeed fanatical, commitment to those decisions and details cannot be adequately understood absent the implicitly genocidal "redemptive anti-Semitism" that motivated them.

Much Holocaust analysis has focused primarily either on the Germans and their collaborators or on the Jews and other victim groups who were trapped in Nazi Germany's lethal web of racism. Indispensable though this work continues to be, it is one-sided insofar as it neglects, for example, the fact that German and Jewish actions and reactions were under way at the same time. Neither the perpetrators nor their victims acted independently; they were always related and intertwined. As obvious as that point may be, the attempt to write the Holocaust's history with that convergence in the foreground is herculean because too much happened all at once. Arguably, no Holocaust scholar knows that predicament better than Friedländer, who, more than any historian thus far, has written a profoundly integrated history of the Holocaust.

~

*Saul Friedländer lived in Nazi-occupied France during World War II; he survived the Holocaust by hiding in a Catholic monastery, while his parents died in Auschwitz. His awards include a prestigious fellowship from the John D. and Catherine T. MacArthur Foundation. Notable among his books are the memoir* When Memory Comes *(1979) and* Nazi Germany and the Jews, 1933-1939 *(1997), the first of a two-volume history of the Holocaust.*

~

No photographs are reproduced in *The Years of Extermination*, but to see what Friedländer's prodigious work required, consider that he begins the book by describing what happened in a picture that was taken at the University of Amsterdam in the Netherlands on September 18, 1942. A medical student named David Moffie is receiving his medical degree. Surrounded by his professors, family, and friends, the young doctor wears a tuxedo. On its left side is a star, the word *Jood* upon it. "Moffie," Friedländer explains, "was the last Jewish student at the University of Amsterdam under German occupation."

Unearthing such details is indispensable for Friedländer's narrative. They contain the interrelationships that he finds so important for documenting and delineating the Holocaust's years of extermination. There is much that the Moffie photograph does not reveal. It is silent, for example, about the words that were spoken at his graduation. Probably they are completely lost, and no history of the Holocaust will ever contain them. Further research indicates, however, that shortly after Moffie's graduation, he was deported to Auschwitz-Birkenau. His survival put him in the 20 percent of Dutch Jews who lived through the Holocaust. Most of the Jews in the Moffie photo, Friedländer observes, were among the other 80 percent of Dutch Jewry, those killed, one way or another, by the Germans and their collaborators.

Friedländer helps his reader to see that the window on the Holocaust provided by the Moffie photograph opens still wider if one pursues key questions implicit in that image. How, for instance, was it possible that a Jewish medical student could receive a degree at a Dutch university in September, 1942? German forces had occupied Dutch soil since the spring of 1940. By 1942, the Nazis' continental "final solution" was under way. Deportations of Dutch Jews to Auschwitz and other places of death in the East had started on July 14 of that year. Later, on September 8, a German decree excluded Jews from Dutch universities. Nevertheless, Moffie's graduation took place in an official ceremony ten days later. It did so, Friedländer's meticulous research shows, because the calendar provided a loophole that allowed some Dutch and Jewish resistance against German power. In Dutch universities, the 1941-1942 academic year ended on Friday, September 18. The 1942-1943 academic year started on

Monday, September 21. The exclusionary decree of September 8 was not effective until the beginning of the new academic year. In conferring Moffie's degree, the Dutch university took an action that was clearly contrary to the spirit if not the letter of German intentions. The photograph, says Friedländer, "documents an act of defiance, on the edge of the occupier's laws and decrees."

In receiving his degree, Moffie, his family, and their Jewish friends were going forward with their lives as best they could. For the Dutch Jews in the early autumn of 1942, as Friedländer's analysis also shows, living as best they could was immensely precarious. With deportations already in full cry, Jews were regularly rounded up by Germans and the Dutch police who helped them to fill the weekly transport quotas. Amsterdam's Jewish Council, leaders required to comply with German orders, were also implicated in the deportations. Moffie and the Jews who attended his graduation ceremony would not have been there if they had not received certificates that exempted them, albeit only temporarily, from deportation.

According to Friedländer, there were seventeen thousand of these special certificates for Amsterdam's Jews—by no means enough to go around. Thus, deep probing of the Moffie photograph reveals the gray zone in which some Dutch Jews found themselves. German authority gave Jewish leaders the opportunity to reprieve, if only for a time, some but not all of their fellow Jews from slave labor and death in the East. Saving a few meant condemning others. In the end, however, there were no exemption certificates, because while Moffie received the degree that certified him to be an individual trained to restore health and entrusted to save life, German authority had affixed a Jew-labeling star to his chest. That emblem stole Moffie's individuality and virtually sentenced him to death because "the Jew" had to be wiped off the face of the earth.

The Moffie photograph illustrates what an integrated history of the Holocaust entails. It has to include much more than German decisions and measures alone. It has to go beyond a singular focus on Jewish perceptions, initiatives, and reactions. In addition, such history writing requires attention to what was happening concurrently and simultaneously as well as concentration on intermediate and long-term relationships of cause and effect. Still further, Friedländer's project reaches overwhelming proportions when one realizes how many Holocaust-related artifacts await the same careful scrutiny that he gave to a single photograph.

Just as the words spoken at Moffie's commencement ceremony are unlikely to be retrieved, there are countless documents pertaining to the Holocaust that are lost forever. The number that remains is large, however, and more documents and artifacts are still being recovered. They include German records that chronicle the years of extermination and Jewish diaries that recall the onslaught day by day. The amount of Holocaust-related evidence is matched by its complexity because these sources cover vast geographical terrain and more places than any single map can identify. Interpreting these Holocaust data also involves understanding of the cultural and religious differences that contextualize them, as well as expertise in the diverse languages in which Holocaust-related experiences are recorded. No matter how extensive, Friedländer's attention could never encompass all the important moments, their interrelationships and juxtapositions. To some extent, Friedländer's project was destined to be self-defeating. Odds in favor of that outcome even increased as he tackled other integrative problems—narration, contextualization, and comprehension—that are related to but beyond detail gathering.

No history of the Holocaust, especially an integrated one, can be only a collection of episodes, even if they are interpreted as well as Friedländer handles the Moffie photograph. Friedländer had to put the episodes together so that a sustained narration resulted. This work required careful and difficult decisions about where to start and stop a particular thread, such as the one about Moffie. It entailed complicated judgments about how to connect Holocaust moments in ways that show accurately, not for literary effect, how one thing led to another in the destruction process.

Putting the episodes together was not enough. To get the compelling narrative he wanted, Friedländer had to keep context in mind as well, for just as one Holocaust moment relates to others, these events unfolded in social, economic, political, and religious settings that were larger than the individual episodes and arguably more than the sum of their parts. Assuming that all of these tasks could be handled satisfactorily, there would still be the problem of what, if anything, to conclude about the Holocaust, how to end an integrative and integrated two-volume work that is well over a thousand pages in length. In this area, Friedländer had to decide what, if anything, to do about lingering questions that elude closure and that further historical analysis may not be able to answer. Friedländer's best accomplishment is that his Holocaust history brims with integrated detail. Friedländer's project was self-defeating, but his refusal to give up produces significant light that has never before been shed on the Holocaust.

*The Years of Extermination* ends without a definitive summing up or conclusion. As though exhaustion intervened, Friedländer's account stops rather abruptly with events in May, 1945. While he has little to say about the Holocaust's aftereffects, his final paragraph concentrates on the few hundreds of thousands of Jews who stayed in Nazi-occupied Europe and survived the Holocaust. Probably with his own experiences in mind, he notes that the years of destruction "remained the most significant period of their lives. . . . Recurrently, it pulled them back into overwhelming terror and, throughout, notwithstanding the passage of time, it carried along with it the indelible memory of the dead." Friedländer's conclusion is no more—or less—than that. If it leaves his reader wanting still more, perhaps the author's wisdom, and his appropriate modesty about the all-but-impossible task he set for himself, is simply to recognize that while one can know much about the Holocaust, how and why it happened, there is no closure for an event that leaves one staring into an unacceptable abyss.

Friedländer's nonconcluding ending circles back to the beginning and, in particular, to the book's governing epigraph, whose sense is more intense and ominous after one reads *The Years of Extermination*. Stefan Ernest, the epigraph's author, lived in Warsaw, Poland. Like Friedländer, he was a Jew in hiding in 1943. Ernest wrote his version of Holocaust history, hoping that the narrative would survive although he would not. Ernest imagined readers asking him whether his account was the truth. "I reply in advance," he says. "No, this is not the truth, this is only a small part, a tiny fraction of the truth. . . . Even the mightiest pen could not depict the whole, real, essential *truth.*" With those words, Friedländer's awesome research and mighty pen find a fitting place for study of the Holocaust to stop momentarily, but not end, and then to begin again.

*John K. Roth*

## Review Sources

*Booklist* 103, no. 16 (April 15, 2007): 18.
*First Things: The Journal of Religion, Culture, and Public Life* 177 (November, 2007): 62.
*Los Angeles Times*, July 15, 2007, p. F6.
*The New Republic* 237, no. 5 (September 10, 2007): 51-55.
*The New York Times Book Review* 156 (June 24, 2007): 16-17.
*Newsweek* 149, no. 17 (April 23, 2007): 52-54.
*The Times Literary Supplement*, January 4, 2008, pp. 3-5.

# THE YIDDISH POLICEMEN'S UNION

*Author:* Michael Chabon (1963-      )
*Publisher:* HarperCollins (New York). 432 pp. $26.95
*Type of work:* Novel
*Time:* An alternate 2007
*Locale:* An alternate Sitka, Alaska

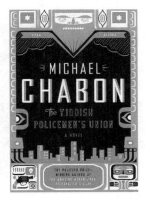

*In this alternate history, in which surviving European Jews settled in Alaska instead of Israel after World War II, Meyer Landsman is a detective who investigates a murder, discovers the victim was the estranged son of a local crime boss, and uncovers an international conspiracy to destroy an important religious shrine*

*Principal characters:*
MEYER LANDSMAN, homicide detective, forty-four years old
BERKO SHEMETS, Landsman's partner and younger cousin,
    half-Jewish, half-Native American, member of the Tlingit nation
BINA GELBFISH, Landsman's ex-wife and superior in the homicide squad
MENACHEM-MENDEL SHPILMAN, also known as Emanuel Lasker
    and Frank, murder victim and heroin addict
HESKEL SHPILMAN, Mendel's father, rabbi, leader of the local
    Hasidic Jews, and organized crime boss
HERTZ SHEMETS, Meyer's uncle, Berko's father, and disgraced
    FBI agent
ESTER-MALKE SHEMETS, Berko's wife
ISIDOR LANDSMAN, Meyer's father
FREYDL LANDSMAN, Meyer's mother
NAOMI LANDSMAN, Meyer's sister

The premise of the alternate history genre is that changing certain key events will radically alter the course of history. In Philip Roth's *The Plot Against America* (2004), a faction of isolationist Republicans succeed in securing the party's 1940 presidential nomination for Charles Lindbergh. He then goes on to defeat Franklin D. Roosevelt in the general election and adopts a pro-Axis foreign policy and an anti-Semitic domestic one. In *The Man in the High Castle* (1962), Philip K. Dick postulates that an attempt to assassinate Roosevelt in 1933 was successful. Therefore, the United States was unprepared for and loses World War II. By 1962, the United States is divided into three countries, one neutral, one pro-Japan, and one pro-Germany.

The premise of this alternate history novel, *The Yiddish Policemen's Union*, is that a proposal made by Roosevelt's Secretary of Interior Harold Ickes in the late 1930's became law. He had offered to settle Alaska with European Jews fleeing from the Third Reich. The key event was that the nonvoting congressional delegate from Alaska, who opposed the proposal, died in an automobile accident. Millions of

*Michael Chabon won the Pulitzer Prize for his 2000 novel* The Amazing Adventures of Kavalier and Clay, *the Mythopoeic Fantasy Award for Children's Literature for his 2002 young adult novel* Summerland, *and the Aga Khan Award and the National Jewish Book Award for his 2004 Sherlock Holmes pastiche* The Final Solution.

Jews accepted the invitation and settled in and around Sitka, a small town of fewer than ten thousand people in the Alaskan Panhandle. There was still a Jewish Holocaust, but "only" two million were killed rather than six million, and it is called "The Destruction." Although it is not clear how these events followed, Nazi Germany defeated the Soviet Union in World War II. Presumably, the resources used against the Jews were applied against the Russians instead. Germany was itself defeated when the United States dropped the atomic bomb on Berlin in 1946. The state of Israel only lasted three months before the Arabs destroyed it in 1948, so the Jews were granted a sixty-year lease on what is officially called the Federal District of Sitka and unofficially "Alyeska." The lease is only a few months from expiring, so the Sitka police department is under pressure to close its open cases, and most people are making plans to stay or move to other countries such as Madagascar, voluntarily or not. By 2007, more than three million people, sometimes called the "Frozen Chosen" or "Sitkaniks," live there, and Yiddish rather than English or Hebrew is the official language. Instead of the Palestinians, the Jews displaced a Native American nation known as the Tlingits, who lived in the land surrounding Sitka. However, there were only fifty thousand Tlingits, and, unlike the Palestinians, none of the other Native American nations were in any position to support them.

The main point-of-view character is Meyer Landsman, a detective in the tradition of Philip Marlowe, Lew Archer, and Sam Spade. (There is a minor character in the novel named Spade, and the local crime boss is an even more obese version of the actor Sidney Greenstreet, who played the Fat Man in the best film version of *The Maltese Falcon*, 1930.) Having moved out of the house he shared with his former wife, for the last nine months Meyer has been living in the seedy Hotel Zamenhof when the night manager informs him that a dead body has been found in one of the other rooms. Although Meyer is off duty, he investigates. Known as Emanuel Lasker, the murder victim had a chess set in his room as well as two books on the subject. Meyer knew enough about chess to tell that he was in a complex endgame. He also knew that Emanuel Lasker was the name of a famous Jewish chess player in the early twentieth century and concluded that it was not the victim's real name. The victim was also a heroin addict, as evidenced by needle marks and devices. He must have been a devout Jew at some point in his past, because he used a tefillin, a leather strap attached to a box containing passages from the Torah used in prayer, as a tourniquet. Lasker was shot in the back of the head, and the killer used a pillow to muffle the sound, so Meyer concludes that it was a professional hit. Meyer has the feeling, correctly as it turns out, that the arrangement of the chess pieces is an important clue.

Meyer's father, Isidor, and uncle Hertz Shemets were both serious chess buffs, but their attempts to teach him the game only resulted in his hating it. Hertz and his sister Freydl had arrived in Sitka in 1941 and Isidor, a survivor of a concentration camp, in 1948. Isidor and Freydl were married in 1953. Freydl worked for a local newspaper while Isidor wrote articles on chess and drew a pension from the German government. Besides Meyer, they had one daughter, Naomi, who grew up to be a bush pilot. Isidor committed suicide when Meyer was a teenager, Freydl died of cancer while Meyer was in college, and Naomi died when her plane flew into a mountain under mysterious circumstances the year before. Meyer eventually discovers a connection between Naomi and Lasker.

Hertz Shemets attended law school in Seattle after the war and then joined the Federal Bureau of Investigation (FBI). He eventually rose to head their counterintelligence program in Alaska but was forced into retirement because of a scandal. A newspaper reporter discovered that he had been working on a private agenda to secure permanent status for Sitka as a homeland for the Jews and had been using illegal means such as bribing and blackmailing congressmen. Years previously, Hertz had had an affair with a Native American woman, a member of the Tlingit nation whose family claimed descent from their raven god, and the result was their son, Berko, whom Hertz adopted after she died. Berko, known as Johnny "the Jew" Bear to the Tlingits, converted to Judaism, became a police officer, and married Ester-Malke Taytsh, a Jewish woman. They have two sons, and Ester-Malke is pregnant with their third child at the beginning of the book. They provide Meyer with the closest thing he has to a family, although the elder Shemets is still alive and married to another Tlingit woman.

Berko and Meyer's relationship is reminiscent of the one between the title characters in Michael Chabon's earlier novel *The Amazing Adventures of Kavalier and Clay* (2000). Not only are they cousins but they are also partners in their professional lives and best friends. As teenagers, Meyer was supposed to teach chess to Berko, but his hatred of the game stopped him, so Berko has little knowledge of it. Berko's Native American ancestry also suggests a connection with Chabon's young adult fantasy *Summerland* (2002).

Meyer was married to Bina Gelbfish for twelve years, and they had been dating for five years before that. They also worked in the homicide squad together for four. However, they were partners on only one case, which they failed to solve, and they aborted their only child, a boy, after the doctor informed them he might have birth defects. After their divorce, she left for a year to train as a supervisor. When she returned, she became Meyer's boss. It makes for a complicated relationship, to say the least. Because of the impending reversion of Sitka back to Alaska, she wants Meyer to flag the Lasker investigation as a cold case. He does not so much refuse as ignore her.

The investigation leads Meyer to the Einstein Chess Club, which meets regularly at the Hotel Einstein. The players recognize the man from his picture, but to them he is known as Frank. Meyer and Berko eventually identify the victim as Mendel Shpilman. He was the estranged son of the Hasidic rabbi and organized crime boss Heskel Shpilman. Mendel was a child prodigy at chess, Torah studies, and foreign languages. Healing miracles were associated with him, so many people hoped he was the Tzaddik Ha-Dor, the one man in his generation with the potential to become the Messiah. Another of his peculiarities was that his body temperature was two degrees warmer than normal. Twenty-three years previously, he angered his father when he refused to marry the nice Jewish girl his parents had chosen for him, and he disappeared. Meyer and Berko's interview with the elder Shpilman goes badly, and they suspect the gangster already knew that Mendel was dead.

Meyer eventually discovers a conspiracy to destroy the Dome of the Rock in Jerusalem. This is the third holiest shrine in Islam and, according to tradition, the place where Abraham almost sacrificed his son Isaac. More important, it is known to be on the site where Solomon's Temple stood. In Judaic tradition, the temple must be rebuilt before the Messiah can come. Furthermore, according to the book of Revelation in the New Testament, the temple must be rebuilt before the second coming of Christ. The conspirators, Meyer learns, are an alliance of fundamentalist Jews and Christians. While the fundamentalist Jews are very richly characterized, the fundamentalist Christians are poorly and thinly drawn.

Some readers might be put off by the Yiddish slang, inspired by the 1958 phrase book *Say It in Yiddish* by Uriel and Beatrice Weinreich, and the jargon Chabon has invented for the novel. However, such language usually can be understood from the context. Uniformed police officers are called "latkes," and plainclothesmen are called "nozes." "Black Hats" refers to Hasidic Jews, who also control organized crime in Sitka, "rebbe" to rabbi, "yids" to Jews living in Sitka, "Mexicans" to Jews living in the continental United States, "shtarkers" to muscle men, and "schlossers" to contract killers. They have cell phones, which they called "shoyfers," cigarettes are called "papiroses," and guns "sholems."

Despite the convoluted plot, Chabon explores the issues of identity and assimilation in a world where people are not what they seem. The most devout ones are among the most corrupt, and the sleaziest are the ones with the most integrity. Many of the Sitkaniks want to become Americans, but the most they can hope for in the coming year is a green card. Meyer is more alienated than most, because he does not believe in God, which puts him at odds with the Orthodox Jews who compose most of the Sitkaniks. The reader will also see that he will have trouble becoming an American, if that is what he is allowed and chooses to do after Sitka reverts back to the United States, because he has trouble belonging to anything.

*Thomas R. Feller*

## Review Sources

*Booklist* 103, no. 13 (March 1, 2007): 38.
*Commonweal* 134, no. 16 (September 28, 2007): 26-27.
*Esquire* 147, no. 5 (May, 2007): 44.
*Kirkus Reviews* 75, no. 5 (March 1, 2007): 185.
*Library Journal* 132, no. 4 (March 1, 2007): 68-69.
*London Review of Books* 29, no. 16 (August 16, 2007): 26-27.
*The New York Times Book Review* 156 (May 13, 2007): 10.
*Time* 169, no. 19 (May 7, 2007): 85.
*USA Today*, May 1, 2007, p. D4.
*The Washington Post*, May 13, 2007, p. BW03.

# YOUNG STALIN

*Author:* Simon Sebag Montefiore (1965-    )
*Publisher:* Alfred A. Knopf (New York). 496 pp. $30.00
*Type of work:* Biography, history
*Time:* 1878-1953
*Locale:* Primarily Georgia, Russian Empire

*New sources revise the understanding of Joseph Stalin's early years and, hence, his personality*

> *Principal characters:*
> JOSEPH STALIN (JOSEPH VISSARIONOVICH
>     DZHUGASHVILI), known in his youth as
>     Soso and Koba
> EKATERINA "KEKE" GELADZE
>     DZHUGASHVILI, his mother
> SIMON "KAMO" TER-PETROSIAN, a psychopathic gangster
>     who was Stalin's right-hand man
> EKATERINA "KATO" SVANIDZE DZHUGASHVILI, Stalin's first wife
> LUDMILA STAL, fellow Bolshevik and girlfriend, from whom
>     he may have taken his alias
> VLADIMIR ILICH LENIN (VLADIMIR ILICH ULYANOV), founder of
>     the Bolsheviks
> LEON TROTSKY (LEV DAVIDOVICH BRONSTEIN), Stalin's principal rival
> NADYA ALLILUYEVA, daughter of old friends from his youth and
>     his second wife

Historians have often deplored the lack of information available regarding people and events in the Soviet Union, especially about the early life of Joseph Stalin. The gap was filled with myths and speculations, some provided by Stalin's enemies (Leon Trotsky foremost among them) and some by Stalin himself. Following the collapse of the Soviet Union, Simon Sebag Montefiore had access to police records and political archives in Russia and Georgia, and to prepare *Young Stalin* he was able to interview persons previously unreachable or unwilling to talk.

It is surprising that Stalin survived his childhood. He was born with two toes webbed together, suffered numerous bouts of illness, was twice badly injured by carriages racing down the narrow streets of his hilly hometown, and was periodically beaten by his father. These left him with a pock-marked face, a slight limp, and a crippled arm. Nevertheless, he had impressive physical strength and even more powerful psychological skills that made him the center of whatever group he entered.

His mother was important in many ways but not those normally associated with mothering. Her voracious sexual appetite undoubtedly hurt her husband's self-esteem, worsening his tendency to drink excessively and to beat her. Seeing that her son was exceptionally bright, she determined that he would be more than a cobbler like his father. Believing that he might even become a bishop in the Russian Orthodox

Church, she sought his admission into a seminary; since entry was reserved for the children of priests, she arranged for one of her lovers to claim Stalin as one of his illegitimate children. Later, Stalin benefited from the aid of another of his rumored fathers.

*Simon Sebag Montefiore is a British journalist and historian. He is the author of* Stalin: The Court of the Red Tsar *(2004), one of the most widely praised biographies of recent years.*

This background prepares readers, in a way, for Stalin's own sexual adventures. Not up to Grigori Yefimovich Rasputin's standards, perhaps, but in both macho Georgian culture and the world of radical politics, lax standards were accepted and expected. Stalin indulged himself freely, laughingly taking away the mistresses of close friends, using them, abandoning them, then indulging in high-spirited drinking bouts with both the women and the men. There were no hard feelings, and no thought of caring for the illegitimate children.

The one exception, to the extent it was an exception (his gangster politics always came first), was his wife, Ekaterina Svanidze Dzhugashvili, known as Kato. He was so distraught at her death that he threw himself into her grave for a last embrace of her coffin. He ignored his son so completely that even when Yakov was captured by the Nazis, he refused to contemplate any kind of exchange. No one doubts that Stalin, a master of underhanded and secretive maneuvers, could have arranged something discretely.

One of the most enduring stories of Stalin's early life is that he was a police spy. Montefiore sorts through the contradictory evidence to refute the rumors in their baldest form, but since Stalin was trying to infiltrate the police himself, he undoubtedly had close ties to many policemen. It is easy to imagine that he used these contacts to dispose of rivals, just as they sought to have him arrested. This would not be the only time in world history that gangsters and policemen have made mutually comfortable arrangements.

His personal life was irregular. He kept in contact with his mother, his former lovers, and his friends, but Marxism always came first. In a world of transitory relationships, only the inevitable triumph of the revolution could be counted on.

He sometimes dressed like a dandy, sometimes like a bum, but he always enjoyed having his photo taken, especially with groups of revolutionary friends. He moved around the Caucasus easily, avoiding arrest, extorting capitalists and encouraging kidnappings, setting fires, robbing banks, and perhaps even taking over ships carrying money. Unlike other political gangsters, he did not take much for himself, only enough for one lavish party. Then it was back to Communist Party work, borrowing money from friends (never repaying them), and living in their homes and apartments. This behavior was apparently never resented, even when he seduced the women of the house or provoked police raids.

He was arrested numerous times but usually talked his way out of custody. In 1902, however, he was sentenced to internal exile in Siberia. Wherever he was, he quickly made himself the head of the most violent criminal elements; he disliked the political exiles, suspecting them of ratting out true revolutionaries. Three years later he escaped.

The carefully organized 1907 bank robbery in Tblisi (Tiflis) was bloodier and more chaotic than expected, but Stalin's gang came away with enough loot to finance Bolshevik activities. With the police long unable to determine who was responsible, it was the perfect crime. It also brought Stalin to Vladimir Ilich Lenin's attention.

Stalin was more widely traveled than most realize. He was in London, Paris, Berlin, Kraków, Vienna (at the same time as Adolf Hitler and Tito), Stockholm, and Finland. He was not much of a tourist, though he seemed to have visited the Louvre, and he was more interested in party business than in soaking up local culture. However, with Stalin's intense study of English and German, it seems likely that he made his way around easily. Between 1905 and 1912, he met Lenin (instant mutual admiration), Trotsky (instant mutual detestation), and all the Bolsheviks who became important later. He became friends with some, his blunt manners offended others, but all recognized that he had genuine talent and was willing to work hard. It was not true, as was later alleged, that he had few abilities beyond intrigue, but few people recognized that he was, at heart, a gangster. For these reasons, he was underestimated by those Bolsheviks who later went to the firing squad; those who recognized what he was, and approved, later became his closest associates.

After years of dealing with secret police spies, either to avoid their clutches or to bribe them, Stalin became cynical and mistrustful. Still, he was unready for the terrible betrayal of Roman Malinovsky, a member of the central committee and one of the party's two deputies in the Duma. Malinovsky was a paid informer for the secret police, responsible for arresting the party's key members (including Stalin, whom in 1912 he lured to a public entertainment where Stalin was easily captured) or causing them to flee abroad. If such a trusted man could be an agent of the enemy, who could not be? This story goes far to explain Stalin's later paranoia about spies and wreckers, but it is perhaps less important than Stalin's realizing that revolutions spawn people just like himself.

This time, the secret police finally found a place from which he could not escape— a tiny remote village north of the Arctic Circle. Stalin managed to adapt. He was an entertaining guest, singing, telling stories to the children, seducing a thirteen-year-old girl and fathering two children (one of whom survived), fishing, hunting, making long trips over the ice to visit friends, and thinking, planning, plotting. When the war came in 1914, he was sure it would bring down the monarchy, but that did not happen quickly. At length, however, the bloodletting in the army became so extreme that in 1917 an offer was made to the exiles—amnesty for military service. Stalin volunteered, knowing that his crippled arm would exempt him from service. That, however, was not discovered until he took the physical exam, and the police were too busy to return him to the north. Instead, he was assigned to a new location, near Petrograd (later St. Petersburg). When the February Revolution freed all political prisoners, he hurried to the capital and quickly made himself one of the principal figures in the Bolshevik Party.

His principal responsibility was to publish *Pravda*. In this period, as earlier, he advocated working with the Mensheviks, Julius Martov's rival faction to Lenin's Bolsheviks. Lenin, out of touch in distant Switzerland, was outraged; he demanded immediate efforts to overthrow the new democratic government. When Lenin finally reached Petrograd, he dismayed his comrades by urging an armed uprising. Quickly, however, he realized that the situation was not yet favorable for success; by July, he disapproved when overly eager comrades rose against Aleksandr Fyodorovich Kerensky, and the latter's leadership was confirmed when their effort was utterly crushed. All the Bolshevik leaders went into hiding. It seemed that the party had no future, except for Stalin, who had been so confined by the democratic political process. In underground activities, he was in his element again.

The July debacle was not the total catastrophe it had appeared, however, but led directly to the revival of the Bolshevik Party. Kerensky had called on a courageous but stupid general, Lavr Kornilov, to put down the rising. Kornilov began reading books on Napoleon, decided that he fit the role, and ordered his troops to Petrograd. Kerensky called on the Soviets to stop the coup, after which the Bolsheviks had both an important political role and arms.

The October Revolution, in Montefiore's telling, was not much of a revolution. Kerensky's government melted away much as the czar's had. The cadets guarding the Winter Palace went off to find something to eat, the Cossacks left in disgust, the women's battalion panicked at the sound of the first shells, and Kerensky's government surrendered. However, there had been such disorganization in the Bolshevik ranks that any resistance might have been successful. In short, it had no resemblance to the climatic moment immortalized by director Sergei Eisenstein.

The handful of Bolshevik leaders then laughingly divided up the ministerial posts among themselves. Stalin reluctantly accepted responsibilities for nationalities, but his main concern was to win the war that followed. Lenin, Trotsky, and Stalin shared responsibilities in the great struggle—Lenin directing politics, Trotsky commanding the Red Army, and Stalin employing his gangster skills to consolidate the party's power.

Almost as an afterthought, Stalin took up with Nadya Alliluyeva. He had known her family in Tblisi before 1905, after which they had moved to St. Petersburg. In 1912, while hiding in their apartment, he had become attracted to the lively daughters; in 1917, he became Nadya's lover. It was a long-term mistake. The entire family was borderline bipolar, and Stalin never changed his habits: Marxism came first, his numerous short affairs second, his friends next, and his family last. It should not have come as a surprise when she committed suicide in 1932.

Stalin's importance grew during the revolution, and that of the moderates diminished. Just as the czarist and democratic forces had abdicated power, their poorly coordinated military efforts eventually confirmed the Bolsheviks' victory, and Lenin achieved an iron control of the country that he could perhaps not have attained otherwise. Montefiore's *Young Stalin* is not only a "must read" but also a good read.

*William L. Urban*

## Review Sources

*The Economist* 383 (May 19, 2007): 88.
*History Today* 57, no. 8 (August, 2007): 63-64.
*Kirkus Reviews* 75, no. 17 (September 1, 2007): 911-912.
*Library Journal* 132, no. 17 (October 15, 2007): 74.
*London Review of Books* 29, no. 21 (November 1, 2007): 27-29.
*The New York Review of Books* 54, no. 17 (November 8, 2007): 36-38.
*The New York Times Book Review* 157 (November 25, 2007): 21.
*The Times Literary Supplement*, August 17, 2007, p. 10.

MAGILL'S
LITERARY ANNUAL
2008

# BIOGRAPHICAL WORKS BY SUBJECT

## 2008

BAHĀDUR SHĀH ZAFAR II
  Last Mughal, The (Dalrymple), 415
BEAH, ISHMAEL
  Long Way Gone, A (Beah), 455
BERNSTEIN, HARRY
  Invisible Wall, The (Bernstein), 376
BEWICK, THOMAS
  Nature's Engraver (Uglow), 524

COLERIDGE, SAMUEL TAYLOR
  Friendship, The (Sisman), 282
COLTRANE, JOHN
  Coltrane (Ratliff), 169
COOPER, JAMES FENIMORE
  James Fenimore Cooper (Franklin), 384
CUNARD, NANCY
  Nancy Cunard (Gordon), 519

DANTICAT, EDWIDGE
  Brother, I'm Dying (Danticat), 114
DAY, DORIS
  Considering Doris Day (Santopietro),
  182
DIANA, PRINCESS OF WALES
  Diana Chronicles, The (Brown), 216
DONNE, JOHN
  John Donne (Stubbs), 392
DOYLE, ARTHUR CONAN
  Arthur Conan Doyle (Doyle), 36

EINSTEIN, ALBERT
  Einstein (Isaacson), 236

GODWIN, PETER
  When a Crocodile Eats the Sun
  (Godwin), 845
GORDON, MARY
  Circling My Mother (Gordon), 156

GRASS, GÜNTER
  Peeling the Onion (Grass), 578

HEINRICH, BERND
  Snoring Bird, The (Heinrich), 685
HEINRICH, GERD
  Snoring Bird, The (Heinrich), 685
HIRSI ALI, AYAAN
  Infidel (Hirsi Ali), 366

JAMES, HENRY
  Henry James Goes to Paris (Brooks),
  326

KAPUŚCIŃSKI, RYSZARD
  Travels with Herodotus (Kapuściński),
  772
KESHAVARZ, FATEMEH
  Jasmine and Stars (Keshavarz), 388
KINGSOLVER, BARBARA
  Animal, Vegetable, Miracle
  (Kingsolver), 27
KIRSTEIN, LINCOLN
  Worlds of Lincoln Kirstein, The
  (Duberman), 872
KISSINGER, HENRY
  Nixon and Kissinger (Dallek), 533
KOZOL, JONATHAN
  Letters to a Young Teacher (Kozol),
  434

LATUS, JANINE
  If I Am Missing or Dead (Latus), 344
L'ENFANT, PIERRE CHARLES
  Grand Avenues (Berg), 296
LINCOLN, ABRAHAM
  Land of Lincoln (Ferguson), 406

MAO ZEDONG
  Nixon and Mao (MacMillan), 538

# CATEGORY INDEX

## 2008

ANTHROPOLOGY. *See* SOCIOLOGY, ARCHAEOLOGY, and ANTHROPOLOGY

ARCHAEOLOGY. *See* SOCIOLOGY, ARCHAEOLOGY, and ANTHROPOLOGY

AUTOBIOGRAPHY, MEMOIRS, DIARIES, and LETTERS
Animal, Vegetable, Miracle (Kingsolver), 27
Arthur Conan Doyle (Doyle), 36
Brother, I'm Dying (Danticat), 114
Circling My Mother (Gordon), 156
If I Am Missing or Dead (Latus), 344
Infidel (Hirsi Ali), 366
Invisible Wall, The (Bernstein), 376
Jasmine and Stars (Keshavarz), 388
Letters to a Young Teacher (Kozol), 434
Long Way Gone, A (Beah), 455
Mother Teresa (Mother Teresa), 491
Notebooks (Williams), 543
Peeling the Onion (Grass), 578
Prime Green (Stone), 605

Reagan Diaries, The (Reagan), 619
Snoring Bird, The (Heinrich), 685
Touch and Go (Terkel), 759
Travels with Herodotus (Kapuściński), 772
When a Crocodile Eats the Sun (Godwin), 845

BIOGRAPHY. *See also* LITERARY BIOGRAPHY
Alexis de Tocqueville (Brogan), 13
Alice Waters and Chez Panisse (McNamee), 18
Being Shelley (Wroe), 68
Coltrane (Ratliff), 169
Considering Doris Day (Santopietro), 182
Death and the Maidens (Todd), 203
Diana Chronicles, The (Brown), 216
Einstein (Isaacson), 236
Grand Avenues (Berg), 296
Land of Lincoln (Ferguson), 406
Last Mughal, The (Dalrymple), 415
Leni (Bach), 429
Life of Picasso, A (Richardson), 442
Mother Teresa (Mother Teresa), 491
Nancy Cunard (Gordon), 519

# TITLE INDEX

## 2008

# AUTHOR INDEX

## 2008